EARLY RABBINIC CIVIL LAW
AND THE SOCIAL HISTORY OF ROMAN GALILEE

Program in Judaic Studies
Brown University
BROWN JUDAIC STUDIES
Edited by
Shaye J. D. Cohen, Wendell S. Dietrich,
Ernest S. Frerichs, Calvin Goldscheider, David Hirsch, Alan Zuckerman

Project Editors (Projects)

Lenn Evan Goodman, University of Hawaii (Studies in Medieval Judaism)
David Hayes, Coe College (Studia Philonica)

Number 307
EARLY RABBINIC CIVIL LAW
AND THE SOCIAL HISTORY OF ROMAN GALILEE
A Study of Mishnah Tractate *Baba' Meṣi'a'*

by
Hayim Lapin

EARLY RABBINIC CIVIL LAW
AND THE SOCIAL HISTORY OF ROMAN GALILEE
A Study of Mishnah Tractate *Baba' Meṣi'a'*

by

Hayim Lapin

Scholars Press
Atlanta, Georgia

EARLY RABBINIC CIVIL LAW
AND THE SOCIAL HISTORY OF ROMAN GALILEE
A Study of Mishnah Tractate *Baba' Meṣi'a'*

© 1995
Brown University

Library of Congress Cataloging-in-Publication Data
Lapin, Hayim.
    Early Rabbinic civil law and the social history of Roman Galilee :
a study of Mishnah tractate Baba' Meṣi'a' / by Hayim Lapin.
        p.   cm. — (Brown Judaic studies ; no. 307)
    Revision of author's thesis: Columbia University, New York, N.Y.
    Includes bibliographical references and index.
    ISBN 0-7885-0204-2 (cloth : alk. paper)
    1. Jewish law—History. 2. Mishnah. Bava meẓia—Criticism,
interpretation, etc. 3. Jews—History—70–638. 4. Jews—Israel—
Galilee—Social conditions. 5. Jews—Israel—Galilee—Economic
conditions.   I. Title. II. Series.
LAW <GENERAL Lapin 1996>   95-45154
                                              CIP

Printed in the United States of America
on acid-free paper

In memory of my father
Shmuel Lapin

Table of Contents

Preface	ix–x
Chapter I: Introduction: The Social Study of the Mishnah	1–34
A. Definitions and Historical Background	2
1. *The Mishnah.*	2
2. *The historical background.*	5
3. *Rabbis in Palestine.*	13
B. Methodology	19
1. *The Mishnah as a literary artifact.*	20
2. *The Mishnah as a historical document.*	27
3. *The limitations of this study and areas for future research.*	31
Chapter II: Mishnah Tractate *Baba' Meṣi'a'*: Literary and Redactional Problems	35–118
A. Sources in the Mishnah	37
1. *Context, terminology, style.*	40
2. *Parallels.*	50
B. The Shape of Sources	59
1. *Strategies.*	60
2. *Nominative absolute (article + participle) series.*	67
C. Traces of the Redactional Process	83
1. *Codas.*	84
2. *Glosses, revisions, corrections.*	86
3. *Redaction as literary creation.*	94
D. The Problem of Attributions	98
1. *Catalogue of attributed statements.*	101
2. *Attributed statements in m. Baba' Meṣi'a'.*	105
3. *Attributions and the nominative absolute series.*	113
E. Conclusions: The Mishnah as a Literary Artifact	115

Chapter III: Institutions and Relationships in Mishnah Tractate
Baba' Meṣi'a' 119–235

    A. Economic Institutions 121
        1. Money. 122
        2. Markets. 134
        3. Banks. 147

    B. Economic and Social Relationships 155
        1. Finder and loser. 157
        2. Deposits. 164
        3. Buyer and seller. 175
        4. Lender and borrower. 186
        5. Laborer and employer. 201
        6. Lessor and lessee. 218

    C. Conclusions 232

Chapter IV: Conclusions: Rabbinic Civil Law and the Social
History of Roman Galilee 237–241

Appendix I: Mishnah Tractate *Baba' Meṣi'a'*: Text, Translation,
and Annotation 243–310

Appendix II: Mishnah Tractate *Baba' Meṣi'a'* and Other "Tannaitic"
Corpora 311–329

Abbreviations and Bibliography 331–347

Index of Primary Sources 349–363

Index of Subjects 365–368

~ PREFACE ~

This study began as a doctoral dissertation written at Columbia University. I am pleased to acknowledge the generous help that I received from Columbia University during my tenure there as a student, as a Faculty and President's Fellow, during the years 1987–91. In addition, I have benefited from doctoral fellowships from the National Foundation for Jewish Culture, the Memorial Foundation for Jewish Culture, and the Lane Cooper Memorial Trust. The late Dr. Norma Furst, President of the Baltimore Hebrew University during my year of teaching there (1993–4), took a personal interest in my work and progress for which I am deeply grateful. Professor James Harris, the Chair of the Department of History at the University of Maryland, and Professor Bernard Cooperman, Director of the Meyerhoff Center for Jewish Studies, have provided an atmosphere of collegiality and support, which have made research as well as the final production of this book possible. Publication was further supported by a generous grant from the Lucius N. Littauer Foundation.

No research, especially that of a junior scholar, is undertaken in isolation. I should like to take the opportunity to thank the numerous people (too numerous to mention by name) who have in innumerable ways helped this work to take shape. Dr. Steven Rubenstein, currently of Georgetown University, served as a sounding board for ideas at various points during the preparation of this material. Ms. Rachel Brodie was a kind friend and helpful reader. Dr. Lauren Granite of Drew University was an ever-present support during the final stages of writing this study and throughout the painful process of revision. In addition, Dr. Granite was kind enough to assist me with the thankless task of editing and indexing the book. Professor Linda Safran of The Catholic University of America offered editorial help when it was almost too late to heed it. Professors Daniel Boyarin, Eliezer Diamond, Edward Greenstein, Jay Harris, Kenneth Holum, David Kraemer, Dirk Obbink, James Rives, Seth Schwartz, Alan Segal, Robert Somerville, and Burton Visotzky read and commented upon portions of this study at various stages of its preparation. Professor Shaye Cohen, as the editor of this series, offered sharp and instructive criticism of my manuscript as only he can. The help that I have received from Professor Roger Bagnall of Columbia University is evident on every page of Chapter III, and, more subtly, throughout the whole book. What is not clear enough from the pages that follow is the guidance that Bagnall unstintingly offered me in my forays into ancient history and papyrology. Finally, I wish to thank Professor David Weiss Halivni, who was the sponsor of the original thesis. Halivni took a personal interest in my progress while I was still a first-year student in college, and oversaw this project from its inception. His support is all the more valuable in that it was offered even when I found myself disagreeing with him over fundamental issues.

My mother, Evelyn Lapin-Reich, has been my most consistent reader and perhaps my most trenchant critic, and for this, in addition to her support and her affection, I wish to thank her publicly. I dedicate this work to the memory of my father, Shmuel Lapin, whose books I appropriated and read, and whose presence I continue to feel some twenty-three years after his death. I hope he would have been pleased.

CHAPTER I

Introduction: The Social Study of the Mishnah

> "That is a good joke!" replied Don Quixote. "Books which are printed by royal license and with the approval of those to whom they are submitted, and which are read with universal delight and applause by great and small, poor and rich, learned and ignorant, plebeians and gentlefolk—in short, by all kinds of persons of every quality and condition—could they be lies and at the same time appear so much like the truth? For do they not specify the father, the mother, the family, the time, the place, and the actions, detail by detail, of this or that knight? Be silent sir, do not speak such blasphemies; and, believe me, if you take my advice you will be acting like a man of sense...."[1]

The history of the Jews in Roman Palestine, indeed the history of Palestine in general, in the late second and third centuries CE is only poorly known. The Mishnah is one of the few texts of Palestinian origin from this period, and nearly the only Jewish one whose provenance and date are generally acknowledged as placing it squarely within this region and in this period. In addition, in contrast to literature written in Greek and Latin, and therefore capable of circulating widely within the Roman empire (and presumably written with this intention), the Mishnah was composed in Hebrew and therefore constrained to circulate primarily among Jews, and, in the first instance, in Palestine. The Mishnah therefore offers a remarkable opportunity for the study of how a highly articulate group (the Rabbis) within a subject people of the Roman empire presented itself to itself and to a local audience. This study focuses on tractate *Babaʾ Meṣiʿaʾ* of the Mishnah, which deals primarily with contracts of various kinds. Chapter III, which constitutes the heart of this project, is an attempt to tease out some of the implications of the tractate's depiction of social and economic relationships for an understanding of the history of later Roman Palestine. The purpose of this chapter is to provide the historical and methodological background for the study as a whole.

Some presuppositions which will be further explicated below, must be stated at the outset. First, we have few controls for the authority of early

---

[1] Miguel de Cervantes Saavedra, *Don Quixote*, tr. J. M. Cohen (London: Penguin, 1950), 440.

Rabbinic law. That is to say, there is no way of knowing the extent to which the legal practices of the Jewish population of Roman Palestine corresponded to Rabbinic laws. Even if we were to grant that Rabbinic law does reflect the common practice of at least a large portion of the Palestinian Jewish population, we would still not be in a position to determine whether that is because Rabbinic authority directed legal praxis, or because Rabbinic legal texts have recast after their own fashion the legal practices of the world in which Rabbis lived and worked. Second, the Mishnah is a literary artifact produced by Rabbis and expresses specifically Rabbinic concerns. As a result, the Mishnah cannot be read as if it were a straightforward map of social relationships. Instead, the Mishnah offers depictions of these interactions informed and filtered by a particular world view. The ideological factors that shape this world view, of which explicitly religious or exegetical considerations are only one dimension, include more mundane notions such as dignity, property or fair play, and are firmly rooted in the way in which power and wealth were produced and distributed in Galilean society, and in the Rabbis' own place in that distribution.

A. Definitions and Historical Background

1. *The Mishnah.*

The Mishnah is a legal compendium produced by a religious group in roughly 200 CE and the first text of the Rabbinic canon. Traditionally the final redaction of the Mishnah is ascribed to the circle of R. Judah the Patriarch (*ha-nāśîʾ*, "the prince"), in Galilee.[2] This ascription, which fits with the rough chronology of those people cited as transmitting traditions within the Mishnah itself, as well as traces in the Mishnah and elsewhere for a Galilean provenance of the latest of these tradents, has never seriously been challenged.[3] Thus, in contrast to the other texts that purport to present "Tan-

---

[2] The Rabbinic traditions associating R. Judah the Patriarch with the redaction of the Mishnah are collected in Epstein, *Siprût*, 200–5. Medieval traditions place the redaction of the Mishnah in 500, 510 or 530 of the Seleucid era (187, 197 or 217 CE). See G. D. Cohen, *Sefer ha-Qabbalah: The Book of Tradition* (Philadelphia: JPS, 1967), 211 n. 15.

[3] For some of the evidence for the Galilean (and urban) provenance of the later Tannaim see H. Lapin, *Text, Money and Law: The Social and Literary Background of Mishnah Tractate Babaʾ Meṣiʿaʾ* (Diss.: Columbia University, 1994), Chapter III.B.1; see also L. I. Levine, *The Rabbinic Class of Roman Palestine in Late Antiquity* (Jerusalem: Yad Izhak ben Zvi and JTSA, 1989), 23–42. M. S. Zuckermandel, *Gesammelte Aufsätze. Erster Teil. Zur Halachakritik* (Frankfurt, 1911), 86–7, expressed the view that the Mishnah is a later Babylonian recension of a text of which the Tosepta forms the original Palestinian version. This is not a view that

naitic" material, about whose respective dates and origins there is a variety of opinions, the Mishnah is relatively firmly fixed in time, place, and redactional setting.[4] For that reason, this study takes early Rabbinic civil law as it is depicted in the Mishnah as its point of departure. At the same time, extra-Mishnaic literature, both "Tannaitic" and "Amoraic," offers a wealth of complementary, contradictory and exegetical material that is essential for elucidating the Mishnah itself, as well as some of the range of possible opinions and conflicts that are not necessarily expressed in the Mishnah.

The Mishnah as a whole is divided into six *sĕdārîm* ("orders") which are in turn subdivided into *massektôt* ("webs [on a loom]"), or tractates. The orders are as follows: (1) *Zĕrāʿîm*, "Seeds," dealing primarily with agricultural gifts to the poor and to priests, and including one tractate on blessings and prayers; (2) *Môʿēd*, "Appointed Times," concerned with rules for festivals, overwhelmingly centered on the cult of the Jerusalem Temple; (3) *Nāšîm*, "Women," which, in addition to treatment of marriage, divorce, and special levirate marriages, includes special tractates on vows, nazirite status, and the ordeal of a wife suspected of adultery; (4) *Nĕzîqîn*, "Damages," including three tractates on "private" law (e.g., damages, contracts, property), another on the relations between Jews and gentiles, a series on courts and oaths (including those taken in a judicial context), and two miscellanies; (5) *Qodāšîm*, "Holy Things" concerned with the Temple and its cult; and (6) *Tohorôt*, "Purities," the longest of the six, dealing with ritual purity. The present study focuses on one of these tractates, *m. Babaʾ Meṣiʿaʾ*, "The Middle Gate," in the order of Damages. This tractate is the second of the three private law tractates which seem originally to have made up a single

---

has gained wide appeal; in fact, the relationship between the Mishnah and the Tosepta actually appears to be the reverse.

[4] The Rabbis who lived before the first decades of the third century CE are traditionally known as *tannāʾîm* ("reciters") and those who lived after are known as *ʾamôrāʾîm* ("staters"); hence the conventional periodization "Tannaitic" and "Amoraic." Outside of the Mishnah, "Tannaitic" material is presented in one of two types of texts: (a) texts that are themselves "Tannaitic" (i.e., they attribute statements almost exclusively to tradents who are dated to before the third century), namely the Tosepta and the Halakic Midrashim; (b) *bāraîtôt* ("external [i.e., extra-Mishnaic 'Tannaitic'] traditions") cited in Amoraic texts, namely the Yerushalmi (Palestinian Talmud) and Babli (Babylonian Talmud). The relationship of *m. Babaʾ Meṣiʿaʾ* to the Tosepta and the various Halakic ("Tannaitic") Midrashim with which it overlaps is briefly discussed in Appendix II. For the various dates of the "Tannaitic" texts see the relevant headings in H. L. Strack, *Introduction to Talmud and Midrash*, ed. G. Stemberger, tr. M. Brokmuehl (Minneapolis: Augsburg Fortress, 1992). The *bāraîtôt* of the Yerusalmi and Babli come by definition from post-Mishnaic contexts, and, according to some scholars and particularly in the case of the Babli, reflect Amoraic reworking at the very least (see Appendix II, n. 1).

tractate *Nĕzîqîn*.⁵ Hence the name: the middle gate is preceded by a first gate (*m. Babaʾ Qammaʾ*) and followed by a last gate (*m. Babaʾ Batraʾ*).⁶ *M. Babaʾ Meṣiʿaʾ* itself consists of rules for lost objects, deposits, sale, loans of various kinds, hiring and leasing of labor and property, and conflicts arising between neighbors.⁷

In terms of genre, the Mishnah is difficult to pin down. It is, like other ancient texts, an anthology of sorts. Although laws were an important area of speculation and literary activity in ancient Judaism, the Mishnah is rather unlike pre- (or non-) Rabbinic Jewish texts: it neither retells nor mimics the Bible, putting its words in the mouth of some ancient prophet, patriarch or sage; it is not explicitly and formally a work of exegesis of Scripture; and, unlike the "law codes" associated with the Qumran community (the Manual of Discipline and the Damascus Covenant), the Mishnah does not have a single authorial and authoritative voice.⁸ It is, instead, a highly stylized presentation of legal materials punctuated by disputing opinions, and at times full-blown debates. In some ways its closest analogue is the sixth-century Digest of Justinian, since in that text, too, legal traditions of various origins are collected, organized by headings, and brought "up to date."⁹ On the other hand, the Digest is explicitly the result of a literary undertaking and the editors have identified the authors and books from which the material is

---

⁵ In the Kaufman, Parma and Cambridge (Lowe ed.) manuscripts of the Mishnah, and in the Genizah fragment published by Ginzberg the chapters are numbered sequentially through all three tractates, although in the Cambridge ms. Chapter 11 (i.e., *m. B. Meṣ.* 1) is labeled *Bābāʾ tinyānāʾ* ("second gate"). The Escorial ms. of the Palestinian Talmud on these three tractates uses both systems of numeration. (For references to these mss., see Appendix I.) The stammaitic explication of an Amoraic debate in *b. B. Qam.* 102a (*b. ʿAb. Zar.* 7a) already presupposes the separation of the three *bābôt*, but attributes the view that the three make up a unit to one of the disputants. *Lev. Rab.* 19.2 (*Cant. Rab.* 5:8, to 5:11) states, as an example of the vastness of Torah, that tractate *Nĕzîqîn* has thirty chapters. See Epstein, *Nûsaḥ*, 982–3.

⁶ Compare the analogous division of tractate *Kelim* in the Tosepta into three "gates."

⁷ The entire text of the tractate is transcribed, together with a translation and annotation, in Appendix I.

⁸ I am grateful to Prof. Eliezer Diamond of the Jewish Theological Seminary of America for reminding me that the comfortable dichotomy between Second Temple Jewish literature (either mimicking or commenting on Scripture) and the Mishnah (utilizing its own organization and language) is overly simplistic. The "newness" of the Mishnah as a genre and text nevertheless remains.

⁹ See, e.g., F. Schulz, *A History of Roman Legal Science* (Oxford: Clarendon, 1946), 318–22; H. F. Jolowicz, *A Historical Introduction to Roman Law*, ed. B. Nicholas (Cambridge: Cambridge, 1972), 480–92. The problem of "source criticism" in the Digest (i.e., the incorporation of pre-formed masses of material into the work, apparently through the work of committees), and the process of "interpolation" offer important grounds for comparison with the Mishnah.

excerpted. By contrast, although the Mishnah does attribute views to individuals in the case of disputes, it does not label its sources. At the same time, by incorporating and speaking through disparate (and occasionally contradictory) source material, the Mishnah effaces the individuality or authority of the composers or arrangers of material (see further Chapter II). Moreover, the Mishnah may have emerged in a pointedly oral setting, despite the fact that Roman Palestine had a long history of literate culture and that Rabbis themselves participated in that culture, at least to the extent of their study of a written Scripture, and their comfort with, and on occasion insistence upon, written deeds. This too may have contributed to the form of some of the material in the Mishnah (e.g., the use of mnemonic devices), as well as the organization of the Mishnah as a whole as a kind of single but multivocal, codified "tradition" rather than a collection of extracts from books.[10]

2. The historical background.

There is a largely conventional narrative history of the Rabbinic movement in Roman Palestine: in the wake of the destruction of the Jerusalem Temple in 70 a new center in Yabneh (Iamnia) was founded by R. Yohanan b. Zakkai, and later was led by R. Gamaliel (II). The group of sages (who were now identified by the title "Rabbi") who met at Yabneh set about (according to the particular reconstruction, more or less effectively) rebuilding the national and religious life of Palestinian Jewry. In the wake of the Bar Kokhba revolt, the Rabbinic movement, in fits and starts, regrouped in Galilee, eventually under the leadership of R. Simeon b. Gamaliel, and worked towards restoring centralized governmental institutions led by Rabbis, although always in some conflict with the wealthy elites of Palestine. A centralized Rabbinic organization reached the height of its authority under the leadership of R. Judah the Patriarch, whom we have met above as the figure

---

[10] The problem of orality and literacy in early Rabbinic literature is beyond the scope of this study. I wish to point out, however, that analytically, and perhaps historically as well, the problem of orality as a mode of transmission (either parallel to written preservation of the Mishnah, as was suggested in different ways by Z. Frankel, *Darkê ha-mišnâ* [Leipzig, 1859], rev. ed. I. Nusbaum [Tel Aviv: Sinai, n.d.], and Albeck, *Mābô*, 111–5, or entirely orally, as S. Lieberman, "The Publication of the *Mishnah*," in *Hellenism in Jewish Palestine* [Texts and Studies 18: New York, JTSA, 1950], 83–99 has argued; see also J. Neusner, *Oral Tradition in Judaism: The Case of the Mishnah* [New York and London, 1987], reworking earlier material on the Mishnah), is different from the notion of an "oral law" as a theological principle (for which see P. Schäfer, "Das 'Dogma' des mündlichen Torah im rabbinischen Judentum," in idem, *Studien zur Geschichte und Theologie des rabbinischen Judentums* [Leiden: Brill, 1978], 153–97). At any rate, the repertoire of technical terminology and typologized stories of study and transmission all have oral referents: reciting a tradition, sitting before a sage and hearing, asking a sage; but whether this really presupposes oral transmission remains open.

traditionally credited with the redaction of the Mishnah. Afterwards, the Patriarchate became increasingly "secularized" and beholden both to the urban elites and the Roman government. The Rabbis were relegated to a more "religious" role as teachers but were able nevertheless to be effective judges and leaders of the people, as well as to exert considerable pressure on the elites and the Patriarch to observe their norms.[11]

In the present study, I have purposely avoided such narrative reconstructions. Rabbinic stories are typically brief (rarely longer than a few paragraphs), and are told for a variety of purposes of which none corresponds to the modern project of historiography. To string these episodic narratives, which are scattered about the Rabbinic canon in works of various date and provenance, into a single coherent narrative is to risk inventing histories out of the narrative intentions and choices of Rabbinic narrators, tradents and redactors. Moreover, these stories can be contradictiory. Thus, only in one version of the story of the removal of R. Yohanan b. Zakkai to Yabneh is the Rabbi credited with founding a Rabbinic center there;[12] in another pair of sources the general/emperor allows R. Yohanan at most to teach his own disciples there as a personal boon;[13] in still a third version, Yabneh is not mentioned at all.[14] In sum, the historian is forced into a potentially thankless search for "historical kernels" whose plausibility is measured against the limits of his or her own credulity.[15]

---

[11] The reconstruction is roughly that of G. Alon, *Tôldôt ha-yĕhûdîm bĕ-ʾereṣ yiśrāʾēl bitĕqûpat ha-mišnâ wĕ-ha-talmûd* (Tel Aviv: Hakibutz Hameuchad, 1953–7). Although an English version of this work has appeared (*The Jews in their Land in the Talmudic Age*, tr. G. Levi [Jerusalem: Magnes, 1980–4]), it has been substantially reworked (not always for the better) and much detailed discussion has been omitted. I therefore cite the Hebrew edition throughout.

[12] See *b. Giṭ.* 56a-b: "Give me Yabneh and its sages, and the chain [i.e., the hereditary line] of R. Gamaliel, and doctors to cure R. Sadoq."

[13] *ʾAbot R. Nat.*, version A Ch. 4 (ed. Schechter, p. 23): "... that I might teach my disciples there ...;" cf. version B Ch. 6 (ed. Schechter, p. 19): "... that I might study (ʾelmôd) Torah there ...." Based on the reading of Version B printed in Schechter (ʾlmwd, rather than ʾlmd which can be pointed ʾalamēd, "(I will) teach"), R. Yohanan b. Zakkai does not even ask for the ability to teach disciples.

[14] *Lam. Rab.* 1:32 (to Lam. 1:5). The classic study of this episode is still G. Alon, "The Removal of R. Yohanan b. Zakkai to Yavneh," in G. Alon, *Meḥqārîm bĕ-tôldôt yiśrāʾēl* (Tel Aviv: Hakibutz Hameuchad, 1976), 1, 49–52 [Appendix] = idem, *Jews and Judaism in the Classical World*, tr. I. Abrams (Jerusalem: Magnes, 1977), 269–313. See also J. Neusner, *The Development of a Legend* (SPB 16: Leiden: Brill, 1970), 228–33; and P. Schäfer, "*Die Flucht Johanan b. Zakkais aus Jerusalem und die Gründung des 'Lehrhauses' in Jabne*," ANRW 2.19.2 (1979), 43–101.

[15] In the example cited above, not only are there multiple versions of the story, but all are difficult to reconcile with the chronology of the war (most notably that Titus and not Vespasian

The Social Study of the Mishnah

Nevertheless, since much of the ensuing study of *m. Babaʾ Meṣiʿaʾ* presupposes a particular interpretation of the history of Roman Palestine and the place of Rabbis in it, some discussion of this background is necessary. The two centuries between the middle first and middle third centuries CE saw the transformation of Roman Palestine.[16] On the level of imperial and governmental politics, the most significant development was the transition from client kingdom to garrisoned province.[17] During the first part of this period there were at least two major Palestinian Jewish revolts against Rome (66–70 CE and 132–5).[18] Information for the second part of this period is less full,

---

carried out the siege of Jerusalem) and the troubled succession to Nero (for a summary see A. Saldarini, *The Fathers according to Rabbi Nathan* [SJLA 11: Leiden: Brill, 1975], 60 n. 1). How much "history" is left here? That someone might escape to the Romans and proclaim a Roman general emperor is not implausible (Josephus describes himself as having done exactly the same thing, *BJ* 3.399–408), but even granting that this is what R. Yohanan b. Zakkai did, the details and outcome of that desertion and proclamation are, at best, shrouded in legend. To take one more example: if, as most modern historians are likely to do, we do not suppose that Honi ha-Maagel succeeded in bringing rain down through his own prayer in the first century BCE (*m. Taʿan.* 3:8), what shall we take as the "historical kernel" of the story? Since the existence of a rain-making Onias in the first century BCE is independently confirmed by Josephus, *Ant.* 14.22–4, that he existed is a possibility. However, if we assume that Honi was not successful, neither Josephus' story nor the Rabbinic one have much point. More suggestive is the criticism (and grudging admiration) of the Rabbinic story, which articulates a discomfort with charismatics who draw circles in the ground and deliver ultimatums to God, without questioning (as moderns do) the fact of the rain-making itself. But at this point, we have veered from the events themselves as "history" to the historical dimension of the telling and retelling of stories. The story might have been told at any time between the first century BCE and approximately 200 CE. The historicist question then becomes who, and at which time, would narrate the story in a particular way, and which details would seem to the narrator ro be pertinent, self-evident, redundant, or lacking (and therefore to be supplied)? See, on this story, W. S. Green, "Palestinian Holy Men: Charismatic Leadership and the Rabbinic Tradition," *ANRW* 2. 19. 2 (1979), 619–47; cf. G. Vermes, *Jesus the Jew* [corr. ed.] (Philadelphia: Fortress, 1981), 69–72.

[16] In addition to the material cited below, see, for all the following, F. G. B. Millar, *The Roman Near East* (Cambridge: Harvard, 1993), 337–86 and much of part I; B. Isaac, *The Limits of Empire* (Oxford: Clarendon, 1990), 78–96, 104–18 and *passim*.

[17] The last Roman experiment with governing the bulk of Herod's kingdom as a client kingdom was in the last years of Agrippa I (44–6 CE); in addition to Gaulanitis, Trachonitis, Auranitis, and other territories, part of Galilee was given to Agrippa II who remained a major player in first-century Judean politics (see E. Schürer, *A History of the Jewish People in the Age of Jesus Christ*, rev. ed. G. Vermes, *et alii* (Edinburgh: T. and T. Clark, 1973–87), 1, 472–3; S. Schwartz, *Josephus and Judaean Politics* (*Columbia Studies in the Classical Tradition* 18: Leiden: Brill, 1990), 114–9.

[18] For discussion and literature of still another revolt under Trajan (the so-called "war of Qitos" in Rabbinic sources) see Schürer, Vermes, 1973–87, 1, 533–4; E. M. Smallwood, *The Jews Under Roman Rule*, corr. rpt. (SJLA 20: Leiden: Brill, 1981), 421–7.

but based on the evidence that remains, revolts ceased.[19] It seems plausible that Jews in Palestine, like other populations, supported Avidius Cassius against Marcus Aurelius in 175.[20] The conflict between Septimius Severus

---

[19] Cf. the reference in *SHA Ant. Pius* 5.4, referring, in the context of the reign of Antoninus Pius (138–161), to: "Germans and Dacians and many nations and also the Jews, who were rebelling." This is sometimes connected to the rescript of Antoninus Pius permitting Jews to practice circumcision (referred to in D 48.8.11 [Modestinus]; cf. Paul, *Sententiae* 5.22.3–41; texts and discussion in A. Linder, *The Jews in Roman Imperial Legislation* [Detroit: Wayne State, 1987], 99–102, 117–120), that is, as an effort to soothe tensions in Palestine. See the discussion by M. Stern, *Greek and Latin Authors on Jews and Judaism* (Jerusalem: Israel Academy of Arts and Sciences, 1976–84), 2, 622–3, who seems to approve of the association between the Jewish "revolt" and the law on circumcision. E. M. Smallwood, "The Legislation of Hadrian and Antoninus Pius against Circumcision," *Latomus* 18 (1959), 341, favored a late date for the revolt (after 145, and perhaps around 156 [p. 341 n. 3]), but a date early in Antoninus' reign for the rescript; later (Smallwood, 1981, 467–9), Smallwood seems to accept an early date for both events and takes the "revolt" as perhaps "no more than local disorders and demonstrations of protest, easily magnified" in later historiographic tradition (p. 468). Alon, 1953–7, 2, 60–3, took the notice of this revolt as evidence of continued tensions in Palestine stemming from economic and geographical dislocation and concomitant economic and political banditry, as well as a continued policy of persecution well into the reign of Antoninus. The information comes to us as the barest notice, in a catalogue of other wars and revolts successfully fought by Antoninus. Moreover, although the early lives of the *SHA*, including that of Antoninus Pius, are based on good information (R. Syme, *Emperors and Biography: Studies in the Historia Augusta* [Oxford: Clarendon, 1971], 37–41["*Ignotus*, The Good Biographer"]; T. D. Barnes, *Sources of the Historia Augusta* [Collection Latomus 155: Brussels, 1978], 37–78, esp. 39–48), the possibility of fiction cannot be denied (Barnes, pp. 47–8). Thus, no far-reaching conclusions are possible.

Also problematic, and possibly spurious, is the reference to a "Jewish triumph" permitted to Caracalla. See *SHA Septimius Severus* 16.7: Severus gave his son (Caracalla) permission to celebrate a triumph *cui senatus Iudaicum triumphum decreverat idcirco quod et in Syria res bene gestae fuerant a Severo* ("for whom the Senate had decreed a Judean (Jewish?) triumph because of the military successes attained by Severus in Syria"). H. Graetz, *Geschichte der Juden* (Vienna, 1853–76), ed. Fr. Rozenthal (Leipzig, 1893), vol. 4, 208, connected it with a victory over the brigand Claudius (see below). Others referred the triumph to the Samaritan and Judean war mentioned by Jerome (see below n. 22). M. Avi-Yonah, *The Jews of Palestine: A Political History from the Bar Kokhba War to the Arab Conquest* (Blackwell's Classical Studies: Oxford: Blackwell, 1976), 79, taking *Iudaicus* as "Jewish" but not "Judean" referred this notice to the defeat of Adiabene in the context of the Parthian war. Still others have simply rejected the notice: so Alon, 1953–7, 2, 103; Stern, 1976–84, 624–5; Smallwood, 1981, 489 n. 11; in A. R. Birley, *The African Senator: Septimius Severus*, 2. ed. (London: Batsford, 1988) the triumph "may be an invention of the *HA*" in the text (p. 134), and is "highly doubtful" in the notes (n. 11 on p. 250).

[20] See the remark attributed to Marcus Aurelius that "Cilicians, Syrians, Jews, and Egyptians" could not defeat a Roman army (Dio 71.25.1). Stern noted that the passage "may suggest that Jews still occasionally served in the Roman armies" (Stern, 1976–84, 2, 406); and

and Pescennius Niger may have been played out on the local level in Palestine,[21] and it is just barely possible that a "Jewish and Samaritan war" mentioned by Jerome refers to support that these Palestinian populations gave to Severus.[22] This might help explain the apparently exceptionally good relations between the Severan emperors and the Palestinian Jewish community (see below). If, like other local populations, Palestinian Jews took sides in

---

Smallwood thought this was evidence of local levies to supplement the legions supporting Avidius Cassius (Smallwood, 1981, 482). However, it is precisely the casting of the opposing forces as local and provincial that seems to be at issue. Cf. *SHA M. Ant.* 25.6–11; *Avidius Cassius* 8.1–4 for the leniency of Marcus Aurelius in the wake of the revolt during his visit to Syria and Egypt (for which see also Dio 71.27.3^2), and in which special emphasis is laid on that emperor's treatment of Antioch, Cyrrhus (Avidius Cassius' birthplace), and Alexandria.

[21] *SHA Septimius Severus* 9.5: Neapolis lost civic rights due to the revolt of Niger. There is indeed a gap in coinage from Neapolis from Commodus to Julia Domna (and Caracalla) (Hill, *BMC Palestine*, 58, nos. 84–5). If this gap corresponds to a period when the city lost civic rights (cf., however, the gap in coinage at Sepphoris, for which there is no evidence for such a loss of status), the resumption of coinage, and the restoration of the city, may predate the death of Severus (Smallwood, 1981, 487–8, and 490 n. 13; the identification of Julia Domna as *Ioulia Domna Seb(astē)* [i.e., Iulia Domna Augusta] corresponds to her titulature under Severus). It is perhaps to this restoration (and others?) that *SHA Septimius Severus* 14.6 refers: Severus rescinded the penalties imposed on the Palestinians on account of Niger (so Stern, 1976–84, 623). By contrast Sebaste (Samaria) was elevated to colonial status under Severus: D 50.15.1.7 (Ulpian). (The dating of this grant is uncertain: the last non-colonial coin is a coin of Septimius Severus, year 226 according to the urban era [Hill, *BMC Palestine* 79, no. 11; Meshorer, 1984, no. 116], giving a *terminus post quem* for the change in status between 199 and 201: Schürer, Vermes, 1973–87, 1, 290 n. 9, argues that the foundation is to be put in 25 BCE, following Josephus *Ant.* 15.292–8 referring to the thirteenth year of Herod; 27 BCE [the date Octavian took the title Augustus (*Sebastos*,) whence the name for the city] is the date favored by Smallwood, 1981, 77 n. 55; 490 n. 14. The earlier date would allow for the coordination of the re-founding of the city with the visit of Septimius Severus). It is possible that Caesarea, upon whose coins the titles *felix* and *constans* (or *concordia*) appear beginning with Septimius Severus, also was given these titles due to its support for Severus (L. Kadman, *CNP* II *Caesarea*, 46 and no. 63). It has been argued from the fact that the legion VI Ferrata (stationed during the second and third centuries at Kaparkotna [later Legio]) was given the titles *fidelis constans* that it remained loyal; by implication it might seem that the legion X Fretensis at Jerusalem did not (Ritterling, *PW*, *s.v. Legio*, 12, 1312–3, 1592–3, who, connecting this with the "Jewish Samaritan war" in Jerome, suggested that the legions became embroiled in a local conflict). Palestine is not unique in this respect. In this conflict inter-city rivalries in the east played themselves out through the support of one or the other claimant. See, e.g., Herodian 3.2.7–9 (Nicaea and Nicomedia), 3.3 (Laodicea and Antioch, Tyre and Berytus); see also Dio 75.8.3–4, *SHA Severus*, 9.3–11 (Smallwood, 1981, 487 n. 4).

[22] *Iudaicum et Samariticum bellum motum* (Eusebius, *Chronica*, GCS 7, 211, dated by Jerome to year five of Septimius Severus, i.e., 197). The chronology has been questioned. Smallwood, 1981, 488, n. 7 suggests that events of the first Parthian war (195) have been dated in the *Chronica* to the second (6–8 of Septimius Severus, 197–9), so that redating the whole

wider conflicts involving the imperial government, we should not characterize this period as one of political quietism. Yet that same Jewish population was either unwilling or unable to motivate the resources and ideological will for full-fledged revolts proclaiming the "liberation of Israel" or the "redemption of Jerusalem."[23]

The Severan period in Roman Palestine is frequently seen by modern scholars as peaceful and as one of excellent relations between the Jewish population of Palestine and the Roman government, and for this Jerome already provides some attestation.[24] A unique inscription (possibly from a temple) that can be dated to approximately 197, in fulfillment of a vow by Jews (reading *[...ex] eukhēs Ioudaiōn*), records a dedication "for the salvation of

---

cluster places the Jewish Samaritan war in 194, and Smallwood dates it to just after the defeat of Niger. Alon, 1953–7, 2, 95–103, also redates this entry, and sees it as a misconstrued reflex of events in the revolt of Niger. In addition, as worded in the *Chronica*, the war could be one between Samaritans and Jews (as already Orosius 7.17.3, *CSEL* 5, 474), or, as Alon prefers, a conflict in which Jews and Samaritans cooperated, with Septimius Severus against Niger, in the context of the revolt of Niger.

[23] Such were the legends on the coins of the first revolt (L. Kadman, *CNP* III pp. 96–8), and the legends of the coins and the dating formulae of the documents of the second revolt (coins: L. Mildenberg, *The Coinage of the Bar Kokhba War* [Araau: Sauerländer, 1984]; documents: *DJD* II, and Y. Yadin, "Expedition D [to the Judean Desert]," *IEJ* 11 [1961], 37–52; idem, "Expedition D [to the Judean Desert]," *IEJ* 12 [1962], 227–57). Isaac, 1990, 88–9 took a reference to Marcus Aurelius having been accosted by Jews (Ammianus Marcellinus, *Res Gestae*, 22.5.5 [for the text, which requires emendation, see Stern, 1976–84, 2, 607]), together with the mention of the brigand Claudius under Septimius Severus in Dio 75.2.4, as examples of references, preserved only "accidentally," to violence in Palestine (and in the East more generally) and otherwise not regularly discussed in classical authors, and giving the general "impression of strife and turmoil." This seems overstated in the case of the story about the Jews under Marcus Aurelius (where at most Jews appear to have taken advantage of the presence of the emperor to voice grievances). Even widespread, politically motivated brigandage in Palestine (see Isaac, 1990, 82–9), however, is not the same as full-scale revolt. If violence under Gallus in 351 was, properly speaking, a widely supported "revolt" and not more limited and localized unrest, Palestine at any rate saw more than two hundred years without such activity. For the episode see Avi-Yonah, 1976, 176–81; S. Lieberman, "Palestine in the Third and Fourth Centuries," *JQR* 36 (1946), 340–1 (Patricius was possibly a pagan officer; "a local insignificant incident of a Roman usurper supported by some of the Jews," p. 341); J. Geiger, "The Last Jewish Revolt against Rome: A Reconsideration," *SCI* 5 (1979/80), 250–7 (possibly a Roman usurper).

[24] Graetz, 1893, 207, following nineteenth-century conventions of Roman historiography (the volume was first published in 1866), saw the philosophical Marcus Aurelius as the last of the good emperors, and Commodus as initiating a string of wicked and bloodthirsty emperors. Alon, 1953–7, 103–7, 113–25, takes the period as an ideal one in ancient Jewish history, in which, notably, Jewish institutions of self-government achieved recognition from Rome. See also Avi-Yonah, 1976, 39–44; Levine, in T. Baras, *et al.* eds. *Eretz Israel from the*

our lords, emperors, caesars ...," and lists the members of the royal family.[25] It has sometimes been argued that in the wake of the revolt under Hadrian the Jews were displaced from the urban governments of the cities of Palestine, particularly from the administration of Sepphoris and Tiberias in Galilee.[26] The argument is dependent upon explicitly pagan coin iconography on city coins, and takes for granted what Jews would have been willing to depict on their coins, and is thus hardly decisive. If such a policy existed, a law (or laws) of Severus and Caracalla which grants Jews permission to serve in civil governments and requires them to perform liturgies might be taken as its reversal.[27] If, in the early years of the third century, Jews did control the civic government of Sepphoris, two coin types from the reign of Caracalla proclaiming the city the loyal friend and ally of Rome, would provide striking

---

Destruction of the Second Temple to the Muslim Conquest [Hebrew] (Jerusalem: Yad Izhak ben-Zvi, 1982), 94–8; S. Applebaum, *Judaea in Hellenistic and Roman Times* (SJLA 40: Leiden: Brill, 1989), 143–54 ("Syria-Palaestina as a Province of the Severan Empire"); A. Oppenheimer, *Galilee in the Mishnaic Period* [Hebrew] (Jerusalem: Zalman Shazar, 1991), 60–6. In taking this view of the Severan emperors these historians are following Jerome, who reported that the Jews referred the "little help" in Dan 11:34 either to Julian or to Septimius Severus and Caracalla *qui Iudaeos plurimum dilexerunt* ("who most of all held the Jews dear") (Jerome, *Com. in Dan. CCSL* 75a 923–4; more cryptic Rabbinic sources, such as those relating to "Antoninus" and R. Judah the Patriarch, are also cited to show the mutual support of Jews and the Severan emperors). See also *SHA Septimius Severus* 17.1: On his way through Palestine to Alexandria Severus "founded many rights (?) (*plurima iura fundavit*) for the Palestinians," while also prohibiting conversion to Christianity or Judaism. Severus Alexander is said to have preserved the privileges of the Jews (*SHA Severus Alexander* 22.4).

[25] *CIJ* 972, L. Roth-Gershon, *The Greek Inscriptions from the Synagogues in Eretz-Israel* [Hebrew] (Jerusalem: Yad Izhak ben Zvi, 1987), no. 30 (p. 125). For the argument that the text stems from a pagan site see H. Kohl, C. Watzinger, *Antike Synagogen in Galilaea* (Leipzig: J. C. Hinrichs, 1916), 209–10.

[26] A. H. M. Jones, "The Urbanization of Palestine," *JRS* 22 (1931), 18–35 (and again in idem, *The Greek City From Alexander to Justinian* [Oxford: Oxford, 1940], 80–2; idem, *Cities of the Eastern Roman Empire*, rev. ed. M. Avi-Yonah *et al.* [Oxford: Clarendon, 1971], 277–8). See also M. Avi-Yonah, 1976, 46f; idem, *The Holy Land*, rev. ed. (Grand Rapids: Baker, 1977), 111–2. It is difficult to date this transfer of power, if such it was, to the aftermath of the Bar Kokhba war, since the first coin of Tiberias to bear a tetrastyle temple with a seated god dates from the years 118–23 (depending on the beginning of the urban era, see M. Avi-Yonah, "The Foundation of Tiberias," *IEJ* 1 [1950–1], 160–9; A. Kindler, *The Coins of Tiberias* [Tiberias: Hammat Tiberias, 1961], 49), and therefore predates the revolt.

[27] D 50.2.3.3 (Ulpian citing a law of Severus and Caracalla); cf. D 27.1.15.6 (Modestinus) (on the duties of Jews to undertake guardianships and liturgies). Avi-Yonah, 1976, 46–7, dates the restoration of Jewish control in Tiberias to sometime in the second century, and certainly to the period of R. Judah the Patriarch, to which period he also dates the restoration of Sepphoris; although he cites the law of Severus and Caracalla as evidence, his primary support

attestation of the outwardly good relations between that Jewish population and the imperial government.[28]

The redaction of the Mishnah in about the year 200 coincides with the political transformation of Palestine. But these political and military changes had social and religious implications as well. The two wars had left the Jerusalem Temple destroyed and its cult abandoned. The priestly class—a hereditary aristocracy that had ruled Jerusalem, which in turn had dominated all of the province of Judea—was, by 200, on its way to becoming an aristocracy in name alone. Not only was a Roman city built on the site of Jerusalem (Aelia Capitolina), but urbanization progressed in Palestine more generally,[29] and this progress may be expected to have placed power on the local

---

is brought from Rabbinic literature. The specification that Jews were obliged to undertake only those liturgies "which do not transgress their *superstitio*" presupposes a general context for the law (the cities of the empire), and not the particular situation of the Galilean cities with a majority Jewish population. Nor is it clear to what extent this law confirms old custom (which might vary regionally; cf. a law of Constantine from the West, which refers to the old tradition of exemption of Jews from curial duties, *CT* 16.8.3 [321]), and to what extent it legislates a new practice.

[28] A large bronze medallion from the reign of Caracalla added to the now customary legend "holy, autonomous, having right of sanctuary (*asylos*)" the words "loyal, friend and ally of the holy assembled (*synklētos* appears in one type only) Senate and people of Rome (*IER(as) B(oulēs) S(ynklētou) K(ai) D(ēmou) RŌ(maiōn)*)." For the coins see Y. Meshorer, *The City Coins of Eretz-Israel and the Decapolis in the Roman Period* (Jerusalem: Israel Museum, 1984), 36–7. I follow the reading of C. M. Kraay, "Jewish Friends and Allies of Rome," *ANS Museum Notes* 25 (1980), 56–7, against Y. Meshorer, "The Coins of Sephorris (*sic*) as a Historical Source" [Hebrew], *Zion* 43 (1978), 194–9; *idem*, "Sepphoris and Rome," *Greek Numismatics and Archaeology: Essays in Honor of Margaret Thompson* (Brussels: Cultura, 1979), 166–71. Meshorer reads the coins as commemorating a treaty between the holy *boulē* (council) of Sepphoris (which Meshorer further identifies with the Rabbinic Sanhedrin), and the *synklētos* (Senate) and people of Rome. (Meshorer is followed by Y. Ne'eman, "Sepphoris in the Period of the Second Temple, Mishna and Talmud" [Diss. Hebrew University, 1987], 188–9 [Ne'eman has given the expansion for the legend of his no. 10 under no. 9 and of no. 9 under no. 10]; see also E. M. Meyers, "Roman Sepphoris in Light of New Archeological Evidence and Recent Research," in Levine ed., 1992, 327.) This reading seems highly unlikely: for *synklētos boulē* referring to the Roman Senate (in second- and third-century texts, both literary and documentary, and especially in the Severan period), and for the adjective "holy" applied to it, see H. J. Mason, *Greek Terms for Roman Institutions* (*ASP* 13: Toronto: Hakkert, 1974), 121–4. The full expression *hiera boulē synklētos* appears in a context in which it must refer to the Senate of Rome: *IG* XII.1 786 (from Lindos in Rhodes): "By the decrees of the emperors among the gods and of the holy assembled Senate of Rome" (*hypo tōn en theois autokratorōn kai tōn tēs hieras boulēs synklētou dogmatōn*).

[29] See n. 26 above, and Z. Safrai, "Urbanization in Israel in the Greco Roman Period" [Hebrew], in *Meḥqarîm* 5 (1980), 105–29; see *idem*, *The Economy of Roman Palestine* (London: Routledge, 1994), 19–30.

level in the hands of urban elites—a status based on wealth, and hereditary in this period only to the extent that wealth could be maintained between generations[30]—rather than in the centralized hands of a client king, high priest or Roman governor, or their local appointee. The emergence in the third century of synagogues that were institutionalized and architecturally distinctive enough to leave recognizable traces in the archeological record suggests that the localization of power in the Palestinian countryside was mirrored by the rise of local religious institutions.[31] These synagogues, so far as the inscriptions can show, were built, and presumably run, by local lay leaders and not by priests.[32]

3. Rabbis in Palestine.

The rise of the Rabbinic movement during the period between the first and the third centuries is itself symptomatic of the changes in Palestinian Jewish society, since it reflects the emergence of an articulate, self-conscious group of non-priestly sages and disciples who take it upon themselves to collect, guard or construct the tradition of the world of the Temple, and to dictate (with what success we cannot know) the terms of the management of everyday life (e.g., marriage, contracts, torts).[33] Nevertheless, outside of Rabbinic sources we know precious little about Rabbis. It is by no means clear that Palestinian Jewish inscriptions using the title "Rabbi" ("my master") are

---

[30] See P. Garnsey, "Aspects of the Decline of the Urban Aristocracy in the Empire," *ANRW* 2.1 (1974), 229–52.

[31] On third-century synagogues see: D. E. Groh, "The Stratigraphic Chronology of the Galilean Synagogue from the Early Roman Through the Early Byzantine Period (ca. 420 C.E.)," in D. Urman, P. V. M. Flesher, eds. *Ancient Synagogues: Historical Analysis and Archeological Discovery* (SPB 47: Leiden: Brill, 1995), 60–4; see also Y. Tsafrir, "On the Source of the Architectural Design of the Ancient Synagogues of Galilee: A New Appraisal," in Urman, Flesher, 1995, 79–83. These two essays debate the value of the conventional typological dating of synagogues (cf. G. Foerster, "The Ancient Synagogues of Galilee," in L. I. Levine, ed., *Galilee in Late Antiquity* [New York: JTSA, 1992], 289–320), but the significance of the (later) third century seems secure.

[32] For the inscriptions see Lapin, *Text, Money and Law*, Chapter III.A.2; Palestinian epigraphy was also the subject of a paper presented by me at the 1994 SBL/AAR annual meeting. I hope to return to this subject in the near future.

[33] There seems to be little reason to doubt that Rabbis could link their "pedigree" to other non-priestly groups, notably the Pharisees, who predated the destruction of the Temple in 70 CE. Rabbinic traditions link the "patriarchal" house with first-century Gamalielites, who may plausibly be identified with the Gamaliel and Simeon b. Gamaliel known from Acts and from Josephus. The treatment of various legal topics, especially cultic, may stem from controversies from before 70: see, for instance, the preliminary discussions about a controversial Qumran text named *miqṣat maʿaśeh ha-tôrâ* (now published as *DJD* X). However, the connection is

not using an honorific with no specific connection with learning in general or affiliation with the Rabbinic movement in particular.[34] Hence these inscriptions may tell us nothing about the role Rabbis played in the social world of late Roman Palestine. Classical writers who refer to Palestine in this period provide no information about the internal politics and government of the region or its cities, nor, by extension, about the Rabbinic institutions that are the primary concern of this study. To state on the basis of this evidence that Rabbis had no significance in the society of Roman Galilee is, of course, to argue entirely from silence. What is striking, however, is that it is not until the late fourth century that the Patriarch (if this is still to be identified as a "Rabbinic" institution in that period[35]) is referred to by a non-Christian writer, much less a correspondent of someone of the status of Libanius.[36] In Roman legal texts as well, the first unambiguous reference to the Palestinian Patriarch is dated to 392,[37] and it is only from the fourth century

---

not quite as explicit as one might have expected, as S. J. D. Cohen, "The Significance of Yavneh: Pharisees, Rabbis and the End of Jewish Sectarianism," *HUCA* 55 (1984), 36–42, has pointed out. In other words, there existed non-priestly religious groups with claims to authority and greater or lesser appeal (note also Josephus' "fourth philosophy:" *BJ* 2.118; *Ant.* 18.4; and the two *sophistai* who spark an act of pious vandalism against the Temple during Herod's last days: *BJ* 2.248–55; *Ant.* 17.149–163), and a certain amount of continuity between pre- and post-revolt groups. Similarly, synagogues are already attested in first-century Palestine (see L. I. Levine, "The Second Temple Synagogue: The Formative Years," in L. I. Levine, ed., *The Synagogue in Late Antiquity* [Philadelphia and New York: ASOR and JTSA, 1987], 7–31). Nevertheless, sectarian disputes and localized religious gathering places in the period before 66–70 arose in the interstices of a firmly entrenched Temple-based piety.

[34] S. J. D. Cohen, "Epigraphical Rabbis," *JQR* 72 (1981), 1–17; see also H. Lapin, *ABD* s.v. "Rabbi;" and the section of *Text, Money and Law* cited above, n. 29.

[35] For the separation of the "Rabbinic" Sanhedrin from the "secular" patriarchate see Alon, 1953–7, 148–51; A. Oppenheimer, "*Batei Midrash* in the Early Amoraic Period" [Hebrew], *Cathedra* 8 (1978), 80. Cf. H. Mantel, *Studies in the History of the Sanhedrin* (*Harvard Semitic Series* 17: Cambridge: Harvard, 1961), 244–52, who argues against Alon's basic thesis of conflict (and subsequent division) between these two institutions, although the passages cited to show that fourth-century Patriarchs "were anything but mediocre" (p. 252, by which Mantel apparently refers to their quality as Rabbinic sages), do not address the problem: these nearly all refer to the Patriarchs' secular wisdom and political clout, but not the study of Torah. As Alon himself notes, however, the division should not be made too sharply. Although Epiphanius, *Panarion*, 30.7.2–3 (*GCS* 25, 342), can report on the immorality of the lifestyle of the young patriarch (cf. Jerome, *Com. in Esaiam* (3.4, *CCSL* 73, 49), he also knows that what the *apostoloi* of the patriarch do is sit with him regularly, night and day (cf. Josh. 1:8; Ps. 1:3), "in order to advise and report (?) to him according to the law (*dia to symbouleuein kai anapherein autō kata ton nomon*)," 30.4.2 (*GCS* 25, 338).

[36] Libanius, *Epistulae* 917, 973, 974, 1084, 1097, 1098, 1105. See also the letter of the emperor Julian to the Jews (*Ad communitatem Iudaeorum*), who is writing in his official capacity as emperor, and in any case is more properly regarded as "post-Christian" than "pagan."

that we can point to evidence for Patriarchs controlling the Jewish communities in Palestine and beyond.[38] By this time, the position of Jews had become complicated by the fact that the existence of semi-autonomous Jewish

---

The emperor refers to the patriarch as "my brother Ioulos the venerable patriarch." For questions as to the authenticity of this letter see Stern, 1976–84, 2, 508–10. See also the putative "letter of Hadrian" cited in *SHA Quadriga Tyrannorum* 8.4, which refers to a "patriarch," apparently "the" Jewish Patriarch. Syme, 1971, 17–29 ("*Ipse ille patriarcha*"), has persuasively dated this "letter" to the late fourth century.

[37] *CT* 16.8.8 (Theodosius, Arcadius, Honorius, 392): *primates* who hold authority from the renowned and illustrious (*viri clarissimi et inlustres*) patriarchs are upheld as the only ones able to expel Jews from the community. More problematic is the law of Constantine (dated 329–30) which seems to be preserved in two versions: *CT* 16.8.2 (to the praetorian prefect) and 16.8.4 (to the leaders of the Jewish communities). The first ("public") version grants exemption from curial duties to "those who with total dedication have devoted themselves to the synagogue of the Jews, to the patriarchs or to the elders, and living in the aforementioned sect preside over the very law." These "patriarchs" are best taken as local officials (cf. *CT* 16.8.13 [397] in which those subject to the "illustrious patriarchs" are termed "archisynagogues, patriarchs, presbyters and others;" A. Linder, "The Roman Imperial Government and the Jews under Constantine" [Hebrew], *Tarbiz* 44 [1974–5], 119–20, following Mommsen and others, recommends emendation or excision of the second "patriarchs"). If Linder, 1974–5, 123–6, is correct that the goal of Constantine in *CT* 16.8.2, 4 is to institutionalize a Jewish "clergy" parallel in some respects to the Christian hierarchy (cf. the more explicit notice in *CT* 16.8.13), might not a localized "diocesan," rather than a highly centralized model be presupposed? Similarly, another law of Constantine, in which the emperor informs "the Jews, their great men (*maiores*), and patriarchs," to know that the persecution of converts is prohibited (*CT* 16.8.1; *CJ* 1.9.3), seems again to refer to local officials (i.e., to the Jews in their communities, however they are governed). For the so-called "minor patriarchs" (i.e., local synagogue officials by that title) see J. Juster, *Les Juifs dans l'empire romain* (Paris, 1914), I 402–5, with A. M. Rabello, "The Legal Condition of the Jews in the Roman Empire," *ANRW* 2.13 (1979), 717, n. 230. See also Mantel, 1961, 203–6, and n. 219. The existence of these local patriarchs has been denied: see Linder, 1974–5, 119–20; *idem, The Jews in Roman Imperial Legislation* (Detroit: Wayne State, 1987) 130, n. 12 ("highly conjectural").

In *CJ* 3.13.3 (293) Diocletian issues a rescript to one Iuda ruling that the decision of an unofficial judge chosen by the parties does not have the authority of a verdict by an official judge. Some scholars have taken this rescript as addressed to the Patriarch Judah III, and as supporting the authority of the patriarch alone to appoint official judges (see the literature cited in Linder, 1987, 114–7; and L. I. Levine, "The Patriarch (Nasi) in Third Century Palestine," *ANRW* 2.19.2 [1979], 682–3). The identification of this Iuda with the Patriarch cannot be proven, however (G. Alon, "Those Appointed for Money" [Hebrew], in Alon, 1976], 2, 55–7 [Appendix] = *idem*, 1977, 433–5), and this piece of information is probably best left out of consideration. Even granting the identification, however, it is not clear that this rescript is intended to bolster Patriarchal authority rather than weaken it: Diocletian might consider all Rabbinic verdicts as merely private arbitration.

[38] Cf. the account of the *comes* Joseph in Epiphanius, *Panarion*, 30.11.1–5 (*GCS* 25, 346) (written in the 370s about events taking place considerably earlier): Joseph is sent by the patriarch to collect the patriarchal tax in Cilicia, and while there exercises his authority to depose

communities in the Roman empire constituted not only an administrative problem but a theological one as well, so that it is difficult to retroject information pertaining to this late period to earlier centuries.[39]

For the second and third centuries, the period during which the Mishnah was produced, we are on far shakier ground. If the Jewish teachers of Justin Martyr's *Dialogue with Trypho* are not merely Justin's invention building on New Testament polemic, they might perhaps be identified with the Rabbinic movement, although in that case we learn primarily about opposition by Rabbis to Christianity and only indirectly, if at all, about their organization and history.[40] Of greater importance is the testimony of Origen from the first half of the third century. Origen mentions Jewish traditions that sound like Rabbinic teachings, even if they cannot be precisely identified, suggesting that Rabbinic teaching was spreading beyond a limited circle of disciples and adherents.[41] More problematic are his references to individuals "styled wise (*sophos*) among the Jews," and especially to a "patriarch" named Ioullos, who has frequently been identified with a member of the patriarchal

---

communal officials. (For the *apostolē* tax cf. Julian's letter to the community of the Jews; it is referred to in *CT* 16.8.14 [399], and in *CT* 16.8.29 [429] it is called *aurum coronarium*. Eusebius, *Com. in Esaiam*, to 18:1 [*PG* 24, 212–3], refers to apostles with encyclical letters, but not collecting taxes [cf. also Jerome, *Com. in ep. ad Gal.*, *PL* 26, 335]. This patriarchal tax is not referred to directly in Rabbinic literature. For attempts to connect it with Rabbinic accounts of visits to the diaspora for a variety of reasons see Graetz, 1853–76, 442–5; 1893, 482–4; Alon, 1953–7, 1, 147, 156–8, 313)

[39] It is at least in part for this reason that Jews (and their leaders) emerge as a topic for legislation after Constantine. See the table of laws regarding Jews listed in Linder, 1987, 91–4: of sixty-six laws cited, only six precede the reign of Constantine.

[40] See, for instance, Justin, *Dialogue with Trypho* 112.4–5 in which Justin attacks the teachers of the Jews for their (very Rabbinic-sounding) exegeses of Scripture that misperceive the truth of the Bible, and connects these teachers with those called "Rabbi," but with explicit citation of the polemics against the Pharisees in Matthew 23. S. J. D. Cohen, 1984, accepts the identification of these teachers with Rabbis (p. 52 and n. 70) and argues that the depiction by Justin of an orthodoxy among Jews (pp. 34–5, 49) reflects an emerging Rabbinic ideology whose origins Cohen traces to the Yavnean period.

[41] Origen, Commentary to Song of Songs, Prologue, *GCS* 8, 62, who mentions Jewish rules not to teach certain passages of the Bible freely (cf. *m. Ḥag.* 2:1 and related texts). If the reference to *deuterōseis* properly means Rabbinic traditions (i.e., to the Hebrew *mišnâ/mišneh*, cf. Epstein, *Siprût*, 17–18), this particular passage, which comes down to us only in a fourth-century Latin translation, appears garbled since in context *deuterōseis* refers to passages in Scripture (*omnes scripturas ... tradi pueris, simul et eas quas deuterōseis apellant ad ultimum ... observare*, "all the Scriptures ... are given to children, while those they call *deuterōseis* ... they guard until the end"). (N. M. R. de Lange, *Origen and the Jews* [Cambridge: Cambridge University, 1976], 163, n. 66. For Origen's knowledge of Rabbinic tradition see de Lange, 1976, *passim*, and, in addition, R. Kimelman, "Rabbi Yohanan and Origen on the Song of Songs: A

family.[42] Of all the evidence for Rabbis and Rabbinic institutions in Origen's writing, however, the most tantalizing is his description of how the "ethnarch" managed to carry out judgments and death penalties with the tacit approval of the Roman authorities.[43] This account suggests the emergence, by the middle 240's (i.e., when Origen himself was living in Palestine, if Origen's claim to have personal knowledge of such events be taken

---

Third-Century Disputation," *HTR* 73 [1980], 567–89. For a rather less confident assessment about the connections between Rabbis and Origen see R. Brooks, "Straw Dogs and Scholarly Ecumenism: The Appropriate Jewish Background for the Study of Origen," in C. Kannengiessen, W. L. Petersen, eds., *Origen of Alexandria: His World and Legacy* [Notre Dame: University of Notre Dame, 1988], 63–95.) For *deuterōsis* as Rabbinic tradition in later Patristic literature, see Epiphanius, *Panarion* 15.2.1; 33.9.4; 42.11 (*GCS* 25, 209–10, 459; 31, 135–6); Jerome, *Com. in Abacuc* 1 (to 2:15) (*CCSL* 76A, 610) which refers to a tradition transmitted by one "who was called wise (*sapiens*) ... and *deuterōtēs* ("repeater" cf. Aramaic *tanāʾ*)" by the Jews; *Epistulae* 121 (*CSEL* 56, 48–9); *Com. in Esaiam* 3 (to Is. 8:11–5) (*CCSL* 73, 116) (these passages use the names of Rabbis that could only come from some passing knowledge of Rabbinic tradition). By the middle of the sixth century, Justinian could prohibit the use of *deuterōsis* in the context of a ruling on the use of translations in the synagogue (Justinian, *Novellae* 146.1 [553]), which, if the identification with Rabbinic literature is correct, suggests that the teachings of the Rabbis had assumed a liturgical role in synagogues (cf. Jerome, *Epistulae* 121, already cited, in which he refers to "most wise chiefs" [*praepositi sapientissimi*] of the synagogue in the same passage as he discusses *deuterōseis*, but their job is to rule on the menstrual impurity of virgins, and not to run the synagogue).

[42] de Lange, 1976, 23–4, questions whether Ioullos the patriarch (*Frag. Com. on Psalms*, *PG* 12, 1056) should be identified with the Rabbinic patriarch; and tentatively suggests an Alexandrian provenance for the reference; cf. M. Goodman, "The Roman State and the Jewish Patriarch in the Third Century," in Levine, ed., 1992, 132, "an apparently local sage in Caesarea." See further, de Lange, 1976, 23–8, 33–4, for references to "those called sages." One particular passage deserves mentioning: the reference to "a learned Hebrew styled by them the son of a sage, brought up to succeed his father" (*Ep. ad Afric.* 7, *PG* 9, 61–3), suggesting an institutionalized hereditary transmission of the status of sage, which, if this sage is a Rabbi, sheds light on the institutional development of the movement. See G. Alon, "The Sons of Sages" [Hebrew], 1976, 2, 58–73 = *idem*, 1977, 436–57.

[43] Origen, *Ep. ad Afric.* 14 (*PG* 11, 81–4). See M. Goodman, *State and Society in Roman Galilee* (*Oxford Centre for Postgraduate Hebrew Studies*: Totowa: Rowman and Allanheld, 1983), 115–6; *idem*, 1992, 128–9, 132. In this passage Origen writes that the ethnarch is like a king; elsewhere, he is at pains to object to a similar claim made by Jews that the scepter has not left Judah, and that the ethnarch is the Jewish king (*De principiis* 4.1.3, *GCS* 5, 297).

[44] The chronology of Origen's life is a subject of dispute, but the letter to Africanus seems to be datable to approximately 243 or 244 (R. P. C. Hanson, *Origen's Doctrine of Tradition* [London: SPCK, 1954], 15; cf. H. Crouzel, *Origen*, tr. A. S. Worall [San Francisco: Harper and Row, 1989], 231: before 244; cf. P. Nautin, *Origène: sa vie et son oeuvre* [Paris, 1977], 182, shortly before the persecution of 249–250), and Origen had been in Caesarea since at least 238 (so, Hanson, 1954, 4; Crouzel, 1989, 2–3, puts this in 233; Nautin, 1977, 431–2, in 234–5).

seriously[44]), of the Patriarch as a powerful local figure on the Palestinian political scene. It goes beyond the evidence, however, to argue that in this period the Patriarch was the local ruler of the Jews appointed or officially recognized by Rome.[45]

As a result, while it seems likely that by the early third century (specifically, in the writings of Origen), Rabbis (and particularly their primary patron, the Ethnarch or Patriarch) had become prominent in Palestinian society, it is difficult to trace their history or to gauge their religious or political authority. Indeed, with the exception of Origen, Rabbis are almost invisible. On the basis of Rabbinic texts (problematic though they may be) it is possible to argue that Rabbis in the late second and early third centuries were relatively wealthy and that the locus of their activities (e.g., preaching, judging, teaching) and institutions was increasingly the cities of Palestine.[46] It also appears likely that throughout late antiquity Rabbinic authority continued to be unofficial and limited to adherents whose number and social distribution we are in no position to estimate. Rabbinic texts polemicize against other, non-Rabbinic judges ("those who are appointed for money") who have been plausibly identified with the official civic judges of the Galilean cities.[47] Rabbinic narratives about cases judged by Rabbis may similarly be taken regularly as cases of arbitration by a holy (or otherwise significant) man.[48]

On balance, then, there is very little positive evidence that Rabbis served as the governing body of Roman Palestine, or even the class which provided the staff for that government. Such evidence as we do have actually suggests the opposite: that Rabbis at the time of the redaction of the Mishnah (and later) may have been a prominent wealthy group with claims to special authority, but they had little institutional authority and no official standing. In this respect, they may have been like other (frequently religious) figures in the ancient Greco-Roman world who served as judges, miracle workers and

---

[45] Goodman, 1992, 131–4; cf. Levine, 1979, who although he does not necessarily regard the Patriarch as the creation of Rome (p. 679), still sees the Patriarch as "the undisputed representative" of the Jews to the Romans (p. 658).

[46] On Rabbinic wealth in the Tannaitic period see S. J. D. Cohen, "The Place of the Rabbi in Jewish Society of the Second Century," in Levine ed., 1992, 157–73, and below Ch. II, n. 252. For urbanization see Levine, 1989, 23–42; see also Lapin, *Text, Money and Law*, Chapter III.B.1.

[47] G. Alon, "Those Appointed for Money," in Alon, 1976, 2, 15–57 = idem, 1977, 374–435. See also A. Büchler, *The Political and Social Leaders of the Jewish Community in Sepphoris in the Second and Third Centuries* (Oxford: Clarendon, 1909), passim.

[48] See Lapin, *Text, Money and Law*, Chapter III.B.2, and Appendix III. This was the subject of a paper presented by me at the 1994 annual meeting of the Association for Jewish Studies; I hope to return to this topic in the near future.

arbiters of public opinion.[49] Nor does it seem likely that Rabbinic law as such (for our purposes we may focus on the Mishnah) served as the legal code of the Jewish population of Roman Palestine.

B. Methodology

The preceding survey of the evidence for the political history of Palestine and for the place of Rabbis in it has important implications for the historiography of Roman-period Palestine. Palestinian Rabbinic texts are the richest source for the cultural and social history of Roman Palestine (especially Galilee). From the perspective of ethnic and provincial history in the Roman empire, this literature is of particular importance because it constitutes a cluster of expressions of a non-Greek- or Latin-speaking culture that is highly interested in the boundaries between "Israel" and "the gentiles." Moreover, from the point of view of the history of Judaism, the emergence and the rise to prominence of this movement were epoch-making: the Rabbinic movement and its literature came, ultimately, to define the religious, cultural and intellectual history of nearly all Jewish communities. Yet, as has already been suggested, it is difficult if not impossible to use Rabbinic sources to construct a narrative history in the conventional sense either of Roman Palestine or of Rabbis. In addition, Rabbinic legal texts cannot be taken in any simple way to describe what people did. The argument of this study of *m. Baba' Meṣi'a'* is therefore that in order to understand Rabbinic texts in the context of their social and historical background in a way that elucidates that context, and that does not merely presuppose the "givenness" of that background, it is crucial to come to terms with those texts as literature. That is to say, first, that the Mishnah, like other Rabbinic texts, is a literary artifact (and, moreover, one that was not simply authored, but was redacted out of other material, at least in part) and it is essential to try to understand the mechanics of how and by whom it was produced, and how it works as a piece of literature. Second, the statements that the tractate makes about the world (for our purposes, particularly about such matters as property and contracts) are embedded in a "poetics" that constructs relationships

---

[49] For a later period see the classic essay by P. Brown, "The Rise and Function of the Holy Man in Late Antiquity," in *Society and the Holy in Late Antiquity* (Berkeley: University of California, 1982), 103–52. More roughly contemporaneous with our period is Plotinus. See, e.g., Porphyry, *Life of Plotinus* 9, in which the philosopher is said to have acted as arbitrator and as guardian for children; 10, the imperviousness of Plotinus to magic; 11, his ability to discover thieves and to predict the future.

between people in a particular way.⁵⁰ This means that part of the historical investigation of *m. Baba' Meṣiʿaʾ* involves exploring the elusive boundaries between the real world in which Rabbis lived and the constructed one of the Mishnah. It is in these ways that the Mishnah is a "historical" document. The following sections discuss these matters more fully in light of modern study of the Mishnah.

1. The Mishnah as a literary artifact.

The modern study of Rabbinic literature and society, including the Mishnah, has a long history, and one that cannot be surveyed here. In the first place, the undertaking is vast and deserves (and has produced) study in its own right in the context of the intellectual history of modern Europe. The western academic "invention" of ancient Judaism is closely tied to the political and intellectual forces that shaped the "invention" of such other academic fields as "orientalism," and was frequently carried out by the same people.⁵¹ The same forces informed the parallel construction of Jewish history by Jews for internal Jewish consumption as well as for apologetic purposes.⁵² In addition, the publication in recent decades of major study tools addressing this history make a detailed bibliographical review redundant.⁵³ However, to the extent that these very works are the product of ongoing, overlapping debates that have shaped the critical agenda of the study of

---

⁵⁰ Cf. the rather different view taken in the introductory section of Z. Safrai, 1994.

⁵¹ See E. Said, *Orientalism* (New York: Pantheon, 1978). To take one example of the interpenetration of "orientalism" and the study of Judaism among gentile scholars, J. Wellhausen wrote seminal studies on the Hebrew Bible, ancient Jewish history, and the origins of Islam: e.g., *Prolegomena to the History of Israel*, tr. J. S. Black, A. Menzies (Edinburgh: A. and C. Black, 1885); idem, *Die Pharasäer und die Sadducäer* (Greifswald, 1874); idem, *The Arab Kingdom and its Fall*, tr. M. G. Weir (London: Curzon, 1973); idem, *The Religio-Political Factions in Early Islam*, tr. R. C. Ostle, S. M. Waltzer (Amsterdam: North Holland, 1975).

⁵² The intellectual background is discussed in J. M. Harris, *Nachman Krochmal: Guiding the Perplexed of the Modern Age* (New York: NYU, 1991), 210–34 and was developed more fully in a paper given at the Columbia University Seminar on Israel and Jewish Studies (1990), which I have not seen in print.

⁵³ J. Neusner, ed., *The Modern Study of the Mishnah* (SPB 23: Leiden: E. J. Brill, 1975), surveys the major nineteenth- and early twentieth-century Jewish scholars on the Mishnah. See also J. Neusner, ed., *The Study of Ancient Judaism* (New York: Ktav, 1981), 2 vols., incorporating, in volume 2, two important essays by B. M. Bokser ("An Annotated Bibliographical Guide to the Study of the Palestinian Talmud") and D. Goodblatt ("The Babylonian Talmud") first published in *ANRW* 2.19.2 (1979), 139–256, 257–336 respectively; Strack, Stemberger, 1992; S. Safrai, ed., *The Literature of the Sages* (CRINT 3: Philadelphia and Assen: Fortress and Van Gorcum, 1987).

ancient Judaism as a field, a discussion of some of the critical issues raised by these debates is essential.

To be sure, scholarship that challenged the world view of the Rabbinic sources and its latter-day guardians is not a new phenomenon. Nineteenth-century (and later) Christian scholars tended to be interested in *Spätjudentum* ("late Judaism") only to the extent that it helped explicate Christian origins,[54] and tended to treat it as a rather static, stultifying system of "works-righteousness" which the liberating Christ-event and Paul's (or Luther's) doctrines of faith, grace, and salvation came to undo.[55] Jewish scholars, such as I. M. Jost or A. Geiger, might have been prepared to doubt the veracity or historicity of Rabbinic sources, the nobility of Rabbinic intentions, the authority of Rabbis as a religious elite, or the value of Rabbinic piety, in part as a critique of contemporaneous Jewish institutions.[56] In retrospect, however, neither became pivotal figures in framing the critical historical study of Judaism by Jews (although in the case of Geiger such a role would have been well deserved). Instead, it was the more conservative representatives of the *Wissenschaft des Judentums* school such as L. Zunz, Z. Frankel and H. Graetz who came to define the study of Judaism.[57]

---

[54] See, e.g., the massive commentary, H. Strack, P. Billerbeck, *Kommentar zum Neuen Testament aus Talmud und Midrasch* (Munich, 1922–8), which still frequently serves as the sole repository of Rabbinic knowledge for students of the New Testament.

[55] See, e.g., Wellhausen, 1885, in which the late dating of P and the distinction between "natural" Israelite religion and Judaism presupposes this world view; E. Schürer, *A History of the Jewish People in the Age of Jesus Christ*, tr. J. Macpherson *et al.* (Edinburgh: T. and T. Clark, 1885–91), 2.2, 90–128. See the critical discussion by G. F. Moore, "Christian Writers on Judaism," *HTR* 14 (1921), 197–254, and E. P. Sanders, *Paul and Palestinian Judaism* (Philadelphia: Fortress, 1977), 34–59. The same model informs M. Hengel, *Judaism and Hellenism*, tr. J. Bowden (Philadelphia: Fortress, 1974), 1, 308–9, who locates Jews' fixation on the law (which made Judaism forever unable to critique itself) in the repudiation of Hellenistic reform in the second century BCE.

[56] I. M. Jost, *Geschichte des Israeliten* (Berlin, 1820–47); A. Geiger, *Urschrift und Übersetzungen der Bibel* (Breslau: Julius Hainauer, 1857) = *Ha-miqrāʾ we-targûmāyw*, tr. Y. L. Baruk from second ed. (1928) (Jerusalem: Bialik, 1949); idem, *Das Judenthum und seine Geschichte* = *Judaism and Its History*, tr. C. Newburgh (New York: Bloch, 1911). See, on Jost, S. W. Baron, *History and Jewish Historians*, ed. A. Hertzberg, L. A. Feldman (Philadelphia: JPS, 1964), 240–63; I. Schorsch, "Ideology and History in the Age of Emancipation," in H. Graetz, *The Structure of Jewish History and Other Essays*, tr., ed. I. Schorsch (New York: JTSA, 1975), 7 n. 11; Harris, 1991, 214–26.

[57] For the emergence of the *Wissenschaft des Judentums* school, see Schorsch, 1975, 1–62, and idem, "Breakthrough into the Past: The Verein für Kultur und Wissenschaft der Juden," *Leo Baeck Institute Yearbook* 33 (1988), 2–28. N. Rotenstreich, *Tradition and Reality: The Impact of History on Modern Jewish Thought* (New York: Random House, 1974). G. Scholem, "The Science of Judaism—Then and Now," in *The Messianic Idea in Judaism* (New York: Schocken, 1971), 304–13.

What does characterize recent research, however, is an increase in methodological studies exploring and rethinking the compositional and redactional strategies that produced the Rabbinic texts, and, by extension, the historical circumstances in which the texts emerged and were propagated.[58] Through a series of brilliant, but hotly contested, studies addressing literary questions, openly borrowing from New Testament form and redactional criticism, and appealing to anthropological (generally structuralist and symbolist) models, Jacob Neusner has sparked an important and frequently acrimonious debate on method.[59] By challenging assumptions about the history of the traditions behind Rabbinic texts, religious motivations behind their production, the historicity of anecdotal and narrative traditions, and the normativity and authority of legal materials, Neusner has also been a focal figure, although certainly neither the first nor the only one, in subverting the enterprise of the historical reconstruction of Rabbis and Palestinian society on the basis of literary evidence.[60]

---

[58] S. Friedman, *A Critical Study of* Yevamot X *With a Methodological Introduction* (Jerusalem: JTSA, 1978); D. W. Halivni, "Methods of the Study of the Talmud," *JJS* 30 (1979), 192–201; P. Schäfer, "Research into Rabbinic Literature: An Attempt to Define the Status Quaestionis," *JJS* 37 (1986) 139–52; C. Milikowsky, "The *Status Quaestionis* of Research in Rabbinic Literature," *JJS* 39 (1988), 208–11; P. Schäfer, "Once Again, the Status Quaestionis of Research in Rabbinic Literature: An Answer to Chaim Milikowsky," *JJS* 40 (1989), 89–94.

[59] Neusner's most important work on the Mishnah remains his twenty-two volume *A History of the Mishnaic Law of Purities* (SJLA 6: Leiden: Brill, 1974–7). Among other publications, J. Neusner, *Method and Meaning in Ancient Judaism*, first series (BJS 10: Missoula: Scholars, 1979); second series (BJS 15: Missoula: Scholars, 1980); third series (BJS 16: Chico: Scholars, 1980); fourth series (BJS 168: Atlanta: Scholars, 1989), has been used as a forum for exploration of methodological themes (as well as polemics). Neusner's students have also been instrumental in bringing methodological questions to the forefront of the historiographical and literary debates. See. e.g., B. M. Bokser, "Talmudic Form Criticism," *JJS* 31 (1980), 46–60; idem, ed., *Jewish History: The Next Ten Years* (BJS: Chico: Scholars, 1980); W. S. Green, ed. *Law as Literature, Semeia* 25 (1983). The essay "The Abominations of Leviticus" in M. Douglas, *Purity and Danger* (London: Routledge, 1966), 41–57 has had a particularly strong influence on writings about Rabbinic classification of the world (male-female, pure-impure): see, for instance J. Neusner, *The Idea of Purity in Ancient Judaism* (SJLA 1: Leiden, Brill, 1973) with a rejoinder by Douglas herself. Douglas' emphasis on the "anomalous" finds explicit echo in the work of a student of Neusner's, J. R. Wegner, *Chattel or Person?* (Oxford: Oxford, 1988), 168–81.

[60] See, for instance, the transition between J. Neusner, *A Life of R. Yohanan b. Zakkai* (SPB 6: Leiden: Brill, 1962) and idem, 1977, which reworks much the same material, but now traces *The Development of a Legend*, and is no longer a biography. Neusner, *Judaism: The Evidence of the Mishnah* (*Chicago Studies in the History of Judaism*: Chicago: Chicago, 1981), 5–14, describes Neusner's rejection of the characterization of Rabbinic Judaism as "normative" (the term is that of G. F. Moore, *Judaism in the First Centuries of the Christian Era*

Critical to Neusner's view of Rabbinic texts is his treatment of each Rabbinic work as a separate document, each with its own "argument."[61] By focusing attention on whole works, this approach provides benchmarks for the emergence of certain topics, kinds of material, and strategies of organization, and therefore serves as an important corrective to a conception of these texts as containing more or less independent crystallizations of "traditions," any of which might be early or late. However, this treatment of the material, and in particular his identification of the Mishnah's argument as "philosophical," raises serious problems. First, what is most important about the Mishnah, for Neusner, is its interest in hierarchical organization of the world and in such problems as the nature of mixtures that, according to his view, it shares with Aristotelian and late antique Stoic philosophical tradition. In making this claim, however, Neusner subordinates to the document as a whole all of its individual contents which are articulated "in an odd idiom" through a discussion of "pots and pans," "matters of no consequence," and "nothing very much."[62] Thus, Neusner's Mishnah is not about that which it appears to talk about. What Neusner has not accounted for is why what he acknowledges precisely as commonplaces of late antique speculation should be transmitted in the form of esoteric knowledge, accessible only to *cognoscenti*, and so deeply submerged in the structure of the Mishnah that it had never been noticed.[63] Moreover, in utilizing terms such as "essay"[64]

[Cambridge: Harvard, 1927]). In this respect Neusner is hardly innovating: see F. C. Porter's review of Moore in *Journal of Religion* 8 (1928), 30–62, esp. 41–4. E. R. Goodenough, *Jewish Symbols in the Greco-Roman Period* (*Bollingen* 27: Princeton: Princeton, 1954–68), 1, 11–23 and elsewhere (who challenged the limits of Rabbinic influence even in Palestine; see further S. J. D. Cohen, 1981, 1–17). P. Schäfer, *Die Bar Kokhba-Aufstand* (Tübingen: Mohr, 1981) is an exemplary exploration into the limits of narrative Rabbinic traditions for the reconstruction of historical events. For D. W. Halivni see below.

[61] See, e.g., J. Neusner, *The Canonical History of Ideas* (South Florida Studies in the History of Judaism 4: Atlanta: Scholars, 1990), 18–39.

[62] J. Neusner, *A Religion of Pots and Pans?* (BJS 156: Atlanta: Scholars, 1988), 73–4, 108–9.

[63] See Neusner, 1988, 125:

By contrast [to Scripture], the Mishnah's writers spoke into the depths, anticipating a more acute hearing than they would ever receive. So the repetitions of Scripture reinforce the message, while the endlessly repeated paradigm of the Mishnah sits too deep in the structure of the system from the ear that lacks acuity or to attain visibility to the untutored eye.

The "Aristotelian character of the Mishnah" eluded no less an Aristotelian than the twelfth-century philosopher Maimonides, who therefore erred grievously in separating Aristotelian philosophy from Talmudic law (J. Neusner, *The Philosophical Mishnah I* [BJS 163: Atlanta: Scholars, 1990], 5).

It is not the "esoteric" quality of the Mishnah itself that is problematic. Indeed, the notion of Rabbis as a group with specialized and exclusive knowledge is a useful one. What is curious in characterizing the arrangement of his philosophical Mishnah and its text, Neusner is drawing an analogy between specialized forms of discourse that are not precisely comparable: the Mishnah is not "prose" in the usual sense of the term,[65] much less a literary construction whose rhetorical success is measured by its ability to lay out an argument and thereby to persuade, but rather is terse and formulaic to the point of near obscurity; the argument is encoded and must be teased out. Nor has Neusner asked who else besides "philosophers" might be interested in exploring the material implications of deeply held and intersecting principles about the nature of the world (e.g., "lawyers"). Second, the Mishnah frequently can be shown to utilize different sources—a fact that, ironically, Neusner's own work substantiates, but from which he fails to draw important conclusions.[66] As a result, despite the overall coherence and unity of the Mishnah, the Mishnah's "argument" is frequently fragmented and occasionally contradictory. Thus, Neusner's treatment of the Mishnah fails to account for the philosophical and literary

---

is the fact that the "philosophical" agenda of Neusner's Mishnah is entirely "exoteric": the hierarchical organization of earthly phenomena through lists (what Neusner terms *Listenwissenschaft*), and the problem of the dissolution of primary elements into mixtures and the possibility of their later separation. Almost entirely absent in the Mishnah is any sense that "Torah" is truly esoteric (except to state that certain portions of Scripture should not be publicly read or translated, or generally expounded, e.g., *m. Meg.* 4:10; *m. Ḥag.* 2:1) or any discussion of those topics such as the nature of the divine, the glory of God or the makeup and hierarchy of the divine household which were, in different ways, the core of certain kinds of Platonic, "gnostic" and later Jewish esoteric traditions. Arguably, the very idiom of the Mishnah betrays not the overriding interest in mixtures and hierarchy of a philosopher, but the virtuosity and ingenuity of the technical specialist in a legal discourse who can use a handful of "principles" to generate a multitude of cases, ever refining, qualifying, and making more explicit their application.

[64] E.g., Neusner, 1988, 74.

[65] Note J. N. Lightstone, "The Rhetoric of the Mishnah and the Emergence of Rabbinic Social Institutions at the End of the Second Century," Paper presented at the SBL Annual Meeting, 1994 [cited with the author's permission].

[66] See further Chapter II. Here it is necessary to point out that when Neusner denies that the traces of original "sources" can be recovered, he seems to refer to the actual traditions formulated by Rabbis to whom material is attributed. See, for instance, J. Neusner, *A History of the Mishnaic Law of Purities: Part XXI, The Redaction and Formulation of the Order of Purities in Mishnah and Tosepta* (SJLA 6: Leiden: Brill, 1977), 316. On the other hand, Neusner is willing to acknowledge not only that material attributed to earlier sages seems to fit different formal characteristics from those that characterize traditions attributed to later Rabbis (1977, 167), but even that tractates were formed out of "already-formed aggregates of cognitive units," whose pre-existence, and occasional dissolution at the hands of the final redactors, Neusner attempts to show (1977, 113–63, explicitly, 124, 158). Thus, Neusner's redactional model (arguably ancient traditions, but actual materials of relatively recent date handled conservatively) is in some respects quite similar to that of Albeck, *Mābô*, 99ff.

implications of an authorial voice that speaks through the words of others. Third, Neusner's emphasis on whole documents as the only framework in which we can identify the meaning of a tradition (until we find it in a later document in which case it has a new, but equally unique, meaning) naively ignores the problem of the indeterminacy and multiplicity of meaning, especially when "true" meaning is hidden deep below the surface.[67] Finally, the emphasis on the document as a unity despite traces of a complex redactional process ignores the social matrix—who produced these texts, how they circulated, how the redaction was carried out—in which the text itself was produced.

These questions inform the conception and organization of Chapter II, which bears a distinct methodological debt to the procedure that Neusner worked out in his *History of Mishnaic Law* series. On the assumption that different tractates may have different histories that may be obscured if analysis centers on specific topics, or on pericopae reflecting certain stylistic or redactional traits, this study centers on one tractate: *m. Babaʾ Meṣiʿaʾ*. Secondly, I attempt to deal seriously with the Mishnah as a literary artifact of late second- and early third-century Roman Galilee. What is important is not only the broad programmatic purpose of the Mishnah (as a cleverly disguised philosophical discourse, or, as others would have it, a law code,[68] or an authorized compendium of legal materials[69]), but also what the Mishnah betrays about its own composition. This attention to redaction, too, follows Neusner's earlier procedure, but is entirely ignored in his work on the order of *Nĕzîqîn* (Damages) in which *Babaʾ Meṣiʿaʾ* appears.[70]

As a result, Chapter II emphasizes the complexity of the Mishnah as a text. In this respect I have been following important contributions to the study of the Mishnah by David Weiss Halivni (building, in turn, on important studies by J. N. Epstein), who has repeatedly identified the complex redactional seams in various Mishnah pericopae.[71] This approach draws critical attention

---

[67] E.g., Neusner, 1988, 24.

[68] Frankel, n.d. (1859), 206; Epstein, *Siprût*, 225; see also D. W. Halivni, *Midrash, Mishnah and Gemara* (Cambridge: Harvard, 1989), 63–88.

[69] I. H. Weis, *Dôr dôr wĕ-doršāyw* (Vienna, 1871) vol. 2, 183, 208–9; H. Graetz, *Geschichte der Jüden* (Vienna, 1853–76), 3 ed. Fr. Rosenthal (Leipzig, 1893), Heb. ed. tr. S. P. Rabinovitz (Warsaw, 1893), vol. 2, 297; Albeck, *Mābôʾ*, 270–83; A. Goldberg, "Purpose and Method in R. Judah Hannasi's Compilation of the Mishnah" [Hebrew], *Tarbiz* 28 (1958–9), 260–69.

[70] J. Neusner, *A History of the Mishnaic Law of Damages*, 5 volumes (SJLA 35: Leiden: Brill, 1982–5). This series has no equivalent to volume 22 of his *History of the Mishnaic Law of Purities* series, cited above, which deals with structure and redaction, or with his treatment of indvidual tractates in that series.

[71] See Epstein, *Nusaḥ* and *Siprût, passim*. Regrettably, Halivni has not devoted a book-length study to the problem of the Mishnah. Brief analyses may be found in his *Mĕqôrôt û-*

to the way in which material has been utilized in the Mishnah. More importantly, it opens the question of the social or ideological background that is reflected by the existence of a multivocal tradition preceding the Mishnah, and of the only partial suppression of that multivocality in the redaction of the Mishnah itself.[72] By concentrating on a single tractate, I wish to bring sustained inquiry to what has been, on Halivni's part, a sporadic undertaking. In tracing redactional processes, my approach differs from that of Halivni primarily in that I tend to emphasize the fluidity and instability of highly stylized transmitted material where Halivni is inclined to see the codification and occasional alteration of authoritative and highly fixed formulations. Thus, for instance, I do not treat material attributed to individual sages (e.g., "Rabbi X says" or "[The above were] the words of Rabbi Y") as the words of these sages.[73] Rather, these statements are stereotyped formulations, taking the form of more or less tightly controlled rhetorical structures that arise in the context of literary production. What this means is that there is no guarantee that we can accurately reconstruct the legal "policy" of any individual sage.[74] Instead, attributed statements present what contemporaneous or later tradents thought a particular sage might have ruled in a given case. In addition, this may mean that statements attributed to particular

---

mĕsôrôt to the orders of Women (*Našîm*) (Tel Aviv: Dvir, 1968), and of Appointed Times (*Môʿēd*), 3 volumes (New York: JTSA, 1975–82); and tractate *Babaʾ Qammaʾ* (Jerusalem: Magnes, 1993). See also *idem*, 1986, 38–65. Halivni has underscored competing theological motivations underlying literary and redactional strategies (Halivni, 1986, 1–8). In his source-critical studies of the Babli, Halivni has stressed the role of the anonymous, redactional hand in altering the meaning of antecedent materials, and thereby challenged the notion that Rabbinic literature simply freezes in time authoritative traditions that can then be mined for a history of ideas. In a recent study of various Mishnah pericopae Halivni has raised a similar problem for students of the Mishnah (D. W. Halivni, "*Mišnôt še-zāzû mi-mĕqômān*," *Sidra* 5 [1989] 63–88). This last article represents something of a methodological break for Halivni since in it he addresses conscious changes to original sources by the redactor of the Mishnah.

[72] See, e.g., Halivni, 1986, 59–61. However, the Mishnah's sources seem to me to be too fragmented, and the stylistic commonalities (whether or not they are imposed by redactors) too consistent to show, at least in *Babaʾ Meṣiʿaʾ*, that identifiable corpora representing specific schools (e.g., "the mishnah of R. Yose") have been utilized. This is the argument of A. Goldberg, 1958–9, 260–9 and worked out in his commentaries to tractates *Šabbat* (*Commentary to the Mishnah Shabbat* [Hebrew] [Jerusalem: JTSA, 1976]) and *ʿErubin* (*The Mishnah Treatise Eruvin* [Hebrew] [Jerusalem: Magnes, 1986]).

[73] This is an insight stressed by Neusner (see, e.g., Neusner, 1981, 17–20). However, I argue against his use of attributed statements as benchmarks for historical development in the final section of Chapter II.

[74] R. Goldenberg, *The Sabbath Law of R. Meir* (BJS 6: Missoula: Scholars, 1978), 181–212.

sages are subject to freer interpretation and manipulation than Halivni sometimes presupposes.[75]

2. The Mishnah as a historical document.

Where this study clearly breaks with the approach laid out by Neusner is in the attempt to deal seriously with the Mishnah as a document shaped by and reflective of a history. That the Mishnah is in some way a response to the destruction of the Jerusalem Temple (70 CE) or the failure of the Bar Kokhba revolt (ca. 132–5) is something of a commonplace. But whereas most proponents of this view treat Rabbinic tradition as generally quite old, and therefore point to "practical" considerations (for instance, to insure that "the tradition" not be forgotten, or to repair losses that arose due to the destructions[76]), Neusner, who denies the existence or relevance of any "tradition" in the Mishnah, makes response to catastrophe the very point of the Mishnah's production. That is, the Mishnah addresses a shattered world with a utopian fantasy of its own creation, in which the Temple still stands, and all society is still properly ordered.[77] What Neusner does not do is locate the production of the Mishnah within the dynamics of a real society. To be sure, he analyzes the interests of the Mishnah into those of priests, scribes, and householders.[78] However, his failure to link this coalition of interests to what we might possibly know about the priests, scribes, and householders within the social world of Roman Galilee makes it impossible to evaluate the

---

[75] Halivni, 1989, 63–70, 69–84, himself makes this argument in connection *m. Šab.*2:1–2 and *m. Ker.*3:1; see also his reference to assertions in *Měqôrôt û-měsôrôt* (in n. 76) about the redactor's hand in manipulating attributed material. In Halivni, 1979, 194–5, Halivni showed the way in which apparently synonymous formulations could replace one another in the transmission of traditions, but still formulated the problem in terms of what R. Gamaliel "originally said" rather than in terms of the transmission history of the tradition.

[76] N. Krochmal, *Môreh něbûkê ha-zěman*, ed. L. Zunz (Lemberg, 1851), 212–7; I. H. Weis, 1871, 2, 41–2; Albeck, *Mābô'*, 82; Halivni, 1986, 58, for example, all attribute early collections of Tannaitic material to the prevention of loss due to political or religious crises. Such interpretations for the codification and transmission of material are not modern inventions. They begin already with *t. ʿEd.* 1:1: "When the sages entered the vineyard at Yabneh they said: 'The time is coming when a person will seek a word from the words of Torah and not find it, from the words of the sages and not find it ... for no one word of Torah is like its fellow. Let us begin with Hillel and Shammai.'" The scriptural exegesis of Amos 8:11–2 that is incorporated here suggests that it is not merely the multiplicity and variety of Torah that is at issue, but also a universal upheaval that has created this deplorable decentralization of Torah.

[77] See, e.g., Neusner, 1981, 25–42; in *idem, Midrash in Context* Philadelphia: Fortress, 1983), 111–25, Neusner uses a similar rationale for explaining the development of post-Mishnaic literature in Byzantine Palestine.

[78] Neusner, 1981, 230–56.

magnitude of the utopian world of the Mishnah.⁷⁹ Neusner assumes, without substantiation, that the suppression of the Bar Kokhba revolt was perceived as the cataclysmic destruction of a messianic hope.⁸⁰ Yet the messianic claims of the revolt have been questioned, and any connection between Rabbis as a group and the revolt is open to doubt.⁸¹ It is more difficult to question the apparently enormous demographic, and therefore cultural and political, consequences of the revolt (see the brief discussion above, section A.2). This means that even if Neusner is correct in seeing the Mishnah as the response to the revolt and its suppression, it is a response to the revolt as a

---

⁷⁹ In connection with priests and scribes Neusner makes a number of unsubstantiated assumptions. While it may be that priests were particularly interested in preserving (or creating) traditions about the temple, there is no necessary reason to believe that all priests were concerned with personal purity, and that therefore the tractates concerned with ritual purity are the "gift of the priests" (see the table in Neusner, 1981, 240), especially since, as Neusner himself argues, the origins of this material may well be among a lay group insisting on ritual purity (pp. 69–71, 225–9; see also *idem, Rabbinic Traditions About the Pharisees Before 70* [Leiden: Brill, 1971], 304–5). So, when Neusner states that "the Mishnah ... speaks for the program of topics important to the priests. It takes up the persona of the scribes, speaking through their voice and in their manner" (Neusner, 1981, 233), we may ask whether those very "priests" are not priests at all but instead those people whom Neusner calls "scribes" who have a "pseudo-priestly" agenda. On the other hand, to ascribe to scribes, and not to priests, an interest in the running of courts is to ignore the political and governmental power of priests in Judea up to the revolt in 66 CE, the last period before the Mishnah in which the political actors can be identified with some ease, and also to forget that priests were never a monolithic body. Neusner might be correct that the Mishnah reflects "priestly" concerns, but he has failed to tell us which priests he means; at any rate "the priests" is almost an empty signifier.

In outlining the interests and concerns of "scribes" (who, according to Neusner, later become "Rabbis") Neusner assumes that the scribes linked with Pharisees in the New Testament (e.g., Mt 23:2) and referred to obliquely in the Mishnah are equivalent to a professional guild of document and list writers (Neusner, 1981, 233), whose contribution to the Mishnah are tractates concerned with documents and courts. Yet Neusner offers no evidence that this should be so. That professional Jewish scribes existed we have no reason to doubt (see *P. Babatha* I; and M5:11). What needs further clarification is that these scribes (a) formed a guild that (b) shared specific religious and political theories.

⁸⁰ E.g., Neusner, 1981, 40–1.

⁸¹ Mildenberg, 1984, 73–6. Schäfer, 1981, 55–67 accepts the messianic character of the revolt—attested in Rabbinic and Christian tradition—while noting the limitations of the Rabbinic evidence for this (cf. *idem*, "Rabbi Aqiba and Bar Kokhba," in *Approaches to Ancient Judaism II*, ed. W. S. Green [Chico: Scholars, 1980], 117–9), and the absence of any explicit evidence for messianic connections in the documents and coins of the revolt itself. See also D. Goodblatt, "The Title *Nasi*ʾ and the Ideological Background of the Second Revolt" [Hebrew], in A. Oppenheimer, U. Rappaport, eds., *The Bar-Kokhva Revolt: A New Approach* [Hebrew] (Jerusalem: Yad Izhak ben Zvi, 1984), 113–32.

symbol whose meaning was constructed and had been perpetuated for decades before the Mishnah as a whole was completed, by people who lived under specific (and shifting) social and political conditions. It is this context that needs elucidation if we are to understand the particular "argument" of the Mishnah. This is not a positivist historical critique of Neusner's non-positivist text-as-system analysis: it is a critique of his use of simplistic historical assumptions and argumentation under the guise of speaking only of known facts.

The present study attempts to root the Mishnah's civil law in smaller-scale interactions in the agrarian world of Roman Galilee. Thus, the primary focus is not "law" as a coherent system of discourse but rather how individuals deeply interested in legal questions construct and respond to the environment in which they live through their exposition of legal materials.[82] In framing the study in this way, as I have already pointed out, I am not denying the fictional character of the Mishnah in general or *Baba' Meṣi'a'* in particular. The goal of the present study is rather to explore the horizons of this fictional world.[83] We should like to be able to identify those areas in which

---

[82] This is not to say that I have not benefited from the work of legal specialists interested in early Jewish law. See B. Cohen, *Jewish and Roman Law: A Comparative Study* (New York: JTSA, 1966); D. Daube, "Civil Law in the Mishnah: The Arrangement of the Three Gates," *Tulane Law Review* 18 (1944), 352–407, and other studies; B. S. Jackson, *Theft in Early Jewish Law* (Oxford: Clarendon, 1972); A. Gulak, *Lĕ-ḥēqer tôldôt ha-mišpāṭ ha-ʿibrî*, (Jerusalem: 1929), and more specialized studies; B. S. Jackson, *Essays in Jewish and Comparative Legal History* (SJLA 10: Leiden: E. J. Brill, 1975).

[83] Compare the programmatic statement by J. Neusner, *The Economics of the Mishnah* (*Chicago Studies in the History of Judaism*: Chicago: University of Chicago, 1990), 13: "Nor do the Mishnah's authors tell us anything at all about the economy of the Jews in the time of the Mishnah or even reveal economic attitudes that demand attention." Although I agree with Neusner on many issues, such as the utopian character of the Mishnah, and, most pointedly, the insistence of the Mishnah, at least in *m. B. Meṣ.*, on addressing only a rather narrow set of economic topics, shaped by the concerns of a landowning class (cf. Neusner, 1990, 50–71), the preceding quotation underscores the fundamental difference of the approach taken here. I take it as my starting point that any description of an economic system, however utopian, is fundamentally influenced by the economic notions of its authors, and indeed reflects upon the social and economic world of these authors.

For the present, I leave aside what I think are fundamental misreadings of texts (e.g., M4:1 does not cast every sale as a form of barter, but rather sharpens the distinction between money and merchandise; nor does the rest of the chapter presuppose that "price" is a constant corresponding to a "value" that is taken to be inherent). I wish to point out, however, that in order to understand the "systemic" and ideological character of the Mishnah's economics, it is necessary to be as clear as one can about the range of what people may actually have been doing. This Neusner simply refuses to do, preferring, instead, to compare the Mishnah's rules to Aristotle (pp. 32–49), rejecting any comparison with Roman law (pp. 42–3), much less

Rabbis simply mirror the leading ideological assumptions about the nature of economic interactions because they accept them as commonplace and true, and where the authors of the Mishnah actively construct an argument that circumscribes economics within a consciously held and articulated theological, lega,l or other ideological framework. In marking out these areas, the comparability of the Mishnah's exposition of contracts and obligations in tractate *Baba' Meṣi'a'* to other evidence from the Roman world (notably, but not exclusively, roughly contemporaneous Roman juristic writings, and more importantly the actual documentation of transactions from Judea, Syria, and, above all, Egypt) provides the background and some of the conceptual boundaries that can help identify where the Mishnah reflects, distorts, or simply ignores the realities of the world in which the Rabbis who produced it lived. Similarly, attention to implicit differences in power in the way relationships are described, even where actors are nominally free (e.g., when a borrower is free to act with the property on loan, and when the borrower's activity is controlled by the lender) and to topics that do not receive attention in connection with civil law but which may arise in other contexts (e.g., traditional long-term tenant farming) may elucidate the range of assumptions. Although the present study is of necessity incomplete, Chapter III is meant to set the parameters for such an inquiry through my analysis of *Baba' Meṣi'a'*.

If, in Chapter III, I have managed to outline the leading economic and social concepts of the Mishnaic civil law, it has been in part by perpetuating the Mishnah's own fiction: the world of wealthy owners of land. Some ideas

---

documentary evidence, and, to my mind, misunderstanding Finley (pp. 47–8), who offers, in many ways, a depiction of the very economic notions of the Mishnah as the common assumptions of the landed elite in the ancient world (M. I. Finley, *The Ancient Economy*, 2 ed. [*Sather Memorial Lectures* 43: Berkeley: University of California, 1985]). After the statement cited above, Neusner does go on, for instance, to describe the Mishnah's notion of markets and occasionally compares it with what he assumes was the "real" economic world in which the Mishnah was produced. However, Neusner makes no effort to ground these assumptions in any assessment of the evidence for what people may really have been doing. Hence, when he states that the Mishnah has little regard for the importance of the commercial sector of society (e.g., Neusner, 1990, 69, 90–1, 122), he presupposes their "real" importance, without asking to what extent and in what ways commerce functioned at all in the ancient world. Thus he over-emphasizes the play of the "free market" in the world outside the mental one of the Mishnah, surely an anachronism in any discussion of economic ideas in antiquity (see, e.g., p. 82). Similarly, in his discussion of the Mishnah's refusal to take money as an abstract (Neusner, 1990, 80–1, citing M4:1–2), Neusner ignores the fact that in the ancient world money was not merely a system of signs, but also based on the circulation of pieces of metal which, in turn, had fluctuating value in the marketplace which might, and indeed in the late second and third centuries did, undermine the system as a whole.

were likely to fall into the category of the self-evident: that primary actors are free male adults; that wealth comes primarily in the form of land; that marketers and bankers, far from making the economy "work," provide a service to landowners; that to charge interest is to take advantage of need. Others are far less obvious. Given the drastic changes in Palestinian society, and in the political relationship between Palestinian Jewry and Rome, between approximately 50 and 200 CE, just how to define "Israel" as a concept and as a social group, and its proper constitution and leadership, were hardly self-evident. Yet, piety, learning, and the temple, together with the proper management of economic interactions, had become saturated symbols with which Rabbis could articulate a new notion of "Israel," its internal organization, and its relationship with "the gentiles." By working out a detailed program of everyday interactions *m. Baba' Meṣi'a'* reflects a renewed interest in civil law as an aspect of Torah after centuries during which questions of civil law seem to have received no more than sporadic treatment.[84] However, the concerns that they reflected in this articulation to and for all of Israel were consistently those of the wealthy landholder. On the evidence of the Mishnah it is impossible to define or quantify this apparent anomaly. We are unable to measure the extent to which Rabbis themselves were members of the landed elites, or to which the wealthy landowners of Roman Galilee formed a monolithic group whose responses to Rabbis, and to Rome, were likely to be essentially the same. Arguably, the Mishnah might have been targeted at those landowners who were not sufficiently wealthy to be absorbed directly into the Roman establishment, but this is a hypothesis that is probably beyond the evidence of Rabbinic literature and certainly that of the Mishnah itself. Similarly, the Mishnah does not provide information about how far down the social and economic spectrum Rabbinic notions, much less authority and influence, were likely to go. Did the attention to "Israel" really grant only one group in society a true claim to that title, or might Rabbis have taken their rhetorical inclusiveness quite seriously?

3. The limitations of this study, and areas for future research.

The remainder of this study focuses on *m. Baba' Meṣi'a'* almost exclusively. What is still lacking, therefore, in the approach to the Mishnah just outlined, is a way of describing its composition, composers, the means of its formulation and propagation, and its potential audience within the complex web of social relationships that was the world of Roman Galilee. For if it is correct to assume that the composers of the Mishnah have not merely restated that which is "traditional," but have instead staked a claim to the

---

[84] See H. Lapin, "Early Rabbinic Civil Law and the Literature of the Second Temple Period," *JSQ* 2 (1995), 149–83.

control and interpretation of everyday assumptions by means of traditions of lesser or greater antiquity, we should like to understand this self-consciously traditional discourse against the background of wider (but for us largely unrepresented) discussions about the everyday and the contents of "tradition." What is at stake is not merely the history of ideas, but the way in which power and authority are taken up through the appropriation and manipulation of ideas, traditions, and symbols in the form of such institutions as courts, schools, and houses of worship.

I am suggesting, in short, that in order to understand the Mishnah we must be willing to attempt to ask about the world outside of its mental and descriptive boundaries. This will require attention to a growing body of studies (primarily, but not exclusively, produced by scholars working in Israel) that integrate literary evidence (Rabbinic, classical, and patristic) with a growing body of archeological, epigraphic, and papyrological material— much of it only discovered or published in the last decades—into a picture of Palestinian society.[85] In particular, recent study relating to Galilee, the area in which the Mishnah was produced, and in which the Rabbinic movement first rose to prominence, has produced several syntheses[86] and an "International Conference on Galilean Studies in Late Antiquity" under the auspices of a "Center for the Study of the Galilee."[87] In addition, more specialized studies have attempted to assess village layout, regional and market organization, cultural influence, and the emergence of a Rabbinic elite in late

---

[85] E. K. Vogel, "Bibliography of Holy-Land Sites" I-III, *HUCA* 42 (1971), 1–96, 52 (1981), 1–92, 58 (1987), 1–63; and Y. Tsafrir *et alii*, *Tabula Imperii Romani: Iudaea, Palaestina* (Jerusalem: Israel Academy of Arts and Sciences, 1994). Much attention has been paid to synagogue remains, the bibliography for which is collected in F. Hüttenmeister, G. Reeg, *Die antiken Synagogen in Israel* (Wiesbaden, 1977); M. J. S. Chiat, *Handbook of Synagogue Architecture* (BJS 29: Chico: Scholars Press, 1982); partially updated by Foerster, 1992, 317–20 (see also above n. 28). For epigraphic material see above, n. 32. The papyrological remains from the Judean Desert remain only partially published; see, however, *DJD* II, *P. Babatha* I; H. M. Cotton, J. Geiger, eds. *Masada: Final Reports* (Jerusalem: IES, Hebrew University, 1989), and the recent articles in by H. Cotton: *ZPE* 85 (1991), 263–7; 99 (1993) 115–21; 100 (1994), 547–57; 101 (1994), 53–60; 104 (1995), 211–24 (with J. C. Greenfield); *JRS* 84 (1994), 64–86.

[86] Oppenheimer, 1991; cf. Goodman, 1983, who is far more sensitive to the limitations of the Rabbinic literary evidence. See also E. M. Meyers, J. F. Strange, *Archeology, the Rabbis and Early Christianity* (Nashville: Abingdon, 1981). Although none of the following is strictly focused on Galilee the following books deserve mention: G. Hamel, *Poverty and Charity in Roman Palestine, First Three Centuries C. E.* (*Near Eastern Studies* 23: Berkeley, University of California, 1990); Isaac, 1990, and Millar, 1993.

[87] The papers of this conference have been published as *The Galilee in Late Antiquity* (Levine, 1992), cited above.

antique Galilee.[88] Among other sites, Sepphoris (one of the two Galilean cities in the Roman period) has been excavated repeatedly since 1983 and has rewarded excavators with truly stunning mosaics that have contributed to current understanding of the acculturation of the city (or of its urban elites) to Greco-Roman norms.[89] For historians working now, the new resources available for the regional study of Galilee offer opportunities for a new synthesis of both early Rabbinic history and Roman-period Palestinian history. With this, however, we have moved well beyond the limits of this study.

***

The format and presentation of the present essay have been structured around the canons of the academic study of ancient Jewish history and Rabbinic literature, which are committed to the analysis of Jewish communities and literature *sui generis*. However, this project overlaps with several different sets of concerns which have shaped my thinking about the problem, and which I wish to mention briefly, because they merit further study. Rabbis emerged in the late second or early third century as champions of a "discursive practice": a specialized way of speaking about certain topics (discourse) that is closely tied to the appropriation or manipulation of power on the level of government, institution, and, through a specialized way of controlling behavior, the body itself.[90] Rabbinic texts therefore offer an opportunity to

---

[88] For regional and marketing patterns see D. Adan-Bayewitz, I. Perlman, "The Local Trade of Sepphoris in the Roman Period," *IEJ* 40 (1990), 153–72; D. Adan-Bayewitz, *Common Pottery in Roman Galilee: A Study in Local Trade* (Ramat Gan: Bar Ilan, 1993), and the work of Z. Safrai (cited and discussed in section III.A.2, n. 26. (See also Z. Yeivin, "Survey of Settlements in Galilee and the Golan from the Period of the Mishnah in Light of the Sources" (Diss. Hebrew University, 1971); Z. Safrai, *Pirqê galîl bi-tĕqûpat ha-mišnâ wĕ-ha-talmûd* (Tel Aviv: Maalot, 1985). R. S. Hanson, *Tyrian Influence in Upper Galilee* (*Meiron Excavation Project* 2: Cambridge: ASOR, 1980), discusses the economic dominance of Tyre. Levine, 1989, discusses the emergence of a defined Rabbinic class.

[89] See the summary articles by E. M. Meyers, "Roman Sepphoris in Light of New Archeological Evidence and Recent Research," and J. F. Strange, "Six Campaigns at Sepphoris: The University of South Florida Excavations, 1983–9," in Levine, 1992, 321–38 and 339–56 respectively. See also S. S. Miller, *Studies in the History and Traditions of Sepphoris* (SJLA 37: Leiden: Brill, 1984), and the publications of a recently uncovered mosaic depicting a Nilometer motif (E. Netzer, Z. Weiss, "New Mosaic Art from Sepphoris," *BAR* 18 no. 6 [1992], 36–43). Z. Weiss was kind enough to inform me about some of the more recent discoveries at Sepphoris, especially the newly discovered synagogue. Y. Ne'eman, 1987, attempts a synthetic history of Sepphoris.

[90] See, e.g., M. Foucault, *The Archaeology of Knowledge*, tr. A. M. Sheridan Smith (New York: Pantheon, 1972); *idem*, *Discipline and Punish*, tr. A. Sheridan (New York: Vintage, 1979). What is interesting in Foucault's treatment of "discursive formations" is his acknowledgment of political or social effects (indeed these formations are transformative) without tak-

examine the construction of knowledge and its implication in the relations of power.[91] Moreover, Palestinian Judaism itself did not develop in a cultural or political vacuum: Rabbis are an articulate group within a subject people in a province of the Roman empire. As such, Rabbinic literature offers a window into the nature of Roman hegemony from the perspective of non-Romans. The persistence of a non-Greek and non-Latin vernacular as a religious and literary language, and its implications for the politics of religious difference, should be compared with the emergence or persistence of, for example, Syriac, Coptic, and Armenian literatures.[92] This may, in turn, help to better understand the limits and contours of "hellenization" in the eastern Roman empire. I would also suggest that modern anthropological debates on the construction of ethnicity among "colonized" populations through a dialectical process of resistance, appropriation and acculturation offer further material for comparison and a theoretical framework for the study of later Roman Palestine.[93] What such a broadening of perspective may provide is a sense of that which the various forms of Judaism in antiquity share with human communities everywhere. Such an approach does not only "de-center" the history of Judaism, but may also highlight that which is unique in Jewish civilizations as well.

---

ing these as intended (e.g., the "takeover" of the hospital by the physician in the course of the modern transformation of medicine).

[91] Since the summer of 1994 (after much of the preceding chapter was written), I have also begun to consider the relationship of my project as it is envisioned here to the so-called "New Historicism" (or "Cultural Poetics"). While I acknowledge a great deal of overlap in interests (and biases), it seems to me that the New Historicism remains a practice of literary criticism and that its goal is still more or less subversive readings of "Literature." The exercise undertaken here remains, I believe, resolutely historical: it is the elucidation of a real world outside of the Mishnah that is the aim (however unattainable) of this study, and without which the entire undertaking is pointless.

[92] See, for instance, the studies of F. G. B. Millar, "Local Cultures in the Roman Empire: Lybian, Punic and Latin in Roman Africa," *JRS* 58 (1968), 126–34; *idem*, "Paul of Samosata, Zenobia and Aurelian: The Church, Local Culture in Third-Century Syria and Political Allegiance," *JRS* 61 (1971), 1–17; *idem*, "Empire, Community and Culture in the Roman Near East: Greeks, Syrians, Jews and Arabs," *JJS* 38 (1987), 143–65; and his most recent synthesis *The Roman Near East*, cited above.

[93] E.g., F. Barth, ed., *Ethnic Groups and Boundaries* (Boston: Little, Brown, 1969); J. Comaroff, *Body of Power, Spirit of Resistance: The Culture and History of a South African People* (Chicago: Chicago, 1985); J. Comaroff, J. L. Comaroff, *Of Revelation and Revolution* (Chicago: Chicago, 1991); G. Sider, "When Parrots Learn to Talk, and When They Can't: Domination, Deception, and Self-Deception in Indian-White Relations," *Contemporary Studies of History and Society* 29 (1987), 3–23. Also interesting in this context is B. Anderson, *Imagined Communities*, corr. ed. (London: Verso, 1991).

✥ CHAPTER II ✥

Mishnah Tractate *Baba' Meṣi'a'*
Literary and Redactional Problems

> How the Mishnah was written? If the members of the great assembly began to write it and the sages of each and every generation wrote part of it until the generation of Rabbi [Judah the Patriarch] who sealed it—lo, the majority of the Mishnah is anonymous, and "the anonymous Mishnah is R. Meir"! And most of the sages of the Talmud [i.e., the Mishnah] whose names are made explicit, R. Meir and R. Judah and R. Yose and R. Simeon—and they were all the disciples of R. Aqiba; and the general rules that our sages of blessed memory taught us in the Talmud, that the law follows R. Aqiba against his fellow, and R. Yose against his fellow—they are all from the end of the second Temple [*sic*]! Why did the earlier Rabbis leave over the majority to the later, and especially if nothing of the Mishnah was written until the end of the days of Rabbi?[1]

In the preceding chapter, I have attempted to draw attention to the problem of reconstructing "history" from Rabbinic texts, and in particular from the Mishnah. The Mishnah is neither an authoritative archive of laws, practices and events, nor even a mine of "facts" to be uncovered and, if necessary, cleansed, purified or cut to shape. Instead, I suggested that we should pay close attention to the Mishnah, and *m. Baba' Meṣi'a'* in particular, as itself an artifact that must be placed into a historical context. This means unpacking the underlying assumptions and referents of the Mishnah, to the extent that these can be recovered. I will sketch out the outlines of some of these in the next chapter. However, this approach to the Mishnah also requires that we pay close attention to the way in which the Mishnah itself came into being, and it is to this that I now turn. In particular, I wish to draw attention to *m. Baba' Meṣi'a'* as a document that has been edited from sources.

In part, my goal is to problematize what we mean by Rabbinic "texts." Western literary tradition has conditioned us to expect "texts" to represent unities (or, at least, apparent unities whose very integrity must be

---

[1] From the question of the community of Kairouan to Sherira Gaon (late tenth century). B. M. Lewin, ed. *'Iggeret rab šěrîrā' gā'ôn* (1921) rpt. (Jerusalem: Makor, 1972), 5.

deconstructed). If the argument about the redaction of *m. Baba᾽ Meṣiʿa᾽* from sources is correct, the Mishnah reflects a technology and sensibility of text production rather different from that of conventionally "authored" texts, one that betrays the indeterminacies and complexities of meaning on its surface. (How, for instance, should we read apparently contradictory passages?) However, my primary concern here is historiographical. If we are to be able to contextualize the contents of the Mishnah (in this case claims about the way in which the economy ought to work) in the "real" world in which "real" men produced it, we have to take seriously the mechanics by which the Mishnah makes its message known, a process that is not only literary, but social. By focusing on the sources of the tractate, I am attempting to highlight the emergence of the Mishnah within a larger human framework of authors, compilers or transmitters of traditions that conformed to certain conventions and that addressed topics of concern to the Rabbis who produced the Mishnah. What social relations or standards of authority and authenticity are presupposed in this text that uses already existing material, at least in part, to make its statement?

In this chapter, I ask first what evidence there is that suggests that the Mishnah has utilized sources; second, whether there is any evidence that suggests what those sources might have looked like before their redaction into their present context; and third, what traces there are of the process of redaction itself: how sources might have been used, altered, glossed or corrected. Finally, I consider the significance of statements attributed to named individuals. Although these are the only internal markers of chronological development, I point out the secondary or supplementary character of the attributed material, and the limitations of any argument based on attributions for the dating of the ideas or sources of the tractate. At the same time, the attributed material offers some support for the contention of this chapter that the sources of *m. Baba᾽ Meṣiʿa᾽* have undergone a process of revision and editing. Since statements attributed to a particular sage, although apparently supplementary, can link pericopae of disparate material together, such statements may reflect on the process of redaction through circles to whom the traditions of individual sages were particularly important. This last observation is important, since it leads us, however tenuously, into the realm of the social context for the production of the Mishnah. The existence of different and occasionally contradictory source material suggests that different "schools" (or disciple circles) may have existed. The interest in organization and systematization that is manifested in *m. Baba᾽ Meṣiʿa᾽* may possibly correspond to an attempt to centralize and institutionalize the Rabbinic movement.

A. Sources in the Mishnah

The question of the "source criticism" of the Mishnah has a long history. The earliest students of the Mishnah could already use the idea that the Mishnah was not of one piece as an analytical tool. Thus, in the Tosepta an apparent conflict between two passages in *m. Sukka* is resolved by the assertion that they reflect different views, despite the fact that they appear together in the Mishnah.[2] Amoraim, too, suggested similar solutions to such problems, as in the exclamation: "A contradiction: the one who taught this [passage] did not teach this [one]!"[3] Amoraim were acute readers of the text of the Mishnah, and sensitive to the implications of subtle differences in language or formulation. Nevertheless, ancient Rabbinic exegesis of the Mishnah reflects hermeneutical purposes (legal, intellectual or religious) and stance that are those of neither the historian nor the text critic, and reach different results. Thus, to take an example from *m. Baba' Meṣi'a',* M3:9 appears to be internally consistent: the liability of a depositary who moved the deposit is different in a case in which the owner specified that the object (a jar) be kept in a specific place, than when he did not make such specification. Yet the Babli cites the exclamation of R. Yohanan that "whoever explains [the case of the] jar according to one *tannā'* ("reciter"), I will carry his things with him to the bath house" (B41a). This objection attributed to R. Yohanan seems to derive from a specific Amoraic (or Talmudic) exegetical agenda, and not from any "internal" problem with the pericope from the Mishnah.[4]

Similarly, statements are ascribed to Amoraim that attribute whole tractates,[5]

---

[2] *m. Suk.* 5:4–5; *t. Suk.* 4:10. See Epstein, *Siprût*, 39, 351–2.

[3] *Tabrā' mî še-šānâ zô lo' šānâ zô*; see *b. Šab.* 92b; *b. Yeb.* 13a; *b. Ket.* 75b; *b. B. Qam.* 20b, 47a, 48b; *b. B. Meṣ.* 82b; *b. Ḥul.* 16a; *b. Ker.* 24b.

[4] The stammaitic stratum of the Babli, at least, derived the problem in M3:9 (to which the exclamation of R. Yohanan refers), and the suggested resolutions, from a *bāraîtā'* presenting a dispute between R. Aqiba and R. Ishmael over things that have been stolen and returned without the owner's knowledge (B40b–41a; cf. *t. B. Qam.* 10: 33, 35).

[5] See, e.g., the statements that "[Mishnah tractate] *Tamid* is R. Simeon of Mispeh's" (attributed to R. Yohanan), and that "*Middot* is R. Eleazar b. Jacob's" (attributed to R. Hizqiya, R. Aha in the name of R. Abbahu) (*y. Yoma'* 2:3 [39d]; cf. *b. Yoma'* 14b in which the opinion that "*Yoma'* is R. Simeon of Mispeh's" is ascribed to R. Yohanan, in a context in which this attribution contradicts the view that *Tamid* is R. Simeon of Mispeh's). In the Yerushalmi, however, both of these claims are countered (by R. Yaaqob b. Aha, and by R. Yose b. R. Bun respectively) with the assertion "but not all of it, but rather *milîn di-ṣĕrîkîn lĕ-rabbānān.*" The untranslated clause (lit. "words/things that are necessary for the Rabbis") is quite obscure, but at any rate reflects the fact that without this qualification the statements in question would imply that the whole tractates are attributed to these individual Tannaim.

chapters (not necessarily identical with ours),[6] and individual pericopae[7] to specific sages. To be sure, there are good reasons for attempting to locate certain tractates in circles other than those that produced other parts of the Mishnah, as L. Ginzberg has shown.[8] Nor is it implausible that Rabbinic literature preserves valuable traditions about the composition of Rabbinic texts. But where modern arguments about the redaction of the Mishnah are based on later Talmudic traditions (and, in the case of *m. Tamid,* on contradictory traditions)[9] they rely on traditional assertions whose accuracy can generally not be determined. Equally problematic is reliance on other types of traditions supplied by later Rabbinic literature and utilized by scholars to determine the history and nature of the redaction of the Mishnah. To take one oft-quoted example, in *ʾAbot de-Rabbi Natan* (A, ch. 18), R. Aqiba is described as a laborer who has gone out and gathered different kinds of produce, and then proceeded to separate them by kind: "thus R. Aqiba made all the Torah into separate rings [or: coins]." Leaving aside the problems of the reliability of the attribution (to R. Judah the Patriarch), the dating of the tradition itself, and the late date of the text in which it appears,[10] the question remains, to what extent this statement may be used as evidence for R. Aqiba as a redactor of a proto-Mishnah.[11] The context of the passage is a highly

---

[6] E.g., *y. Giṭ.* 8:5 (39c); *b. Ned.* 82a.

[7] See for example Y4:1 (9c) (R. Hiyya b. Ashi): "Who taught it [M4:1]? R. Simeon the son of R. [Judah the Patriarch]"; cf. B44a.

[8] L. Ginzberg, "*Tamid,* The Oldest Tractate of the Mishnah," *Journal of Jewish Lore and Philosophy* 1 (1919), 33–44, 197–209, 265–95, followed in part by Epstein, *Siprût,* 27ff. Compare J. Neusner, "Dating a Mishnah Tractate," in *History, Religion and Spiritual Democracy: Essays in Honor of Joseph L. Blau,* ed. F. A. Martin *et al.* (New York: Columbia, 1980), 97–113.

[9] Ginzberg, 1919, 285–93. See also N. Krochmal, *Môreh nĕbûkê ha-zĕmān,* ed. L. Zunz (Lemberg, 1851), 205–9; D. Hoffman, "The First Mishnah and the Controversies of the Tannaim" (1882), in *The First Mishnah [and] the Highest Court,* tr. fr. German P. Forscheimer (New York: Maurosho, 1977) 27–29; L. A. Rosenthal, *Über den Zusammenhang der Mischna* (Strasbourg, 1909), 42; Epstein, *Siprût,* e.g., 28, 31, 53, 55. Albeck, *Mābô*, 85–6, while disagreeing with the reading of the traditions about Tamid and Middot by Krochmal and others, still feels compelled to accept their basic veracity ("It follows, that since according to the Yerushalmi it is a fixed tradition ... we can only accept it .... However, we have no authority to interpret it in any other manner than that in which it is interpreted in the Yerushalmi ...," p. 86).

[10] On *ʾAbot R. Nat.* see the discussion and literature in H. L. Strack, *Introduction to Talmud and Midrash,* ed. G. Stemberger, tr. M. Brockmuehl (Minneapolis: Augsburg-Fortress, 1992), 245–7 (dates given for the composition of the work as a whole range from the third century to the ninth).

[11] See, e.g., S. Lieberman, "The Publication of the Mishnah," in *Hellenism in Jewish Palestine* (Texts and Studies 18: New York, JTSA, 1950), 95:

stylized classification of sages using similes (a pile of nuts, a filled [*bālûm*] storehouse, a merchant's basket) and their explication. Such an "enumeration of the merits of sages" might have been worked out based on knowledge of the activities that the individual sages undertook during their lives, but remains typological rather than strictly biographical. The present instance, moreover, does not appear to deal with the activity of redaction. The formation of "rings," whatever they were, is a special attribute of R. Aqiba's wisdom and teaching style, to be contrasted with that of two other sages whose teaching resembled the cascading of a pile of nuts or stones (R. Tarfon) or a merchant who always seems to have just the produce his customers want (R. Eleazar b. Azariah).[12]

We are left, at least in the first instance, with literary criteria. How does the tractate, chapter or pericope hold together? Are there persistent patterns or abrupt disjunctures in the text? Can glosses be identified? Are there contradictions in the text?[13] The purpose of this section is to identify some of the criteria for discerning the seams between sources, and to exemplify these through an analysis of *m. Baba' Meṣiʿa'*.

These rings seem to signify general rules, i.e., R. ʿAkiba used to convert case law into abstract general rules. At any rate the part played by R. ʿAkiba as a systemizer of the Mishnah is quite evident from the tradition reported in *Aboth deR. Nathan*. See also Z. Frankel, *Darkê ha-mišnâ* (Leipzig, 1859), rev. ed. I. Nusbaum (Tel Aviv: Sinai, n.d.), who on 123f. cites the passage as a discussion of R. Aqiba's method of study, but on 221 cites it again as an indication that R. Aqiba was instrumental in the redaction of the Mishnah; Epstein, *Siprût*, 72.

[12] "This is what R. Tarfon was like when (*bĕ-šāʿâ šeʿ-*) a disciple of a sage would come in to him and say: 'Recite [i.e., "teach"] to me' ..."; "Thus was R. Eleazar b. Azariah at a time when (*bi-zĕmān šeʿ-*) disciples of sages came in to him: he asked him [a question] in connection with Scripture, he would say [i.e., "answer"] to him ...," *'Ab. Rab. Nat*. A 18 (ed. Schechter, p. 67). After a substantial gap, the other two members of R. Judah's list are dealt with briefly. Again, the images probably refer to wisdom and personal style rather than a "literary" project: R. Yohanan b. Nuri is "a basket of *halākôt*"; Yose the Galilean is "one who picks [produce] well, without arrogance of spirit, for with it [i.e., his spirit?] he seized the measure (*middâ*) of sages from Mt. Sinai, and with it would teach all of the Sages of Israel" (ed. Schechter, p. 68).

[13] This is where the work of Albeck in his *Mābôʾ*, and in his *Untersuchungen über die Redaktion der Mischna* (*Veröffentlichungen der Akademie für die Wissenschaft des Judentums. Talmudische Sektion* 2: Berlin, 1923); Epstein, *Siprût*; A. Weiss, *Lĕ-ḥēqer siprût ha-mišnâ*, *HUCA* 16 (1941), 1–33; and, more recently, the work of D. W. Halivni (see Chapter I, n. 71), excel.

1. Context, terminology, style.

The clearest example of two passages stemming from two different authors is that of a contradiction. For instance, M7:10 [E–G] allows the "four watchmen," connected by the Mishnah to the Biblical discussion of Exodus 22:6–14, to stipulate changes in the level of their liability, while M7:11 [A] prohibits the making of conditions "on [i.e., contrary to] what is written in the Torah."[14] On the face of it, at least, these passages contradict each other, although it is not impossible that a harmonizing interpretation could already be presupposed in the juxtaposition of these passages.[15] M4:5–6 deal with the problem of worn coins: if they are worn beyond a certain point they may not be used. At the end of M4:6, however, the following, apparently contradictory, comment occurs: "and he may give it for [redemption of] second tithe and he ought not hesitate, for this [i.e., failure to accept the coin] is only stinginess" [F–G]. One possible explanation is that the author of M4:6 [F–G] is in disagreement with the various rulings in M4:5 about the permissible amount of wear (ranging from 1/24 to 1/6).[16]

For the most part it is difficult to find outright contradictions.[17] Instead we can point to shifts in frame of reference, that is, to passages that do not

---

[14] For the connection between the Mishnah's concept of deposit with the passage in Ex. 22:6–14 see H. Lapin, "Early Rabbinic Civil Law and the Literature of the Second Temple Period," *JSQ* 2 (1995), 149–83. The contradiction between M7:10 and M7:11 was already recognized by the Babli (B94a) (see the note to M7:11 in Appendix I). The force of the expression "All who make conditions on [i.e., contrary to] what is written in the Torah, his condition is invalid" is that it is the stipulation alone that is invalid, but that the transaction made conditional upon the stipulation retains its validity, as is clear from *m. Ket.* 9:1 (cf. also *m. B. Bat.* 8:5; *t. Ket.* 9:2; *t. Naz.* 2:2; *t. Git.* 9:1; *t. Qid.* 3:7).

[15] A clear attempt at such harmonization that occurs in *t. Qid.* 3:8 suggests a possible way in which this might have been carried out: "This is the general rule: All who make conditions on what is written in the Torah: in a matter of money his claim is valid, in a matter that is not money his claim is invalid."

[16] Compare *m. Kel.* 12:7: "How far may [a *selaʿ*] be worn down and one still be permitted to keep it [for use]? Up to two *denarii* [=1/2]; [if it contains] less than this let him cut it." For the relationship between M4:5–6 and *m. Kel.* 12:7 see T3:8 and the discussion below in Chapter III.A.1. At any rate, it certainly seems clear that there existed a far more permissive view than that found in M4:5, and this may well be what underlies the qualification in M4:6 [F–G]. The interpretation given here is not that favored by the medieval commentators, who tend to explain M4:6 [F–G] as a gloss of M4:5 [A] ("How much may a *selaʿ* be lacking and there [still] not be *hônāyâ* in it?"): as long as the coin is still valid, adds M4:6 [F–G], there is no reason why it should not be accepted as second tithe money. (See the second view in Tos. *s.v. Nôtnāh* [B52b]; Rosh to B52a who cites Rif and Rabad; see also *Nimmûqê yôsēp* to Rif *ad loc.*).

[17] On the possible contradiction between M7:9 [A] and [H] in some manuscripts (but not the Kaufman ms.) see the note to M7:9 in Appendix I. The contradiction between M8:4 [F–S] and [A–E] (a contradiction that may have already appeared in a cluster of pericopae,

quite disagree but were very likely not authored by the same person in the same context. For example, M2:7 [E–H] distinguishes between finding "a thing that produces and eats" and "a thing that does not produce and eat." The latter, since some expense is required for its maintenance, is to be sold and the proceeds kept, rather than maintained. The next pericope proceeds with a series of rules about the care that certain kinds of objects should

---

M8:4–5, utilized by the redactors as a source) is discussed below in Section B.2, in connection with the relationship between M8:1–3 and 4–5. Another possible example of contradiction that is worth noting is M2:2–4. In M2:3 [C–E] a utensil, *kĕlî*, found in a dungheap cannot be appropriated but must be left for the owner (who presumably hid it there) or, if the finder did take it, must be publicly proclaimed. By contrast, M2:3 [F]–2:4 [D] presents a series of cases in which a *kĕlî* (the term does not occur in these cases, but carries over from M2:3 [A]), when found, may be kept. I suggest that M2:3 [C–E] considered a generic utensil as the kind of thing the owner was likely to be able to identify (in agreement with M2:2, which ruled that a *kĕlî* "as it is" [B], i.e., empty, as opposed to filled with produce, must be publicly proclaimed), whereas M2:3 [F]–2:4 [D] considers such an item to be unidentifiable. Otherwise, I see no way of accounting for the difference between, for instance, the rule regarding a dungheap (M2:3 [C–E]) and that regarding a new wall [G–J]. (The question of why in the case of a new wall the finder is not required either to leave the item or, having taken it, to proclaim the find, was already raised by Tos. *s.v. Bĕ-kôtēl* [B26a]; see also Maimonides to M2:3.) The view taken here is not the traditional one. Tos. *s.v. ʾAḥar ha-gapâ* (B25a) understood a dungheap as a "place that is guarded," i.e., where one might leave an object for safe keeping, hence the finder ought to leave it in its place. It is not clear, however, why a dung heap should be any more "guarded" than the other installations mentioned. The case of the old wall was already glossed in the Tosepta: "for he can say that they belonged to the [pre-Israelite] Amorites" (T2:12; cf. Y2:4 [8c]; B25b). That is, the wall must be old enough (according to the Babli the object must be rust-bitten [*šātîk*] enough) to be presumed ownerless, and therefore the finder may appropriate it. The commentaries recognized that the case of a new wall requires the same logical step to distinguish it from that of a dungheap. In the words of Rosh (to B25b): "'In a new wall,' that is, in a wall about which it is known that the forefathers of the present owners built it and it never left their possession ... even in the case of something that has a distinguishing mark ... because it is very rust-bitten" (see also, e.g., Tos. *s.v. Bĕ-kôtēl* [B26a]). This is a rather strange interpretation of "new," and is designed to remove an exegetical difficulty, and does not correctly interpret the passage at hand.

In addition, note that *TYT* and *Mĕlʾeket šĕlomoh* (the latter basing himself on Rosh to B111a, dependent, in turn, upon Rif, although neither make the internal contradiction in the Mishnah explicit) took M9:11 [C] (following the view attributed to Rab in B111a: "a worker hired for hours, [hired] for the day, he collects all through the day ... [for] the night, he collects all through the night") to conflict with [D–F] ("... if he left [work] during the day, he collects all through the [same] day, if he left [work] during the night he collects during the [same] night and the following day"). However, this is neither the inevitable interpretation of the Babli (which, more likely, attributes the dispute of Rab and Samuel, and not the clauses of the Mishnah, to an antecedent Tannaitic dispute), nor is it clear that the views of Rab and Samuel ought to be taken as exegeses of the Mishnah rather than independent legal statements, of which that attributed to Rab apparently conflicts with the Mishnah.

receive (books, fabric, silver or brass, gold or glass; M2:8 [A–G]). The implication of the binary opposition in M2:7 is that there is no middle ground between "every (*kol*) thing that produces and eats" and "that which does not produce and eat." In that case, the items listed in M2:8 should fall into the latter category, that is, they should be sold off rather than cared for. It is clear, however, that the assumption behind M2:7 is that the lost object is an animal whereas the items enumerated in M2:8 are inanimate.[18] This suggests that the same author is not responsible for both passages as they appear before us, even though they may not actually conflict.

In the present instance we can go somewhat further in elucidating the contexts of the two passages. The problem of lost animals is strikingly absent from the discussions of Chapters 1–2. Indeed, with the exception of M2:9–10, M2:7 is the only pericope that deals with domestic animals.[19] This is all the more noticeable in light of the fact that the Pentateuchal verses on the subject deal primarily with animals.[20] It is therefore probably no accident that M2:7 [A–H] is explicitly tied to the exegesis of Deuteronomy 22:1–3, citing portions of 22:2 as prooftexts. The topic of lost animals recurs in M2:9; once again, the passage is tied to Scriptural interpretation. First, Deuteronomy 22:2 is cited as a prooftext. Second, the connection with Scripture accounts for the connection of M2:10 with M2:9. The topic of M2:10 [E–N], the obligation to care for an animal suffering under a burden, is irrelevant to the discussion of Chapters 1 and 2, but the presence of M2:10 is explained by the fact that in both Exodus (23:5) and Deuteronomy (22:4) it is this topic that immediately follows the rule about lost animals. Moreover, there are distinct parallels between parts of M2:9 and M2:10, suggesting that (at least parts of) these pericopae were intended to form a unit:[21]

---

[18] That M2:7 [E–H] is concerned primarily with animals is already implied by T2:20, in which a somewhat different version of the Mishnaic passage includes the gloss "such as a cow or an ass" to "a thing that produces and eats" (M2:7 [E]) and the gloss "such as a goose or a chicken ... in the case of calves or foals ..." to "a thing that does not produce and eat" (M2:7 [F]). (See also Maimonides *Code*, *Gězēlâ wa-ʾabēdâ* 13:15 whose paraphrase of our passage opens: "He found a living thing [lit. 'a thing that has the spirit of life in it'], which, indeed, he has to feed: if it was a thing that produces and eats ....") The expression "produces and eats" is also found in M5:5 where the context once again involves animals.

[19] There are two other passages that deal with finding living things. The deer and birds introduced in M1:4 are wild: the question that arises is merely who has the right of acquisition. Similarly, the bound fledgling birds in M2:3 [A] are presumably birds that have been caught. M2:7 and M2:9, however, are concerned with domesticated farm animals.

[20] Ex. 23:3: "If you should come upon the ox of your enemy or his ass ...." Deut. 22:1: "You shall not see the ox of your brother or his sheep ...." The rule in Deut. is extended, however, to include a garment (22:3); cf. M2:5.

[21] It should be noted that M2:9 [A–C] is in some literary tension with M2:10 [A–B]. M2:9 distinguishes between animals that are grazing on the road (which are presumed not to be

Literary and Redactional Problems 43

M2:9	M2:10
[D] [If] he returned it and it ran away, he returned it and it ran away, even four or five times, he is [still] obligated,	[E] [If] he unburdened and loaded, unburdened and loaded [an animal] even four or five times, he is [still] obligated,
[E] for it is said: "You shall return them" (Deut. 22:1).	[F] For it is said, "You shall help" (Ex. 23:5).

Although in one case the verse cited stems from Deuteronomy and in the other from Exodus, the parallels between the passages extend to the grammatical form of the Biblical lemmata cited (the emphatic construction with infinitive absolute). M2:9–10, I suggest, derives from a source that is concerned with Scriptural interpretation and that allows the order of Biblical verses to dictate its literary structure. A similar argument can be made for separating off M2:7 [A–H] as stemming from a source concerned with the Biblical verses. The rest of Chapters 1–2 are rather unconcerned with Scripture.

---

lost) and those with their burdens turned over or running in vineyards (which are presumed to be lost). In M2:10 [B] the rule is given that if one finds animals in the public domain (of which a road is one example) one is obligated with respect to them. These pericopae need not conflict: M2:9 is concerned with the attitude of the animal; M2:10 with its location. (Rabad, cited by Rosh [to B32a], suggested that the animal in M2:10 is escaping from a loud noise [in contrast to the case of M2:9 where the animal is grazing], or that the finder felt that someone might appropriate the animal if he did not take it in; Rosh himself gave a more general version of the same view, namely, that in M2:10 [B] the animal is clearly lost.) Nevertheless, it would seem that either M2:9–10 was composed with considerable awkwardness, or the awkwardness stems from the process of redaction (either through the combination of originally disparate material or through the modification of M2:9–10 in the process of its removal from its original context). It is worth noting that in *Sipre Deut.* a parallel to M2:9 is cited in connection with Deut. 22:1 ("'... or his sheep straying,' in the manner of its straying. From here they said [*mi-ka*ʾ*n* ʾ*āmrû*]: 'What is a lost object ...' [=M2:9 [A–C]") (*Sipre Deut.* 222 [ed. Finckelstein, pp. 255–6]); but M2:10 is cited in connection with Deut. 22:4 ("'On the road,' and not in the cattle shed. From here they said: '[If he found it in the cattle shed...' [M2:10 [A–B]]") (*Sipre Deut.* 225 [ed. Finkelstein, p. 257]). That is, the passages are taken to refer to different legal problems, the one to lost property, the other to a struggling animal. Since *Sipre Deut.* appears to cite the Mishnah we can, at most, conclude only that there was an ancient exegetical tradition that resolved an apparent conflict between M2:9 [A–C] and M2:10 [A–B]. If this exegesis is correct, and M2:10 properly relates to the question of helping an overburdened animal, M2:10 [D] ("[If] his father said: ... 'Do not return it'"), which apparently refers to a lost animal, becomes problematic. Compare the related tradition in *Mek.*, which may attempt to resolve this problem by recasting 2:10 [D] in terms of an overburdened animal as well: "[If] his father said: 'Do not unburden with him,' [or] 'Do not load with him,' or 'Do not return to him his lost object ...'" (*Mek., Kaspaʾ*, 20 [ed. Horovitz, Rabin, p. 325]). On the relationship of *m. B. Meṣ* and the halakhic midrashim see further Appendix II.

The dependence of both M2:7 [A–H] and M2:9 on Scripture shows itself in terminology as well: M2:7 [A] and M2:9 [A–C] both use the noun *'abēdâ*, "lost object," the noun used in Deuteronomy 22:3. Heretofore in Chapters 1–2 the term *mĕṣî'â*, "found object," has been used.[22] The dependence or independence of a passage on the text of the Torah can be an important indicator of what I have called a shift in frame of reference.[23]

Anomaly of style is another indicator of distinct origin. By far the best example, M2:5, is once again a passage that is dependent upon Scriptural interpretation:

[A] Even the garment was included among all these, and why did it go out [and was mentioned separately]?
[B] So that analogy be made with it:
[C] Just as the garment is unique in that it has identifying marks, and has claimants,
[D] so for everything that has identifying marks and claimants, he is required to proclaim.

The "garment" mentioned in M2:5 [A] is that referred to in Deuteronomy

---

[22] M2:11, with no particular connection with Biblical usage, also uses *'abēdâ*. This suggests that M2:11, literarily and topically independent of the rest of Chapters 1–2, stems from a "source" with little contact with the materials preceding it in the tractate. In using *'abēdâ* M2:11 corresponds to the regular usage of the Mishnah elsewhere. When the Mishnah refers to the obligation to return lost objects the expression used is typically one or another variant of *mēšîb 'abēdâ*, "one who returns a lost object": M3:6; 6:7; 7:4; elsewhere in the Mishnah: *m. Ned.* 4:2; *m. B. Qam.* 5:7; *m. Šebi.* 6:1 *m. Hor.* 3:7; *m. Kel.* 27:12. On several occasions *'abēdâ* clearly echoes Biblical usage as it does in the case of M2:7 and M2:9: M7:8 (=*m. Šebi.* 8:1), echoing Ex. 22:8; *m. Šebi.* 4:5; 5:3, echoing Lev. 5:21–22, 23. Incidentally, the kind of lost object presupposed by the term *'abēdâ* in *m. B. Qam.* 5:7 is an animal.

By contrast, the usage of *mĕṣî'â* as a noun with the concrete sense of "found object" is restricted to the first two chapters of *m. B. Meṣ.* (M1:3, 4; 2:1). Elsewhere, as also in M1:5, the verbal noun *mĕṣî'â* retains the emphasis on the action, approximating "that which [someone] finds" (see Segal, 103–4, §227), especially in connection with the question of who acquires that which someone of restricted legal personhood, such as women, minors and incompetents have found: *m. Yeb.* 10:1; *m. Ket.* 4:1, 4; 6:1; *m. Giṭ.* 5:8; 8:5; *m. Nid.* 5:7 (see also *m. Ṭoh.* 3:5; 4:12; 5:7: *ki-šā'at mĕṣî'ātān*, purity or impurity "according [to its state at] the time of its being found").

[23] It is not, however, the only one. For instance, *'ônēs* in M7:9 bears a somewhat different meaning from M7:10 [A–D] (see Appendix I). Similarly, in Chapter 4, *hônāyâ* can have a technical meaning (overcharge in sale) or retain its root meaning of "oppression" (see Appendix II). It should be noted that the fact that a pericope utilizes or is even structured around a Biblical verse does not *necessarily* imply a different frame of reference from that of another pericope. Thus, for example, although M8:1 is structured around conditions given in Ex. 22:13b–14a, the transition from M8:1 to M8:2–3 does not reflect such a shift.

22:3: "And so shall you do with his ass, and so shall you do with his garment, and so shall you do with every lost object (*ʾabēdâ*) of your brother...." As a passage from the Mishnah M2:5 is quite odd, but the style is quite typical of the "dialectical midrash" form well known from the "Tannaitic" midrashim.[24] Curiously, M2:5 does not explicitly cite the verse upon which it is dependent (the verse is absent in all the versions of the Mishnah checked). Presumably the verse has been omitted in the process of inclusion of the pericope into the Mishnah, but the basic stylistic contours remain unchanged.

It is not only on the level of legal force or literary formulation that the seams between pericopae appear, but also on the level of terminology.[25] I have already noted this in connection with the terms *ʾabēdâ* and *mĕṣîʾâ*. Similarly, M5:1 sets up a binary opposition between two Biblical terms for usury, *nešek* and *tarbît*: "Which is *nešek* and which is *tarbît*? Which is *nešek*?... And which is *tarbît*?..." [A, B, E].[26] The former term is taken to refer

---

[24] A parallel to M2:5 occurs in *Sipre Deut.* 224 (ed. Finkelstein, p. 257). D. W. Halivni, *Midrash, Mishnah and Gemara: The Jewish Predilection for Justified Law* (Cambridge: Harvard, 1986), 53, has called this type of midrash "complex" or (in oral communication) "complex midrashic midrash," to be distinguished from "mishnaic midrash." (Incidentally, the passage in *Sipre Deut.*, like M2:5, has no lemma from the verse, but in the case of *Sipre Deut.* this is to be explained by the broader context in which the verses are cited.) Such interpolated midrashic fragments are not unheard of in the Mishnah: see Hoffman, 1882 (1977), 11, 13; see also the discussion by Halivni, 1986, 47–58 (a clear example of such a passage is *m. Mak.* 1:7). The relationship between the halakic midrashim such as *Sipre Deut.* and the Mishnah is dealt with briefly in Appendix II. For the present it is enough to point out that the form which M2:5 takes is a midrashic one.

[25] See Epstein, *Siprût*, 234–40. Epstein, *Nûsaḥ*, 1129–31 addresses passages where it is precisely the language of Scripture that exerts pressure on the language of the Mishnah. In addition to the examples cited below, see the two disputes between Hillelites and Shammaites in M3:12 [A–C; E–G], which use the Biblical expression *šālaḥ yād* (Ex. 22:7); where related issues are raised elsewhere (M3:9; M3:12 [H–J]) no such terminology is used.

[26] Compare the force of similar rhetorical structures in M2:1–2; a variant of this structure appears in M7:2 (without the introductory question). In both cases, the force of the pericope is to make a single subdivision in the legal field (found objects must either be kept or proclaimed; workers either eat or do not). See, e.g., *m. B. Qam.* 2:4 (distinguishing between the terms *mûʿād* and *tām*; the case is complicated by the fact that this pericope is used to gloss the item "ox" in the list of "five *tamîm* and five *mûʿadîm*"); *m. Zeb.* 11:2 (glossing a rule that mentions sin-offerings that were or were not at one time valid [*še- (loʾ) hāyâ* (sic) *lāh šāʿat ha-košer*]: "Which is it that was at one time valid ?... and which is it that was not at one time valid?..."; this passage has a parallel in *m. Meʿil.* 1:1 in which the opposition is between offerings that did or did not have a time during which they were permitted to priests [*še- (loʾ) hāyâ* (sic) *lāh šāʿat hettēr la-kohanîm*]); *m. Qin.* 1:1 (distinguishing between two Biblical terms for vows [i.e., votive offerings]: "Which is a *neder*?... and which is a *nĕdābâ*?..."; see Lev. 7:16; 22:18, 21, 23; Num. 15:3; 29:39; Deut. 12:6, 17).

to a loan in which the borrower is required to pay back more than he borrowed; the latter to a transaction in which someone sells produce that he does not yet have (so that the appreciation in the value of the produce by the time of delivery is, in effect, paid to the buyer in exchange for his waiting for delivery).[27] Neither word reappears in the chapter or, for that matter, in the Mishnah as a whole; the term utilized everywhere else is the Rabbinic *ribbît*.[28] While this abrupt terminological shift need not necessarily mean that M5:1 stems from a different hand than the rest of Chapter 5, it is suggestive: M5:1 sets up an expectation for a distinction in terminology for types of usury that does not appear elsewhere. If so, the fact that the distinction between *nešek* and *tarbît* seems to underlie the chapter as a whole[29] may imply that M5:1 was an already existing tradition utilized and explicated by the redactors, or, alternatively, that it was formulated to introduce a chapter composed of other materials.

Another example of a shift in terminology also occurs in Chapter 5 (M5:6):

> [A] One may not accept "iron sheep" from an Israelite,
> [B] because it is interest.
> [C] But one may receive "iron sheep" from the nations (*gôyîm*),
> [D] and one borrows from them and lends to them at interest,
> [E] and so too with a resident stranger (*gēr tôšāb*).
> [F] An Israelite may lend [at interest] with the money of a foreigner (*nokrî*),
> [G] with the knowledge of the foreigner (*nokrî*), but not with the knowledge of the Israelite.

[F–G] add a rather more nuanced case (one Jew lending to another with money belonging to a gentile) to a straightforward pericope [A–D] about who is or is not protected by the prohibition of usury. These clauses are

---

[27] For the Biblical use of the terms see Lev. 25:36, Ez. 18:8, 13, 17; 22:12; Prov. 28:8. The commentaries, following the tradition in the Babli attributed to both R. Abbahu and Raba, read *nešek* as divinely (i.e., Biblically) prohibited usury and *tarbît* as a Rabbinic supplement to the Biblical rule (B61a). This seems to be the implication of the view attributed to R. Yannai in the Yerushalmi (Y5:1 [10a]) that *nešek* is "the [type of] interest (*ribbît*) that can be confiscated by the judges," as opposed to others that, although prohibited, may not be confiscated (see also the tradition attributed to R. Eleazar at B61b). This interpretation is quite surprising in that it takes a Mishnaic passage clearly working with Biblical terminology and reads it in terms of a distinction of Biblical and non-Biblical prohibitions.

[28] M5:2, 5, 6, 9, 10; elsewhere in the Mishnah: *m. Roš Haš.* 1:8; *m. Sanh.* 3:3; *m. Šebu.* 7:4; *m. ʿArak.* 9:3.

[29] Neusner, *Damages* V, 66. I return to this subject below, Section C.3.

concerned with "subjective" criteria (knowledge, awareness) and not merely "objective" criteria (Jew, gentile, interest). On these grounds [F–G] might be deemed a later supplement.[30] In this context, the fact that the first part of the passage refers to gentiles by the term "the nations" [C], but the latter part uses "foreigner" [F, G], may be important. While both terms stem ultimately from Biblical usage, one particular usage of the term *nokrî*, "foreigner," is significant in this context: "the *nokrî* shall you charge interest (*taššîk*, cf. *nešek*); your brother shall you not charge interest" (Deut. 23:21). In other words, [F–G] explicitly echo a verse in Deuteronomy that [A–D] do not.[31]

In M4:9 [E], M7:8 [D, G] and M7:10 [G] a paid depositary is called a *nôśēʾ śākār* (wage bearer). In M6:6 [A] (plu.), [C], 7 [A, C], 8 [C], by contrast, the term used is *šômēr śākār* (paid watchman).[32] The clauses of M6:6–7 in which *šômēr śākār* appears all make a similar argument: they attempt to define the liability of someone who holds property belonging to someone else (e.g., an artisan holding raw materials or finished products) in terms of the liability of a paid or unpaid depositary. It follows that (whatever the redactional history of these passages) the terminology of M6:6 persists in M6:7 because the two passages were ultimately meant to be taken together. That the term *šômēr śākār* reappears in M6:8 may be due to the function of M6:6–8 together as a "coda" (see below, section C) to M6:1–5.

M7:8 [C–H] has another terminological feature, and once again Biblical language offers a key. In describing those kinds of loss for which a paid depositary or a renter is not liable and a borrower is liable, M7:8 [G–H] states: "the wage bearer and the renter swear for the break (*šeber*), for the

---

[30] The suggestion that [F–G] stem from a different source than [A–E] is supported by the fact that, like the key clauses in M5:4–5 (M5:4 [A, D, E, G, H]; 5:5 [A, D, E]), M5:6 [A–E] is formulated in an impersonal construction using the plural participle (present) (see Segal, 159, §330). By contrast, the final sentence [F–G] uses the somewhat emphatic *malweh hûʾ yiśrāʾēl*, "an Israelite lends (or: may lend)," using a singular form and a clearly defined subject (see Segal, 163–4, §341), which may have supplementary force ("however he may ...").

[31] In making reference to the resident alien (*gēr tôšāb*), M5:6 [E] also echoes verses in Scripture prohibiting interest, but in this case the Biblical passage is Lev. 25:35–6. This reference is problematic since the rule of [E] apparently contradicts Scripture (the discussion of M5:6 in Appendix I). If [E] is not a later supplement (as formulated, [A–D] form a self-contained unit; [E] explicitly adds to it [*wĕ-kēn*, "and so also ..."], and might be an addition), [A–E] might be conceived of as formulated with reference to Lev. 25:35–7. In this case M5:6 would provide an example of material originating in the interpretation of verses in Leviticus, supplemented (by a different hand) by materials stemming from the interpretation of Deuteronomy. While this is not impossible, there is nothing in [A–D] as a unit that requires that it is the product of exegesis of Lev. 25:35–7 specifically, other than the presupposed prohibition of interest.

[32] In fact, M6:6–8 is the only place in the Mishnah where the term *šômēr śākār* is used. Elsewhere *nôśēʾ śākār* is used (*m. B. Qam.* 4:9; *m. Šebu.* 6:5; 8:1, 6).

captured animal (*šěbuyâ*), and for the dead animal (*mētâ*) [and are exempt from payment], and pay for the loss (*ʾabēdâ*) and for the theft (*gěnēbâ*)." This language clearly reflects Exodus 22:9–10: "(9) If a man gives an ass ... to his fellow to watch, and it dies (*mēt*) or is broken (*nišbar*) or taken captive (*nišbâ*) and no one sees, (10) let an oath of the Lord be between the two of them ...." Furthermore, the ruling with respect to theft (and, from the Mishnah's point of view, loss) corresponds to verse 22:11: "If it should be stolen (*gānob yiggānēb*) from him [the depositary], he shall pay its owners." The Mishnah has manifestly interpreted Exodus 22:9–12 as referring to a paid depositary (and perhaps to a renter as well).[33] The material that follows immediately in M7:9–10 [D] introduces the term *ʾônēs* to cover precisely those acts of force beyond the control of the depositary for which M7:8 had used Biblical terminology.[34] Although M7:8 could circulate independently (cf. *m. Šebu.* 8:1; see Section A.2 below), M7:10 [E–G] corresponds clause by clause to M7:8 [C–H], and there is clearly an intentional connection between them. It is possible that M7:9–10 [D] has been interpolated into an already existing unit to amplify the limits of "accidental" death or damage.

The final example of terminological variance to be discussed here is M9:13.[35] In general, the term used for the distraint of pledges is *maškēn*.[36]

---

[33] On the problem of Biblical derivation for the rule of the renter (*śôkēr*) from Ex. 22:6–14, see the brief discussion in Lapin, 1995, 155–6, n. 16.

[34] However, in M7:9–10 [D], too, Scriptural interpretation seems clear. *Mek. Něziqîn* 16 glosses Ex. 22:9 ("... and it dies [*mēt*] or it is broken [*nišbar*] or it is taken captive [*nišbâ*]") as follows: "'and it dies,' that its death be at the hands of heaven [and not due to human intervention], 'or it is broken,' that an animal broke it, 'or it is taken captive,' that brigands (*lisṭîm*) took it captive" (ed. Horovitz-Rabin, p. 303). While the precise connection between the *Mekilta* and the Mishnah here is far from clear (see the discussion of this passage in Appendix II), the *Mekilta* transmits interpretations of the three key words used in M7:8 [G] in a manner that helps unpack M7:9–10 [E]. Thus, when M7:9 works out under which circumstances damage by an animal [A–F, H–J] or a brigand [G, K] is considered *ʾônēs*, it is apparently using the definition found in the *Mekilta* for *nišbar* (*šeber* in the Mishnah), and *nišbâ* (*šěbuyâ* in the Mishnah) respectively. Similarly, in M7:10 [A–E] what is at issue is whether the animal died (*mētâ*) due to human intervention or due solely to "the hands of heaven."

[35] One additional case of variant terminology should be mentioned, although I am not certain that it shows a redactional seam. In M9:11 [A–D], 12 [H], the term used for a hired laborer is *śākîr*, "wage-earner, hireling." Clearly the term echoes the use of *śākîr* in Lev. 19:13 ("You shall not keep the wages of the wage-earner [*śākîr*] with you overnight until the morning") and Deut. 24:14–15 ("You shall not oppress a poor or impoverished wage-earner [*śākîr*] ..., on his day let him receive his wage, and let the sun not set upon him [unpaid]"). Elsewhere in the tractate (M2:9 [G]; M5:4 [C]; M6:1 [D]; M7:1 [A, G], 4 [F], 5 [A]; 10:5 [G]) and in the Mishnah as a whole, the term used is *pôʿel* (laborer). This may suggest that M9:11–12 together stem from a source (or sources) more dependent upon Biblical terminology than elsewhere in the tractate, a suggestion supported by explicit citation of verses in M9:12 [B–C].

The final section of M9:13, which deals with the distraint of a millstone, uses the term *ḥabol* (M9:13 [L]). The choice of this latter verb is dependent upon the use of precisely the same word in the Bible.[37] This is clear from language of the passage itself:

[L] One who seizes the mill as pledge (*ha-ḥôbēl ʾet ha-rēḥayîm*)—
[M] he transgresses a negative commandment,
[N] and is liable for two utensils,
[O] as it is said: "You shall not seize the upper and lower millstone as pledge" (Deut. 24:6: *loʾ yaḥabol rēḥayim wā-rekeb*).
[P] Not the upper and lower millstone alone did they say,
[Q] but everything with which one makes food for living (*nepeš*),
[R] as it is said: "For it is a life that he seizes as pledge (*kî nepeš hûʾ ḥôbel*)" (Deut. 24:6).

Not only the operative verb *ḥabol*, but also the object of that verb (the millstone), and the term (*nepeš*) from which the general definition of items that may not be distrained is deduced, derive from a Biblical verse. It is precisely the point of this passage to flesh out some of the legal implications of Deuteronomy 24:6. By contrast, the passage immediately preceding this one uses the verb *mašken*, in conjunction with a citation of a verse using *ḥabol*: "A widow [*ʾalmānâ*] ... one does not distrain a pledge from her [*ʾên mĕmaškĕnîm ʾôtāh*], for it is said 'You shall not seize the garment of a widow as a pledge [*loʾ taḥabol beged ʾalmānâ*]" (Deut. 24:17)' [J–K]. The self-conscious echoing of Scripture in [L–R] juxtaposed with its absence in [J–K] makes it possible that [L–R] derives from a different source than the preceding material.[38]

However, when *śākîr* is used in the Mishnah (outside of *m. B. Meṣ.*, see *m. Šebi.* 10:5; *m. Šebu.* 7:1) the subject is always identical: the worker's right to prompt payment of wages. Thus it may also be that the use of *śākîr* is merely a stereotyped way of referring to a particular topic, and may not necessarily imply that the authorship of M9:11–12 is different from that of, say, M7:1–7.

[36] M9:13 [B, J]; elsewhere in the Mishnah: *m. Peʾa* 8:8; *m. Šebi.* 10:6; *m. Maʿaś. Š.* 1:1; *m. Šeq.* 1:3, 5; 7:5; *m. Ket.* 11:3; 13:8; *m. Šebu.* 7:2; *m. Ab. Zar.* 4:5; *m. ʿArak.* 5:6; 6:3.

[37] Two examples are cited in M9:13 itself: Deut. 24:6, 17. Cf. Ex. 22:25; Ez. 18:7, 12, 16; 33:5; Amos 2:8; Prov. 20:16; 27:13; Job 22:6; 24:3–9.

[38] Against this suggestion, is the argument (ultimately unanswerable) that I have demanded too much consistency from Mishnaic terminology. Moreover, in context *ḥabol* in M9:13 [L] could mean distraint by force or against the will of the court or debtor, whereas *mašken* in [J] refers to the authorized seizure outlined in [A–D]. In that case, however, *ḥabol* should have been expected in [C], rather than the comparatively long-winded *loʾ yikkānēs lĕ-bêtô wĕ-yiṭṭol maškônô* ("let him not go in and take his pledge"). In *m. Šebu.* 7:2, too, the Mishnah favors the conventional *mašken*: "They were testifying against him that he entered his [the debtor's]

2. Parallels.

I have been arguing that the Mishnah's redactors made use of heterogeneous materials, and that this process of compilation and redaction has left traces of alternative strategies of formulation and organization. There are times when the use of already existing materials is relatively clear. For instance, when a pericope appears in identical language in two separate tractates, as it does in M7:8 [C–H] and *m. Šebuʿot* 8:1, it is worth asking (a) whether the material originally circulated independently, or at any rate (b) whether one context served as the source for the other. The inference seems secure, however, that one or both of the passages is dependent upon antecedent material. In the example just cited, although both versions of the passage are followed by material that builds on them, there is no reason to grant priority to either *m. Šebuʿot* or *m. Babaʾ Meṣiʿaʾ*.[39] It is possible, therefore, that M7:8 [C–H] circulated independently of both contexts, and has been utilized by one or more redactors in two different places.

From a redactional point of view, those parallel passages that differ somewhat from one another are of particular interest, since they may reflect the

---

house to seize a pledge without authorization (*lĕmaškĕnô še-loʾ bi-rĕšût*)." *Ḥabol*, which only appears in Mishnaic usage in M9:13 [L], therefore appears to be essentially synonymous with *maškēn*. On balance, the rarity of *ḥabol* together with the close connection of [L–R] with Deut. 24:6, and the tendency of the accusative absolute form using the definite article with the participle (*ha-ḥôbēl* ...) to mark the beginning of a pericope or unit (see below Section B.2), lead me to suggest that [L–R] was not authored together with the rest of M9:13.

[39] As already noted above (the end of Section A.1), M7:8 [C–H] is echoed closely by M7:10 [E–G]: the passage in M7:8 outlines the liabilities for depositaries and related "watchmen," and the question of whether these liabilities may be altered by stipulation is addressed in M7:10 [E–G] in clauses that match the order and language of M7:8. Nevertheless, M7:8 can clearly stand by itself, and M7:10 [E–G] could be taken as a later supplement. The independence of M7:8 [C–H] of M7:10 [E–G], despite the close connections between them, suggests a complex process of redaction for M7:8–10. This is true whether or not M7:9–10 [D] is taken to have been interpolated into an already existing unit, as suggested above. *m. Šebu.* 8:1 is followed by several pericopae that explore the liability of the depositary to a sacrifice if he denied or misrepresented the loss of the deposit under oath. While the recurring key forms of loss (theft, loss, death, "breaking" or captivity) echo *m. Šebu.* 8:1, the question of sacrifice is secondary and could easily reflect later supplementation. (Rashi's comment to *m. Šebu.* 8:1 [*b. Šebu.* 49a], that the redactor had already taught this Mishnah in much the same language, "and the reason that R. [Judah the Patriarch] taught it here again is that he wanted to teach their [i.e., these 'watchmen'] liabilities and exemptions for the sacrifice for [a false] oath, and therefore he first taught the monetary liabilities and exemptions ...." implies that the passage in question has its original context in *m. B. Meṣ* 7:8, and is only used secondarily in *m. Šebu.* 8:1. However, Rashi bases his arguments on logical, not literary considerations [thus M7:8 serves as a primary context since M7:8–10 deal with "monetary liabilities and exemptions"], but does not explain why, say, M7:8 [C–H] appears where it does and not before M3:1, which clearly presupposes the rules of M7:8 [C–H].)

treatment of materials at the hands of redactors. The relationship of M3:11 to *m. Meʿila* 6:5 provides a case in point:

	m. Babaʾ Meṣiʿaʾ 3:11		*m. Meʿila* 6:5
[A]	One who deposits money with a banker—	[A]	One who deposits money with a banker—
[B]	if it is bound let him not make use of it;	[B]	if it is bound let him not make use of it.
		[C]	Therefore, if he spent [them] he has stolen sacred property (*māʿal*).[40]
[C]	if it is loose, let him use it.	[D]	If it is loose, let him use it.
		[E]	Therefore, if he spent [them] he has not stolen sacred property.
[D]	[If he deposits] with a householder in any case let him not use it.	[F]	[If he deposits] with a householder in any case let him not use it.
		[G]	Therefore, if he spent [them] he has stolen sacred property.
[E]	"The shopkeeper is like a householder,"	[H]	"The shopkeeper is like a householder,"

---

[40] The logic of this clause as well as [E] and [G] presuppose that in [A] the money deposited was sacred money. If the depositary was not permitted to use the money, when he uses it he does so on his own authority, and he himself is guilty of appropriating Temple funds. Where he was permitted to use the deposited money, he did so with the depositor's authorization (later commentaries saw the depositary here as a kind of agent, as in *m. Meʿil.* 6:1–4), and is himself not guilty of misappropriation. (That in such a case the depositor should be deemed guilty is the implication of a *bāraîtāʾ* parallel to *m. Meʿil.* 6:5 [A–D] at B43a [or perhaps a variant version of *m. Meʿil.* 6:5, as Tos. *b. Meʿil.* 21b, *s.v. Ha-mapqîd* imply], in which [C] and [G] read "Therefore the *gizbār* [i.e., the Temple official in charge of sacred property, who is presumably the depositor] has *not* stolen sacred property," and [E] reads "the *gizbār* has stolen sacred property" [B43a; the citation is attributed to R. Nahman]. However, *m. Meʿil.* 6:5 appears in the context of individuals who are not Temple officials holding Temple funds, and giving them to a second party, and the rule for the depositor might not be identical in the case of a lay depositor and a Temple official [Maimonides, *Code*, *Mĕʿîlâ* 7:9–10, for example, did not deem the depositor culpable, cf. *Kesep mišnâ ad loc.*]. The wording of *t. Meʿil.* 2:11 [Vienna ms.] ("has not stolen ..." [C, G]; "has stolen ..." [E]) agrees with the *bāraîtāʾ* in the Babli, without the word *ha-gizbār*. The Tosepta passage might conflict with the Mishnah, and rule that where the depositary ought not to have used the deposit what he intended was theft from a human and therefore he is not culpable for the misappropriation of Temple property. Arguably, where the parallel in the Babli adds *ha-gizbār*, it might be attempting to resolve two apparently contradictory traditions.)

[F]	The words of R. Meir.	[I]	The words of R. Meir.
[G]	R. Judah says: "Like a banker."	[J]	R. Judah says: "Like a banker."

The pericopae are nearly identical but for three supplementary clauses.[41] The passage from *m. Meʿila* thus seems to reflect the application of a rule originally formulated in the context of civil law (whether one may use deposited money) to the problem of the misuse of Temple funds. Since the parallels include material attributed to figures of the middle to late second century, the redactional process responsible for the reuse of the material (at least in *m. Meʿila*) can be no earlier than that period.[42]

A second example occurs at M4:9 and *m. Šebuʿot* 6:5:

	m. Babaʾ Meṣiʿaʾ 4:9		*m. Šebuʿot* 6:5
[A]	And these are things that do not have [the rule of] *hônāyâ*:	[A]	These[43] are things for which one does not swear:
[B]	slaves, documents, lands and consecrated goods.	[B]	slaves, documents, lands and consecrated goods.
[C]	They have neither [the rule of] two-fold payment nor four- or five-fold payment;	[C]	They have neither [the rule of] two-fold payment nor four- or five-fold payment;

---

[41] Some traditions of *m. B. Meṣ.* 3:11 have analogous supplementary clauses, but these may be later scribal additions (see the note to M3:11 in Appendix I). In *m. Meʿil.* 6:5 the verb in the supplementary clauses has shifted from *šmš* to *yṣʾ*. Although the point of the verb *hôṣîʾ*, "spent" (lit. "took out") (cf. *m. Meʿil.* 6:2, 6) may be no more than to specify what kind of "use" makes the depositary guilty of misappropriation of sacred property (as opposed to that which makes him culpable for misuse of a deposit; it is possible to cite at least one view, M3:6 [A–B], that any intervention with the deposit, even in the interests of the depositor, is prohibited to the depositary), the shift in verb may suggest the activity of a later hand. If all of *m. Meʿil.* 6:5 had been formulated in a single piece, one might have expected the use of *yṣʾ* throughout. (See further, next note.)

[42] The matter is complicated by the fact that M3:11 and *m. Meʿil.* 6:5 have a partial parallel in M2:7 [I–M] and may have been formulated with reference to it. However, whereas M2:7 [K, M] have the supplementary clauses, although they are not required by context (M2:7 [E–H] introduces the problem of the permissibility of use, and not specifically the problem of liability in the case of loss; if the presence of M2:7 [K, M] cannot be accounted for by the immediate context, might these clauses be original here?), and M3:11 appears not to have them at all (see Appendix I), although they would fit with that context (M3:9, 10, 12 deal specifically with liability), *m. Meʿil.* 6:5 would have no point in its current context without the presence of these clauses. Furthermore, M2:7 [I–M] itself may be reworked from a more general formulation about deposits of money (see below, Section D.2). Thus parallels, while suggesting the existence of sources, may not offer sufficient evidence for a nuanced transmission history.

[43] Concerning the presence or absence of the initial *waw* (i.e., "and," as in *m. B. Meṣ.*) in the manuscripts and early editions, see Epstein, *Nûsaḥ*, 429.

[D] an unpaid depositary does not swear,	[D] an unpaid depositary does not swear,
[E] a paid depositary does not pay.	[E] a paid depositary does not pay.
[F] R. Simeon says: "Sacrifices for which he is liable have *hônāyâ*, and [those] for which he is not liable do not have *hônāyâ*."	[F] R. Simeon says: "Sacrifices for which he is liable one swears, and [those] for which he is not liable one does not swear."

Clearly, the differences between the two versions of this pericope reflects their different contexts. Chapter 4 of *m. Baba' Meṣi'a'* is concerned, on the whole, with the question of *hônāyâ*; *m. Šebu'ot* 6:5 appears in the context of a discussion of *šĕbû'at ha-dayyānîm*, "the oath [imposed by] the judges," that is, the oath imposed upon a defendant who admits only part of the debt (or other claim) claimed against him.[44] The situation is further complicated by the following passage in *m. Baba' Qamma'* 7:4 in which the view attributed to R. Simeon appears in still a third context:

[G] He stole [an animal] and consecrated it, and afterwards slaughtered or sold it:

[H] He pays the two-fold payment, but he does not pay the four- or five-fold payment.[45]

[I] R. Simeon says: "Sacrifices for which he is liable he pays the four- or five-fold payment; sacrifices for which he is not liable he is exempt."

The parallel between the version of the statement attributed to R. Simeon in *m. Baba' Qamma'* and those from *m. Baba' Meṣi'a'* and *m. Šebu'ot*, and its

---

[44] Although the formulation of *m. Šebu.* 6:5 applies to oaths in general (see below), the pericope is presumably designed to amplify the problem of *šĕbû'at ha-dayyānîm*. *m. Šebu.* 6:5 has been integrated into the discussion of *šĕbû'at ha-dayyānîm* through 6:6, in which the amplification of a dispute over whether produce still connected to land is considered land (i.e., and exempt from an oath in *m. Šebu.* 6:5 [A–B]) exemplifies the question with a case of *šĕbû'at ha-dayyānîm*. (The terms of the dispute itself are quite general ["there are things that are like land but are not like land ..."]; the amplification ["How (*kēsad*) ..."] may be secondary.)

[45] The point of [H] is that it is only when one steals from a private person and then slaughters or sells, that one is liable for four- and five-fold penalty payments (Ex. 21:37). In the present case [G], however, when the animal was slaughtered or sold it was already consecrated, and was now the property of the Temple, and neither the theft nor the subsequent slaughtering or sale of consecrated goods carries these penalty payments (M4:9 [C] = *m. Šebu.* 6:5 [C]; see also *t. B. Qam.* 7:21). The thief does pay a double payment, since the animal was private property when he stole it.

formulation as a general rule, suggests that in *m. Baba' Qamma'* it was intended to have a wider application than to the rather narrow case of one who has stolen, consecrated and then sold or slaughtered an animal, in connection with which it appears in *m. Baba' Qamma'*.[46] By contrast, in *m. Baba' Meṣiʿa'* and *m. Šebuʿot,* the view attributed to R. Simeon matches the respective introductory clauses of the passages in which it appears. However, in each of these cases the tradition of R. Simeon appears embedded in a pericope that is somewhat problematic in its broader thematic context. In *m. Šebuʿot* 6:5, the general formulation of the pericope as a whole ("These are the things for which one does not swear" [A]; "one does (not) swear" [F]) stands in some tension with its immediate context, the discussion of a specific kind of oath.[47] The questions of double or four- or five-fold payment and of paid and unpaid depositaries are largely irrelevant to both *m. Baba' Meṣiʿa'* 4:9 (on *hônāyâ*) and *m. Šebuʿot* 6:5 (on *šĕbûʿat ha-dayyānîm*).[48] The parallels between these two pericopae are best explained if we assume that a common pericope, formulated to discuss the specific legal qualities of slaves, documents, lands, and consecrated goods (but whose original form cannot

---

[46] That the Babli, for exegetical reasons of its own (whether dedication is equivalent to sale with respect to obligation to pay four- or five-fold payments), could separate the statement of R. Simeon from its context in *m. B. Qam.* and connect it with another text (*'amrê r. šimʿôn 'amiltā' 'aḥarîttî qā'ê wĕ-hakî qā-tānê*), may reflect the fact that the wording of the rule was general enough to be applied to another text (*b. B. Qam.* 76a). Moreover, in this new context (apparently a variant or revision of *m. B. Qam.* 7:1 that includes the case of one who stole already consecrated goods) the tradition attributed to R. Simeon applies not only to four- and five-fold payments for sale or slaughter, but to any penalty payment for theft. (However, in the revised version, the Babli mss., apparently unanimously, have "Sacrifices ... he is liable" where the Mishnah has "Sacrifices ... he pays the four- or five-fold payment," so that the language of the tradition of R. Simeon has perhaps consciously been given less specificity.)

[47] Cf. *TY* to *m. Šebu.* 6:5, who notes that "one does not swear" [A] refers to "any of the three oaths of Biblical authority" (i.e., the oath of a "watchman" [cf. [D]], that required of a defendant denying part of a claim, and that imposed on a defendant who denies a claim entirely, but whose denial is refuted by only one witness; see *TY*'s introduction to chapter 6).

[48] It is possible to argue that *m. Šebu.* 6:5 is the "original" pericope, and that *m. Šebu.* serves as its proper context, since the rule that an unpaid depositary does not swear over slaves documents, lands and consecrated goods [D] is connected with the question of oaths in [A] (the rule about paid depositaries [E] being merely an extension of the thought of [C]). Against this suggestion that the pericope has its proper context in *m. Šebu.* 6:5, is the fact that the pericope, although placed in the context of a unit of material on *šĕbûʿat ha-dayyānîm*, deals with oaths in general, and supplements the opening general rule [A–B] with a specific case [D] that involves a type of oath not dealt with in the surrounding material, and that in any case is already guaranteed by that general rule. What is new in *m. Šebu.* 6:5 [C–E] (the exemption of a thief or a paid depositary from their respective payments) is also irrelevant to the context. Similarly, in M4:9, the whole of [C–E] is largely irrelevant to the immediate context.

necessarily be recovered) stands behind the formulation of both *m. Baba² Meṣiʿaʾ* 4:9 and *m. Šebuʿot* 6:5, which could then be modified in later use.[49] If the tradition attributed to R. Simeon, which is concerned with a distinction between two classes of consecrated animals, was originally formulated in connection with this hypothetical original pericope (as is suggested by its inclusion in both *m. Baba² Meṣiʿaʾ* and *m. Šebuʿot*), *m. Baba² Qammaʾ* 7:4 might reflect the separation and adaptation of the tradition of R. Simeon in still a third passage, or perhaps even a reapplication of a common "original" pericope as a whole.[50] M4:9 and its parallels, then, are an example of the

---

[49] D. W. Halivni, *Mĕqôrôt û-mĕsôrôt: Bābāʾ qammāʾ* (Jerusalem: Magnes, 1993), 291–3, argues that the original core of both *m. Šebu.* 6:5 and M4:9 is [C–E], an "early Mishnah" that served as the source from which the exclusion of slaves, documents, lands, and consecrated goods is derived for both oaths and *hônāyâ*. The exclusion, Halivni contends, is based on exegesis of Ex. 22:6–12; the extension to oaths and *hônāyâ* is derived by analogy. Attractive as this suggestion is (especially its attempt to account for material shared by *m. B. Meṣ.* and *m. Šebu.*), I find it difficult to give it its full force. First, Halivni does not cite (nor have I found) other ancient sources that offer confirmation for the exegetical processes he proposes. By contrast *Sipra, Bĕ-har* III:1–3 (ed. Weiss, 107a), in a context that has much overlap with the Mishnah, derives the exemption for slaves, documents, lands, and consecrated goods from the rules of *hônāyâ* from Lev. 25:14 (see also B47b; B65b). Second, the textual basis for Halivni's claim is not as strong as it might be. Halivni suggests that [C–E] be read as explanatory: "[there is no rule of *hônāyâ*/oaths for slaves ...] *for* these have neither the rule of two-fold payment ...; an unpaid depositary does not swear ...." The *waw*, which Halivni wishes to take as introducing a causal clause, appears only in P; the Rome B ms. of *b. B. Meṣ.*; the Munich ms. of *b. Šebu.*; and the Mishnah text (*m. B. Meṣ.*) of the Meiri as printed in K. Schlesinger, ed., *Beth Habehira* (Jerusalem: Mekize Nirdamim, 1959), 209. Moreover, this use of *waw*, while attested (see, e.g., *m. Nid.* 4:1: *wĕ-hēn yôšbôt*, with the commentary of *TY* and *TYṬ*; T7:1: *wĕ-ʾēnô dômeh ʿôśeh*, Erfurt ms.; Venice and *editio princeps* have *še-ʾênô*), is hardly the most common use of *waw* in Mishnaic Hebrew, and can, in this case, just as easily be taken as merely conjunctive (i.e., adding an additional rule about slaves, documents, lands, and consecrated goods).

[50] Halivni, 1993, 291–3 saw the view of R. Simeon as based on the "original" pericope. However, it remains possible that the legal distinction between two kinds of "holy things" attributed to R. Simeon, was itself a free-standing tradition that could be reapplied in various contexts. At any rate, as it appears in *m. B. Qam.* 7:4 [I] this version of the tradition of R. Simeon too appears to have undergone alteration. Although *m. B. Qam.* 7:4 [I] does have the formal qualities of a general rule, the formulation of the view attributed to R. Simeon in terms of penalty payments over and above the double payments (corresponding to the use of "four- and five-fold payments" in *m. B. Qam.* 7:4 [H]), although from the point of view of law the statement of R. Simeon should apply equally to the more general case of double payments in a simple case of theft, suggests that [I] has been adapted to fit the requirements of its present context. Hypothetically, [I] might stem from an "original" pericope analogous to M4:9 or *m. Šebu.* 6:5, but dealing with the penalty payments for theft (something along the lines of "These are the things for which one pays neither two-fold nor four- or five-fold payments:

fluidity of traditions—even when attributed to named individuals—even as they indicate the basic conservatism towards the textual raw material at hand.

Another example may be found in the parallels between M7:4 [A–C] and *m. Maʿaserot* 2:8 [A–C]:

m. Babaʾ Meṣiʿaʾ 7:4	*m. Maʿaserot* 2:8
[A] If he was working with figs, let him not eat from the grapes;	[A] If he was working with *lĕbasîm*[51] [figs] let him not eat from the *bĕnôt šebaʿ* [figs];
[B] with grapes, let him not eat from the figs;	[B] with *bĕnôt šebaʿ*, let him not eat from the *lĕbasîm*;
[C] but he may hold himself back until he reaches the place of the nice ones, and eats [there].	[C] but he may hold himself back until he reaches the place of the nice ones, and eats [there].

The version in *m. Babaʾ Meṣiʿaʾ* distinguishes between two kinds of fruit, while that in *m. Maʿaserot* distinguishes between varieties of figs. It is presumably no accident, but the product of stylistic choice, that nearly all the cases in *m. Maʿaserot* 2:1–3:4 illustrate the rules of tithing with examples about figs.[52] It is not clear whether *m. Maʿaserot* 2:8 [A–C] should be taken

---

slaves, documents, lands, and consecrated goods [as in M4:9 [C]; *m. Šebu.* 6:5 [C]; cf. also *t. B. Qam.* 7:11, 20; *Mek. Kaspaʾ* 13 (ed. Horovitz-Rabin, p. 295)] ... R. Simeon says: 'Sacrifices ....'"). (Arguably, this hypothetical pericope—focused on the problem that is also shared by M4:9 and *m. Šebu.* 6:5—might form the common stock from which both of these latter pericopae stem. In its broad outlines this suggestion is similar to the view of Halivni discussed in the previous note.) Even if this were so, however, the wording of the view attributed to R. Simeon would still be expected to reflect both double and four- and five-fold payments (or, as the formulation from *b. B. Qam.* 76a cited above has it, simply "liable"/"exempt"). That it does not do so in *m. B. Qam.* 7:4 [I] would still suggest a certain amount of correction.

[51] This word is variously preserved in the mss. (*lbsym*; *lwbsym*; *lwpsym*; *klwpsym*; and others). See the variants cited in *The Mishnah*, ed. N. Sacks (*Institute for the Complete Israeli Talmud: Jerusalem*: Yad Harav Herzog, 1971–), 219.

[52] Three notable exceptions are: (1) *m. Maʿaś.* 2:6, which gives several variations on the following case: "One who says to his fellow: 'Here is an *ʾissār* (as) for ten figs that I will choose" (2:6 [A], developing 2:5 [A]), in terms of clusters of grapes [C], pomegranates [E], and melons [G]; the primary example, however, is one of figs; (2) *m. Maʿaś.* 3:2, which gives illustrations using olives and onions; this pericope amplifies a rule already stated in 2:7 (cf. 2:5, R. Judah) in terms of figs; (3) *m. Maʿaś.* 3:4, which deals primarily with various kinds or by-products of figs (chopped, dried, pressed), supplemented with contrasting cases concerning olives and onions.

as having a direct application to tithing,⁵³ or whether it has roughly the same force as M7:4 [A–C] and is included in *m. Maʿaśerot* only by association with *m. Maʿaśerot* 2:7.⁵⁴ Given that *m. Maʿaśerot* 2:8 [A–C] follows immediately upon material in which the worker's right to "eat according to the Torah" is invoked (cf. M7:2 [A]), it seems likely that *m. Maʿaśerot* 2:7–8 has been formulated with material now in M7:2–4 in view. However, below (Section C.2) I will suggest that M7:1–8 [B] shows traces of a complex process of redaction. Since these traces do not appear to be reflected in *m. Maʿaśerot*, I am inclined to think that the two traditions have independently used material common to both. Since it does not appear that either formulation is dependent upon the other it seems likely that the pericope circulated independently, and was incorporated in slightly different forms in the two tractates.⁵⁵

---

⁵³ See, e.g., R. Yehosep Ashkenazi in *Mĕlʾeket šĕlomoh* to *m. Maʿaś.* 2:8 and *TY* to *m. Maʿaś.* 2:8, who suggest that *m. Maʿaś.* 2:8 deals with a case where the owner permits the worker to eat even from produce that the worker is not working on, but rules that the exemption from tithes is valid only for produce that the worker is working on. (Albeck, to *m. Maʿaś.* 2:8 raises the issue of tithes here as well.)

⁵⁴ So, explicitly, R. Solomo Sirillo, as cited in *Mĕlʾeket šĕlomoh* to *m. Maʿaś.* 2:8. R. Samson of Sens, following *y. Maʿaś* 2:7 (50a), treated the passage from *m. Maʿaś.* as dealing with a case in which the two varieties of fig were planted together; Bertinoro, *TYT*, and *TY* (with some misgivings) are dependent upon R. Samson of Sens or directly upon the Yerushalmi.

⁵⁵ There are other examples that should be mentioned:

(1) M4:7, to be discussed below, has a number of parallels.

(2) M1:6–8 and *m. Moʿed Qaṭ.* 3:3. M1:6–8 deals with documents that are found; *m. Moʿed Qaṭ.* 3:3 presents a list of documents that may be written on the intermediate days of a festival. Although the pericopae are not formally similar to one another, the order in which the documents are presented in the two passages is strikingly similar:

m. B. Meṣ. 1:6–8	*m. Moʿed Qaṭ.* 3:3
loan documents	
divorce documents for women	divorce documents
	receipts
emancipation documents for slaves	
wills	wills
[deeds] of gift	[deeds] of gift
receipts	
letters of estimation	letters of estimation
letters of alimony	letters of alimony
documents of *ḥalîṣâ* and of refusal of marriage	documents of *ḥalîṣâ* and of refusal of marriage
documents of selection [of judges]	documents of selection [of judges]

Somewhat more ambiguous is the relationship between M7:7 and *m. Maʿaśerot* 1:8. M7:7 reads as follows:

[A] If someone hires workers—
[B] to work with him on his fourth-year produce,
[C] lo, let these not eat;
[D] but if he did not inform them,
[E] he redeems [the produce] and feeds them.
[F] His fig-rounds broke up, or his jars were opened (*niptĕḥû*), his gourds were cut (*nithatkû*)[56],
[G] lo, let these not eat,
[H] but if he did not inform them,
[I] he separates the tithe and feeds them.

m. Maʿaśerot 1:8 has the following tradition:

[F] Dried figs [are liable to tithing] from the time that he threshes them (i.e., presses them into jars).

---

any act of the court
decrees of the court
letters of authorization

Loan documents are absent in *m. Moʿed Qaṭ.* because the writing of them is prohibited on the intermediate days of the festival (*m. Moʿed Qaṭ.* 3:4). The reading "letters of authorization" (i.e., *ʾiggĕrôt šel rāšût*) in *m. Moʿed Qaṭ.* follows the context (court-related documents) and the responsum of the Gaon [Isaac] Zadok (appt. 816) (see B. M. Lewin, *ʾÔṣār ha-gĕʾônîm* [Jerusalem: Hebrew University, 1928–43; rpt. Jerusalem, 1984] vol. 4, sec. 3, pp. 23–4): "a writing that the exilarch writes to a judge to go and teach Israel [that which is] permitted or prohibited and to make rulings for them ..."; and Rashi and Tos. *ad loc.* [*b. Moʿed Qaṭ.* 18b]: royal orders). Compare, however, the reading of the Yerushalmi (*y. Moʿed Qaṭ. [Mašqin]* 3:3 [82a]; followed by, e.g., R. Hananel, Rif, Maimonides, Rabad [*Haśāgôt*]): *ʾiggĕrôt šel rĕšût*, i.e., a personal letter. Although there is no question here of dependence between *m. B. Meṣ.* and *m. Moʿed Qaṭ.*, the parallels between these two sources may be significant: is it not possible that a common stock catalogue of documents is being utilized in both tractates?

(3) M7:11 [A] reads: "All who make conditions of [i.e., in contradiction to] what is written in the Torah, his condition is invalid," to which there is a partial parallel at *m. B. Bat.* 8:5 (technically the same tractate as *m. B. Meṣ.*) and a full parallel at *m. Kel.* 9:1 (see Section A.1 above).

(4) M9:12 [H], "A hired worker (*śākîr*) at his proper time swears and takes [his payment] (*nišbaʿ wĕ-nôṭēl*)," finds an echo in *m. Šebu.* 7:1: "All those who swear according to the Torah swear and do not pay. And these swear and take (*nišbaʿîn wĕ-nôṭlîn*): the hired worker (*śākîr*) ...." While there is no doubt that there is material in common, the use of *śākîr* together with *nišbaʿ wĕ-nôṭēl* may reflect standardized terminology rather than the use of sources (cf. n. 35 above).

[56] For the words "his gourds were cut" see the note to M7:7 in Appendix I.

[G] [Figs to be stored in] a storage jar, [are liable] from the time that he presses them.[57]

[H] He was threshing into a jar or pressing into a storage chamber:

[I] the jar broke or the storage jar was broken through (*niphatâ*),

[J] let him not eat [even] casually from them.

[K] R. Yose permits.

The language and case of M7:7 [F–G] and *m. Ma'aserot* 1:8 [F–J] are strikingly similar, yet these two pericopae remain quite different. The one passage explores the middle ground between the time that the labor on the produce that renders produce liable to tithing (the "completing of its work") and prohibited from consumption has begun, and the time that it is finished (*m. Ma'aś.* 1:8); the other, the problem of produce whose work has been "completed," but that, due to an accident, appears not to have been "completed" (M7:7).[58] Although it is possible that the most closely parallel material (M7:7 [F]; *m. Ma'aś.* 1:8 [I]) merely conforms to a common rhetorical pattern,[59] these two pericopae may share a common source, or, perhaps, the author of M7:7 may have carried the material of *m. Ma'aserot* 1:8 forward by considering the case in which the produce only looks like it is not liable to tithing.

B. The Shape of Sources

The argument of the preceding section was that the redactor or redactors of the *m. Baba' Meṣi'a'* have demonstrably utilized already existing materials as sources. Whatever revision and adaptation of materials occurred in the process of redaction, a deep conservatism towards utilized materials is in evidence. This conservatism allows us to see the traces of various alternative strategies for presenting material and for organizing it. Before addressing the question of the process of redaction itself, it is worth asking to what extent we can determine what some of the sources available to the redactors may have looked like.

---

[57] "Storage jar" translates the Hebrew *mĕgûrâ* (also "storage chamber"; cf. Appendix I, note to M4:12). "From the time that he presses" corresponds to the Hebrew *mi-še-ya'aggēl*, from the same root as the term for a pressed fig-round, *'iggûl*, used in M7:7. Maimonides, in his commentary to *m. Ma'aś.* 1:8, takes the verb to mean "smooth with a trowel (*'iggûl*)." This usage of *'iggûl* is unattested in the Mishnah.

[58] Despite the parallels in language, the prohibition "let him not eat" in *m. Ma'aś.* 1:8 [J] applies equally to householder and worker; in the analogous prohibition in M7:7, the antecedent of "these" is by definition the workers.

[59] Cf. *m. 'Orl.* 3:8, and the note to M7:7 in Appendix I.

1. Strategies.

In the context of the discussion of pericopae in *m. Baba' Meṣiʿa'* paralleled in other tractates, I have suggested that in general the material that can plausibly be identified as source material is not original in one Mishnaic tractate as it has come down to us, and reused in another Mishnaic context, but rather seems to reflect the independent use by the redactors of the two (or more) places where the material appears. In the case of parallels the only material that can be shown to have served as a source is that which actually appears in both locations, and we are given no explicit information about the wider literary context of these source-pericopae. It is possible that some of these circulated singly.

On the other hand, it stands to reason that some of the materials utilized in the Mishnah were available in the form of clusters of pericopae. At least some passages concerned with the exegesis of Scripture conceivably stem from sources that were organized around verses. Unfortunately, at least in the case of *m. Baba' Meṣiʿa'*, it is possible at most to point to pericopae that presuppose exegesis of Scripture;[60] it does not seem possible to reconstruct a "midrashic source," much less to demonstrate the reliance of the Mishnah on an extant midrashic collection (see Appendix II). However, if it could be shown that the redactors of the Mishnah did indeed use exegetical sources, and chose, for the most part, to recast that material independently of Scriptural authority even where that authority could easily be cited, this conclusion would be potentially significant for uncovering the development of Mishnaic discourse. The Mishnah, after all, while claiming to present "Torah," is, paradoxically, largely free rhetorically, topically, and structur-

---

[60] Passages that cite verses (e.g., M4:10; 5:11), that echo the language of Scripture (e.g., M3:12; 7:8), or even that reflect conscious exegesis in their wording (e.g., M3:1), do not necessarily give evidence of a larger source that is dependent for its organization and structure upon Scripture. M7:9–10 [D], for instance, may reflect exegesis of "death," "capture" and "breaking" in Ex. 22:9–13 (see above Section A.2), but may nevertheless form an isolated unit interested in a question deriving from Scripture. M2:5 is a fragment using midrashic style, and may, but need not, imply the existence of a Scripture-based source. M8:1 seeks to divine in its two parts the implications of two verses in the same Biblical passage [Ex. 22:13, 14], and might be taken as an example of how a pericope in Mishnaic style can be structured around verses, but it need not be part of a larger exegetical source. We are perhaps on stronger ground with M2:7, which offers exegesis of successive phrases of Deut. 22:2. In M2:9–10, which, I have argued above, derives from a source different from that of the rest of Chapters 1–2, the topics (including that of the animal struggling under its load, irrelevant in its present context) and their order are accounted for by Ex. 23:4–5 and Deut. 22:1–4. Similarly, the material in M9:12–13 is determined by that in Deut. 24:6, 10–15, 17–18. There are better examples of the phenomenon of clusters of Mishnaic pericopae organized around the exegesis of a passage of Scripture in other tractates, such as *m. Soṭ.* 8:1–7; 9:1–8; *m. Sanh.* 10:4–6.

ally, of the one unambiguously acknowledged source of authority that the Mishnah cites: the Pentateuch (Torah) itself.

There is, however, other material in *m. Baba' Meṣi'a'* that betrays different strategies of organization. Consider, for example, M4:7–8. The first three clauses of M4:7 give a series of three brief rules setting out the minimum value involved in a particular kind of claim. (Actually, M4:7 [B–C] are linked in that they refer to a single case in which the plaintiff claims that he is owed money, but the defendant only admits to a lesser amount.[61]) All three clauses have parallels: the first [A] in M4:3 [A], and the second and third [B–C] in *m. Šebu'ot* 6:1. Strikingly, in their other contexts, the three statements of M4:7 [A–C] appear with what appears to be secondary interpretation. In M4:3 the rule that a case of *hônāyâ* must involve overcharge of at least four silver coins (*mā'ôt*) is generalized as a proportion: "one sixth of the purchase." One implication of the formulation of M4:3 is that the rule of *hônāyâ* applies even when the value of the purchase as a whole is less than twentt-four silver coins. In *m. Šebu'ot* 6:1 the rules about claim and (partial) confession are taken to mean not that the amount of the claim itself must be two *mā'ôt*, but that the difference between the amount claimed by the plaintiff and the amount admitted by the defendant must equal that amount.[62]

---

[61] See Appendix I. Curiously, Neusner, *Damages* II, 60, has translated M4:7 [C]: "An admission *[as at M. 1:1]* must be for at least what is worth a *perutah*" (my italics). In other words, Neusner has taken [C] quite literally (although there is no case of admission at M1:1; he may, perhaps, be referring to M1:2 [E], taking *môdîm* as "confess" or "admit"). In his translation of *m. Šebu.* 6:1 Neusner read the two clauses as linked, as the context there requires (*Damages* IV, 51–2). Since Neusner's treatment is under-documented, it is unclear whether he has purposefully translated literally in *m. B. Meṣ.* or whether he has simply missed the parallel with *m. Šebu.*

[62] *m. Šebu.* 6.1 reads as follows:
   [A]   The oath that the judges [impose]:
   [B]   the claim is two silver coins,
   [C]   and the confession is a *pĕrûṭâ*-worth,
   [D]   and if the confession is not of the same kind as the claim he is exempt.
   [E]   How (*kēṣad*)?
   [F]   [The plaintiff said:] "You have two silver coins of mine," [and the latter said:] "I only have a *pĕrûṭâ*-worth of yours,"
   [G]   he [the defendant] is exempt [from an oath]
   [H]   [The plaintiff said:] "You have two silver coins and a *pĕrûṭâ* of mine," [and the latter said:] "I only have a *pĕrûṭâ*-worth of yours,"
   [I]   he [the defendant] is liable [to an oath].

In [F], the first illustration of [A–C], the plaintiff claims two silver coins, but the defendant admits to only a *pĕrûṭâ*-worth, to all appearances the very case of [B–C] (= M4:7 [B–C]). However [G] rules that the defendant is exempt from an oath. In the second illustration [H], the difference between the claim and the amount admitted by the defendant equals two silver

This cluster of three rules, referring to amounts in descending order of size, could easily be taken as a self-contained pericope that catalogues claims and the minimum values for which legal action on these claims may be brought. The other pericopae where these rules appear may be revisions of the earlier cluster of rules.[63]

The remainder of M4:7–8 consists of two units: (1) a set of five cases in which the value of a *pĕrûṭâ* is determinative ("There are five *pĕrûṭôt* ...," M4:7 [D]), and (2) one of five cases in which a charge of an added fifth applies ("There are five [added] fifths ...," M4:8 [A]). Once again, we can point to multiple parallels with other passages in the Mishnah, frequently attributed to early figures.[64] I suggest that, like the first part of M4:7, these

---

coins. That *m. Šebu.* 6:1 [A–D] is immediately glossed suggests that it itself may have constituted an independent unit utilized in the redaction of *m. Šebu.* 6. Moreover, the only attributed statements that appear in Chapter 6 that relate directly to *m. Šebu.* 6:1 deal with the rule in [D] and are attributed to Yabnean figures and might reflect a relatively early date for *m. Šebu.* 6:1 [A–D] (see, however, Section D below). The placement of [B–C] itself within *m. Šebu.* 6:1 [A–D] may be secondary ([D] is clearly supplementary, and [A] serves as an introduction), and may reflect the "contextualization" of the bare rule [B–C].

[63] See Weiss, 1941, 12–13, who argued that M4:7 [A–C] (and more generally M4:7–8) form an early source that is partially cited and then developed in M4:3–6.

[64] M4:7 [E] corresponds to M4:7 [C] and *m. Šebu.* 6:1 [C]. [F] corresponds to the Hillelite view in *m. ʿEd.* 4:7: "'The woman is betrothed with a *dînâr* or a *dînār*-worth,' in accordance with the words of the house of Shammai; the house of Hillel says: 'With a *pĕrûṭâ* or a *pĕrûṭâ*-worth.'" (The introductory words of the Shammaite view together with the ruling of the Hillelites [itself formulated as dependent upon the opening words] closely parallel M4:7 [F]. Incidentally, compare Neusner, *Purities* XXI, 196–7, who sees dispute forms as typically formed out of two independent declarative sentences. While such a reading is attractive here, it is hardly necessary to conclude, as Neusner does, that the dissolution of a dispute form into two declarative sentences will show "the traits of the several cognitive units that, in theory, serve as primary components of the dispute ...." There is no reason why a dispute form should not originally have been formulated as such.) Compare also *m. Qid.* 1:1. M4:7 [G] is paralleled, in somewhat expanded form in *m. Meʿil.* 5:1 where it is attributed to R. Aqiba: "'One who benefits by a *pĕrûṭâ*-worth from consecrated property, even though he has not marred [it] [*pāgam*, i.e., decreased its value], he has stolen sacred property (*māʿal*),' the words of R. Aqiba." [H] does not have an explicit parallel in the Mishnah (for similar language cf. M2:1; the rule appears, e.g., T2:14). [I] is paralleled in *m. B. Qam.* 9:5.

To M4:8 [B] compare *m. Meʿil.* 4:2 (itself part of a highly formalized series dealing with combinations of different substances that together add up to a minimum bulk; *miṣṭārpîn zeh ʿim zeh* occurs repeatedly in Chapter 4): "Heave offering, the heave offering from tithes, and the heave offering from tithes from produce suspected of not having been tithed, the priest's portion of the dough, and first fruits combine with one another to make up a forbidden [amount] and to obligate [the eater] to an [added fifth] over them." In *m. Meʿil.* 4:2, the minimum amount is presupposed and not specified, and the legal problem may be a development of the mere list of M4:8 [B]: the combination of small amounts of the items that make up a

two units, essentially catalogues of rules sharing a particular characteristic, constitute relatively early formulations, that could be utilized in other contexts.[65]

The link between the three parts of M4:7–8 is entirely associative: M4:7 [C] refers to the value of a *pĕrûṭâ*; [D–I] presents a set of rules involving the *pĕrûṭâ*, of which the first [E] is a restatement of [C]. M4:8 is structurally analogous to M4:7 [D–I] (opening title, followed by five cases each beginning with a definite article with the participle), but topically quite unconnected. With the exception of the first clause of M4:7, this whole cluster of rules is thoroughly unrelated to *m. Baba' Meṣi'a'*, and it is precisely this first clause that serves as the link with the preceding material. The question that needs to be answered is at what point in the process of redaction this cluster of materials was put together. While it is certainly possible that the editor of the tractate as a whole appended each of these units of material to M4:3–6 as a sort of coda, we would then have to explain why a redactor who is interested in setting materials according to a general topical arrangement should here append not one "tangential" tradition, but three. It seems more likely that these materials stood together as a group before their inclusion into the

---

minimum bulk. (The same list recurs in *m. 'Orl.* 2:1: see the critical apparatus in Sacks, 1971–, 2, 374 and n. 2, and the discussion of Frankel, n.d. [1859], 267.) The remaining items in M7:8 do not have explicit parallels, but are generally presupposed elsewhere in the Mishnah: [C], on the produce of the fourth year, corresponds to the Hillelite view in *m. Pe'a* 7:6; *m. Ma'aś. Š.* 5:3; *m. 'Ed.* 4:3; [D], concerning the redemption of dedicated property, is presupposed, among other places, in *m. 'Ar.* 3:2, where the rule is referred to by the "Yabnean" R. Eliezer; the language of [E] bears a strong resemblance to M4:7 [G], although the rule is not explicitly referred to (it is, however, clearly based on Biblical authority: cf. Lev. 5:15–16); [F] is presupposed by *m. B. Qam.* 9:6–7.

[65] There is a tendency among scholars to see pericopae organized along formal or mnemonic lines (e.g., "five rules concerning X") as early. See, e.g., Krochmal, 1851, 202–3; Graetz, 1893 (1853–76) 162; Frankel, n.d. (1859), 12, 123; and much more recently D. Zlotnick, *The Iron Pillar: Mishnah* (Jerusalem: Bialik, 1988), 45–50; see also the view of Weiss, 1941. As such, this is an *a priori* judgment and no more valid than Neusner's stated but unsubstantiated assumption that M4:7 [D–I] and M4:8 are "formal exercises" dependent upon earlier passages from which they have derived materials (Neusner, *Damages* V, 53, 60). In the present case, at least, there are no linguistic or stylistic criteria (outside of that of the formulation of M4:7 [D–I] and M4:8 as "mnemonic catalogues") such as archaic language or grammar that would necessitate an early date. What I mean by referring to M4:7 [D–I]–8 as "relatively early" is (1) that on the basis of the parallels between these pericopae and other material attributed to Yabnean (or earlier) figures, these pericopae could conceivably date from the end of the first century at the earliest; and (2) that these passages and M4:7 [A–C] should at the latest have been early enough to allow for two stages of redaction (the joining of M4:7 [D–I]–8, which are formally connected with one another, with M4:7 [A–C], and the inclusion of the whole cluster into the Mishnah as we have it).

tractate. Admittedly, this does not explain why or when someone did string these materials together, nor elucidate the social setting in which such a cluster of rules has meaning or utility. However, if this is correct, then one of the possible shapes that a source for the Mishnah could take is an "associative cluster."[66]

---

[66] We may, perhaps, make a similar argument for M10:4 [E]–10:5. Note the following outline of M10:4–6:

a. M10:4 [A–D]: a rule that gives an analogous case to that of M10:2, and explicitly amplifies preceding material (wĕ-kēn).
b. M10:4 [E–L]: a wall or tree that has fallen (še-nāpālû; cf. M10:1 [B], 3 [B]) into the public domain and caused damage.
c. M10:5 [A–F]: the owner of a wall that has fallen (še-nāpal) into his neighbor's garden tries to get his neighbor to clear the stones.
d. M10:5 [G–M]: analogous negotiations to those of [A–F] in the case of a householder and his laborers (note the language of [G]: ha-śôkēr ʾet ha-pôʿēl; cf. M6:1–5; 7:1).
e. M10:5 [N–Aʾ]: the deposit of dung or building materials in the public domain, and the liability for damage that ensues.
f. M10:6 [A–H]: two terraced gardens (zô ʿal gabbê zô; cf. M10:4 [A]: wĕ-ginnat ʾaḥēr ʿal gabbāyw), and the produce that grows between them.

The first section (a) is clearly connected with M10:2, as noted. The place of the last section (f) in this context seems to stem from the fact that like M10:4 [A–D] (with which it has slight verbal links, as noted), and M10:1–3 in general, it deals with conflicts that arise due to properties that are shared or are in close proximity to one another. This subject is continued in *m. B. Bat.* 1–2. However, the second (b) deals with damages and is irrelevant to the predominant interest in problems of property in Chapter 10. Moreover, the following three sections (c–e) are also unrelated to their general context in Chapter 10, but are connected either directly (c, by the case of the fallen wall; e, by the problem of damages) or indirectly (d, by analogy with c) to (b) (M10:4 [E–L]) itself. (To the cases of damage in these pericopae (b, e), cf. *m. B. Qam.* 3:1–3. Albeck, 1923, 137–8, noted the analogy with *m. B. Qam.* and argued that M10:4–5 as a unit are brought in *m. B. Meṣ.*, rather than *m. B. Qam.* where they belonged because of the analogy between M10:4 [A–D] and the subject of the preceding material. D. Daube, "Civil Law in the Mishnah: The Arrangement of the Three Gates," *Tulane Law Review* 18 [1944], 393, arguing [correctly] against the view that M10:4–5 are a displaced fragment that belongs in *m. B. Qam.* 3, took as separate categories of Mishnaic law the damage done by a collapsing house or other property [falling under property law and therefore belonging in Chapter 10 of *m. B. Meṣ.*] and that done by items left in the public domain [falling under the category of delict, and belonging in *m. B. Qam.* 3]. In fact, the relationship between *m. B. Qam.* 3:1–3 and M10:4–5 are closer than Daube supposes: *m. B. Qam.* 3:2 deals with a fence that has tumbled and caused damage, as in M10:4 [E–L]; *m. B. Qam.* 3:3 involves the case of refuse brought out into the public domain to be put on the dungheap, as in M10:5 [N–O]. It is redaction by associative links rather than by legal categorization that accounts for the presence of sections (b) and (e) in M10:4–5.) As in the case of M4:7–8, the links that unify these sections are entirely associative. I am inclined to suggest that at least M10:4:[E]–5 constitute a cluster of materials that was utilized whole by the redactor of the

In M3:2–5 there are traces of another kind of organizational strategy. M3:2 deals with the case of a lessee of a cow who lends the cow to a third party in whose possession the animal died. M3:3 is concerned with the matter of a thief who comes forward to admit liability but is not sure who the victim was. In M3:4–5 the problem of two householders claiming the more valuable of two deposits (whether in the form of money, M3:4, or objects, M3:5) from the depositary is discussed.[67] On formal grounds, M3:2–5 can

---

Mishnah. In the absence of unambiguous criteria by which to determine whether this cluster of material constitutes a source, this suggestion must remain only a suggestion. Still, I find it striking that the four sections in this cluster can be associated more easily with one another than with any other pericope in the tractate. As in the case of M4:7–8, it seems more reasonable that the redactor of the tractate has utilized a source composed of irrelevancies, than that he has purposely assembled them. Nevertheless, it remains difficult to account for the inclusion of this cluster into the Mishnah by the editor who utilized it, except by the admittedly associative link of fallen houses with fallen trees and walls, and once this is admitted there is no *a priori* reason to exclude the assembly of other material based on further associative links.

[67] To M3:3–5, compare *m. Yeb.* 15:7:
  [Q] "[If] he robbed one of five people
  [R] "and he does not know which he robbed,
  [S] "each one says: 'It is me that he robbed,'
  [T] "he leaves the property between them and departs,"
  [U] the words of R. Tarfon.
  [V] R. Aqiba says: "this is not the way that removes him from sin:
  [W] "[he cannot acquit himself] until he pays the robbed object to each one."

On the face of it, M3:3 agrees with the rule of R. Aqiba (which requires that every claimant be given the full payment claimed if the robber is to have fulfilled his obligation). But we should note that in M3:3 it is the thief's own confession that is significant and claims of the victims are not stated and perhaps irrelevant (see the motive clause in M3:3 [D]: "because he has admitted it by his own mouth"; similar logic seems to underlie *m. B. Qam.* 10:7), while in *m. Yeb.* 15:7 it is precisely the fact that there are multiple claimants that determines the ruling. (See *t. Yeb.* 14:2, which links M3:3 to *m. Yeb.* 15:7 with the connecting words: "And R. Tarfon concedes that if he said: 'I robbed one of you ....,'" [this led Lieberman to claim that M3:3 is according to (!) R. Tarfon, Lieberman, *TK*, 6, 171 to *t. Yeb.* 14:2; *TK*, 9, 70 to T3:5]. In other words, the author of *t. Yeb.* 14:2 considered M3:3 to be concerned with the specific problem of confessed liability, as opposed to *m. Yeb.* 15:7.)

More interesting is the relationship between *m. Yeb.* 15:7 and M3:4–5. The cases are analogous. Yet neither ruling in M3:4–5 corresponds to either of the rulings in *m. Yeb.* 15:7. In M3:4–5 the defendant returns the amount that definitely belongs to each (or according to R. Yose none of it), but on the basis of *m. Yeb.* 15:7 we expect the defendant to leave the whole sum for the plaintiffs to divide (R. Tarfon) or to pay the maximum amount to both parties (R. Aqiba). One possibility for the distinction may be that *m. Yeb.* 15:7 deals specifically with willful robbery, whereas M3:4–5 considers a case of deposit, in which there may have been no purposeful wrongdoing on the part of the defendant. If this is correct, then it is not necessarily self-evident that the author of M3:3, which deals with both robbery [A] and deposit [B], is the same as that of M3:4–5, who might rule differently in cases of robbery and of deposit.

be distinguished from M3:1, 6–11 in which some variant of the formula *ha-mapqîd ʾēṣel ḥabērô*, "one who deposits ... with his fellow," recurs no fewer than six times to introduce new pericopae.[68] While a partial parallel to this formulaic pattern may be found in M3:2 [A], which deals with another type of contract,[69] in M3:3–5, in which unpaid deposit is specifically invoked, the formula is not in evidence. While it is possible that the redactor of the chapter or tractate as a whole has brought together pericopae more or less unconnected to one another, I wish to suggest another possibility: that M3:2–5 has been utilized as a unit. What links these passages together is the series of traditions attributed to R. Yose (dated to the middle to late second century) (M3:2: [C–E], M3:4 [D–E]; M3:5 [D–E]). The statements of R. Yose, moreover, are structurally similar (although, admittedly, those from M3:4–5 are identical glosses to parallel pericopae): each consists of an exclamation challenging not the underlying principles of the antecedent ruling but the moral implications of the rule itself, followed by a new ruling. If my suggestion that tradental glosses can serve as the common link for clusters of material is correct, it is possible that we have a window, however opaque, into the social and literary processes that produced the Mishnah. First, the attributed statements in such cases are not merely "minority" dissenting views, but in fact provide the organizing principle. This presupposes a redactor or author

---

(That a distinction between claims of robbery and other kinds of claims might make sense in ancient Palestinian Rabbinic circles may perhaps be seen from *t. Yeb.* 14:2: "Said R. Simeon b. Eleazar: 'R. Tarfon and R. Aqiba did not dispute ... over one who purchased something from five [people] and does not know .... Over what did they dispute? Over one who robbed ....'" However, as noted above, the Tosepta here connects this rule (analogous to *m. Yeb.* 15:7) to the case of M3:3 that includes both deposit and robbery. In addition, note T3:5–6, which includes analogues to M3:4 for both deposit [T3:6] and robbery [T3:5].)

[68] M3:1 [A]: *ha-mapqîd ʾēṣel ḥabērô*, followed by the object of *ha-mapqîd*; M3:6 [A]; M3:7 [A]; M3:9 [A]; M3:10 [A]: *ha-mapqîd pērôt (ḥābit, māʿôt) ʾēṣel ḥabērô*, i.e., with the object following the verb (participle); M3:11 [A]: *ha-mapqîd māʿôt ʾēṣel ha-šulḥānî*, i.e., following the word order of M3:6–10, but with a different indirect object. (On this material see Section B.2 below.)

[69] *Ha-śôkēr pārā mē-ḥabērô*, "one who leases a cow from his fellow." However, the subject of the verb (participle) is now not the owner of the object, but the renter, and "his fellow" (*ḥabērô*) is now the owner. The significance of the shift in aspect (from owner to contractor as subject) in the formulaic introduction is limited, however. The formula *ha-śôkēr* is typical in pericopae about the hiring of animals (e.g., M6:3–5) or labor (e.g., M6:1–2, 7:1; 10:5 [G]), as opposed to a house (M8:6–9, *ha-maśkîr*). However, the use of *mē-ḥabērô* in M3:2 [A], echoes the use of *ḥabērô* throughout the *ha-mapqîd* series in Chapter 3, in contrast to the examples of the formulaic *ha-śôkēr* used elsewhere in the tractate in connection with animals (cf. also M8:1–3, *ha-śôʾēl*), where this element of the formula is absent. If M3:2–5 originates in a different source from the rest of the chapter, it is possible that M3:2 [A] is meant to serve as a redactional link to the *ha-mapqîd* pericopae of Chapter 3.

for whom the traditions of a particular sage (in this case R. Yose) were significant. I suspect (although the evidence falls short of proof) that what we have in such cases is the product of particular "schools" or "disciple circles," which "annotate" traditions (perhaps already in existence) by reference to the view of the sage who is particularly important to them.[70] Second, to the extent that the tractate incorporates several such clusters, from different "schools," these clusters may offer some insight into how source material came into being and how it could be incorporated into the wider structure of the tractate. I will return to this problem below in Section D.3.

2. Nominative absolute (article + participle) series.

In the end, the strategy that is utilized by *m. Baba' Meṣi'a'* for the organization of its materials as a whole is that of topical arrangement. From the point of view of the redactional history of the Mishnah it is therefore important to ask to what extent the sources utilized by the Mishnah reflect this kind of organization. On methodological grounds, however, this sort of inquiry is quite problematic. The preceding section has relied on the observation that it is precisely where the Mishnah presents materials that do not seem to conform to the redactional patterns of the tractate as a whole (e.g., where it is organized by verse, by association, or by tradent) that it is possible to hypothesize that a source has been utilized. In the case of material arranged topically, however, we are faced with a redactional strategy that approximates that of the final product. How, then, are we to isolate such sources, if they exist? There is at least one class of passages in *m. Baba' Meṣi'a'* that is susceptible to analysis: passages that are linked to each other not only by content but also by formulaic patterning. In such cases distinct series of pericopae can be identified, and we can then proceed to ask whether these series betray signs of secondary redaction, which might show that they have been utilized as sources. In what follows, I examine the most prominent example of this type: series in which the protases of the member pericopae take the form of a nominative absolute construction (specifically, the article

---

[70] In the rest of the chapter the tradents of R. Yose's generation are R. Simeon b. Gamaliel (M3:6 [C]); R. Judah (M3:7 [I]; 8 [B, F]; 11 [G]); and R. Meir (M3:11 [F]), whereas R. Yose does not appear again. If the unit comprising M3:2–5 is the product of a "circle" ("school") interested in R. Yose, the rest of the chapter is not. Neusner, *Damages* II, 41, 43–4, already noted the linkage of M3:2–5 through the traditions of R. Yose, but his comment "Yose's involvement in the matter explains the inclusion of an appendix" does make explicit how Neusner thinks the material got into the Mishnah, whether as a "formal exercise" or through the interpolation of a pre-existing source. Epstein, *Siprût*, 143, cited these traditions as examples of "the Mishnah of R. Yose," but does not specify how these traditions constituted what he considered an early Mishnah.

+ participle [present]).⁷¹ Consider the following catalogue of occurrences of this form (brackets [ ] designate examples of the article + participle (present) that appear singly and not in series):⁷²

---

⁷¹ See Segal, 210-1, 212-5, §§439, 442-7. This is not, however, the only type of series in the tractate. For instance, a short series occurs in M1:3-4, where three cases dealing with the acquisition of lost objects are each opened with the verb *rāʾâ*, "he saw," and where terminological links connect all three passages (see Section C.3 below).

In M10:1-3 there is a series linked by the formula *ha-bayît wĕ-hā-ʿaliyyâ šel šĕnayîm*, "the house and upper storey belonging to two people ..." (M10:1 [A], 2 [A], 3[A]). In this case the opening formula that links the pericopae uses a nominative absolute construction with a definite subject. This series was, I believe, available for use as a source. After M10:1-3, M10:4 [A-C] illustrates an analogous case (*wĕ-kēn* ...) involving a below-ground olive press with a garden above it and gives a ruling similar in content and language to that of M10:2 (especially [B, D]). The rather motley assortment of materials that follows (M10:4 [E]-6 [H]; see above n. 66) contrasts with the three closely linked pericopae that constitute M10:1-3, and suggests that the same hand has not produced both the first three and the last three pericopae of the chapter. In addition, the resumption in M10:4 of a topic dealt with in M10:2, and the failure to bring this material immediately after M10:2 (which would have been quite expected based on the kinds of redactional choices made in M10:4-6) makes M10:4 [A-C] appear to be a coda to the already completed M10:1-3.

Another example of such a series may be found in M1:6-8. In this example each member, dealing with the rules relating to the finding of documents, opens with the verb *māṣāʾ*. I have already shown that the order in which the documents is presented is based on some sort of stereotyped format (see above, n. 55). Moreover, the legal question throughout these three pericopae is identical (does one return documents that one finds?), and the cases are mere variants of one another (see, however, the discussion of M1:6, Section D.2 below). Thus, although it cannot be proved that M1:6-8 constitute a source used by the redactor, since there is no evidence that a redactor made use of these three pericopae as a whole, the interconnection between these passages is such that they are clearly one unit (even if one can make the case that all or part of M1:8 [C-K] has been added to it). The same formulaic pattern recurs in M2:1 [C, G], 2 [B]; 2:4 [A, C, F, G], 3 [A], 8 [A, D, H], 9 [B], 10 [A]. However, in the case of these passages from Chapter 2, there is far less that holds these materials together. The examples from M2:1-2 are part of the rhetorical structure introduced at M2:1 [A] and reiterated at 2:1 [B] and 2:2 [A]. M2:9 [B-C] is subordinate to the opening rhetorical question in M2:9 [A], and, in addition, stands in some tension with M2:10 [A-B] (see above, Section A.1). Both of these deal with domesticated cattle, which is not mentioned in the other passages opening with *māṣāʾ* (Section A.1). Moreover, as I noted previously, the ruling of M2:3 [C-E] stands in apparent contradiction to M2:3 [F]-4 [D] (Section A.1). Thus, the rhetorical patterning in Chapter 2, if it is not accidental, may reflect redactional shaping of disparate materials rather than the existence of a source. (On the other hand, this redactional activity itself could conceivably antedate the redaction of *m. B. Meṣ.* as a whole.)

⁷² Note also the following usages: M4:7 [H, I], M4:8 [B-F]; M7:4 [F], in which the form is used to express a rule briefly. The participle introduced by the article also serves to illustrate rules: M5:1 [C, F]; M7:2 [B, F].

Literary and Redactional Problems 69

M3:1 [A]	ha-mapqîd ʾēṣel ḥabērô	One who deposits with his fellow
[M3:2 [A]	ha-śôkēr pārâ mē-ḥabērô	One who rents a cow from his fellow]
M3:6 [A]	ha-mapqîd pērôt ʾēṣel ḥabērô	One who deposits produce with his fellow
M3:7 [A]	ha-mapqîd pērôt ʾēṣel ḥabērô	One who deposits produce with his fellow
M3:9 [A]	ha-mapqîd ḥābît ʾēṣel ḥabērô	One who deposits a jar with his fellow
M3:10 [A]	ha-mapqîd māʿôt ʾēṣel ḥabērô	One who deposits money with his fellow
M3:11 [A]	ha-mapqîd māʿôt ʾēṣel šulḥānî	One who deposits money with a banker
[M3:12 [A]	ha-šôlēaḥ yād ba-piqādon	One who appropriates a deposit]
[M3:12 [E]	ha-ḥôšēb lišloaḥ yād ba-piqādôn	One who intends to appropriate a deposit]
[M5:2 [A]	ha-malweh ʾet ḥabērô	One who lends to his fellow]
M6:1 [A]	ha-śôkēr ʾet ha-ʾummānîm	One who hires artisans
M6:2 [A]	ha-śôkēr ʾet ha-ʾummānîm	One who hires artisans
M6:3 [A][73]	ha-śôkēr ʾet ha-ḥāmôr	One who hires an ass
M6:3 [K]	ha-śôkēr ʾet ha-ḥāmôr	One who hires an ass
M6:4 [A]	ha-śôkēr ʾet ha-pārâ	One who hires a cow
M6:5 [A]	ha-śôkēr ʾet ha-ḥāmôr	One who hires an ass
[M6:7 [A]	ha-malweh ʿal ha-māškôn	One who lends on security]
[M6:8 [A]	ha-maʿabîr ḥābît mi-māqôm lĕ-māqôm	One who was moving a jar from place to place]
M7:1 [A]	ha-śôkēr ʾet ha-pôʿalîm	One who hires workers
M7:7 [A]	ha-śôkēr ʾet ha-pôʿalîm	One who hires workers
M8:1 [A]	ha-šôʾēl ʾet ha-pārâ	One who borrows a cow
M8:2 [A]	ha-šôʾēl ʾet ha-pārâ	One who borrows a cow
M8:3 [A]	ha-šôʾēl ʾet ha-pārâ	One who borrows a cow
[M8:4 [A][74]	ha-maḥalîp pārâ bĕ-ḥāmôr	One who exchanges a cow with an ass]
[M8:5 [A]	ha-môkēr zêtāyw lĕ-ʿēṣîm	One who sells his olive [trees] for wood]
M8:6 [A]	ha-maśkîr bayît lĕ-ḥabērô	One who leases a house to his fellow
M8:7 [A]	ha-maśkîr bayît lĕ-ḥabērô	One who leases a house to his fellow
M8:8 [A]	ha-maśkîr bayît lĕ-ḥabērô	One who leases a house to his fellow
M8:9 [A]	ha-maśkîr bayît lĕ-ḥabērô	One who leases a house to his fellow

---

[73] See also the discussion of M6:3 [F] in Appendix I.
[74] Note M8:4 [B]: wĕ-kēn ha-môkēr šipḥātô, "... and so too, one who sells his female slave."

M9:1 [A]	ha-mĕqabbēl śādeh mē-ḥabērô	One who receives a field from his fellow
M9:2 [A]	ha-mĕqabbēl śādeh mē-ḥabērô	One who receives a field from his fellow
M9:3 [A]	ha-mĕqabbēl śādeh mē-ḥabērô	One who receives a field from his fellow
M9:4 [A]	ha-mĕqabbēl śādeh mē-ḥabērô	One who receives a field from his fellow
M9:5 [A]	ha-mĕqabbēl śādeh mē-ḥabērô	One who receives a field from his fellow
M9:6 [A]	ha-mĕqabbēl śādeh mē-ḥabērô	One who receives a field from his fellow
M9:7 [A]	ha-mĕqabbēl śādeh mē-ḥabērô	One who receives a field from his fellow
M9:8 [A]	ha-mĕqabbēl śādeh mē-ḥabērô	One who receives a field from his fellow
M9:9 [A]	ha-mĕqabbēl śādeh mē-ḥabērô	One who receives a field from his fellow
M9:10 [A]	ha-mĕqabbēl śādeh mē-ḥabērô	One who receives a field from his fellow
[M9:13 [A]	ha-malweh ʾet ḥabērô	One who lends his fellow]
[M9:13 [L]	ha-ḥôbēl ʾet hā-rēḥayim	One who distrains a millstone]
[M10:5 [G]	ha-śôkēr ʾet ha-pôʿēl	One who hires a worker]
[M10:5 [N]	ha-môṣiʾ ziblô bi-rĕšût hā-rabbîm	One who takes out his dung to the public domain]
[M10:5 [T]	ha-bôneh bi-rĕšût ha-rabbîm	One who builds in the public domain]

The series of passages utilizing these formulae are found in some thirty pericopae out of a total of one hundred and one (based on the division of the text in the standard printed editions), a sizable proportion. If we include only those chapters in which these traditions appear (i.e., those with shared subject mattter, excluding chapters 1, 2, 4, 5, and 10) the passages account for more than half of the pericopae (thirty out of fifty-three). It is reasonably self-evident that the disproportionately large number of these passages, and their arrangement in series is not accidental. What does need elucidation is whether these series are the work of the final redactors of *m. Babaʾ Meṣiʿaʾ* as a whole, or whether they were already available to the redactors for secondary use. In what follows, I review the evidence in favor of considering these series as sources utilized in a more or less complete form in the process of redaction.

The *ha-mapqîd* series in chapter 3 consists of six passages. This series is interrupted by another series linked, as I have argued above, by attribution to

R. Yose (M3:2–5). While it is attractive to see this as indicating that a redactor has broken up an existing series to interpolate another, the case is hardly secure. M3:2–5 cannot be shown to refer to the contents of the *ha-mapqîd* series in Chapter 3; hence, we have no evidence that the series as a whole was known to the person (whether "redactor" or "author") who placed M3:2–5 after M3:1. Some support may be gleaned from the similarities between the opening formula of M3:2 and those of the *ha-mapqîd* series (see Section B.1, above). More suggestive is the return to use or appropriation of the deposit in M3:12, a topic already raised in M3:9. It is possible that M3:12, in its various parts, serves as a coda to the already existing *ha-mapqîd* series.[75]

The relationship between M3:6, 7, and 8 is complex. After an introductory statement that a depositary may deduct the losses incurred to the produce (*ḥesrônôt*) in his care [A–B], M3:7 lists acceptable amounts of loss arranged in order of increasing proportions (4.5/180 = 1/40 [C]; 9/180 =1/20 [D]; 18/180 = 1/10 [E]).[76] The second part of the pericope follows with two attributed traditions (M3:7 R. Yohanan b. Nuri [G–H]; R. Judah [I]), which both echo the language of the introductory statement and respond to the general conclusion to the first part: "All is [assessed] according to the measurement and all is [assessed] according to the amount of time" [F].[77]

---

[75] M3:12 [A–D] and [E–G] share formal characteristics and common terminology (both use forms of *šālaḥ yād*; Ex. 22:7, 10), and are clearly designed to be taken together (whether or not both parts were composed at the same time). Together these passages deal with the use or appropriation of a deposit, a topic already dealt with in M3:9 and 11. The placement of M3:12 [A–G] might be due to the topic of M3:11, and does not reflect awareness of any other items in the *ha-mapqîd* series of Chapter 3, so it is hardly necessary to take M3:12 [A–G] as the coda to an existing series. If M3:12 [I–J], which deals more specifically with jars on deposit that are moved and broken, as in M3:9, should be taken as an independent pericope (it could circulate separately, *t. B. Qam.* 10:34; and some versions of the Mishnah do not include [H], *kêṣād*, which links [I–J] directly to [A–G]; see Appendix I), M3:12 [I–J] may serve as a supplement to M3:9, and hence as a coda to an already existing *ha-mapqîd* series. If M3:12 [A–G] and [I–J] made their way into *m. B. Meṣ.* together as a unit (with [I–J] amplifying the Hillelite position), all of M3:12 might serve as a coda to M3:11. If the *ha-mapqîd* series in Chapter 3 were composed by the redactor of the Mishnah as it has come down to us, should we not have expected all or part of M3:12 (especially [I–J]) earlier in the tractate?

[76] M3:7 [C–E], like M4:5, presents a geometric progression of ratio 1/2 (in M4:5: 1/24; 1/12; 1/6). Neusner's translation and commentary for this passage are wrong (*Damages* II, 46–7). First, Neusner misread "nine half *qabbîm*" [B] as "nine *qabbîm* and one half," which he gave as 5.2% (properly, it rounds off to 5.3); second, he came up with a figure of 16.6% (i.e., 16.7) for the proportion "three *sěʾîn* to the *kôr*" [E], apparently by dividing 30 *sěʾîn* by 180 *qab*, i.e., by merely giving the ratio of the *sěʾâ* to the *qab*. (Since one *kôr* equals 30 *sěʾîn*, the actual ratio is 3/30 = 1/10.)

[77] Neusner, *Damages* II, 47, stated that M3:7 [F] conflicts with [C–E] since these latter clauses require fixed proportions, and suggested that [F] and the tradition attributed to R.

Without any transitional material, M3:8 gives a list of deductions for wine and oil. In contrast to M3:7, in which the opening sentence [A–B] provided the verb for all three elements on the list [C–E] with which they are syntactically connected, the list in M3:8 consists of two independent but parallel sentences [A, C]. Moreover, whereas the cases of grains are worked out quite tersely in M3:7, the case of oil in M3:8 [C] is expanded with both an explanatory clause [D] and two qualifications [E–F]. In short, M3:8 is a less tightly controlled pericope than M3:7. There is some tension between the two pericopae in terms of content as well. From the objection and gloss of R. Yohanan b. Nuri [G–H] it would appear that at least one possible reading of the "losses" in [B] took them to be the result of vermin alone, and not spoilage, although by itself, that [A–E] refers to spoilage as well seems likely.[78] In M3:8 the kind of loss for which one makes deduction is the absorption by the container, and not for consumption by vermin (since M3:8 deals with liquids) or for spoilage. It is possible, therefore, that the lists in M3:7 and M3:8 derive from different hands. This possibility becomes important when we consider the relationship of both these pericopae to M3:6. In particular, while M3:7 can be seen as referring to the same general problem as M3:6, M3:8 cannot: M3:8 is not concerned with the loss of all or part of the deposit due to spoilage, but only with the standard amount of wine or oil that a depositary returns at the end of the term. At the same time, the topical as well as linguistic (specifically the use of the expression *yôṣî' lô* in M3:8 [A, C, F]; cf. M3:7 [B]) links between M3:8 and M3:7 suggest that M3:8 was intended to supplement M3:7.

Significantly, the presupposition behind M3:8 is that the depositary is not returning jars of oil or wine that the owner has left with him, but pours the liquid out of his own jars: hence the concern for the deduction for sedimentation and absorption. A similar argument can be made with respect to the various types of produce mentioned in M3:7. It is at least possible in such

---

Yohanan b. Nuri [G–H] together form an interpolated dispute concerning only the topic sentence [A–B] but not [C–E]. However, [F] does not conflict with [C–E], but supplements it with the observation that the deductions in [C–E] are deductions and not fixed amounts, and that they are dependent upon the duration of the deposit (presumably in years) and the amount of produce deposited. It remains possible that [F–H] form an added dispute, but [G–H] could easily be taken as a gloss disputing with the whole of [A–F], a hypothesis that requires less "surgery."

[78] Cf. the reply to R. Yohanan b. Nuri in T3:10 (cf. B40a): "Rather [Lieberman, *TK*, 9, 174, reading *'l'* for *l'* in the Vienna ms.] because they become scattered; rather because they perish (*'ôbdôt*; cf. M3:6 [B])"; i.e., the produce is thought to perish not merely because of vermin. Compare the more humorous response in the Yerushalmi: "There [in Babylonia] they say: 'Those wicked mice [are meant who] when they see much produce call their friends and eat with them'" (Y3:8 [9b]).

cases that the depositary is not returning the produce that he received.[79] If this is so, M3:8 (and, by implication, perhaps M3:7 as well) stands in striking tension with M3:6, which presupposes that the owner's produce is readily identifiable, and, according to the anonymous opinion, that the depositary may (indeed, must) sit by and watch the produce go to waste.[80] At any rate, if the rules of the anonymous opinion of M3:6 applied generally, there should be no reason to invoke acceptable percentages of loss in M3:7–8: it should be enough that the depositary returns the very same produce in whatever state it now is (perhaps with guarantees by oath, if necessary, that there was no wrongdoing on the part of the depositary).

While the mutual tensions among the various pericopae of M3:6–8 are rather clear, just what bearing this has on the redaction of the *ha-mapqîd* series in Chapter 3 is far from self-evident. Several possibilities present themselves. First, M3:8 may have been added to M3:6–7 as a supplement. In support of this possibility is the fact that some of the tension between M3:6 and M3:7 is relieved if M3:8 does not inform our reading of M3:7.[81] Second, it is

---

[79] That the depositary returns different produce than he received is proposed explicitly by the gloss to M3:7 [B] in T3:9: "In what context are [these] things said? When he mixed it with his own produce; but if they were set by themselves let him [the depositary] say to him: 'Lo, yours is before you.'" That is, where the produce of the owner is readily identifiable the depositary returns it in whatever state it may be (for this use of *harê šelkā lĕ-pānêkā* cf. *m. B. Qam.* 9:2; 10:5; *m. B. Meṣ.* 6:3).

[80] It is tempting to see the gloss to M3:7 [B] in T3:9 (cited in the previous note) as an attempt to resolve the tension between M3:6 and M3:7 (and 8) by proposing that M3:7 is a special case where the rules of the anonymous view of M3:6 do not apply. However, the language of T3:9 (*harê šelkā lĕ-pānêkā*, "lo, yours is before you") implies that the depositary is merely not liable for certain kinds of expected damage, but M3:6 [B] (*harê zeh loʾ yiggaʿ bāhen*, "lo, let him not touch them") conveys prohibition and actual culpability for taking action to prevent damage. If T3:9 does indeed respond to an apparent contradiction between M3:6 and M3:7, it may be that "lo, yours is before you" is intended to correct the language of M3:6 [B].

Incidentally, the conception of M3:8, at least, of deposited produce returned by pouring it out of the depositary's own jars, does not dovetail well with pericopae that consider the liability of a depositary who has broken a jar that is on deposit. See M3:9, 3:12 [I–J]; 6:8. Arguably (although this is unlikely), M3:9 and M6:8 might refer to the deposit of an empty jar, and have no bearing on the way the authors of the pericopae assumed that deposit of produce was carried out. Compare, however, M3:12 [H–I], where "a jar" is assumed to be full (cf. *m. B. Qam.* 3:1).

[81] At the very least, both M3:6 and M3:7 can be taken to be concerned with spoilage. Moreover, without M3:8, it is not necessary to see M3:7 as a case where the depositary mixed the deposited produce with his own. M3:7 could be taken as qualifying M3:6 by giving acceptable rates of loss in produce: above the rates in M3:7, both disputants in M3:6 might agree that the depositary should sell the produce; below those rates, the depositary does not

conceivable that M3:7–8 together were interpolated into the series. In support of this it should be noted that the presence of three glosses attributed to R. Judah within these two pericopae suggests that they be marked off as having a common origin. In either case, moreover, the joining of these problematic materials may have been the work of the redactor of Chapter 3 as it appears before us, or may already have been present in a source. On balance, the latter possibility, that M3:6–8 together were part of the *ha-mapqîd* series, strikes me as promising.[82] If this is correct, the process of the combination of material that may not quite agree, or of the supplementation of material, is not merely the product of the final redaction but has a longer and more complex history.

The next series of the type that I have been discussing occurs in Chapter 6 (M6:1–5), with a possible continuation in M7:1, 7.[83] Here we are on somewhat stronger grounds than in Chapter 3. To begin with, M6:6–8 together seem to form a coda to M6:1–5. The common link within M6:6–8 is the liability of depositaries.[84] What links the material in this unit to M6:1–5 is

---

sell (according to the anonymous view of M3:6), and is not responsible to make up the losses. (Something akin to this interpretation was suggested by *Nimmûqê yôsēp* to M3:6 in connection with that pericope, in keeping with the Babli's discussion of whether the case disputed in M3:6 is one where the produce has suffered the usual amount of spoilage or more than the usual amount [B37a]. However, *Nimmûqê yôsēp* also followed the Babli in taking M3:7 as a case where the depositary had mixed the produce with his own.) If M3:7 is properly a qualification of M3:6, the subject of the expression *harê zeh yôṣîʾ lô ḥesrônôt*, literally: "lo, let this one take out diminutions (or: losses)" (M3:7 [B]) should perhaps be taken to refer to the owner and the whole phrase to read: "let him [the owner] make allowance for" (and not "let him [the depositary] make deductions," i.e., when he returns the produce). By contrast, the reference to sedimentation in M3:8 [D] forces the conclusion that it is the depositary who, upon returning the deposit by pouring oil out of his own jars, makes appropriate deductions. (In M3:8 *yôṣîʾ* may plausibly be taken to have the depositary as subject ["let him deduct"]; cf. [G]: it is the seller, the one who is pouring out oil, who "accepts upon himself" a certain volume corresponding to the sediments [cf. Epstein, *Nûsaḥ*, 1017–8].)

[82] One of the arguments in favor of seeing M3:6–8 as part of the *ha-mapqîd* source is the link constituted by the glosses attributed to R. Judah. I shall argue in Section D that the "definite article + participle" series are characterized by attributions to both R. Simeon b. Gamaliel and R. Judah.

[83] See also M10:5 [G]: "*ha-śôkēr ʾet ha-pôʿēl*," One who hires a worker," which is remarkably similar to the protases of M7:1 and 7. It should be noted, however, that in M10:5 the formula refers to one worker, whereas in M7:1, 7, as in M6:1–2, the workers are referred to in the plural.

[84] M6:6 [A–B] correlates the liability of an artisan with respect to the work in his possession to that of a paid or unpaid depositary, depending on circumstances (see the discussion of S. Friedman, *Talmud Arukh: BT Bava Meziʿa VI, Commentary* [Hebrew] [Jerusalem: JTSA, 1990], 241–2); M6:7 [A–C] considers an analogous problem in connection with a lender and the pledge that he holds (cf. *m. Šebu.* 6:7). M6:6 [C–D] deals with the legal force of certain

Literary and Redactional Problems   75

solely the rule that opens M6:6 that "all artisans (ʾûmānîm) are paid depositaries," which connects with the topic of the opening formulae of M6:1–2: "One who hires artisans (ʾûmānîm) ...." Considering M6:6–8 a coda to an already existing M6:1–5 accounts at once for why the traditions of M6:6–8 appear in their present context at all, and why they appear after M6:5 and not M6:1.[85]

In addition to this possible coda, it is possible to point to revisions of pericopae in Chapter 6. Consider M6:3 [A–E] and [K–R]:

[A]	One who leases an ass—	[K]	One who leases an ass—
[B]	to walk it on the mountain and he walked it in the valley,	[L]	to walk it on the mountain and he walked it in the valley,
		[M]	if it slipped he is exempt,
		[N]	but if it became overheated he is liable;
	in the valley and he walked it on the mountain	[O]	in the valley and he walked it on the mountain
		[P]	If it slipped he is liable,
		[Q]	but if it became overheated he is exempt,

---

kinds of statements between owner and (potential) depositary. M6:8 rules, for the third time in this tractate, on the question of a depositary who has broken a jar in his care. The rule of Abba Shaul in M6:7 [D–E] does not connect directly with the question of deposit, but does build on the problem of the creditor who holds a pledge considered in an earlier part of the same pericope.

[85] Of course, this argument is hardly probative. It does not *necessarily* follow that M6:1–5 constituted a source available to the redactor of the chapter: the *ha-śôkēr* series in Chapter 6 could have been constructed by the final editors of the chapter who, for their own reasons of formal consistency, did not want to break up the series they were constructing in order to present what they considered a related or relevant source (on M6:6–8 as a source see above Section A.1). One problem with the argument that M6:1–5 is a pre-existing series followed by a coda is that the *ha-śôkēr* series seems to be picked up again by M7:1, the pericope following M6:8. Why break the series after M6:5 and not after M7:1+7? If M7:1 and M7:7 concluded the *ha-śôkēr* series of Chapter 6, the redactors might have considered the shift in topic from the hiring of animals to the hiring of workers to be a sufficient break to warrant interpolation at that point, but in that case surely the break between the hiring of artisans (M6:1–2) and hiring of animals (M6:3–5) would have been more appropriate. Another possible explanation is that M7:1, 7 were not originally part of the *ha-śôkēr* series. However, while it is possible to argue that M7:7 deals with the right of workers to eat produce in the fields, and dependent upon M7:2–3 and therefore a later insertion to the chapter, there is no necessary reason to doubt the connection of M7:1 to M6:1–5. Cf. M9:1[A–E] (from another nominative absolute series), which serves as a near analogue to M7:1 [A–F].

		[R]	but if [it became overheated]
			due to the height, he is liable.
[C]	even [if] this was ten miles		
	and this was ten miles		
[D]	and it died,		
[E]	he is liable.		

M6:3 [A–E] ruled simply that a renter who specifies a certain kind of use and deviates from that specified use has broken the contract and is liable for whatever damage may occur.[86] M6:3 [K–R] has revised this rule to find the renter liable only when it can be presumed that it is precisely the renter's deviation from the stated terms that has caused the damage to the rented animal.[87] Strikingly, all of M6:4 follows the line of reasoning introduced by

---

[86] Cf. M6:2: [F]: "anyone who alters [the contract] is in the inferior position." The expression *yādô la-taḥtônâ*, literally: "his hand is lower" (compared with its antithesis *yādô la-ʿelyônâ*, "his hand is higher"), typically means that the party so described is required to absorb loss (*m. Šeq.* 4:9; 5:4), or at any rate has a weaker legal claim (M4:2, 6; *m. Šebu.* 7:6).

[87] The tension between M6:3 [A–E] and [K–R] was already noted by Amoraim. The opening question of the Babli concerning this pericope reads: "What is the difference between the first and last parts [of the Mishnah] (*maʾî šānāʾ rēšāʾ* ... *û-maʾî šānāʾ sēpāʾ*...) that the first part makes no division [between slipping and overheating] and the last part makes a distinction?" (B78a). This opening question is followed by several harmonizing suggestions (e.g., that the animal died by some other means in [A–E]) and finally by the view attributed to R. Hiyya b. Abba in the name of R. Yohanan (R. Yohanan alone in the Yerushalmi parallel, Y6:3 [11a]) that: "This [first part [A–E]] is according to whom? It is according to R. Meir ..." (following the language in the Babli; the Yerushalmi tradition is slightly different). What the solution proposed by (R. Hiyya b. Abba in the name of) R. Yohanan does not account for, however, is why the wording of the two parts of the pericope is so closely linked. (Cf. a closely parallel commentary on the Mishnah in Y6:3 [11a] the text of whose opening question is somewhat uncertain and obscure: "'In the valley and he walked it on the mountain' [M6:3 [B]] is understood [*nîḥâ*], [why does M6:3 [B] state] 'on the mountain› and he walked it in the valley' [as well]?" [The text is quoted from the Escorial manuscript, slightly emended; see Lieberman, *Yerushalmi Neziqin*, 164 to l. 26 and Friedman, 1990, 133–5.] The Yerushalmi's question is apparently attached to M6:3 [A–E] alone: granted that the lessee is liable in the case of death for walking an animal on the mountain against the terms of the agreement because of the stress on the animal due to the climb, why should the lessee be liable for walking the animal in the valley, where the stress is less? As Friedman notes, all the answers given in the Yerushalmi, including that attributed to R. Yohanan, which assigns [A–E] to R. Meir, may be read as addressing that question. Arguably, the use of likely causes of death as criteria for liability in [K–R] may underlie the question about [A–E]. [Lieberman, *Yerushalmi Neziqin*, 164 to l. 26, sought to explain the question of the Yerushalmi as based on the rule about slipping in [O–R]: granting that the lessee who walked the animal on the mountain instead of in the valley is liable, because slipping is likely, why should that person be liable in the reverse case when slipping is not likely?] However, it is possible that the Yerushalmi, and the authors of the Palestinian

the latter part of M6:3, suggesting that it too was part of the process of revision and supplementation that produced M6:3 [K–R].[88]

In light of this alteration of M6:3 in the direction of giving greater emphasis to the specific circumstances of the case, it is worth asking whether a similar process has taken place in M6:5 as well:

[A] One who leases an ass—
[B] to bring wheat and he brought barley,
[C] grain and he brought straw [and the animal was damaged]
[D] he is liable,
[E] for volume is as difficult as load.
[F] To bring a *letek* [a measure of volume] of wheat and he brought a *letek* of barley,
[G] he is exempt;
[H] and if he added to its load he is liable.
[I] And how much shall he add to its load and [thus] be liable?
[J] Symmakhos says in the name of R. Meir: "A *sĕʾâ* for a camel; three *qabbîm* for an ass.

It is possible that M6:5 [A–D] together with [F–G] formed a core pericope concerned with the implications of the stated terms of the agreement. Without the explanatory clause in [E], [A–D] can be taken as roughly analogous to M6:3 [A–E] (and M6:2[F]): any non-compliance with a contract makes the renter liable.[89] [F–G] may add only that if the parties agreed to a specific

---

Amoraic traditions, did not have [K–R] as part of the Mishnah [cf. Friedman, 1990, 135, n. 33, who rejects this possibility].)

[88] Two additional points should be noted regarding M6:4. (1) It deals with the renting of a cow, whereas M6:3 and M6:5 both deal with renting an ass. (2) In M6:4 [A–F] the damage is not damage to the animal, as in M6:3; 6:4 [G–L]; 6:5, but to the plow. These two factors strengthen the supposition that M6:4 was added in the process of revision.

[89] This may have already been hinted at by Nahmanides, *Ḥiddûšîm*, s.v. Abayye ʾāmar (to B80a). Commenting on the reading of the M6:5 [E] attributed to Abbaye ("for volume is as difficult as load"; this is also the reading in nearly all Mishnah texts, see Appendix I) as interpreted in the Babli, Nahmanides notes that an ass can carry several times the volume of straw that it can carry of grain, and that the reading "for volume is as difficult as load" is therefore problematic, and comments: "For Abbaye 'anyone who alters [the contract] is in the inferior position' [= M6:2 [F]]." See also Epstein, *Nûsaḥ*, 380, who takes the first part of M6:5 as prohibiting any change in the kind of load. Compare Friedman, 1990, 223–5, 232–6, who does not see the two parts of M6:5 in their present form as conflicting. Friedman sees M6:5 [A–B] as referring specifically to a case where the renter used the ass to carry the same *weight* in barley (but a greater volume, see Appendix I); by contrast, in [F–G], where the renter is exempt from liability, the ass has carried the same *volume* in barley (and less weight). Friedman's argument

volume to be carried, it is that volume, and not the type of material, that is decisive for determining whether the lessee has deviated from the contract. If this is so, the "core pericope" (M6:5 [A–D + H–G]) reflects a concern with the implications of the wording of contracts that is expressed in other pericopae in the tractate, especially in the nominative absolute series under consideration here.[90] The other material in the pericope [E, H–J] is explanatory or serves to quantify rules, and may well consist of later additions. What this supplementary material has in common, however, is that it introduces two circumstantial factors, the stress of weight and volume, which might lead to damage to the animal.

Alternatively, it is possible that [F–G] stands in some tension with [A–D]: unlike [A–D] (and M6:3 [A–E]; cf. M6:2 [F]), it allows variation in content, as long as the specified volume is maintained. [H], which may have been a later supplement to [F–G], sets a limit on the kinds of changes permitted in [F–G] by making the renter liable if the change involved a greater weight than that of the initially specified load (in the case of the Mishnah, the weight of a *letek* of wheat).[91] [F–H] may be intended to recast [A–D] in a manner that gives greater specificity (the volume of the load is explicitly stated) and takes into account the factors of weight and volume (i.e., in much the same way that M6:3 [A–E] has been revised in [K–R]).[92] The

---

focuses, in part, on the gloss "for volume is as difficult as load" (M6:5 [E]), which he takes as prohibiting additional volume. Even if this interpretation of M6:5 [E] is correct, this clause remains a gloss that may have been added to reduce conflict between the first and second parts of M6:5; without it M6:5 [A–D] is inexplicit and open to both interpretations.

[90] Cf. M6:3 above; M8:8: the implications of renting "for a year" as opposed to "for twelve months"; M9:10: leasing a field "for seven years" or "for a week of years." See also M9:8: leasing a field and specifying a particular kind of produce to be grown. Cf. M7:1; M9:1, concerned with what needs to be specified in the face of "local custom"; and M6:6 (not a member of the *ha-śôkēr* series), concerned with the kinds of statements that assign the liability of a paid or unpaid depositary to the person who stated them.

[91] Cf. Friedman, 1990, 225, who took [H] more generally and as applying equally to [A–D] and [F–G] (i.e., "if the animal was made to carry more than its conventional load," no matter what type of load it was carrying).

[92] Cf. Epstein, *Nûsaḥ*, 380, who saw M6:5 [A–E] and [F–G] as coming from different and conflicting sources, the former prohibiting any change in kind, but the latter an increase in weight. Friedman, 1990, 223–5, also saw M6:5 as derived from two sources that initially conflicted, but that no longer do. M6:5 [F–J], according to Friedman, 1990, is a revised version of the tradition in T7:10 (cf. the *bāraîtāʾ* at B80a, according to the version of R. Hananel, as cited by Nahmanides, *Ḥiddûšîm*, s.v. *Ha-śôkēr* [to B80a]; see Epstein, *Nûsaḥ*, 380f; Lieberman *TK* 9, 254 [to T7:10; l. 45]; Friedman, 1990, 225–7): "If someone rents an ass to bring a *letek* [= 15 *sěʾîn*] of wheat and he brought sixteen *sěʾîn* [= 1 *letek* + 1 *sěʾâ*], he is exempt ...." The rest of T7:10 largely parallels M6:5 [G–J]. According to Friedman, 1990, the pericope from the Tosepta, despite its close parallels to the Mishnah, conflicts with M6:5 [A–D] taken together

insertion of [E], then, is also part of this process of revision and sets the ruling of [A–D] in terms of the stress of weight and volume rather than narrowly on the fact that the lessee said one thing and did another. [I–J] carry this process further by defining how much additional weight is considered non-negligible, and therefore makes the renter culpable.

The process of revision in M6:3–5, if such it was, indicates that at least some pericopae in M6:1–5 have been subjected to editorial alteration at some point. In and of themselves these corrections cannot constitute proof that the series M6:1–5 was utilized as a source. (Even if it is assumed, for instance, that M6:1–5 did constitute a source used by the redactor of the Mishnah, the corrections might already have been present in that source; cf. the discussion of M3:6–8 above.) However, if I am correct in suggesting that the series was utilized as a source that was available for use by the redactor of the Mishnah on other grounds (the "coda" in M6:6–8, as well as the formal literary links of the opening formulae), these revisions, which were carried out along the same conceptual, if not literary, lines, are suggestive of the kind of redactional work that may have gone into constructing a tractate out of sources.

In M8:1–3, the Mishnah takes for granted the rule that a borrower is liable for nearly any kind of damage that might occur; the three cases presented in M8:1–3 deal with when and how this liability applies.[93] There is no internal evidence that implies either that these pericopae were used as a pre-existing source or that they are the product of the redactor of the tractate. There is, however, a small amount of evidence to be gleaned from the context of these pericopae. While the end of Chapter 7 does deal with "watchmen," including the borrower, and one could argue that M8:1–3 has been brought here to follow this discussion, I shall argue below that M7:8–11 are better explained as a coda or supplement to the discussion of workers in M7:1–7.[94] The two pericopae that follow M8:1–3 consist of four cases. The first three are cases of sale or exchange, and the fourth is an analogous extension of the

---

with [E] ("for volume is as difficult as weight"), which Friedman takes as prohibiting any increase in volume (Friedman, 1990, 223; see above n. 89). Friedman therefore suggests that T7:10 served as the source for M6:5 [F–J], but that its opening (M6:5 [F]) has been modified to resolve overt contradictions with M6:5 [A–E]. T7:10, however, could just as easily be seen as a revision of M6:5.

[93] M8:1 interprets Ex. 22:14 as exempting the borrower from liability where the owner of the animal was hired or "borrowed" with or before the animal itself; M8:2 examines a case where it is not clear whether the animal that died was borrowed or rented (the renter is exempt in cases of accidental death, M7:8 [G–H]); M8:3 considers under what circumstances the borrower is already liable while the animal is still being delivered to him.

[94] See below, Section C.1.

third case.[95] All four of these cases are linked by the fact that they involve disputes over ownership resolved (in part, at least) through division of the disputed property, and by the formulaic manner in which this is expressed: (1) introductory case, (2) "this one says ... and this one says ...," (3) "let them split [it]." It is this that constitutes the only link between M8:1–3 and 4–5, since M8:2 works out a similar kind of dispute (over liability) in similar language. By far the closest connection is that between M8:2 and M8:4 [F–S]:

M8:2		M8:4	
[A]	One who borrows a cow—	[F]	He had two manservants, one big and one small:
		[G]	and so too, two fields, one large and one small:
[B]	he borrowed it for half a day and leased it for half a day,		
[C]	he borrowed it today, and leased it on the next day,		
[D]	borrowed one and leased one:		
[E]	the lender says: "The borrowed one died," [or] "It died on the day it was borrowed," [or] "It died at an hour when it was borrowed,"	[H]	the purchaser says: "I bought the big one,"
[F]	and the latter says: "I do not know,"	[I]	and the latter says: "I do not know,"
[G]	he is liable.	[J]	he has gained the big one.
[H]	The renter says: "The leased one died," [or] "It died on the day it was leased," [or] "It died at an hour when it was leased,"	[K]	The seller says: "I sold the small one,"
[I]	and the latter says: "I do not know,"	[L]	and the latter says: "I do not know,"
[J]	he is exempt.	[M]	he only has the small one.
[K]	This one says: "The borrowed one [died],"	[N]	This one says: "The big one [is mine],"

---

[95] M8:4 [A–E]: an animal or slave has given birth in the process of sale, and it is not clear in whose possession the mother was when she gave birth; M8:4 [F–S]: the sale of two items (slaves [F]; fields [G]), one large and one small; M8:5 [A–G]: olive trees were sold for wood, and produced olives; M8:5 [H–K]: olive trees were washed by a river into the field of another, where they were replanted and produced olives.

[L]	and this one says: "The leased one,"	[O]	and this one says: "The small one,"
[M]	let the renter swear that the leased one died.	[P]	let the seller swear that he sold the small one.
[N]	This one says: "I do not know,"	[Q]	This one says: "I do not know,"
[O]	and this one says: "I do not know,"	[R]	and this one says: "I do not know,"
[P]	let them split [it].	[S]	let them split [it].

The two pericopae are clearly worked out along parallel conceptual and linguistic lines: definite claims and uncertainty ("I do not know") are balanced against each other and against themselves. These two passages are significantly different from the other cases of M8:4–5. Formally, M8:2 and M8:4 [F–S] involve four different sets of claims and rulings culminating in the case where the parties split the disputed amount, whereas the remaining cases in M8:4–5 each have only one set of claims. Legally, M8:4 [F–S], like M8:2, introduces the problem of definite and indefinite claims and the requirement of oaths. Furthermore, by ruling that the disputed property is only divided in the case of indefinite claims (M8:4 [N–P]; cf. M8:2 [K–M]; the remaining cases allow this even in the case of definite claims), M8:4 [F–S] appears to be in some tension with M8:4 [A–E] and M8:5, which rule that money over which there are conflicting claims is to be divided among the claimants.[96] If, despite this tension, M8:4–5 as a unit has been added as a coda to

---

[96] See Epstein, *Nûsaḥ*, 384–5, and compare T8:23 in which the same case as M8:4 [A–E] (the offspring of an animal being sold) is cast in terms of M8:4 [F–S] and attributed to R. Meir (with two disputing views that, as Epstein has noted, seem to agree neither with R. Meir nor with the Mishnah as we have it). One could argue that M8:4 [A–E] (and M8:5) does not conflict with [F–S], but rules differently for a different kind of case. [A–E] deals with uncertainty over the "objective" status of a particular item of property (in whose possession was the mother when the offspring was born; in M8:5 both cases deal with the status of the olives grown); [F–S] is concerned with the "subjective" aspect of the terms assumed in the agreement (was the big field or slave meant, or the small one). For the Mishnah itself this may well be true (and may be the implicit legal exegetical rationale behind the inclusion of M8:4 [F–S] in this context). However, both the view attributed to R. Meir in T8:23 (treating the "objective" problem of M8:4 [A–E] in the same way as the "subjective" problem of [F–S]) and M8:2 (also treating an "objective" question of status: was the animal rented or borrowed when it died) suggests that Rabbis did not inevitably make this distinction, and that the difference between M8:4 [A–E] and [F–S] may instead reflect a disagreement over the questions of whether claimants are required to take an oath, and whether the property claimed should be split. (The formulation of T8:23 as a dispute also testifies that in antiquity precisely the case of M8:4 [A–E] was thought to be subject to a dispute in the Ushan period.)

M8:1–3, it suggests that the redactor responsible for compiling M8:4–5 was tolerant of contradictions in the composition, or that some implied exegetical rule allowed for the resolution of the tension. If the latter is the case, it is not impossible that the inclusion of M8:4 [F–S] in M8:4–5 is the work of the person who joined M8:1–3 and 4–5 and reflects a conscious effort to "update" M8:4–5, that is, to apply to the cases of disputed property the rules of conflicting claims from M8:2.

There is no unambiguous evidence in the pericopae in M8:6–9, linked by the opening formula *ha-maśkîr bayît lĕ-ḥabērô*, to show that this series has been used as a source.[97] Immediately following M8:9 is the last series of this type in *m. Babaʾ Meṣiʿaʾ* (M9:1–10). This is followed by a cluster of three pericopae dealing with material unrelated to M9:1–10 (the right of a worker to his pay, M9:11–2; the distraint of pledges, M9:13), which, I have argued earlier, is shaped by the juxtaposition of topics in Deuteronomy 24:10–5.[98] One could argue, therefore, that a redactor has appended one cluster of materials at the conclusion of another. This argument would be stronger if we could show how M9:11–3 constitutes an appendix to specific materials that precede it. In that case one could hypothesize that the appendix or coda was added only at the end of a body of already existing material rather than interrupting that body of material. Unfortunately, there are no direct links between M9:11–3 and M9:1–10. On the whole, however, the conclusions regarding earlier series (in Chapters 3, 6 and in M8:1–3) should inform our understanding of the redaction of M8:6–9 and 9:1–10. Thus, although there is no specific way of proving that 8:6–9 or M9:1–10 were used as pre-existing sources, despite the suggestiveness of the opening formulae, it remains distinctly possible that these last two series were available to the redactor of the tractate for use as sources.

The only candidates for connecting M9:11–3 with preceding material are M7:1, 7, which deal with workers, and M8:1–3, which are concerned with

---

[97] Epstein, *Nûsaḥ*, 338–9, argued on the basis of a comparison of M8:6 and a *bāraîtāʾ* in T8:27 (cf. Y8:8 [11d]; B101b), which apparently glosses M8:6 ("When they said, 'Thirty days,' and when they said 'Twelve months,' [this is] not that he may live in it for thirty days, and not that he may live in it for twelve months, but that [the landlord] must inform [the tenant] [of his eviction] thirty days before, and that he must inform him twelve months before"), that the passage of the Tosepta glosses a different version of the pericope in M8:6 (a version that only had cases stated in terms of "thirty days" and "twelve months," but not our M8:6 [B]), and that our M8:6 is composed of two strands. This conclusion is not necessitated by the text or language of M8:6 itself. Even if correct, however, this conclusion need not imply that M8:6–9 constitutes a source that has undergone a revision in the process of inclusion in the Mishnah, but could as easily reflect the original composition of the series out of sources (whether at the hands of the final or of earlier redactors).

[98] See above, Section A.1.

borrowers of animals. Neither of these candidates is entirely satisfying.[99] If M9:11–3 were a coda to an article + participle (present) series that appears substantially earlier in the tractate, it would follow that not only each individual series, but an agglomeration of such series, perhaps all of them taken together, constituted a source for the redactor of the tractate. Although direct demonstration of this admittedly is impossible, there are certain impressionistic reasons to accept the possibility of one large nominative absolute series. First is the formal parallel between the several series, of which some, at least, appear to have preceded the redaction of the *Baba' Meṣi'a'*, and to have been utilized as sources. A second reason is the rather limited range of topics that are covered by these series: they all deal with contracts. I take it as no accident that in *Baba' Qamma'* and *Baba' Batra'*, originally part of the same tractate as *Baba' Meṣi'a'*, the only full-blown example of this type of series has the opening formula *ha-môkēr*, "one who sells ..." (*m. B. Bat.* 4–6). I am inclined to suggest, therefore, that the redactor of our tractate has used a collection of pericopae on contracts as a source (see further Section D.3 below). If this is so, the redactor of *m. Baba' Meṣi'a'* had at least one extended source organized according to topic available for use.

C. Traces of the Redactional Process

If the argument of the preceding sections is correct, the redactors of *m. Baba' Meṣi'a'* had before them a variety of materials, which they used to compile the tractate as we have it. The purpose of this section is to examine some of the evidence that can be used to identify the processes that these materials have undergone in their incorporation into the Mishnah. Once again, the methodological approach is to examine the literary evidence presented by the text of the Mishnah itself. Anecdotal testimonies about the redaction of the Mishnah from elsewhere in Rabbinic literature, and extra-Mishnaic Rabbinic legal and interpretative dicta, properly constitute separate bodies of evidence and deserve studies of their own, but are not discussed here.[100]

---

[99] I have noted above possible objections to including M7:1 + 7 as part of the series begun at M6:1. If they are not connected with M6:1–5, M7:1 and M7:7 are too far separated in the chapter and too different in content to be considered automatically part of a series that has been disassembled. Moreover, the specific question of the laborer's right to his wages is not dealt with in Chapter 7. As for M8:1–3, these pericopae deal specifically with the problem of the liability of a borrower of an animal when that animal has died. This is considerably different from the matter of distraint of a pledge in the case where the debtor has defaulted on a cash loan.

[100] By "anecdotal" evidence I mean traditions that describe, or at least may be taken to

1. Codas.

One of the ways in which the Mishnah betrays its use of sources is the supplementation of passages with what I have been calling "codas," borrowing the term from D. Daube. I use the term coda to designate passages that supplement one element in a preceding body of material and that "logically" would have fit better if they were presented together with that element. In such cases it is distinctly likely that the reason that the supplement does not occur at the location where it belongs is that the body of material to which the coda is appended existed as a unit before the supplement, and that the person responsible for the coda chose not to interrupt it with an interpolation.[101] Since I have repeatedly referred to examples of codas in *m. Baba' Meṣi'a'*, I discuss only one such passage here.[102] M7:1–7, which deals with the rights of workers, falls into two parts: (a) M7:1, that workers be treated

---

describe, some aspect of the redaction of the Mishnah, such as the passage from *'Abot R. Nat.* A 18 discussed above, Section A (introduction). For an example directly connected with *m. B. Meṣ.* see the discussion of both the Yerushalmi and the Babli concerning M4:1: the son of R. Judah the Patriarch asks why he taught one version of the M4:1 ("silver acquires gold") in his youth, and another in his old age ("gold acquires silver") (Y4:1 [9c]; B44a–b; see Appendix I). As an example of a "legal or interpretative dictum" see the comment attributed to (R. Hiyya b. Abba in the name of) R. Yohanan that: "R. [Judah the Patriarch] saw the words of R. Meir in [the rule] '[As for an ox or a sheep, you shall not slaughter] it and its offspring [in one day]' (Lev. 22:28), and formulated them as the words of the sages [i.e., in *m. Ḥul.* 5:3]; and the words of R. Simeon [in the rule of] covering the blood [of non-domesticated animals when slaughtered] (Lev. 17:13), and formulated them as the words of the sages [in *m. Ḥul.* 6:2]" (*b. Ḥul.* 85a). One dictum that has been the crux of various interpretations of the redactional process of the Mishnah is the principle *mišnâ loʾ zāzâ mi-mĕqômāh*, "the Mishnah [as originally formulated] has not moved from its place," even though the law is not in accord with the rule as formulated (*b. Yeb.* 30a, 32a; *b. Qid.* 25a; *b. Šebu.* 4a; *b. ʿAb. Zar.* 35b; *b. Ḥul.* 32b, 116b; see the recent article by Halivni on precisely this dictum, [1989], 63 and *passim*; see also Epstein, *Siprût*, 212; Albeck, *Mābôʾ*, 105).

[101] D. Daube, "Codes and Codas" in *Studies in Biblical Law* (New York: Ktav, 1969 [rpt.]), 74–101, suggests five reasons for the failure to modify the existing source of which four are relevant to the redaction of the Mishnah: inertia (laziness), the complexity of the technique required to fit in an interpolation, the facilitation of memorization (by leaving existing sources relatively unchanged), and the force of tradition (i.e., a conservatism with regard to altering traditional documents). In particular, the last two reasons are likely to be of greatest importance to our question (after all, laziness or reluctance to undertake a difficult task are likely to be justified by a redactor in terms of a more positive reason). The problem of the oral or written transmission of the Mishnah is beyond the scope of the present study (cf. Chapter I, n. 10), but, written or not, the earliest method of study and "performance" of the Mishnah seems to have been oral. I discuss the problem of "conservatism" with respect to traditional materials below.

[102] See the discussion above of M4:7–8; M6:6–8; M10:4; and, more speculatively, of M3:12; M9:11–13.

according to the customary terms of work contracts; and (b) M7:2–7, that they are permitted to eat of the produce with which they are working. M7:2 introduces the second part of M7:1–7 with a distinction between workers who eat produce *mi-dibrê tôrâ*, "according to the Torah" [A–D], and those who may not eat [E–H]. M7:8 [A–B] returns to this theme: "watchers of produce may eat according to the local custom (*mē-hilkôt mĕdînâ*), but not according to the Torah (*min ha-tôrâ*)."[103] Moreover, the expression *mē-hilkôt mĕdînâ*, "according to local custom," echoes M7:1 [F, M] (*minhag ha-mĕdînâ*), and, more generally, the rule of [A–E] (*māqôm še-nāhagû*). Had all of M7:1–8 been composed by one redactor or author at one time, we might have expected the rule of M7:8 [A–B] to be more neatly incorporated after M7:2 (perhaps in M7:3). It is possible that M7:8 [A–B] serves as a coda: a later supplement to an already existing body of material.

The situation appears to be more complicated, however, since M7:8 [A–B] serves as the hinge between M7:1–7 and M7:8 [C]–11 whose respective contents are irrelevant to each other. As a whole, M7:8 [C]–10 [G] deals with "depositaries" (including borrowers and renters). M7:8 [C–H] and M7:10 [E–G] are closely matched pericopae that show terminological links with Scripture.[104] The intervening material (M7:9 [A]–10 [D]) abruptly introduces the problem of *ʾônes* (in its usage here, a Rabbinic term), which is directly relevant only to the paid depositary and the renter. The passage is formulated in connection with the kinds of damage that might occur to animals in a person's care (i.e., some sort of shepherding arrangement, with liability rules approximating that of a paid depositary), but this is nowhere made explicit. This abrupt shift makes it possible that these passages were interpolated between M7:8 [C–H] and M7:10 [E–G].[105] While it is impossible to account with any degree of specificity for the failure of the redactors of *m. Babaʾ Meṣiʿaʾ* to incorporate M7:8 [C]–10 with the material on deposits from Chapter 3 and M6:6–8 (beyond, as I have been suggesting, the origins

---

[103] A tradition attributed to R. Ashi that M7:2 distinguishes between those who may eat according to the Torah, and those who may not eat at all, while M7:8 [A–B] gives a case where local custom alone (but not the Torah) allows the worker to eat (B93a), may well describe the legal relationship between the passages. (R. Ashi glosses a dispute attributed to Rab and Samuel over the interpretation of M7:8 [A–B], of which a parallel dispute [between R. Huna and Samuel] is presented in the Yerushalmi, Y7:9 [11c].)

[104] See above Section, A.1.

[105] In addition, it is possible that M7:9 [A]–10 [D] stems from two separate sources: M7:9 and M7:10 use *ʾônes* in two related but distinct ways. See the discussion of the term *ʾônes* in the note to M7:9 in Appendix I. It was noted above that the links between M7:8 [C–H] and M7:10 [E–G] do not prove that they came from a single source: the second pericope could quite easily be a supplement (indeed, a coda as defined above) referring back to and echoing the earlier passage.

of this material in different sources), it may be possible to account for the presence of this cluster of material here: the rule of M7:8 [A–B] permitting those who watch produce (šômrê pērôt; cf. M7:8 [C]: "There are four šômrîm") to eat. The final pericope of Chapter 7 (M7:11), dealing with the validity of special stipulations in contracts, connects with M7:10 [E–G], which considered the kinds of special stipulations that depositaries might make.

Even if both claims made above, that M7:8 [A–B] (1) serves as a coda to M7:1–7, and (2) accounts for the juxtaposition of M7:1–7 and 8–11, are correct, it remains unclear whether the same person is responsible for both the addition of M7:8 [A–B] and the remainder of M7:8–11, and whether the cluster of traditions in M7:8–11, which may itself have been composed of disparate materials, was available more or less in its present state to be used by the redactor or whether it was assembled by the redactor. If it should be the case that M7:8–11 was also a single block of material used by the redactor, the present passages would not only offer an example of amplification or supplementation of a source through the use of codas, but also the juxtaposition of whole clusters of material through the use of codas. This sort of juxtaposition based on single elements in two separate sources suggests that although topical and logical organizational strategies dominate the tractate as a whole, the principle of redaction by associative logic was also used.

2. Glosses, revisions, corrections.

Those passages that have been glossed, revised or corrected comprise another crucial area for examining the process of redaction of *m. Baba' Meṣi'a'*. If the redactional use of codas suggests by definition a reluctance to alter sources, the evidence for glosses and revision suggests both analogous and opposite tendencies. On the one hand, cases of correction can be identified precisely because both the "original" and the text that amplifies or corrects that "original" are present in the text, rather than a single recast text. (Cases where revised texts alone are presented in the Mishnah are by and large difficult to identify on the evidence of the Mishnah itself, although by comparison to other Tannaitic sources it is sometimes possible to hypothesize such revisions.[106]) On the other hand, these corrections demonstrate at the same time the willingness on the part of the redactors to modify or alter transmitted material.

---

[106] See, e.g., D. W. Halivni, *'Al herkēbāh šel ha-mišnâ ha-ri'šonâ bĕ-bābā' qammā'*, in *Studies in Rabbinic Literature, Bible and Jewish History* [Hebrew: Festschrift for E. Z. Melamed], ed. M. Gilat *et al.* (Ramat Gan: Bar Ilan, 1982), 108–14 (now revised in *idem*, 1993, 1ff.), and 1989, 63–88; and more generally in Epstein, *Siprût*, 205–27. Friedman, 1990, 223–5 argued on the basis of the Tosepta that M6:5 [F–J] was the product of just this sort of revision (above, n. 92; cf. however my suggestion above, Section B.2, that M6:5 [F–H] may consciously revise [A–D]).

Unfortunately, identifying cases in which the Mishnah preserves the kind of glosses or revisions under consideration is not always easy. The rhetoric of the Mishnah tends to be based on short strophic patterns. Individual sentences are largely syntactically independent of one another, and it is therefore sometimes difficult to determine, for instance, whether one has found a gloss or a syntactically independent sentence carrying the idea of a preceding sentence forward. M1:8 [C–F] offers a case in point:

[C] If he found, in a bag or a chest, a bundle of documents or a bunch of documents,
[D] lo, let him return it.
[E] And how much is a bunch of documents?
[F] Three documents tied one to another.

The question and answer in [E–F] give greater specificity and precision to the rather vague term "bunch" in [C]. While this may mean that [E–F] constitutes an added gloss, it may equally reflect the "strophic" composition in the dialectical question-and-answer style that the Mishnah frequently utilizes.[107]

The clearest example of revision has already been discussed at some length (section B.2, above). M6:3 [K–R] restates [A–E], adding greater nuance and specificity to the ruling: a renter is not automatically liable after any deviation from the terms of the contract, but only when that deviation could be presumed to have precipitated the damage to the rented animal. That both parts of the pericope have remained in the text suggests that the last part of M6:3 was intended to be taken as a "commentary" on the first.

Another reasonably straightforward example of a gloss occurs at M4:2. That M4:2 supplements the material that preceded it is announced by its opening expression (*kêṣad*, "how ...?" [A]).[108] M4:1 [A–E] consists of a series

---

[107] Much the same may be said about the tradition attributed to R. Simeon b. Gamaliel that follows in M1:8 [G]. However, the problem of statements attributed to named Rabbis is reserved for a later discussion (Section D below).

[108] *Kêṣad* regularly designates some sort of explanation or amplification. This does not mean, however, that in every case the material introduced by *kêṣad* is automatically an added gloss (cf. Epstein, *Nûsaḥ*, 1032, who states generally that *kêṣad* "as a rule serves to interpret a *halākâ* that preceded it [*še-qādmâ lô*; i.e., preceded temporally?]"). In particular, the Mishnah's regular use of a dialectical rhetoric of questions and answers should be noted (e.g., M2:1–2; M5:1). In M5:10 [E–N], for instance, *kêṣad* [F] introduces illustrations of a rule attributed to R. Simeon b. Gamaliel ("there is interest in advance and interest delayed" [E]), each concluding with the formula *zô hî³ ribbît muqdemet* [J]/ *mᵉ³uḥeret* [N], "this is interest in advance [J]/delayed [N]." It seems likely that the whole of [E–N] is meant to be one single rhetorical unit. Similarly, in the case of M2:1 [E–G], it is not clear whether [F–G] ("How? He

of rules outlining whether one type of item in an exchange "acquires" (*qôneh*) the other. The language of this entire pericope is quite formulaic and repetitive, and is far from self-explanatory. M4:2 supplies a gloss to this material by explaining that what is meant by the expression *qôneh* is that transfer of the object for sale without transfer of money obligates the parties to uphold the sale, but transfer of money alone does not obligate the parties. While this is presumably meant to apply to all the clauses of M4:1, the part of M4:1 with the most immediate connection to the supplementary rule of M4:2 is M4:1 [E]: "Moveable goods acquire the coin but the coin does not acquire moveable goods." Yet it is here that we notice a peculiar shift in language between M4:2 [B–C] and M4:1, for whereas M4:1 [E] uses the terms *miṭṭalṭĕlîn*, "moveable goods," and *maṭbēʿa*, "coin," M4:2 [B–C] uses *pērôt*, "produce," and *māʿôt*, "money." Moreover, in M4:2 the idiom has changed from one of "acquisition" to one of "withdrawal from the contract," and emphasis is placed not only upon transfer of goods, but also on *mĕšîkâ*, the acquisition of the money or produce by means of the formal possessory act of drawing it. While it is possible to account for these shifts along other lines,[109] it is worth suggesting that the differences noted between the two

---

found a fig-round and in it there was a potsherd, a loaf and in it there was money"), which connects the statement attributed to R. Judah [E] explicitly to the list of items in [B], is part of the literary formulation of R. Judah's view itself, or whether [E] has been supplemented by a later hand in order to correlate it with [B]. In connection with M5:2 [D–K] it can be argued that *kêsad* [E] is part of a single rhetorical structure analogous to M5:10 [E–N].

A likely example of later material introduced by *kêsad* can be found in M5:1[F–L], in which [H–L] comprises a far more complex example of the principle of "increasing with produce" than the context requires. Perhaps [H–L] originally circulated as an independent pericope (it requires only the participle *ʾāsûr*, "it is prohibited" [cf. M5:2 [H, K]] to make the passage fully independent). (See *m. Neg.* 7:2 in which, according to Frankel, n.d. [1859], 298–9, explanatory material based on the view attributed to R. Meir in *m. Neg.* 1:1 has been added after the formulaic question *kêsad*. See also *m. ʿEd.* 3:1 = *m. ʾOhal.* 3:1, in which a dispute involving the power of a roof [a "tent"] under which there are human remains to transmit impurity to people and objects also under that roof when the contaminating material is in two pieces, neither of which alone is large enough to qualify as contaminating, is recast, following *kêsad*, in terms of touching, carrying and overshadowing [i.e., where the person involved has become a "tent" over the impure material] as well. Moreover, the problem has been complicated by the question of whether one can contract impurity by a combination of methods. See Epstein, *Nûsaḥ*, 1039.)

[109] In particular, the use of the rather general term "movable goods" in M4:1 [E] might stem from the fact that M4:1 is giving general rules; but M4:2 [A–C] gives an illustration and therefore uses a noun with greater specificity, "produce." On the other hand, had the author of M4:1 been responsible for M4:2 [B–C] the language in M4:2 might have matched its antecedent more closely. Compare, for example, the language of T3:13:

pericopae result from the fact that M4:2 constitutes a later gloss to M4:1.[110]

M7:4 [D–H] requires some comment in the context of this discussion of glosses and revisions, since that passage seems to refer to and to gloss M7:2, but in a way that is quite curious. M7:2 reads as follows:

[A] These [workers in the field] eat according to the Torah:
[B] one who works on [produce still] attached to the ground, at the time of the completion of the work,
[C] and on [produce] detached from the ground, while its work has not yet been completed,
[D] as long as its growth is from the earth.

[A] "Gold acquires silver [=M4:1:1 [A] according to the "Babylonian" tradition (see Appendix I)]
[B] How (kêṣad)?
[C] He gave him a golden dînār (cf. Latin aureus) for twenty five silver [dînārîm], lo, this one has acquired [the silver coins] wherever they may be.
[D] But if he gave him twenty five silver [dînārîm] for a golden dînār, lo, this one has not acquired [the gold coin] until such time as he draws it.

The text of T3:13 continues with a parallel exposition of M4:1 [B]. In both parts of T3:13, the idiom of "acquisition" is retained, and the notion of possessory acts is absent. At the same time, however, the general terms "silver" and "gold" have been replaced with coin denominations that show the relative values of the metals.

[110] Other possible examples of later revisions or expansions include the following passages. M5:4 opens with a negative indefinite construction in the participle (present): ʾên môṣîbîn [A]. The negative construction repeats in [D, E], and a positive indefinite construction is found in [G, H]. By contrast, 5:4 [B] has a verb with a definite subject ("he," i.e., the householder), in the imperfect (future): loʾ yittēn. Moreover, while this pericope uses technical jargon for the contracts in [A, D, E, G], the language of [B] is quite explicit: "let him not give him money in order to buy fruit with it." The grammatical and linguistic shift is matched by one in content: while M5:4–5 (and M5:6 [A–C], also using an indefinite construction) as a whole is concerned with giving raw materials to a contractor to work with: M5:4 [B] adds the case of a shopkeeper given money to buy produce. M2:9 [H–J] may also be a supplement. One of the difficulties in understanding this passage is that there seems to be a shift in the time to which the clauses are referring: [I–J], and perhaps [H], focus on the time at which the finder first comes upon the object; in [F–G] the finder, having already cared for the find wishes to be reimbursed for outlay (see the discussion in Appendix I). It seems possible that [H–J], giving an alternative means for the finder to retrieve the money, has been added to M5:4. Two passages already referred to in different contexts should be noted here: M4:6 [F–G] seems to conflict with the rules that precede it about the value of worn coins, but the inclusion of [F–G] in M4:5–6 seems to serve the purpose of revising these rules: although a coin may be worn more than the maximum amount, one may still be permitted to use it (see above, Section A.1); M10:4 [A–D] was described above as part of a coda to M10:1–3, with particular reference to M10:2; the opening word, wĕ-kēn, "and so [too]," shows that what follows in M10:4 is meant to supplement M10:2.

[E] And these do not eat:
[F] one who works on [produce still] attached to the ground at a time that is not the completion of the work,
[G] and on [produce] detached from the ground after the work has been completed,
[H] and on something whose growth is not from the earth.

The expression *nigmĕrâ mĕl'ākâ* [C, G] apparently means "at the time when the work [necessary to make the produce a finished product] has been completed."[111] In context, then, the related phrase *bĕ-šā'at gĕmār mĕl'ākâ* [B, F] must mean something analogous, perhaps "at the time when the produce is ripe."[112] At any rate, it seems clear that [B] and [F] refer to a stage in the preparation of produce, and not a part of the work day. Compare, however, M7:4 [D–H]:

[D] And [regarding] all of them, they only said: "At the time of the completion of the work (*bĕ-šā'at gĕmār mĕl'ākâ*),"
[E] but because of [the principle of] returning lost property to the owners they said:
[F] "Workers eat while walking from row to row,

---

[111] This may be seen from T8:7 (of which versions are cited at Y7:2 [11b] = *y. Ma'aś.* 2:6 [50a]; B89a; cf. *Sipre Deut.* 287 [ed. Finkelstein, p. 305]), in which threshing is done to something *še-lo' nigmĕrâ mĕl'aktô*, "whose work is not complete"; as opposed to the preparation and baking of dough, which is carried out on already milled grain, i.e., material *še-nigmĕrâ mĕl'aktô*, "whose work has been completed." The relevance of the determination of when "the work has been completed" is clearest in connection with such agricultural obligations as tithes, where it is important to know at what point the produce is liable to tithing (with which T8:7 and the general tenor of the Babli's discussion, B89a–b, correlate the rules of M7:2). See, e.g., *m. Ma'aś.* 2:4; what is meant by this is outlined in *m. Ma'aś.* 1:5–7 (although using different terminology): "What is the [stage at which produce is considered to have reached] the *gôren* for tithes? For cucumbers and gourds, from the time that he has removed the coils of blossoms (*mi-še-yĕpaqqēs*, Jastrow, s.v. *pqs*), and if he does not remove the coils of blossoms, from the time that he makes a stack...." Even the term *gôren*, "granary" or "threshing floor" (cf. M5:9 [A]), is suggestive of the fact that work has been completed, and the produce now put up for storage. See also *m. Pe'a* 5:8; *m. Ter.* 1:10; *m. Ma'aś. Š.* 3:6. More explicit testimony for the use of the expression meaning "completing a finished product" can be found in the Mishnah outside of the realm of agriculture (e.g., *m. Šab.* 22:2 in connection with the question of when an object first becomes susceptible to impurity; *m. Kel.* 5:1: "What is the *gĕmār mĕl'ākâ* [of an oven]? From the time that he [first] heats it to bake *supgānîm* in it...."; see also *m. 'Ed.* 2:5; *m. Kel.* 2:6; 4:4; 5:2; 20:7; *m. Toh.* 9:1, 3).

[112] See the note to M7:2 in Appendix I. Alternatively: "at the time when the work [leading up to the preparation of the crop for harvest] has been completed."

[G] "and on their way back from the winepress,
[H] "and an ass [may eat] until it is unburdened."[113]

What is meant by M7:4 [D–H] seems to be that an existing rule only stated that the workers may eat at the time of the completion of their work [D], but in the interest of curtailing the amount of time that workers take out to eat [E], workers were permitted to eat while they are walking from place to place, but not while they are actually engaged in the work of the harvest [F–G].[114] The expression ʾāmrû, "they said" [D], regularly refers to an anteced-

---

[113] I have followed the Kaufman ms. in reading bĕ-šāʿat gĕmār mĕlʾākâ (not bĕ-šāʿat mĕlʾākâ) in [D] and ʿad še-tĕhēʾ (not kĕ-še-tĕhēʾ) in [H]. See the note to M7:4 in Appendix I, and nn. 114 and 116 below.

[114] That M7:4 [D–H] assumes that the workers ought in principle to be prohibited from eating while they are actually working was stated explicitly by Maimonides in his paraphrase of our Mishnah, Code, Śĕkîrût, 12:2; but compare Nahmanides, Ḥiddûšîm, s.v. Hāʾ dĕ-ʾāmrî to B87b (see Appendix I). At least two factors militate against this reading. First, [E] might make more sense if [D–H] recognized the technical right of workers to eat only while engaged in work (i.e., reading bĕ-šāʿat mĕlʾākâ in M7:4 [D]), but in practice allowed workers to eat even while not actually working on harvesting, but merely walking, so that they will waste less time by eating when they ought to be working. Compare, e.g., T8:8: "R. Judah says: 'He may only eat when he is unburdening and burdening [an animal?]' (bĕ-šāʿâ še-pôrēq û-bĕ-šāʿâ še-tôʿēn) because [of the prevention] of the robbery of the work of the householder.'" While R. Judah's rule in the Tosepta corresponds to that of M7:4 [E, H] in that loss to the householder is prevented by having the worker eat only during restricted times (during "down time"), the wording of that tradition implies that it responds to a rule that allows the worker to eat at any time. (This is also the implication of the anonymous tradition preceding the tradition of R. Judah in T8:8: "One who works with his whole body eats at any time that he wants." Since the significance of "with his whole body" is not clear, it is difficult to be certain whether and how the tradition of R. Judah is intended to respond precisely to this anonymous tradition.) Secondly, if the correct reading in M7:4 [H] is "until it is unburdened" (as in the Kaufman ms.), and not "while it is being unburdened," [H] presupposes permission, at least for animals, to eat continuously until that moment. Of course, if Epstein, Nûsaḥ, 543–4, is correct that "until" is a post-Mishnaic corruption, this argument from this variant fails. Nevertheless, even without this textual argument, the rule of allowing an animal to eat (M7:4 [H]) is presumably based on Deut. 25:4: "You shall not muzzle an ox *while it is threshing* (bĕ-dîšô)." If so, whatever the wording of [H], the permission to eat is presumably granted while the animal is engaged in work: that, by right, permission extends only to eating during work itself, but for practical reasons permission was granted to other times. The juxtaposition of the rule about animals and the rule about workers in M7:2 suggests that the same assumptions are being made in both cases (see T8:7 [cf. *Sipre Deut.* 287 (ed. Finkelstein, p. 305), Y7:2 (11b); y. Maʿaś. 2:6 (50a); B89a], in which rules for workers are derived from precisely this verse about oxen, suggesting that other "Tannaitic" texts could associate the rules for oxen and for animals). On the other hand, it is not impossible that Deut. 25:4 was interpreted narrowly to refer to threshing and not to other activities, so that an animal too may be restricted from eating in other cases. It is also conceivable that M7:4 [H] has been added parenthetically as a

ent rule (cf. M3:1 [C] "For they said: 'an unpaid depositary swears and is exempt'"), and frequently is used in the context of a gloss or revision.[115] In the present case the parallel between M7:2 [B] and M7:4 [D] is close enough to suggest that M7:4 is referring to the rule in M7:2. However, in M7:4 the straightforward translation of *bĕ-šāʿat gĕmār mĕlʾākâ* is "at the time when the workers complete their work," that is, a time in the worker's day and not a phase of the ripening or processing of the produce.[116] It is striking, then, that

---

supplement to the rules about persons in a slightly inappropriate place (see the commentaries cited in Appendix I who see [H] as an independent clause). In that case the author of [D–G] may have considered the rule of workers eating distinct from that concerning animals (compare *Sipre Deut.* 287 [p. 305] [cf. *y. Maʿaś.* 2:6 (50a); B82b]: "'You shall not muzzle an ox' (Deut 25:4) .... If so, why has "ox" been said [explicitly]? It is an ox that you may not muzzle, but you may muzzle a person").

[115] Frankel, n.d. (1859), 304 (Rule 27) stated as a general principle that *ʾāmrû* indicates an "ancient *halākâ*." At most, all that can be established is that the expression refers to an antecedent rule: presumably that rule is prior chronologically, but its "antiquity" is not thereby fixed. In M4:2 [D] the expression is used to invoke a warning to (or curse on) those who profit by holding to the letter of the law rather than doing what is equitable. In M9:3 [P–Q], *ʾāmrû* introduces a comment on Scripture following the citation of a verse [O]. In neither of these cases is that which "they said" necessarily early. By contrast, in M3:1 [D], *ʾāmrû* introduces an underlying principle that may predate the formulation of the pericope as a whole. In M4:9 *ʾāmrû* appears in the context of a dispute over whether the list of items in M4:9 [A–B] can be expanded: "they said to him: 'they only said these things'" [H]. That is: the list that "they said" is assumed to include only certain items, and is taken by a later tradent to have referred to those few items exclusively. Here, then, *ʾāmrû* introduces a tradition that is subsequently glossed.

To take an example from outside the tractate in which the rule introduced by *ʾāmrû* is not merely referred to but commented upon see *m. Peʾa* 4:5: "There are three *ʾabʿāyôt* (times for the gleaners to come and pick gleanings?) in the day: dawn, noon and [the time of] the offering of meal (nine and one half hours into the day). R. Gamaliel says: 'They only said [this] so that [householders] not do less;' R. Aqiba says: 'They only said [this] so that they not add more.'" More interesting (and, arguably, pointing to a rule that is indeed quite early) is the case of *m. Pesaḥ.* 1:1:

[A] On the eve of the fourteenth [of Nisan] they inspect [for] the leaven by the light of the lamp.
[B] Any place in which they do not introduce leaven does not require inspection.
[C] And why did they say: "Two rows in the cellar"?
[D] [This refers to] a place in which they introduce leaven.
[E] The house of Shammai says: "Two rows across the entire face of the cellar";
[F] the house of Hillel says "The two outer rows, which are the top ones."

The antecedent rule "two rows in the cellar" is glossed in two ways: first, what kind of cellar is meant by the rule [D], and second, what is meant by "two rows" [E–F].

[116] Following Nahmanides, *Hiddûšîm*, s.v. *Hāʾ dĕ-ʾāmrî* (to B87b), it remains possible to take *bĕ-šāʿat gĕmār mĕlʾākâ* in M7:4 [D] as identical in meaning to *nigmĕrâ mĕlʾākâ* in M7:2

if M7:4 [D] introduces a gloss and revision of M7:2 as we have it, the author of M7:4 seems to have misread that source. This may have been due to an error, or to a conscious "misreading" in order to provide a contextual hook upon which to hang a supplementary ruling. It is also possible that M7:2 itself is an amplification of a rule that read more simply that workers may eat *bĕ-šāʿat gĕmār mĕlʾākâ*, and that M7:2 and M7:4 involve differing interpretations of this rule.[117]

[G, C] (i.e., the completion of the processing of the produce) and to read M7:4 as stating that although M7:2 permitted workers to eat produce "at the time of the labor that completes it" (*bĕ-šāʿat mĕlʾākâ še-hûʾ gĕmār*, Nahmanides) it did not permit eating while the workers were not actually working, "but because of [the principle of] returning lost property to the owners" (M7:4 [E]), the sages also permitted workers to eat while they are merely walking from place to place [F–G], "in order that they not eat while they are working" (Nahmanides). However, Nahmanides' preferred reading in M7:4 [D] is still *bĕ-šāʿat mĕlʾākâ*, "at the time of work" (without *gĕmār*, i.e., at the time that the workers are actually working), which fits his interpretation of the Mishnah more closely, and he explicitly interprets the version attested in our manuscripts, *bĕ-šāʿat gĕmār mĕlʾākâ*, in terms of his preferred reading. Moreover, M7:4 [D] sounds most like M7:2 [B, F], which seem to refer to the state of the produce (its readiness for harvest), and not to [C, G], referring to work being done by the workers (i.e., that labor that completes it), although it is in light of [C, G] that Nahmanides interprets M7:4 [D]. (Here it may be objected that *bĕ-šāʿat gĕmār mĕlʾākâ* [M7:2 [B, F]] and *še-[loʾ] nigmĕrâ mĕlʾaktô* [C, G] are sufficiently close that M7:4 [D] could, as Nahmanides argued, in fact be referring to M7:2 [C, G]. However, if M7:4 [D] responds to M7:2 [A–H], two expressions, with somewhat different meanings, were available, and we should have expected the authors of M7:4 [D] to utilize the expression that most closely suited their purpose [M7:2 [C, G]], rather than the other.) Even if Nahmanides is correct in his reading of *bĕ-šāʿat gĕmār mĕlʾākâ* in M7:4, the use of this expression to refer back to the rule of M7:2 requires some sort of "misreading" in order to make sense in M7:4.

[117] Just how M7:2 might be amplifying a rule that said simply "the worker may eat at the time of the completing of the work," is not clear. It may perhaps be harmonizing rules concerning workers with those involving tithes (i.e., that workers may eat produce until it is liable to tithing). In fact, the problem is probably more complicated than merely the relationship between M7:2 and M7:4 [D–H], since other traditions from outside the Mishnah and using much the same terminology appear to come to different conclusions. T8:7 (and, with differences in *y. Maʿaś.* 2:6 [50a] and Y7:2 [11b]) derives the rules for workers from Ex. 25:4, which deals with muzzling oxen (see above n. 114), and allows the worker to eat "(1) whose work has not finished (*še-loʾ nigmĕrâ mĕlʾaktô*) ... (2) whose growth is from the earth,... (3) that is separated from the earth,... (4) whose work is not finished with respect to tithes (*še-loʾ nigmĕrâ mĕlʾaktô lĕ-maʿaśĕrôt*)." The fourth part adds something we have not seen in the Mishnah, while parts (1–3) only permit eating produce that has been detached from the earth (cf. M7:2 [C]). T8:7 does not explicitly permit what M7:2 [B] permits.

3. Redaction as literary creation.

Codas, glosses, interpolations, and revisions in Mishnah tractate *Babaʾ Meṣiʿaʾ*, to the extent that these can be recovered, give some indication of the way in which the redactors of the Mishnah used their sources, and illustrates some of the tensions between the reliance on extant material and the desire to present a collection of material reflective of the redactors' own particular viewpoint. Thus far, however, the analysis of the redactional traces has not focused on how various traditions could be used to build up a broader redactional structure. I have argued that on the whole *m. Babaʾ Meṣiʿaʾ* is organized in clusters of pericopae connected by topic. Although there is occasional overlap in content between our tractate and other tractates in the Mishnah, there can be little doubt about which range of topics is appropriate to *Babaʾ Meṣiʿaʾ* and which to other tractates.[118] However, the standards of literary or redactional cohesion are different from our own, with the result that it is probably impossible to discern an overarching logical pattern of organization that will account for all the material in the tractate as a whole.[119] If, for instance, the nominative absolute series did constitute a source on contracts, in the course of the inclusion of this material into the tractate codas and interpolations added to the parts of this source have broken it up, and have, at least occasionally, added material that seems rather extraneous (for example the inclusion of material about deposits following the discussion of hiring workers and animals in Chapter 6 and again in Chapter 7).

At the same time, there are passages in *m. Babaʾ Meṣiʿaʾ* that show a remarkably subtle structure. M1:1–4 may offer a useful example of creative redaction:

M1:1 [A] Two people are holding a garment:
  [B] this one says ... and this one says ....
M1:2 [A] Two people were riding on an animal ...
  [B] this one says ... and this one says ....

---

[118] Compare, for instance, the contents of *m. Babaʾ Meṣiʿaʾ* with those of tractates *Babaʾ Qammaʾ* and *Babaʾ Batraʾ*. Even if these tractates originally constituted a single tractate on civil law, the fact that this "meta-tractate" could be broken down rather neatly into three parts dealing with delict, contracts and property respectively (with some argument about the proper place of the final chapters of the first two of these tractates), indicates that care was taken to group material by appropriate subject matter, however unsatisfactory the organization might be by modern standards (see the rough outline by Daube, 1944, 356–7; cf. Neusner, *Damages* II, 5–15; III, 4–17).

[119] There are tractates, or parts of tractates, which do clearly follow an overarching redactional pattern. For instance, the greater part of *m. Šebu.* is clearly a systematic working out of the different kinds of oaths and the rules connected with them. The whole of *m. Sanh.* is a logically organized tractate on the rules and procedures to be followed in court cases.

M1:3 [A] He was riding an animal,
     [B] and he saw the found object ....
M1:4 [A] He saw the found object ....
     [D] He saw them running ....

The four pericopae are easily separated into two units: the first (M1:1–2) is made up of two largely parallel pericopae about disputed claims to found property argued out in court;[120] the second (M1:3–4) is constructed out of three independent cases each dealing with the acquisition of found objects, and which are linked by common terminology.[121] What is striking in this example is the participial phrase "He was riding an animal" in M1:3 [A]. While the fact of riding or leading an animal is essential to the legal problem of M1:2 ("Two people were riding an animal, or one was riding and one was leading") since both actions demonstrate possession of the animal, in the same way that "holding" (*ôḥazîm*) demonstrates possession in M1:1, it is entirely irrelevant to the matter at hand in M1:3. I suggest that this phrase has been added to M1:3 to form a verbal bridge between M1:1–2 and M1:3–4, thus linking the two units of information into a single structure with possible legal implications.[122]

---

[120] The problem with which M1:1–2 deals is how to rule in a case involving conflicting claims brought by the claimants; the rulings themselves are given in the jussive imperfect (future). M1:2 [E–F] offer an alternative ruling when the conditions of the case are somewhat different. The *Sitz im Leben* of M1:1–2 clearly appears to be the court. That this was the ancient understanding of these pericopae as well is proved, for instance, by the (first version of the) tradition attributed to R. Hiyya, which is linked to M1:1–2 (with the formula *wĕ-tānnā᾿ tûnā᾿*, "the tanna [reciter of the Mishnah] teaches"; see Epstein, *Nûsaḥ*, 887): "[The plaintiff says:] 'You have a *maneh* belonging to me,' and the latter says: 'I have nothing belonging to you,' *and the witnesses testify that he has fifty* zûz (= *dînārîm*, one half of a *maneh*) ...." (B3a). By contrast, M1:3–4 presents the rules that govern the acquisition of found objects at the moment and in the context in which they were found.

[121] These pericopae use the verb *zky/h*, here in the sense of "gain possession," in the apodoses to the cases (M1:3 [E], 4 [C, G]), and in the description of the cases themselves (M1:3 [F], 4 [F, I]). The verb *᾿mr*, "say," features in the first and third case as a significant element in both the circumstances (M1:3 [C, D], 4 [F, I]) and in the rulings (*lo᾿ ᾿āmar kĕlûm*, "he has not said anything," M1:3 [G], 4 [J]). Finally, as the summary of the pericopae given above in the text shows, each of the cases is introduced with the verb *rā᾿â*, "he saw."

[122] On the face of it, the importance of the fact that the claimants in M1:2 are holding or riding an animal is that the sole evidence before the court is that both parties equally demonstrate their ownership of the animal in question (riding or leading is something that someone with a legal right to an animal does with it). However, in T1:3 (cf. B8b–9a) a tradition attributed to R. Judah, if not the anonymous opinion to which it is attached, gives preference to one form of directing the animal and may presuppose that what is at issue for the view attributed to R. Judah, and by implication for M1:2, is the effectiveness of leading and riding as possessory acts:

Perhaps the clearest example is Chapter 5. Earlier in this chapter I pointed to the terminological shift between M5:1, which used the terms *nešek* and *tarbît*, and the remainder of Chapter 5 (and, indeed, of the Mishnah) in which the term *ribbît* is used, and suggested that the author of M5:1 is not the same as the author(s) who produced the remainder of the chapter.[123] Here I wish to explore the redacted structure of the chapter as a whole. The rhetorical force of M5:1 at once links this pericope to the language of Scripture, and suggests that the field of usury as a whole is divided into two fields: outright usury on a loan in money or in kind (*nešek*) (M5:1 [B–D]), and (possible) increase accruing to the lender because of the rise in value of the produce that the borrower has agreed to pay (*tarbît*). The very next passage (M5:2 [A–C]) introduces a third type of usury, a gift to the lender (in the form of a reduction of rent) in consideration of a loan, and uses the term *ribbît*. Nevertheless, there are signs that M5:2 [A–C] was designed or altered to follow and supplement M5:1: the case is introduced *ha-malweh*, "one who lends ..." (M5:2 [A]; cf. M5:1 [C]) and concludes with the explanatory formula *mi-pĕnê še-hûʾ ribbît*, "because it is interest (M5:2 [C]; cf. M5:1 [D], *mi-pĕnê še-hûʾ nôšek*, lit. "because it bites"). In M5:2 [D], the syntax moves away from the nominative absolute construction of M5:1 [B, F] and M5:2 [A], but the wording of the rule *marbîm ... wĕ-ʾên marbîn ...*, "one may increase ... but one may not increase ..." echoes *ha-marbeh bĕ-pērôt*, "one who increases [his return by means of] produce" in M5:1 [F].[124] Moreover, the two cases that exemplify M5:2[D], and the cases of M5:3, have clearly parallel structures.[125] Whatever their separate origins, the various parts of

---

[A] Two people were pulling [*môškîn*] a camel, or leading [*manhîgîn*] the ass,
[B] or one person was pulling and one was leading,
[C] [the rule] follows the same manner [*ka-middâ ha-zoʾt*, referring to a text (presumably T1:2 or M1:2) of which T1:3 is a continuation].
[D] R. Judah says: "One who is pulling the camel or one who is leading the ass, lo, this one has gained possession (*zākà*)."

It is possible that the juxtaposition of M1:1–2 to M1:3–4, in which the force of possessory acts is explicitly discussed (M1:4), also presupposes this interpretation (the Babli, B8b, certainly assumed this). If this is so, this is a good example of the process of reinterpretation and supplementation of materials in the process of redaction.

[123] See above, Section A.1.

[124] As far as I know M5:1 [F] and M5:2 [D] are the only passages in the Mishnah that use the root *rby/h* as a verb to mean to make usurious gain. Compare the expression used in M5:6 [D]: *lôwîm mē-hen u-malwîm ʾôtān bĕ-ribbît*, "one borrows from them and lends to them at interest."

[125] (1) Case, in perfect (past) (M5:2 [F, I]; M5:3 [A, D]); (2) "(and) he said to him" (M5:2 [G, J]; M5:3 [B, E]); (3) ruling: it is permitted/prohibited (*muttār/ ʾāsûr*) (M5:2 [H, K]; M5:3 [C]); cf., however, M5:3 [F]: "lo, it is his." In M5:1 [H–L] a similar kind of case is brought,

M5:1–3 as they appear before us in the Mishnah seem crafted so as to form a single unit.

With M5:4 the dominant syntactical pattern changes from perfect (past) tense verbs with definite (if assumed) subjects, to indefinite constructions in the participle (present) and from casuistic presentation of cases to apodictic rules (for instance *ʾēn môšîbîn*, "one may not set up [lit. seat] ...," M5:4 [A]). In M5:8 the syntactical pattern shifts again to a definite construction with the subject *ʾādām* supplied: *malweh ʾādām*, "a person may lend ..." (M5:8 [A]); *lōʾ yōʾmar ʾādām*, "let a person not say ..." (M5:9 [A]); *ʾômēr ʾādām lĕḥabērô*, "a person may say to his fellow" (M5:10 [A]). M5:10 [E–P] contains two sub-units that follow still another rhetorical structure.[126] Finally, the syntax, structure, and contents of M5:11 (which lists the verses that the various participants to a usurious loan have transgressed) mark this pericope off as separate from the preceding. These syntactical shifts might reflect the juxtaposition of sources.

In terms of content, the major breaks in the chapter seem to be at M5:2 [D]; M5:4 [A]; M5:7 [A]; M5:8 [A]; M5:10 [E]; and M5:11 [A].[127] To a great extent, these shifts in subject matter correspond to shifts in language and syntax that I have already noted.[128] This gives a measure of support to the hypothesis that the various clusters linked by common syntax stem from different sources. As Neusner has already noted, however, the contents of M5:2 [E]–10 [D] can be broken into two more general categories: the prohibitions of M5:2 [D]–6 seem to conform, by and large, to the definition of

---

to explicate M5:1 [E–F] (note *kēṣad* [G]; however a somewhat more complex case is presented, and no final ruling is offered). Thus similarly presented cases exemplify rules that use language unique to M5:1 [F] and M5:2 [D] (see previous note).

[126] M5:10 [E–N] as a whole is structured similarly to M5:1: a statement proclaiming the existence of two categories [E], exemplified in subsequent clauses (see M5:10 [J, N]). The two cases themselves may follow the pattern of the cases in M5:2 [F]–3 (see previous note): (1) case in perfect (past): [G–H], [K–L]; (2) "... he said" [I, M]; (2) ruling: lo, this is interest in advance/delayed [J, N]. M5:10 [O–P], attributed to R. Simeon, supplements [E–N].

[127] The topics of these sections are as follows: M5:2 [D]–3: intersection between sale and loan; M5:4–6: aspects of usury in giving raw material to contractors to work with (e.g., animals to be raised); this is at least the opening topic of M5:6, although that pericope includes subsidiary issues as well; M5:7: payment in advance for produce (whose price is liable to rise); M5:8–10 [D]: lending of produce or service measure for measure (and not by monetary value); M5:10 [E–P]: interest in advance, interest delayed; verbal interest; M5:11: the verses for which participators in usury are liable.

[128] The major exception is M5:7 [A]. It is perhaps not accidental that in M5:7 the plural indefinite construction (*pôsqîn*, [A]) with which the pericope opens quickly gives way to the singular (*pôsēq*, [C, H, I, K]; cf. [L]). It is possible, then, that M5:7, too, constituted its own source.

nešek in M5:1: transactions in which the nature of the contract is such that the lender receives more than the amount of the loan. By contrast, the cases of M5:6–10 [D] are all concerned with the implications of fluctuations in value (especially of produce, but also of work, M5:10 [A–D]), which is one of the essential characteristics of the definition of *tarbît* in M5:1.[129] If I am correct in seeing M5:2 [A–C] as defining a third kind of interest (a gift, not specified in the contract itself), we can find the echo of this form of interest in M5:10 [E–P] in which extra-contractual gifts of money [E–N] or information [O–P] are deemed usurious.[130] Thus the redactor of this chapter of *m. Baba' Meṣiʿaʾ* may have set out at the beginning of the chapter a set of definitions, whose contents define the structure of nearly all the rest of the chapter. This is followed by M5:11, which linked the prohibition of interest back to its Scriptural roots. If the opening précis, and, as suggested above, the raw material of M5:2 [D]–10, are constructed out of a variety of sources, Chapter 5 is an example of how redaction can shape already existing sources into a body of material with an overarching thematic organization.

D. The Problem of Attributions

As far as possible, I have avoided until now a discussion of statements attributed to named sages. These statements, as the catalogue below will show, are quite numerous, and deserve a discussion in their own right. On the one hand, since we can place Rabbis into a general chronological framework, attributed statements constitute almost the only internal benchmarks for assigning a rough dating of individual rules in the Mishnah. On the other hand, the attributed statements are no less stylized than the rest of the Mishnah, and this makes it hard, if not impossible, to assume that the person to whom a statement is attributed actually said those words. If so, we are dealing in each case with a literary representation of someone's opinion, which has inevitably altered (whether greatly or slightly, and whether knowingly or unknowingly) the view that that person held. Neusner's procedure in his *History of the Mishnaic Law* series was to group the attributed statements by generation, and to see whether the material belonging to particular generations coheres.[131] Neusner went further by asking to what extent the topics or

---

[129] Neusner, *Damages* II, 66–7. Neusner makes the argument more generally for all of M5:2–10.

[130] Here I am assuming that in M5:10 [P] it is the debtor who is not to give information, and not the creditor who is not to ask for information. Analogy with [E–N] supports the interpretation taken here. Unfortunately, [P] is not as clear as it might be. See Appendix I.

[131] While he was neither the first nor the only person to recognize the implications of these traditions (see, e.g., Frankel, n.d. [1859], 21ff.; Weiss, 1941, 1–33), Neusner has made this

problems assigned to a particular generation were generative or determinative of the issues covered in the tractates (and by extension the Mishnah) as a whole.

In the case of *m. Baba' Meṣiʿa'*, where the traditions assigned to the "Ushan" generation (i.e., middle to late second century CE) outnumber those of earlier generations by a factor of approximately four,[132] and where the Ushan traditions do indeed correspond to the legal concerns of the tractate as a whole, it is easy to see why Neusner concluded that this tractate is largely the product of this generation.[133] Elsewhere I have made much the same argument: that *m. Baba' Meṣʿaʾ* is not the product of the second Temple period, and is more likely to be the work of the second century.[134] This argument is based on the distribution of attributed statements, the general evenness of the tractate as a whole in terms of style, syntax, and language (suggesting that its various parts were not composed over extremely long periods of time),[135] and the general absence of interest in questions of civil law from texts that did demonstrably come from the second Temple period. Here, however, I wish to point out that this argument, plausible though it may be, is neither self-evident nor conclusively provable. The argument from numerical distribution alone is problematic because we cannot control for literary processes that might skew the distribution. Labeling a tradition as coming from a particular sage is a literary convention, and we have no way of

---

material a central aspect of his approach to the Mishnah. See his *Purities* III, 237–44, and his summary statement in *idem*, 1981, 14–22. Neusner, 1981, *passim* presents the results of the procedure worked out in the studies of Mishnaic law.

[132] The breakdown by generation can be presented in tabular form as follows:

Early: 4
Yabnean: 6
Ushan: 38 (or 40 if we include M2:4 [E–F] and M4:12 [I–J])
Ushan/Late: 2
Late: 2

"Early" refers to figures thought to have flourished before 70 CE; "Yabnean" those between roughly 70 and 135; "Ushan" after 135; and "Late" those who flourished in the generation of Judah the Patriarch (late second or early third century).

[133] Neusner, *Damages* V, 48–9.

[134] Lapin, 1995.

[135] To this extent I concur with Neusner, *Purities* XXI, 234–46, in which he argues that the Mishnah (or at least the order of Purities) was composed by "tradent redactors," that is, the same people who are responsible for transmitting the material have also formulated it and organized it. However, in the same section (pp. 245–6), Neusner makes it clear that he is talking about "intermediate divisions" that, earlier in the volume (e.g., p. 124), he treats as having preceded the redaction of whole tractates. That is to say, there is still substantial room for the manipulation of sources (e.g., these "intermediate divisions") in the formulation of tractates in their final form.

knowing the extent to which such a convention might have developed over time, with the result that later material was more likely to be assigned to a sage than earlier material.[136] Alternatively, traditions, however recast or revised in their present form, may have survived a long period of transmission during which the names with which they were once associated have been lost. Moreover, I will argue below (Section 2) that much of the attributed material, particularly of the Ushan generations, is largely supplementary in character, and can be taken as secondary glosses or amplifications. In that case, it is very difficult to argue that the Ushan material in the tractate can conclusively date it. If the attributed material mostly supplements the Mishnah, the first attributed reference to a particular concept in the Mishnah cannot conclusively date the concept since the concept could have been current long before the attributed view was expressed (whatever relationship this bears to its literary representation). In fact, the concept might have been current only in the period in which the attribution was made to the sage, perhaps falsely (again, whether knowingly or unknowingly), but long after the death of that individual. It is still less possible to date the tractate as a literary work on the basis of attributions, since we cannot account for the date of the texts that the attributed material supplements.

The following survey of attributed statements in *m. Baba' Meṣiʿa'* yields largely negative results in terms of the fixing of the date of the Mishnah and its materials. However, there is at least one possible positive conclusion to which I wish to draw attention. In Section 3, below, I will argue that the

---

[136] It is perhaps no accident that although traditions are associated with Hillel and Shammai, the generations following them are remembered only by their affiliation to one of these two sages (the House of Hillel; the House of Shammai). Rabbinic tradition places Hillel and Shammai after Shemaiah and Abtalion (*m. Ḥag.* 2:2; *m. 'Ab.* 1:10, 12), who may correspond to the Samaias and Pollion who were contemporaries of Herod the Great and active in the second half of the first century BCE (Josephus, *Antiquities*, 14.175 [events in 47 BCE]; 15.3 [37 BCE], 370 [20 BCE]; the literature and problems concerning the identification are reviewed in E. Schürer, *A History of the Jewish People in the Age of Jesus Christ*, rev. ed. G. Vermes, *et al.* [Edinburgh: T. and T. Clark, 1973–87], 2, 362–3). Hillel and Shammai themselves would have been active at the end of the first century BCE or the beginning of the first century CE, leaving several decades (roughly as long as the period between the conventional date of the beginning of the Ushan period and the redaction of the Mishnah, 135–200) in which there are remarkably few attributions to, or stories about, named individuals, with the notable exception of Gamaliel I. If the "Houses" material generally reflects the views of this period (cf., however, Neusner's argument that much of this material is pseudepigraphically attributed to these first-century schools: Neusner, 1981, 20–1, worked out in greater detail in *idem*, *Purities* XVII, 202–22 in connection with *m. Makš.*), the absence of individual attributions is striking, and may reflect a shift in the methods of transmission, regardless of the date in which the traditions themselves were put in their present form.

distribution of attributed statements may help elucidate the redactional history of some material in the Mishnah.

1. Catalogue of attributed statements.[137]

	Tradent	Gen.	Form	Topic
1:6 [G–I]	Meir + Sages	U	Reverse dispute form (includes qualifiers)	Return deeds (does court collect?)
1:8 [G]	Simeon b. Gamaliel	U	Gloss—qualifying	Return documents (ʾagudâ of lender? borrower?)
2:1 [E–G]	Judah[138]	U	Independent sentence (followed by explanatory clause, kēṣad ...)	What things must be proclaimed
2:1 [H]	Simeon b. Eleazar	L	Independent sentence	What things need not be proclaimed
[2:4 [E–F][139]]	[Judah]	U	Gloss—supplement (ʾap)?	Money (loose/bound) found in produce
2:6 [C–E]	Meir, Judah	U	Reverse dispute form (includes qualifier to R. Judah)	How long to proclaim?
2:7 [I–M]	Tarfon, Aqiba	Y	Standard dispute form	What to do with the proceeds from the sale of a lost object
2:10 [K]	Simeon	U	Gloss—disputing (ʾap)	Loading, unloading animal
2:10 [L–N]	Yose ha-Gelili	Y	Gloss—disputing	Loading, unloading animal

---

[137] I have used the following abbreviations: in the column labeled "Tradent": BŠ (*bêt šammaî*, the Shammaites); BH (*bêt hillel*, the Hillelites); in the column labeled "Gen." (generation): E ("Early"); Y ("Yabnean"); U ("Ushan"); and L ("Late"). The abbreviation U/L, which appears twice in the table, means that a late tradent is stating a tradition in the name of an Ushan figure. In the column headed "Form" I have distinguished between independent traditions, glosses, and dispute forms. The latter, in turn are divided into three types: (a) the "standard dispute form," in which a heading is followed by the rulings of the disputants; (b) the "reverse dispute form," where a statement is followed by the attribution "the words of (*dibrê*) R. N," which is in turn followed by a disputing tradition; and (c) the "rejoinder dispute form," in which a rule is introduced by an attribution to a sage, and followed by a disputing tradition attributed to a specific individual or to "the Sages" or an unspecified "They."

[138] See the note to M2:1 in Appendix I.

[139] See the note to M2:4 in Appendix I and Epstein, *Nûsaḥ*, 1017. If we follow the reading "R. Judah says: 'Even one who acquires ...,'" the tradition is supplementary. Without ʾap, the tradition is independent in form.

3:2 [D–F]	Yose	U	Gloss—objection + dispute	Renter who lends	
3:4 [D–E]	Yose	U	Gloss—objection + dispute	Thief does not know from whom he stole	
3:5 [D–E]	Yose	U	Gloss—objection + dispute	Depositary does not know who deposited	
3:6 [C–D]	Simeon b. Gamaliel	U	Gloss—disputing	Deposited produce is rotting	
3:7 [G–H]	Yohanan b. Nuri	Y	Gloss—objection + dispute	Deductions for perishing produce	
3:7 [I–J]	Judah	U	Gloss—qualifying? disputing?	Deductions for perishing produce	
3:8 [B]	Judah	U	Gloss—disputing	Deductions for losses in produce	
3:8 [G]	Judah	U	Gloss—correlation (ʾap)[140]	Deductions for losses in produce	
3:11 [F–G]	Meir, Judah	U	Reverse dispute form	Shopkeeper; deposits of money	
3:12 [A–C]	BŠ, BH	E	Standard dispute form	Appropriating, using deposit: value for which liable	
3:12 [D]	Aqiba	Y	Gloss—dispute? Third member of a dispute form?	Appropriating, using deposit: value for which liable	
3:12 [E–G]	BŠ, BH	E	Standard dispute form	When does liability for appropriation, use begin	
4:2 [E]	Simeon	U	Gloss—disputing? Independent tradition?	Recision of sale	
4:4 [C]	Judah	U	Gloss—disputing	*Hônāyâ* does (not) apply to merchants	
4:5 [A–D]	Meir, Judah, Simeon	U	Standard dispute form	Short-weight coins and *hônāyâ*	
4:9 [F]	Simeon	U	Independent statement?	Things that do not have *hônāyâ* (sacrifices)	
4:9 [G–H]	Judah + "They"	U	Rejoinder dispute form	Things that do not have *hônāyâ*	
4:12 [D–H(?)]	Judah + Sages	U	Rejoinder dispute form	Equitable market practice	

---

[140] Reading ʾ*ap* as in RLMPN; ʾ*ap* is absent in K (cf. Appendix I). Without the word the tradition is formally independent.

[4:12 [I–J]]	Abba Shaul (?)[141] + Sages	U	Reverse dispute form ("and they concede ..." follows)	Equitable market practice
5:5 [D–E?]	Simeon b. Gamaliel	U	Gloss—supplementing?	Raising of cattle for a share
5:7 [I–J]	Yose + Sages	U	Rejoinder dispute form	Sale of produce (dung) one does not have
5:7 [L]	Judah	U	Gloss—disputing	Stipulation for lowest price for advance sale
5:9 [C]	Hillel	E	Gloss—disputing (*ʾôsēr*)	Loans of produce
5:9 [D–G]	Hillel	E	Independent tradition	Loans of produce
5:10 [E–N (?)][142]	Gamaliel	Y	Independent tradition	Advanced and delayed interest
5:10 [O–P]	Simeon	U	Independent tradition	Verbal interest
5:11 [C]	Sages		Gloss—disputing	Who transgresses the prohibition of usury
6:5 [J]	Symmakhos in name of Meir	U/L	Gloss (anonymous question + attributed ruling)	How much may be added to load of animal before liability
6:7 [B–C]	Judah	U	Gloss—disputing	Secured loans of money or produce and the liability for security
6:7 [D–E]	Abba Shaul	U	Independent tradition	Special rights of lender with respect to security
6:8 [D]	Eleazar[143]	U	Gloss—objecting	Liability of depositary with respect to a broken jar
7:1 [L–M]	Simeon b. Gamaliel	U	Gloss—disputing (commentary)	Specific stipulations for rights of workers to food, etc.

---

[141] See the note to M4:12 in Appendix I. I am inclined to follow the reading of K (*kĕ-dibrê*, "according to the words of ..."), which takes the reference to Abba Shaul in [I] as a sort of cross-reference, and not as an attribution of [H] to him.

[142] It is possible that only the opening statement [E] is, properly speaking, attributed to R. Gamaliel, and that the remainder of the tradition is a later elaboration. I am inclined, however, to see the whole of [E–N] as a single tradition.

[143] I have followed the tradition of the Babli in taking the name intended here as Eleazar (b. Shamua) despite the strong attestation of the form "Eliezer." See the notes to M6:8 in Appendix I.

7:3 [E]	Yose b. R. Judah	L	Gloss—disputing	Circumstances under which a worker may eat
7:5 [C–D (?)]	Eleazar Hisama + Sages	Y	Rejoinder dispute form	Eating more than the value of the wages
7:9 [C]	Judah	U	Gloss—disputing, qualifying	Wild animals as ʾônes
7:9 [E–F]	Yadua the Babylonian in the name of Meir	U/L	Gloss—disputing, qualifying	Wild animals as ʾônes
8:6 [H]	Simeon b. Gamaliel	U	Gloss—supplementary	Notice of eviction for shops
9:5 [E–F]	Judah	U	Gloss—objection + dispute	Minimum amount of produce for tenant to work
9:6 [G–H]	Judah	U	Gloss—qualifying, disputing	(No) deduction for tenant due to locust or blight if leased for cash
9:8 [D]	Simeon b. Gamaliel	U	Gloss—disputing (ʾôsēr)	Growing produce different from agreed upon
9:8 [G]	Simeon b. Gamaliel	U	Gloss—disputing (ʾôsēr)	Growing produce different from agreed upon
9:13 [H–I]	Simeon b. Gamaliel	U	Gloss—disputing (ʾap)	Selling pledge after 30 days
10:2 [E]	Yose	U	Gloss—disputing	How much responsibility for residents of storeys with damage between them
10:3 [F–H]	Judah	U	Gloss—objection + dispute (reformulation)	Upper resident's recourse if lower refuses to rebuild
10:5 [A']	Simeon b. Gamaliel	U	Gloss—disputing? (ʾap)	Builder may prepare for building for thirty days (with no liability)
10:6 [A–H]	Meir, Judah, Simeon (?)	U	Standard dispute form (reworked; Simeon is a third member of the dispute?)	Produce growing between terraced fields

2. Attributed statements in m. Baba' Meṣi'a'.

If one may take all of M3:12 [A–G] as a single unit, two of the three traditions attributed to the earliest tradents of the tractate ("E" in the catalogue)[144] are formulated as independent statements. The third (M5:9 [C]: "Hillel prohibits"), although dependent upon the preceding material, is likely to be redactional, since it merely serves as the transition to the independent rule attributed to Hillel in M5:9 [D–G]. That these traditions are formulated as independent, in contrast to the bulk of the material ascribed to the Yabnean or still later generations, is striking. Moreover, in the case of M3:12 [A–G], the two Hillelite-Shammaite disputes encapsulate the entire discussion of the Mishnah on those subjects, with the result that if we removed the disputes, we would also remove the mention of the problem of how to value the deposit, and the implication of intention alone for liability.[145] Perhaps these traditions assigned to the generations before 70 derive from a redactional strategy in which material assigned to the earliest generations is handled differently from other material. On formal grounds, this strategy need not reflect an "early" redactional layer: the differences might be due to the way in which late formulators of material cast traditions (perhaps pseudepigraphically) in the name of the earliest Rabbinic tradents. M3:12 [A–C] is supplemented with a statement attributed to the Yabnean R. Aqiba (M3:12 [D]), so that this passage, at least, can be seen as reflecting early concerns that have been subsequently developed. If this is so, then the possibility that we actually have an early text incorporated with a gloss into the Mishnah is strengthened.[146] The case is harder to make for the other two "Early" traditions, since in neither case do we have explicit development or comment on the "early" material, as we do in the preceding example.[147] In any

---

[144] The "early" traditions are: M3:12 [A–C], [E–G]; M5:9 [C], [D–G].

[145] This is especially the case if, with C. Levine, "The Concept of 'Sheliḥut Yad' in the Mechilta De Rashbi" [Hebrew] *BIA* 18/19 (1981), 101–4, we take the case of "reaching of the hand" to the deposit as specific to deposit, and involving the temporary use of the deposit. If so, we cannot assume, for instance, that the rules of robbery, as in *m. B. Qam.* 9:1–2, would apply. See further Section III.B.2. (n. 108).

[146] Neusner, *Damages* V, 63–4, neglects to treat the tradition of R. Aqiba. See further Lapin, 1995, 177–8, n. 85.

[147] The concern in M5:9 [D–E] with the potentially usurious outcome of loans of produce is echoed in a story about R. Gamaliel (Yabnean) in M5:8. Neusner, *Damages* V, 69 minimizes the significance of this intersection of concerns. It is also worth noting that both M5:9 [D–E] and M3:12 [A–C] attribute concerns with shifting market values to early tradents, and to that extent these passages support one another. Neusner, *Damages* V, 64, argued that M3:12 [E–G] is a late passage falsely ascribed to the "Houses," and reflects the common Ushan concern for intention. However, since in the case of the treatment of deposit the issue of intention is not raised in material attributed to later generations, it is possible to argue that

event, since there are so few statements attributed to the earliest generations of tradents and since they deal with such a restricted range of topics (appropriation of deposits, M3:12 [A–G], and loans of produce, M5:9 [C, D–E]), it is impossible to argue that material composed (or even more or less accurately reflecting the views from) before 70 CE underlies *m. Baba' Meṣi'a'* as a whole.

In the case of traditions assigned to the "Yabnean" period, we have a somewhat wider range of topics covered (in addition to usury and deposits, the Yabnean traditions address lost objects and the right of workers to eat of the produce with which they are working), although, again, the traditions are few enough that it is hard to substantiate a claim that in its basic outlines, much less in substance, *m. Baba' Meṣi'a'* comes from this period.[148] Assuming that M5:10 [E] and [F–N] were composed together as a unit, M5:10 [E–N] is the one Yabnean tradition that is both formally independent and encapsulates the entire discussion of the legal problem involved: without this statement we would have no discussion of "interest in advance" and "interest delayed." Also perhaps originally independent is the dispute between the "Sages" and R. Eleazar Ḥisama (M7:5 [C–D]). The tradition of R. Eleazar Ḥisama [C], although somewhat abrupt, is comprehensible by itself, and in its present context the view ascribed to the "Sages" is redundant, since it agrees with M7:5 [A–B].[149] However, this last passage, in its present position, serves as a parenthetical supplement to M7:5 [A–B + E–F]. The remaining Yabnean traditions come at the end of the units in which they appear, and similarly supplement the stock pericopae.[150] Thus, in the case of

---

this dispute reflects a question raised early on and, following the Hillelite position, left behind (in which case, it is possible that such passages as M3:9 and M3:11 actually develop an older Hillelite view).

[148] The traditions are as follows: M2:7 [I–M]; M2:10 [L–N]; M3:7 [G–H]; M3:12 [D]; M5:10 [E–N (?)]; M7:5 [C–D (?)].

[149] Cf. the question raised in the Babli: "The Sages are the same as the first reciter [i.e., [A–B]]," *ḥakāmîm haynû tannā' qammā',* B92a (on this formula see D. W. Halivni, *Měqôrôt û-měsôrôt: Mô'ēd* [New York: JTSA, 1975–82], *Šabbat,* 75). In addition, the dispute is articulated in different terms than those of M7:5 [A–B]: the tradition of R. Eleazer states the problem in terms of the amount of the worker's wages for the day; in [A–B] a specific monetary amount, a *dînār,* is discussed. (Does the juxtaposition of M7:5 [A–B] and [C] allow us to conclude that a "typical" day's wage should be identified with a *dînār*? Cf. Mt. 20:1–16, and see below, Chapter III.B.5) It is also possible that [E–F] extends the view of the sages in the dispute form (i.e., the sages permit eating more than one's wages, but rule that workers ought to be taught not to do so), in which case the rather extended dispute form occurs at the end of the pericope, much as the other Yabnean materials cited do.

[150] M2:7 [I–M] and M2:10 [L–N] come at the end of the pericopae, according to the standard division of the Mishnah. M3:7 [G–H] clearly comes at the end of the unit discussing

the problem of deductions made for produce on deposit, the tradition attributed to R. Yohanan b. Nuri (M3:7 [G–H]) clearly objects to the reasoning of the preceding material ("What does it matter to them? Mice eat [as much as they eat] whether from much or from little," [G]) and echoes the language directly: "Let him deduct losses only for a *kôr*" [H] (cf. [B]: "Lo, let this one deduct losses"; in [C–E] the losses are calculated per *kôr*).

As noted above, the vast bulk of the attributed statements are assigned to the "Ushan" period. A cursory glance at the catalogue above will show that the majority of the Ushan traditions are what I have termed (somewhat loosely, perhaps) "glosses." Some traditions are merely the brief expression of

---

deductions for dry produce; together with the tradition attributed to R. Judah (M3:7 [I–J]) it comes at the end of a pericope as well. M3:12 [D] may be seen as either coming at the end of the dispute form [A–C] or as a parenthetical insertion. Since the conventional division of *m. B. Meṣ.* into paragraphs is a printers' convention (which differs from that of earlier manuscripts), I make no claim that the coincidence of attributed statements with ends of pericopae reveals the original subdivision of the Mishnah into units (although more work could be done on this). My point is only that the stylistic, linguistic, or thematic criteria used by copyists or printers for identifying where new "paragraphs" begin often leaves attributed statements at the end of units.

Although in their present form all of these passages serve as supplements, in the case of M2:7 [I–M] and M2:10 [L–N] it is possible that (as proposed above in connection with M7:5) the Yabnean material originates in independent traditions that have been reapplied here. (1) As formulated, the subject of the "standard dispute form" attributed to R. Aqiba and R. Tarfon in M2:7 [I–M] supplements the topic of the main part of the pericope: [E–G] considers the circumstances under which a found animal should be sold; in [I–M] R. Aqiba and R. Tarfon dispute the secondary question of the handling of the proceeds of that sale. However, the dispute between R. Tarfon and R. Aqiba could easily be generalized to deposits of (loose) money, with R. Tarfon permitting use of such money. It is possible that M2:7 [I–M] originated as just such a dispute, which was later reapplied in a more narrow context: money resulting from the sale of a found object. (M3:11, using similar language, addresses just this issue of deposited money and rules that bankers may use loose money, but householders [as in M2:7] may not. Might M3:11 reflect the application of the view of R. Aqiba? For the question of using a deposit, compare the concept of *depositum irregulare* in Roman law, in which a banker might use loose money on deposit, having contracted to return the value of the deposit but not the coins themselves. Although this concept may be a "post-classical" one in Roman law, classical jurists were aware of how the concept of deposit might shade into that of a loan [see, e.g., D 12.1.9.9; 12.1.10 (Ulpian); 16.1.24 (Papinian)]. Moreover, Hellenistic legal traditions did allow for such "irregular" deposits. See further Chapter III.B.3.) (2) The tradition of R. Yose the Galilean, M2:10 [L–M] by itself is a fragment. However, it uses different terminology than [E–I] (*zāqûq* is used in [L]; *ḥayyāb* appears in [E] and [I], as well as [A–B]). Is it possible that what was originally an independent Scriptural exegesis (perhaps something along the lines of "'Under its load' (Ex. 23:5), R. Yose ha-Gelili says ...") has been recast in Mishnaic form (i.e., with the verse, preceded by *še-neʾemar*, following the Rabbinic statement)?

a dissenting view.[151] Others include clear reference to, and commentary on, preceding material. For instance, in the tradition attributed to R. Judah in M9:5 [E–F], R. Judah's objection is directed both at the rule and the wording of the material to which it refers and supplies a clause to replace the one that R. Judah opposes.[152] The language attributed to R. Eleazar in M6:8 [D], "I question whether this one or this one can swear" (*tāmēha ʾanî ʾim yĕkôlîm zeh wĕ-zeh lĕhiššābēʿa*) expresses doubt about the correctness of a tradition as it has been passed down.[153] The attributions in M4:9 [G–H] may be instructive (the pericope has been cited in full above, Section B.2). The dispute of R. Judah and "They" is over the interpretation of a list: is the list of items in [B] to be taken exclusively or not? The language of R. Judah certainly echoes that of [A] (*ʾên lāhem hônāyâ*), and the wording of the rejoinder by "They" presupposes a preexisting list. These examples of attributed traditions that treat the preceding material as already existing and as susceptible to commentary may be explained as a rhetorical convention. Yet, as I have already argued, versions of M4:9 [A–F] circulated independently in the Mishnah, varying according to context.[154] Here, then, there are independent grounds for considering the dispute a secondary addition to an already existing literary formulation.[155] R. Simeon's tradition (M4:9 [F]), which may have been

---

[151] See M2:10 [K] ("R. Simeon says: 'Even to load'"); M3:8 [B] ("R. Judah says: 'One fifth'"); M4:4 [C] ("R. Judah says: 'A merchant has no *hônāyâ*'"); M9:8 [D, G] (in both: "R. Simeon b. Gamaliel prohibits").

[152] R. Judah objects: "What amount is a *kĕrî* ('pile')?" [D]; cf. [C]. In addition, where [C] reads "If there is in it to enough to erect a pile with it" (*ʾim yēš bāh kĕ-dê lĕhaʿamid kĕrî*), [G] reads "Rather [*ʾelāʾ*]: 'If there is in it sufficient for falling'" (*ʾim yēš lāh kĕ-dê nĕpîlâ*).

[153] This is even clearer in the Babli's version of this pericope ("R. Eliezer says: 'This one and this one swear, but (*wĕ-*) I question whether this one or this one can swear"; see the note to M6:8 in Appendix I). Compare Rashi, *ad loc.* (B82b): "That is to say, 'I, too, have heard thus from my masters, ... but (*ʾabāl*) I question ....'" The Babli's version testifies, at the very least, to an early interpretation of R. Eleazar's tradition as glossing a previously existing one.

[154] See *m. Šebu.* 6:5; *m. B. Qam.* 7:4; and above, Section A.2.

[155] Arguments of this kind are clearly subjective. Thus, for instance, in the case of M4:2 [C] ("R. Simeon says: 'Whoever has the money in his hand, his hand is in the superior position'") can plausibly be taken as a disputing gloss to M4:2 [B–C]. However, it could conceivably be taken as a legal aphorism that could circulate separately; cf. the rules in M6:2 [F–G], which have a similar form. Nevertheless, a reasonable case can be made for the following as referring back to existing text: M1:8 [G] (R. Simeon b. Gamaliel); M2:1 [E–G] (R. Judah; [F–G], however, could conceivably be a gloss added to the pericope already including R. Judah's statement in [E]); M3:2 [D–F], 4 [D–E], 5 [D–E] (R. Yose, echoing [C] in all three pericopae); M3:7 [I] (R. Judah, echoing [B]); M3:11 [E–G] (R. Meir, R. Judah); M5:5 [D] (R. Simeon b. Gamaliel, referring back to [A]; alternatively M5:5 [D–F] can be taken as attributed to R. Simeon b. Gamaliel, and the whole taken as an originally independent statement); M5:7 [L–M] (R. Judah); M6:7 [B–C] (R. Judah); M7:1 [L–M] (R. Simeon b. Gamaliel,

used as a gloss as well, but which already circulated with the core pericope, serves to underscore the complicated process of transmission and modification of the materials that went into the Mishnah.

That attributed statements may be redactional and added to already existing texts is suggested also by the placement of these passages. A substantial number of Ushan traditions appear at the end of pericopae;[156] others at the end of internal units of material;[157] others still are parenthetical.[158] In fact, if we were to remove all of the material attributed to the Ushan Rabbis, the basic structure and contents of the tractate would be altered only very slightly.[159] This is not only because these attributed materials act formally as supplements (as I have been arguing), but their content frequently reflects secondary or supplementary concerns. Several traditions supply qualifications

---

commenting on a story, and citing a rule presented *verbatim* in [F]); M7:9 [C] (R. Judah); M9:6 [G–H] (R. Judah, with [H] echoing [F]; the use of *ḥakôrô* in R. Judah's statement explicitly for rent paid in money, despite the conventional meaning of the term *ḥakôr* as payment in kind, can be taken to suggest that the author of [H] is consciously echoing an already existing formulation despite the inapplicability of the terminology [see Appendix I, notes to M9:2, 3, 6]); M10:3 [F–H] ([F] objects to the preceding ruling; [G–H] recast [D–E]). These passages, together with the three mentioned above in the text, make up seventeen of the attributed statements, a sizeable proportion.

[156] M2:6 [C–E]; M3:2 [D–F], 4 [D–E], 5 [D–E]; M3:6 [C–D]; M3:7 [D]; M3:8 [G]; M3:11 [F–G]; M4:2 [E]; M4:9 [G–H]; M5:7 [L]; M6:7 [D–E]; M6:8 [D]; M7:1 [L–M]; M7:9 [C]; M8:6 [H]; M9:5 [E–F]; M9:6 [F–G]; M9:8 [G]; M10:2 [E]; M10:3 [E–H]; M10:5 [A']. If the view attributed to R. Simeon b. Gamaliel in M5:5 [D] extends to [F], this passage should be listed here as well. Otherwise this tradition should perhaps be classed as "parenthetical." See above, n. 150.

[157] M2:1 [E] (if [F–G] is part of the original tradition, the statement attributed to R. Judah, together with that attributed to R. Simeon b. Eleazar ["Late"], appear at the end of the pericope); M2:10 [K]; M4:4 [C] ([D] begins a new, if related, problem); M6:7 [B–C] (the statement attributed to Abba Shaul in [D–E] deals with a new problem about pledges); M9:13 [H–I] (alternatively, M9:13 [J] continues the basic question of M9:13 [A–G], and the tradition attributed to R. Simeon b. Gamaliel is "parenthetical"). If, as I have suggested above, M4:9 [F] circulated together with [A–G], M4:9 [F] should probably be categorized as coming at the end of a unit as well.

[158] M1:8 [G] ([H] continues with the same basic question, and the same formal patterning [*māṣā*...], as [C–D]); M3:8 [B]; M9:8 [D]. M2:6 (formulated as an Ushan "reverse dispute") can be taken in its entirety as interrupting between M2:5 [D] ("so for everything that has identifying marks and has claimants, he [the finder] is required to proclaim") and M2:7 [D] ("[If] he [the loser] said the lost object, and did not say its identifying marks ...").

[159] If in the case of the Ushan "reverse dispute form" (M1:6 [G–I]; M2:6 [D–F]; M3:11 [F–G]; depending on the textual history of the Mishnah, M2:1 [E–G] and M4:12 [I–J] might be examples of this as well) we were to remove the second disputing view and the formula "[the preceding were] the words of (*dibrê*) R. N" as well, but leave the initial view as anonymous, we would remove still less from the tractate.

or rule on special cases. For instance, the tradition attributed to R. Simeon b. Gamaliel in M1:8 [G] qualifies the preceding definition given for an *'agûdâ* of documents ("three tied to one another" [F]) as follows: "R. Simeon b Gamaliel says: 'One borrowing from three lenders, let him return it to the borrower. Three borrowing from one lender, let him return it to the lender." Other traditions are concerned with quantification. Thus, R. Meir and R. Judah dispute the amount of time that a finder must proclaim the find (M2:6), and R. Meir, R. Judah, and R. Simeon dispute the permissible amount of wear in a short-weight coin (M4:5).[160] M3:7–8 are interesting in this regard: the three traditions attributed to R. Judah offer examples of qualification (M3:7 [I–J]: the rule "lo, let this one deduct losses [B] ... all is assessed according to the measurement .... [F]" does not apply when the measurement was large), of quantification ("Let him deduct one sixth for wine. R. Judah says: 'One fifth.'" M3:8 [A–B]), and—still a third type of supplementary material—of cross-reference (the rules cited in connection with the absorption of wine in casks apply equally to sale, M3:8 [G]). One "reverse dispute" questions whether a shopkeeper is covered by the rules for a householder or for a banker with respect to deposits of loose money; that is, it explores the grey area of a rule that is itself taken for granted (M3:11 [E–G]). Another tradition, already cited, questions the correctness of a transmitted rule, without, notably, explicitly disputing with it (M6:8 [D]). Attributed traditions addressing these kinds of "secondary" questions easily account for nearly half (if not more) of the Ushan traditions.[161]

By contrast, only a very few traditions encapsulate the entire treatment of a given rule. M10:6, a dispute about produce growing from the divider between two terraced gardens, can clearly stand by itself; and although it is possible to account for its presence here by associative logic,[162] the pericope is not carrying forward a problem dealt with previously in the tractate. If one may read all of M4:12 [D–M (?)] as the words of R. Judah, with parenthetical comments attributed to the "Sages" and a cross-reference to the views of Abba Shaul, we have here a discussion of market practices entirely attributed

---

[160] See also M7:5 [C–D] (How much may a worker eat?); M9:5 ("What amount is a 'pile'?"); M9:13 [H–J] (For how long must a borrower return the pledge nightly?); M10:5 [A'] (How long may a builder put building materials in the public domain?).

[161] In addition to the eight passages cited above in the text and the three in the preceding note, see, e.g., M4:9 [F] (qualifying "consecrated goods" [B]?); M4:9 [G–H] (whether the list in [B] is exclusive); M5:7 [L] (the rule of [K] applies even if the buyer has not stipulated); M7:1 (whether the son of Yohanan b. Mattia was required to make the stipulation that his father demanded); M7:9 [C] (an exception to the general rule in [A–B]); M9:6 ([G–H] (an exception to the rule in [A–F]). There are, thus, at least seventeen such passages.

[162] See above, n. 66.

to a named figure, without which we would have no mention of these rules. M4:5 addresses the amount by which a coin may be short in weight and still be valid, and, although somewhat abrupt, clearly can stand by itself.

Other material, which appears to be formally independent or which seems to encapsulate an entire discussion, nevertheless may be supplementary. Thus, for instance, the tradition attributed to R. Simeon in M5:10 [O–P] is formally an independent statement on verbal interest (not dealt with elsewhere), but as it is formulated, it seems clearly to develop M5:10 [E–M].[163] Since in the "rejoinder dispute" in M5:7 [I–J] the view of the "Sages" seems redundant,[164] the dispute was possibly originally independent of the pericope in which it is now embedded. M1:6 is harder to assess. On the one hand, the pericope is an independent Ushan dispute that encompasses the entire dispute about the criteria for when one returns loan documents. Possibly the fact that this passage is part of a series of pericopae dealing with documents that have been found may be taken to imply that M1:6 is the work of "tradent redactors" (to use Neusner's expression) who have incorporated attributed views into their formulation of the series. In fact, the situation may be more complicated. In the pericopae that follow, if the document found is considered valid one returns it to the nominal owner (M1:8), but if it can be presumed never to have been delivered, and therefore not valid, one does not return it (M1:7). In M1:6, however, the legal problem is different: the dispute focuses on the effectiveness of a specified or implied lien on property in a loan document.[165] Moreover, in contrast to M1:7, the two disputants agree that it is precisely when the document would be fully effective (i.e., where a court would exact payment on the basis of such a document) that one does not return the document. The discontinuities are explained if

---

[163] "There is verbal interest" (M5:10 [O]; cf. E: "There is interest in advance and there is interest delayed"). Moreover, like [E–M], [P] appears to focus on what the borrower "says" to the lender (cf. Appendix I, note to M5:10). Note also M5:10 [B, D], which like [P] use the formula *loʾ yoʾmar lô*, "let him not say to him ..." (see also M5:9 [A–B]).

[164] Cf. the Babli's question (B74a): *ḥakāmîm haynû tannāʾ qammāʾ* ("The Sages are the same as the first reciter").

[165] This led both Talmuds to consider why it was the lien itself that was problematic. One view, attributed to R. Yohanan, is that the Mishnah was concerned with shady dealings (*qĕnunyāʾ*) between debtor and creditor: the creditor will collect the alienated property on the strength of the document and split it with the debtor (Y1:6 [8a]; B14b; cf. *m. B. Bat.* 10:7; *m. ʿArak.* 6:1 where precisely such a transaction is described). The Babli cites another reason: the debtor may have used a predated document, so that property alienated between the date of the document and that of the actual loan would be subject to unjust seizure on the basis of the document (this may be related to the view of R. Yassa in the name of R. Yohanan, Y1:6 [8a]). Predated documents are considered invalid at *m. Šebi.* 10:5.

we take M1:6 as a secondary elaboration of the problem of liens in the case of loan documents.[166]

The traditions of the "Late" generation may be dealt with quite briefly. They are all dependent traditions. Two are statements made in the name of R. Meir (M6:5 [I–J]; M7:9 [E–F]). Of these, the first is a striking example of the supplementary character of attributed material:

[H] ... and if he added to its load he is liable.
[I] And how much shall he add to its load and [thus] be liable?
[J] Symmakhos says in the name of R. Meir: "A sĕ'â for a camel; three qabbîm for an ass."

This Symmakhos/R. Meir tradition appears in the context of an explicit gloss to [H], and, notably, is concerned with quantification. The tradition of Yaddua the Babylonian in the name of R. Meir (M7:9) supplies a qualification of a rule. The remaining two late traditions are both mere notices of a disputing position (M2:1 [H]; M7:3 [E]). As in the case of the statements attributed to the earliest sages, there are too few examples here to show the dependence of the tractate on the work of this generation. However, the traditions are certainly consistent with the idea that attributed statements are frequently supplementary.[167]

---

[166] Note that in M1:8 [C–K] (and especially [G], which explicitly deals with loans) there is no mention of the problem of liens. On analogy with M1:7, an original pericope on loan documents might have read something like: "He found loan documents, let him not return them." Cf. the Amoraic rule attributed to R. Eleazar: "For I say: 'He wrote it to borrow, but did not borrow'" (Y1:6 [8a]), which echoes M1:7 [C], and may presuppose an existing tradition of a rule for loan documents parallel to that for the documents listed in M1:7 [A]. See m. B. Bat. 10:3, which allows someone to write a document obligating himself to make some kind of payment in anticipation of the transaction itself, without the "creditor" of the particular transaction being present, since it is delivery of the document that makes it effective.

[167] This assumption is in some tension with the traditional view that material attributed to individuals (yāḥîd, "[the opinion of a] single [person]") is less authoritative than that of an anonymous opinion, presumed to reflect the majority (rābbîm, "[opinion of the] many"). Already within the Mishnah itself, there are traces of a concern with the majority and minority opinion: "And why do they mention the words of the individual (dibrê ha-yāḥîd) among the majority (ha-mĕrubbîm), inasmuch as the law is only according to the words of the majority?... Said R. Judah: 'If so why do they mention the words of the individual among the majority for naught?...'" (m. ʿEd. 1:5–6). It does not necessarily follow that what is meant here is cases where an anonymous view is glossed with a named tradition: dibrê ha-mĕrubbîm does not automatically imply an anonymous view. The question that begins the discussion in m. ʿEd. ("And why do they mention the words of Shammai and Hillel for naught?..." [1:4]) suggests by analogy that what might be at issue is a case where two views are presented, in whatever form, and one is known (or can be shown) to be a majority opinion, and the other a

3. Attributions and the nominative absolute series.

I have been arguing in the preceding section that the attributed traditions, especially those of the Ushan and later periods are largely supplementary both in form and in content. Admittedly, it is impossible to argue conclusively that such traditions are in fact supplements added by redactors, although such passages as M4:9 (with its parallels in *m. Šebuʿot* 6:5 and *m. Babaʾ Qammaʾ* 7:5) support such an argument. Nor is it clear, even granting this argument, who would have done this and for what reasons. Earlier (Section B.1), I noted that the underlying link between the various parts of M3:2–5 was a series of attributions to R. Yose, and proposed that this might mark out this string of passages as the product of a person or persons (a "school"?) for whom the traditions of R. Yose were particularly important.[168] If correct, this proposal suggests one possible setting and rationale for adding attributed statements.

In the present section, I would like to carry this proposal forward by examining briefly the distribution of attributed statements in the nominative absolute (article + participle) series already discussed in some detail above

---

minority opinion (see, e.g., those disputes in which an individual opinion is opposed to "the sages," or simply "they").

At any rate, the traditional view that the anonymous opinion is authoritative is reflected in the later interpretive and legal dicta about the Mishnah such as the rule that "the law follows the anonymous [opinion in the] Mishnah" (*halākâ ki-sĕtam mišnâ*; see the sources cited in C. J. Kasowski, *Thesaurus Talmudis* [Jerusalem: JTSA, 1954–81], vol. 27, 363 col. b–c) or the pair of rules resolving the problem of a rule presented anonymously in one place and again later as a matter of dispute (in which case the law does not [automatically] follow the anonymous tradition), or presented first as a dispute but later anonymously (in which case the law follows the anonymous formulation) (*sĕtam wĕ-ʾaḥar kāk maḥlôqet ʾēn halākâ ki-sĕtam; maḥlôqet wĕ-ʾaḥar kāk sĕtam halākâ ki-sĕtam*; see *y. Taʿan.* 2:14 = *y. Meg.* 1:6; *y. Yeb.* 4:11; *b. Yeb.* 42b; *b. B. Qam. b.* 102a = *b. ʿAb. Zar.* 6b–7a; *b. B. Bat.* 122b; *b. Nid.* 11b). These dicta are the product of an exegetical program that took the Mishnah as an authoritative code, and required standards for judging cases where the Mishnah presents more than one opinion. As such, they do not necessarily reflect the process of redaction itself (both rules cited, in particular the first, are associated with R. Yohanan who flourished in the middle third century; other such dicta are attributed to R. Yohanan: see, e.g., *y. Dem.* 2:1 [22d]: how to resolve a dispute between R. Judah the Patriarch and others).

[168] On this particular matter, my view is close to that of A. Goldberg, "Purpose and Method in R. Judah Hannasi's Compilation of the Mishnah" [Hebrew], *Tarbiz* 28 (1958–9) 260–69; and more recently, "The Mishnah—A Study Book of Halakah," in S. Safrai, ed., *The Literature of the Sages* (CRINT 3: Philadelphia and Assen: Fortress and Van Gorcum, 1987), 211–51. On the whole, however, Goldberg relies too heavily on the assumption that literary or thematic criteria can be used to isolate the work of individual tradents even when the material in question is presented anonymously (see the application of his method in *idem, Commentary to the Mishnah Shabbat* [Hebrew] [Jerusalem: JTSA, 1976] and *The Mishnah Treatise Eruvin* [Hebrew] [Jerusalem: Magnes, 1986]).

(Section B.2). In that discussion I suggested on formal and other grounds that these series originated as a source on contracts that was used by later redactors. A comparison of the pericopae that are members of these series with the list of attributions (above, Section D.1) yields the following results:

3:6 [C–D]	U	Simeon b. Gamaliel
3:7 [G–H]	Y	Yohanan b. Nuri
3:7 [I–J]	U	Judah
3:11 [F–G]	U	Meir, Judah
6:5 [I–J]	U/L	Symmakhos in name of Meir
7:1 [L–M]	U	Simeon b. Gamaliel
8:6 [H]	U	Simeon b. Gamaliel
9:5 [E–F]	U	Judah
9:6 [F–G]	U	Judah
9:8 [D]	U	Simeon b. Gamaliel
9:8 [G]	U	Simeon b. Gamaliel
9:13 [H–J]	U	Simeon b. Gamaliel

Nearly all of the attributions belong to either R. Judah or R. Simeon b. Gamaliel. Exceptions are one attribution to the Yabnean generation (M3:7 [G–H]), and one to a member of the later generation, to whom is attributed a statement in the name of R. Meir. The only direct attribution of a statement to an Ushan who is neither R. Judah nor R. Simeon b. Gamaliel is to R. Meir in a dispute with R. Judah.[169] What is striking here is that material that on formal grounds appeared to be distinct from other parts of the tractate is consistently glossed by traditions attributed to the same two individuals.[170] This differential distribution of attributed statements, it seems to me,

---

[169] It was suggested earlier that the *ha-môkēr* ("one who sells...") series in *m. B. Bat.*, which deals with a form of contract (sale), might be part of an original source on contracts. It is therefore interesting to note the distribution of attributed material in that series. If we consider only those pericopae that together constitute the series, we find, for the Yabnean generation, attributions to R. Eliezer (*m. B. Bat.* 4:4, 5) and to R. Aqiba and R. Ishmael (6:4), an entirely different distribution than *m. B. Meṣ.* For the Ushan generation there are repeated attributions to R. Judah (4:1; 5:2, 8, 9) and R. Simeon b. Gamaliel (4:7; 5:10, 11, 6:1, 4, 8), but only one pericope with attributions to R. Simeon (6:8, twice). (I do not include *m. B. Bat.* 4:9, since the final section of this pericope may easily be taken as an independent pericope [although, admittedly, opening with the nominative absolute *ha-maqdîš*] on the dedication of landed property.) The prevalence in *m. B. Bat.* of traditions of the two tradents who predominate in the series in *m. B. Meṣ.* as well suggests that these two series may have passed through the same hands.

[170] It should also be pointed out that inasmuch as these pericopae account for some 30% of those in the tractate, the concentration of attributions is disproportionately high. This is

is not accidental, and reflects the activity of redactors, whether or not these statements are secondary additions, and constitutes an area that would reward further form-critical and redactional-critical study. If, as I have been arguing, such attributed material (especially Ushan material) derives from redactional additions, the nominative absolute series may not offer us the identity of the original authors of specific traditions, but—equally important—the attributions may serve as an indicator of the hands through which this material has passed.[171]

E. Conclusion: The Mishnah as a Literary Artifact

The purpose of this chapter was to show traces of a complex redactional process that produced the *m. Baba' Meṣi'a'*. I have attempted to demonstrate this, first, by stressing disjunctures in the Mishnah: places where sources contradict, or are at least in tension with one another. Second, I examined passages that seemed to have circulated independently of their present contexts, and that therefore seem to have been used as sources by a redactor or redactors. Next, I asked whether it is possible to recover strategies for organizing and presenting material that preceded the final redaction of the tractate. Several possible forms were identified, including organization based on Scripture, associative logic, formal patterning, or common content. Fourth, the traces of the adaptation of material were investigated: glosses, corrections,

---

not the case with R. Judah, of whose seventeen attestations four (less than 25%) appear in these pericopae (although if the attributions to R. Judah in M3:8 are included the number rises to 35%); but among the traditions of R. Simeon b. Gamaliel six out of nine attestations (approximately 67%) are accounted for. A rough calculation of the *ha-môkēr* series in *m. B. Bat.* also shows this: the series accounts for some seventeen of eighty-six pericopae in the tractate (approximately 20%), but five out of thirteen pericope in which there are attributions to R. Judah (approximately 38%) and six out of eleven pericopae involving R. Simeon b. Gamaliel (some 55%) occur in this series. (Two out of five traditions attributed to R. Simeon [i.e., 40%] occur in this series as well; however, since these occur in one pericope this may be something of a special case.) These statistics in and of themselves are not probative, but together with other criteria they are highly suggestive. Furthermore, they mark out an area for further study.

[171] In my earlier discussion of the nominative absolute series (for instance in connection M3:6–8; M6:3 and M6:5) I suggested that the "source" on contracts, if such it was, may have already included material from different sources as well as revision of material. If the argument here about the secondary character of attributed statements is correct, supplementation of existing traditions with attributed statements, together with collecting and shaping earlier material, may be part of the redactional procedure used by the people who produced that source.

supplementation, and the structuring of disparate material around broad themes (e.g., Chapter 5). Finally, I assessed the significance and utility of the traditions attributed to individuals, and found that much of this material supplemented the texts in which they were embedded.

I make no pretense of having fully answered any of these problems, or that every case to which I have drawn attention has been, or even can be, "proved." My goal has been to identify a sufficiently large number of wrinkles in the fabric of *m. Baba^ʾ Meṣiʿaʾ* to point to a complex process of redaction that worked with two somewhat contradictory principles: to transmit material with a great degree of conservatism, retaining the language, style, form, and content of the sources, but at the same time to gloss, correct and above all organize and group the material. One implication of this result is that analyses of the "meaning" of the Mishnah (as Chapter III will attempt for *m. Baba^ʾ Meṣiʿaʾ*) will have to take into account the indeterminacies built into the very structure and rhetoric of the Mishnah itself. In the process, I hope, this chapter has also succeeded in making some substantive contributions to the elucidation of the redactional history of the tractate and, by extension, of the Mishnah.

On the evidence of *m. Baba^ʾ Meṣiʿaʾ*, there is frustratingly little that can be used to reconstruct the immediate social and institutional frameworks in which this first literary artifact of the Rabbinic movement was produced. On the basis of the material discussed in the preceding sections of this chapter (and on the assumption that the redactional history of *m. Baba^ʾ Meṣiʿaʾ* mimics the social setting and literary practices of the people who produced it), I would like to propose the following model for its redaction. By the time of the redaction of the Mishnah (or at least tractate *Baba^ʾ Meṣiʿaʾ*) there were various circles ("schools") with their own material (traces of whose redaction can sometimes be found in the distribution of attributed materials). The traditions of these various "schools" shared certain common characteristics (specific legal and theological interests, as well as a highly stylized language and tradition of transmission; the language of all the material in the tractate that is not a citation of Scripture is characteristically "Rabbinic"). Yet these circles or schools were different from one another, and their traditions were (at least sometimes) different as well; hence the differing strategies for formulating or organizing material. If the redactors of the Mishnah appear to take an active role in consolidating and organizing material (whether as a law code, or as some sort of approved collection), this is not to be explained solely as an exercise in philosophy or legal theory, although it may be that as well. I suggest that the redaction of the Mishnah was, at least in part, an effort to increase the centralization and institutionalization of the Rabbinic movement.

One last body of material in *m. Baba' Meṣi'a'* helps elucidate the nature of some of the claims that Rabbis made on the world around them in producing the Mishnah: stories.[172] Two things are common to all of the stories presented in the tractate: (1) they involve Rabbis; and (2) they assume that what is at issue is not merely correct opinion, but proper practice. Clearly, we are not in a position to evaluate the extent of Rabbinic authority to enforce their legal program, and that program itself clearly has utopian elements (see Chapter I). However, the rhetoric of these stories is that Rabbinic rules make demands upon the property and the day-to-day activities of its audience. How a Rabbi adjudicates cases and, more interestingly, what a Rabbi does in his own practice (how he treats his workers or tenants) is offered as evidence for how the world should be run. This "evidence" is not in every case presented unilaterally and decisively. The merchants oppose R. Tarfon's ruling (M4:3 [G–H]); R. Gamaliel's practice is immediately marginalized as supererogatory piety (M5:8 [F]: "not because such is the law, but because he wanted to be strict with himself"); and R. Simeon b. Gamaliel undercuts the authority of the story of R. Yohanan b. Mattiah and his son (M7:1 [L–M]). Nevertheless, however we imagine the Mishnah as a document (as law code, school text, philosophical document, or something else), and whatever the limits of Rabbinic influence or authority, there is at least one strain represented in *m. Baba' Meṣi'a'* in which there is far more at stake in Rabbinic "discourse" than talk alone. Rabbinic Torah is to be played out in the practice of men and women. To go beyond this picture, will be necessary to take seriously the kinds of claims that the Mishnah makes, and root those claims in the "real" world in which the Rabbis who produced the Mishnah lived and worked. It is to this that I wish to turn next.

---

[172] M4:3 [D–H] (R. Tarfon's ruling is opposed by merchants because of the way it will effect them); M5:8 [C–E] (R. Gamaliel's customary practice with his tenant farmers); M7:1 [G–K] (R. Yohanan b. Mattia orders his son to make specific stipulations with the workers he has hired); M8:8 [F–H] (R. Simeon b. Gamaliel and R. Yose rule on a bath house in Sepphoris).

◆§ CHAPTER III ?◆

Institutions and Relationships in Mishnah Tractate *Baba' Meṣiʿa'*

> That evening Sancho spent drawing up some ordinances touching the good government of what he supposed to be his isle. He decreed that there must be no cornering of provisions in the state, and that wine could be imported from anywhere at all, on condition that its place of origin was declared so that it could be priced according to its value, goodness and reputation; and anyone watering it or changing its name should pay for it with his life. He lowered the price of all footwear, especially of shoes, the current price seeming to him exorbitant. He fixed the rate of servants' wages, which were mounting unchecked at a headlong pace. He imposed the heaviest penalties on singers of lewd and disorderly songs either by night or by day. He decreed that no blind man should sing miracles in rhyme unless he could bring unquestionable evidence that they were true, as most of their tales were, in his opinion, fictitious and brought discredit upon the genuine ones. He created and selected an inspector of the poor, not to persecute them but to examine whether they were genuine; for under the disguise of poverty and counterfeit sores go sturdy thieves and hale drunkards. So good, in fact, were the laws he ordained that they are kept in place to this day under the name of "*The Constitutions of the great Governor Sancho Panza.*"[1]

The previous chapter reviewed the evidence for the use of sources and for redactional strategies in the composition of *m. Baba' Meṣiʿa'*. This evidence, I have argued, suggests that the materials that make up our tractate were subjected to an editorial process of collection, adaptation, revision, and glossing. This, in turn, may reflect an effort at centralization and institutionalization of the Rabbinic movement. In the present chapter, I wish to turn to the contents of the texts themselves, and to consider the kinds of economic assumptions and interests that *m. Baba' Meṣiʿa'* expresses in its discussion of rules relating to property and contracts. The chapter falls into two parts. The first considers economic and social institutions: money, markets, and banks. The second deals with such relationships as that between lender and borrower, or lessor and lessee.

The argument of this chapter proceeds on a number of levels. First, I am interested in identifying and elaborating the legal issues that the texts raise.

---

[1] Miguel de Cervantes Saavedra, *Don Quixote*, tr. J. M. Cohen (London: Pengiun, 1950), 804.

In this context I have tried not to efface redactional problems (for instance, places where contradictions remain, or where earlier material is glossed and thereby limited or extended). Moreover, considerable attention is focused on placing the tractate's rules about civil law within the context of a wider field of early Rabbinic discourse, in particular within the Mishnah itself. This approach emphasizes the range of possible views within the Rabbinic communities who produced the Mishnah, as well as inherent inconsistencies or contradictions in the treatment of matters of property and contract within the Mishnah.

Second, this chapter addresses the extent to which the Mishnah's civil laws can be used as a source or map for the social history of Roman Galilee in which it was finally edited. If Mishnaic "law" neither effectively proscribes nor simply describes economic practice in Roman Palestine, how are we to understand these rules? One dimension of this problem is the relationship between Mishnaic material and other, non-Jewish, evidence for economic practices and relationships. While a full discussion of this relationship would swell this chapter beyond its already unwieldy size, I have attempted (especially in the notes) to give attention both to the broad commonalities and the differences between the way the same institutions and relationships are reflected in our tractate and in Roman juristic texts and papyri from Egypt, Dura Europus, and the Judean Desert. The Digest and other juristic texts are hardly less "ideological" than the Mishnah, and not necessarily any more true to practice. In documentary remains we have evidence of what people claim to have done, but it is only occasionally possible to tease out underlying negotiations, deceptions or legal fictions. What is significant about these materials for the present discussion is that despite important differences, *m. Baba' Meṣi'a'* presents a battery of economic institutions and relationships that would be wholly familiar to the authors of the non-Rabbinic texts. Thus, for instance, while the Mishnah clearly prohibits interest and distinguishes between Jews and gentiles in the scope of its prohibition, the contracts that *m. Baba' Meṣi'a'* uses to illustrate the prohibition (e.g., loans to be repaid in money or in kind, sales for advanced or delayed delivery, or various kinds of work contracts) are all well attested in Greco-Roman documents. This means that the Mishnah, however utopian its ultimate picture, responds to economic structures (fundamentally, an agrarian economy) and works with assumptions about those structures that were common throughout the Roman world.

My goal, therefore, has been to understand how Rabbis imagined the proper working of Jewish economic practices in such an economy. Moreover, in an effort to identify whose interests and concerns within the agrarian economy of Roman Galilee *m. Baba' Meṣi'a'* reflects, I have paid attention to the scale and settings of transactions as they are described and to the kinds of relationships that are presupposed. Which sales, for instance, take place in markets at the hands of professional marketers, which between private individuals? What kinds of items are lent or borrowed? Are loans assumed to take place between wealthy individuals or between a wealthy lender and poor borrower? What kinds of tenants or landlords are presupposed in discussions of tenant farming? The answers to these questions do indeed offer insight into such matters as the distribution of currency, the role of markets, or the social relationships in which economic transactions are embedded. However, ultimately, and disappointingly, we are on firmest ground in taking the Mishnah as a legal and religious program.

Thus, and this is the third level on which this chapter proceeds, I have attempted to outline some of the ideological choices made by the Rabbis who produced *m. Baba' Meṣi'a'*. On the whole, the legal materials themselves, their organization, and their selection suggest that the audience to whom the redactors of our tractate addressed their work was by and large that of wealthy, town-dwelling landholders. In a broad sense, this is confirmed by the universe of discourse that Rabbis shared with, for example, the authors of Roman legal texts. At the same time, where literary sources from the Greco-Roman world in general (and the Roman legal texts are no exception) are quite comfortable with assumed distinctions between rich and poor, large landholders and peasants, *honestiores* and *humiliores*, *m. Baba' Meṣi'a'* makes a conscious choice to present their materials as inclusive: its rules pertain to all Israelites, as opposed to gentiles. This insistence of the Mishnah to speak to and for all of Israel (and, elsewhere, to draw the primary distinguishing lines within Israel between those who do and do not observe rules incumbent upon all), indeed the attempt to construct a "Jewish" civil law at all, opens up the question, ultimately beyond the scope of this study, of how early Rabbinic discourse mapped the boundaries of Jewish ethnicity in late antiquity.

A. Economic Institutions

This section considers the three primary institutional economic frameworks that are dealt with in *m. Baba' Meṣi'a'*. The first, quite simply, is money, a good that is produced in this period by the state, and distributed, at least initially, through state institutions (payments to soldiers, for example).[2]

---

[2] For a recent discussion of coinage in the Roman economy, together with bibliography, see C. Howgego, "Coin Circulation and the Integration of the Roman Economy," *JRA* 7 (1994), 5–21.

As a result the Mishnah can more or less take the existence of money for granted, although not without puzzling over some of the inconsistencies of a system of coinage in which coins function both as symbols (they represent relative units of value in a graded hierarchy) and as commodities in their own right. The other two areas to be discussed are markets and banks, two arenas of economic practice where the use of money is central. In all three cases, I am interested in elucidating how the Mishnah expected these institutions to function, and what this might tell us either of actual money, markets, and banks in Palestine, or (more securely) about Rabbis and their audience.

1. Money.

Money functions in *m. Bābā' Meṣi'ā'* as a general medium of transaction and exchange. Thus, in general, a sale is thought of as involving the payment of coins.³ Similarly, transactions such as loans, leases, and the hiring of labor can be characterized as effected through the transfer of money.⁴ Nevertheless, in essentially all of these transactions payment can be, and is, described as taking place in kind.⁵ The notion that much economic interaction takes place without the transfer of coinage is hardly unique to the Mishnah: the

---

³ E.g., M4:2 [B–C], 5–6; M5:2, 3, 4.

⁴ Loans: M5:1 [B–F], 10 [K–N]; 6:7; similarly, pledges are assumed to be not merely appropriated by the creditor, but sold for cash to pay back the monetary amount of the loan (M9:13 [I]). Leases: M8:8 [F–H] (lease of a house); M9:3, 6 [G], 10 (lease of farmland; of the examples cited, the first two are somewhat exceptional: in M9:3 we are dealing with assessment of penalty in a case where there was no produce from the leasehold; in M9:6 payment of money is raised as a special case). Hire: M7:5; 9:12 [G]; 10:5 [G–M] (hire of labor); the hire of a paid depositary is not explicitly said to be paid in money in the Mishnah, although this is implied by the term *śākār* (wage) in *šômēr śākār* or *nôśē' śākār* (but the comparison of paid deposits with other types of contracts, as in, e.g., M6:6–7, especially M6:6 [C], suggests that the "payment" could be understood as some other form of non-monetary benefit). The characterization of the renter of an animal as a *śôkēr* similarly reflects the presumption of a transaction based on the payment of money (M6:3–5).

⁵ All of these contracts will be discussed below in greater detail. For the present, the following may be noted. An example of barter (the exchange of a cow for an ass) occurs in M8:4; see also M4:1 [F]; M5:1 [H–K]. The problem connected with loans of commodities (especially produce) for consumption, for food or for seed, to be repaid in kind, is dealt with in M5:8–9; a related problem is raised in M5:1, 7. Leases of land are more characteristically thought to be contracted in terms of payment in kind (see M9:1–8, and the notes to M9:1 and 2 in Appendix I). The hire of labor seems to involve both payment in money (this is presumed to be the worker's right unless specifically waived, M10:5 [G–M]) and supplementary payments in kind (subject, among other things, to local custom, M7:1–8 [A]). For paid deposits see the preceding note.

prevalence of payment in kind is well documented, for instance, in Roman Egypt.[6]

Even where money is not described as changing hands, it serves as a measure of value. Thus, for instance, M4:7 gives minimum values above which liabilities or obligations apply. This role of money in the Mishnah's conception of transactions is perhaps best illustrated by the following dictum attributed to Hillel (M5:9):

[D] For thus Hillel used to say:
[E] "Let a woman not lend a loaf to her fellow until she has calculated its monetary value,
[F] "lest wheat become more expensive,
[G] "and they will come to commit usury."

In a world in which prices are assumed to vary in the marketplace, calculating the amount of a loan in terms of money protected the parties from engaging in a potentially usurious loan. This is because Hillel's dictum presupposes another assumption about money: money creates a standardized scale against which the value of commodities is measured.[7] A loan of money,

---

[6] The relationship between these contracts as described in the Mishnah and papyrological remains will be discussed later in this chapter. For the time being, see, for instance, the discussions of labor and leases in D. Rathbone, *Economic Rationalism and Rural Society in Third-Century Egypt* (*Cambridge Classical Studies*. Cambridge: Cambridge University, 1991), chapters on "Permanent labour" (88–147), "Occasional labour" (148–74) and "Lessees and other contractors" (175–212) and, more generally, A. C. Johnson, *Roman Egypt*, in *An Economic Survey of Ancient Rome* II, ed. T. Frank (Baltimore: Johns Hopkins, 1936), 83–105 (leases), 306–10 (wages, showing payment in money, in kind and a combination), 460–6 (loans of seed grain).

[7] The idea that money serves as a stable marker of value underlies M5:8–9 more generally. That informal and customary rights of workers might be rethought in monetary terms is shown by M7:5 (whether a monetary ceiling is placed on the right of the worker to eat in the fields), and by M7:6 (a head of household can agree to receive a higher wage for members of his family, in exchange for their waiving their right to eat). The way in which the authors of the Mishnah conceive of the execution of transactions involving commodities is neatly illustrated by M5:1 [H–K]:

[H] He bought wheat from him at a golden *dînār* to the *kôr*, and such was the market price.
[I] Wheat [later] stood at thirty *dînārîm* [to the *kôr*].
[J] He said to him: "Give me wheat, for I am going to sell it and buy wine with it."
[K] He said to him: "But lo, your wheat is valued with me at thirty *dînārîm*! And lo, you have a claim against me with them for wine."

After an initial payment of cash, the amount of wheat owed to the buyer is reevaluated in terms of the higher price of wheat, and this new amount is converted into an amount of wine.

paid back in money, is not subject to appreciation or depreciation, according to this conception, but a loan of produce is (e.g., grain is more expensive at certain times of the year than others). The conceptual distinction between "money" and "commodities" (Hebrew, *miṭṭalṭĕlîn*, "moveable goods" or *pērôt*, "produce") is made explicit in our tractate at the beginning of Chapter 4: "moveable goods acquire the coin, but the coin does not acquire moveable goods" (M4:1 [E]). That is to say, in any non-barter transaction it is clear which party is the buyer and which is the seller: it is the delivery (symbolically or actually) of the commodity that effects completion of the sale.[8]

The pericope just cited is fascinating because it deals also with the exchange of coins in precisely the same terms: certain types of coins are "commodities" with respect to the "money" with which they are purchased. By and large the Mishnah assumes a standardized system of exchange for an equally standardized set of coin denominations for coins of gold, silver, and bronze:[9]

A tradition in the Babli that expands upon this Mishnah adds an additional step in which the money owed is now reevaluated and equated to oil (B63a; it is introduced *tĕnî R. ʾŌšaʿyāʾ*, and assumed to be R. Oshaya's own opinion, B62b–63a). Compare the analysis of analogous "credit" transactions on the Appianus estate in Egypt, in Rathbone, 1991, 318–30.

[8] See M4:2, and the discussion of sale below (section B.3). The rigid conceptual distinction between "money" and "commodity" occurs also in the Roman jurists: Gaius, 3.139–41, D 18.1.1.pr. (Paul); 18.1.2.1 (Ulpian). The treatment of the question of the relationship of barter to sale (which requires an item for sale and a price) both in terms of the views of traditional schools, and also through the exegesis of Homer (*Iliad*, 7.472–5; Gaius, *loc. cit.*, D 18.1.1.1 [Paul]) forms a fascinating parallel to Rabbinic procedure.

[9] This system of coinage can be worked out from the various places within the Mishnah in which relative values of coins are referred to. An example of this kind in *m. B. Meṣ.* is M4:2 [A]: "*Hônāyā* is four silver coins at twenty-four silver coins to the *selaʿ*." (The "silver coin" is identical with the *māʿâ*.) For a survey of the Rabbinic and secondary literature see E. Schürer, *A History of the Jewish People in the Age of Jesus Christ*, rev. ed. G. Vermes *et al.* (Edinburgh: T. and T. Clark, 1973–87), 2, 62–7. The most complete tabulation of relative values of coins comes from the Tosepta (*t. B. Bat.* 5:11–12, cf. *y. Qid.* 1:1 [58d]; *b. Qid.* 12a):

5:11

[A] [The] *pĕrûṭâ* that they said (*še-ʾāmrû*) [is] one of eight to the *ʾissār*.

[B] [The] *ʾissār*: one of twenty-four to the *dînār*.

5:12

[A] Six *māʿâ* of silver: a *dînār*.

[B] A *māʿôt* of silver: two *pôndiônîn* (cf. Lat. *dupondius*).

[C] A *pôndiôn*: two *ʾissārîn* (cf. Lat. *as*, Gk. *assarion*).

[D] An *ʾissār*: two *mismesin* (cf. Lat. *semis*).

[E] A *mismes*: two *qôntresîn* (var. lect. *qôntrônq*, cf. Lat. *quadrans* and *teruncius*, Gk. *kodrantēs*).

[F]   A *qôntres*: two *pĕrûtôt*.
[G]   R. Simeon b. Gamaliel says: "The *pĕrûṭâ* that they said [is] one of six *pĕrûṭôt* to the *'issār*."
[H]   Three *hadresîn*: a *māʿâ*.
[I]   Two *hanṣîn*: a *hadres*.
[J]   Two *šamînôt*: a *hinṣ*.
[K]   Two *pĕrûṭôt*: a *šamîn*.

[I suspect that these pericopae are the product of some sort of redactional revision. *t. B. Bat.* 5:11 and 5:12 [G] together form a perfectly matched anonymous rule with a disputing attributed tradition, and are worded differently than the rest of *t. B. Bat.* 5:12 (they express the smaller denomination as a fraction of the larger [e.g., "one of eight to the *'issār*," 5:11 [A]]). 5:11 itself adds nothing to 5:12 [A–F], and 5:11 [A], at least, circulated elsewhere without connection to 5:12 [A–F] (cf. *m. Qid.* 1:1). If *t. B. Bat.* 5:12 introduces [H–K] (as Sperber and Ben David have taken it; see the next paragraph) it fits awkwardly into that scheme (in [G] the *pĕrûṭâ* is valued in terms of the *'issār*, which does not appear in [H–K], and which is three quarters of a *hadres* and one and one half times a *hinṣ* whereas all other coins are in a ratio of one to a whole number with one another). As a disputing position to that of [A–F], the view attributed to R. Simeon b. Gamaliel [G] is awkward as well, and may not presuppose the values for the *mismes* and the *qôntrônq* given in [D–F]. The two lists of coins in *t. B. Bat.* 5:12 are also worded differently from one another. *t. B. Bat.* 5:12 [A] and [H–K] (which picks up where [A] left off) list smaller denominations first (n x A = B), whereas [B–F] lists the larger coins first (B = n x A), and may reflect the joining of two separate lists (perhaps the interpolation of the conventional list [B–F] into an already existing, but now non-standard, list). I suggest, therefore that *t. B. Bat.* 5:11–12 reflects the joining of at least two, if not more, units of material.]

In *t. B. Bat.* 5:12 [A–F] and [H–K] two different systems of coins are presented. The second [H–K] is otherwise unattested and therefore somewhat mysterious. Sperber has surmised that this text corresponds to the coinage system of the Hasmonean kings. (D. Sperber, "Palestinian Currency Systems During the Second Commonwealth," *JQR* 56 [1965–6], 284. Sperber's suggestion is dependent, in part, on the use of "purely Semitic terms" in [H–K]; but since what these terms mean in any language, Semitic or other, is far from clear, it is difficult to use the names of the denominations as linguistic "evidence" of age. For possible Greek and Latin derivations for some of these denominations see Sperber, 274 n. 2; Lieberman, *TK*, 10, 394 [to *t. B. Bat.* 5:12].) Following the attribution in [G], A. Ben-David took this currency scheme to be the official one of "Jewish Palestine in the time of Rabban Shimʿon son of Gamaliel II (135–160 C.E.)" (A. Ben-David, "Jewish and Roman Bronze and Copper Coins: Their Reciprocal Relations in the Mishnah and Talmud from Herod the Great to Trajan and Hadrian," *PEQ* 103 [1971], 115). However, the attribution of the list in *t. B. Bat.* 5:12 [H–K] to R. Simeon b. Gamaliel seems unlikely in light of the redactional problems discussed in the preceding paragraph. See also F. M. Heichelheim, *Roman Syria* in (*An Economic Survey of Ancient Rome* IV, ed. T. Frank: Baltimore: Johns Hopkins, 1938), 212–3.

The first system of denominations, 5:12 [A–F], corresponds to the system used most commonly in the Mishnah, although the denominations *qôntres* and *mismes* are not attested in the Mishnah. (Their Roman namesakes, the quadrans, and semis seem to have disappeared by the early third century as well: see M. H. Crawford, "Finance, Money and Coinage from the Severans to Constantine," *ANRW* 2.2 [1975], 561.) The terms used clearly correspond to Roman terminology for coins (Sperber, 274, and the literature cited there; Ben-David, 113–4;

Roman analogues	Golden dînār aureus [denarius]	selaʿ	šeqel	dînār denarius	māʿâ	pôndiôn dupondius	ʾissār as	pĕrûtâ
	1	6	12	24[10]	144	288	576	4608
				1	6	12	24	192

Despite terminological and denominational links with the official Roman coinage, the two systems are not identical. The scale of bronze to silver and gold is different: the Roman as was officially worth one sixteenth of a denarius, not one twenty-fourth. While it is possible that the monetary system is entirely a theoretical construct, I suspect that it is based on actual practice, although streamlined for computational ease. That the bronze to silver exchange rate differs from the official one need not prove an unsurmountable obstacle (in our case, perhaps the difference reflects a "correction" for the relative value of bronze to silver in Palestine as opposed to Rome).[11] References to a "Tyrian" standard that is based on the silver tetradrakhma of the independent Tyrian mint (coinage which ceased in the early part of the second half of the first century CE), or the frequent use in the Mishnah of the *pĕrûtâ*, a coin that is not part of the official Roman system, need not imply that the Mishnah's monetary system is entirely theoretical (in that it is based on essentially non-existent coins), or that it is the persistence in literary form of a coinage system that was once, but is no longer, current. In both cases it is possible that the coins in question are used as "units of account," and in

---

Lieberman, *TK*, 10, 393–4). Moreover, the absence of denominations above the *dînār* (such as a *selaʿ* [tetradrakhma] and *šeqel* [didrakhma]), suggests that what we have in [A–F] is an explicit presentation of a Roman scheme of coinage. However, the absence of the Roman sestertius, and the presence of the *māʿâ* (corresponding to the Greek obol) shows that the system is somewhat more complex.

[10] Properly speaking, the golden *dînār* is worth 25 *dînārîm* (e.g., *m. B. Qam.* 4:1, in which half of 50 *zûz* are said to equal a golden *dînār*), as in the Roman system. But in other passages (e.g., *m. Meʿil.* 6:4; and the *bāraîtāʾ* cited in *y. Qid.* 1:1 [58b]), the ratio is said to be 1:24. This latter ratio is clearly the more convenient for the "theoretical" purposes to which the system is put in the Mishnah since all of the denominations can be expressed as simple fractions of the golden *dînār*.

[11] See, for instance, *OGIS* II 484 = *IGR* IV 352, a letter (from Hadrian?), which rules concerning the abuses of money changers in Pergamum. What is not in question, and at no point prohibited, is that the money changers were changing copper to silver coinage at the rate of 17 or 18, and not 16, assaria to the denarius, depending on the direction of the exchange (the money changers took a surcharge of one assarion to the denarius when they gave out silver coins). The text is quoted in full and translated in T. R. S. Broughton, *Roman Asia* in (*An Economic Survey of Ancient Rome* IV, ed. T. Frank: Baltimore: Johns Hopkins, 1938), 893–5; see also the discussion in S. Bolin, *State and Currency in the Roman Empire to 300 AD* (Stockholm: Almqvist and Wiksell, 1958), 238–42. Further variations from the "official" exchange rate are cited by M. H. Crawford, "Money and Exchange in the Ancient World," *JRS* 60 (1970), 43.

the case of the "Tyrian" coinage it is quite conceivable that "Tyrian" is another way of saying "quality."[12]

---

[12] The problem of establishing correlations between literary denominations and actual coins discovered through survey, excavation or less methodical means is a vexing one which it is impossible to discuss here. See E. W. Klimowsky, "Monetary Function of City Coins," in A. Kindler ed., *International Numismatic Conference (1963)* (Jerusalem: Schocken, 1967), 129–79.

As for the *pĕrûṭâ*, the fact that in the official Roman system no such denomination existed does not mean that such coins (the product of local city mints) did not circulate. Mk. 12:42 tells of a poor woman who cast *lepta duo ho estin kodrantēs* ("two lepta, which are a quadrans") into the treasury. Thus, Mark's lepton corresponds to the Rabbinic *pĕrûṭâ*. A denomination by the name of a lepton appears in *P. Babatha* II 16. 20, 27, 32 (127 C.E.) as a division of a hitherto unattested denomination (*melas*, "black"; perhaps a Nabatean denomination; N. Lewis takes melas to be a corruption of mina, and translates lepton as "sixtieth," line notes *ad loc.* and *P. Babatha* II 5 introduction) so there is probably no connection between this lepton and our *pĕrûṭâ*. Despite the fact that Sperber (perhaps correctly) minimizes the importance of the evidence, he does recognize the existence of city coins that are arguably small enough to correspond to the *pĕrûṭâ* (1965–6, 277–8 and n. 16, building on Heichelheim, 1938, 212). L. I. Levine argues that in the second century Caesarea supplied "minims" for use as *pĕrûṭôt* throughout Palestine (L. I. Levine, *Caesarea Under Roman Rule* [SJLA 7: Leiden: E. J. Brill, 1976], 41–2). Even if coins of the *pĕrûṭâ* denomination did not circulate in Roman Palestine (Schürer [rev. ed. Vermes *et alii*], 2, 66), however, the term *pĕrûṭâ* could easily persist as a unit of account.

In *m. Bek.* 8:7, certain obligations based on prescribed payments outlined in the Pentateuch are pegged to a Tyrian standard: "The five *sĕlāʿîm* for [the redemption of] the son [are calculated] according to the Tyrian *māneh*. The thirty [*šĕqalîm*] of the slave ... [are] all according to the sacred *šeqel*, according to the Tyrian *maneh*." All of the obligations are taken to be payable in "sacred *šeqel*" (cf. Num. 18:16), which is in turn taken to be equivalent to a Tyrian tetradrakhma, four *dînārîm* (as opposed to a mishnaic *šeqel*, which is equal to two *dînārîm*). See also *t. Ket.* 12 (13):6: "Money about which the Torah speaks in every case (*bĕ-kol māqôm*): this is Tyrian money (*kesep ṣôrî*). Tyrian money, this is Jerusalemite money."

That the Mishnah, or, for that matter, documents from the second century continue to calculate in *sĕlāʿîm* or the equivalent does not imply as Ben-David concluded (1971, 120), "that this currency [referring to the actual silver coins from the independent city mint of Tyre] continued to be used for business purposes for more than a century after the closure of the mint ...." since tetradrakhmas (four denarius coins) continued to be minted in Syrian and Phoenician mints well into the third century (witness the many tetradrakhmas found at Dura Europus from various cities including Tyre, although these seem to have been minted at Antioch: see A. R. Bellinger, *Dura Europus Final Report VI: The Coins* [New Haven: Yale, 1949], and Bellinger's note in C. B Welles *et alii Dura Europus Final Report V, Part I: Parchments and Papyri* [New Haven, Yale, 1959], 9 n. 14). (A very fragmentary Aramaic document from the Judean desert may have a reference to *kĕsap sĕlāʿîm DJD* II 23.5; *DJD* II 30.20–1 reads, in Hebrew, "I have sold it to you for money, eighty-eight *zûz* [i.e.,] twenty-two *sĕlāʿîm*"; analogues appear in the documents published by Milik in *Biblica* 38 [1957], 259, lines 7–8; 264, lines 5–6; and in a document reported but not published in full by Y. Yadin, "Expedition D" *IEJ* 12 [1962], 244–5 [presumably to be published as *P. Babatha* I 44]; Greek analogues [the

The idea that one form of currency "acquires" another raises the question of how Rabbis understood money to function. In M4:5, the maximal amount that a coin may vary from its appropriate weight is placed between one sixth and one twenty-fourth (this is the subject of the debate in this pericope). In other words, a valid coin circulates according to its face value, and the disputants in M4:5 debate how far from the face value the metallic value of the coin may vary before the party giving the short-weight coins is deemed to be deriving unfair profit (*hônāyâ*). By contrast, in *m. Kelim* 12:7 the permissible range of variation is considerably higher: "How much may a *selāʿ* [=4 *dînārîm*, i.e., denarii] be worn and he will [still] be able to uphold it? Up to two *dînārîm*; more than this let him cut it." It is certainly possible that the sole point of contradiction between these two pericopae is the amount by which a coin may be underweight. I wish to suggest, however, that *m. Kelim* 12:7 implies an entirely different approach to the value of coins: the reason that one may accept a coin weighing as little as one half of its appropriate weight is that its value is taken to be proportional to its weight, and not fixed by its face value.[13] If *m. Kelim* 12:7 nevertheless sets an upper limit for wear

---

value in *denarii* also stated in terms of the stater] appear in *P. Babatha* II 11.3, 15; *DJD* II 114.5; cf. 114.10–11 and verso; this documentary practice is referred to in *m. B. Bat.* 10:2: "If he wrote [in a document] 'One hundred *zûzîm*, which are twenty *sĕlāʿîm* [and not twenty-five],' he has only twenty [*sĕlāʿîm*]; 'One hundred *zûzîm* which are thirty *sĕlāʿîm*' he has only a *māneh* [i.e., 100 *zûz*].").

More tantalizing are references to Tyrian coins (Yadin, 1962, 244–5 [=*P. Babatha* I 7?]; *P. Babatha* II 5 b i. 5; 11, 3, 15; *DJD* II 114.10–11 [171 CE?]; 115.5 [124 CE]; cf. *P. Dura.* 17 D.42, restored [180 CE]; 20.6 [121 CE]; 23.4–5 [134 CE]). This does not mean, that actual Tyrian coins were in regular circulation. It is quite possible that a "Tyrian" denomination was a unit of account, against which circulating coins would be valued, or even that it was a way of saying that the document ought to be paid in "good" coin (Bellinger in the note to Welles *et alii*, 1959, 9 n. 14, cited above, suggests that the expression was nearly meaningless at Dura). Compare the analogous references in Egyptian documents from the second half of the third century to old Ptolemaic coins (*P. Coll. Youtie* II 71.25; 72.8; *P. Oxy.* XXXI 2587.6–8; XLI 2951.25; *P. Stras.* VI 557.20; *P. Vind. Bosw.* 12.7–8; *Stud. Pal.* XX 71.11–12; 72.10–11). Opinion on the references to Ptolemaic coins ranges from the assumption that actual Ptolemaic coins are referred to (C. Wessely, *MPER* IV 144ff.; Grenfell and Hunt, *P. Oxy.* XII 1411 [introd.]; M. Rostovtzeff, *Social and Economic History of the Roman Empire*, rev. ed. P. M. Fraser [Oxford: Oxford University, 1957] 2, 737 n. 5); to the suggestion that "Ptolemaic" refers to a standard of value (J. Rea, *P. Oxy.* XXXI 2587 [introd.]), or "merely a conventional wish that the coins are of good quality" (M. Crawford, cited in the note to *P. Oxy.* XLI 2951.25).

[13] See above, Chapter II.C.2. Alternatively it is possible that *m. Kel.* 12:7 and M4:5 deal with different issues: the former may be concerned with visibly worn (or clipped) coins, while the latter rules on coins that appear to be of full size or weight. However, the interpretation proposed here may underlie T3:17–8 (also cited above) as well. T3:17–8 adds to a parallel to

of the coins, this is presumably because they remain "coin" and have not been demonetized.[14] If this interpretation is correct, *m. Kelim* 12:7 attests to a refusal to accord coins their nominal value, without, however, rejecting the currency system entirely. It is attractive to see this refusal as a reflection of the debasement of currency that began in the later second century (and therefore, perhaps, an attestation to an early stage in the monetary crisis of the third century).[15] This takes us beyond the evidence the Mishnah can

---

M4:5 ("How much may a *selaʿ* be lacking and there not be *hônāyâ* in it? '[For a] *selaʿ*, four *ʾissārôt* ...,' the words of R. Meir....") the following comment: "More than this he would spend it according to its [intrinsic] value (*šiwyāh*): the *selaʿ* [until it weighs as much as] a *šeqel* ..." (i.e., as in *m. Kel.* 12:7). The Tosepta's harmonization implies that coins lacking one sixth (or one twelfth or one twenty-fourth) the proper weight are taken at face value (T3:17), but beyond that amount they are accepted only by weight (T3:18). For this interpretation see Lieberman, *TK*, 9, 180; D. Sperber, *Roman Palestine, 200–400: Money, Prices*, 2ed. with supplement (Ramat Gan: Bar Ilan, 1991), 80, 375. Whether this merely removes an apparent conflict from two contradictory traditions (as I believe) or whether it reflects the correct relationship between M4:5 and *m. Kel.* 12:7, it is striking that the Tosepta implies that one is constantly weighing the coins in a transaction to see how to value them.

[14] According to Lieberman, *TK*, 9, 180 and Sperber, 1991, 80, 375–6, this is because at a certain point worn (or clipped) high denomination coins may be confused with full-value smaller denomination coins.

[15] See, in general, A. H. M. Jones, "Inflation Under the Roman Empire," *Economic History Review* 5 (1953), 293–318. Documents dating from around the turn of the century have been taken to imply a failure of confidence in currency beginning around 200. Some possible examples follow. (1) In a bilingual (Palmyrene and Greek) dedicatory inscription from 193 we know that the honoree was thanked for having expended "three hundred old golden *denarii*" for expenses for those travelling in a caravan with him, reflecting, perhaps, unwillingness among people outside of the Roman empire (Hyspasinou Kharax) to receive debased imperial coinage (*IGR* III 1050 = *CIS* III.3.1 3948; see G. A. Cooke, *North Semitic Inscriptions* [Oxford: Clarendon, 1903], no. 115). See F. Heichelheim "New Light on Currency and Inflation in Hellenistic-Roman Times From Inscriptions and Papyri," *Economic History* 10 (1935), 8–9. However, this might only mean that pure metal, and gold in particular, rather than "coin" was preferable outside the empire. (2) At the very end of an inscription from Mylasa in Asia Minor detailing a decree of the council concerning unauthorized trade in currency (*OGIS* II 515. 208–9), there may be an (unfortunately fragmentary) reference to a lack of coins. This Bolin, 1958, 246, takes as a reference to the hoarding of copper coins because "a stage was reached at which the metallic value of copper coins corresponded to or exceeded the value given them by the official rate of exchange" (Bolin, 1958, 245). This inscription may refer to a local crisis. Moreover, if copper coins had mere token value in the empire even a light wash of silver on "silver" coins would prevent copper coins from exceeding their nominal value relative to "silver" coins. (3) In the *apokrimata* of Septimius Severus there is a record of a decision prohibiting the payment in silver of taxes that were owed in kind (*P. Col.* 123.43–4). Just why this is so is not entirely clear but it has been suggested that it is related to the government's interest in receiving full value for its taxes (see Westermann's commentary on pp. 33–4; R. S. Bagnall, personal communication, argued that this had nothing to do with

provide, however, especially since *m. Kelim* 12:7 deals with the wearing of coins, a normal process in the use of coins.[16] At any rate, it is striking that neither passage takes the value of a coin as simply that of the face value.[17]

The very fact that one type of coin "acquires" another suggests, moreover, that the authors of M4:1–2 are aware that the actual market value of coins may vary. This is substantiated from the gloss to M4:1 in M4:2 (admittedly talking only generally about *māʿôt*, "money," and *pērôt*, "produce"), which explains the legal significance of a commodity "acquiring" the money in terms of the right of the buyer to withdraw from the sale—presumably because the price was no longer to the buyer's advantage. If the official value of coins were taken to be the actual value, the exchange of coins would, in a sense, be a kind of barter between bigger and smaller units of the same type of thing[18] (with the legal implication that in an exchange, after one side

---

currency problems). Later in the third century (260) we hear of bankers having closed their doors, and being ordered to open and receive all but the most debased coinage (*P. Oxy.* XII 1411.10–3; it is not entirely certain whether what is at issue here is the refusal of the bankers to receive the coinage of Quietus and Macarinus for more or less political reasons [Johnson, 1936, 449], or whether this was a refusal to accept Roman Imperial coinage, which by this time was highly devalued, in exchange for Egyptian coinage at the official exchange rate [Bolin, 1958, 287–8]). See also Crawford, 1975, 566 n. 27, who cautiously cites D 46.3.99 as possible evidence of "disquiet over the coinage." In general, however, Crawford (p. 568) argues that in the first part of the third century there is no inflation, but merely the adjustment of prices for the actual metalic value of the debased coins.

[16] The weighing or testing of coins in the case of doubt was likely to be common practice even in periods of stable currency (the production of ancient mints was never entirely uniform, and coin testing was one of the standard tasks of bankers, see, for instance J. Andreau, *La vie financière dans le monde romain* [*Bibliothèque des écoles françaises d'Athènes et de Rome*: 265: Rome: École Française, 1987], 485–525 and *passim*, and the discussion below in Section A.3). It is striking that the Mishnah, in both *m. B. Meṣ.* and *m. Kel.*, discusses the variations in the value of coins in terms of diminution of weight and not the debasement of currency.

[17] A rather more positive view is expressed by Epictetus, *Diss.* 3.3.3 where the requirement on the part of the grocer or banker to accept official coinage (*to tou Kaisaros nomisma*), whether willing or not, is compared with the soul, whose nature it is to recognize the good. That money could shift in value, and not only in the third century, is clear from *P. Bad.* II 37 (ca. 110 CE), in which a letter-writer informs his addressee that the price of a *khrysous*, presumably an aureus, had fallen from "15" to "11" (whether the figures should be taken as shorthand from 115 and 111 or as something else is debated, see Johnson, 1936, 425–6, Bolin, 1958, 92–3). The writer goes on to say that the prefect of Egypt had promised that he would interevene and fix the price (*timēn stēsein*), but that he had not yet done so.

[18] A pericope that might reflect this attitude towards coinage occurs in *m. Šebu.* 6:3 [A–G]:
    [A] [Plaintiff:] "There is a pound (*liṭrāʾ*) of gold of mine in your hand (*yēš lî bĕ-yādĕkā...*)."
    [B] [Defendant:] "There is only a pound of silver of yours in my hand (*ʾēn lāk bĕ-yādî ʾelāʾ...*)."

transfers the coin to be exchanged both sides would immediately be bound by the contract[19]). Moreover, since values would be guaranteed not to change in such a case, the importance of being able to withdraw from the contract would diminish, since with minimal difficulty one could find someone else with whom to conduct the reverse transaction.

An early variant to M4:1 [A] underscores the historical importance of the idea that one form of coinage is considered a commodity with respect to another. In the manuscripts of the Babli the opening clause of M4:1 reads "Gold acquires silver." That is, in an exchange between gold and silver coinage it is the gold coin that is considered a commodity. Since passages in the Tosepta already reflect the tradition "gold acquires silver," and both the Babli and Yerushalmi preserve traditions attributing both variants to R. Judah the Patriarch, under whose auspices the Mishnah is traditionally thought to have been redacted, it stands to reason that this is an early variant.[20] It is possible to explain the variant "gold acquires silver" as stating that

[C] He is exempt [from taking an oath].
[D] [Plaintiff:] "There is a golden *dînār* of mine in your hand."
[E] [Defendant:] "There is only a silver *dînār*, a *těrîsît* (cf. Lat. *tressis* = 3 asses/ *'issārîm*), a *pôndîôn*, and a *pěrûtâ* of yours in my hand."
[F] He is required [to take an oath],
[G] for all [of the coins listed in [D] and [E]] are forms of one coin.

Without entering into the legal issues of this pericope (see the discussion of M4:7 [A–C] and *m. Šebu.* 6:1 in Chapter II.A.2), it should be noted that the Mishnah makes a sharp distinction between claims and denials stated in terms of unminted metal, and those made in terms of coins. Whereas unminted metals of different types are considered different types of property [A–C], when coins of gold are claimed, and the denial put in terms of both silver and copper coinage [D–E], both parties are considered to be talking about the same type of property: coins.

[19] On barter, see M4:1 [F]: neither party is exchanging money, and therefore, on the principle of M4:2, neither may withdraw. The classic, but difficult, assessment of the rules of barter occurs at *m. Qid.* 1:6: "... once this one has gained possession, this one has become obligated with respect to it" (see below Section A.3, and *t. Qid.* 1:9; Rashi and Tos. to *b. Qid.* 28a.)

[20] T3:13; Y4:1 (9c); B44a-b. The Yerushalmi tradition reads:
Said R. Hiyya b. Ashi: "Who taught it? R. Simeon b. R. [Judah the Patriarch]."
Said his father to him: "Recant, and teach thus: 'Gold acquires silver.'"
Said he to him: "I will not recant; for while your vigor was still upon you [i.e., while you were young], you taught me: 'Silver acquires gold.'"

See also *t. Maʿaś. Š.* 2:7, involving a dispute between R. Judah the Patriarch and R. Eleazar b. Simeon over whether one may redeem second tithe money in the form of gold that now cannot be used (e.g., it has become mingled with sacred money) with silver coins (whereas there is no disagreement over the redemption of silver coinage with gold). At issue in the dispute seems to be the status of some coins as "commodities" with respect to one another (see Lieberman, *TK*, 2, 734; Sperber, 1991, 81–3.)

silver coinage, in light of its general utility as a coin, is always considered "money."[21] In light of the increasing debasement of coinage in the late second century and beyond, however, it is possible that the variant "gold acquires silver" reflects the operation of Gresham's Law: debased silver coinage was forcing gold coinage out of circulation. People might indeed wish to buy gold coins, not for use as money, however, but rather as a commodity to be hoarded (because it could be counted on to retain its value) or to be melted down and sold as bullion.[22]

---

[21] Cf. the explanation given in the Babli for this version of M4:1 [A]: "silver, which is current (ḥārîp, lit.: "sharp"), is 'coin'; gold, which is not current, is 'produce.'"

[22] This seems to have been the view of Heichelheim, 1938, 220–1, although this passage is not quite as explicit as it might be. See E. Kleiman, "Bi-Metalism in Rabbi's Time: Two Variants of the Mishna 'Gold Acquires Silver,'" [Hebrew] *Zion* 38 (1973), 48–61. While recognizing that the conditions for the "de-monetization" of gold had long been in the making, and were greatly advanced by the devaluation of the silver coinage by Septimius Severus, Kleiman attempts to date the variant "gold acquires silver" to the introduction of the new Antoninianus by Caracalla in 215 (pp. 56–9). Kleiman further suggests that the "Palestinian" variant, "silver acquires gold," assigned according to tradition to R. Judah the Patriarch's youth, similarly reflects the de-monetization of silver during the course of the middle second century due to the influx of gold into the economy after Trajan's conquest of Dacia in 107 (pp. 55–6). Kleiman himself notes that silver never was truly de-monetized in the second century. Moreover, in context, the rationale for the variant "silver acquires gold" is reasonably straightforward, and does not need to be related to a specific event: M4:1 treats coins of less precious metal as "commodities" with respect to coins of more precious metal. In the language of the Yerushalmi: "This is the principle of the matter: Everything that is inferior to its fellow acquires its fellow" (Y4:1 [9c]). What does require explanation, and Kleiman has persuasively suggested one, is the variant that disrupts the obvious logic of the passage: "gold acquires silver."

Compare Sperber, 1991, 69–83. On the basis of internal evidence from the Babli and Yerushalmi Sperber suggests that R. Judah the patriarch held that "gold acquires silver" for at most twenty-four years (195–219) (pp. 75–6), and concludes that it is precisely the *confidence* in silver coinage (resulting from the tremendous output of silver under Septimius Severus [!]) that led to the variant, before inflation created lack of confidence and R. Judah reverted to the opinion that "silver acquires gold" (pp. 77–8). According to Sperber, there are other, Ushan (ca. 135–70), traditions that also echo the idea that gold is "coin" with respect to silver, precisely because of the strength of silver during this period (pp. 79–81). Sperber's analysis is problematic (1) because it starts with the premise that we can use anecdotal material in Rabbinic literature to reconstruct accurate biographical chronologies; and (2) because it borrows the Babli's criteria of whether one coin is "money" with respect to another because it is "current" (ḥārîp) or of higher inherent value (ḥāšîb), which may not be relevant to the analysis of the Mishnah itself. (3) As Kleiman, 1973, 61 noted, Sperber seems to miss the fact that issuing vast amounts of debased silver will make silver more "current" as coinage, but not because of the "strength" of silver. Finally (4) his evidence that it is stable currency in the middle of the second century that yields the ruling "gold acquires silver" is somewhat weak:

The discussion of the treatment of money in *m. Baba' Meṣi'a'* leaves room for a number of tentative suggestions. The tractate uses a standardized system of coinage, but at the same time reflects an awareness that using that standardized system to serve as a marker of value is complicated by the fact that coins themselves may vary with respect to one another. Here we have an important point of contact with a functioning Roman provincial economy. The rather rigid formal distinction between "commodity" and "money," which becomes extremely important in connection with the problem of usur, suggests a conceptualization of a purchase not as an investment but as the acquisition of goods for use or consumption. However, this should not be overstated. M5:1 reflects the fact that Rabbis were indeed capable of

---

a. T3:19 (Sperber p. 80): "... In [connection with] what are these things said? [In connection] with [silver] *sĕlā'îm* and *dînārîm*. But [in connection] with golden *dînārîm* and copper coins he would spend them according to their weight [i.e., even if worn past half their weight]." At best this pericope glosses an Ushan tradition (T3:17 presents a version of our M4:5, which is an Ushan dispute form; T3:18 is related to the anonymous *m. Kel.* 12:7; the construct T3:17 + 18 is presumably later; moreover, it is not quite clear to which clause in the preceding material the cited passage from T3:19 refers: in the version in the Yerushalmi the clauses in question appear in a different position; and where the Tosepta reads "copper coins," the Yerushalmi reads "silver coins" [Y4:4 (9d)]; see Lieberman, *TK*, 9, 181–2). Furthermore, the passage cited may well imply that as opposed to silver, copper and gold are essentially demonetized, since due to the debasement of silver people are unwilling to use copper or gold coinage as if they had only their face value. If this is so, and if it is to be linked to a specific historical situation, T3:19 would appear to reflect a later (i.e., ca. 200, or later still given the uncertainty of the date of materials in the Tosepta), rather than earlier (135–70), situation.

b. T3:23 (Sperber p. 81). This passage explicitly glosses the variant "gold acquires silver." Once again, the passage cited is anonymous and, since it otherwise appears only in connection with R. Judah the Patriarch or members of his generation, is likely to be late.

c. Sperber is on strongest grounds with *t. Ket.* 6:5 (cf. *b. Ket.* 67a) (Sperber pp. 80–1): "Said R. Simeon b. Gamaliel: 'And the matter is thus: in a place where it was customary (*še-nāhagû*) not to exchange golden *dînārîm*, he [the groom] leaves them as they are, and the gold, lo, it is like utensils.'" This is admittedly an Ushan text, and seems to imply that gold coin might not be readily exchangeable for silver. The matter is not as unambiguous as it might be, however. First, the formulation of the tradition of R. Simeon b. Gamaliel suggests that this might be a local phenomenon, and does not reflect the general circulation of coinage. Second, as Lieberman suggested (with no connection to the problem of monetary policy), what is at issue here is a place where it was customary to not use gold coins brought into the marriage as part of the bride's dowry (*TK*, 6, 276). If Lieberman is correct, the passage may be dealing specifically with localized practices concerning the bride's property, but may not be relevant to the circulation of coinage in general. If this is so, what this reflects is not the strength of silver currency, but confidence in gold to retain its value over the long term (that is, some of the property brought by the wife is not for consumption but for storage). A preference towards gold might occur in periods of relative monetary stability, but is certainly also consistent with what one might expect in a period of uncertainty.

conceptualizing the profitability of trading in futures, and—assuming that the distinction between "commodities" and "money" (M4:1 [E]; M4:2) underlies the exchanges of coins in M4:1 [A–C] as well—silver coinage can be either "produce" or "coin" depending on the kind of transaction. Finally, a preliminary observation on the distribution of money is in order. Although I noted above that many transactions can be effected either in kind or in cash, it is striking that, as these relationships are described in the Mishnah, agricultural workers receive at least part of their wage in kind (through meals, or the right to eat in the fields) and leases of agricultural land generally do not involve the payment of cash (although these cases are raised), while landowners sell their produce for cash, and tenants of dwellings pay in cash. Thus, the Mishnah may presuppose a distinction between people who have a greater use for money as well as greater means for gaining wealth in the form of coin, and others, further down the economic scale, for whom physical wealth in the form of coins plays a relatively small part in their day-to-day lives.[23]

2. Markets.

Markets involve the meeting of people for the exchange of goods and services, and as such form a primary area for the study of human interactions against the background of the distribution and circulation of wealth. Analyses of the regional distribution of markets and their hierarchical articulation can provide considerable information about social and economic structure: the extent to which trade is carried out "horizontally" between peasants on a local level to cover individual shortfalls or surpluses, or to which markets are used to funnel agricultural produce to towns for the use of an urban, non-farming class, are important indicators of the level of dominance the town has over the surrounding agricultural territory.[24] Similarly, the way in which peasant communities are oriented towards the market (e.g., whether all the farmers in a region produce the same goods or different goods) has implications for how "closed" (i.e., exclusive of outsiders, "conservative" in agricultural practice, and distinctive in religious practice) or "open" the peasant society is.[25] Unfortunately, *m. Baba' Meṣiʿa'*, and the Mishnah more generally,

---

[23] Cf. F. Millar, "The World of the *Golden Ass*," *JRS* 71 (1981), 72–3 who argues that monetization seems to have reached quite far down the social scale.

[24] See C. A. Smith, "Regional Economic Systems: Linking Geographical Models and Socioeconomic Problems," in *Regional Analysis*, ed. C. A. Smith (*Studies in Anthropology*. New York: Academic, 1976), 1, 3–63.

[25] See E. R. Wolf, "Closed Corporate Communities in Mesoamerica and Central Java," *Southwestern Journal of Anthropology*, 13 (1957), 1–18; *idem*, *Peasants* (Englewood Cliffs: Prentice Hall, 1966); C. A. Smith, "Exchange Systems and the Spatial Distribution of Elites,"

provide little information on these matters.[26] An examination of the tractate, asking how the people who produced it perceived markets and how they wanted them to be run, shows essentially three things: first, that the Rabbis who produced the Mishnah treated agricultural produce as the basic stuff of the marketplace; second, that trade was carried out at least in part by specialists; third, and finally, that markets are assumed to have a "market price," that is, a legally enforceable ceiling on prices. On one level, this restricted range of material is as it should be: the Mishnah is not an ethnographic study, nor a regional survey, nor even a practical guide for doing business; it is a compendium of legal materials on topics that raised legal questions. Still, we will have to ask, after a survey of the information that is available in the

---

in Smith, 1976, 2, 309–74; F. Cancian, "Economic Behavior in Peasant Communities," in *Economic Anthropology*, ed. S. Plattner (Stanford: Stanford University, 1989). R. MacMullen, *Roman Social Relations* (New Haven: Yale, 1974), 28–56; P. Brown, "The Rise and Function of the Holy Man in Late Antiquity," in *Society and the Holy in Late Antiquity* (Berkeley: University of California, 1982), 103–52; and M. I. Finley, *The Ancient Economy*, 2 ed. (*Sather Memorial Lectures* 43: Berkeley: University of California, 1985), 104–10, among others, try to place the peasantry within the society and economy of the ancient world.

[26] For methodological reasons, the present study focuses on the evidence that can be provided from the Mishnah itself. Some hints of market articulation are found in M4:6 (which distinguishes between a city [kĕrak] and a village [kĕpār] on the basis of the availability of a banker) and *m. ʿArak.* 6:5 (which recognizes that "a pearl, if they take it up to the city [kĕrak] it increases in value," presumably because there is greater demand—as well as concentrated wealth—in urban centers). It should be pointed out that a careful study of the legal and anecdotal material inside and out of the Mishnah, combined with archeological and geographical surveys, can yield important results for the economic history of Roman Galilee. Z. Safrai, in particular, has done important work in this area. See the following publications: "*Lĕ-šĕʾēlat ha-mibneh ha-merḥābî šel ha-yiššûb ba-gālîl bi-tĕqufat ha-mišnâ wĕ-ha-talmûd*," in *In the Lands of Galilee* [Hebrew], ed. A. Shemueli *et alii* (Haifa: University of Haifa, 1983), 269–88 [cited below as "*Ha-mibneh ha-merḥābî*"]; "*Ha-kĕpār bi-tĕqûpat ha-mišnâ wĕ-ha-talmûd*," in *Nation and History* [Hebrew], ed. M. Stern (Jerusalem: Zalman Shazar Center, 1983), 1, 173–95 [cited below as "*Ha-kĕpār*"]; "Fairs in Eretz Israel in the Mishnah and Talmud Period" [Hebrew] *Zion* 49 (1984), 139–58 (with a critique by E. Kleiman, and a rejoinder by Safrai, *Zion* 51 [1986], 471–84, 485–6 respectively); "*Ha-mishar bĕ-ʾereṣ yiśrāʾēl ba-tĕqûpâ ha-rômît*," and "*Ha-ṭippûl bĕ-maʿareket ha-dĕrākîm ha-kĕpāriyyôt bi-tĕqûpat ha-mišnâ wĕ-ha-talmûd*," in *Commerce in Palestine Throughout the Ages* [Hebrew], ed. B. Z. Kedar *et alii* (Jerusalem: Yad Izhak Ben Zvi, IES, 1990), 108–39 and 159–180 respectively. Much of this is now reworked in Z. Safrai, *The Economy of Roman Palestine* (Routledge: 1994). A thorough critique of Safrai's method is beyond the scope of this study. In general, however, Safrai emphasizes the necessity and wide diffusion of trade due to the "development" and "sophistication" of the economy of Palestine and of the Roman empire in general, a view that may be somewhat anachronistic. Secondly, his analysis of regional structures in Galilee tends to break regions into sub-units rather than emphasizing the integration of these units into a regional system. See also I. W. J. Hopkins, "City Regions in Roman Palestine," *PEQ* 112 (1980), 19–32.

tractate, to what extent the "topics that raised legal questions" are themselves products of a particular social or economic perspective.

We should at the outset distinguish between "markets" on a conceptual level and material marketplaces. To speak of markets merely in the conceptual sense (a framework for exchanging goods, or, in more doctrinaire terminology, an institution for allocating limited resources) does not tell us which members of the society participated in markets as physical and social institutions, whether as buyers or sellers, and what the implications of a differential participation in the marketplace had for the distribution of wealth and power in the society. Moreover, to ask how the Mishnah viewed "the market" is to risk asking a question for which the Mishnah can supply no answer. However, it is precisely about physical marketplaces, which people congregated there, and what was permissible or forbidden there, that the Mishnah, with the basic casuistic approach of its legal traditions, offers us information, or at the very least, offers us a picture we are asked to take as information.

Turning first to the evidence outside of *m. Babaʾ Meṣiʿaʾ*, it should be noted that the Mishnah refers to essentially two market institutions: the *ḥānût*, "store," and the *šûq*, "market place."[27] The *ḥānût* is located in some

---

[27] Within the Mishnah itself we find reference to an additional institution, the ʾiṭlis (or ʾiṭliz; the spelling and pointing of this word are variable). That it is a place and not the description of a function seems clear from *m. Ker.* 3:7, a story about two Rabbis in the ʾiṭlis of Emmaus, where one of the Rabbis was buying an animal to slaughter for a feast. In two other passages in which the term appears it is in the stereotyped expression "they are sold in the ʾiṭlis, and slaughtered in the ʾiṭlis, and sold by the pound (*bĕ-liṭrāʾ*)" (*m. Bek.* 5:1; *m. Tem.* 3:5). Finally, *m. ʿArak.* 6:5 refers to the increase in price one receives by waiting to sell one's cow at the ʾiṭlis. One suggestion is that the term may transliterate the Greek *katalysis*, which, though it may refer to a camping spot (and arguably to a caravan station), does not seem to carry the sense of "market" in Greek (for this view see S. Krauss, *Griechische und lateinische Lehnwörter im Talmud, Midrasch und Targum* [Berlin, 1898–9], vol. II, s.v. [p. 30]; criticism by S. Lieberman, "*ʿEśer milîn*," *ʾEškolôt* 3 [1959], 75–81). (*Katalysis*, incidentally, is not an inappropriate translation of the Hebrew *ḥānût*, literally a camping or stopping spot.) Lieberman, 1959, 77 (followed by Z. Safrai, 1984, 139) took the term to be the Greek *atelēs*, for *panēgyris atelēs*, a fair in which taxes (presumably market taxes) had been remitted (cf. *IGR* IV 144 [Cyzicus, I CE], cited by Broughton, 1938, 870, in which reference is made to the *panēgyris kai ateleia*, "fair and tax-freedom," taking place in the city; see also *IG* V.2 18 B.9–12 [under Trajan]). Since all that the Mishnah states about the ʾiṭlis is that animals were sold there, particularly for consumption, neither explanation is altogether satisfactory, although a periodic encampment of local herders with their flocks may not be inappropriate. (In later sources the term has a more generic sense: *Pesiq. Rab Kah.*, *ʿAśśēr taʿaśśēr* [ed. Buber, 98b; ed. Mandelbaum, 162]: one selling a garment in the ʾiṭlis. *Gen. Rab.* 79, to 33:18 [ed. Theodor, Albeck, 940]: Jacob "began to erect ʾiṭlĕśîn, and sell cheaply." In light of the suggested reading as *katalysis*, it is notable that the Rabbinic comment glosses the Biblical expression, "And he

passages of the Mishnah in a public place,[28] and is the locus for small purchases[29] of foodstuffs.[30] *Šûq* is a somewhat more generic term: it can mean merely "out of doors," "in public." Here too, the basic material for sale is agricultural produce and related goods.[31] A review of the sources that deal with marketing in *m. Babaʾ Meṣiʿaʾ* confirms that in our tractate as well, it is basic foodstuffs largely deriving from agricultural production (together with such general requirements as pottery utensils) that make up the core of marketed goods.[32] One of the Mishnaic terms for "commodities" is simply *pērôt*,

---

camped ... (*wa-yiḥan*)"; it will also be remembered that Jacob was a shepherd and that in verse 13 he has just protested that his children and animals prevent him from joining Esau, so that even in this case *ʾiṭlis* as a place to sell animals, and not a "fair," may be the intended meaning.) Kleiman, in his response to Safrai, 1984, 475, also suggests that the term may represent the Greek *katallassis*, which can have the connotation "exchange."

[28] *m. Maʿaś. Š.* 2:2 locates the store *ba-šûq*, "in the marketplace," although this can mean merely "in public," "out of doors"; *m. B. Qam.* 6:6 places the store on a public thoroughfare. Cf. *m. B. Bat.* 2:3 [F–H] that places a *ḥānût* (here, in the sense of workshop) in a residential courtyard, whose occupant goes out to sell in the marketplace (the text is translated in full below n. 38).

[29] *m. Dem.* 2:4 (the shopkeeper, by implication, sells by small measurements); *m. ʿErub.* 7:11 (purchase on the scale of a *māʿâ* [obol; but here, as frequently, perhaps simply "a coin"]); *m. B. Bat.* 5:9 (an *ʾissār* worth of oil). *m. Meʿil.* 6:3–4 discusses purchases worth a half or a whole *pĕrûṭâ*, but this may be dictated by the legal definition of *mĕʿîlâ* (misappropriation of sacred property, see M4:7 [G]) rather than the scale of purchase. Shammai, in *m. Maʿaś Š.* 2:9, is credited with a rule that one does not change a *selaʿ* (tetradrakhma) of second tithe money in Jerusalem but sets up a substantial tab with a shopkeeper; this, again, may be a special case (since it describes, even if accurately, the long defunct practice of carrying second tithe to Jerusalem, rather than contemporaneous market practices) and at any rate gives no sense of the scale of individual purchases.

[30] Foodstuffs: *m. Maʿaś. Š.* 2:9; 4:2; *m. Dem.* 2:4 (implied); *m. ʿErub.* 7:11; produce (*pērôt*): *m. Ned.* 11:2; *m. Šebu.* 7:5–6; nuts, eggs: *m. Beṣa* 3:8; oil: *m. B. Bat.* 5:9; wine: *m. ʿAb. Zar.* 5:4. If *m. Meʿil.* 6:3–4 refer to a store (as does 6:2), and not merely to the problem of agency in establishing misuse of sacred property, then we have references to lamps, wicks, and fruit, but also a garment worth a golden *dînār* (*aureus*).

[31] Produce (*pērôt*, with specific fruits mentioned): *m. Dem.* 8:3; vegetables: *m. Peʾa* 3:3; *m. Dem.* 3:2; 5:7; *m. Šebi.* 7:3; *m. Maʿaś.* 1:5; eggs: *m. Ḥul.* 2:9; wheat and other grain supplies: *m. Men.* 10:5; *m. Makš.* 6:2; prepared bread: *m. Ḥal.* 1:6; 2:7; *m. Pes.* 2:5; grapes: *m. ʾOhal.* 18:1 (although this particular passage may be something of a special case). In addition there are references to slaughtering of animals in the marketplace (*m. Ḥul.* 2:9); a tradition about spice and wool dealers in Jerusalem (*m. ʿErub.* 7:9); and references to the sale of slaves (*m. B. Qam.* 8:1) and utensils (*m. B. Bat.* 2:3). *Šûq* can apparently cover a wider range of transaction than that characterized by the term *ḥānût*.

[32] That this is a product of the economic world of antiquity and not the mere accident of preservation of materials can be seen from comparison with a document from Oxyrhynchus. Compare J. Rea, "P. Lond. Inv. 1562 Verso: Market Taxes in Oxyrhynchus," *ZPE* 48 (1982), 194–6, which lists, in addition to brothels, tinsmiths, clothesmakers, shoemakers, and sellers

"produce."[33] In M4:11–2, the rules regarding how merchandise is to be handled by merchants (whether it can be mixed, dressed up, or given away free as a promotion) are stated in connection with produce (*pērôt*), wine, grain, parched grain, nuts, and beans (although a final note about slaves, animals and utensils is added).[34] Similarly, the rules of advanced payment for goods are worked out for grain, grapes, olives, pottery, and dung (M5:7), and the example given of a usurious "increase" (*tarbît*) is based on the shift of market prices for grain and wine (M5:1). This is not to say that other, non-agricultural merchandise is not thought of as being sold or exchanged (slaves have already been mentioned), but that, at least in *m. Baba' Meṣi'a'*, transactions involving land, trees, animals,[35] and slaves are not usually described as taking place in a marketplace (M5:3; M8:4, 5).[36] Such transactions require considerable outlay, may involve a more or less lengthy period of negotiation

---

or makers of yarn: bakers of two kinds; butchers; sellers of rushes, wood, fruit, olives, garlands, and vegetables; dealers in crops, wool and grain; and importers of spices, beans, natron, rock salt, pottery, fodder, wood, dung, and dates. The paucity of "manufactured" goods in comparison with agricultural produce and raw materials, even in a nome metropolis, is remarkable. Since the document records the taxes for a specific market (lines 3, 5: the market of the Serapeion at Oxyrhynchus), it may be that these other activities are carried out elsewhere. The document may suggest, however, that it took fewer (and less diversified?) "manufacturers" to supply the needs of a town than it did sellers of produce.

[33] E.g., M4:2; compare the language of M4:1 and see the discussion of these pericopae in Chapter II.C.2. See also M5:4 [B]: "let him [the householder] not give him [the shopkeeper] money with which to purchase produce for half profit ...."

[34] M4:11–12. The reference to slaves, animals and utensils, M4:12 [G], may be a supplementary note to these pericopae (the syntactical pattern shifts to an impersonal negative construction: *'ēn mĕparsĕqîn* ...; this is, however, the same construction as used in M4:11 [A, D]).

[35] Cf. P. Lond. Inv. 1562 verso, line 15 (Rea, 1982; see his comment to this line, p. 202), which lists a market tax for the guild of shepherds, who presumably sell sheep in the market and the discussion of *'itlis*, above, n. 27.

[36] Compare *m. B. Qam.* 8:1: in calculating damages to a human, "they evaluate him as if he is a slave being sold in the market (*šûq*)." See also *t. 'Ab. Zar.* 1:8, in which real estate purchases seem to take place at still another market institution, a fair:
- [A] One may go to the fair (*yārîd*) of the gentiles, and be healed by them a monetary healing (*rippûi māmôn*),
- [B] but not a personal healing (*rippûi nepeš*)
- [C] and one may purchase from them houses, fields, vineyards, male slaves and female slaves,
- [D] because he is like one saving [this property] from their [the gentiles'] hands,
- [E] and he writes it and deposits it in the archives (*'erkā'îm*; cf. Greek *arkheia*).

[I have followed S. Lieberman, *TR*, 2, 186, *ad loc.*, in reading "and one may purchase" in [C], against the reading "and one may not purchase" in the mss. The reading adopted here is also that of the Tosepta in the parallel at *t. Mo'ed Qaṭ.* 1:12 (2:1 in the Erfurt ms.), and of the citations of *bāraîtôt* parallel to *t. Ab. Zar.* 1:8 at *y. 'Ab. Zar.* 1:1 (39b); 1:4 (39c); *b. 'Ab. Zar.* 13a.

Institutions and Relationships 139

before a deal can be made, and are likely to be recorded in a deed.[37] Thus, such purchases constitute a different order of magnitude from those involving, say, the buying of produce from a grocer, and are pictured as taking place in a different institutional framework. This may, perhaps, be one of the reasons that the rules of *hônāyâ* (over- or under-charge) do not apply to "slaves and documents and lands and consecrated goods" (M4:9 [B]).

In the treatment of markets in *m. Bab͗a͗ Meṣi῾a͗*, at least some market activity is attributed to market specialists, of which the two most common in the tractate, and in the Mishnah in general, are the *ḥenwānî* (shopkeeper) and the *tāgār* (merchant).[38] The shopkeeper can be an independent marketer

---

On the problems of the interpretation of this passage see Lieberman, *TK*, 5, 1240–3 (to *t. Mo῾ed Qaṭ.* 1:12).]

In light of the fact that the literary sources tend to place fairs (*yĕrîdîm*) predominantly in large towns (see Safrai, 1984, 152–5 who lists as "attested" *yĕrîdîm* in the first four centuries CE: Botnah, Gaza, Gadara, Ashkelon, Akko [Ptolemais], Tyre, Bet Gubrin [Eleutheropolis], and Bet Shean [Scythopolis]; all but the first of these are major towns), it may be that what is at issue in this pericope is not so much a "marketplace" for selling landed and other property, but a convenient opportunity to register such purchases with the proper office, the requirement for which is noted in *t. ῾Ab. Zar.* 1:8 [F]. Cf. S. Krauss, *Talmudische Archäologie* (*Grundrisse der Gesamtwissenschaft des Judentums V.* Leipzig, 1911), 2, 357. *P. Dura* 17 (ca. 180 CE) is an example of a registry of contracts (although none are specifically sales); see also *P. Oxy.* I 72, an Egyptian example of a declaration of purchase. On registration of real property (including its transfer) see P. M. Meyer, *Jur. Pap.* 195–9; R. Taubenschlag, *The Law of Greco Roman Egypt in Light of the Papyri* (Warsaw, 1955), 222–30 (on the *bibliothēkē enktēseōn*). The requirement to register real property existed not only in Egypt; see *P. Babatha* I 16; H. Cotton, "Fragments of a Declaration of Landed Property from the Province of Arabia," *ZPE* 85 (1991), 263–7; eadem, "Another Fragment of a Declaration of Landed Property from the Province of Arabia," *ZPE* 99 (1993), 114–21, for examples from Roman Arabia. For registration of slaves see, e.g., *P. Oxy.* II 263.

[37] For examples from the Judean Desert see *DJD* II 22, 25, 26, 27. See also *P. Dura* 25–8, and the list of documents in Johnson, 1936, 150–4, 157. The Hebrew letter from the heads (*parnāsîn*) of Bet Meshiko to Joshua b. Galgula about a cow that Yehosep b. Ariston bought from Yaaqob b. Yehudah, *DJD* II 42, may have been necessitated by the failure of Yehosep to draw up or hold on to a deed.

[38] There are references to still more specialized sellers: a baker (*naḥtôm*) (M2:1); potter (*qaddār*) (M6:1 [D], according to the text of the Kaufman ms. [see Appendix I]) and so on. *m. B. Bat.* 2:3, for example, presupposes this further specialization:

[A] Let a man not open a bakers' shop (*ḥanût šel naḥtomîm*) or a dyers' (*sabbā῾îm*) [shop] below the storehouse of his fellow,

[B] and not a cattle shed.

[C] Indeed, in the case of wine [i.e., of a wine merchant] they permitted, but not a cattle shed.

[D] A shop (*ḥanût*) that is in the courtyard:

[E] He [a neighbor who shares the courtyard] may prevent him and say to him:

who buys produce from the producers and resells it in a store (*ḥānût*) for a profit.³⁹ Alternatively, the shopkeeper may be a kind of agent of the householder, as in the following pericope (M5:4):⁴⁰

[F] "I cannot sleep from the sound of those entering, and from the sound of those leaving."
[G] One who makes utensils goes out and sells them in the market (*šûq*);
[H] but he [the neighbor] cannot prevent him and say to him:
[I] "I cannot sleep from the sound of the hammer, or from the sound of the millstones, or from the sound of the children [at a teacher's 'shop']."

This kind of specialization is seen in far greater detail in papyri from Egypt. See, once again, P. Lond. Inv. 1562.9–20 (Rea, 1982), which lists rate of market taxes for some eighteen categories of selling establishments, from bakeries to brothels; *W. Chr.*, nos. 311–21; Johnson, 1936, 361–76, and nos. 234 (*P. Bour.* 13), 237 (*P. Oxy.* III 520) and 241 (*P. Oxy.* XII 1461). Compare *PSI* VI 692 (Oxyrhynchite nome, I CE), which records the cession of a *pantopōlikon ergastērion*, loosely, a "general store" (Johnson no. 233, p. 383).

Z. Safrai, "*Ha-mibneh ha-merḥābî*," 271, has stressed the role of the ass driver (*ḥammār*) in the local trade of Palestine. Within the Mishnah itself I have found only one unambiguous reference to a *ḥammār* as merchant, *m. Dem.* 4:7 (see, however, references to a *rôkēl, m. Maʿaś.* 2:3; *m. Šab.* 9:7). More typically, the *ḥammār* is simply a porter. Nor are all the sources from outside the Mishnah cited by Safrai probative. For instance, in T3:25 (telling ass drivers to go to a certain person who will sell them wine or oil when one knows that this person does not have it to sell is a form of verbal *hônāyâ*), the ass drivers are not necessarily buying up local produce; they may be seeking provisions for themselves (i.e., they may function here as "travelling strangers" and not "marketers"). Granting Safrai's contention about assdrivers and donkey caravans in the local trade of Galilee, Safrai has tended to minimize the traditions presupposing a Monday-Thursday market pattern as reflecting an earlier, and, less economically developed, period ("*Ha-kĕpār*," 181–4). In this connection it should be pointed out that a marketing system characterized primarily by rotating traders (as Safrai depicts it) is likely to reflect a less developed system than one in which the marketplace is fixed (since in the former case demand is not high enough to support fixed markets, and merchants must rotate to meet their "minimum demand threshold"; see S. M. Plattner, "Periodic Trade in Developing Areas Without Markets," in Smith, 1976, 1, 72–81). Nor is it necessarily the case that the economy of Palestine progressed from one "stage" to another: different models of trade may reflect the development of different localities.

³⁹ References in the Mishnah to the *ḥenwānî* selling his own produce are not as self-evident as one might like. The shopkeeper discussed in M4:12 [D–L] may own the produce being sold, although this is hardly self-evident. Similarly, the shopkeepers in *m. Dem.* 2:4 may own their own stock (which might explain why they are not permitted to sell *dĕmaî* [produce that is suspected of not having been tithed], rather than requiring them to inform the purchasers [cf. M4:11 [E–F]; cf. *t. Dem.* 3:15]).

⁴⁰ A reflex of the institution of using a *ḥenwānî* as agent appears in *m. Ket.* 9:4, in which a man sets up his wife as shopkeeper (*ha-môšîb ʾet ʾištô ḥenwānît*). The demands that a householder who sets up a shopkeeper is permitted to make of that shopkeeper according to T4:12–13 (not pursuing a craft; not buying or selling anyone else's produce) suggests that a kind of agency is envisaged. On the seller as agent, compare the discussion of D. Rathbone, 1991, 278–306, esp 287–93, of the role of wine merchants on a well documented estate in Egypt.

[A] One does not set up (*'ên môŝîbîm*) a shopkeeper [to sell merchandise] at half profit;

[B] let him not give him money with which to purchase produce for half profit;

[C] unless he gave him his wage as an idle laborer.

Similarly, the emphasis on a store in the rule that one whose wine has become mixed with water ought "not sell it in a store unless he informs" (M4:11) may imply a case where the owner has turned the wine over to a shopkeeper, although it is possible that what is meant is that it is the owner who will "set up shop" to sell the adulterated wine.[41] One of the functions attributed to the *ḥenwānî*, however the stock is received, is that of a credit institution. Thus, for instance, an employer might send a worker to a shopkeeper who is to advance payment (in coin or in produce).[42]

The *tāgār* figures in M4:3 [C] as one who has the expertise to know the market price for an item in a case where one party (on the basis of [D–H], apparently the buyer) suspects the other of cheating, just as the *ŝûlḥānî* ("banker") is the expert to whom one appeals to evaluate a coin (M4:5 [B]). In M4:4, however, just whether a *tāgār* himself can bring a claim of *hônāyâ* is disputed [B–C]. Over and against this image of *tāgār* as expert is the image of *tāgār* as cheat: "Whoever's wine has become mixed with water—let him not sell it ... to a merchant (*tāgār*) even if he informs him [the merchant?], for it is only to cheat with it" (M4:11 [E–H]). That is, as opposed to a shopkeeper [F], in this instance, the *tāgār* is presumed to misuse information on

---

[41] See the note to M4:11 in Appendix I. That the shopkeeper also owns the produce may be implied by the language of the Tosepta: "Let the shopkeeper not mix them [i.e., wine and water as in M4:11] and sell them in his store, unless he informs them" (T3:27). The Mishnah dealt with an accidental case where water and wine have become mixed (M4:11 [E]); in the Tosepta the presumption is that the shopkeeper might do this on purpose. Such liberality with produce may suggest (but hardly proves) that the produce belongs to the shopkeeper (since it is presumably not good business practice to do things that might reflect badly on one's suppliers or lead them to believe that they are being cheated; it is, after all, the shopkeeper, and not the producer, who pockets the increased revenues from selling diluted wine as full strength wine).

[42] M9:12 [G]. See *m. Šebu.* 7:1, 5–6 (the case of *ha-ḥenwānî ʿal pinqěŝô*, "the shopkeeper [swearing] on [the basis of the entry in] his ledger (*pinqas*; cf. Greek *pinax*)"). See also *m. Maʿaś. Š.* 2:9 (=*m. ʿEd.* 1:10); *m. Beṣ.* 3:8; *m. Ned.* 4:7. In this connection it is interesting to note a letter from Egypt sent to a "retail trader" (*kapēlos*), in which the trader is asked to recover a debt from a baker and to use it to buy provisions for the sender (*P. Oxy.* VII 1158). Note also the question raised about the status of a deposit of money with a shopkeeper in M3:11 and *m. Meʿil.* 6:5: are shopkeepers who accept deposits "bankers" or "householders"?

the true quality of goods.[43] More important for understanding the Mishnah's conception of the economic function of the *tāgār* is the following passage (M4:12 [A–C]):

[A] The merchant (*tāgār*) takes from five threshing floors and puts them in one bin,
[B] from five wine presses and puts them in one cask;
[C] so long as he does not intend to mix them.[44]

The impression given is one of a merchant who deals in large quantities of

---

[43] Shopkeepers, too, are accused of cheating. In M4:12 [D–L (M?)] the sages are presented as disputing (with R. Judah throughout?) the permissibility of certain practices of shopkeepers that are considered "misleading" (free distribution of nuts to children, undercutting, and dressing up merchandise to attract customers) while they agree that other practices are downright deceitful (literally, they "steal the eye" [L]). See R. A. O. Ohrenstein, "Economic Thought in Talmudic Literature in the Light of Modern Economics," *American Journal of Economics and Society* 27 (1968), 190–1, who discusses this passage in terms of Rabbinic awareness of "analytic criteria in dealing with market forces of supply and demand," without stressing that the major analytical distinction the Mishnah makes is between "honest" (or, according to the Sages, useful), and "deceitful"; cf. E. Kleiman, "'Just Price' in Talmudic Literature," *History of Political Economy* 19 (1987), 34, who took the view of R. Judah as reflecting "an anti-market, competition-restricting sentiment." Yet, R. Judah's view is not "anti-market" in the sense that the view attributed to him necessarily requires that all prices be set centrally and be conformed to (as Kleiman seems to take it); rather, it expects competition to be based on the quality and price of the goods and not on practices that attract attention by other means.

The theme of the deceitful merchant appears elsewhere in Rabbinic literature:
Let a man not teach his son [to be]: an ass driver, or a camel driver, or a ship's pilot, a waggoner (*qārār*), a shepherd [or] a shopkeeper, for their craft is the craft of brigands (Hebrew *liṣṭîm*; cf. Greek *lēstēs*).

[The text is introduced as a *bāraîtā'* in *y. Qid.* 4:11 (66b); the passage appears in some texts of the Mishnah in *m. Qid.* 4:14; see *Mĕl'eket šĕlomoh ad loc.*, and Epstein, *Nûsaḥ*, 977. Before "a waggoner" (*qārār*) the Yerushalmi text includes also "a potter" (*qaddār*), which may stem from an erroneous duplication of *qārār*, "waggoner," which are easily mistaken for one another.] With the exception of the shepherd, all of the "crafts" mentioned are at least related to commerce (cf. n. 38 above). On Rabbinic disapproval of trade see Krauss, 1911, 350, and 687 n. 307 (who minimized the importance of this disapproval). Such attitudes towards merchants are quite conventional in the Greco-Roman world: see Aristotle, *Politics*, 1256b–1258a, *Econ.* 1343a; and, more strikingly, Cicero, *de Officiis*, 1.150–1 who lists among livelihoods that are *sordidus* ("dirty," "dishonorable"): "... those who buy from merchants to sell immediately. Indeed, they would not be successful unless they were to lie very much. In truth, nothing is more repulsive than falsity."

[44] This clause is slightly problematic. See the discussion in Appendix I.

produce (a wholesaler) as opposed to the *ḥenwānî*, who deals in retail sale.⁴⁵ This image of the *tāgār* as wholesaler may also be reflected in *m. Baba' Batra'* 6:6: "One who has a garden within his fellow's garden ... may not bring merchants (*tāgārîm*) into it [i.e., across the neighbor's field]."⁴⁶ Presumably, the merchant has come to buy up produce to sell elsewhere, such as a nearby large town.⁴⁷

The third aspect of the system of markets and marketing that emerges clearly from *m. Baba' Meṣi'a'* is the notion of the market price. According to one passage, one cannot contract to pay in advance for later delivery of produce unless there is an existing market price at which this contract can be negotiated (M5:7). It is presumably this price that is meant when the Mishnah states that over- (or under-) charge by one sixth constitutes *hônāyâ* (M4:3–4). This is not to say, however, that the Mishnah views the market price as an absolute fixed amount reflecting the inherent value of the thing itself.⁴⁸ On the contrary, speculation in futures is prohibited in M5:1 precisely because the market price is variable. Acknowledgment of this capacity of the market price to shift underlies the explicitly supererogatory care with

---

⁴⁵ For the *ḥenwānî* as small-scale trader see *m. Dem.* 2:4 in which the *ḥenwānî* is opposed the "grain merchants (*sîṭônôt* ; cf. Greek *sitōnēs*) and sellers of grain" who sell with a "large measure" (*middâ gassâ*).

⁴⁶ The implication of *m. B. Bat.* 6:6 is that the *tāgār* is contracting for produce still unharvested. Cf. the reference to a *karpōnēs* ("produce purchaser"), P. Lond. Inv. 1562 verso, line 13 (Rea, 1982, 202, note thereto); and *P. Oxy.* IV 728 (142 CE) the sale of crop (*karpōneia*) in which a buyer agrees to harvest and dispose of a crop of hay on 20 arourai of land. For the use of *kapōnai* in the management of estates in Egypt see D. Kehoe, *Management and Investment on Estates in Roman Egypt* (Bonn: Habelt, 1992), 84–6 and index, *s.v.*

⁴⁷ It is perhaps not accidental that in the interchange presented between R. Tarfon and a group of merchants, the merchants are located in Lydda (M4:3 [D–H]). In the same pericope, the clause stating that the time limit for verifying the price of merchandise, "long enough to show it to a merchant or to his relative" [C] corresponds to the analogous rule in the case of coins "long enough to show it to a moneychanger," which is set specifically in a city (*kĕrāk*) as opposed to a village (M4:6 [C]).

⁴⁸ This is the view of J. Neusner, *The Economics of the Mishnah* (*Chicago Studies in the History of Judaism*: Chicago: University of Chicago, 1990), 82–9. Throughout this book, Neusner sees the Mishnah's treatment of economics as the product of a conscious and ideologically motivated insistence on subordinating what he assumes to be a real flourishing "free market" economy (despite laudatory references to studies by M. I. Finley, A. H. M. Jones, R. MacMullen, Karl Polanyi, and Max Weber all of whom limit the importance of trade and markets in the ancient world) to the "redistributive" conception of the world stemming from the belief that God owns it. While Neusner presents a fascinating, and indeed, useful, interpretive model for the theology of the Mishnah, he fails to note that the Mishnah's attitude towards the economy largely corresponds to that of the ancient wealthy classes (as described, e.g., by Finley, 1985), who are surely not subject to the Mishnah's theological constraints.

which R. Gamaliel is said to have lent his tenants seed grain (M5:8). In addition, the Mishnah is aware that there may be different price levels running simultaneously (presumably reflecting the level of the transaction, such as whether produce is bought wholesale or retail).[49] What the Mishnah does not tell us explicitly is how this price is to be determined, although there is no inherent reason why the price upon which the rules of the "just price" are based should not be thought to derive from the practice of marketing, that is, from the balancing of supply with demand.[50]

Sale can take place on a number of levels and at a number of different venues. To be sure, the *ḥenwānî* sells in a store (*ḥanût*). What of the producer? When a farmer sells to someone other than a market specialist (such as a *tāgār*) where does this take place, and, more importantly, to whom is the produce being sold? In *m. Baba' Meṣi'a'* itself, there are no unambiguous

---

[49] E.g., M5:7 [K]: once the market price has been determined "he may make a bargain with him according to the lower market price (*ša'ar ha-gabôha*)." See also *m. Ma'aś. Ś.* 4:2 [A–B], in which the "cheaper market price" (*ša'ar ha-zol*) is defined: "such as the shopkeeper buys, not such as he sells." (On *m. Ma'aś. Ś.* 4:2 see Section A.3. [on banks] below.)

[50] See E. Kleiman, 1987, 35–9. In at least one story in the Mishnah, attributed to Temple times, the price of doves necessary for certain sacrifices was reduced by a revision of the law stating how many offerings were necessary, i.e., by a reduction of demand, rather than by an administrative ruling on the appropriate price (*m. Ker.* 1:7). Compare T6:14: "There were *agoranomoi* (*'igranmîn*) in Jerusalem, but they were not appointed for market prices, but rather for measurements alone." On the other hand, T11:23 records the tradition that "the members of the town (*'îr*) are permitted to stipulate (*lĕhatnôt 'al*) prices, measurements, and the wages of workers."

On the intervention of the city (and occasionally the provincial) government in the functioning of the marketplace, especially the availability and affordability of staples, see A. H. M. Jones, "The Economic Life of the Towns of the Roman Empire," *Receuils de la Société Jean Bodin*, 6 (1954), rpt. *The Roman Economy* ed. P. A. Brunt (Totowa: Rowman and Littlefield: 1974), 46–51, and *idem*, *The Greek City from Alexander to Justinian* (Oxford: Oxford University, 1940), 215–9. In general, the documents adduced by Jones reflect not the direct control of prices, but attempts to guarantee supply (see *P. Oxy.* XII 1454 [117 CE]: bakers receive grain with which to mill flour and bake bread, and undertake to supply a certain amount of bread; and although the amount that the bakers may receive is specified, far from setting the market price, the government here uses the difference between the market price and the bakers' commission as a source of revenue). This presumably motivates the requirements of authorized merchants to take an oath that they will faithfully pursue their business (e.g., *P. Oxy.* XII 1455, cited above, and *PSI* III 202; for oaths see also *BGU* I 92; II 649, III 730; compare, however, *Syll.*[3] 799 [Cyzicus, 38 CE], which empowers the *agoranomoi* to prevent sellers from raising prices, and outlines severe penalties; with respect to the relative price of gold to silver, at least, *P. Bad.* II 37 expresses the hope that the prefect will intervene to fix the falling price of gold). One interesting example of this type (admittedly, relatively late for our purposes, 327 CE) records the oath of an egg seller to sell eggs daily, and to refrain from selling them secretly or in his house (*P. Oxy.* I 83).

examples of direct sale from producer to consumer.[51] More explicit testimony comes from elsewhere in the Mishnah, for instance *m. Demai* 5:7:

[E] A householder who was selling vegetables in the marketplace:
[F] when they were bringing him [stock] from his gardens he tithes from one [basket of produce] for all of them.
[G] But [if] from other gardens, he tithes from each and every one.

This pericope is interesting in this connection because it not only allows for the possibility of a householder selling the produce he has grown on his own land, but also suggests the ease with which a householder can turn into a marketer engaged in selling other people's produce.

In *m. Babaʾ Meṣiʿaʾ*, however, and in the Mishnah more generally, direct sale from producer to consumer through a marketplace is conspicuous for its absence,[52] and we are in no position to evaluate the actual extent to which

---

[51] In addition to M5:5 and M5:1, which are referred to below, the following passages should be noted. M4:4 [A–B] can be taken to imply that a non-specialist, such as a producer, might be seller as well as buyer ("Whether [it is] the buyer or whether [it is] the seller, they have *hônāyâ*. Just as a non-professional (*hedyôt*) has *hônāyâ*, so a merchant (*tāgār*) has *hônāyâ*"). While it is possible that M4:11 [A–D] originates in the context of rules for traders by profession (M4:11 [F–H] discusses only sale "in a store" [see below] or to a merchant, and M4:12 is concerned with the practices of these specialists), the rules in [A–D] could as easily apply to householders selling wine as to traders. The proposed sale of deposited produce that is going bad (attributed to R. Simeon b. Gamaliel in M3:6 [C–D]), in which the depositary stands in for the owner, may be something of a special case necessitated by the spoilage of the produce. Notably, the transaction takes place "before the court," and makes more sense as a lump sale to a buyer than as retail sale in a market.

[52] One apparent example is *m. Babaʾ Batraʾ* 5:8:
[A] One who sells wine or oil to his fellow—
[B] and they became more expensive or cheaper:
[C] [if the price changed] before the measuring utensil was filled: [it changed] for the seller;
[D] [if] after the measuring utensil was filled: [it changed] for the buyer.
[E] If there was a broker (*sirsûr*) between them [and] the jar broke: [it broke] for the broker.
[F] And he is required to let three drops drip [from the measuring utensil].
[G] [If] he bent and drained [the measuring utensil afterwards], lo, it is the seller's.
[H] And the shopkeeper is not required to let three drops drip.
[I] R. Judah says: "On the eve of the Sabbath at dusk, he is exempt [from letting three drops drip]."

This pericope seems to describe sale for consumption which takes place between one householder (the context presupposes that he is not a shopkeeper) and another ("his fellow"). In addition, the fact that in mid-transaction the parties are informed that the price has changed suggests that the transaction takes place in the marketplace (although this is hardly a necessary

small farmers marketed their own produce in Roman Galilee (although the passage just cited from *m. Demai* suggests that this was at least possible, and to the extent that land was held by freeholding peasants and not tenants [and even in such a case] it seems likely). To be sure, it is the householders on whose land the produce in question was grown who are presupposed in the discussion of a potentially usurious transaction in M5:7: "If he was the first of the reapers he may make a bargain with him [to accept payment now for later delivery] for [grain on] the threshing floor" [B–C]. It is by no means clear, however, that the buyer in this case is envisioned as a consumer: he may be a merchant (professional or occasional) buying up produce. At any rate, the buyer has sufficient disposable capital to pay now for later delivery. We are given no indication of the economic position of the seller: he may be a small farmer producing primarily for subsistence and selling off surplus production or a small cash crop, but a larger householder producing primarily for the market is not excluded. (It is worth noting that in the kind of transaction depicted the seller presumably sells at a discount [cf. M5:7 [K–

---

reading). However, [E] envisions a scale of transaction in which a broker might be involved. Moreover, *m. B. Bat.* 5:8 should be compared with the other pericopae with which it appears. In *m. B. Bat.* 5:6–7, there is nothing to place the case described specifically in a marketplace. Indeed, in 5:7 the Mishnah recommends renting the place in which the produce is located to guarantee transfer of ownership without a possessory act, and considers the case of produce that has not been harvested yet. Neither of these sound like small "retail" consumer transactions. In *m. B. Bat.* 5:10–11, a discussion of proper care for weights and measures (cf. Lev. 19 35–6; Deut. 25:13–19), a householder (*baʿal ha-bayit*) needs to clean his measuring utensils of residue only once yearly as opposed to the grain merchant (once monthly) and the shopkeeper (twice weekly). Since the point of this differential ruling is not merely the presumptive honesty of the seller but also the actual volume of buildup of residue, the householder seems to be involved in more casual selling. Finally, in *m. B. Bat.* 6:1–3 there is no necessity to locate the transactions in a marketplace. In particular, *m. B. Bat.* 6:2 includes the case of one who sells a cellar full of wine.

Elsewhere in the Mishnah, producers appear at first glance to be likely to market their produce themselves. These cases are not unambiguous, however. *m. Peʾa* 3:3: "One who harvests moist onions for the market, and maintains dry ones for the threshing floor [i.e., for storage]...." In this passage there is no way of knowing that the way the vegetables will make it to market will not be through the agency of a specialist. *m. Šebi.* 7:3: "let him not be one who picks (*lôqēṭ*) field [i.e., wild?] vegetables [in the Sabbatical year] and sells them in the marketplace (*šûq*)" (the reading *lôqēṭ* follows Epstein, *Nûsaḥ*, 229; Lieberman *TK*, 2, 554 [to *t. Šebi.* 5:10]). Since unsown seventh year produce is at issue and not regular agricultural produce, this may be something of a special case. *m. Maʿaś.* 1:5: "What is the threshing floor [of vegetables] for tithes [i.e., when are vegetables considered "completed," and thereafter prohibited for the lay Israelite until tithed]?... When are these things said? When he brings [them] to the market; but if he [brings] them to his house...." The language "he brings them" (*môlîk*) suggests that it is the owner who will actually bring them to the market, but this may be a way of expressing the choice of destination for the produce.

L]] in order to guarantee a purchaser for the produce and to minimize risk. Thus if M5:7 presupposes producers oriented towards market sale, these may be householders who can afford the luxury of taking a lower price.) Similarly, the transaction in M5:1 [H–K], in which a buyer who has acquired produce later wishes to sell it at a profit, may be seen as a transaction between relatively wealthy actors. If nothing else, the transaction is described in terms of wheat priced at a golden *dînār* to the *kôr* (a substantial measure, some 400 liters), and not in terms of *qabîm* of wheat per *ʾissār*. Neither party in the series of transaction in M5:1 need be a professional marketer: both may engage in this sort of trade only when the opportunity arises. In this case, too, since the sale does not involve immediate delivery, there is no reason for it not to occur in some other place.

If the Mishnah is relatively unconcerned with the questions of small farmers selling their produce when it deals with the rules for markets—although such farmers undoubtedly did[53]—this may betray something of the worldview of the Mishnah's framers. The primary foci of legislation on markets reflects ambivalence towards market specialists, who are both experts in valuing merchandise and cheats, and a concern for fair pricing. In contrast to the kind of speculative transactions described in M5:1, the marketplace is where basic consumer goods are acquired—i.e., a place that is conceived of as primarily providing a service, goods at an appropriate cost—and our tractate reflects a distinct interest in keeping it running fairly. Beyond this, as *m. Demai* 5:7, cited above, suggests, Rabbis are concerned with small farmers and markets primarily when questions of ritual are raised.[54] It may be worth suggesting that the people about whom the rules of *m. Babaʾ Meṣiʿaʾ* speak, whatever the source of their wealth (it may well have been land), did not live directly from the produce of fields, but bought their food from marketers, and stored their disposable wealth in the form of money.

3. Banks.

A "banker" (*šulḥānî*, from *šulḥān*, "table"; compare the Greek *trapezitēs* and the Latin *mensularius*), in *m. Babaʾ Meṣiʿaʾ*, as elsewhere in the Mishnah, is a professional handler of money. Bankers evaluate the quality of coins,

---

[53] Cf. R. MacMullen, "Market Days in the Roman Empire," *Phoenix* 24 (1970), 333–41.

[54] Indeed, outside of *m. B. Meṣ.* there are only two passages (*m. B. Bat.* 5:8, 10) that deal with the marketer in connection with the rules of the marketplace. The bulk of the contexts in which references to markets appear are related to ritual (tithing, oaths, etc.), with a few cases where markets are discussed in the context of the rules of damages or property relations (e.g., *m. B. Qam.* 8:1 [valuing the damage done to a person by considering the damaged person a slave for sale in the market]; *m. B. Bat.* 2:3 [where an artisan may open a shop; and whether neighbors can prevent or restrict an artisan]).

exchange coinage, accept deposits, and act as agents in the transfer of money.[55] With the exception of the lending of money at interest, which we ought not to expect in the Mishnah's exposition of the role of banks since this is prohibited by the Mishnah in general, these functions correspond quite closely to the patterns of the professional handling of money in the Greco-Roman world.[56] This is one of those many situations in which we should like to know to what extent the Mishnah's understanding of civil law was determinative for a more or less broad sector of Jewish society in Galilee—or at least expresses assumptions about what civil law consisted of

---

[55] In addition to the passages from *m. B. Meṣ.* cited in the text, the following should be noted: *m. Maʿaś Š.* 4:2 (exchange); *m. Šebu.* 7:6 (exchange). *m. Meʿil.* 6:5 basically parallels M3:11 (deposit) (see Section II.A.2). If the "nail of the *šulḥānî*" referred to in *m. ʿEd.* 3:8 and *m. Kel.* 12:5 refers to a nail upon which the moneychanger's scale was hung (as Maimonides took it) and not to some other fixture (as Rabad understood it) we have reference in these pericopae to the practice of exchange or testing. The reference to showing betrothal money "on the table" (*m. Qid.* 3:2) presumably refers to a "banking" establishment; the gloss in the Tosepta: "For he said only that he would show her [betrothal money] from his own" (*t. Qid.* 3:3), implies that the bridegroom in question is a banker who holds other people's money. More ambiguous is the reference to the man who says to his wife: "Lo, your divorce document is placed on the table" (*m. Ket.* 8:8), which may be a reference to documents deposited with a "banker." See also *t. Maʿaś. Š.* 1:1 (deposit); 3:3 (a variant of *m. Maʿaś S.* 4:2, dealing with exchange); *t. B. Qam.* 10:10 (exchange); the passages from *t. B. Meṣ.* are discussed below. See also *Sipre Deut.* 13 (ed. Finkelstein, p. 22) (examination of money).

In this section I refrain from discussing passages that deal with the "temple bankers" as they are described in the Mishnah (*m. Šeq.* 1:3; cf. *t. Šeq.* 1:8; 2:13; compare the references to the *trapezai* of the *kollybistai* that Jesus overturns [Mk 11:15; Mt. 21:12; Jn. 2:15; also a variant to Luke 19:45]; see A. Gulak, "Banking in Talmudic Law" [Hebrew], *Tarbiz* 2 [1931], 165–71) since these sources, even if historically accurate, describe an institution that had been destroyed with the destruction of the Jerusalem Temple itself in 70, and that was, at any rate different from that of moneychangers not tied to a temple or governmental institution.

[56] See L. Mitteis, "*Trapezitika*," *ZRG* (*Röm. Abteilung*), 19 (1898), 198–260; R. Bogaert, *Banques et banquiers dans les cités grecques* (Leiden: Sijthoff, 1968); R. S. Bagnall, R. Bogaert, "Orders for Payment from a Banker's Archive: Papyri in the Collection of Florida State University," *Ancient Society* 6 (1973), 108; Andreau, 1987. For the relationship of Rabbinic tradition to ancient banking practice see, in addition to the article by Gulak cited above, S. Krauss, 1911, 411ff. (I have not found the corresponding section in *idem*, *Qadmôniyôt ha-talmûd* [Berlin, Vienna, 1924], the Hebrew translation); and S. Ejges, *Das Geld im Talmud* (Vilna/Vilnius, 1930). The question of the extent, role, and economic significance of bank loans in the ancient world in general is currently debated, with the minimalist position articulated by M. I Finley (e.g., 1985, 141–2). Bogaert is inclined to limit the importance of bank credit in the Greek speaking world to consumer loans; Andreau argues that in the Latin part of the Empire the bankers were involved in commercial loan but limits the clientele of the bankers to those below the wealthiest members of society. For a more positive evaluation of the extent and role of banking, at least in fifth century Athens, see E. Cohen, *Athenian Banking* (Princeton: Princeton, 1992).

shared with other, non-Rabbinic groups in the society —and to what extent, from the point of view of actual praxis, Rabbinic legislation developed in a vacuum. While it is quite possible that the Mishnah chooses to overlook the existence of moneychangers who might lend money at interest, it is worth noting that when the Mishnah lists those people liable in any given transaction involving interest, there is nothing about the list to suggest that it is professional money handlers who are particularly involved in lending at interest (M5:11).[57] This may reflect the greater interest in non-professionals on the part of the people who produced the Mishnah (a tendency noted in connection with markets above), but may also point to a limited role for the *šulḥānî* in matters of credit in general.

To begin with the question of evaluation of coins, in the case of a coin suspected of being underweight, it is to a moneychanger, and not to a magistrate, that one brings the questionable coin (M4:6):

[A] Until when can one return [such a coin]?
[B] In the towns (*ba-kĕrākîm*), long enough to show [it] to a moneychanger;
[C] and in the villages (*ba-kĕparîm*) until Sabbath eves.

This pericope points out another feature pertaining to bankers: they are thought to be concentrated in towns, or rather, they can be expected to be found functioning in their official capacity every day of the week in towns, but not in villages.[58]

---

[57] Similarly, in the documents from the Judean Desert, there is no indication that the lenders are professional money lenders (see. *DJD* II 18, 114 [fragmentary]; *P. Babatha* 11; H. M. Cotton, "Loan With Hypothec: Another Papyrus from the Cave of Letters?" *ZPE* 101 [1994], 53–9 [fragmentary]).

[58] Cf. the versions of M4:6 in T3:20 and *Sipra Bĕ-har* 3:8 (107d) which add after [D]: "For it is the manner of the marketplace (*šûq*) to stand (*ʿômēd*) in the small towns (*ʿayyārôt*) from eve of Sabbath to eve of Sabbath." (Jastrow, *s.v.*, *ʿîr*, is presumably correct in listing *ʿayyārôt* as a variant plural of *ʿîr*; I could find no examples in ancient Rabbinic literature to the *ʿayyārâ* in the singular.) This gloss (it begins with an explanatory formula, *še-kēn*, and has a shift in terminology: the Mishnah discusses the *kĕrāk* and the *kĕpar*, but these *bāraîtôt* explain [A–D] in terms of an *ʿîr*) requires that *ʿômēd* be taken as "be suspended" (as argued by Krauss, 1924, vol 1.1, 74), although the language itself might be taken to imply that the market "continues" from Friday to Friday. At any rate the testimony of the *bāraîtôt* with respect to M4:6 [A–D] seems to place the availability of "bankers" in clear relationship to the articulation of marketplaces. Safrai's claims (Z. Safrai, 1994, 292), that "the *shulhani* was found only in the *polis*," and that "In the rural sphere ... there was no *shulhani*," citing M4:6 and T3:20, seems to me a misreading of these passages.

Although not referred to in *m. Baba' Meṣi'a'*, a closely related aspect of professional money handling attributed to the *šulḥānî* is the exchange of coins.[59] This is best expressed by *m. Ma'áser Šeni* 4:2:

[A] They redeem second tithe according to the cheaper market price (*kĕ-ša'ar ha-zol*):
[B] as the shopkeeper (*ḥenwānî*)[60] buys, and not as he sells;
[C] as the moneychanger (*šulḥānî*) breaks up (*pôrēṭ*), and not as he combines (*mĕṣārēp*).[61]

---

[59] Compare, once again, *OGIS* II 515 (Mylasa), illustrating the role of *trapezitai* in exchange, but also their official status: only they may exchange (foreign) currency, and they maintain a special right of exaction against unofficial exchangers in accordance with special guarantees (*exousia pratesthai katha ēsphalistai*; partially restored); and *OGIS* II 484 (*IGR* IV 352; Pergamum) in which, too, the official character of the professional moneychangers, and their apparent power over the marketplace are notable.

[60] In a citation of this pericope (but not in the text of the Mishnah itself preceding the chapter), the Leiden ms. of the Yerushalmi, and following it the Venice *editio princeps*, read *šulḥānî*, "moneychanger," here (*y. Ma'aś. Š.* 4:2 [54d]). This is presumably an error since (1) this citation retains the terminology of buying and selling in *m. Ma'aś. Š.* 4:2 [B] and of coin exchange in [C], and (2) the passage is cited again shortly afterwards using *ḥenwānî* in [B].

[61] Clause [C] is difficult to translate. The transaction presupposed is that the owner of second-tithe money in small denomination coins may "redeem" them for an equivalent value in higher denomination coins (just as one may redeem second tithe produce, Deut. 14:22–7), and take these coins to Jerusalem (see, e.g., *m. Ma'aś. Š.* 2:7–8). [A] states that second tithe is redeemed at "the cheaper market price," and the parallel construction between [B] and [C] suggests that they are both explications of the same principle, the former ruling in the case of second tithe produce, and the latter in the case of second tithe coins. The problem is that if we understand the terms *pôrēṭ* and *mĕṣārēp* to take their expected meanings of "give change" and "give a higher denomination coin for several lower value coins" respectively (as Gulak, 1931, 155 and n. 3 insists we must) [B] and [C] appear contradictory. (On *pôrēṭ* see: *m. Šebi.* 5:8; *m. Ma'aś. Š.* 2:9 [*m. 'Ed.* 1:9] [cf. *m. Ma'aś. Š.* 2:8 = *m. 'Ed.* 1:10]; in *m. B. Qam.* 10:1 *pôrēṭ* may have as its subject one who wishes to receive change, but the basic sense of "breaking up" a high denomination coin is retained; see also *t. Ma'aś. Š.* 4:13; *t. Ket.* 6:5; *t. B. Qam.* 10:22. For *mĕṣārēp* as "combining" coins [i.e., and replacing them with a higher denomination coin] see *m. Šeq.* 2:1. See further below, however.) If *OGIS* II 484 (*IGR* IV 352) is any indication, moneychangers accept more copper coins when selling *denarii* (i.e., when they are *mĕṣārēp*), than they give out when they give change (*pôrēṭ*) (this was also the view of the traditional commentaries, e.g., Maimonides, R. Samson of Sens, Bertinoro, *TY*, and *TYṬ, Mĕl'eket šĕlomoh ad loc.*). Thus, [C] states that one who redeems second tithe money (corresponding to the "produce") does so at a rate at which the purchasing power of the higher denomination coin (the "money") is relatively low (i.e., a rate at which one will need to spend more silver to redeem the same amount of copper). By contrast [B] rules that one exchanges second tithe produce for coins at a wholesale rate, where the purchasing power of the coin is high. The introductory clause [A] also implies that we should expect in [C] a ruling that

It is this difference in exchange rates that constitutes the wage of the moneychanger. As in the case of markets, there is no discussion of governmental administration of moneychangers. It is impossible to tell to what extent this reflects the reach of economic administration in Roman Galilee on the part of either the local or imperial government, and to what extent it reflects the absence of concern for (or, indeed, the conscious and ideologically motivated removal from consideration of) this topic.[62]

As the Mishnah has come down to us, a central distinction is made between professional money handlers and non-professionals with respect to deposits: when money is deposited, unbound moneychangers may make use

---

works to the advantage of the householders (i.e., by assigning a relatively lower value to the second tithe coins to be exchanged), and not to their disadvantage. (Cf. Gulak, 1931, 155, who argued that "the lower market price" in [A] works to the disadvantage of the householder undertaking the redemption; compare *m. Maʾaś. Š.* 4:1.)

It should be noted that the traditional commentaries on this pericope unanimously took *pôrēṭ* and *mĕṣārēp* to mean the exact opposite of their expected definitions: *pôrēṭ* is taken to refer to the purchase of copper coins by the banker, while *mĕṣārēp* is understood as "when the moneychanger combines *pĕrûṭôt* in order to give them to people in exchange for a *selaʾ*" (Bertinoro; in addition to the commentaries cited above, see Lieberman, *TK*, 2, 751 to *t. Maʿaś. Š.* 3:3 [ll. 6–7]). In favor of this interpretation is the fact that the terms *pôrēṭ* and *mĕṣārēp* are not entirely stable in Tannaitic literature. For instance, in *m. Maʿaś. Š.* 2:8, *pôrēṭ* is used to mean "combine second tithe coins into a larger coin (*selaʿ*); while in a closely parallel pericope in 2:9 the same verb means "to change into smaller denominations." Similarly, in *t. Maʿaś. Š.* 3:2–3 the same transaction (exchanging smaller second tithe coins for a larger denomination) is described with the participle *pôrēṭ* when exchange for silver coins is concerned, and again with *mĕṣārēp* when gold coins are involved (see Lieberman, *TK*, 2, 751, n. 2) (It is possible that *t. Maʾaś. Š.* 4:9 uses *pôrēṭ* in the sense of accept small coins in exchange for a larger.) If we wish to retain the sense of "give change" for *pôrēṭ* and "combine [in exchange for a higher denomination coin from the banker]" for *mĕṣārēp* in [C] and still resolve the problems associated with [C], we might perhaps consider [C], like [B], to deal with the exchange of *produce* for (copper) coins and to rule that one values the copper coins at the higher rate at which the banker values them when making change (see Maimonides, Code, *Maʿaśēr Šēnî* 4:18: "... and he should provide the coins [for the redemption of produce] as the banker gives change (*pôrēṭ*)"; see also *t. Maʿaś. Š.* 3:2–-3, which, despite the problematic usage of *pôrēṭ* and *mĕṣārēp* noted above, and assuming that it agrees with the rule in *m. Maʿaś. Š.* 4:2 and echoed in *t. Maʿaś. Š.* 3:1, may offer an analogous case: where one redeems second-tithe money with higher denomination coins it is that higher denomination coin that is to be converted into second-tithe that is valued "as the shopkeeper buys ... as the moneychanger breaks up ...."").

[62] Compare three documents to which reference has already been made: (1) *P. Oxy.* XII 1411 (Oxyrhynchus, 260), in which the strategos intervenes to force moneychangers to open their doors and receive coins; (2) *OGIS* II 515; and (3) *OGIS* II 484 (*IGR* IV 352), in both of which the running of the banks and the charge that the moneychangers charge for exchange are intimately tied to the town administration.

of it while lay depositaries in the same situation are prohibited from using the deposited money.[63] Since in the passage in which this distinction arises the non-professional depositary with whom the banker is compared is not paid, it follows that the banker, too, is assumed not to be paid directly for his care. It follows, too, that when the Mishnah explicitly distinguishes between the cases of bound and unbound money on deposit in connection with a *šulḥānî* (M3:11 [B–C]), the permission to use the unbound deposit should carry with it an increase in liability[64] corresponding to the increased risk to the deposit, but perhaps also in compensation for the benefit that the moneychanger is thought to derive from this use. Unfortunately the Mishnah does not specify what this benefit consists of.[65]

---

[63] M3:11, with a close parallel at *m. Meʿil.* 6:5. See above, Chapter II.D.2, n. 150, in which I suggest that the Yabnean dispute in M2:7 may have originally been a general dispute about the use of deposited money by non-professional depositaries. At any rate, this dispute is now localized in a discussion of the proceeds of the sale of a lost object, and in M3:11 (and *m. Meʿil.* 6:5) that a "householder" may not use money deposited unbound is taken as settled. Compare the institution of *depositum irregulare* in Roman law: see the passages from the Digest cited in Chapter II, and Mitteis, 1898, 209–12; F. Schulz, *Classical Roman Law* (Oxford: Clarendon, 1951), 519–20; W. W. Buckland, *A Textbook of Roman Law*, 3 ed., P. Stein (Cambridge: University Press, 1963), 469–70 (these last two argue that the institution was a post-classical one in Roman law); and the detailed review by Andreau, 1987, 533–44 (who tries to locate the institution within the classical law). Reference should also be made to the interest bearing account with a *trapezitēs* referred to in the Gospel parable of the talents (Mt. 25:14–30) or of the pounds (*mnai*; Lk. 19:12–27). The matter-of-fact assumption that the servant ought to have given the money to a banker and derived interest is fascinating in light of the later Christian understanding of usury (and of medieval Jewish moneylending).

[64] This increase in liability is made explicit in some manuscripts of the Mishnah, which add: "Therefore if they were lost he is liable for them" after M3:11 [C]. See the note to this pericope in Appendix I (and brief discussions in Sections A.2 and D.2 of Chapter I), and cf. the language of M2:7 [J–M], which also makes the principle of greater liability explicit and may be the source for the interpolations (if they are such) into M3:11.

[65] One possibility is investment of funds in a "partnership" that avoids the prohibition of usury. See, e.g., M5:4 [B–C]: "let him [the householder] not give him [the shopkeeper] money with which to purchase produce for half profit, unless he gave him his wage as an idle laborer" (see also T4:14–22). The other transactions in M5:4–6 (and Chapter 4 of *t. B. Meṣ.*) involve the provision of raw materials (produce, animals to be raised) and not liquid capital, which implies that the party providing the capital is thought to be a householder and not a professional money handler. Nevertheless, this possibility is an interesting one, especially in light of the current debates about the role of bankers in the commerce of the ancient world in general.

The Tosepta offers another possibility, in connection with funds designated second tithe money (*t. Maʿaś. Š.* 1:1):

> [G] And let him not give them to the banker [so that the latter might] adorn himself with them (*lĕhitnāʾôt bāhen*), or lend them to glory in them (*lĕhitʿaṭṭēr bāhen*);

In M9:12 [G], the *šulḥānî* has on deposit money belonging to a householder, but the issue at hand is not whether the money is bound or not but the keeping of accounts by the professional money handler for the householder, and, in particular, the authorization of the moneychanger to make payments on behalf of his client. Alternatively, the banker or shopkeeper advances money to the worker (cf. n. 68). The passage is especially important since it is one of the few occasions on which the arcana of Rabbinic law have found their way into the work of classical historians: it has been asserted that for specific legal reasons Jews developed the institution of the check.[66] In the context of a discussion of the liability of an employer to pay the wages of the laborer (and, according to M9:12 [A], any payment covered by the word *śĕkār*) "on that day" (Deut. 24:15; see also Lev. 19:13) the ruling is given

[H] [but] if [the householder gave them] so that rot might not arise on them, lo, this is permitted

It is the status of the money as second tithe that raises the possible prohibition in [G]; by implication, bankers are permitted to engage in these activities with profane money. In this passage, the *šulḥānî* is not deriving direct monetary benefit from his use of the money, but prestige by lending money interest free, or by appearing to be wealthy. A related tradition is worth citing in this context (T4:2):

[F] How does a person lease (*maśkîr*) money to a banker?

[G] To adorn himself with them (*lĕhitnāʾôt bāhen*), or to teach himself with them (*lĕhitlammēd bāhen*), or to glory in them (*lĕhitʿaṭṭēr bāhen*).

[H] If they were lost or stolen he is not liable for them.

[I] If they were taken from him by violence (*bĕ-ʾônes*), lo, he is like a paid depositary.

[J] If he was made a third party trustee (*ništallēš*) on their basis (*ʿalēhem*), it is prohibited because of [prohibited] interest.

[K] And if he [the householder (?)] did thus with sacred goods [i.e., leased out sacred money], lo, this one has stolen sacred goods (*māʿal*).

[J] is difficult to interpret. The reading *ništallēš* follows Gulak, 1931, 163, and Lieberman, *TK*, 9, 193–4. Lieberman took [J] to mean that if, because of the money that the banker leased (i.e., because of his apparent wealth), he became a paid trustee for another persons' property, he has used the initially leased money as security for the trusteeship, and put it at risk. Therefore the banker would become liable for any accidental or violent loss (*ʾônes*), as in any case of loan, and would no longer be "renting" the money, but borrowing it at interest. If Lieberman is correct, we have here reference to another source of income for bankers: paid deposits. At any rate, the kinds of uses to which a banker is thought in [G] to put money—for which, in fact, the banker is considered willing to pay a fee [F]—are either related to prestige (which, if Lieberman is correct, leads in turn to a banker's ability to receive fees from others), or to furthering his knowledge of coins in circulation. In neither of these two passages is lending money at interest, or investment in commercial enterprise one of the expected uses to which a *šulḥāni* might put money deposited with him.

[66] Bogaert, 1968, 52, n. 130 340–1, n. 206, citing Ejges, 1930, 83–4; Bagnall, Bogaert, 1973, 103, n. 82 and Andreau, 1987, 562 make reference to this note in Bogaert.

that: "If he sent him over[67] to the shopkeeper or to the moneychanger he has not transgressed it [the Scriptural commandments]." First, it should be noted that there is no inherent connection between the "sending over to a shopkeeper or banker" and the specific Scriptural obligation to pay one's worker. Rather, the pericope merely considers whether an employer's obligation has been fulfilled if rather than handing over coins the householder has sent the laborer to a banker. Second, while it may well be that the transaction in question does not take place with all three parties (banker, employer, and employee) present,[68] this does not mean that the institution involved was what we conventionally call a check: a document addressed to the payee in place of payment, which the recipient can redeem for money at the bank. There is no hint in our pericope that the transaction involves a written document on the part of the employer (although the professional presum-

---

[67] Hebrew: *himḥahû*. Ejges, 84, n. 5, reading the verb as "erase," took it to be the translation of the Greek *diagraphō*, with the sense of both "cross out" and "pay" (*überweisen*). This identification is difficult in light of the use of the verb in Greek in connection with banking practices. Although the imperative *diagrapson* is used in Ptolemaic orders for payment up to the middle of the third century (Bagnall, Bogaert, 1973, 94–5) the use of the verb or of the noun *diagraphē* in the context of banking does not convey the sense of "erasure" (on these terms see Mitteis, 1898, 213–18; Bogaert, 1968, 51–4, 57–9; and P. Drewes, "Die Bankdiagraphe in den gräco-ägyptischen Papyri," *JJP* 18 [1974], 103, who argues that *diagraphē* as the term for a document does not refer to orders for payment, the closest analogy to the transaction in M9:12). The root *mḥḥ/y* can also have the sense of "hit, strike" and in this context probably means "shoved him off."

[68] Certainly, the Babylonian tradition (B112a, views attributed to Rabbah and Rab Sheshet), which asks whether having been refused by the banker the worker can now go back (*ḥôzēr*) to his employer, makes most sense if the worker appears unaccompanied with his employer. Nevertheless, as Gulak noted (1931, 159), elsewhere transactions through a money specialist take place with all three parties together. One particular example, very similar to ours is worth citing, because it offers a rather different version of paying workers through a *šulḥanî* (T4:9; Y5:2 [10b]; cf. B73a):

[A] Ass drivers and workers were standing over him (*ʿômdîm ʿālāyw*) in the marketplace,
[B] and he said to the moneychanger:
[C] "Give me a *dînār* worth of coins (*māʿôt*) and I will see to them (*ʾaparnēsēm*),
[D] "and I will pay you the equivalent of a *dînār* and a *ṭĕrîsît* (cf. Latin *tressis*), which I have in my pouch."
[E] If he had [that much] in his pouch, it is permitted.
[F] But if not, it is prohibited.

The employer appeals to the banker on the spur of the moment, to advance money to him for workers who are present at the time. This transaction is, it should be noted, not one based on an "account" at the bank, but a short term loan. (Gulak, 1931, 163–4, thought that this passage is evidence of credit and clearing transactions for traders removed from their residences. The context, however, implies a local householder and not a trader, and the instant credit that the employer receives reflects local and personal, as opposed to institutional, trust.)

Institutions and Relationships 155

ably has a written register), nor is there any reason why the moneychanger or shopkeeper should not be considered to be acting on direct instructions from the employer. Third, even if the form of payment outlined in M9:12 [G] should be taken to be a check, it is likely that this reflects not financial development, but the rather narrow scope of transactions involving bankers or shopkeepers who are familiar with both payer and payee, and (in light of the fact that a shopkeeper is as good an example as a moneychanger) of the small scale of the transaction as well.

If nothing else, the discussion of banks in *m. Baba' Meṣi'a'* presupposes a society, or at least an audience within the society, for whom use of money, especially verification, exchange, and deposit, are important parts of everyday life. The absence of discussion of the involvement of moneychangers in loans may reflect the theological program of the Rabbinic movement, but if it may also be taken to result from actual practice, this absence also sheds some light on the real scale of activities available to the *šulḥānî*, who may conceivably have been incapable of making loans for more than small amounts or beyond the very short term because of the risks involved. (If wealthy householders did typically borrow money from bankers, it may be argued, we should have expected rules about when such loans are or are not prohibited.) One by-product of a system in which loans are undertaken by individuals is that economic obligations take on a personal character, so that the differential distribution of wealth and power is played out in a very immediate way. Another possible indication of the scale of banking is the proximity of rules concerning moneychangers and shopkeepers, and parallel discussions of these professionals, in a number of sources.[69] This suggests that for the producers of the Mishnah, bankers played the same role in society as did shopkeepers: the provision of a service that allowed the "householder" to live the appropriate life style. This same proximity also suggests that when we use the word "banker" we should not imagine a powerful institution controlling substantial assets, but a rather limited establishment involved in "retailing" money.

B. Economic and Social Relationships

The previous section focused on the extent, and especially the limitations, of economic institutions as they are described in *m. Baba' Meṣi'a'*. In part,

---

[69] M2:4 [A–D]; 3:11 (*m. Me'il.* 6:5); 9:12 [G]; see also *m. Ma'aś. Š.* 2:9 (which, although it does not refer to bankers, opposes the exchanging of coins with the establishment of an account with a shopkeeper); *m. Ma'aś. Š.* 4:2; *m. Šebu.* 7:6.

but only in part, this forms the background for an examination of the economic and social relationships in the tractate: for example, which transactions are executed by means of money, take place in the marketplace or are mediated by professionals? In the present section, I review these relationships to elucidate their connection to economic institutions, but also, and more importantly, as face-to-face relationships both between equals and between non-equals in which divisions of order, status or class may be played out.[70] Where possible, I have also examined the economic interests that may be reflected in the rules of the Mishnah. Since this study focuses on relationships described in the *m. Baba' Meṣi'a'*, I have chosen to leave out of consideration for the present relationships within the household (such as husband-wife, parent-child, or master-slave), which are referred to only sporadically in *m. Baba' Meṣi'a'*.[71] This exclusion is not meant to minimize the importance of household relationships, or to imply that one type of relationship is more "economic" or less "social" than the other. Indeed, in Rabbinic law a marriage is nothing if not a contractual relationship, while in relationships outside the household personal status can have legal implications.[72] The distinction does take into account the fact that the forces that play a role in structuring relationships of both kinds do so differently within the household than outside of it. To take one example: relationships between buyers and sellers, especially where trade is mediated between professionals, can become impersonalized in a way that household relationships, in particular where wives and slaves are few, are far less likely to. Thus, manifestations of hatred, love, fear or loyalty may be expected to be different in the context of a marriage than in an arrangement to buy or sell produce, and it is the latter type of relationship that *m. Baba' Meṣi'a'* deals with. The discussion roughly follows the order of presentation in the tractate.

---

[70] A useful discussion of the concepts of order, status and class occurs in P. Garnsey and R. Saller, *The Roman Empire: Economy, Society and Culture* (Berkeley: University of California, 1987), 109–23. See also G. E. M. de Ste Croix, *The Class Struggle in the Ancient Greek World*, 2 ed. (Ithaca: Cornell, 1989), 31–111 ("Class, Exploitation and Class Struggle"), especially 81–98 ("Alternatives to class" [i.e., status etc.]).

[71] See, e.g., M1:5; 3:10; 7:6. The last of these is particularly interesting, since it implies that even adult male children could be described as financially part of the household of their father. See further, J. R. Wegner, *Chattel or Person: The Status of Women in the Mishnah* (Oxford: Oxford, 1988); P. V. M. Flesher, *Oxen, Women or Citizens? Slaves in the System of the Mishnah* (BJS: Atlanta: Scholars Press, 1988).

[72] See e.g., *m. B. Qam.* 8:6 (where a list of compensations for various kinds of abuse is glossed: "This is the general rule: it all follows his [the planitiff's?] honor").

1. Finder and loser.

The discussion of the treatment of lost objects in *m. Baba' Meṣi'a'* is surprisingly long: it comprises the first two chapters of the tractate. As the numerous references to passages from Chapters 1–2 in the previous chapter indicate, the material on lost objects seems to show traces of considerable redaction from sources, sources that seem at times to approach the legal problems from rather different perspectives. There are essentially two legal issues that are dealt with in connection with lost objects: (1) whether and how one can acquire an object that one has found; and (2) what obligations arise for the finder who may not acquire the object, but must care for it instead. The first of these two topics shares a good deal with the way Roman jurists deal with similar problems and suggests a common set of concepts for discussing possession, ownership, and how they are acquired. Notably, these rules are discussed in *m. Baba' Meṣi'a'* without recourse to Biblical citations. The second topic derives ultimately from Scripture and is particularly characteristic of the Jewish legal traditions.[73]

The first two pericopae of Chapter 2 form a rhetorical frame in which objects that one finds are distinguished by whether one may acquire them, or whether one is obligated to proclaim the find publicly ("Which found objects are his, and which is he obligated to proclaim?" M2:1 [A]). The core of the pericopae consists of two matched lists of objects (M2:1 [C]; 2:2 [B]). The principle that determines the distinction is not made explicit, and seems to be a rather loose one: if an object can be presumed to have been consciously placed where it was found, it is considered not to be lost and must be proclaimed; and if it is readily identifiable, even if it can be presumed lost, it cannot simply be appropriated.[74] An Ushan gloss to M2:1 (M2:1 [E])

---

[73] There is some analogy between the obligation to care for a lost object and the Roman institution of *negotiorum gestio*, the intervention into the affairs of another person for that person's benefit and without their knowledge (see Buckland, 1963, 537–9; Schulz, 1951, 620–4). However, as Schulz already noted (p. 624, drawing an explicit contrast with the same verses that form the Scriptural basis of the Mishnaic rulings) the Roman institution protects the one who intervenes to save another's property, but does not require it. Moreover, the original focus of the Roman rules seems to have been the management of the affairs of individuals who were absent (see Schulz, 1951, 621) or dead (cf. D 3.5.3.pr. [Ulpian] quoting the praetorian edict), and the kinds of intervention imagined on the part of the *gestor* (see, e.g., D 3.5.1 [Ulpian] and throughout the title) are hardly so mundane as the feeding of a lost animal or the dutiful rolling or unrolling of a scroll.

[74] Presumably, if the finder is required to proclaim the find, the loser will be required to identify it in some way. What is not clear, however, is what criteria the finder is supposed to use in determining his obligation. (Any item might have distinguishing marks, but these may not be apparent to the finder.) For some items on the lists in M2:1–2 the reasoning seems to be that there are clear identifying marks (e.g., home made loaves, in contrast to bakers' loaves,

emphasizes that items that have some variation (this is exemplified by variations in such typically "generic" articles as fig rounds or loaves, M2:1 [G]) must be proclaimed. While the rhetorical and legal presupposition of M2:1–2 is that found objects fall into two categories, those that must be proclaimed and those that may be appropriated, M2:3 [A–E] introduces a third category: those things that one should leave where they are. Presumably this is because they have no distinguishing marks, but clearly have been placed where they are: if the finder removes them the loser will be unable to identify them.[75] More explicit is the tradition presented in M2:5:

[C] Just as the garment [in Deut. 22:3] is unique in that it has identifying marks and has claimants,

[D] so everything that has identifying marks and has claimants, he is required to proclaim.

This pericope invokes two criteria. The first is that the found object have identifying marks (this criterion is picked up in M2:7 [A–D]). The second, that the object have "claimants," seems to imply that the object be something (a) that the previous owner would want to retrieve,[76] but also (b) something that the owner should still expect to be able to retrieve. This is as close as the Mishnah gets to articulating the principle of *yēʾûš*, despair on the part of the owner of ever regaining his lost object, as determining lapse of possession or ownership.[77]

---

which are standardized). For at least one item, the small sheaves (*kĕrîkôt*), the determining factor is place: were these found in a public domain or a private one? As for bundles of coins or produce, or a stack of coins, distinguishing marks such as number or place (as Babli understood from this passage, B25a) or perhaps the knots themselves (cf. B25b, in connection with "bound fledglings," M2:3 [A]) are hardly the most stringent of criteria (cf. the dispute attributed to Rab Judah and R. Leazar in Y2:3 [8b] in which the former insists that the stack of coins in M2:2 [B] be made of "three coins from three kings," and the latter that the stack be made "like a tower" [*gôdālîn*; E: *gôdālôn*; cf. T2:7 *migdalôt*; see Lieberman, *Yerushalmi Neziqin*, 134 n.1]; both seem to require some distinctive characteristic for the stack itself). If nothing else, however, a stack of coins has clearly been placed where it is; scattered coins may well have fallen.

[75] So B25b.

[76] Cf. the minimum value of a *pĕrûtâ* assigned to a lost object for the requirement of proclaiming the find to arise, M4:7 [H].

[77] In a disputing gloss attributed to R. Simeon, *m. Kel.* 26:8, the criterion of *nityāʾašû habeʿalîm*, "the owners have despaired," is used to correct a rule distinguishing between property in the hands of a thief and that in the hands of a robber. *m. B. Qam.* 10:2 invokes the concept in connection with tax collectors, robbers, military forces, and brigands (*lisṭîm*), property washed away in a river (cf. *t. B. Qam.* 10:24 = *t. Ket.* 8:4), or a flock of bees that migrates. Roman jurists also considered the problems of possession in similar cases (see, e.g., D

Institutions and Relationships   159

From the perspective of the loser, the issue of intention or will is only hinted at in M2:5. In M1:3–4 this same problem is approached from the perspective of the finder, with the result that the determinative power of human will is greatly limited. When a person picked up a lost object on the demand of another, the one who picked it up can only claim it as his own if he did not hand it over (M1:3 [C–E]). Where the one who picked it up has already handed it over, the mere statement "I have gained possession over it first" is not sufficient (M1:3 [F–G]).[78] Similarly, the owner of property cannot

---

41.1.5.2–4 [Gaius], the ability to possess a flock of bees; 41.1.44 [Ulpian], retention or loss of possession of property carried off by force [wolves]).

Elsewhere in Tannaitic literature explicit connection between "despair" and lost objects occurs only rarely. See T2:2 (attributed, perhaps not accidentally, to a late Tannaitic figure, R. Simeon b. Eleazar), which includes "one who finds [something] on the road (*'rty'*, cf. Latin (*via*) *strata*) or the street (*pĕlaṭayyā'*, cf. Greek *plateia*)," together with one who saves something from wild animals or the surge, with the general ruling: "lo, these are his, for the owners despair of them." In the Amoraic literature, the concept is further fleshed out in terms of lost objects (see, e.g., Y2:1 [8b], a tradition attributed to R. Yohanan in the name of R. Simeon b. Yehosadaq that derives "despair on the part of the owners" from Deut. 22:3; and the stories about sages who lost coins in the market place and did not take them back when offered because of *yĕ'ûš*, Y2:3 [8c]). The notion of *yĕ'ûš* is somewhat analogous to the principle articulated in a number of Roman juristic texts, such as D 41.2.3.13 (Paul), which distinguishes between objects that diligent search would turn up (*quia praesentia eius sit et tantum cessat interim diligens inquisitio*, "because it is still present for him, and merely a diligent search in the meantime is lacking"), and those that are so lost that they cannot be found, for which possession lapses; and 41.2.25.pr. (Pomponius), which states that possession ceases when the object is so lost that it cannot be found; see also the text by Ulpian cited above (D 41.1.44). Although the tradition attributed to R. Yohanan in the name of R. Simeon b. Yehosadaq, cited above, identifies "despair" as a case where the object is "lost from him and from everyone" (not unlike the Roman juristic texts just noted), the Rabbinic concept of despair tends to have a distinctly subjective point of view (note the case cited from Y2:3 [8c], and see B26a-b [attributed to R. Nahman]): what is at issue is not only whether the object can be found, but whether the owner is (or can be presumed to be) still looking for the object. Compare D 41.1.57 (Javolenus): someone who finds something in the sea cannot get ownership until the original owner considers it abandoned.

[78] Lieberman, *Yerushalmi Neziqin*, introduction, p. 33, offers another interpretation of this pericope: in [F–G] the one who picked up the object hands it over thinking that it belonged to the one who asked him to pick it up; but in [C–E], he hands it over knowing that it was a found object. Thus, Lieberman locates the statement "I have gained possession over it" [D, G], in both cases, after the delivery of the object, and therefore in both cases the "finder" claims the object despite the fact that he has already handed it over. I confess that I do not understand this interpretation. (Is the claim "I have gained possession of it *first*" specific to [F–G], or is this implied in both cases [cf. *TYT*; Lieberman cites only "*'aḥarônîm*"]? On what basis should the "finder" in [C–E] retain a claim to the object after having turned it over? Lieberman's wording is quite terse, but he apparently concluded that it is from the request of the rider, "Give it to me" [C], that in [C–E] the one who picked up the object realized that it did

will wild animals (gazelles or birds) that are on his property into his possession, and preempt others who were actually chasing the animals, unless the animals cannot move freely enough to run or fly off the property (M1:4 [D–JJ]).[79] In the case of inanimate objects (such as money or utensils) the property on which they were found is partially determinative of who now owns the find (M2:3 [C] –4).[80] In this case, too, it is not the property owner's intention that establishes ownership of, for example, a utensil that someone else has found in the innermost part of a wall of a house (M2:4 [H]), but the fact that the property owner owns the house.

As noted above, the second aspect of the Mishnah's treatment of lost objects is the obligation to care for items that are not deemed open for appropriation. In a sense, the finder of a lost object becomes a kind of depositary.[81] Unlike a depositary, M2:7 [E–H] implies that the finder has limited rights to the use of the find, at least to set off the expenses of maintenance ("Let everything that produces and eats produce and eat ..."").[82] On the other

---

not belong to the rider.) At any rate, however, the pericope seems to turn on what the finder does or says, and not on the information that he receives from the other party. Nor does the distinction that Lieberman makes between [C–E] and [F–G] follow from M1:3 itself in which both [D–E] and [F–G] deal with the implications of the same case [C].

[79] For the ownership of wild animals, and the requirement that they be physically captured, compare, e.g., Gaius, 2.67–8; D 41.1.3.1; 41.1.5.1 (Gaius); 41.2.3.14 (Paul). The Mishnaic rule differs in that it considers animals that cannot get away to be acquired by intention if the finder owns the land on which they were found.

[80] Compare *thesauri inventio* (i.e., finding a treasure) in Roman law. See Buckland, 1963, 218ff.; and D 41.1.31.1 (Paul); 41.1.63 (Tryphonius); 41.2.3.3 (Paul); 41.2.44 (Papianus); 49.14.3.10–11 (Callistratus). It should be noted that although the Roman jurists did not pay much attention to the obligation to "proclaim" treasures that one has found, there are traces of this kind of obligation, explicit in at least one case (D 49.14.13.11 [Callistratus]), in connection with finds in which the Roman treasury has an interest (treasures on imperial or public property, or funeral treasures). In addition, passages that distinguish treasures buried for safe keeping (for which appropriation is actionable for theft) from those that are ancient and ownerless presuppose some sort of mechanism for making the distinction.

[81] This is not explicit in the Mishnah, although if, as I have argued, M2:7 [I–M] properly pertains more generally to deposits, the idea that a find is considered a kind of unpaid deposit is implied. Compare T2:22 (cf. Y2:10 [8d]; B30a), which, after a series of rules closely related to M2:8 (T2:21–2), makes the correlation of finds and deposits explicit: "Just as you say in [the case of] a lost object so do you say in [the case of] a deposit" (T2:22 [I]). This is followed by a parallel to M2:8 [D–E], now introduced: "One who *deposits* a garment with his fellow ..." (T2:22 [JJ]).

[82] M2:7 [G–H] makes it clear that the reason the finder is entitled to sell the object is that the finder thereby prevents loss (due to expenses) to the owner. On the other hand, when the found animal does "produce and eat" it is not automatically clear that the permission to benefit from the animal was strictly limited to the value of the labor expended by the finder (as according to, e.g., T2:20 [cf. B28b]; so also Maimonides, *Code, Gĕzēlâ wa-ʾabēdâ* 13:15). A

hand, this pericope does not openly stipulate that the finder is entitled to compensation for expenses. Indeed, the requirement to sell unproductive finds [F] (and the verse exegesis that follows [G–H]) may be taken as aimed at preventing a situation where the finder might legitimately claim compensation.[83] By contrast, M2:9 [F–G] allows for compensation, but only to a limited extent:

---

possible interpretation of M2:7 [E–F] is that the finder of a productive animal is considered a kind of borrower with general permission to use the animal for personal benefit. Some slight support for this reading comes from the dispute over what to do with the proceeds of the sale of the unproductive find [I–M], which follows in the pericope. I have already suggested that this dispute may originally have been concerned with the deposits of money in general (see Chapter II.D.2, n. 150, and above section A.3, n. 63). In context, however, the inclusion of this dispute form here may be connected with the idea that the finder was entitled to use the find, which the money in question now replaces. Indeed, since in M3:11 the prohibition of householders using deposited money seems settled, the appearance of the Yabnean dispute in M2:7 may reflect a specialized reinterpretation of the dispute, which centers on the proceeds from the sale of found objects alone. Since an animal does require feeding and maintenance, but the money replacement does not, the dispute might then center on whether the money is like the find itself (R. Tarfon) or like a deposit (R. Aqiba). Since the use of the money in question benefits the finder alone (i.e., since money requires minimal upkeep) and yet according to one view the finder is permitted to use it, it is possible that in [E] as well, the found animal was considered a kind of loan, to be used for the finder's benefit.

[83] M2:7 [H]: "See how [i.e., at what value?] you return it to him." Although in principle the finder may be entitled to claim compensation, this comment, it seems to me, instructs the finder not to accrue expenses or otherwise diminish the find (see further the note to M2:7 in Appendix I). M2:8 also does not explicitly refer to compensation, but here there is nothing in particular that suggests that the author of M2:8 did not intend for the finder to be eligible for compensation. Compare the related pericope in the Tosepta, T2:22 (referred to above):

[I] Just as you say in [the case of] a lost object so do you say in [the case of] a deposit.
[J] One who deposits a garment with his fellow—
[K] he should shake it out once in thirty days (=M2:8 [D]),
[L] and he should spread it in accordance with its needs, but not for his honor (=M2:8 [E]).
[M] If it was great, he takes his wage (*śĕkārô*) from it (*mi-menāh*).

Since [M] discusses reward (*śākār*), "it was great" refers to the labor involved with the upkeep of the deposit. Lieberman, TK, 165, took [M] to refer to depositaries only (citing M2:9 [F–J] as the law for lost objects), but the implication of the introductory clause that the rules for deposits and finds are analogous (T2:22 [I]) makes this difficult. More problematic is the rule that the finder takes his wage *mi-menāh*. The feminine pronominal ending presumably agrees with *kĕsût*, "garment," in the previous sentence (and M2:8 [D]). This may imply that at a certain point the finder is entitled to sell the deposit to recoup "wages" (at which point the depositary or finder will no longer be caring for the object and henceforth not eligible for a wage). Another possibility is that the wage consists of the use of the garment for the finder's benefit, in which case this ruling sees the found object as a kind of loan (see the discussion of

[F] [If] he had given up a *selaʿ* let him not say: "Give me a *selaʿ*."
[G] but he gives him his wage as an idle laborer.

This passage is in tension with the material that follows it immediately (M2:9 [H–J]), which allows the finder to guarantee himself full compensation, or to evade the obligation. This last tradition may be a later supplement intended to resolve a perceived inequity in the law.[84]

In considering the social background of the treatment of lost objects, it is worth considering the kinds of objects people are thought to lose or find: garments,[85] domestic animals,[86] wild animals,[87] written deeds,[88] a variety of goods available in the marketplace,[89] articles of considerable value (books; vessels of gold, silver or glass),[90] and baskets or sacks.[91] Where Roman jurists, for instance, talk about finding a "treasure," the scale of Rabbinic legislation is rather more homey. This does not mean that the people who produced *m. Babaʾ Meṣiʿaʾ* were poor; indeed, the general argument of the first part of this chapter is that they (or their target audience) were not. It is important to

---

M2:7 in the previous note). (Alternatively, *mi-menāh* may refer to *běhēmâ*, "animal," and may be the beginning of the discussion of a rule pertaining to animals without making the transition explicit; note that T2:23 follows immediately with rules pertaining to animals.)

[84] On the textual and literary problems of M2:9 [F–J] see the note to M2:9 in Appendix I. Whether or not we read the word *ʿimmô* in [H], the point of [H] is that the finder can guarantee himself full compensation either by means of self help (reading *ʿimmô*) or by stipulation at the outset (omitting *ʿimmô*). Properly speaking, [G–H] may refer to the opportunity costs lost in the time-consuming activity of returning an animal that repeatedly escapes (M2:9 [D]), and not to the expenses of long term care, and arguably discusses a different kind of problem than M2:7 [E–H]. But to the extent that [H–J] (or at least [I–J], if we read *ʿimmô* in [H], see Appendix I) can be set at the moment of the find, where no distinction can yet be made between out of pocket expense and lost time, the implication is that the author of [H–J], at least, made no such distinction.

[85] M1:1; 2:5 (citing Deut. 22:3).

[86] M2:9–10 (the relationship of these pericopae with each other is discussed in Chapter II.A.2); the discussion of M2:7 implies rules concerning an animal (which "produces and eats"). M1:2 also deals with a domesticated animal, but may not be dealing with found objects at all but rather with the more general problem of claims at court. This may underlie the statement (with problematic attribution) in B2a, 8a: "The first part [of this pericope] deals with found objects, the last with buying and selling," that is, M1:2 deals with disputed ownership of things bought and sold, and not merely lost objects. Compare the discussion of M1:1–4 in Chapter II.C.3.

[87] M1:4.

[88] M1:6–8.

[89] M2:1–2; M2:3–4.

[90] M2:8.

[91] M2:8 [H].

note that this list does have its *Sitz im Leben* in the town: there is a great emphasis on market goods, on things found in a store or at a banker's table (M1:4), and on written deeds. Domestic animals are mentioned, but do not make up the overwhelming focus of attention, and it is not impossible for a town household to keep a domestic animal or two.

A second important point concerns the question of social equality and hierarchy. In principle all people (or at least all adult males) are equal before the law: in the court setting of M1:1 there is no hierarchical distinction made between parties; similarly, not even the divinely sanctioned authority of a father can nullify the finder's obligation towards the lost object and its owner (M2:10 [D]), because the law falls on all Israelites equally. However, there are breaks in this equality. The rule, "If he found a sack or a basket, if it is not his habit to take up [such things], lo, let him not take it up" (M2:8 [H]), introduces an aspect of personal honor and dignity: the finder is not asked to undertake something that would be unseemly. Considerations of ritual purity are taken to exempt the finder from having to deal with an animal found in a cemetery (M2:10 [C]). Whether this passage deals with priests or with lay Israelites observing priestly purity, it presupposes a particular hierarchical division between those people who are prepared to become impure and those who are not.[92] Finally, Chapter 2 ends with an interesting pericope in which the obligations of sons and disciples to their fathers and teachers are compared, in favor of the teachers. Thus M2:11 hints at a social code (theoretical or not) in which, when given a choice between saving one's own property, or that of one's father or teacher, or of a stranger, there is a scale of values that determines to whom one's obligations lie first.

---

[92] G. Hamel discusses purity rules and observance in the context of social status; see, e.g., G. Hamel, *Poverty and Charity in Roman Palestine, First Three Centuries C. E.* (*Near Eastern Studies* 23: Berkeley, California, 1990), 82–6. In a passage related to M2:10 [C], *Sipre Deut.* 222 and 225 (ed. Finkelstein, pp. 256, 257–8) reads: "... if he was a priest and it was in the cemetery, or an elder and it is not in accord with his dignity (*ʾēnāh lĕpî kĕbodô*) ... he is exempt." Thus *Sipre Deut.* explicitly connects this tradition with priests, (although it, too, cites a tradition about "dignity" to which compare M2:8 [H]). In the Mishnah, however, as in the close parallel to our Mishnah cited in *Mek. Kaspāʾ* 20 (ed. Horovitz-Rabin p. 325), the person who is permitted to avoid becoming impure is not explicitly a priest. It is not impossible that a non-priest maintaining a high level of priestly purity is intended M2:10 [C]. This may mean that the pericope (or fragment) is relatively early (since material dated to the earlier period is consistently interested in lay purity) but this is hardly necessary, and in any case does not mean that at the end of the second century lay purity was not an important form of piety. For the literature see A. Oppenheimer, *The ʿAm Ha-aretz: A Study in the Social History of the Jewish Period in the Hellenistic-Roman Period* (Arbeiten zur Literatur und Geschichte des hellenistischen Judentums 8: Leiden: Brill, 1977), 114–6 and *passim*.

2. Deposits.

The rules for deposit take up nearly all of Chapter 3 in *m. Baba* Meṣi'a*, and are referred to elsewhere in the tractate as well.[93] The most systematic exposition of the liabilities of depositaries is given in M7:8 [C–H] (=*m. Šebu.* 8:1):

> [C] There are four watchmen:
> [D] the unpaid depositary (lit. watchman), and the borrower, and the paid depositary (lit. wage-bearer) and the renter.
> [E] The unpaid depositary swears for everything;
> [F] and the borrower pays for everything;
> [G] the paid depositary and the renter swear for the break, for the captured [animal], and for the dead [animal];
> [H] and they pay for the loss and for the theft.

These rules are supplemented by a rejoinder (M7:10 [E–G]) that allows any of these "watchmen" to alter their liabilities by stipulation in the contract. What links the rules of M7:8 [C–H] together is the fact that all four "watchmen" hold property that belongs to another, and are responsible, to varying degrees, for the safekeeping of that property.[94] In addition, all of these categories derive on some level from the exegesis of Exodus 22:6–14.[95] The requirement that the depositary who is exempt from payment must take an oath derives, for instance, from Exodus 22:7 and especially 22:10.[96] The connection with Scripture defines the choice of terminology for describing

---

[93] Outside the tractate, unpaid depositaries are referred to by title in *m. Šeq.* 4:1; *m. B. Qam.* 4:9; 7:6; *m. Šebu.* 8:1 (parallel to M7:8 [C–H]), 2; see also references to the verb *hipqîd*, "deposit," or the noun *piqādôn*, "an object on deposit," *m. Dem.* 3:4; *m. Ket.* 9:2; *m. Soṭ.* 7:1; *m. Giṭ.* 3:5; *m. B. Qam.* 9:7, 8; 10:6, 7; *m. Šebu.* 4:5, 8; 5:1–3; 7:4; *m. Ker.* 2:2; *m. Meʿil.* 6:5 (close parallel to M3:11); *m. Toh.* 8:2; *m. Makš.* 6:3. Paid depositaries are mentioned in M6:6–7; 7:8, as well as *m. B. Qam.* 4:9; *m. Šebu.* 6:5 (a near parallel to M4:9); 8:1, 6. See also the use of *piqādôn* in *m. Šebu.* 6:7, in the context of a discussion of loans against a pledge, and cf. M6:7 in which one who lends against a pledge is a paid depositary with respect to it.

[94] Cf. the Roman juristic texts in which deposit can shade into a form of loan (D 16. 3. 24; 16. 3. 25. 1 [Papinian]; 16. 3. 26. 1 [Paul]; 16. 3. 28 [Scaevola]; 16. 3. 29. 1 [Paul]; in addition to the passages cited above in Chapter II.D.2 and the discussion of *depositum irregulare* in Section A.3 above) or hire (e.g., D 16. 3. 1. 8–10 [Ulpian]).

[95] See Chapter II.A.1. For the problem of the derivation of the "renter" (*śôkēr*), see H. Lapin, "Early Rabbinic Civil Law and the Literature of the Second Temple Period," *JSQ* 2 (1995),155–6, n. 16.

[96] M3:1 goes further in granting the double payment required of a thief to the depositary if the latter paid although the depositary was entitled to take an oath.

the levels of liability for the renter and wage-bearer: theft, breakage, capture, and death.⁹⁷

Systematic though this passage may be, it leaves out certain important details. First, nowhere in the passage, or in *m. Baba' Meṣi'a'* in general, are we told what form the oath that the depositary swears takes. Certain passages elsewhere in the Mishnah may be taken to mean that the oath supports the counter-claim of the depositary against the owner who comes to retrieve the deposit.⁹⁸ Other passages, outside of the Mishnah, seem to imply that the depositary takes a more formulaic oath corresponding in some way to the Biblical oath "that he did not stretch out his hand (*šālaḥ yādô*) to the property of his fellow" (Ex. 22:7, 10), and echoing the language of Exodus 22:8: "For every matter of transgression (*pešā'*) ...."⁹⁹ Second, we are not told what

---

⁹⁷ To the terms in M7:8 (*gĕnēbâ, šeber, šĕbûyâ, mētâ*) compare the terminology of Ex. 22:6–14 (*gunnab*/*gānob yiggāneb, nišbār, nišbâ, mēt*). See also *Mek. Nĕzîqîn* 16 to Ex. 22:9 (ed. Horovitz-Rabin, p. 303), and the brief discussion of that passage in Chapter II.A.1.

⁹⁸ See *m. B. Qam.* 9:7 [G–J], 8 [A–D]:
 [G] [Owner:] "Where is my deposit,'
 [H] [Depositary:] "It was lost (*m. B. Qam.* 9:8 [B]: stolen)."
 [I] [Owner:] " I demand an oath from you (*mašbiʿak ʾanî*)."
 [J] [Depositary:] "Amen."
While the contents of this oath are not stated, the context implies that the depositary swears that the deposit was lost (or stolen) to satisfy the owner. See also *m. Šebu.* 8:1–6.

⁹⁹ See *y. Šebu.* 8:1 (38b): "What does he swear? 'I did not transgress (*lōʾ pāšaʿtî*)'" (it is not clear whether this is the conclusion of the *bāraîtāʾ*, which precedes this tradition, or an anonymous later gloss to the *bāraîtāʾ*, on the word *pšʿ* see below). This same oath is presupposed by the Babli B82b, 83a: "It is all well (*bi-šĕlāmāʾ*) that an unpaid depositary swears that he did not transgess (*lōʾ pāšaʿ*) with respect to it, but as for a paid depositary ...." (It should be noted that this statement arises in a discussion of whether a certain act falls under the heading of *pĕšîʿâ*—by this time a term for "negligence"—and it may be that it is this that determines the form of the oath. Nevertheless, it remains possible that the Babli is saying that in this case the unpaid depositary can take the conventional oath, but asks about the paid depositary in the same case). The same formula may also be presupposed by *Mek. Nĕzîqîn* 16 (ed. Horovitz-Rabin, p. 300) to Ex. 22:7 (= 17 [p. 304], to Ex. 22:10), which glosses "[and swears] that he did not (*ʾim lōʾ*) stretch out his hand to the property of his fellow" with the following:
 [1] "Reaching out the hand" is said here (Ex. 22:7) and "reaching out the hand" is said there (22:10);
 [2] just as here an oath [is referred to], so there an oath;
 [3] just as there [the oath uses the divine name spelled] with *Y-H* [Ex. 22:10: "An oath of the Lord [*YHWH*] shall be between them..."], so here with *Y-H*.
 [4] just as here in a court, so there in a court;
 [5] just as here ["reaching out the hand" refers to use] for his own needs, so there for his own needs.
 [6] just as here "On every matter of *pešaʿ*" (Ex. 22:8), so there "On every matter of *pešaʿ*."

the positive responsibilities of the depositary are.[100] Third, the liability for a depositary who does not live up to (unstated) responsibilities is left unspecified.

To a certain extent, liability for failure to perform one's responsibilities is discussed in the two supplementary pericopae that follow M7:8 (M7:9–10 [D]). In M7:9 [A–G], the absence of *ʾônes*[101] implies a kind of passive negligence: failure to prevent the death of the deposited animal. In [J–K] active negligence is introduced: leading an animal to a place where it is likely that it will be hurt.[102] In M7:10 [A–D], in addition to active negligence ("He took

---

The final clause [6] certainly implies that the oath referred to in Ex. 22:7, 10 is somehow related to the subject matter of 22:8: it is at least possible that the oath form *še-loʾ pāšaʿtî*, "that I did not commit *pešaʿ*," is intended. More complicated is the oath attributed to Rab Sheshet (*b. B. Qam.* 107b; B6a): "One makes him [an unpaid depositary] swear to three oaths: [1] '[I swear] an oath that I did not transgress with respect to it;' [2] '[...] an oath that I did not stretch out my hand to it;' [3] '[...] an oath that it is not in my possession.'" Maimonides, *Code, Šĕʾēlâ û-piqādôn*, 6:1 took this to mean: "[1] That he watched it in the manner of watchmen, [3] and that such and such happened to it and it is not in his possession, and [2] that he did not stretch out his hand to it before that event happened which made him exempt [from paying but obligated to take an oath]." Maimonides' paraphrase reflects a combination of a preset formula with a requirement for the depositary to swear to the truth of his claim (previous note). Notably, without Maimonides' interpretation (and ignoring the insistence in the Talmudic text that there are three separate oaths, which for the Babli could have different implications, as the material that follows immediately at *b. B. Qam.* 107b shows) Rab Sheshet's triple formula utilizes terminology that overlaps considerably in meaning (Rashi, in his comment to M3:1 itself [B33b] cites only a double formula: "That he did not transgress with respect to it and that he did not reach out his hand to it"), and may reflect the amplification of a tradition according to which the depositary swore only "that he did not transgress." In this connection, it is worth noting that already Josephus, *Ant.* 4.287, thought that the depositary had to swear that he did not lose the deposit through his own intention (*boulēsis*) or malice (*kakia*) and that he had appropriated no part of the object.

[100] In M3:6, what is disputed is whether the depositary in charge of rotten produce is required to let them rot ("lo, let him not touch them" [B]) or whether he should sell it in a court authorized sale. But neither view gives any indication of what is normally required of a depositary (even one who holds "let him not touch them" must surely have in mind a basic norm of expected activity). As noted in the previous section, M2:8 gives instructions for the care of certain types of lost objects; closely related material in the Tosepta is supplemented: "and just as you say in [the case of] a lost object, so do you say in [the case of] a deposit" (T2:22).

[101] On this term see the note to M7:9 in Appendix I.

[102] M7:9 [I–K] is clearly a supplementary form ("When [does this apply]?...) that is intended to introduce what I have termed active negligence. The precise relationship between M7:9 [I–K] and the rest of the pericope is not obvious, however. The reference to brigands in [K] suggests that [I–K] refers back to [G] and thus supplements the entire pericope [A–H]. Alternatively, [H–K] could be read as an independent pericope that has been added to supplement [A–G]. In support of this is the inclusion of the word *ha-zĕʾēb*, "the wolf" in [H] in some manuscripts of the Mishnah, an inclusion that brings [H] into some tension with [A] (see the note to M7:9 in Appendix I).

it up to the tops of the peaks ..." [D]), mismanagement or mistreatment is introduced ("[If] he afflicted it [*sigpāh*] and it died ..." [B]), although the parallel structure of [A–B] and [C–D] suggests that the Mishnah may not be making a clear distinction between these forms of "negligence." The clear implication of these passages is that the exemption from payment for the unpaid and paid depositary and for the renter in a case of breaking, capture or death applies only when the damage or loss arose due to *ʾônes*; in the absence of *ʾônes* the depositary would be liable. The three forms of culpable handling of a deposit, active or passive negligence and mistreatment, are all termed in later Rabbinic literature *pešîʿâ* ("transgression," although generally translated "negligence").[103] The concept of negligence itself, however, remains undeveloped in Tannaitic literature.[104]

---

[103] The use of the noun *pešîʿâ* (Aram. *pešîʿûtāʾ*)in connection with some sort of failure on the part of the depositary is at least in part determined by Ex. 22:8. Appearing in the context of a passage dealing with deposits that verse reads "For every matter of *pešaʿ*, ... to the divine tribunal (*ha-ʾelôhîm*, lit. "god(s)") shall come the matter of both [parties], and he whom the divine tribunal finds wicked (*yaršîʿun* [plural]) shall pay double to his fellow." The root meaning of *pešaʿ* is transgression, and since Ex. 22:8 follows a verse dealing with an oath "that he did not extend his hand," reflecting some kind of use or appropriation, and refers to a double payment as penalty, as in the case of theft (Ex. 22:3), it is presumably a charge of theft or misappropriation that is at issue in Ex. 22:8, and not negligence (for *pešaʿ* as sin see the ancient translations: Tg. Neofiti, *ḥiṭayyāʾ*; a Genizah Targum [T–S 20. 155. col. 3, in M. L. Klein, *Genizah Fragments of the Palestinian Targum to the Pentateuch* (Cincinnati: HUC, 1986), 1, 291], *ḥṭy* [i.e., *ḥaṭāʾê?*]; Pešiṭta, *ḥṭʾ*; LXX, *adikia*; the same meaning is likely to be behind the use of a form of *ḥôb*, "debt," but also "sin" [cf. Tg. Onk. to Gen. 20:9, where *ḥābît* translates *ḥaṭāʾtî*]: Tg. Neofiti, margin; Tg. Onk.; cf. U. Cassuto, *A Commentary on the Book of Exodus*, tr. I. Abrahams [Jerusalem: Magnes, 1967], 285 who took *pešaʿ* as negligence; see also M. Fishbane, *Biblical Interpretation in Ancient Israel*, rpt. corrected ed. [Oxford: Clarendon, 1985], 172–3, n. 23, who saw Ex. 22:8 as a charge of theft, but took *pešaʿ* in this case to mean "contestation" at court). The connection between the verb *pāšaʿ* and extending one's hand to the deposit is also made in *Mek. Nĕzîqîn* 15, to Ex. 22:7, and 16, to Ex. 22:10 (ed. Horovitz-Rabin, 300 ll. 9–10; 304 ll. 1–5; cited above) and *Mek. Nĕzîqîn* 15 (300, ll. 12–15) (see also the other passages linking the dispute about the inception of *šĕlîḥût yād* in M3:12 to the exegesis of the word *pešaʿ* listed by Horovitz in the notes thereto).

In later Talmudic usage the term *pšʿ* can continue to mean theft or misappropriation (see, e.g., *b. B. Qam.* 54b, commenting on the tradition in *m. B. Qam.* 5:7 that the rule of double payment for theft [among other rules] applies to all animals, glosses *ʿal kol dĕbar pešaʿ* with *ʿal kol dĕbar pešîʿâ*, where the context requires that it mean theft [note, however, that the context of this gloss is the rule of theft, and not precisely that of deposits]). A related usage, also connected to the use of *pešîʿâ* as "transgression," is that of misuse or improper treatment (e.g., B83a: a rule that porters who use a kind of pole [*ʾagdāʾ*; on the text see S. Friedman, *Talmud Arukh: BT Bava Meziʾa VI, Commentary* (Jerusalem: JTSA, 1990), 403–7] to carry jars and broke the jars are liable is glossed: "What is the reason? [The load] was [too] much for one and [too] little for two, [and the case is thus] near to *ʾōnes* and near to *pěšîʿâ*." Since the load was too much for a single porter, what makes this a case of *pěšîʿâ* may be something more than a kind of "active negligence," but actually an improper procedure that in and of itself endangered the load. (See also Tosafot, *s.v. sîgpāh* [B93b], who question the significance of the rule of M7:10[B] ["[If] he afflicted it and it died, it is not *ʾōnes*"]: "... for it is obvious that this is a case of outright *pěšîʿâ*..."; see preceding note.) Thus, it is possible that the oath formula *še-loʾ pāšaʿtî*, is to be translated "that I did not treat it improperly [i.e., make improper use of; perhaps also "steal"]" (especially if the tradition of the oath formula predates the articulation of the later Rabbinic use of *pěšîʿâ* as "negligence"). In the more general usage of the term *pěšîʿâ* as "negligence," it is frequently difficult to tell whether what is meant is a kind of passive failure to take protective steps, or an act that puts the deposit in an environment of potential risk (e.g., Y3:1 [9a], "He had witnesses that it was stolen due to *pěšîʿâ*"; B5a, "...and one died due to *pěšîʿâ* ...").

In connection with this discussion of terminology, mention should be made of the term *bûsyāʾ*, which may be a Tannaitic term for "negligence" (T5:10–2 [cf. Y5:6 (10b) (Aramaic paraphrase); *b. B. Qam.* 116b; some traditions have *kûsyāʾ*; on the reading *bûsyāʾ* see Lieberman, *TK* 9, 214–5)]; T10:25–6). In the passages in which *bûsyāʾ* occurs, it is used in the context of indemnity or insurance: in T5:10–2 one who contracts to raise an animal agrees to pay full damages if the animal dies *bě-bûsyāʾ*, but only half if not *bě-bûsyāʾ*; in T11:25–6 a guild of ass drivers or of pilots will not replace an ass or a ship for a member who loses it *bě-bûsyāʾ*. What the term refers to precisely is not clear: it may be negligence (failure actively or passively to take proper care; e.g., Lieberman *TK*, 9. 215; M. Sokoloff, *A Dictionary of Palestinian Aramaic* [Ramat Gan: Bar Ilan, 1990], *s.v.*), but it could also refer to a form of misuse or mistreatment. Note that Tg. Ps. Jon., to Ex. 22:8 translates *pešaʿ* with *bûsyāʾ* (emended from *kûsyāʾ*; Lieberman, *Yerushalmi Neziqin*, 159 [to l. 79]). In light of the testimony of the other ancient translations of this word, cited in the previous note, which tended to take the Hebrew word as a form of "sin," a similar meaning for *bûsyāʾ* is attractive in here (transgression, and in the Tosepta passages perhaps misuse). However, Ps. Jon. explicitly reads in other Rabbinic rulings in Ex. 22:6–14 (notably the distinction between a paid and unpaid depositary), and may be projecting a Rabbinic concept of negligence onto the Biblical text. At any rate, the absence of any other Tannaitic word for negligence, the limited range of use that this one term has, and the fact that the word *bûsyāʾ* seems to derive from the language of Aramaic contracts (T5:10) remain striking.

[104] See D. Daube, "Negligence in Early Talmudic Law of Contract (*Peshiʿa*)," *Festschrift F. Schulz* I, ed. H. Niedermeyer, W. Flure (Weimar, 1951), 124–47, who comes to similar conclusions about the chronological development of the concept of *pěšîʿâ* to that taken here. The problem of liability for "negligence" in early traditions is complicated by the apparent multiplicity of traditions that might be taken to rule on cases of negligence. Those in *m. B. Meṣ.* are discussed in the text, but the problem is worth brief further examination.

In *Mek. Nězîqîn* 16, to Ex. 22:10 (ed. Horovitz-Rabin, p. 303, ll. 5–9). R. Eliezer (b. Hyrcanus) is represented as having held initially that a depositary is exempt from "breaking" and "capture" because, like "death," it is something that the watcher could not prevent. In response to a challenge attributed to R. Aqiba (who points out that only "death" takes place "at the hands of heaven" but that "breaking" and "capture" can occur "at the hands of a human"), "[R. Eliezer] recanted and considered them a kind of theft." One possible reading of this revised view attributed to R. Eliezer is that in general cases of "breaking" or "capture" cannot be classed with "death" (as M7:9–10 [D] and the first view attributed to R. Eliezer

Institutions and Relationships 169

The closest that we come to a general principle of liability for negligence on the part of the depositary is M3:10:

[A] One who deposits money with his fellow—
[B] [if] he bound it and cast it behind him,
[C] [or] gave it to his minor son or daughter,
[D] and locked [the door] before them[105] in an inappropriate manner,

---

apparently do), but must be defined as a kind of theft. If, for the sake of argument, we take "negligence" as the failure to prevent damage that should have been prevented, the *Mekilta* here may reflect a different organization of negligence than in M7:9–10 [D]. That is, unlike the Mishnah, the *Mekilta*, according to the interpretation suggested here, apparently treats such failures differently, putting "breaking" and "capture" into a separate category. As a result, whereas the Mishnah does not appear to treat paid and unpaid depositaries differently in this regard, the designation in the *Mekilta* of "breaking" and "capure" as "theft" has the legal implication that a paid depositary will be liable but an unpaid depositary will be exempt in such cases (cf. M7:8 [H] and elsewhere in the *Mekilta*). If this is correct, how the rule of the *Mekilta* might be applied is not clear. Perhaps, unlike the Mishnah, the *Mekilta* does not hold depositaries who fail to prevent "death" liable at all ("for 'death' can only come about at the hands of heaven"). This interpretation of the *Mekilta* as treating the failure to prevent "capture" and "breaking" in particular as a "negligent" view may be echoed in other passages in the *Mekilta*, which compare theft with loss, and loss with attack by wild animal on the grounds that all involve "a lack of watching (*ḥesrôn šěmîrâ*)" (*Mek. Nězîqîn* 16 to Ex. 22:12 [pp. 305–6]).

Alternatively, what is at issue in *Mek. Nězîqîn* 16 (ed. Horovitz-Rabin, p. 303, ll. 5–9) may be not the conceptualization of what constitutes culpable failure to prevent damage, but rather how one assigns liability. As noted above, this passage implies (but does not state) that paid and unpaid depositaries should be treated differently. Perhaps, according to the *Mekilta*, one expects a higher degree of care, and therefore greater liability, from a paid depositary. Similarly, the passages in *t. B. Qam.* 10:8–10 and T7:15 hold artisans liable for damage done to the material on which they are working (as in *m. B. Qam.* 9:2) "because he is like a wage bearer (*nôśē' śākār* [i.e., a paid depositary])." This explanatory comment implies that in order to understand why the artisan is liable for what appears to be a kind of "negligence" one has to compare his case to that of a paid depositary, in contrast, no doubt, to an unpaid depositary. See also the *bāraîtā'* cited at *b. B. Qam.* 45a, which states that all four "watchmen" assume liability in place of the owners for damage that animals in their charge do (cf. *m. B. Qam.* 4:9) "except the unpaid depositary." Compare the Amoraic tradition at *y. Šebu.* 8:1 (38c), attributed to R. Leazar in the name of R. Hoshaya, in which liability for "stretching out one's hand" begins for the unpaid depositary only when he has formally taken possession by a possessory act, but at the mere derivation of benefit for a paid depositary (cf. an analogous view in the Babli, B41a, attributed to R. Yohanan in the name of R. Yose b. Nehorai, taken by the stammaitic expansion to refer to whether liability for "stretching out one's hand" occurs only if the deposit has been damaged). These last passages, although not connected with "negligence" resulting in damage to the deposit, reflect differential rulings for paid and unpaid depositaries.

[105] See Appendix I, note to M3:10.

[E] he is liable,
[F] for he did not watch in the manner of watchmen.
[G] But if he watched in the manner of watchmen,
[H] he is exempt.

The second part of this pericope makes it clear that the reason that the depositary is liable is that there is a basic level of care that is expected even of the unpaid depositary "who swears for everything" (M7:8 [E]). This minimal standard of care is based on a social norm that is not articulated in detail, and may support more than one definition.[106] Thus, M3:6 [A–B] states that a depositary is required not to touch [B] rotting produce in order to save it. The view attributed to R. Simeon b. Gamaliel in the same pericope [C–D], that the depositary should sell the produce before the court, does not disagree in principle but in practice recognizes the importance of another rule: "returning a lost object to its owners" [D]. At the same time, in M3:9 and M6:8 the depositary who breaks a jar while handling it for the purposes of caring for it (explicit in M3:9, implicit in M6:8) is exempt from paying for it, although precisely this exemption is a matter of surprise in the view attributed to R. Eliezer (Eleazar) in M6:8.[107] All of these views can be reconciled with a standard of care "according to the manner of watchmen,"

---

[106] Compare the equally "social" definition of *culpa* (negligence) by Gaius in the Digest: "*culpa*, however, is absent if everything was done, which every very diligent man (*diligentissimus quisque*) would be likely to attend to (*observaturus fuisset*)" (D.19.2.25.7). See also D 10.2.25.16 (Paul); 13.6.18.pr. (Gaius); 50.16.223.pr. (Paul). In all of these texts, however, the standard is not what is expected of anyone bound by the same contract (e.g., "in the manner of watchmen") but either the same care one would exercise on one's own property, or the care of a diligent (or very diligent) *pater familias*. See Schulz, 1951, 515–6; Buckland, 1963, 556–8.

[107] According to the view attributed to R. Hiyya b. Abba in the name of R. Yohanan at B83a, "This oath [of M6:8 [C]] is an enactment of the sages (*taqānat ḥakāmîm*), for if you do not say this no one will move a jar from place to place for his fellow." This statement resolves the objection by R. Eliezer (Eleazar) by explaining that the oath in [C] is a special one, and not the standard oath (considered Biblically ordained) of exemption for an unpaid depositary (see Friedman, 1990, 369–70). Thus, this Amoraic tradition presupposes (a) that in principle both paid and unpaid depositaries should be liable—that there is some sort of negligence here—and (b) that some kind of intervention with a deposit (moving a jar for his fellow) is generally expected of the depositary. However, the wording of the Mishnah itself (and the *bāraîtā'*, B82b, cited below) does not imply that this is a special kind of oath. Hence, although the reasoning attributed to R. Yohanan (i.e., that M6:8 [A–C] does not hold the depositary liable so that the depositary will not refrain from necessary tasks) may well be correct, M6:8 [D] does not appear to question a special relaxation of the rules of liability, but the rules themselves.

but the differences among them (although not all irreconcilable with one another) seem to turn on how much active care is demanded.

The very concept of breaching the contract, of "reaching out one's hand" to the deposit, is somewhat unstable in the Mishnah as well. The Hillelite position in the Houses (and Yavnean) debate about how to value the loss to the owner ("[the price] at the time of taking it out") is somewhat parallel to

---

M6:8 and the related *bāraîtāʾ* that occurs at B82a (see the note to M6:8 in Appendix I) read as follows:

	M6:8	B82b
[A]	One who moves a jar from one place to another,	"One who moves a jar for his fellow from one place to another,
[B]	and broke it:	"and broke it:
[C]	whether he is an unpaid depositary or a paid depositary let him swear.	"whether he is an unpaid depositary or a paid depositary, let him swear," the words of R. Meir. R. Judah says: "Let the unpaid depositary swear, and the wage bearer pay."
[D]	Said R. Eliezer: "I question whether this one or this one can swear."	R. Eliezer says: "This one and this one swears, but I question whether this one or this one can swear."

If we may plausibly interpret these passages within the framework provided by M7:9–10 [D] (i.e., that which is not *ʾônes* has happened because of the depositary, who is therefore "negligent" and liable), these disputes arguably deal with whether or not the breakage was a form of *ʾônes* (cf. B82b, in which the problem is characterized as one of whether "one who trips [*nitqal*] [and breaks what he carries] is negligent [*pôšēʿa*]"; and see Friedman, 1990, 376–7). The first view (M6:8 [A–C]; R. Meir in the *bāraîtāʾ*) would then rule that the breakage of the jar was an unpreventable accident, and therefore constitutes *ʾônes*, and the depositary is exempt. By contrast, the surprise attributed to R. Eliezer presupposes that on the face of it the depositary ought not to be exempt for this kind of accident, and by implication this is a kind of negligence. The view attributed to R. Judah in the *bāraîtāʾ* could be taken in one of two ways: either (a) distinctions are made between various kinds of "negligence" (and for some, an unpaid depositary is not liable while a paid depositary is) or (b) that paid and unpaid depositaries in general have different rules in the case of negligence (see the discussion above, n. 104).

In fact, however, although both M6:8 and the *bāraîtāʾ* attribute the damage to the depositary (*û-šĕbārâ*, "and he broke it"), neither makes it possible to distinguish between "negligent" breaking and "accidental" breaking. I would like to suggest that what is at issue in these passages is entirely separate from negligence, and relates to the question of whether a depositary acting in the interests of the owner should ever be liable, even when it is the depositary who actually caused the damage (compare M3:9, in which a depositary who breaks a deposit while moving it *lĕṣorkāh*, "for the needs [of the jar]," presumably the case of M6:8 as well, and explicitly that of the *bāraîtāʾ* ["One who moves ... for his fellow"], is always exempt from payment). M6:8 [A–C] (R. Meir in the *bāraîtāʾ*) holds that he is never liable; the view attributed R. Eliezer (Eleazar) responds that the depositary ought, in theory, to be liable for the damage [D]; with a mediating position attributed to R. Judah in the *bāraîtāʾ*.

m. Baba' Qamma' 9:1–2 ("[the price] at the time of the robbery") and suggests that, as in the latter passage, what is at issue is a kind of robbery. Yet M3:9 seems to imply that liability for use lasts only as long as the depositary made use of the object, while M3:12 [I–J] (although not necessarily in conflict with M3:9) introduces the concept of possessory acts and distinguishes between liability for the whole and liability for only part of the deposit.[108]

There is relatively little material in the Mishnah about paid depositaries. In a number of passages they are mentioned only in the context of other "watchmen," with or without differentiation in terms of rules (*m. B. Qam.* 4:9; M4:9 [cf. *m. Šebu.* 6:5]; M7:8 [cf. *m. Šebu.* 8:1], 10; *m. Šebu.* 8:6). In some ways, the most interesting pericopae that involve the paid depositary are M6:6–7, which use the framework of liability for the paid and unpaid depositaries as a way of working out liability for other individuals who hold

---

[108] In reading M3:9 in this way, I am following C. Levine, "The Concept '*Shelihut Yad*' in the Mechilta De Rashbi" [Hebrew], *BIA* 18/19 (1981), 103, who bases his argument on two passages from the *Mek. dĕ-rašbi*: a comment to Ex. 22:7 (ed. Melamed, pp. 201–2) and one to Ex. 22:10 (p. 205). The way in which the *Mek. dĕ-rašbi* combines the cases and language of M3:9 and M3:12 in the first of these passages is relatively clear. (The passage from the *Mek. dĕ-rašbi* concludes "... and if after he put it down whether for his needs or for its needs he is exempt [M3:9 [D]], as it says: 'For every matter of transgression [*peša'*],' this one is excluded *mi-pĕnê še-lo' pāša'*"; the context seems to require the translation "because he was not transgressing," i.e., at the time of the breakage.) The second passage is not as explicit as Levine, 1981, 102–3, takes it to be. This second passage distinguishes between a case in which an animal was grazing when appropriated by a military force (the depositary is exempt), and one in which the depositary rode on the animal that was seized (the depositary is liable). The tense of the verb in the second case (*rākab*, "he rode") can mean that the riding had taken place in the past, but that the depositary is nevertheless liable, and not, as according to Levine, that the animal was seized while the depositary was riding it. (Note, however, that an analogous problem of tenses occurs in the first passage where the meaning is nevertheless clear).

The relationship between M3:9 and M3:12 [H–J] is complicated. Clearly the author of the first passage of the *Mek. dĕ-rašbi* considered that both could be interpreted in the same manner. The two pericopae may stem from different authors. If we were to cast M3:12 [I–J] in terms of M3:9, we would describe it as a case where no specific place has been specified for the deposit and in which the depositary has handled it for its own use. However, M3:12 [I–J] does not clearly distinguish between cases in which damage happened before or after the depositary put down the deposit as M3:12 [I–J] does. Still, we have no idea whether the M3:12 [I–J] makes a distinction between breakage before or after he stopped handling it (the same passive verb, *wĕ-nišbĕrâ*, is used in M3:12, and for both cases in M3:9; contrast *šĕbārāh*, "he broke it," M6:8 [B], which implies both causality and immediacy). In addition, M3:12 [I–J] introduces the problem of possessory acts, which is absent in M3:9. (C. Levine, 1981, 104, took M3:12 [I–J] as dependent upon M3:9 and claimed that as a result, the language of M3:12 [I–J] is highly condensed. However, it seems to me that one of the points of introducing possessory acts in M3:12 [I–J], may be precisely to consider the depositary liable from that moment forward.)

property belonging to another: artisans, and lenders holding a pledge.[109] In both of these cases, as well as the case of M6:6 [C–D], which distinguishes between two depositaries who agree to watch for one another and one who merely said "leave it before me," the Mishnah reflects a theory of liabilities that correlates benefit to both parties with the assumption of risk.[110]

It has long been noticed that in the Greco-Roman world contracts of deposit often mask other transactions.[111] Although this is hardly the main concern of the Mishnah there are traces of this phenomenon in the *m. Baba' Meṣiʿaʾ* as well. As formulated, M3:11 prohibits the use by non-bankers of loose money on deposit—a kind of loan—but the fact remains that it recognizes the concept. In addition, I have argued in Chapter II that M3:7–8 presuppose that the depositary has mixed the depositor's produce with his own.[112] If this is correct it appears that in these pericopae (but not in M3:6) a deposit is actually a permitted kind of loan of produce. This is particularly

---

[109] On these pericopae see Friedman, 1990, 239–40, 295–7.

[110] See Lapin, 1995, 156–7, n. 18 and the text thereto. Compare Gaius, 3.206, who specifically links the liability for *custodia* for both an artisan and a borrower for use to the benefit they derive: a wage on the one hand, and use on the other.

[111] See *M. Grz.* 257; Taubenschlag, 1955, 350–1. For the use of deposit to mask the dowry of Roman soldiers see *BGU* I 114 i. 5–13 (*M. Chr.* 372), in which the prefect of Egypt refuses to grant a trial to a woman who wishes to claim a deposit from the property of a dead soldier, on the grounds that "we presume that the deposits are dowries" (ll. 9–10). Mitteis considers *M. Chr.* 167 (=*BGU* III 729), 334 (=*P. Lond.* II 310 [p. 208]) and 335 (=*CPR* I 29) possible examples of such transactions. For a contract of deposit serving to document a loan, see *M. Chr.* 332 (=*P. Lond.* II 298 [p. 206]), 333 (=*BGU* III 704), 338 (=*P. Tebt.* II 392). Closer to the world of the Mishnah is a papyrus from the Judean Desert (*P. Babatha* 5 a i.5–16) in which the Jesus' share (in money, loan documents and other forms, including produce) of his deceased father's partnership is held by the former partner "on deposit" and valued as an amount in cash, over and above Jesus' mother's dowry, which was apparently also "on deposit." The depositor's "deposit" clearly allows his father's former business partner to continue to participate in the same business and with the same capital.

[112] See above Chapter II.B.2. See also *m. Dem.* 3:4:
  [A] One who takes wheat—
  [B] to a Samaritan miller or an ʿam hā-ʾāreṣ miller:
  [C] [it remains] in its status with respect to tithes and the sabbatical year;
  [D] to a gentile miller, [it is] *dĕmai* ["doubtfully tithed produce"].
  [E] One who deposits his produce—
  [F] with a Samaritan or an ʿam hā-ʾāreṣ:
  [G] [it remains] in its status with respect to tithes and the sabbatical year.
  [H] with a gentile,
  [I] [it becomes] like the gentile's produce.
  [J] R. Simeon says: "[It is] *dĕmai*."
Produce deposited with a gentile is presumed to have been exchanged with other produce, and is therefore considered to no longer have the ritual status it had before the deposit [H–I].

notable in light of prohibitions of loans of produce elsewhere in the tractate in order to avoid potential usury (M5:8–9).

By and large the rules of deposits are worked out in *m. Baba' Meṣi'â* in terms of relationships between equal parties.[113] While it may be that the Mishnah here purposefully avoids a discussion of social distinctons, it is also possible that the Mishnah devotes its attention to interactions between members of the same social group.[114] The selection of objects described as deposits, occasionally money or utensils, but also animals, wine, oil, grain, and other agricultural produce, reflect the agrarian world in which the Mishnah came into being. At least sometimes, the amounts or values given for deposits presuppose individuals with considerable wealth as well.[115]

If the Tosepta is any indication, the issue is not the likelihood that gentiles, but not *'amê hā-'āreṣ* or Samaritans, would exchange produce on deposit (i.e., presumptive unscrupulousness of gentiles), but rather a gentile's inability to make the claim "I took them [i.e., the produce] and I put in their place old [i.e., pre-sabbatical–year] and tithed (*mĕtuqqānîm*) [produce]" (*t. Dem.* 4:22, 24; cf. *y. Dem.* 3:4 [23d]).

[113] Other social divisions, not automatically of an economic kind, are raised elsewhere in the Mishnah. See, e.g., *m. Dem.* 3:4 (previous note) and *m. Toh.* 8:2 in which the Jewishness or piety of the depositary become factors in the ritual status of the deposited foodstuffs. In *m. Makš.* 6:3, the force of: "And for all of them the *'am hā-'āreṣ* is believed when he says 'They are clean,' except for small fish, because they deposit it (*'ôtāh* [i.e., the small fish]) with the *'am hā-'āreṣ*," is that there are certain kinds of items that the people in whom the Mishnah is interested will deposit with an *'am hā-'āreṣ*—and that are therefore suspected of having been made impure by the depositary—and others that they will not. [I take the explanatory clause as dependent on "small fish," about which the *'am hā-'āreṣ* is not believed, reading *'ôtāh* with the witnesses KRLMPN and following, e.g., Maimonides, *Code, Ṭûm'at 'ôkalîm*, 16:3; R. Elijah of Vilna, *ad loc.*; so also Albeck *ad loc.* Cf. R. Samson of Sens, and Rosh, and, following them, Bertinoro and *TYT ad loc.*, who read "they deposit them (*'ôtān*)." That is, depositaries are believed precisely about things that are deposited with them.]

[114] Compare J. A. Crook, *Law and Life of Rome* (Ithaca: Cornell, 1967), 209, who takes the Roman insistence that *depositum* be free of charge (as in the case of loans) as a form of *noblesse oblige*. Cf., however, *t. B. Qam.* 11:1, which deals with the deposits by individuals who are under the authority of the householder (slaves, women, minors).

[115] An animal, such as an ass or an ox, is a substantial piece of property (see M3:1, 9–10; *m. Šebu.* 8:2–6; cf. *m. B. Qam.* 4:9; 7:6, which also deal with animals, but this may be the influence of Biblical terminology). Deposits of one or two hundred *dînārîm* (M3:3–4; cf. *m. Šebu.* 4:8, which compares a case of a promise [unfulfilled] to lend 200 *dînārîm* to one of deposit) or of utensils worth a hundred or a thousand *dînārîm* are also examples of this kind (M3:5). Similarly, the way in which amounts of acceptable loss are calculated in M3:7–8 presupposes individuals with considerable holdings in the form of produce: dry goods, such as wheat and linseed, are calculated by the *kôr* (M3:7; something under 400 liters), and wine and oil by the 100 *lôg* (M3:8; where the *lôg* is roughly equivalent to 13 liters). (For a discussion of measurements see Hamel, 1990, 243–6.) Compare, however, *m. Šebu.* 6:7, in which the value of a loan and pledge (termed, at the end of the pericope, a *piqādôn*), is disputed: the order of magnitude is that of a *sela'* (tetradrakhma).

3. Buyer and Seller.

Chapter 4 of *m. Baba' Meṣi'a'*, which contains a sustained discussion of sale, opens with the pericope "Silver acquires (*qôneh*) gold, but gold does not acquire silver" (M4:1 [A]). The implications of this passage for the Mishnah's treatment of money have already been discussed above (section A.1). This pericope ends:

> [E] Moveable goods acquire the coin, but the coin does not acquire moveable goods.
>
> [F] This is the rule:[116] all moveable goods acquire one another.

The operative verb in M4:1, *qny/h*,[117] used in its specialized sense of "acquire," "gain possession" (as distinct from "buy"[118]), suggests that what is at issue is the transfer of ownership in the context of sale. However, M4:1 is extremely terse and does not specify when or how the formulaic "A acquires B" is thought to apply. Moreover, the verb (participle) *qôneh* in M4:1 is somewhat awkward since its subject is not one of the actors, but one or the other of the two items in the exchange.[119] To the extent that *qôneh* implies an

---

[116] On these words (which should perhaps be deleted) see the note to this pericope in Appendix I.

[117] The root *qnh/y* can take the meaning "buy" in the Mishnah. See, for example, *m. Ber.* 9:3; *m. Ḥal.* 4:1; *m. Bik.* 1:6,11; 3:12; *m. B. Bat.* 1:5; *m. Ohal.* 18:7. In other passages, the required sense is "acquire:" *m. Qid.* 1:1–5 is the most important example; see also *m. Šebi.* 10:9, *m. Nid.* 5:4. In *m. Ma'aś.* 5:5 the act of buying is juxtaposed to the attendant change in ownership ("One who buys [*ha-lôqēaḥ*] a field of vegetables .... Said R. Simeon b. Gamaliel: 'When are these things said? When he acquired [*qānâ*] the land [with the crop], but when he did not acquire the land...."); so also *m. B. Bat.* 5:7 ("One who sells [*ha-môkēr*] ... [the buyer] has acquired [*qānâ*]; ... has not acquired"). A hybrid passage of this type is *m. B. Bat.* 5:4: "One who buys (*qôneh*) ... trees ... has (not) acquired [*(lo') qānâ*] the land." (Compare also *m. Ma'aś Š.* 1:5, which juxtaposes "buying" with the somewhat difficult expression *lo' qānâ ma'aśēr*, in context perhaps "that which he acquired is not tithe"; cf. *m. Ma'aś Š.* 3:12.) On wives being "acquired" in *m. Qid.* 1:1 (as well as *m. Ned.* 10:6; *m. Nid.* 5:4) see Wegner, 1988, 42–5 and 227 n. 84. (Wegner has misunderstood D. W. Halivni, *Měqôrôt û-měsôrôt: Našim* [Tel Aviv: Dvir, 1968], 614–5 [to *b. Qid.* 2a] as saying that the Mishnah only uses *qnh* for betrothal when the *marriage* involves a property transaction: Halivni is seeking to explain why *qnh* is used in *m. Qid.* 1:1, whereas in other contexts the root *qdš* is used, and argues that the *literary context* of *m. Qid.* 1:1 involves property transactions.)

[118] "Buy" is usually covered in Mishnaic Hebrew by *lqḥ*. On the semantic shift of the root *lqḥ* to the sense of "buy" in Mishnaic Hebrew see E. Y. Kutscher, "Marginal Notes to the Biblical Lexicon [III]" [Hebrew], *Leš.* 30 (1966), 21–3, rpt. in *idem, Hebrew and Aramaic Studies*, ed. Z. Ben-Hayyim *et al.* (Jerusalem: Magnes, 1977) 351–3.

[119] Cf. the language of T3:13, glossing a variant of M4:1 [A] (see Appendix I and the discussion in Section A.1 above):

obligation (i.e., if the coin has been acquired, the buyer, who still holds it, now owes it to the seller), M4:1 [A–E] operates from the perspective of the seller: it tells how the buyer comes to owe the seller the price, and not the reverse.

Immediately following this passage, M4:2 [A–C] adds the following explanation, which I take to be a later supplement:[120]

[A] How?
[B] [If] he drew produce from him but did not give him money he cannot withdraw [from the sale.]
[C] [If] he gave money but did not draw produce he can withdraw.

This explanation introduces the concept of possessory acts (specifically, drawing the merchandise in order to complete the sale), a notion that is not referred to explicitly in M4:1.[121] In doing so, M4:2 shifts attention to the buyer who is the subject of the verbs in [B–C]. M4:2 [A–C] restricts the buyer in that it gives the seller some guarantee that the sale of the merchandise is final. At the same time, the passage grants the buyer comparatively wide power not only to withdraw, but also to determine by a unilateral act whether the seller can withdraw or is legally bound.[122] In light of the

---

[A] Gold acquires silver [but silver does not acquire gold]:
[B] How?
[C] He gave him a golden *dînār* for twenty five silver [*dînārîm*],
[D] lo, this one has acquired [the silver] wherever it may be (*hārê zeh qānâ bĕ-kol māqôm še-hû*).
[E] But if he gave him twenty five silver for a golden [*dînār*],
[F] lo, this one has not acquired (*loʾ qānâ*) [the gold] until he draws it.

In [G–L], the Tosepta repeats a parallel gloss to M4:1 [B]. In the first place, in T3:13 [C, F] (and [J, L]) the subject of *qny/h* has been shifted from material to person. Secondly, the passage from the Tosepta illustrates, as does M4:2 [A–C], how much must be read into the bare formulae of M4:1 to give them context.

[120] See above Chapter II.C.2.

[121] See *m. Qid.* 1:5 cited in full below, and, e.g., *m. Šebi.* 10:9; *m. B. Bat.* 5:7.

[122] Although the language of M4:2 [A–C] focuses on the buyer alone, it seems that the expression "he can (not) withdraw" should apply equally to both buyer and seller (so, e.g., Rashi *ad loc.*, B44a). Although it is impossible to prove from the passage itself that the seller is bound by the buyer's act, and unbound as long as the buyer has not taken it, this is consistent with *m. B. Bat.* 5:7. In that passage, a straightforward rule that it is drawing and not measuring of produce that constitutes the formal transfer is supplemented by the note: "If he was bright, he [the buyer] rents the place [of the produce]." (Since what a person rents temporarily belongs to the renter, one can acquire what is in it by an act of will, and not by a formal possessory act alone.) This note, it seems to me, assumes that it is within the rights of the seller to withdraw as long as the buyer has not drawn the produce, and offers the buyer a way

Institutions and Relationships

preoccupation with purchases in the marketplace in Chapter 4 of the tractate,[123] I am inclined to see this pericope as protecting the power of a buyer of goods for consumption (see the discussion of markets above, Section A.2) to bargain and shop around for a better price.[124] Nevertheless, the warning that God will demand payment from people who do not stand by their words (M4:2 [D]) reflects a certain discomfort with this latitude to bargain.[125]

By itself, however, M4:1 is far from explicit. In the first place, it is not clear whether M4:1 presupposes the rules of possessory acts.[126] It is possible

---

to effect the transfer of ownership immediately even if the produce cannot be drawn. (This is not the traditional understanding of *m. B. Bat.* 5:7, the interpretation of which in the Babli [B84bff.] is complicated by a complex set of rules about the efficacy of various forms of possessory acts. The matter requires further study.) See also the end of T3:16, which, if it refers to M4:2, equates the case of seller and buyer ("just as the seller can withdraw, so can the buyer" [this passage, and the statement attributed to R. Simeon that follows do not fit in context, and seem to be a misplaced reference to M4:2, Lieberman, *TK*, 9, 179]).

[123] M4:3, M4:4 [B], perhaps M4:5–6, and certainly M4:11–2. I return to this matter below.

[124] In addition to the advantage to the buyer in a market situation, another advantage for the buyer is alleged in the following Palestinian Amoraic tradition (Y4:2 [9d]):

R. Yohanan gave money to his relative for oil.
Oil went up in price.
He went and asked R. Yannai.
He said to him: "According to Scripture money [alone without a possessory act] acquires,
"And why did they say 'It does not acquire'?
"So that [the seller] not tell him [the buyer] 'your wheat has burned in the cellar.'"

[Lieberman, *Yerushalmi Neziqin*, 148–9, to ll. 41–2, suggests that the case itself is problematic in that it is already covered by M4:2 [C] (God will punish one who withdraws from a contract), and a rule applying M4:2 [C] is attributed to R. Yohanan himself; but this does not concern us here. The answer attributed to R. Yannai is given, with minor variations, in the Babli (B47b and elsewhere) in the name of R. Yohanan himself.] In the answer of R. Yannai, the rule that drawing alone ends the transaction by passing ownership to the buyer was perceived as a Rabbinic enactment resulting from a conscious choice to increase security for the buyer (i.e., since as long as ownership had not passed the buyer assumed no risk for the maintenance of the merchandise).

[125] In the Mishnah, as also in the Tosepta (T3:14), this is clearly a warning. In later traditions, however, this statement seems to be taken as a reference to a court-invoked curse (as in the expression "give (*msr*) him over to 'He who exacted payment'," Y4:2 [9c] [attributed to R. Hiyya b. Yosep, R. Yohanan]; 4:3 [9d]; 4:4 [9d] [attributed to R. Yose]). Even according to this later interpretation, however, it is clear that the agreement in M4:2 [D] creates a moral, but not a legally enforceable, obligation to follow through on one's promise.

[126] If it is true that the notion of possessory acts is not presupposed by M4:1, it is an attractive suggestion that M4:1 is a relatively early formulation of a rule for sale (cf. B. S. Jackson, *Theft in Early Jewish Law* [Oxford: Clarendon, 1972], 81–7, who argued that possessory acts are a late development in tannaitic law). Nevertheless, that a view rejecting the concept could

that "moveable goods acquire the coin" only when all of the merchandise has been delivered, and not upon a symbolic act of drawing it. Second, the obligation created may be either bilateral (i.e., just as the buyer now owes the money, the seller cannot withdraw from the sale and demand the merchandise back) or unilateral (once one has received merchandise one has committed oneself, but the other party may withdraw). If the obligation created is bilateral, the opposition between sale and barter[127] in M4:1 [E–F] (if [F] is not a later addition) creates the following distinction: while in the case of sale a binding contract from which neither can withdraw can only be instituted by an act of the buyer (as in M4:2 [A–C]), in a case of barter both sides are obligated by an act of either party.[128]

Nevertheless, this is not the only possible reading of M4:1. The statement attributed to R. Simeon, "Whoever has the money in his hand, his hand is in the superior position" (M4:2 [E]), rejects the idea stated in M4:2 [A–C] that it is the buyer's possessory act that completes the transaction. The words of the tradition imply that it is up to the party that holds the money to decide whether to force the other party to honor the agreement to buy or sell.[129] The statement attributed to R. Simeon can be read, however, as ruling that as long as both money and merchandise have not changed hands the sale is

---

be attributed to R. Simeon (an Ushan) in M4:2 [E] suggests that it was conceivable to the redactors of the Mishnah that the rule was not universally held in the mid to late second century.

[127] Compared to sale and purchase, discussion of barter is quite rare in the Mishnah: see M8:4 and *m. Ma'aś. Š.* 1:1; *m. Qid.* 1:6. Like the Roman jurists (cited in Section A.1. above), early Rabbis seem to have had a certain amount of conceptual difficulty with barter. Hence, in *m. Qid.* 1:6 the Mishnah uses an odd formulation:

[A] Everything that is made [to serve as] money with respect to another [thing]:
[B] once (*kēwān še-*) this one has gained possession (*zākâ*), this one has become obligated with respect to that with which it has been exchanged (*bĕ-ḥalipāyw*).

The expression "made money with respect to another" analyzes barter in terms of sale. While M5:1 [H–K] gives an example in which one thing is indeed "made [to serve as] money with respect to another," since the cash value of the objects traded is constantly noted and made the basis of the exchange, and this interpretation could apply to *m. Qid.* 1:6 [A–B], the case is glossed in [C–E] with the example "one who exchanges [*ha-maḥalîp*] an ox for a cow ..."; that is, with a simple case of barter.

[128] However we understand M4:1, it seems relatively clear that in contrast to Roman law, sale is not a "consensual" contract (i.e., one created by mere agreement) but requires some action to make it binding. For this aspect of Roman law see, e.g., Gaius 3.135, D 18.1.2.1(Ulpian) and F. de Zulueta, *The Roman Law of Sale* (Oxford: Clarendon, 1945), 7, 20–1. F. Pringsheim, *The Greek Law of Sale* (Weimar: Hermann Boelhaus, 1950), 14ff. discusses the differences between Roman and Greek legal traditions in this regard.

[129] For this force of "his hand is in the superior position" see M4:4 [D–E], where the expression is glossed: "Give me my money or give me the amount whereby you have oppressed me," and cf. T3:16.

Institutions and Relationships 179

not fully complete and bilaterally binding: where the buyer has given money or where the seller has given merchandise that party is bound, but the other party is not.[130] If this is so, the idea that delivery of merchandise in M4:1 (like the delivery of money in M4:2 [E]) creates only a unilateral obligation is conceivable within the Mishnah itself.

Although one can speak of sale as binding, at least once both parties have made the exchange, the Mishnah also has provisions, the rules of *hônāyâ* ("oppression"), for voiding the sale should one of the parties claim that they have been cheated.[131] M4:3, which defines *hônāyâ* as "one sixth of the

---

[130] In the Mishnah, R. Simeon's rule is not framed in terms of permission to withdraw, but in terms of which party has the upper hand. This may presuppose that legally the sale is not fully binding, but the one who has the money has an enforceable claim. (Alternatively, however, the tradition may reflect a more nuanced view of contracts in which what one "may" do is less important than what kind of legal recourse the parties have.) Cf. T3:16, in which a tradition attributed to R. Simeon that may be a version of the rule attributed to him in M4:2 is formulated in terms of permission: "The seller can withdraw, but the buyer cannot withdraw, for that one [the seller] has already received his money." That is, by paying the price the buyer is obligated to go through with the sale, but this has not bound the seller. (The tradition attributed to R. Simeon may be out of place [Lieberman, *TK*, 9, 179], as has been noted above. The interpretation of this rule in the Tosepta is further complicated by the fact that in T3:14 what appears to be a restatement of the principle of M4:1 [A–D] together with a version of M4:2 [D] are attributed to R. Simeon, who, if I have read M4:2 [E] correctly, should disagree with M4:1 as well.)

J. Neusner, *The Economics of the Mishnah*, 1990, 82, noticed, quite correctly, that R. Simeon has an entirely different conception of sale, but he is absolutely incorrect in his assessment of the Mishnah's system of sale as an (Aristotelian) system of barter keyed to an abstract quantity called money. I have already argued in the first part of this chapter that Rabbis have a clear sense of money as a commodity to be bought, sold, and hoarded; moreover, they make a clear distinction between barter and sale (in fact, it is this distinction that, in part, motivates, the discussion M4:1 [A–D]).

[131] See P. Dickstein, "*Mĕḥîr ṣedeq wĕ-ʾônāʾâ*," *Ha-mišpāṭ ha-ʿibrî* 1 (1926) 15–55, E. Z. Melamed, "*Hitpathût dînê ha-ʾônāʾâ*," *Yabneh* 3 (1942–3), 33–56; D. Sperber, *Roman Palestine 200–400: The Land* (*Bar Ilan Studies in Near Eastern Languages and Cultures*. Ramat Gan: Bar Ilan, 1978), 136–59; Kleiman, 1987, 23–45. On the relationship between the rules of *hônāyâ* and the Roman institution of *laesio enormis* (lit. "great injury") see Dickstein, 1926, 28–9, and Sperber, 1978, 153–9; H. F. Jolowicz, "The Origin of *Laesio Enormis*," *Juridical Review* 49 (1937), 50–72. The source for *laesio enormis* in Roman law comes from two rescripts of Diocletian (*CJ* 4.44.2 [dated 285] and 4.44.8 [dated 293]; see below n. 142), in which the rule in question has long been suspected as an interpolation (it is rather obvious in the second of the two rescripts, less so in the first). The documentary examples cited by Taubenschlag, 1955, 330–1 and n. 40, as relevant to the issue of *laesio enormis* or *iustum pretium* ("just price") are all late. The medieval development of the problem is discussed by J. W. Baldwin, "The Medieval Theories of the Just Price," *Transactions of the American Philosophical Society*, New Series, 49, part 4 (1959), 1–92.

purchase" (šĕtût la-meqah), allows the party that has been "oppressed" "long enough to show it to a tāgār or to his relative" to return the object [A–C]. In the story that follows (and by implication in [A–C], which the story supplements) the rules of hônāyâ are clearly perceived to protect the buyer from overcharge at the hands of the marketer. M4:5–6 together supplement M4:3:[132] M4:6 presents a substantially analogous formulation to M4:3 [B–C], while M4:5 [A] clearly extends the definition of hônāyâ to coins: "And how much may a selaʿ be lacking and there [still] not be hônāyâ in it?" I am inclined to think that these pericopae, too, are designed to protect the consumer in the marketplace.[133] Between M4:3 and M4:5 is inserted an interesting set of rules supplementary to M4:3 (M4:4):

[A] Whether [it is] the buyer or whether [it is] the seller, they have hônāyâ.
[B] Just as a non-professional has hônāyâ, so a merchant (tāgār) has hônāyâ.
[C] R. Judah says: "A merchant has no hônāyâ."
[D] Whoever has been imposed upon, his hand is in the superior position.
[E] For he says to him: "Give me my money or give me the amount whereby you have oppressed me (še-hônētānî)."

The three anonymous rules [A, B, D–E] reflect an attempt to impose a degree of consistency and systematization on the rules of overcharge: the

---

[132] Dickstein, 1926, 33–4, argued that the bare rule of hônāyâ defined as one sixth (M4:4 [A]; 4:7 [A]) constitutes the earliest stratum of the law. Dickstein's argument is based mostly on the language and style of M4:7, which, he argues, must stem from second Temple times. M4:7 may indeed contain a series of early rules, but these appear concentrated in the list that follows (M4:7 [D–I]; see Chapter II.A.2). In any case, his argument that the reference to Media in M4:7 [I] implies a time of current or recent Persian domination (i.e., before or not long after Alexander's conquest) is mistaken; on the contrary, a time when Media is considered the other end of the world is presupposed. By contrast, Melamed, 1942–3, 37–8 considered M4:3 and M4:5–6 as apparently coeval and as together making up the earliest stratum of the rules of hônāyâ. He prudently avoids assigning a date to these passages, although he apparently considered them quite early. Melamed's observation that the Yerushalmi does not refer to M4:4 is at best an argument from silence, and in any case has no bearing on the dating of M4:3 and 4:5–6; moreover M4:5 is entirely an Ushan pericope [rare in *m. B. Meṣ.*, see Chapter II.D.2] and arguably relatively late. Moreover, since M4:5 is formulated as an elaboration of the rule of hônāyâ it makes sense to see it as supplementary. This suggests (but does not prove) relative priority for M4:3 (it is suggestive that M4:3 includes a tradition involving the Yabnean R. Tarfon), but even if this is so, no fixed date can be given. As for the relative dating of M4:4 and M4:5–6, there does not seem to be any way of deciding one way or another.

[133] I.e., to protect someone who has received a suspect coin from a local shopkeeper or money changer. Cf. Melamed, 1926, 36, who understood this passage to grant equivalent

Institutions and Relationships

rules involved are balanced, and apply equally to both parties and, apparently to sales between two householders as well. If the view attributed to R. Judah [C] backs away from giving the right to an action on *hônāyâ* to a professional merchant,[134] it is presumably because it is precisely the *tāgār* who is expected to know the correct prices (and who, according to M4:11 [G–H], is in any case of doubtful integrity). These three rules are clearly to the advantage of the professional marketers (in comparison with M4:3). However, we should not automatically conclude that it is these people in whom M4:4 is particularly interested. As a concomitant to the rule that buyers and sellers are equally protected from excessive overcharge, landowners engaged in selling crops or trading in large amounts of produce outside the marketplace would be as well protected as sellers as they are as buyers in the marketplace.[135]

---

protection to the seller, stated in terms of coins, to that of the buyer in M4:3, stated in terms of a proportion of the price.

[134] This seems to be the most straightforward explanation of M4:4 [C] (see Appendix I) (it is also supported in the Babli by the view attributed to R. Nahman, and a *bāraîtāʾ* cited in defense of this view), but in the view attributed to Rab Ashi (B51a) the expression *ʾên la-tāgār hônāyâ* means "the merchant is not subject to the rules of *hônāyâ* (*ʾênô bě-tôrat ʾônāʾâ*) and can therefore void the sale even if the overcharge has been less than one sixth (see B51a).

[135] This is consistent with the rule of R. Judah (M4:4 [C]) as well. One of the roles of the *tāgār* is to buy up produce in bulk and market it out to the retail *ḥenwānî*. Thus, R. Judah may be seen as rather baldly protecting the interests of the householder against the interests of the *tāgār*, while maintaining the balance of interests in transactions between householders.

Another step in this direction may be seen in the tradition attributed to R. Judah the Patriarch at T3:16. After a citation of M4:4 [D] ("Whoever has been imposed upon is in the superior position") the Tosepta works out a case in which the buyer can withdraw (in the manner of M4:4 [E]) when overcharged, as can the seller who has undercharged the buyer. To this is added: "R. [Judah the Patriarch] says: 'The seller is always (*lě-ʿôlām*) in the superior position.'" It seems highly unlikely (although still possible) that this statement gives a blanket right to a marketer to withdraw, and none to the buyer, and it may well be correct that this statement presupposes sale between householders. However, this statement of R. Judah the Patriarch appears also in B50b without the word *lě-ʿôlām*, and on B51a the contradiction with our Mishnah [M4:4 [D]] is resolved by the suggestion (attributed to Raba, supported by a tradition attributed to Rab Ashi) that the Mishnah gives a case in which the buyer may withdraw (i.e., M4:4 [E] gives the claims the buyer might make), and in the *bāraîtāʾ* R. Judah the Patriarch adds the case of a seller who has undercharged ("that which he left out of the Mishnah, he made explicit in the *bāraîtāʾ*"). This interpretation is hardly necessitated by the wording of the tradition of R. Judah the Patriarch itself, and is clearly designed to resolve a contradiction with the Mishnah; moreover it is impossible to apply this interpretation to the version preserved in the Tosepta (*lě-ʿôlām*). The version in the Babli is further complicated by the fact that it is appended to a tradition attributed to R. Natan that is treated as a *bāraîtāʾ* in the Babli, but may be a Palestinian Amoraic tradition. See Y4:3 [9d]), in which the view of R. Natan in the Babli is attributed to "R. Judah the Patriarch," and an opposing view to R. Yohanan, and see *Yěpê ʿênayîm* to B50b; Lieberman, *TK*, 9, 178–9. Epstein, *Nûsaḥ*, 300 n. 5

One last pericope on *hônāyâ* should be noted. In M4:9 [A–B] "slaves and documents and lands and consecrated goods" are listed as "things for which there is no [rule of] *hônāyâ*." In a conceptual world in which loans are interest-free, it only makes financial sense to buy a loan document (and with it the right to collect the debt) if one buys at a discount. Similarly, if the "consecrated goods" are sacrificial animals (as seems a distinct possibility from R. Simeon's disputing view [F]), it would follow that what is at issue is the sale of animals that have become blemished and can no longer serve the purpose for which they were consecrated, and are being sold off at a discount. By implication, in the sale of land and slaves as well, the force of "there is no [rule of] *hônāyâ*" is that the seller cannot void the sale by claiming that he has undercharged the buyer.[136] While this rule no doubt applied to a buyer claiming overcharge as well, the formulation of the pericope, and indeed the rule itself, seem to presuppose a general reluctance to sell off land (except, perhaps, due to need), and protect the buyer from having the sale voided by the seller.[137]

---

argued that in the Yerushalmi the full expression "R. Judah the Patriarch" never refers to the redactor of the Mishnah, but always to later descendants, and that Yohanan (second generation Amora) there is a corruption for [Yo]natan (first generation Amora) in the Yerushalmi.

[136] Compare Sperber, 1978, 153–9, who argues that the later view attributed to R. Yohanan in allowing a claim of *hônāyâ* in cases of sale of land in which the difference in price was excessive (*mûpleget*) (*y. Ket.* 11:4 [34 d]; cf. B57a, *b. Tem.* 27b), refers to a case in which the seller undercharged the buyer.

[137] Certain other passages of the Mishnah have been taken to imply that there was a tradition that held that *hônāyâ* did apply to land (Melamed, 1942, 51–2), but none of them are quite decisive:

(a) *m. B. Bat.* 7:3. 7:2–3 discuss the implications of formulae that the seller uses in designating the land to be sold: "measured by a cord," "whether more or less," "by its [geographical] marks and boundaries (*mĕṣarāyw*)" (cf. H. H. July, *Die Klauseln hinter den Massangaben der Papyrusurkunden* [Diss. Cologne, 1966]). In the case of the last of these *m. B. Bat.* 7:3 rules that if the actual size of the plot of land turned out to be more than one sixth smaller than the amount stated, the seller deducts (*mĕnakkeh*) from the price. It should be noted, however, that there is no permission to the party "imposed upon" to withdraw, but only to retrieve the difference in price. Moreover, what is at issue is an error in the description of the land involved and therefore a mistaken sale, and not a case of overcharge. (Cf. *t. B. Bat.* 6:26.)

(b) *m. Ket.* 11:4. R. Menahem Meiri took the rule that "[If a wife's] *kĕtubbâ* was worth a *māneh* and she sold [land worth] a *māneh* and a *dînār* for a *māneh*, her sale is invalid," as a form of *hônāyâ*, in which, since the wife was merely an agent of the husband's heirs and not the principal owner, the sale could be considered void due to any overcharge whatsoever (*Bêt ha-bĕḥîrâ ʿal masseket kĕtubbôt*, ed. A. Sofer [Jerusalem: 1947–8], 451). The real issue, however, is that in contrast to the first two cases given in *m. Ket.* 11:4 the wife has sold more than she was entitled to.

(c) *m. Ket.* 11:5. The first part of the pericope reads:

[A] The evaluation [of property to be sold by the widow to recover her *kĕtûbbâ*]

The distinction between "real" and "moveable" property raised in M4:9 also has important implications for sale, as the following passage shows (*m. Qid.* 1:5):

> [A] Property against which there can be a lien [when sold] (*še-yēš lāhem ʾaḥarāyût*)[138] is acquired by money, or by document, or by [act of] possession (*ḥazāqâ*),[139]
>
> [B] and that against which there can be no lien is acquired only by drawing (*mešîkâ*).

The implication of this pericope is that the actual ownership of moveable goods (that against which there can be no lien) may be transferred only by the formal possession of the goods by the buyer, while in sale of real property mere delivery of the money or a unilateral act of the seller (the writing of a document) without prior payment can also transfer ownership.[140] Any

---

by judges who subtracted a sixth or who added a sixth, their sale is invalid.
[B] R. Simeon b. Gamaliel says: "Their sale is valid,
[C] "for if [the rule in A] is] so, what is the power of the court worth?"

For both views given in the pericope the limit of a sixth for overcharge or undercharge in the sale of land seems to be a general principle. Here too, however, what is at issue is not a straightforward case of "overcharge" but one in which one or both parties acted on the basis of an official valuation by a court, only to find that the official valuation was incorrect. This may therefore also be a case of mistaken sale and not *hônāyâ*. (Cf. *t. Ket.* 11:3; *t. B. Bat.* 6:26)

[138] See Appendix I, note to M1:6. The reference is to land, slaves and documents (cf. M4:9 [A–B]).

[139] The term *ḥazāqâ* does not refer, in this case, to usucaption (as in *m. B. Bat.* 3:1–3), but a formal act of possession. See, e.g., *t. Qid.* 1:5, in which *ḥazāqâ* for land is defined: "he locked, or built a wall, or breached [a wall], to any extent (*kol še-hû*)" (cf. the end of *m. B. Bat.* 3:3), and that for slaves: "he tied on his shoe, or loosened his shoe, or took clothing (*kēlîm*) after him to the bath." This conception is precisely analogous to the acquisition of a wife (i.e., binding betrothal) by "money, by deed or by intercourse (*bîʾâ*)" (*m. Qid.* 1:1) although the specificity of intercourse as an act of possession for betrothal left room for a distinction between *ḥazāqâ* for slaves and *bîʾâ* for wives (e.g., *y. Qid.* 1:1 [58b]).

[140] That the writing of a sale document could be taken as a unilateral procedure is indicated by *m. B. Bat.* 10:3, which considers a deed of sale written for the seller in the absence of the buyer valid, in the same way that a borrower may write a loan document in the absence of the lender. In both cases the documents were to be given over to the beneficiary of the document who could then use them to collect on the basis of their contents. See also characterization of the operative clause in a loan document in *b. Qid.* 26a: "My field is sold to you" (on traces of the formulae of the sale document see A. Gulak, 1929, *Lĕ-ḥēqer tôldôt ha-mišpāṭ ha-ʿibrî* [Jerusalem, 1929], 67–8). Gulak, 69–70, argues that in the Mishnah sale by deed was ineffective unless accompanied by payment in full, and treats the Amoraic traditions to the contrary (e.g., the tradition attributed to R. Yona and R. Yose, *y. Qid.* 1:1 [60c]) as later developments. However, the Yerushalmi supports the view that ownership passes with a document alone

attempt to explain this distinction is bound to be speculative, especially since we have almost no information about actual custom, and have no way of determining to what extent the Mishnah's rules approximate usual practice. It is worth observing, however, that while from a contractual point of view the sale of real property is easier to effect, practically it is likely to be more difficult: the costs are higher, the negotiations therefore more careful, and (in the real world outside the Mishnah) the steps involved perhaps more complicated (involving, for instance, registration of the transfer of property[141]). Thus the Mishnah's rule about real property may reflect the recognition that by the time that the actual transfer takes place the two parties are both resolved to go ahead with the sale.[142] It also implies that for the

---

from a *bāraîtā'* with parallels in *t. Ket.* 2:1: "But if he gave him the money for one of them [one of ten fields being sold simultaneously], or (*'ô*) wrote him a document for one of them, he has only acquired that one field," in contrast to *ḥazāqâ*, by means of which one can take possession of ten fields with the formal possession of one (cf. *t. B. Bat.* 2:12, which has a partial parallel to *t. Ket.*; in both *t. Ket.* and *b. Qid.* 27a, the tradition is part of a larger rhetorical structure comparing the relative strengths of money, documents and *ḥazāqâ* [in the Babli, however, the *bāraîtā'*, reads quite differently; see *Yĕpê ʿênayîm* to *b. Qid.* 26a, 27a]). The implication of the specification of both sale by deed and sale by money is that sale by deed is not dependent upon payment, and that property can be considered fully "sold" by a deed from the seller alone. Similarly, unless *t. B. Bat.* 2:13, which glosses *m. Qid.* 1:5 [A], implies that all three elements are required, the conjunction *waw* must be taken as disjunctive: "... since he wrote a document *or* received the money, *or* took possession of one of them, he has possessed all of them" This follows also from the treatment of *m. Qid.* 1:1, on betrothal "by money, by document or (*û-*) by intercourse" (analogous to *m. Qid.* 1:5 [A]) in *t. Qid.* 1:1–3, which treats each element separately. (See also *y. Qid.* 1:1 [58b]: "The Mishnah [should be read] thus: 'Either (*'ô*) by money, or (*'ô*) by document or (*'ô*) by intercourse,' and R. Hiyya taught: 'The end of the matter is: not by means of all of them, but even by means of one of them.'") Thus, it appears that both the apparent meaning of the Mishnah, and early witnesses to its interpretation support the idea that sale could be completed by the writing (and delivery) of a deed of sale, before the payment of the price.

[141] See Pringsheim, 1950, 232–42; this was discussed briefly in n. 36, above.

[142] The reasoning in a rescript of Diocletian (*CJ* 4. 44. 8 [293]) is apposite here:

For this alone, which you express, that the land was sold at a somewhat lower price, is not effective for the rescission of the sale. It is plain that had you considered the nature of a contract of buying or selling, and that the buyer comes to this contract having in mind to buy at a lower price and the seller to sell at a higher price, and that with difficulty, after many disagreements, little by little, the seller subtracting from that which he had asked, the buyer adding to that which he had offered, they agree to a fixed price, you would perceive, undoubtedly, that neither good faith (*bona fides*) allows ... nor any other reason permits, the rescission of a contract finalized by consensus because of this ....

[The rescript goes on to allow voiding the sale if the price given was less than half the full value, but this is patently against the argument of the rescript as a whole]. The legal principles

authors of the Mishnah, in a sale of real property for deferred payment or for deferred delivery, ownership was assumed to pass, and the transaction to be binding, even though one of the parties had not yet been satisfied (cf., e.g., M5:3 [A–C]). By contrast, the sale of moveable goods is probably likelier to be contracted quickly (e.g., to take advantage of what one thinks is a bargain) and less likely to require administrative or customary complications such as registration. On the other hand, prices for moveables (especially such commodities as produce) are subject to wider and more volatile variation, and there may be greater impetus for one of the parties to want to get out of a contract. It is in this latter case, therefore, that the Mishnah specifies a single and clear-cut formal criterion for when the contract has become binding.

With the exception of M4:11–12 (which were dealt with above in connection with markets), the remaining pericopae in *m. Baba' Meṣi'a'* concerned with sale do not deal with markets but with large-scale transactions between householders. In M3:8 [G] R. Judah extends the rule of acceptable deductions for absorption, articulated for a case of deposit of wine and oil, to a case of selling. In both the tradition ascribed to R. Judah and in the case of deposit the scale envisaged is that of one hundred *lûggîn* (some 50 or 60 liters). M5:1[H–K], I have already suggested, is one of large-scale speculation in commodities; here too the order of magnitude is large (25–30 *dînārîm*). The initial transaction that set the case of M5:1 [H–K] in motion is apparently one of advance payment for deferred delivery. The reverse is the case in M5:2 [I–J] in which the seller is permitted to accept a higher price for later payment, although the property (a field, again relating to the concerns of landholders) changes hands immediately. Similarly, in M5:3 the implicit rule is that in a sale (of a field) in which the buyer gives only partial payment, the property is to be transferred immediately. M5:7 gives another case of advanced payment for produce for deferred delivery, focusing on the question of how early in the production of the produce the material can be sold. Here too, the context is large-scale purchases between land owners.[143]

---

may be different (notably the emphasis on consensuality), but (especially since the rescript deals explicitly with land) the logic is the same: after an extended process of negotiation it would be difficult for either side to say that they did not know what they were getting into.

[143] In these four cases from Chapter 5 we have references to more complex transactions than simple cash sales, since in a contract for delayed delivery the buyer needs guarantees that the produce will be delivered, and in a contract for delayed payment the seller requires guarantees of payment. The Mishnah does not develop these further (although these and other transactions are dealt with in post-Mishnaic literature). Compare, the documents cited in Pringsheim, 1950, 259–65 for papyri from the Roman period dealing with sales on credit; 279–81 for sales with deferred delivery (see, e.g., *BGU* I 223; IV 1015); and see Taubenschlag, 1955, 336–9.

M8:4 deals with the sale or exchange of animals or slaves (both expensive items) and M8:5 with the sale of olive trees for wood. In general, then, outside of Chapter 4 the tractate focuses on the concerns of landholders.[144] Within Chapter 4, the primary focus is on consumers in their relationship to marketers, but the rules have been expanded in a way that reflects a concern for systematization and consistency. There are also indications, I believe, of amplification in a direction that gives greater play to the role of the landholder as seller.

4. Lender and Borrower.

The Mishnah distinguishes between two different types of contracts of loan: *šĕʾēlâ*, a loan for use, with the object borrowed itself to be returned, and *milwâ*, a loan of money or some other fungible good for consumption, with the value of the loan to be returned.[145] Since in the case of *šĕʾēlâ* the borrower

---

[144] In this respect *m. B. Meṣ.* is consistent with the Mishnah as a whole. In most of the tractates of the Mishnah in which questions of sale arise what is at issue most frequently is a ritual problem (e.g., whether produce may be used), and the focus is therefore usually on the sale or purchase of foodstuffs for use. However, even in connection with ritual matters, sale of real property, large scale transactions, and transactions reflecting the concerns of landholders are considered (e.g., *m. Bik.* 3:12; *m. Peʾa* 1:6; *m. Maʿaś.* 5:1, 5; *m. Maʿaś. Š.* 1:7). Where what we would call "civil" or "private" law is at issue the objects for sale are likely to reflect the interests of this same wealthy stratum (e.g., *m. Qid.* 1:1–5: modes of acquisition for wives, slaves, animals, real estate [opposed to moveables]; 1:6 exchange exemplified by an ox and a cow; *m. B. Bat.* 2:5: buying a house with a pigeon coop; 3:7–8: houses; 4:1–4: houses, courtyards, olive presses, bath houses, villages [*ʿîr*, perhaps an isolated farm settlement, see S. Applebaum, "Economic Life in Palestine," in *The Jewish People in the First Century*, ed. S. Safrai *et alii* (CRINT 1: Philadelphia: Fortress, 1976), 641–6; but ownership of villages is not impossible: G. M. Harper, "Village Administration in the Roman Province of Syria," *YCS* 1 (1928), 160ff.; R. MacMullen, *Roman Social Relations* (New Haven: Yale, 1974), 38–9 and notes thereto], fields, ships, asses, and produce for seed; but also trees, slaughtered animals and produce). See also the passages in *m. Ket.* in which money belonging to the wife is left in the care of the husband who is to buy land with it, this being the only acceptable investment (e.g., *m. Ket.* 6:1; 8:3, 5, 7). The rules for how a widow may claim her *kĕtûbbâ* assume that she will sell land now belonging to the heirs of the husband (e.g., *m. Ket.* 11:4–5). In addition, as noted previously, to the extent that ritual restrictions or prohibitions of certain kinds of transactions with gentiles were observed, the Mishnah gives us a window into another set of social interactions.

[145] See, e.g., Rashi to *m. ʿAb. Zar.* 1:1 (*b. ʿAb. Zar.* 2a):

Šĕʾēlâ [is transacted] with something that returns in the form [in which it was lent] (*bĕ-ʿayîn*), such as an animal or vessels, as it is written: "If a man borrows (*yišʾal*) from his fellow ..." (Ex. 22:13 [Rashi's citation of the verse depends on context: Ex. 22:6 refers to "silver (*kesep*) or vessels"; 22:9 to animals; and 22:13 itself refers to the "breaking" or death of the object borrowed, i.e., an animal as in 22:9]). *Milwâ* [is given] with a thing that does not return in the form [in which it was lent], such

has an obligation with respect to the object of the loan itself, and because the connection is already made in Exodus 22:6–14, the Mishnah frequently considers this form of loan under the rubric of "depositaries" (*šômrîm*).[146] From the point of view of law, the pericopae in *m. Baba' Meṣi'a'* that deal with loans for use are concerned with liability: at what point it begins or ends

---

as money (*māʿôt*), as it is written "If you should lend (*talweh*) silver to [one of (?)] my people (*ʿamî*) ..." (Ex. 22: 24), for a *milwâ* is given for expenditure, and he pays him other money.

An analogous distinction between loan for use (*commodatum*) and loan for consumption (*mutuum*) occurs on Roman law (see on *commodatum* D 13.6 and Schulz, 1955, 513–6; Buckland, 1963, 470–3). That the distinction in Rabbinic usage is not merely between loans of objects and of money (although it may have been this in origin) may be seen, for example, in M5:9 [H, E] where *lwy/h* is used for the loan of a commodity, apparently for consumption.

Occasionally the Mishnah uses the verb *šʾl* in a less technical sense for a "neighborly" loan for consumption. For instance: "The woman who has borrowed (*še-šāʾalâ*) from her fellow spices and water and salt for her dough ..." (*m. Beṣ.* 5:4). In the present case, the rule follows one in which "One who borrows (*šôʾēl*) a vessel from his fellow ..." and may use parallel language for formal reasons. More interesting, because it seems consciously to utilize the terminological distinction, is *m. Šab.* 23:1:

[A] A person may borrow (*šôʾēl*) from his fellow jars of wine and jars of oil,
[B] as long as he does not say: "Lend to me (*halwēnî*)."
[C] And so also a woman [borrows] loaves from her fellow.

The continuation, as well as the correlation of [A–B] with [C], make it clear that a loan for consumption is meant. In a tradition attributed to R. Zera in the name of R. Yonatan in the Yerushalmi (*y. Šebi.* 8:4 [38a]) this pericope is explained as an example of a (permissive) rule going against the strict application of a prohibition (*mē-halākôt šel ʿimʿûm hûʾ*). Strictly speaking, a loan is a business transaction and a typical weekday activity and should be prohibited, but this pericope allows the parties to evade the prohibition in the case of a "neighborly" loan by specifically refraining from the language of *milwâ*. (See Albeck, *Mišnâ*, 2 [*Môʿēd*], 423–4.) According to the Babli (*b. Šab.*148a), in a dialogue between Abbaye and Raba b. Rab Hanan, the issue at hand is that when the language of *halwāʾâ* is used, the lender might be led to record the transaction. The medieval commentaries sought reasons why this should be so (Rashi, *b. Šab.* 148a: *halwēnî* implies a loan of some duration, thirty days, and the lender might therefore be inclined to write the loan down; cf. the objection of Tos. *ibid. s.v. Šôʾēl ʾādām*, who add according to R. Isaac that since *šē-ēlâ* is typically a loan for use, the object of which is therefore always "there," one is less likely to record the transaction; see also Meiri to *m. Šab.* 23:1 [*Beth Habehira on the Talmudical Treatise Shabbath*, ed. I. S. Lange [Jerusalem, 1968], 587), who adds that *šēʾēlâ* implies that the borrower will return it shortly, or whenever the lender demands it; but that *milwâ* implies a lengthy loan).

[146] M7:8, 10; *m. Šebu.* 8:1, 5. See also *m. B. Qam.* 4:9, 7:6 in which all four "watchmen" are listed together as a group. Similarly, the R. Yose series in Chapter 3 (M3:2–5) includes pericopae about unpaid deposit (M3:3–5), as well as one on renting and borrowing for use (M3:2). Compare, e.g., D.16. 3.18.1 (Gaius), which similarly considers the analogy between pledging, lending for use and deposit.

(M8:3), what the level of liability is (M3:2; 7:8; 8:1), whether one can alter the legal liability by stipulation (M7:10), and how one resolves the problem of liability in cases of uncertainty (M8:2) or where the borrower has borrowed from a renter (M3:2). A review of the objects described as loaned affords two interesting observations. First, the objects, when they are not articles of clothing, are connected with the production or storage of agricultural produce, or the making of bread.[147] For the most part, then, the loans that the Mishnah considers are tied to basic activities of production within an agrarian economy, and not "prestige" or "life-style"–oriented loans. This might be taken to imply that the Mishnah is concerned here with the economic lives of relatively poor farmers, especially given the kinds of objects loaned for use in the treatment of *commodatum* in the Digest of Justinian.[148] However, this observation need not necessarily conflict with my argument that overall *m. Baba' Meṣi'a'* speaks to the concerns of a wealthier landholding class. In the first place, emphasis on the household and on production may be a conscious choice to focus on loans common to a broad spectrum of households. Secondly, wealth need not imply the absence of active interest in the maintenance and exploitation of one's assets—and in fact may imply the reverse.

The second point worth noting is an apparent division in the text between objects that women borrow and objects that men borrow: while men borrow agricultural implements, women borrow articles of clothing and implements for the transformation of grain into bread.[149] This suggests a division, cer-

---

[147] Clothing: *m. Ta'an.* 4:8; *m. Ned.* 4:1; *m. Nid.* 9:3; animals: M3:2; 8:1–3; *m. Šebi.* 8:5–6 (see also *m. B. Qam.* 4:9; 7:4, in which the case of borrowing an animal is part of a formulaic working out of hypothetical cases); utensils for storing produce: *m. Ma'aś. Š.* 3:12; implements for the preparation of grain and the baking of bread: *m. Šebi.* 5:9; *m. Ned.* 4:1; *m. Giṭ.* 5:9 (*m. Beṣ.* 5:4 refers to *kĕli* without specification, although the continuation may imply food production).

[148] An impressionistic survey of the title in the Digest on *commodatum* (D 13.6) suggests that the majority of objects considered in this context are connected with the maintenance of a certain standard of living: 5.6: a slave; 5.7: a horse to take to one's villa or to war, a slave to perform manual (but not agricultural) labor; 5.8: a codex; 5.9: a mare with its foal (the use is not specified); 5.13: a slave with a dish (presumably a domestic slave); 5.14: the material to outfit a dining room; 5.15: a vehicle (Ulpian); 13.1: beasts of burden (arguably for agricultural work) (Pomponius); 17.3: writing tablets (*pugillares*), and timbers to support a building; 17.4: a coach (*carruca*) and a litter (*lectica*) (Paul); 18.pr.: silver plate; 18.2: a slave; 18.3: vessels for wine or oil (Gaius); 20: silver (Julian); 21.1: vessels (Africanus); 22: a slave (Paul); 23: a horse for a journey (Pomponius).

[149] Both *m. Ta'an.* 4:8 and *m. Nid.* 9:3, which deal with the borrowing of clothing, specifically picture women as borrowers. (It should be noted however that in both cases there are other reasons for the rule to be formulated in connection with the women. *m. Ta'an.* 4:8 involves the description of a ritual equalization of women through the wearing of garments

tainly not unique to Rabbis or Jews, in the spheres of economic activity open to women and to men. Papyrological remains, such as the archives of Babatha in the Judean Desert, imply that this kind of distinction could be largely ideological, and not reflected in actual practice, in which women, if they had the means, and although working within the framework of legal restrictions, could carry on a diversified economic life on their own.

The archetypal loan for use is one between status equals. In theory people lend freely to their neighbors and can expect to borrow in turn when the need arises, and on balance there is no structured inequality between those who are able to lend, who gain prestige or power (by being able to ask for favors in return), and those who are forced to borrow. Thus the Mishnah

---

that are both white and borrowed "so as not to embarrass one who does not have." In *m. Nid.* 9:3 the legal problem is one of a menstrual stain, and of necessity involves women.) It is striking that *m. Šebi.* 5:9 = *m. Git.* 5:9 chooses to discuss the lending of winnowing fans, sieves, millstones, and ovens in connection with women (and continues by discussing women of different ritual status baking together). This observation is consistent with other loans, for consumption, attributed to women in the Mishnah, for example: *m. Šab.* 23:1; M5:9 [E–G] (loaves); *m. Beṣ.* 5:4 (note that the first part of this passage, dealing with an unspecified *kĕlî*, has a masculine subject, but that the second part concerns "the woman who has borrowed spices and water and salt for her dough"). If I am correct in my general assessment of the differentiation—at least in theory—between women and men in the economy of the household, *m. Ned.* 4:1, a notable exception, deserves comment:
  [B] One who is under a vow [not to benefit from] his fellow's food:
  [C] let him not lend him [i.e., to the one under the vow] a winnowing fan, a sieve, millstones, or an oven.
  [D] But he may lend him a tunic (*ḥalûq*) or a ring or a cloak (*ṭallît*) or earrings,
  [E] or anything that one does not use for the means of sustenance (*še-ʾên ʿôśîn bô ʾôkel nepeš*).
[See G. Hamel, 1990, 58–64 for a discussion of and literature on *ḥalûq* and *ṭallît*.] In this pericope, it is precisely the man who is pictured as lending garments and implements of food production. Perhaps this pericope should be seen as focusing on the master of the household who can dispose at will any or all its contents.

In the Tosepta, too, women are presented as borrowing clothing (*t. Nid.* 9:12), as well as winnowing fans, sieves, millstones, and ovens (*t. Ket.* 7:4). In the latter case the passage from the Tosepta states that if a woman is under a vow not to lend these implements to neighboring women she is to be divorced: if imposed by the husband "he gives her a bad name before her female neighbors"; if she took the oath on her own, "she gives him a bad name before his female neighbors," and therefore receives no *kĕtubbâ* settlement. The lending of such implements on the part of women is thus pictured as part of the expected activity of women. However, in the Tosepta the emphasis on loans by men of material for agricultural production is less pronounced: men are seen as lending or borrowing not only animals (*t. B. Qam.* 5:4; 6:14; 11:1; *t. B. Meṣ.* 8:20–2; *t. Šebu.* 6:7), axes (*t. Ned.* 4:6; *t. Nid.* 6:14), and containers for produce (*t. B. Meṣ.* 2:18), but also clothing (*t. Beṣ.* 4:6; *t. B. Meṣ.* 8:28), a kerchief to cover a Torah scroll (*t. Meg.* 3:2), and wicker vessels for a wedding or funeral (*t. Kelim B. Meṣ.* 5:3).

pictures loans for use as taking place between householders or between women. Similarly, the Mishnah's assessment of loans for consumption (*milwâ*) considers loans between status equals (although, unlike *šeʾēlâ*, *milwâ* is typically perceived as a consumer loan, i.e., a loan that allows the borrower to buy goods that he needs to live or to maintain a certain standard of living and not for production). This goes a certain distance towards explaining the rulings on interest, which are the focus of Chapter 5 of *m. Babaʾ Meṣiʿaʾ*.

In economic terms, the concept of interest can be analyzed in at least two directions. On the one hand, we can describe interest as compensation to the lender for the risk that is incurred by making the loan, and for loss to the lender of the benefits that would have accrued had the lender been able to make use of the money. On the other hand, interest is also a function of the balance of supply and demand. This is true not only in the broad sense in which the price for money (the interest rate) is tied to the amount of money in circulation, but also in the narrow sense in which an individual's demand for money may force that person to pay a premium for it. I believe that the Mishnah's rules on usury focus on this last aspect: to charge interest is to take advantage of the borrower's need and to impose an inequality where in principle there ought to be none. In other words, the authors of our tractate, in setting out the rules for lending at interest, choose to see all of Israel as equal, and structure the rules of interest accordingly.[150]

---

[150] That the rules apply to Israel, as opposed to any other group, is quite clear from M5:6 [C–D]: "But one may accept "iron sheep" from the gentiles, and one borrows from them and lends to them at interest." That is, the rules prohibiting interest apply only between Jews. In this respect, the Mishnah follows the Deuteronomic legislation of Deut. 23:20–1: "You shall not lend to your brother at interest (*taššîk*).... To the foreigner (*nokrî*) you may lend at interest, but to your brother you shall not lend at interest." That the Mishnah consistently prohibits interest should not be taken for granted simply because the Bible prohibits it: Rabbinic tradition is capable of remarkably flexible interpretation, and the other two Pentateuchal passages prohibiting interest are susceptible to a more "refined" exegesis. Both Ex. 22:24 ("If you should lend money to [one of (?)] my people—to the poor person who is with you—do not be an oppressor to him ...") and Lev. 25:35–6 ("And if your brother should be brought low ... do not take *nešek* or *tarbît* from him ..."; compare however vs. 37, which states the prohibition as a general rule, and may be a supplementary expansion [Fishbane, 1985, 174, n. 32]) specifically describe the borrower as poor: it would not take tremendous creativity to exclude loans to borrowers who are not poor from the prohibition. Moreover, it is always possible to define "usury" as interest that exceeds some acceptable rate. The choice taken in the Mishnah to uphold the rules of interest bespeaks an ideological decision to view all Israel as "brothers" and a *milwâ* as a loan between equals. Whether this choice further reflects the limitations of ancient economic thinking (e.g., an inability to conceive of loans as a form of capital investment), or the ideological refusal to see loans in any other manner than personal favors, is a question to which the Mishnah does not afford an easy answer.

The basic form of interest in the Mishnah is expressed in M5:1 [B–D]:

[B] What is *nešek*?
[C] One who lends a *selaʿ* for five *dînārin*, two *sāʾin* of wheat for three,
[D] because he bites (*nôšēk*).

What is prohibited is the receipt by the lender of more than he gave out. The rate of interest given in this example is quite high: 25% for loans in money and 50% for loans in kind, although what relationship this bears to rates of interest as actually charged is far from clear.[151] It is a corollary of the Mishnah's assumption that loans for consumption are given between equals that

---

[151] In an uncharacteristically ingenuous and "historicizing" gesture, Neusner, *Economics of the Mishnah*, 1990, 102, states "the going rate of interest appears to have been 25 percent for a loan in cash, and 50 percent for a loan in kind." The matter is not so simple. The rate of 50% on loans in kind was quite conventional in Egypt (see Johnson, 1936, 460–1). If similar economic conditions existed in Palestine during the time of the Mishnah it would be a reasonable assumption that in Palestine too this was a conventional rate. As for loans of money, under Roman law, and in Egypt in the Roman period, the legal rate of interest was 12% for loans of money, and this is reflected in documents from Egypt (the rate is set in the Gnomon of the Idios Logos par. 105 [dated to the middle of the second century]; for documents see Johnson, 1936, 450 n. 58, who cites examples of variation from 24% to 6%). In at least one of the documents from the Babatha archive, involving a loan by a Roman soldier (therefore, in theory, bound by Roman law) and a Jew, the rate of interest charged is 12% (*P. Babatha* 11.7, 21–2 [124 CE]; N. Lewis, in noting the erasure in line 3 of "forty" and the interlinear insertion of "sixty," suggests that the loan was actually for forty *denarii* and the document falsely records the loan as sixty as a way of charging a higher rate of interest as well as a higher "principal"). *DJD* II 114 (again involving Roman soldiers) refers to an official rate of interest (*ton eg (l. ek) diatagmatos tokon*). From *P. Babatha* 15, S. Lieberman, "The Importance of the Bar Kokhba Letters for Jewish History and Literature," in *Masada and the Finds from the Bar Kokhba Caves* (New York: The Jewish Museum, 1967), 42–3, rpt. *idem, Texts and Studies* (New York: Ktav, 1974), 208–9, concluded that the going rate of interest varied between 6% and 18%. However, if Lewis' analysis of the relationship between *P. Babatha* 14 and 15 is correct, the statutory rate of interest was 12%, and the point of the proceedings against the guardians is that Babatha accused them of withholding half of the income from their ward's money. The elevated rate of 18%, which Babatha proposes to provide for her son's upkeep, is explicitly expansive and may be a special case of "interest" paid for the upkeep of a minor. It may be, therefore, that in the Judean Desert documents, as in Egyptian papyri, a 12% statutory provincial interest rate is presupposed. However, both sets of documentation come from different administrative units (Egypt and the province of Arabia) than that in which the Mishnah was produced, and cannot offer direct evidence for Galilee in the late second century. These documents do indicate, however, that statutory rates of interest need not necessarily prevent lenders from charging higher rates. However, when and where (or even whether) 25% was the going rate for loans is beyond our knowledge. It may even be that the figure of 25% was chosen for ease of presentation (a *dînār* is one fourth of a *selaʿ*).

the traditions attributed to R. Gamaliel (Yabnean) and R. Simeon (Ushan) in M5:10 [E–P] prohibit extra-contractual gifts of money or service as a form of interest: it is precisely the giving of a "gift" that expresses inequality and residual obligation.[152] The emphasis on equality between lender and borrower is also emphasized by the insistence on parity in M5:10 [A–D]: the labor that one person does for another has to be balanced by the "loan" of labor that that person receives in return, or the exchange of unpaid labor is usurious.

The rule that the lender ought not to receive more than he gave out is used as a systemic principle to structure other permissible or prohibited transactions. Hence, M5:2 allows the lessor of a property to charge more if the lessee pays on a month-by-month basis, and less if he pays for a full year in advance [F–H], but prohibits a seller from charging a higher price for deferred payment [I–K].[153] In the sale of land where partial payment is made, the seller is not permitted to retain possession (and usufruct) of the property

---

[152] I have argued (Appendix I, note to M5:10) that M5:10 [O–P] refers to information that the debtor offers to the lender as a gift. If the reading supported by the Sifre to Deuteronomy (*Sipre Deut.* 262, ed. Finkelstein, p. 284) is correct, that the information is specifically requisitioned by the lender, the built-in inequality inherent in this form of "interest" is even more emphatic.

A similar prohibition of extra-contractual gifts occurs, I believe, also at M5:2 [A–C], which prohibits letting one's lender live in one's courtyard for free or for a reduced rent (Chapter II.C.3). However, in light of papyri from Egypt and elsewhere documenting loans on *antikhrēsis* where the service was provided explicitly instead of interest, it is possible that M5:2 [A–C] considers a contractual form of interest, and not an extra-contractual gift (see below on security). (For loans involving personal service, cf., e.g., *P. Dura* 20, 21 and the documents listed by Johnson, 1936, 452–4; for documents involving housing see, e.g., the contracts of *enoikēsis* such as *P. Fouad* 44 [44 CE]; *BGU* I 260 [90 CE] [=*M. Chr.* 137]; *P. Oslo* III 118 [111/2 CE]; *P. Mich.* III 188 [120 CE], 189 [123 CE]. See further Taubenschlag, 1955, 286–91; B. Cohen, "Antichresis in Jewish and Roman Law," in *Jewish and Roman Law: A Comparative Study* [New York: JTSA, 1966], 433–56.)

[153] Note that in this case the rate of "interest" is 20%. The case of sale is clearly understandable as one of usury: payment is due immediately, and by charging more for deferred payment the seller is charging interest. The case of renting requires some explanation. According to the Babli (B65a), the reason that the transaction is permitted in the case of lease is that in a lease payment is due at the end of the term (this rule is attributed to Rabbah and Rab Yosep), in this case at the end of each month, so the lessor is seen as charging the fair value for a month by month basis, and as willing to deduct from the rent in exchange for the money in advance, and not as charging a fee for the use of the money by the lessee. At the end of Y5:2 (10b) there are two traditions that seem to be comments upon M5:3 [I–K] (see Lieberman, *Yerushalmi Neziqin*, 156 and the commentaries cited there). (1) "R. La said: 'He gives him the fee for his walking (*śěkār raglô*, lit. "the wage for his feet")." That is, the lessee compensates the lessor for having to come monthly and collect the rent. (2) "R. Zera said: 'He becomes like one renting

Institutions and Relationships 193

until full payment is made since this would constitute interest (M5:3 [A–C]). By contrast, in a loan against a field as security, possession of the field remains with the borrower (the "seller") (M5:3 [D–G]).[154]

It is a measure of the Mishnah's dependence on a money economy, and on the use of coins to mark the value of commodities, that loans of produce that are liable to price fluctuations are restricted even when they do not involve an outright charge of interest. According to the dictum of Hillel, even loans of a loaf between women must be made according to the cash value of the loaf at the time of the loan (M5:9 [D–G]). (Note once again the kinds of loans depicted as taking place between women.) Even in traditions that do not conform to Hillel's strictures,[155] loans of produce may not be made for a

---

his dwelling for a high rate.'" In other words, in the case of leases, one is simply permitted to charge what one wants (perhaps because of the view underlying the Babli's interpretation as well).

[154] Arguably, if the point of M5:3 [D–G] is to rule on the problem of who may enjoy the use of the field in the interim, its conclusion is trivial: if the field remains in the hands of the borrower surely there is no problem of unlawful gain by the lender. Furthermore, the terms of the agreement, "If you do not give me [payment] from now until three years [from now], lo, it is mine" [E], may imply that possession is not transferred until the borrower defaults. At any rate, [E–F] seems to be particularly concerned with the transfer of ownership, and not with interim use. It may be that M5:3 [D–G] (unlike [A–C]) does not deal with the possession and enjoyment of the property, but with a field whose value exceeded that of the loan (so that the eventual transfer of the house will give the lender more than was lent out). That possession and use of the property used as security stays with the borrower need not be contradicted by the view attributed to R. Judah in T4:2 (cf. Y5:3 [10b] [on the text see Lieberman, *Yerushalmi Neziqin*, 156], and B63a; *b. ʿArak.* 31a). That passage appears to presuppose a different case, despite the clear overlap with M5:3 [D–G] (both deal with a field used as security, and both refer to Boethos b. Zenon). The wording of the passage from the Tosepta ("he sold him his field in writing") may imply that the document transferred ownership immediately, and not, as in M5:3 [D–G], only upon default (cf. the Greek institution of *ōnē en pistei*, "purchase on trust"; see Taubenschlag, 1955, 272–5). Thus, should the lender make use of the field (as according to R. Judah) and the borrower fail to pay, the lender will have been enjoying the use of a field that he bought and was his own all along. A similar suggestion was attributed to Rab Nahman in the Babli as an explanation of M5:3 [D–G] itself (B66b), and was accepted by the commentaries, but is not required either by the wording of the Mishnah itself or by its ruling on interest. In the Tosepta, however, this reading seems very likely (it is suggested, e.g., by Ritba in *Šiṭṭâ mĕqubbeṣet* to B63a, s.v. *Û-šĕmûʾēl*, and may be implied in the comparison in the Yerushalmi [attributed to R. Yohanan, R. Eleazar, and R. Hoshaya] of this case to the Biblical rule of redemption of urban property [Lev. 25:29–30; *m. ʿArak.* 9:3]: i.e., both are immediate sales subject to redemption).

[155] Cf. the tradition attributed to Rab Judah in the name of Samuel, which sees Hillel's rule as a kind of supererogatory legalistic pietism that can only lead to trouble (B75a).

term long enough for the price to fluctuate in the interim (M5:9 [A–B]).[156] Similarly, where one buys produce for later delivery, the seller must either have produce, or the produce must currently be available in the marketplace (i.e., there is a "market price") so that either buyer or seller could get the produce immediately if they wanted; otherwise the seller owes a debt of a certain volume of produce, which, since the produce is subject to fluctuation in price, is prohibited (M5:1 [H–L]; M5:7).[157]

I have been arguing that the treatment of interest in *m. Baba' Meṣi'a'* reflects the assumption that loans are consumer loans between equals. Yet the world in which the Mishnah took shape was one in which loans were also given as business investments. The Mishnah refuses to grant legitimacy to such loans when the lender charges interest, and is willing to permit them only when they can be perceived as another form of transaction. This is quite clear in one of the passages just referred to above (M5:1 [H–L]):[158]

---

[156] The language of this pericope is worth noting. First, the prohibition is applied although the borrower promises to pay at the harvest, when prices are likely to be at their lowest [A]. Second the permitted case [B], "but he [the borrower] may say to him: '[Lend me produce] ... until my son comes,' or '... until I find the key,'" may presuppose not only that the loan must be for a short term, but that the borrower actually has produce but is currently unable to get at it (so, e.g., Rashi, *s.v.* *'Abāl* [B75a]). If so, this pericope is working with the same principles as M5:1 [H–K] and M5:7. If this is the case, loans of produce, "neighborly" loans between equals, can only really be carried out in an informal manner between two parties who have a measure of wealth in the form of produce. (In [A], too, the stipulation "I will give it to you at [the time of] the threshing floor," is consistent with a picture of a land holding borrower who expects to have produce down the line, although admittedly it would apply equally to small freeholding or tenant farmers as well.) A loan to a poor person who does not have stores of produce would have to be made on the basis of the cash value. This is potentially a strikingly divisive element in what is ostensibly an egalitarian system.

[157] Compare the Gnomon of the Idios Logos, par. 104, which prohibits selling produce until it is harvested. R. S. Bagnall, "Price in 'Sales on Delivery,'" *GRBS* 18 (1977) 85–96, describes how these kinds of sales, at least in Egypt, can mask loans that are decidedly not interest free by misrepresenting the sale price. The Mishnah, however, seems to be concerned with increase resulting from the "natural" fluctuations in prices.

[158] See on this pericope S. Lieberman, "*Mišnat bābā' mešī'a' rēš 'ēzehû nešek û-pērûšāh,*" in *Yad R. '. M. Lifshitz* (Jerusalem, 1975), 217–23, rpt. in *idem, Studies in Palestinian Talmudic Literature,* ed. D. Rosenthal (Jerusalem: Magnes, 1991), 12–8. Lieberman seems to suggest (p. 14 [219]) that in [H–K] what is referred to is a wheat merchant re-selling produce that he had bought for twenty five *dînārîm* for thirty *dînārîm* (i.e., precisely the limit allowed by the rules on *hônāyâ*, if the sixth is calculated as a fraction of the market price plus the overcharge [on this method of calculation see Y4:3 [9d]; B49b; Melamed, 1942–3, 45–6]). This is a rather strange reading of the Mishnah, since the pericope states explicitly that the market price had gone up [I], and not that the original purchaser, now the seller (Lieberman's "wheat merchant," although there is no reason why this transaction should not be seen as taking place between householders, as I have argued above in my discussion of markets) wishes to raise the price.

[H] He bought wheat from him at a golden *dînār* to the *kôr*, and such was the market price.
[I] Wheat [later] stood at thirty *dînārîm* [to the *kôr*].
[J] He said to him: "Give me my wheat, for I am going to sell it and buy wine with it."
[K] He said to him: "But lo, your wheat is valued with me at thirty *dînārîm*! And lo, you have a claim with me against them for wine"—
[L] but he does not have wine.

Where M5:7 depicts a straightforward purchase, this pericope adds the element of speculation: buying at a low price to sell high and converting the proceeds into a new investment in produce. What makes the transaction prohibited in this pericope is the fact that the borrower (the "seller") does not have wine. Since the transaction cannot be construed as a sale, it must be a loan and is prohibited.[159]

---

[159] The restriction is even more explicit in a *bāraîtā'* in T4:23 (with parallels Y5:8 [10c]; B62b):
[A] He owed him money,
[B] and he came to take produce from him at the threshing floor.
[C] He [the borrower] said to him: "Go out and value them against me at the market price, and I will give [the produce] from now to twelve months [from now],"
[D] lo, this is *ribbît*,
[E] because it did not come to him like his *'issār*.
[F] He came and said: "Lend me a *kôr* of wheat and I will give it to you at the market price at which you sell it,"
[G] it is permitted.

[Nahmanides, *Hiddûšîm* to B65a concluded that the Yerushalmi's version of [F–G] read *'āsûr*, "it is prohibited," in [G] (see Lieberman, *TK*, 9, 208), and sees [F] as a reference to a contract to pay according to some future price. Even if correct, this does not mean, however, that the Tosepta should be emended accordingly, since traditions often circulated with variations. In the context of the Tosepta, [F] may mean simply "I will give it to you at the market price at which you could sell it [now]," i.e., the current price.] In [A–E] the transaction is prohibited [D], even though the borrower ("buyer") had produce (cf. M5:1 [L]), "because it did not come to him like his *'issār*" [E], i.e., because the transaction did not begin with the transfer of a coin given as a purchase (see Rashi, s.v. *Dě-lo' kě-'issārô*, B62b). According to this tradition, not only must the transaction appear to be a sale, but it must actually be a sale. By contrast, a *bāraîtā'* at B63a (*těnî R. 'Ôša'yā'*), begins (as does T4:23) with a debt, but allows a succession of conversions of the debt to new forms of produce, much as does M5:1 [H–L].

Since M5:1 does not specify whether there existed a market price for wine in [K–L], it is possible that the author of [H–L] would have permitted the transaction—even though the borrower had no produce—if such a price existed. In that case, M5:1 would make no distinction between actual sales for delayed delivery (cf. M5:7) and a fictive "sale" that converts a debt of one commodity into another. While this may be, this view is not attested in the Tannaitic material cited in the preceding paragraph. T4:23 clearly would prohibit such a transac-

In the transaction just described, the parity between the parties is maintained. It is otherwise with the other form of investment described in Chapter 5 of our tractate, in which one party gives money or raw materials (produce or animals) to a borrower and shares the profits.[160] M5:4 [A–B] discusses transactions with a shopkeeper. In [A] the principal gives actual produce to the borrower. The next clause [B] considers an investment of "money with which to buy produce." Since this latter transaction, too, is contracted "for half profit" (*lĕ-maḥaṣît śākār*), it follows that the produce is to be bought for reselling. In connection with animals, two types of contractors "for half profits" are considered in *m. Babaʾ Meṣiʿaʾ*:[161] (1) one who assesses (or: receives on assessment) (*śām*) the value of the animal (M5:4 [E]; M5:5 [A, D]; the "setting up" of chickens, M5:4 [D], is presumably a contract of the same type since the same ruling, M5:4 [F], applies to both);[162] and (2) one who receives (*mĕqabbēl*) (M5:4 [G]).[163] In all of these cases, the

---

tion (in [B–C] there exists a market price and the borrower has produce). The *bāraîtāʾ* of R. Oshaʿya, which permits conversion of a loan, nevertheless specifies at each phase: "value them against me at the current market price" (*ka-šaʿār šel ʿakšayw*), and concludes that the transaction is permitted only if the borrower ("seller") actually had produce. If the expression "he has no wine" in M5:1 [L] specifies that [K–L] would only have been permitted had the borrower had wine, even if there existed a market price, the Mishnah, like T4:23 and the *bāraîtāʾ* of R. Oshaʿya, makes a sharp distinction between these two contracts.

[160] It is perhaps an indication of the limitations of the Mishnah as a workable law code and of its incompleteness as a compendium of materials, that this subject is discussed in no more than two pericopae in the Mishnah (M5:4–5; three, including M5:6), but takes up the better part of twenty-nine pericopae in the Tosepta (T4:11–25; 5:1–14, with some exceptions).

[161] For the material from Egypt see S. von Bolla, *Untersuchungen zur Tiermiete und Viehpacht in Altertum* (*Münchener Beiträge zur Papyrusforschung und antiken Rechtsgeschichte* 30: Munich: C. H. Beck, 1940), 28ff. (on leases of animals for their "produce" rather than their labor, *Viehpacht*) and especially 93ff. (on proportional arrangements). For contracts on shares see *SB* V 7814 (K.S. Gapp, "A Lease of a Pigeon-House with Brood," *TAPA* 64 [1933], 90–1; 256 CE) in which the lessees pay a specific (and increasing) number of birds and a proportion of the dung produced (one half in the first year, two thirds in successive years); *P. Thead.* 8 (306 CE) = *P. Sakaon* 71 similarly involves both payments of fixed amounts and proportional shares of the flocks (see the discussion by von Bolla, 1940, 102–4).

[162] T5:10, dealing with receipt on assessment ("One who assesses (*ha-šām*) an animal from his fellow") presents the following fragment of a documentary formula: "if it should die at [my] fault (*bĕ-bûsyāʾ*) I will pay the whole [of its value], [if] not at [my] fault I will pay half" (cf. the discussion of the term *busyāʾ* in connection with negligence in section B.2 above). The implication is that under normal circumstances (i.e., not *bĕ-busyāʾ*) the "borrower" assumed only half the risk for loss, damage, or depreciation from the initial valuation (cf. the expansion on this in T5:11–2).

[163] T5:1–2, in two pairs of cases, distinguishes between a contractor who receives (*qibbēl*) animals "for a hundred gold [coins], for a half, for a third or for a quarter," (a prohibited

borrower is permitted to use the "loan" for personal profit. However, since half of the profits go to the owner, the borrower returns more to the lender than the lender gave out as an investment. Therefore, the lender must compensate the borrower so that the latter not appear to be providing free service (or value) to the lender in exchange for use of the money or raw materials (unless the borrower receives some other form of supplementary compensation).[164] In discussing these contracts, the Mishnah does not deal with status

---

contract) and one takes on the contract "for a half, for a third or for a quarter, half for food and (or?) half for idleness [i.e., from other activities, in modern terms "opportunity costs"]" (a permissible contract). According to Lieberman, *TK*, 9, 209, the valuation "for a hundred gold [coins]" applies to the first case alone, and the primary distinction between the cases is the assignment of risk: in the prohibited case the contractor is liable for the entire initial value. If this is correct, it is possible to take "receipt" as a contract in which there is no liability at all for the "borrower" (as did Rashi, for instance [see the note to M5:4 in Appendix I]; see also Lieberman, *TK* 9, 210, n. 4). However, even if the initial valuation referred to in T5:1–2 applies only to the prohibited case, it remains possible that some liability (e.g., a proportion equivalent to the share of the profits) is undertaken by the "receiver" in the permitted case. Moreover, it is possible that "for a hundred gold [coins]" applies to both cases, and what distinguishes the two cases is solely the specification "half for food and half for idleness" in the second: i.e., by making the compensation explicit one has met the requirement of "paying a wage." If that is so, it should be noted that in contrast to the Mishnah, in the permitted contract it is the proportion of the appreciation that is the functional equivalent of labor costs and wages (cf. M5:4 [C, F]) and the payment per head that serves as the "share" in the contract. Nevertheless, this passage from the Tosepta may explain why the requirement to pay a wage is not specified in connection with a *mĕqabbēl* (M5:4 [G–I]).

[164] The traditional assessment of the contracts in M5:4 [A–F] is that the recipient of the materials is partly a borrower (and liable with respect to damage and loss) and partly a depositary (i.e., bearing only limited liability) (see B74b, in the name of the "Nehardeans"), and that the share of the profits that the contractor makes from the portion on "deposit" and delivers to the "lender," is the product of labor offered free of charge in exchange for the use of the portion that is a "loan." It is this labor that is "interest" unless it is compensated. (See Rashi *ad loc*. B68a). In the Tosepta there is a dispute about how high the compensation is to be, with the view attributed to R. Judah that the compensation need be only nominal (the "borrower" ate some of the "lender's" bread and vinegar or dates); and a further distinction between "full payment" (attributed to R. Simeon) and the wage of "an idle laborer" (*pôʿēl bāṭēl*, attributed to R. Meir). (On the expression "an idle laborer," compare J. Heinemann, "The Status of the Labourer in Jewish Law and Society in the Tannaitic Period," *HUCA* 25 [1954], 278–83, who understands the phrase to refer to a worker duly hired but unable to work because of circumstances such as inclement weather, who is therefore entitled to partial compensation for the wasted day [T4:11; see also the note to M2:9 in Appendix I]; alternatively, the expression may refer to an unemployed worker willing to take work even at reduced wages). According to the reading of the manuscripts KRLNP in M5:4 [C], our Mishnah agrees with the view of R. Meir; according to the variant that leaves off the word "idle," M5:4 is in agreement with the view of R. Simeon (see Appendix I, note to M5:4). In M5:5 [A], the fact that during the term of the contract the animal can be made productive (it "produces and

equals making a mutually beneficial business arrangement, but rather transactions in which one party works for another and is directly answerable to the principal party: workers who will sell the produce of a householder, or will raise his animals, as well as tenant farmers receiving loans of seed or of money for improvements (M5:5 [E–F]; M5:8).[165]

Loans are everywhere a risky undertaking. Despite the apparent ability of the debtor to pay there is always the risk that borrowers will default on loans. If the Mishnah refrains from compensating the lender for undertaking this risk (i.e., through interest), it does recognize the need of lenders to secure their loans. One way of doing this is for the debtor to put forward a third party who is willing to guarantee payment (*ʿārāb*, "surety," "guarantor") (M5:12 [B]).[166] The other form of security that the Mishnah recognizes is that of pledged property.[167] This may take the form of landed property, as in M5:3 [D], which refers to a case in which one party lends to another against the value of a field.[168] (Although the Mishnah does discuss the "Hebrew slave" who sells himself for a limited period of time, it does not use the category

---

eats") apparently obviates the need for an additional wage. M5:4 [G–I] may not specify payment for the "receiver" (*mĕqabbēl*) because it is presupposed by the definition of that kind of contract (see the preceding note). Alternatively, [G–I] depends on the rule of [C, F].

On the prohibition of the contract of the *ṣoʾn bārzel*, "iron sheep" (M5:6 [A, C]), see Y5:7 (10c) and T5:14 (on the text of which see Lieberman, *TK*, 9, 217–8). The passage from the Yerushalmi presents a case where the recipient of animals accepts all of the risk for the animals, but receives all of the profits less a charge per animal. A. Gulak, "*Ṣoʾn bārzel bi-dînê ha-talmûd*," *Tarbiz* 3 (1932), 137–46 surveys the material and discusses it in connection with Greek (especially the "*athanatos*" contracts; see von Bolla, 1940, 17–27) and Roman legal traditions.

[165] As I have already noted in my discussion of markets, the Tosepta greatly expands on M5:4 [A–C] (investment with a shopkeeper), and, in particular, emphasizes the demands that the principal may make on the shopkeeper's time and activities (T4:12–3, 19–21). For the tenant farmer see M9:1–10 and the discussion in Section B.6 of this chapter.

[166] Cf. *m. B. Bat.* 10:7, 8. The latter passage (in a tradition attributed to Ben Nannas [Yabnean]) makes a distinction between a surety who is assigned after the giving of the loan ("after the signature of the documents") and one who undertakes the responsibility before the money is loaned ("lend to him and I will give it to you").

[167] Compare Taubenschlag, 1955, 271–91; for the Roman legal traditions see D 13.7; and D 20; and Schulz, 1955, 406–27; Buckland, 1963, 473–81.

[168] Compare, e.g., papyrus documents referring to loans on hypothec (*P. Oxy.* III 485 [178 CE]; XVII 2134 [170–1]; from the Judean Desert comes a fragmentary document [it is listed by the editors as an *acte de vente*] that refers to a piece of property that is "liable for payment of a debt" [*ʾaḥarāʾî bĕ-pērāʿôn*], *DJD* II 22. 1–2; and a fragmentary Greek document, *P. Seʾelim Gr.* 3, published in H. M. Cotton, 1994, 53–60); compare also the institution of *hypallagma*, in which the debtor retains possession of the security but is prohibited from alienating it (e.g., *P. Ath.* 21; *P. Vind. Worp* 10; and the two documents in J. G. Keenan, "Two Loans from Tebtunis," *BASP* 7 [1970], 77–84).

Institutions and Relationships 199

of personal security of a loan.[169]) In general, when the Mishnah uses the noun *maškôn*, "pledge," it refers to moveable goods that the borrower hands over to the lender in exchange for the loan.[170] In M9:13 [B] the noun is used to refer to a pledge seized for the lender by the court. In either case, the pledge is considered to be in the hands of the lender, hence the level of liability that the lender bears with respect to the pledge becomes an important issue, discussed in M6:7.[171] In M9:13 [E–I], however, the Mishnah discusses the Pentateuchal rule that the pledge of a poor person be returned so that the

---

[169] See E. E. Urbach, *The Laws Regarding Slavery as a Source for the Social History of the Period of the Second Temple and the Mishnah and Talmud* (*Ancient Economic History*. New York: Arno, 1979), 91–2.

[170] For instance, M6:7. Cf. also *m. Maʿaś. Š.* 1:1 (produce as pledge; the context, which involves selling and exchanging second tithe produce [as well as using it as a weight (?)], suggests that it has been transferred to the lender); *m. Šebu.* 6:7 (the rule worked out about the pledge presupposes that the lender had possession of it and lost it). *m. Šebi.* 10:2 is not explicit in this regard. Compare *P. Lond.* II 193 (p. 205), the account of a pawn broker who makes small loans (to women) in exchange for articles of clothing, jewelry or furniture; *P. Oxy.* III 530.

The verbal use of *maškēn* in the Mishnah applies to land as well as moveable property, and can mean both to "distrain" (especially by a court: M9:13 [B, J]; see also *m. Šeq.* 1:3; 7:5; *m. Ket.* 13:8; *m. Šebu.* 7:2; *m, ʿArak.* 5:6; 6:3; 8:2) and "to give up as a pledge" (e.g., the formula "sold it or gave it as a pledge [*miškěnāh*]," *m. ʿAb. Zar.* 4:5; *m. Ket.* 11:3 [in both cases real estate is referred to], which seems to presuppose that the object is no longer in the borrower's possession). However, the context of the passive participle *měmuškan* in *m. Peʾa* 8:8 and *m. Šebi.* 10:6 may imply that the object so described is still in the possession of the borrower.

[171] See on this pericope Friedman, 1990, 296–7, and the glosses of the Yerushalmi to M6:7 [B–C] ("R. Judah says: '... [if] he lent him produce [against a pledge] he is a paid depositary'") (Y6:7 [11a]):
Said R. Yohanan: "How much is a person willing to give to sell his produce on the [security] of a pledge."
Said R. Abbahu in the name of R. Yohanan: "How much is a person willing to give to sell his produce to someone who will appease him by means of a pledge."
On the basis of the Yerushalmi traditions, Friedman took M6:7 [B–C] to refer to a sale for delayed payment, with the payment secured by a pledge (hence the "lender" receives the additional benefit of disposing of the produce, and therefore has a higher liability with respect to the pledge). Indeed, given the discomfort with loans of produce in the Mishnah, and the dictum of Hillel (M5:9 [D–G]) that loans of produce were to be made for the current monetary value of the produce, it is not impossible that what is envisioned in M6:7 [B–C] is a loan in which the lender will receive cash in repayment of the loan. Nevertheless, M6:7 is framed in terms of a loan, and not a sale. This may be merely because the view attributed to R. Judah amplifies a tradition involving loans. However, since loans of produce to be repaid in kind do appear in the Mishnah, at least within limits (see M5:8–9 and the discussion of M3:6–8 in Chapter II.B.2), it may be that M6:7 [B–C] is working with the case of real loans. In that case, the increased benefit to the lender is that the lender now has an unpaid caretaker for the produce.

borrower may use it. In focusing on the Biblical rules (Ex. 22:25–6; Deut. 24:10–13, 17), M9:13 as a whole emphasizes the potential real poverty of borrowers, and demonstrates an interest in protecting paupers from rapacious creditors: distraint can only be undertaken by the court [A–D]; the pledge must be returned for the debtor's use [E–F], and something upon which the sustenance of the debtor depends may not be seized at all [L–R]; for reasons of sexual morality or reputation, rather than economic ethics, the pledge of a widow may not be seized at all [J–K] (cf. Deut. 24:17).[172] Once again, the model of parity is allowed to break down, and in its place a picture in which a creditor may have substantial power over his debtor is recognized. This is especially striking in the tradition attributed to R. Simeon b. Gamaliel (M9:13 [G–K]), which limits the amount of time that the borrower can rely on receiving his pledge back for use before it is sold off.[173] In this rule the power of a creditor over the property of the borrower is not only noted but enforced (within limits). The same theme, that of the power that the lender has over the borrower, recurs in M6:7 [D–E]:

[D] Abba Shaul says: "A person may rent out the pledge of a poor [debtor] in order to continually assign it to him [i.e., against his debt],
[E] "because he is like one returning a lost object."

On the one hand, this tradition is clearly in the interests of the poor person, since it reduces the debt. At the same time, however, the passage also presupposes that this renting out of the pledge is undesirable (whether because of

---

[172] M9:13 [J–K] is glossed in T10:10 as follows:
[C] "It is the same (ʾaḥat ... wĕ-ʾaḥat ...) whether she is poor or wealthy."
[D] the words of R. Judah.
[E] R. Simeon says: "[In the case of] a poor woman he is not permitted to seize the pledge [at all],
[F] "[In the case of] a wealthy woman, he takes [a pledge] but he does not return it,
[G] "so that he not [regularly] go in and out of her house (hôlēk û-bāʾ ʾeṣlāh),
[H] "so as not to cause her a bad name."
[G–H] make the issue of sexual reputation quite clear. Notable in this context is also the question of the interpretation of "authorial intent" in Deut. 24:17: "You shall not seize the garment of a widow as pledge."

[173] By contrast, in M9:13 [E–F] the time limit is unstated, and presumably open. It is probably in this connection that T10:9 adds explicitly "but if he returns it [i.e., if the creditor is required to return the pledge to the debtor for the debtor's use] he returns it forever." (Note, however, that in T10:9 the specific case is somehat different than in M9:13. In the Tosepta, the loan is secured by two pledges: "one that he [the debtor] needs, and one that he does not need."

wear and tear on the object, or the loss of dignity involved in having one's property in the hands of a stranger), and that poor people are subjected (against their will?) to something from which wealthy borrowers are exempt.[174]

5. Laborer and employer.

The Mishnah considers the rights of workers to be protected from unilateral deviations from customary practice, to eat of the produce of the field, to demand their wage and, in fact, entitles workers to an extraordinary procedure to secure their payment. This concern with the privileges of workers is remarkable in light of the general attitude towards laborers in Greek and Latin literature and, in particular, the relative absence of concern for this topic in Roman legal texts.[175] The recurrent description of manual labor as "servile" and of laborers as slave-like in classical literature is by and large absent in Rabbinic tradition.[176] It will not do, however, to romanticize the

---

[174] This is made explicit in T7:18, in which a version of Abba Shaul's tradition ends "but he is not permitted to touch [the pledge] of the wealthy man."

[175] This lack of interest was noted by Schulz, 1951, 344–5. See also Crook, 1967, 192–200. There are, however, occasional references in the Digest to the rights of a worker. For example, D 19 2.38.pr. (Paul) rules that a worker is entitled to his wage if it was not his fault that he did not do his job (cf. T7:3–4); cf. D 19.2.19.9 (Ulpian), which cites an imperial rescript that gave a similar ruling for a copyist (cf. T7:1, to be discussed further below). In both cases the texts refer to workers who have leased out their labor (*operas suas locare*) and not to a situation in which the worker (typically an artisan) has accepted a contract to do a job. In D 38.1.50.1 (Neratius), a worker is entitled either to food (cf. M7:1) or to time off to eat, and time to take care of physical requirements.

[176] See, e.g., Aristotle, *Politics*, 8.1337b.19–21 (performing even "liberal" activities on account of another is both *thētikos* [like a hired worker] and *doulikos* [slave-like]); *Nicomachean Ethics*, 4.1124b.31–5a.2 (for the noble person [*megalopsykhos*] to live for another is *doulikos*; that is why all flatterers [*kolakes*] are *thētikos* and humble people are flatterers); Cicero, *De officiis*, 1.150–1 (the occupations of hirelings [*mercenarii*] are all illiberal and dirty [*sordidus*]: "the very wage [they receive] is the recompense for their servitude"); Lucian, *Apology*, 10 (entering the imperial service is different than entering the service of some rich man in order to serve [*douleuein*]). It is not accidental that the closest thing in the Digest to a discussion of contractual relations between employer and employee does not occur in the context of a discussion of *locatio conductio* (lease and hire) (D 19.2) but in the title *De operis libertorum* (D 38.1, "Concerning the Work of Freedmen"), that is, in the context of the obligations a nominally free, but not independent, person owes his or her patron (cf. also D 47.2.90; 48.19.11.1). See Finley, 1985, in particular 62–94; de Ste Croix, 1981, 179–204.

That the status of a laborer might also be seen as "servile" in Rabbinic tradition is made quite clear in *Sipra Bĕ-har* 7:3 (ed. Weiss, 109c), to Lev. 25:39–40 ("If your brother should be brought low and is sold to you, you shall not have him perform the labor of a slave. He will be with you like a hired laborer [*śākîr*], like a resident [alien] ...."). The *Sipra* notes that "like a hired laborer" the "Hebrew slave" is also entitled to his wage at the proper time. More

Rabbinic attitude towards labor.[177] To be sure, the relationship of laborer to employer can be used in tractate ʾAbot as a model for the relationship of humans to God (m. ʾAb. 2:14–16), but so can the relationship of slave to master (1:3). At best, we can say that the Mishnah reflects an appreciation of skilled artisanship (although not without some ambivalence),[178] and this appreciation perhaps extends to small independent farmers who had to work hard to make ends meet. Both artisan and small farmer, however, are independent producers; the same cannot be said of unskilled wage labor, and it is

---

interesting, however, is the immediately preceding tradition that "you shall not have him perform the labor of a slave" implies that this special class of bondservants is exempt from doing servile work, but free laborers do not share in this exemption. (In light of this, it seems that the rule brought in the continuation of 7:3 [109c–d], that "with you" means that the bondservant is to be maintained at the standard of living that the master enjoys, need not be taken as extending also to the hired laborer. Cf. M. Ayali, *Pôʿalîm wě-ʾûmānîm: mělʾaktān û-maʿamadām bě-siprût ḥzl* [*Yād la-talmûd*: Jerusalem: Masada, 1987], 77, who concludes that this passage expresses the hope that workers be treated as equals.) It should be noted, however, that this passage does not attribute servile status to workers merely because they perform work for others, but rather requires duly contracted laborers to perform whatever duties they are assigned even if those duties are servile. In this connection, it is worth noting the Amoraic tradition attributed to Rab and connected in both Talmuds to the contractual relationship of the worker to his employer that glosses the verse "for unto me are all the children of Israel slaves" (Lev. 25:55): "[They are] my slaves and not slaves to [my] slaves" (B10a; cf. *b. B. Qam.* 116b; B77a–b; compare Y6:2 [11a]: "Israelites do not acquire [*qônîn*] one another"). It is presumably in the context of an easy association between hired laborers and slaves or bondservants that this passage explicitly denies any such connection.

[177] See, e.g., Krauss, 1911, 2, 104; 1954, 265–6; Ayali, 1987, 79–101 (who collects and evaluates many of the Rabbinic traditions about labor; additional material is collected in an appendix, 157–68).

[178] In a gloss to a reference in *m. Qid.* 1:7 to obligations of fathers with respect to their sons, the Tosepta includes teaching one's son a trade (*ʾûmānût*), followed by a series of traditions about how knowing a trade establishes both financial security and morality (*t. Qid.* 1:11). More ambivalence is reflected in the Mishnah itself in a late supplement that appears in standard editions of *m. Qid.* 4:14 (see Epstein, *Nûsaḥ*, 977–8: most mss. do not include this material and several medieval commentaries testify that it is not properly part of the Mishnah; Epstein suggests that the material comes from *t. Qid.* 5:14–7, with which the supplement to *m. Qid.* 4:14 does indeed have multiple parallels). A tradition attributed to R. Meir instructs a father to teach his son an "easy and clean trade" (surely because some trades were beneath one's dignity if one could avoid them) and continues with the recommendation that the father pray for his son's sustenance "for there is no trade in which there is not [both] poverty and wealth …," a theological position that is rather less confident in the advantages of trades than the passages from *t. Qid.* 1:11 referred to above. More striking is the passage attributed to R. Simeon b. Eleazar that follows immediately in the supplement to *m. Qid.* 4:14 (= *t. Qid.* 5:15), which describes the necessity of trade in human experience as the regrettable result of the fall of Adam in terms strongly reminiscent of Mt. 6:25–33 and Lk. 12:22–31.

unclear to what extent Rabbis' appreciation of labor extended to include these workers.[179]

Traditions about workers (*pô'alîm*) in the Mishnah associate them with agricultural labor,[180] in contrast to slaves, who are regularly associated with domestic work.[181] If this differential treatment of free and unfree labor is reflective of the forms and distribution of labor in Roman Galilee (this is far

---

[179] In *m. ʾAbot* 1:10 the dictum "love work (*mĕlʾākâ*)" is attributed to Shemaʿyah. How this was taken by later tradition may be seen from the way in which the dictum is glossed in *ʾAbot R. Nat.* B 21, in which the work referred to is repeatedly assumed to be skilled crafts, or independent agricultural activity, for instance:

(1) R. Yose says: "Great is work, for the Divine Presence did not descend upon Israel until they did work [in the building of the Tabernacle (i.e., the work of carpenters, weavers, and metalsmiths)]" (cf. A 11).

(2) R. Eleazar b. Azariah says: "Great is work, for every single artisan (*kol ʾûmān wĕ-ʾûmān*) goes out and glories himself in his craft."

(3) R. [Judah the Patriarch] also used to say: "Great is labor, for even if a man has a courtyard or a vineyard in ruins he should occupy himself with them so that he will be occupied with work."

If Rabbis made the distinction I am suggesting between independent production and wage labor they were merely conforming to more or less common upper class values in the ancient world. This is precisely the difference that Cicero, for example, makes in the passage referred to above between those workers who are paid for their labor (*operae*) and those for their skill (*artes*) (*De officiis* 1.150–1). See also the discussion of de Ste Croix, 1981, 198–9, of the terminology of *locatio conductio operarum* (the hire of one's services) and *locatio conductio operis* (the hire of a job) in Roman legal sources.

[180] See, e.g., *m. Peʾa* 5:6, 7; *m. Kil.* 7:6; *m. Šebi.* 5:8; 8:4; *m. Ter.* 3:4 (treading grapes); *m. Maʿaś.* 2:7–8; 3:1–3; 5:5; *m. Moʿed Qaṭ.* 2:1–2 (production of wine and oil); *m. Ned.* 4:7 (agricultural labor, but also building a house or wall); *m. B. Meṣ.* 7:2–7 (cf. M6:1 [D], processing of flax); *m. ʿAb. Zar.* 5:1 (wine production).

[181] See *m. Pes.* 7:2 (roasting the paschal lamb); 8:2 (slaughtering the paschal lamb); *m. ʾAbot* 1:3 (personal service, as a model for humans' service of God); *m. ʾOhal.* 18:7 (watching a house). See also the passages in which a slave is listed among the members of a household (e.g., *m. Ter.* 3:4; *m. Maʿaś. Š.* 4:4; *m. ʿErub.* 7:6; *m. Šeq.* 1:3; *m. B. Meṣ.* 1:5; *m. ʿArak.* 8:8; *m. Neg.* 14:12), or in which he appears as the representative of the householder, like his wife or agent (*m. Bik.* 1:5; *m. B. Meṣ.* 8:3; *m. Menaḥ.* 9:8). In *m. B. Qam.* 6:5, the slave who is killed in the burning of a stack of grain may (but need not) have been used for agricultural labor. Similarly, in *m. B. Bat.* 10:7 (whether slaves are automatically sold along with an *ʿîr*), even if *ʿîr* is taken to be an agricultural installation and not a village, the slaves may (but again, need not) be thought be doing work in the fields. In M7:6, the implication is that the slave performs agricultural labor, but this is perhaps to be explained by the fact that the pericope is interested in the status as competent adults of the various members of a household (including slaves) rather than in the type of labor these members perform. See G. Alon, *Toldôt ha-yĕhûdîm bĕ-ʾereṣ yiśrāʾēl bi-tĕqûpat ha-mišnâ wĕ-ha-talmûd* (Tel Aviv: Hakibutz Hameuchad, 1953–4), 1, 97; Ayali, 1987, 82, who stress the relative infrequency of slaves in agricultural work in Rabbinic literature. See, more generally, Urbach, 1979.

from clear, but it is at any rate consistent with observations about Roman Egypt[182]), it suggests that slaves were not involved with "production" but rather contributed to the standard of living and, no doubt, the personal status of those people wealthy enough to afford them. Free laborers are also to be distinguished from artisans (ʾumānîm), who perform a more or less skilled trade, own their own tools (or, in the case of porters, their own animals), and are located in "town" and not in the fields.[183]

It is about artisans that m. Babaʾ Meṣiʿaʾ formulates its rules about contracting for labor (M6:1–2). M6:2 [A–E] reads as follows:

[A] One who hires artisans—
[B] and they withdrew,
[C] their hand is in the inferior position.
[D] And if the householder withdrew,
[E] his hand is in the inferior position.

In other words, employer and employee are considered equal contracting parties, subject to the same penalties for withdrawal from the contract: if either party withdraws that party has a weaker legal standing.[184] This rule is further generalized to penalize any alteration of, or withdrawal from, any

---

[182] See Rathbone, 1991, 89 (also Johnson, 1936, 277f.).

[183] m. Ber. 2:4 (working on a course of stones; the pericope also refers to ʾûmānîm atop a tree, although this may result from the Mishnah's compressed language [cf. the emendation in y. Ber. 2:4 (5a): "[Read] the Mishnah thus (kēnî, for mānî in the Leiden ms. and the Venice editio princeps): 'The pôʿalîm read atop a tree, and the ʾûmānîm atop the course of stones;'" see Epstein, Nûsaḥ, 444–5]; m. Šebi. 5:6 (sellers [and presumably makers] of farm equipment); m. Pes. 4:6 (tailors, barbers, launderers and shoemakers are identified as workers in ʾûmāniyyôt, "crafts"); 4:7 (one gets "vessels" [kēlîm; perhaps clothing, cf., e.g., m. Beṣa 1:10] from the house of the ʾûmān); m. Beṣa 1:10 (repairing shoes); m. Moʿed Qaṭ. 1:8 (a professional tailor); 1:10 (construction work); 2:4 ("vessels" from the house of the ʾûmān); m. B. Qam. 9:3 (carpenters and builders are given as examples of ʾûmānîm); m. B. Meṣ. 2:2 (wool that is processed in the house of the ʾûmān); 8:7 (doors and locks are the work of artisans); m. ʿArak. 6:3 (carpenters); m. Kel. 5:4, 9 (makers of ovens); 26:1 (repairing baskets). In a Yabnean gloss to m. ʿArak. 6:3 an ass driver and ʾikkār (an agricultural worker) are mentioned. Ass drivers are also mentioned in M6:1 [D] in the context of hiring artisans. The case of the ʾikkār is especially important because it is apparently the latter's possession of a team of oxen that takes this worker out of the class of mere laborer ("If he was an ʾikkār they give him [i.e., allow him to retain] his team [of oxen]," m. ʿArak. 6:3; see also the sources cited in Ayali's catalogue of types of labor, Ayali, 1987, 105 s.v. ʾikkār).

[184] It is frequently assumed that the view attributed to R. Dosa in T7:1 (cf. Y6:1 [10d–11a]; B76b) corresponds to that of M6:2 (Rashi to B76b, s.v. šāmîn lāhen; see also Heinemann, 1954, 299–300; S. Friedman, 1990, 88). That view holds that if workers withdrew half way through a job and the cost of completing the job had gone up the employer can

Institutions and Relationships 205

type of contract [F–G]. However, M6:1 [A–C] rules that where the parties have "deceived one another" (*hiṭʿû zeh ʾet zeh*) they have no legal claim against each other (cf. M4:6 [E]). Just what is meant by deceit is not entirely clear, but the interpretation of the Yerushalmi[185] is probably correct, that the

---

deduct the added cost to himself from the amount owed to the workers for the half that they completed (and perhaps, if the cost of labor had gone down, the employer could pay the workers for the work already done at the new lower rate, rather than at that originally contracted; see Lieberman, *TK*, 9, 247, citing *Ḥasdê dāwîd* and *Merkebet ha-mišnâ*). Since, however, the tradition of R. Dosa only explicitly considers withdrawal by workers, there is no guarantee that according to this view employers were penalized if they withdrew, whereas the wording of M6:2 [A–E] states that the position of the employer who withdraws is analogous to that of the workers if they withdraw.

[185] See Y6:1 (10d) (and Lieberman, *Yerushalmi Neziqin* 163; see also Albeck, *Nĕzîqîn*, 426):

(1) What is "and they deceived one another" [=M6:1 [C]]?
(2) [Employer:] "Come work for me (*ʿimmî*; Escorial ms. *ʿimmān* [plural])."
(3) [Workers:] "How [i.e., at what rate] do you (pl.) work?"
(4) "For five *rbn* (?),"
(5) and it turned out that they worked for ten *rbn* for the job.
(6) "Come work for me."
(7) "How [i.e., for how long] do you (pl.) work?"
(8) "For ten days,"
(9) and it turned out that they worked for five.
(10) What is "They deceived (*hiṭʿû*) the householder?" (ms. Escorial; Leiden ms., Venice *editio princeps*: "The householder deceived them (*hiṭʿan*)").
(11) "Come work with your fellows,"
(12) "How do they work?"
(13) "For ten *rbn*,"
(14) and it turned out they worked for five *rbn* for the job.
(15) "Come work with your fellows,"
(16) "How do they work?"
(17) "For five days,"
(18) and it turned out that they worked for ten.

The interpretation of this passage is problematic. Following the text of the Escorial ms. in (2) and (11), Lieberman, *Yerushalmi Neziqin*, 163, took (1–9) as describing deceit by the employer of the laborers, and (10–18) deceit by the laborers. Friedman, 1990, 4–5 and n. 14 followed the Leiden ms. in (10) and saw (10–18) as describing a case where the workers deceived the employer, although in order to make this reading make more sense, he proposed the readings "five" and "ten" in (13) and (14) respectively (i.e., the workers accept a lower wage thinking it is the going rate, as in Lieberman's interpretation of (1–9)). Lieberman could rely on citations of the Yerushalmi in medieval commentaries (see Rabad, cited in a comment attributed to the Ritba in *Šiṭâ mĕqubbeṣet*, *s.v. Wĕ-rêšaʾ* [to B71a]; Rashba, in the same collection, *s.v. Ḥāzrû*); but Friedman, n. 15 argued that the version cited by the commentaries was simplified and revised. Friedman, 1990, 4–5 (see also nn. 12, 13, 18) interpreted (1–9) as referring to groups of workers deceiving one another, and saw this as the basis of the Babli's

parties misrepresented the going rate or the expected duration of the work in order to get advantageous terms.[186] The material that intervenes between this passage and M6:2 (M6:1 [D–G]) supplements the material that precedes it and may be a later addition.[187] At any rate, whereas M6:1 [A–C] and M6:2 deal with the rights of contracting parties at court,[188] M6:1 [D–G] offers a form of self-help ("he hires [others] at their liability or deceives them") to the householder in the case of "time-sensitive" matters.

---

analogous interpretation of M6:1. In doing so Friedman depended on the use of the plural in (4) and (7) (and in (2) and (6) in the Escorial ms); but as Lieberman, *Yerushalmi Neziqin*, 163 (to ll. 2–3) noted, this evidence is hardly probative. The most obvious antecedents for the pronouns in the expression *hiṭʿû zeh ʾet zeh* in the Mishnah are the workers and the employer, and not two groups of workers, and this seems to be the most straightforward interpretation of the Yerushalmi tradition (with some of the ambiguities in the passage stemming from the fact that the author has chosen to use a highly repetitive and laconic style). At the very least, what is clear in the Yerushalmi is that "deceived" refers to misrepresentation of wages or conditions, and not to withdrawal from the contract.

[186] Compare the use of same verbal form (the *hipʿîl* of *tʿh/y*) at the end of this very pericope ("in a place where there is nobody [else], he hires [others] at their liability or deceives (*matʿān*) them," M6:1 [G]): here the use of "deceive" is explicitly "lie about what one is willing to pay" (cf., e.g., T7:1: "How [does he deceive them]? 'I made a deal with you for a *selaʿ*, I will hereby give you two,'" but the employer only pays the one originally agreed upon).

However, Friedman, 1990, 7–8, took *hiṭʿû* in M6:1 [B] as equivalent to "withdrew," which is the sense that it has in *m. Moʿed Qaṭ.* 2:1–2 (the Babli raises this as one of two possible interpretations [*ʾî bāʿît ʾēmāʾ*], B76a-b; this is also the view of Maimonides, *ad loc.*), and resolved the apparent contradiction between M6:1 and M6:2 (they are both now dealing with cases where parties withdrew) temporally: M6:1 [A–C] discuss the contract before the workers have begun working, and M6:2 after they have begun (see also Heinemann, 1954, 306; cf. T7:1: "When are these things said [i.e., that one has only "anger"]? When they [the workers] did not go .... When are these things said? When they did not begin ....").

[187] Note the shift in verbal form from the participle (present) *ha-śôkēr* to the perfect (past) *śākār* in [D], which has the force of a supplement ("but if he hired ..."); cf. M6:3 [A] *ha-śôkēr* ... [F] *śākār* .... ("One who rents ... but if he rented ...."); M9:9 [A] *ha-mĕqabbēl śādeh* ... [E] *qibbĕlāh* ("One who receives a field ... but if he received ..."). However, the relationship of M6:1 [D–G] with [A–C] is somewhat awkward. If "deceived" in [B] means merely that, [D–G] is dealing with an entirely different case (where one party withdrew) and is out of place (the rule would have fit better after M6:2 [E]). Even if, with Friedman, we take "deceived" to mean "withdrew," we nevertheless have to distinguish between a case where work has begun [D–G] and one where it has not yet begun [A–D] (see previous note), a distinction that is by no means self evident from the language of the text itself. If M6:1 [A–C] + M6:2 [A–E] were formulated together as a unit ("deceit" is not actionable, but "withdrawal" is), the awkwardness of M6:1 [D–G] may suggest that it was a later interpolated amplification.

[188] This is the force of the opposition of "They have only anger against one another" M6:1 [C], and "Their/his hand is in the inferior position" M6:2 [C, E; also F, G].

Since all of this is formulated in terms of artisans, or at least workers hired to take on a particular job (M6:1 [D] mentions "workers (*pôʿalîm*) to take his flax out of the infusion"), it is worth asking to what extent the rules of M6:1–2 are thought to apply to casual labor, especially day labor.[189] Even if

---

[189] The traditional commentaries took M6:1 as referring to any worker, but M6:2 as referring specifically to workers hired for a contract. This seems to be at least partially implied in Maimonides, *Code, Śĕkîrût*, 9:4, who distinguishes between a day laborer and a contract worker who withdrew (the latter is penalized according to the view of R. Dosa in T7:1; i.e., "they are in the inferior position," M6:2 [C]); but discusses M6:1 [D–G], at least, in connection with both day laborers and contract workers (see also *TY, TYT*); *Tos. s.v. Ha-śôkēr* [B75b] clearly takes M6:1 to refer to any labor contract; *Tos. s.v. Ha-śôkēr... wĕ-ḥāzrû* [B76a], in connection with M6:2, only addresses the problem of contract labor. For the possible origins of this view, in connection with the tradition of Rab (see below) see D. W. Halivni, *Mĕqôrôt û-mĕsôrôt: Bābāʾ mĕṣîʿāʾ* (in preparation). Friedman, 1990, 89, questioned whether the expression "their/his hand is in the inferior position" in M6:2 should even apply to laborers hired on a day to day basis, since they are not contracted for a specific job. (i.e., the whole question of future labor costs and leaving a job in the middle should not apply). Part of Friedman's argument depends on his view that the Mishnah already assumes that the rules pertaining to workers are different than for artisans, i.e., that day laborers can, by the law presupposed in the Mishnah, quit at any time. Friedman is probably correct in his argument that the views attributed to Rab and R. Yohanan in the Yerushalmi (Y6:2 [11a]) and to Rab alone in the Babli (B77a), that the worker (*pôʿel*) (and according to the interpretation given to Rab's tradition in the Yerushalmi, the employer as well) may withdraw "even at mid-day," assume different rules for a *pôʿel* (Friedman, 1990, 87–8). Nevertheless, that Amoraim make a distinction between day laborers and artisans or other workers hired for a particular job does not necessarily mean that this distinction is implied in the Mishnah itself. Moreover, Friedman's argumentation, at least from the Yerushalmi, seems problematic. First, he suggests that the views of Rab and R. Yohanan apply not to the Mishnah [he argues that the lemma from M6:2 [A] is erroneous in the Yerushalmi] but to the *bāraîtāʾ* that appears in different forms in T7:1, Y6:1 [10d–11a] and B76b. Yet in the Yerushalmi the clause to which Friedman attaches these Amoraic views is stated in terms of classic "contractors," and should apply to them as well ("He saw [other] ass drivers coming along ... or ... [in the case of a shipper] he said to him: 'Go and hire one of all of these'"), although the whole clause is introduced using the word *pôʿel*. It is only in the Babli that this clause is phrased in terms of "workers" without further qualification. Second, in all three versions of the *bāraîtāʾ* what is at issue is that workers who withdraw in a case where there is no lack of other workers (cf. M6:1 [G]) ought not to be penalized (as in M6:1 [D]) since there are other workers immediately available to work at the same price. The same logic should apply whether the workers had contracted for an extended job or had been hired for the day. I do not see how this tri-form *bāraîtāʾ* is the Tannaitic basis for special rules for casual laborers. (Indeed, if "workers (*pôʿalîm*) to take the flax out of the infusion," M6:1 [D], refers to day laborers [note, however, that the significance of the job description here may be to stress the pressing need of the employer [E] rahter than the technical character of the contract], M6:1 [D] mentions "artisans" and day laborers together suggesting that the Mishnah could treat them together.)

we do take these rules to apply to day laborers,[190] the choice to articulate the rules in terms of *ʾûmānîm* is significant. First, M7:1 assumes that workers typically take a customary contract.[191] If they had negotiated a special contract they might be considered analogous to the *ʾûmān*, but in the general course of business it may well be that this kind of dispute with mere casual laborers is not expected to arise. Second, to the extent that it is artisans who take the householder's raw material who are referred to by the term *ʾûmānîm*, these workers have a certain amount of leverage against the householder. It is easier to see how, in a case where the employer decided to withdraw or to pay a lower wage, an artisan could force a settlement (or at least an appearance in court) by withholding the material or the finished product, than a day laborer could in an analogous situation.[192]

By contrast, the remaining contractual issues dealt with in *m. Babaʾ Meṣiʿaʾ* arise in the discussion of "workers" (otherwise unqualified; presumably day

---

[190] So Heinemann, 1954, 271–2 and n. 13; Ayali, 1987, 69–70 and 188–9 n. 11. In favor of this argument is the fact that the Tosepta (T7:1, cf. Y6:1 [10d–11a]; B76a) glosses M6:1–2 using the word *pōʿēl*. However, the second part, at least, of T7:1 uses the language of "laborers" but refers to the work of "artisans" (cf. the discussion of a clause from the Yerushalmi parallel in the previous note). (In the first part of T7:1, the reference to workers who find the field unworkable may refer either to casual labor or to an extended work contract.) Similarly, the explication of "They deceived one another" in Y6:1 (10d), cited above, presupposes a contract where workers are paid so much money "for the job" (5), (14) or in which the work contract is for a specific number of days (8–9), (17–18). It may be that the author of T7:1, in using the term *pōʿēl*, is introducing a new category of labor not considered directly in this context in the Mishnah: a laborer with a specific contract.

[191] Compare the parable of the workers in the vineyard in Mt. 20:1–16. Although the first workers are contracted for a specific wage, later workers are promised payment according to "what is right" (*ho ean ē dikaion dōsō hymin*, 20:4). It is possible that this is a reflex of "customary practice" (so, e.g., Heinemann, 1954, 276). That is, since the workers knew the going wage and that they only worked a partial day, they left it to some unspecified standard to determine what proportion should be paid to them. Notably, the determination is left to the landowner (and workers are chastised for questioning his judgement, 20:12–15): within the context of the parable this makes perfect sense since it is God alone who decides what is just recompense; what is less clear is the extent to which day laborers were in practice dependent on unilateral decisions by their employers.

[192] This distinction holds for the cases of contract workers dealt with in the Tosepta: the employer can, according to R. Dosa in T7:1, withhold his expected loss from the wages of his workers; but in the situation where the employer withdrew, the Tosepta can only assign a suitable settlement (T7:1, "he gives him the wage [for] idle [laborers]"). Cf. T7:3–4: (a) a worker with a month's contract who had to stop work due to illness or a period of mourning is paid the completed portion of the contract (with no penalty); (b) a worker hired to perform a service and was unable to complete the service (e.g., the worker was hired to bring food to a sick person who became well or died), is entitled to a complete wage. In all of these cases workers may be entitled to a certain settlement, but have no leverage to enforce it.

laborers).[193] These issues are (1) the protection of the worker from unilateral changes in the customary contract, (2) the right to eat produce in the fields, (3) the right to payment at the proper time, and (4) the right to payment in the form in which it was agreed upon. In principle, all of these matters should pertain to *ʾûmānîm* as well[194] (except perhaps that of eating the produce of the field, to the extent that "artisans" are not engaged in this kind of activity). In this case, it may be precisely the assumption of the relative vulnerability of the worker that underlies the framing of these rules (which are concerned with the protection of rights in an unequal relationship) in terms of *pôʿălîm*, while M6:1–2 (which depict a contract between equals with balanced rights) is worked out in terms of *ʾûmānîm*.

Of these four contractual issues, the last can be disposed of quickly. According to M10:5 [G–M], a worker who was working "in hay and straw" and who was promised payment in cash cannot be told at payment time: "Take what you produced as your wage" [J]. Similarly, if the worker agreed to this arrangement the employer cannot later state: "Here are your wages, and I am taking what is mine" [L]. The point of this pericope does not seem to be to prohibit payment in kind, but rather the unilateral decision on the

---

[193] The Mishnah uses two terms for a laborer: *pôʿēl* and *śākîr*. Krauss, 1911, 102, saw the former as a landless worker who lived on daily wages and the latter as a poor landowner supplementing his income with wage labor. See also Alon, 1953–7, 95–6, who correctly identified the *śĕkîr yôm* with the *pôʿēl*, but who took the mention of "a worker (*śākîr*) [hired for] a Sabbath [i.e., a week] ... a month ... a week [of years]" (M9:11 [D]) to refer to workers who undertake to become dependents of landowners for a particular length of time. (Such arrangements existed in Egypt: see J. Hengstl, *Private Arbeitsverhältnisse freier Personen in den hellenistischen Papyri bis Diokletian* [Diss. Freiburg, 1971] [Bonn: Rudolph Habelt, 1972], 9ff. [*paramone* contracts]; 35ff. [service contracts], and D. Rathbone's discussion of *metrēmatiaioi*, 1991, 116–8; for later documents see the studies of A. Jördens, published in *P. Heid.* V.) However, in the Mishnah at least, *śākîr* only occurs in the context of the Biblical obligation to pay the laborer's wages on time (in addition to M9:11–12, see *m. Šebi.* 10:1; *m. Šebu.* 7:1), and cannot be distinguished from a *pôʿēl*. In the Tosepta *śākîr* is used more generally to refer to a worker, and in particular where a contract for a specific amount of time is referred to (*t. Šebi.* 5:21; *t. Ter.* 1:6; *t. B. Meṣ.* 7:3; 8:1; 9:1; *t. B. Bat.* 2:5; *t. ʿAb. Zar.* 1:3) but this does not mean that what is referred to is bound labor. The Tannaitic midrashim reflect the same usages; however in these works the situation is complicated by the Biblical use of *śākîr* for a dependent laborer (e.g., Lev. 25:50; see *Mek. Boʾ* 15 [ed. Horovitz-Rabin, p. 54] [here *śākîr* is taken to refer to a gentile]; *Sipra ʾEmor* 4:17 [97a]; *Bĕ-har* 8:7 [110b]). In the non-exegetical works (Mishnah, Tosepta) this meaning of *śākîr* does not seem to appear.

[194] See, e.g., T10:7, which specifically discusses the requirement to pay the worker on time in connection with an artisan. See also M9:12, which, although not mentioning the *ûmān* explicitly, extends the application of Lev. 19:13 and Deut. 24:15 beyond the limits of a contract for day labor alone.

part of the employer to change the mode of payment.[195] Moreover, it may be significant that the pericope is formulated in terms of a worker "in hay or straw": if the worker has no use for hay or straw (if the worker does not own animals), in order to receive a usable wage the worker has to sell the materials as well, while the owner, if he too had no use for the straw or hay, has effectively had the field cleared for free.[196]

M7:1 guarantees the workers protection from changes to their customary work standards ("... in a place where it was customary not to rise early or not to work late he cannot force them ... all follows the custom of the province" [C, F]). In particular, it is the practice of feeding the workers a meal that is most developed both in this pericope [D–E] and elsewhere in the Mishnah.[197] The gloss to the story about R Yohanan b. Mattya and his son ("R. Simeon b. Gamaliel says: 'he did not have [to specify bread and pulse only [K]], [for] all follows the custom of the province'" [L–M]) indicates how custom might work in the interests of the householder as well: having specified "a meal" the employer was certainly not obligated to feed the workers more than the customary fare.

Related to the practice of feeding a meal to workers is their right to eat the produce of the fields in which they are working.[198] On the one hand, there are passages that treat this privilege expansively. Most notable in this regard is M7:8 [A–B], which grants the privilege to eat to watchers of produce (who

---

[195] Cf. Heinemann, 1954, 284 (and n. 32), who was uncertain "whether the ruling of the Mishnah means to prohibit payment in kind altogether or only payment with inferior products, such as straw," but took it as self evident that it was payment in kind that was prohibited in this pericope. Here we must distinguish between employers who give their workers a measure of certain basic staples (e.g., wheat, oil, or wine), but little or no cash wage, and the "payment in kind" described in M10:5. It is not impossible that in those pericopae in which workers get paid through a grocer (*ḥenwānî*, M9:12 [G]; *m. Šebu.* 7:5) what is at issue is not merely that on the village level these individuals are likeliest to have stores of coins, but perhaps also that part of the payment is in the form of staples. However, in *m. Šebu.* 7:5 at least, the only payment explicitly envisaged is one of money.

[196] Compare T7:4 [D–G], in which this rule is extended to rather more valuable produce (and cf. Heinemann, cited in the preceding note):

[D] One who hires a workman to bring grapes, apples, and Damascene plums (*darmasqanôt*, cf. Greek *Damaskēna*) for a sick person—

[E] he went, and found him dead, or recuperated,

[F] let him not say to him: "Take what you brought as your wage,"

[G] rather, he pays him his complete wage.

Here, again, however, the employer attempts to dispose of goods for which he no longer has any use.

[197] See *m. Dem.* 3:1; 7:3; *m. Ter.* 6:3; *m. Maʿaś.* 2:7–8; 3:1–3; *m. Ned.* 4:4.

[198] On the apparent Pentateuchal derivation see Deut. 23:25–6; 25:4 see Lapin, 1995, 161–3 and notes thereto.

are not involved with its actual production or harvesting) "according to local practice" (*mē-hilkôt ha-mĕdînâ*), despite the fact that these should not be permitted "according to the Torah" (*min ha-tôrâ*) (M7:2 [A]). The anonymous view in M7:3 that a worker who "was working with his hands, but not with his feet, his feet, but not with his hands, even [if only] on his shoulder" [A–C] is permitted to eat, is presumably intended to extend the privilege of eating to a variety of types of agricultural workers.[199] Finally, for those workers permitted to eat, there was, according to the anonymous first view of M7:5 [A–B] and that attributed to the sages [D], no limit to the amount that the worker could eat.[200]

On the other hand, there is a distinct tendency to limit the privilege. In M7:5, the permissive ruling that set no upper limit to the amount the worker may eat [A–B] is countered by the view attributed to R. Eleazar Hisama that sets the upper limit as that of the worker's wage [C]. The note that closes the pericope ([E–F]; either anonymous and continuing [B], or attributed to the sages [D]) qualifies the permissive rulings by agreeing with R. Eleazar Hisama in practice if not in law: "one teaches a person not to be a glutton ...." More importantly, M7:2 distinctly limits the privilege of eating to those workers actually involved with the work of the harvest, but excluding, say, workers engaged in hoeing or weeding in fields where the produce was ripe and ready for harvesting (and perhaps guards as well, against M7:8 [A–B]).[201] Similarly, M7:4 [A–C] limits the right to eat to the produce on which one is actually working (cf. *m. Ma'aś.* 7:8). If the correct reading of

---

[199] Just what division between activities is intended in this pericope is not immediately clear, and may reflect a conventional division of labor. The Yerushalmi's comments on this passage (*y. Ma'aś.* 2:6 [50a]; Y7:2 [11b]) gloss "with his hands" as "binding [fruit together]," "with his feet" as *mĕqammēṣ* (*y. B. Meṣ.*) or *masmîk* (*y. Ma'aś.*) (Lieberman, *TK*, 9, 261, to T8:7, took these as synonymous terms referring to the stamping on produce [e.g., figs] in order to press it together), and "with his shoulder" as "loading [an animal] (*tô'ēn*)." Presumably, the Yerushalmi's glosses are not meant to be exclusive, but merely examples, and analogous divisions of labor could be found in the harvesting and preparation of any crops.

[200] On the redaction of this pericope see Chapter II.D.2. The context suggests that "even as much as a *dînār*" [A, B] was taken to mean that workers could eat more than the value of their wages [C–F] (see below). In addition, the expression also implies that "cucumber ... figs as much as a *dînār*" is intended as a fantastically high sum. If the prices given for figs in *m. Ma'aś.* 2:5–6; *t. Ma'aś.* 2:11 (ranging from three to four to the *'issār* to ten to the *'issār*) is any measure of the real price range, a worker would have to eat between 72 and 240 figs to match the value of one *dînār* (and presumably more since the cost to the producer is lower than the market price). How many workers could consistently eat that many figs day after day?

[201] M7:2 could conceivably apply to any labor and not just to harvesting and processing. However, the restriction to these activities is implied by the language of the pericope ("one who works on [produce while it is still] attached to the ground ... and on [produce] detached

M7:4 [D] is "and [regarding] all of them, they said only '[Workers may eat] at the time of the completion of the work,'" we have a traditional rule that limited the right of workers to eat (perhaps to the end of the day, or to other pauses in the workday), the strictures of which are explicitly relaxed because it is in the interests of the householder to do so [E] (presumably to limit the amount of time that workers might take out of the workday to eat the produce).[202]

Finally, the Mishnah recognizes the Biblical right of a worker to be paid "on that day."[203] One of the most interesting features of the Mishnah's legislation is an exception to its normal rules of oaths. As a general rule an oath in court (in lieu of evidence) can only exempt one from liability, but does not entitle one to exact payment. However, workers, together with a select group

---

from the ground ..."), and by other passages in the chapter: M7:4 [F–G] refers to workers who make their way between the rows of vines, and back and forth to the winepress. Guards of produce (presumably during the time that it is harvested and exposed) are given a special dispensation in M7:8 [A–B] that may or may not be presupposed by M7:2 (cf. the Amoraic disputes in the Yerushalmi [Y7:9 (11c), Rab Huna, Samuel] and Babli [B93a, Rab and Samuel] that center on whether certain kinds of guards might be considered permitted to eat even according to M7:2) but the language of M7:2 suggests the active handling of produce itself. This understanding is consistent with other passages as well. See, e.g., *m. Ma'aś.* 3:3:
  [E] [One who hires a worker] to weed among his onions
  [F] and said to him: "On condition that I have the right to eat vegetables,"
  [G] he pulls off one leaf at a time and eats,
  [H] but if he combined [two leaves together] he is liable [to tithe what he eats].
Because the worker was weeding, he could only eat with the owner's permission (hence the stipulation that he be permitted to eat [F]), and therefore became liable for tithes. (The same reasoning applies to the other cases in *m. Ma'aś.* 3:1–3, but this is the only case where the form of labor is specified.) By contrast, a laborer working with the harvest would have been automatically permitted to eat and would have been exempt from tithes (see *m. Ma'aś.* 2:7; *t. Ma'aś.* 2:14; T8:7; *y, Ma'aś.* 2:6 [50a]; Y7:2 [11b]; B89a).

[202] See the note to M7:4 in Appendix I and Chapter II.C.2. If we read *bĕ-šā'āt mĕl'akâ*, i.e., "while the work is going on" in M7:4 [D], the pericope is subject to two interpretations. (1) It is possible to see M7:4 [D–H] as expansive: the permission was given to eat even when not actually working, in addition to that granted by tradition, because in that way the workers would take up less time eating during real work. However (2), it is still possible to take M7:4 [D–H] as restrictive, [F–H] now prohibiting eating during work-time, which according to the traditional rule was permitted. In this case the revision of the traditional rule in [D–H] would more or less agree with the view of R. Judah in the Tosepta: "R. Judah says: 'He may eat only at a time when he is unloading [an animal], and at a time when he is loading [an animal] [i.e., and not during the harvesting itself] because of the robbery of the work of the householder'" (T8:8). (Compare Nahmanides, *Ḥiddûšîm* to B87b, s.v. *Hā' dĕ-'amrî[nān]*, who saw M7:4 as expansive [interpretation (1)], and saw the view attributed to R. Judah in the Tosepta as in conflict with the M7:4.)

[203] See Lev. 19:13; Deut. 24:14–5.

Institutions and Relationships 213

of other claimants, are entitled to exact payment on the basis of their oath ("the hired worker (*śākîr*) swears at his [proper] time and takes [his payment]," M9:12 [H]; cf. *m. Šebu.* 7:1). The only limitation imposed within the Mishnah is that the claim must have been made, and the oath taken, at the time that the worker should have been paid, or the worker must at least have witnesses that the claim was indeed made at the proper time.[204] Leaving aside the question of whether the Mishnah describes or legislates actual judicial practice, or of the effectiveness of court procedures once formally instituted, this limitation itself is potentially insurmountable since it was the worker who had to manage to get the employer quickly before a court (or at least before a group of people who could serve as a court).[205]

Studies of workers in the Mishnah typically assume that the worker was poor, and that day laborers in particular had a standard of living quite close to the subsistence level.[206] While this seems to be a safe assumption based on

---

[204] M9:12 [F], [H–J]. The reading of [H] in all the Mishnah texts checked (see Appendix I) makes it clear that the oath too takes place "at his time," and this seems clear from the exception brought in [J] (expanded T10:6) as well. The statement that the employer has not transgressed if he personally did not pay the workers but sent them to a banker or grocer (M9:12 [G]) is not a limitation of the worker's privilege unless the banker or grocer is exempt from the obligation to pay "on that day." See T10:5:
  [A] He sent him over to a shopkeeper or to a banker, they transgress it [the commandment],
  [B] but he [the employer] does not transgress them.
  [C] But if he made a stipulation with him on this condition from the beginning, even they do not transgress it.
  [D] And if he told another to hire [workers] for him, neither this one [the employer] nor this one [the agent] transgress it.
In [A–B], the grocer or banker takes the place of the employer, and the worker is protected. On the basis of the rather technical standpoint that the Biblical rule only applies when the relationship is an unmediated one between worker and employee, [D] rules that where employment (and payment) was not carried out by the employer himself neither the employer not hiring agent are liable. [C] is obscure, but if it follows the same principle as [D], where the workers agreed to accept payment from an intermediary they have lost their right to payment "on that day." [C–D], then, would substantially limit the worker's enforceable privilege to prompt payment, but these limitations do not appear to underlie the rulings in M9:11–2. (Alternatively, [C] rules that if the employer hired the workers on condition that he need not pay them immediately, he is exempt [so Rabad, to *Sipra Qědôšîm* 3:11 [88d], citing the Tosepta, Lieberman, *TK*, 9, 299; cf. *Sipre Deut.* 279 (ed. Finkelstein, p. 297), with textual comments by Lieberman in *TK*].)

[205] See Heinemann, 1954, 288–9: "... the actual purpose of the law, to ensure prompt payment of the labourer, is almost entirely whittled away."

[206] See, e.g., Krauss, 1911, 102; Alon, 1953-7, 2, 94–7; Ayali, 1987, 43–50; Hamel, 1990, 53. See *m. Pe'a* 5:6 (in which the implication is that the worker is poor); *m. Dem.* 3:1

analogies from elsewhere in the ancient world, it should be pointed out that on the basis of the Mishnah (or Rabbinic literature more broadly), there is simply not enough material to quantify the social and economic position of free labor in Roman Galilee, for a number of reasons.[207] To begin with, there are the problems of the literary evidence. First, we can never be sure that when a figure (a price, a wage level) is given in Rabbinic literature that it is not merely a "round" figure pulled more or less out of thin air. Second, even if we could be sure the figures given in Rabbinic literature had to meet some test of believability, the complex redactional history makes it difficult to assign a wage or price to a particular date and time. Third, the evidence of wages and prices, such as it is, is sporadic and not nearly complete enough to work out a household budget. Beyond this, however, is a set of imponderables such as the availability of labor, the proportion of labor used in agricultural and other production taken up by wage earners, the structure of households, the number of incomes and their sources, and the way they needed to be spent to meet subsistence needs. An example may best illustrate the limits of the evidence. If we assume that the daily wage of a worker is one *dînār* per day,[208] and that the price of wheat is on the order of one *dînār* to the *sĕ'â* (some 13 liters),[209] in one day's work workers can earn a *sĕ'â* of wheat if they buy nothing else. Now assuming a 300-day work year (leaving off time for Sabbaths and festivals; perhaps this is too optimistic?),[210] the annual wage of one worker in terms of wheat is approximately 3,900 liters, or roughly eight and one third times the minimum caloric requirements of a

---

(although here the inclusion of workers among poor people and "guests" may be due either to (a) the assumption that they are not fastidious about doubtfully tithed produce, or to (b) the fact that these are groups of people to whom one typically serves food, cf. *m. Ter.* 6:3).

[207] For scholars who have tried to use this material to quantify the standard of living on the basis of the Rabbinic sources see, e.g., Heichelheim, 1938, 178–38; A. Ben-David, *Talmudische Ökonomie* (Hildesheim: Georg Olms, 1974), 1, 291–311; Ayali, 1987, 57 pays particular attention to the evidence for laborers. Sperber, 1991, 101–11, also gives a table of prices.

[208] This seems to be the assumed figure in M7:5 (cf. Mt. 20:1ff., and see one of the two glosses to M7:5 [A–B] at Y7:6 [11b]: "R. Leazar b. Antigonos says in the name of R. Eleazar b. R. Yannai: 'That is to say a worker may eat more than his wage'"), but compare *m. Šebi.* 8:4, which gives an *'issār* (= 1/24 *dînār*) as a daily wage (cf. *y. Šebi.* 8:4 [38a], which quotes the Mishnah pericope but uses *dînār* where the Mishnah uses *'issār*), and *m. Šebu.* 7:1 in which the dispute between a *śākîr* and his employer is over a wage of 50 *dînārîm*.

[209] For the size of the *sĕ'â* I have followed Hamel, 1990, 244. The price of wheat is that of *m. Pe'a* 8:7; *m. 'Erub.* 8:2; *m. Kel.* 17:11; see also M5:1 in which the price of wheat shifts from 25 to 30 *dînārîm* to the *kôr* (=30 *sĕ'â*), i.e., from 5/6 to one *dînār* to the *sĕ'â*.

[210] R. S. Bagnall (personal communication) points out that an annual wage of 300 *denarii* was substantial: it was the equivalent of a soldier's wages.

very active male, age 20–39, as calculated by Foxhall and Forbes.[211] How meaningful is this figure, however? First, how many workers were there who relied entirely on wage labor? Second, how likely is it that a worker whose sole income came from wages could find 300 days of work? Third, how does this figure relate to a household economy? We do not know to what extent women—especially a woman with several children—could rely upon finding paid work, or to which a gender-based division of labor, depicted in the Mishnah and no doubt a widely held social ideal, was maintained at the very lowest level of the economic scale.[212] For a family (such as the sample family outlined by Foxhall and Forbes) depending on one income, the amount of the yearly wage necessary to pay for food alone (in the form of wheat) might come to some 56 percent.[213] However, the size and structure of a household in Roman Galilee is a complete mystery. Even if correct, this figure of 56 percent is presumably a minimum, first, because I have assumed that the caloric minimum is met only with wheat, whereas where it was available and when it could be afforded, families probably ate such other foods as oil,

---

[211] See L. Foxhall, H. A. Forbes, "*Sitometreia*: The Role of Grain as a Staple Food in Classical Antiquity," *Chiron* 12 (1982), 41–90. For the daily caloric minimum (3337 calories) see 49, n. 26; kilograms of wheat per liter are given on p. 43 (Foxhall and Forbes's sample had a weight-to-volume ratio of 0.782 kg/L); caloric content is given on the table on p. 48 (3340 cal./kg). Taken together these figures give the following calculation of the number of calories earned per year: 3900 L/year x 0.782 kg/L x 3340 cal/kg = 10,186,332 calories. This figure divided by the caloric minimum for the extremely active adult male (3337 cal./day x 365 days/year = 1,218,005) gives 8.36.

[212] *m. Ket.* 5:5 requires a woman to grind, bake, launder, cook, nurse, make up the bed, and work with wool, but her possession (*hiknîsâ lô*, "she brought in to him," i.e., as part of her dowry) of servants allows her to forgo some or all of these activities ("... four [servants], she sits on her seat (*qattedrā*ʾ, cf. Greek *kathedra*)"). The pericope has two supplementary attributed statements that even the wealthiest women must work with wool. *m. Ket.* 5:9 quantifies the amount of work required of the wife (just as 5:8–9 quantify the wife's basic maintenance), and the pericope ends with the gloss: "In connection with what are these things stated? In connection with the poorest (m.) of Israel, but with an honored [man (the participle is in the masculine)], all is according to his honor." Clearly, there is an expectation that suitable activity for women ranges from domestic chores to the idleness of wealthy matrons. Granting that outside of the literary world of the Mishnah itself this reflects the social norm for the families of secure landowners, we are in no position to determine at what point economic pressure will overcome this expectation.

[213] Using the same total number of calories earned per day (10,186,332) derived in n. 211, but dividing by the caloric requirements of a household consisting of one elderly adult female, one male 20–39, one woman of the same age and three children (15,495 cal./day x 365 days/year =5,655,675 cal./year) (Foxhall, Forbes, 1982, 49, n. 26) yields 1.8 times the caloric minimum of that household; in other words some 56 percent of the income went to meeting food requirements alone.

wine, and fruit, and second, because I have assumed no loss to the wheat in processing or due to spoilage or vermin.[214] Beyond this, it is not clear how effectively the remaining 44 percent of the wages (132 *dînārîm*) could meet such other needs as clothing or housing: Did workers have to pay rent somewhere? Did they own their own homes? Did they make do in makeshift residences? Were they housed by employers? If every member of a six-person household received the same thirty-*dînār* outfit that is said in *m. ʿArakim* 6:5 to increase the value of a slave, the sample salary would not have met the household needs. However, since this outfit was for someone who was to do domestic service in the home of a relatively wealthy person, it may have been of better quality than a day laborer could afford.[215] In addition, a family with a single income is a mere assumption: at what point and how much would children or the worker's wife be able to contribute to the household income? This kind of investigation opens more questions than it answers. At best we can say that for a small farming family that met all or most of its requirements through production on its own land, the income of a *dînār* per day for some part of the year would have been a substantial supplement, but for a family relying on one income from wages the situation may have been quite precarious. It may be worth noting in this context that a 300-*dînār*-per-year income is only half again as much as the yearly income per person given in *m. Peʾa* 8:8 as the cutoff for an individual recipient of certain gifts to the poor.

The rules concerning workers in *m. Babaʾ Meṣiʿaʾ* do not translate simply into either a description of the social and economic position of free labor, nor even into the place they took in the ideological world of the Mishnah. As I have noted, the Mishnah's rules, and the way they are formulated, show considerable sensitivity to the potential vulnerability of workers in their relationship with their employers. These rules go a certain distance towards securing the position of workers (at least in principle) by such means as allowing them to use an oath to claim their pay or protecting them from

---

[214] For extraction rates for wheat see Foxhall, Forbes, 1982, 76, who calculate an extraction rate of 94.6 percent; cf. Hamel, 1990, 247, who estimated a somewhat lower rate (90 percent). M3:7 [C–E] assumes that during long term storage (a year?) losses for rice, grain, and linseed will range from 1/40 to 1/10 per year.

[215] Compare *m. Ket.* 5:8, in which the clothing allocation for a wife is given as 50 *dînārîm*, exclusive of a head covering, a belt, and shoes; again, perhaps a higher standard than workers could afford. Sample prices for a *ṭallît* (*m. Meʿil.* 6:4; *t. Šeq.* 2:8; *t. Bek.* 6:13; *t. ʿArak.* 4:3; *t. Meʿil.* 1:23; 2:10) or for a *ḥallûq* (*m. Meʿil.* 6:4; *t. ʿArak.* 4:3; *t. Meʿil.* 2:10) range from 8 to 50 *dînārîm*. Ben-David, 1974, 312, considered a full set of clothing somewhere on the order of 100 to 200 *dînārîn*, citing *Mek. Kaspaʾ* 19 (ed. Horovitz, p. 317). Even if the passage were a reliable indicator of the scale of prices, it would still reflect the prices that could be afforded by wealthier people. On the question of clothing in general see Hamel, 1990, 57–93.

unilateral changes in agreements. At the same time, however, we should try to place the achievement of the Mishnah into its proper perspective. It is worth noting that the same Rabbis who set minimum standards for charity distribution and for the maintenance of one's wife refrained from setting minimum wages for hired labor. The rules about workers eating in the fields show a considerable tendency towards limiting who can eat the produce of the fields (if not how much). In a case of potential loss to the employer, the Mishnah empowers the employer simply to cheat. With the exception of tithes (*m. Maʿaś.* 2:7), workers remained restricted by ritual prohibitions of produce[216] while, according to a story told of R. Gamaliel, an employer need not scruple over feeding his employees doubtfully tithed foodstuffs (*m. Dem.* 3:1).[217] This permission not only allows the householder to cut corners, but also reinforces a social distance between pious householders and the people of doubtful integrity in their employ. In this regard, the rules of *m. Babaʾ Meṣiʿaʾ* reflect the interests of the landholders and employers, and not of their laborers. In doing so, the Rabbis who produced the Mishnah presumably relied on the fact that a work contract was, after all, a contract between "equals," and was in any case guided by customary practices. Indeed, the Mishnah avoids describing labor contracts where the employee was fully economically dependent upon the employer (e.g., where the employee was bound for a long or short period of time to perform labor for the householder in exchange for maintenance). That such contracts existed seems likely, but is impossible to prove from the Mishnah itself. In depicting the relations of free labor with householders, the sages who produced the Mishnah made a choice to see these relations as between equal Israelites and not between such categories as free or honorable and servile or dishonorable. At the same time, both through the rules themselves and through their presentation, these same Rabbis showed themselves sensitive to inherent inequalities in these relations, without trying to create rules to erase the inequalities. This is an ideological choice, if a realistic one, and one that reflects the interests of the householder and not that of the laborer.

---

[216] In M7:7 workers remain prohibited from fourth-year and second tithe produce (cf. the formulation in T8:7). By informing the workers that the produce was prohibited to them the employer was exempt from his obligation to allow them to eat in the fields, and only became obligated when he neglected to inform them. Similarly, according to both views in *m. Ter.* 6:3 if workers were fed produce separated for priests (*těrûmâ*) they are required to make up at least part of the penalty payment.

[217] The suggestion in the Yerushalmi that the householder tithes the produce (*y. Dem.* 3:1 [23a]) surely cannot be what the author of the pericope of the Mishnah intends. Cf. *m. Dem.* 7:3, which discusses a worker who does not trust the employer to have put tithed food before the workers.

6. Lessor and Lessee.

Under what we would consider the rubric of leasing, the Mishnah considers two distinct kinds of contract.[218] The first is rental of an object for use, for instance, an ox for threshing or an ass to carry a load (what students of Roman law would call *locatio conductio rei*, "lease and hire of a thing"). In this case the relationship between the parties is relatively straightforward: a lessee pays the owner a fee for the privilege of using an object. The second involves letting out the productivity of a thing (an animal to produce offspring or wool, a field to produce crops). The relationship of lessor to lessee in this case is necessarily more complex: the lessee is acting only partly in his (or her) own interests; on a certain level the lessee is also working for the lessor. From the point of view of the lessor, a lease of this type is one of the ways of exploiting the economic productivity of his property, and the lessor therefore retains an interest in how the property is managed. For the first type of contract the Mishnah uses forms of the verb *śkr*.[219] For the second type, forms of *śkr* do occur, but more frequently a different set of terms is used, of which the one with the widest application is *qbl*, "receive."[220]

That the Mishnah itself attributed this two-fold character to *qablānût*-type contracts may be seen from a brief examination of two texts from outside *m. Babaʾ Meṣiʿaʾ*. In *m. Babaʾ Batraʾ* 10:4 land leases (*šĕṭārê ʾarîsût wĕ-qablānût*)

---

[218] See the brief discussion by von Bolla, 1940, 3–5, who notes that both the Greek *misthōsis* and the Latin *locatio conductio* cover these two types of contracts.

[219] *Śākar* ("hire", "lease [from]"), used of animals: *m. Ter.* 11:9; *m. B. Meṣ.* 3:2, 3; 6:3, 4, 5; 8:1, 2; see also references to the *śôkēr*, the renter: *m. B. Qam.* 4:9; 7:6; *m. B. Meṣ.* 7:8, 10; *m. Šebu.* 8:1, 6; used of real estate (e.g., a house, but not a field): M8:7, 8; cf. *m. B. Bat.* 5:7 (a place where produce is stored). Curiously, *hiśkîr* (the causative form, "lease [out to]") does not occur in connection with animals, and only occasionally in connection with other objects (*m. Ned.* 4:1; *m. B. Meṣ.* 6:7 [an unspecified pledge]); but more frequently of real estate (*m. Šebi.* 9:7; *m. B. Meṣ.* 2:3; 5:2; 8:6–9; *m. ʿAb. Zar.* 1:8–9; cf. *m. Maʿaś. Š.* 5:9 [a place where produce is stored]). On *m. Ned.* 5:3, see the discussion below in the text.

The verb *śkr* is used only rarely for the lease of productive land. The only textually secure occurrence is *m. ʿAb. Zar.* 1:8, where, however, the permissibility of leasing of fields (*śādôt*) is compared to that of houses, and the use of a single verb may suit the Mishnah's rhetorical purposes. (In M9:2 [B] the manuscripts KRMP and the Naples *editio princeps* read *haśkēr/haśkîr*, where L and the Babli manuscripts have *ḥakôr*; see Appendix I.) This usage is reflected in the Tosepta as well: in addition to T9:3, 4, 6, 7, 8, 33, see *t. Dem.* 6:2, 3; *t. B. Bat.* 2:12; *t. ʿAb. Zar.* 2:8, 9).

[220] On the use of *qbl* for a variety of different contracts see Maimonides to M9:2. For the use of this term for contracts involving animals see, e.g., M5:4 [G]; M5:6 [A, C]; as well as *m. Bek.* 1:1; 2:4. For land see M9:1–10, where *ha-mĕqabbēl* is used for all the lease contracts discussed, despite the differences in the way rent (and risk) is determined (see Appendix I, notes to M9:1 and 2). Sometimes, however, *qablānût* is used technically for a sharecropping arrangement, to be distinguished from leases for fixed payment in kind (*m. Dem.* 6:1–5).

are grouped with betrothal and marriage documents and documents for the selection of lay judges (*šĕṭārê bĕrûrîn*) preparatory to a trial (cf. M1:8 [A]), as documents that can only be written with the knowledge of both parties.[221] All of these documents create obligations on both sides (and in the case of marriage and lease documents, privileges as well). By contrast, documents for a one-sided obligation (e.g., sales, in which the point of the deed is to transfer ownership, and loans) can be written with the knowledge of the party that obligates itself (the seller, the borrower) alone (*m. B. Bat.* 10:3). In general, *qablānût*-type leases are discussed in terms of animals or agricultural land; leases of a business installation, such as a bath, are treated like leases for use (e.g., M8:8 [F–H]). For this reason, *m. Nedarim* 5:3 is especially interesting:

[A] One who is prohibited by oath from enjoying benefit from his fellow—

[B] and he [his fellow] has a bath or an olive press leased out [to a third party] in the village:

---

[221] Note, however, that the fragments of lease formulae cited in Tannaitic literature are formulated in the first person, from the side of the lessee: M9:3 [D] (see the note to this pericope in Appendix I); T9:13; *t. Ket.* 4:10; see Gulak, 1929, 116 and n.3. Compare also the following tradition from the Tosepta (*t. B. Bat.* 11:6):

[A] Wills (*diyātikā'ôt*, cf. Greek *diathēkai*), mortgages (*hipôtiqā'ôt*, cf. Greek *hypothēkai*), and gifts—

[B] [are written] without the knowledge of the giver,

[C] but one may not write them without the knowledge of the receiver.

[D] Sale documents and documents of land tenancy (*'arîsût*) and the receipt of animals (*qabbālat bĕhēmâ*)—

[E] [are written] without the knowledge of the giver,

[F] but one may not write them without the knowledge of the receiver.

I have cited the entire pericope because the text is problematic. All of the documents listed in [A] are unilateral acts of transfer, and following the rule of *m. B. Bat.* 10:3 we should expect [B] to read "without the knowledge of the receiver" and [C] "without the knowledge of the giver" (so Lieberman, *TK*, 10, 456–7, citing Rashba). Indeed, in T1:8 the same documents, if found, are to be returned to the receiver only if the giver consents, for precisely the same reason: it is the giver alone who obligates himself through the contract. In [D] the Tosepta deals with both deeds of sale and deeds of lease and gives the same ruling for both of them. [D–F], too, is problematic. First, unlike *m. B. Bat.* 10:3–4, the Tosepta here treats both *qablānût* leases and sale together. Moreover, the ruling of *m. B. Bat.* 10:3 is that "one may write a sale document for the seller, even though the buyer is not with him," because the sale document is a unilateral transfer of ownership to the buyer. The text of *t. B. Bat.* 11:6 [D–F], however, presupposes just the opposite. Lieberman proposes reading "[are *not* written (assumed in [D]?)] ... without (*'l* for *bl'*) the knowledge of both of them (*šnyhn* for *nwtn*)" in [E], and omitting [F] altogether (Lieberman, *TK*, 10, 457). In support of this emendation is the fact that T1:8 also discusses the documents listed in [D] and rules that when found they are not to

[C] if he [the owner] has a handhold (*těpîsat yād*) in them,
[D] it [i.e., use of the bath or press by the one prohibited by oath] is prohibited.
[E] If he does not have a handhold in them,
[F] it is permitted.

The distinction between the cases of [C] and [E] seems to be precisely whether the installation is simply leased out (*sěkîrût*), or whether the owner maintains some sort of interest in the management and profitability of the installation.[222] Therefore, in the latter case [C] use of the press or the bathhouse constitutes a benefit derived from the owner, and is prohibited. In a case of lease for use, the lessor, although retaining ownership, is not thereby considered to have maintained an interest in its operation.[223]

It is difficult to get a clear sense of the scale of these transactions and of the social and economic position of owners and lessees. In connection with the lease of animals, it is possible that the picture that the texts presuppose is that of property owners who own animals making them available to people

---

be returned at all, presumably because they are not considered merely one-sided documents. In this way, [D–F] would disagree with *m. B. Bat.* 10:3–4 in the case of sale, and *t. B. Bat.* 11:6–7 would agree clause by clause with T1:8–9. However, and this is the reason for citing this tradition, it is possible that the same emendation as suggested for [B–C] should apply to [E–F], with the result that this pericope would agree with *m. B. Bat.* 10:3–4 in the case of sale, but disagree in the case of *qablānût* leases, because, since they are formulated only from the point of view of the lessee, they may be viewed as documents obligating only the lessee.

[222] That this is the way this pericope was taken in antiquity is indicated by the gloss in both the Yerushalmi and the Babli: "How much is 'a handhold'? For a half, for a third, for a quarter" (*y. Ned.* 5:2 [39a]; *b. Ned.* 46b). [In the Yerushalmi the tradition is cited anonymously, in the Babli it is put in the mouth of R. Nahman; it is possible that it is a *bāraîtā*' being cited in both cases, and in the Babli the dispute between R. Nahman and Abbaye is whether to take the proportions given literally.] The formula "for a half, for a third, for a quarter," is regularly used to describe a sharecropping arrangement in the lease of land (e.g., *m. Pe'a* 5:5) and of animals (e.g., T5:1, 2). This gloss implies that where the rent paid to the owner was dependent upon the money taken in, the owner maintained an interest, and the lessee was, at least in part, the agent of the owner. Whether these same commentators would apply the rule of *m. Ned.* 5:3 [C–D] only in the case of a proportional rental arrangement, or whether in taking any kind of active part in management (however the rent was to be paid) the owner was considered to have "a handhold," is not clear.

[223] Compare, however, *m. Ter.* 11:9, in which one who leases (*sôkēr*) an animal for use from a priest can feed it priestly produce (*těrûmâ*), whereas one who has made a contract for production (*šām*, cf. M5:5 and the note thereto in Appendix I) cannot feed it priestly produce. The implication is that in the case of the contract for production, at least in the present case where the contract depends on a valuation of the animal, the animal becomes (partially?) the property of the lessee, whereas in a lease for use the animal remains entirely the property of the priestly owner.

who otherwise could not afford them. This makes particular sense in the context of a *qablānût*-type loan (see the discussion below and section B.4 of this chapter), and especially if flocks or herds and not single animals are leased.[224] As in the case of tenant farming, the owner turns the exploitation of the property over to someone else in whose interest it is to work effectively; in principle this both affords security and absolves owners of the need for direct and minute management of the property. The discussion of letting out animals for use (*śĕkîrût*) might similarly reflect wealthier landholders exploiting (and paying for the upkeep of) extra animals. However, the texts may presuppose another pattern: relatively poor people (perhaps small farmers) who can improve their position if they can buy, say, an ox and a yoke and lease them out with or without their own labor.[225] The relative availability of such animals might allow other landowners to economize by not maintaining their own livestock.[226] The lessee of a bathhouse (for twelve golden *dînārîm*, i.e., three hundred *dînārîm*, per year) is presumably not among the very poorest (M8:9). Similarly, the lessee of an entire courtyard (presumably to sublease individual units) (M5:2 [F–H]) is probably not to be taken for a pauper, although in absolute numbers the rent given in [G] is not extremely high (ten to twelve *sĕlā'îm*, i.e., forty to forty eight *dînārîm*).[227] Indeed, there is no reason to exclude at the outset the idea that lessees of houses—in

---

[224] E.g., T5:1–2 (discussed above, n. 163, and the note to M5:4 in Appendix I), which deal with a lease of one hundred sheep or calves.

[225] See, e.g., *m. 'Arak.* 6:3, which refers to an *'ikkār*, who owns his own yoke of oxen. Arguably, this is presupposed by M8:1 in which both worker and animal are "borrowed." (According to those versions of M8:1 that include the case "he hired the cow and hired its owners with it" [see the note to this pericope in Appendix I, see also T7:20], the case is explicitly raised). However, this may equally be a hypothetical working out of the implications of the wording of Ex. 22:14. See also T8:4:

[A] A householder [here, the owner of an animal] is permitted to starve and afflict his cow so that it may eat much at the time that it is threshing;

[B] and the renter [who rents it for the purpose of threshing] may feed it bunches of sheaves so that it not eat much at the time that it is threshing.

Hamel, 1990, 122, assumed that this text implies endemic poverty and chronically malnourished animals (as well it might), but careful economizing at another's expense (not to say miserliness) is hardly the preserve of the poor.

[226] For this strategy on the part of estate owners see Kehoe, 1992, 63–5 and index *s.vv.* "draft animals" and "livestock."

[227] T8:31 gives a figure that works out to three hundred *dînārîm* per year, but this is clearly a doublet of M8:9, which deals with a bathhouse. If it could be taken to reflect the possible range of domestic rental rates, T8:31 would imply that some residences, at least, were well beyond the means of anyone close to the subsistence level, which must have included a large portion of the population.

particular the lessees about whom the Mishnah is concerned—should not be members of the propertied classes.[228]

Of particular interest is the position of tenant farmers, since this goes directly to the question of the exploitation of free (at least nominally), independent peasant producers on the part of larger landowners in Roman Galilee. To be sure, there are passages that imply that tenant farmers might be poor and vulnerable, and that particular tenants or their families might hold the same leasehold for many years or for generations.[229] On the other hand, the discussion of leases in M9:1–10 presupposes rather short terms (M9:9 [B, E] opposes "for a few years" to "seven years"). It is certainly possible that the system the Mishnah envisages is one in which the same tenants repeatedly negotiate new leases, that is, in practice, one of permanent tenancy. It is

---

[228] For comparison see B. W. Frier, *Landlords and Tenants in Imperial Rome* (Princeton: Princeton University, 1980), 52 and *passim*, who argues that in Rome a large proportion of the aristocracy leased homes, and it is with precisely these leases that the Roman jurists were concerned.

[229] *m. Peʾa* 5:5 discusses the rights of a tenant farmer to the gleanings and other agricultural gifts for the poor; cf. *t. Peʾa* 3:1. The story in *Sipra Bĕ-ḥuqôtai* 3:3 (111b) about a king (i.e., God) and his *ʾārîs* (the righteous of Israel) who used to quake before the king until he reassured him ("I am like you") makes use of both the vulnerability of the tenant farmer and his nominal freedom (such a story could not have been told about a king and his slave, who was not free and therefore not "alike") as a trope to illustrate a theological point. See also the story in *y. B. Qam.* 5:7 (5c); *y. Šebu.* 7:2 (37d), describing a case of a tenant who deposited something and then both tenant and landlord died. The judge (R. Ishmael b. R. Yose, of the last Tannaitic generation) is said to have assigned the deposit to the heirs of the landlord and not to the heirs of the tenant with the explanation: "Is there anyone who does not know that that which belongs to bar Ziza's tenant belongs to bar Ziza?" If this tradition does not presuppose an exceptional relationship between a specific landlord and his tenant, truly dependant tenants were imaginable in late antique Palestine.

On traditional tenancy see the discussion of Gulak, 1929, 124–36 (who notes that the best Rabbinic evidence for "eternal tenancy," such as it is, comes from Babylonian sources). At any rate, *m. Dem.* 6:2 refers to one who receives "the field of his fathers" as a leasehold. It is at least possible that what is presupposed here is a farmer now permanently leasing land that his family once owned (see also *t. Dem.* 6:7; *t. Ter.* 2:11). *t. Maʿaś.* 3:13, discusses one "to whom were appointed *ʾarîsîn*," apparently because they came with the land that the landlord bought or inherited (Lieberman, *TK*, 2, 706). While this could occur in the case of short term leases, it is also possible that a longer (and traditional) leasehold is implied. Such an institution is also implied by the story told of a king (God) who was displeased with his tenants and replaced them with the next generation, and then the next generation after them (*Sipre Deut.* 312 [ed. Finkelstein, p. 353]). Cf. the inscription from Ağa Bey Köy in early third-century Asia in which tenants on an imperial estate threaten to leave their "ancestral hearths and family tombs" (*hestias patrōas kai taphous progoniko[u]s*) and move to (i.e., take up tenancy on?) private lands (text with translation in Broughton, 1938, 656–8). Even allowing for melodramatic language, the traditional possession of these lands as leaseholds seems presupposed.

worth suggesting, however, that whether or not such a system of tenancy existed in Roman Galilee (and presumably it did), it is not these tenants that *m. Baba' Meṣi'a'* is concerned with, but rather with wealthier tenants, perhaps landholders of some substance in their own right, who supplement their income from their own holdings by taking up the lease of other land.[230]

---

[230] M9:10 discusses a lease whose yearly rent is one hundred *dînārîm* per year, which by the typical valuation of wheat in the Mishnah of one *dînār* to the *sĕ'â* (see the preceding section) comes to 1300 liters of wheat (or approximately 33 artabas of wheat in Egyptian measures). This fits quite well with the evidence collected by H. J. Drexhage, *Preise, Mieten/Pachten, Kosten und Löhne im römischen Ägypten bis zum Regierungsantritt Diokletians* (St. Katharin: Scripta Mercaturae, 1991), 141–54, 158, on Egyptian leaseholds of grain land: in the second and third centuries these were for the most part smaller than ten arouras, and of those most were smaller than five arouras. A rental yield of 33 artabas (our Mishnaic example), at a rent varying between, say, 3.5 and 9 artabas/aroura would have implied a leasehold of between 9.4 and 3.7 arouras. (For Egyptian rental rates see the table in D. Hennig, *Untersuchungen zur Bodenpacht im ptolemäisch-römischen Ägypten* [Diss. Munich, 1967], after p. 26, for the second and third centuries; I have taken the maximal range given by Hennig without attention to regional differences since what I am interested in is an impression of the range of possibilities). How taxes were allocated, the rates of rents, and differential yields between Palestine and Egypt might alter this result considerably. If anything, yields in ancient Palestine will have been considerably lower than those of second century Egypt (see B105b, which gives a range of 1:3.75 to 1:7.5, cf. yields from the Negev from the seventh century as reflected in *P. Ness.* III 82 [an account recording yields of approximately 1:7] and 83 [from which yields of 1:3.6 and 1:5.6 can be reconstructed]; see the discussion by Hamel, 1990, 127–32; within Palestine conditions were also quite variable), which means that to extract the same rent a larger plot would have to be sown. What is important here, however, is that the rent itself, as it is presented in M9:10, implies a scale of leaseholds that would yield rents comparable to those of Egypt for the owners. According to the material collected by Drexhage, 1991, 167, leases tended to be in the range of one to four years (three to four years in the Arsinoite nome; one or four years in the Oxyrhynchite), which also accords well with the implication of M9:9 that a seven year lease is a long one.

Certainly, not all of the lessees represented in the papyri at this scale are poor. For instance, in *SB* IV 7468 (221 CE) a Lucius Nonius Casianus (a Roman citizen whose citizenship does not derive from the Constitutio Antoniniana, and presumably not poor) asks to be released from an eleven aroura leasehold. (It should be pointed out, however, he had been leasing for a number of years; in his words "a long time.") In other leases the scale of operations and of rents are considerably more substantial (e.g., *P. Oxy.* XIV 1630, which records a bidding war for a lease in which the final offer made by the author is one talent and three thousand drakhmas; see also the Oxyrhynchite agricultural leases involving multiple forms of cultivation and production, vast sums of money and substantial payments in kind, e.g., *P. Ross. Georg.* II 19; *P. Oxy.* IV 729; *P. Oxy.* XIV 1631). For landholders also engaging in the leasing of property, see, e.g., Kehoe's discussion of Aurelius Isidorus (Kehoe, 1992, 158–65). Compare also D 19.2.25.6 (Gaius): although greater damage to the crops than is bearable should not be at the lessee's liability, "the tenant, whose substantial profit (*immodicum lucrum*) is not lost, must bear with equanimity moderate damage (*modicum damnum*)." Unless this is sheer perversity

In *m. Babaʾ Meṣiʿaʾ*, the material pertaining to the lease for use (*śĕkîrût*) of animals is scattered throughout the tractate. On the side of the lessee, there is, first of all, the obligation to pay rent on time (M9:12 [A–B]). Secondly, the lessee is expected to take proper care of the animal, and to assume a certain level of liability (M3:2; M6:3–5; M7:8).[231] From the point of view of the lessor, the one requirement that is mentioned is the requirement to supply an animal for use during the entire term of the lease if the animal "died or was broken," but not if "it was blinded or carried off for the *angareia*" (M6:3 [F–J]). Death and "breaking" are standard terms for accidental damage for which the renter is not liable;[232] here M6:3 adds that not only is the lessee not liable, but it is the lessor's responsibility to allow him to finish his lease. Perhaps the reason that in the case of an animal that has become blinded the owner is under no obligation to replace it (he may say to the lessee "Lo, yours is before you" [H][233]) is that the animal is still of some utility

---

on the part of Gaius, surely some agricultural lessees gained substantial income from their leaseholds. It should not surprise us, then, that in M9:7 a lease is presented whose rent is some three times that of M9:10 (ten *kôr*, i.e., three hundred *sĕʾâ* [ca. 3900 liters]; cf. also T5:13, increase in rent from ten *kôr* to twelve [ca. 4680 liters]). T9:26 refers to someone who leases an *ʿîr*, which contains multiple fields.

[231] See also M7:9–10 [D], in which it is not clear whether a shepherd (i.e., a paid depositary) or a renter is referred to. The implication of the Tosepta is that these pericope were taken in connection with paid depositaries. The end of T8:15 (perhaps an introduction to the parallel to M7:9, which follows in T8:16) reads "Which are the forms of *ʾônes* for which a paid depositary is exempt?..." T8:17 and 18 both discuss the case of a shepherd. In the Babli, too, both in a narrative attributed to Abbaye and in an anonymous question, M7:9–10 are fleshed out by referring to the person in whose possession the animal is, as a shepherd (B93b). Since M7:8 [G–H] makes no distinction in liability between the renter and the paid depositary it should follow that the rule is nevertheless the same. Liability of the renter is also discussed at *m. B. Qam.* 4:9; *m. Šebu.* 8:6. See also *m. Ter.* 11:9 and *m. B. Qam.* 7:6, where other aspects of the effects of transferring property to a renter (or, in *m. B. Qam.* 7:6, any of the "watchmen") are discussed.

[232] Cf. Ex. 22:6–14; M7:8 [C–H]; *m. Šebu.* 8:1; and the opening discussion of the section of this chapter on deposits (above, section III.B.2).

[233] That it is the lessor who is presumed to speak (see Rashi, *ad loc.* B78a) seems implied by other examples of the opposition "he is liable to supply ..." and "he says to him: 'Lo, yours is before you,'" e.g., *m. B. Qam.* 10:5 in which the same person is the subject of both verbs ("he is liable," "he says"). In T7:7 (and in the citation of the parallel *bāraîtāʾ*, Y6:3 [11a]), the analogous opposition is between "he is liable to supply" and "he is not liable," implying that the latter expression (where the subject is clearly the lessor) is the functional equivalent of "he says to him, 'Lo, yours is before you.'" (See the discussion in Friedman, 1990, 153–4.) Compare H. Danby, *The Mishnah* (Oxford: Oxford University, 1933), 358: "he [the lessee] may say to the owner 'Here before thee is what is thine.'"

(depending, of course, on the task for which it was hired).²³⁴ An animal requisitioned by the government cannot be understood as still useful to the lessee unless we assume that the animal would eventually be returned, and this may indeed lie behind the rule of the Mishnah.²³⁵ However, it is also possible that in this case the author of the pericope considers the seizure of the animal at least partially the fault of the lessee.²³⁶

---

²³⁴ Cf. T7:7 (with parallels Y6:3 [11a]; B78b), which, on the face of it contradicts M6:3: "And thus R. Simeon b. Eleazar used to say: 'One who says to his fellow: "Lease me your ass that I may ride on it ..." [if] it became blind, or mad, he is liable to supply him with an ass.'" The view attributed to Rabbah b. Rab Huna (B79a) that this passage deals with riding specifically, and M6:3 with leading a pack animal may well be correct. Although the use of the animal is not specified in M6:3 [F–J], it occurs between two passages dealing with hiring an ass *lĕ-hôlîkāh*, "to lead it" (see also M6:5, in which the ass serves as a pack animal).

²³⁵ The problem of the animal seized for the *angareia* is further complicated by the following traditions in T7:7 (both with parallels Y6:3 [11a]; B78b): (1) "One who rents an ass .... [if] it died, or the *angareia* took it (*nĕṭaltāh*), he is liable to supply him with an ass"; (2) "R. Simeon b. Eleazar says: 'If [the *angareia*] takes it (*nôṭlāh*) on the road on which it (fem.) was going, he is not liable to supply him with an ass; if [the *angareia*] takes it not on the road on which it (fem.) was going, he is liable to supply him with an ass.'" The first tradition (1) seems clearly to contradict M6:3 [G–H] (see Epstein, *Nûsaḥ*, 199). It is to resolve this contradiction that the view attributed to Rab at B78b proposes that M6:3 deals with "an *angareia* that returns," that is, one in which the animal will eventually come back (Friedman, 1991, 157–8, proposes that the animal has been seized for a round trip), while the *bāraîtāʾ* deals with "an *angareia* that does not return." The tradition attributed to R. Simeon b. Eleazar (2) may be taken to make the same kind of distinction between (possible) retrieval and permanent loss, if we take the expression "the road on which it (fem.) was going" to refer to the animal. This seems to have been the understanding of the second of two glosses to this tradition, attributed to R. Abbahu in the name of R. Yose b. Hanina in the Yerushalmi (the owner is liable to supply an animal if the lessee was going to Lydda [in the south] and the animal was taken to Tyre [in the north], but not when he and the animal went to Lydda; it follows that the lessee needed the animal for carrying on the return journey [see Tos. s.v. *ʾIm*]). The view attributed to Samuel (B78b), which closely parallels tradition (2), was taken by Rashi in essentially the same way (see also the Geonic commentary cited by Friedman, 1990, 165, n. 76).

²³⁶ An anonymous comment in the Yerushalmi (Y6:3 [11a]) on the contradiction between M6:3 [G–H] and the anonymous view preserved in T7:7 (cited as tradition (1) in the previous note) distinguishes between a case where the lessee could have bribed the official requisitioning the animal (where it ceases to be the lessor's problem) and one in which the lessee could not have bribed (see on this passage Epstein, *Nûsaḥ*, 119; Lieberman, *TK*, 9, 251–2; Friedman, 1990, 163–4; all three [Lieberman and Friedman with some misgivings] follow the reading of the Yerushalmi given in Nahmanides, *Ḥiddûšîm*, s.v. *Pē(rûš) ʾangāryāʾ ḥôzeret* [B78b]). In a somewhat similar vein, the first gloss attributed to R. Abbahu in the name of R. Yose b. Hanina to the view of R. Simeon b. Eleazar (tradition (2) in the previous note) distinguishes between a case where the lessee was on a major road (*basîlkî*, i.e., Greek *[hodos] basilikē*), and one in which the lessee was on a shortcut (*qapendāryāʾ*; cf. Latin *[via] compendiaria*). Apparently, by failing to stay on the major road the lessee became liable for mishaps such as

In Chapter II, I suggested that M6:3 [K–R] appears to be a revision of [A–E], and that a similar case can be made for the relationship between M6:5 [F–H] and [A–E].[237] In both of these cases what seems like a simple exposition of the principle that anyone who alters a contract is in a weaker legal position (M6:2 [F]) has been revised to take account of "probable cause." The same concern underlies M6:4 as formulated as well. The revised pericopae are not only more nuanced (animals slip on steep mountains, and become overheated in the valley), they decidedly take the interest of the lessee to heart. It is interesting to note that M6:3 [F–J] is formulated as a supplement but seems to be in some tension with its present surroundings, suggesting that it may constitute a later addition to an already existing pericope.[238] If I am correct in taking the force of M6:3 [F–J] as extending (and not limiting) the obligations of the lessor, this passage, too, revises the *ha-śôkēr* series in the interests of the lessee. The process is evident in the final form of the Mishnah, and may extend back to an earlier redactional level of the *ha-śôkēr* series, before it was utilized as a source.

Contracts for the raising, reproduction, and by-products (e.g., wool or dung) of animals are dealt with in *m. Baba' Meṣi'a'* in the context of loans (M5:4–6), where what is at issue is the possible usury in such transactions if perceived as loans (See the discussion above, in section B.4. of this chapter). Here it should be recalled that in the sources themselves such transactions are also considered types of leases.[239] It should also be noted that in all of these arrangements the lessee acts as the agent or worker of the lessor; hence, the obligation of the principal to compensate the contractor in order to avoid the taint of usury receives the most attention. Even in these pericopae,

---

these, and the lessor is no longer required to supply another animal. (Cf. also the interpretation of R. Hananel [cited Tos. *s.v. 'Im*, and Nahmanides, *ibid.* (both B78b)] of the traditions of Samuel and R. Simeon b. Eleazar, which distinguished between officials happening to requisition animals on their way, and those making a sustained search for animals. This comment takes the expression "on the road on which it [fem.] was going," to refer to the progress of the officials making requisitions [the "angareia"], and not to the animal.)

[237] Chapter II.B.2

[238] The shift of tense from the participle (present) [A] to the perfect (past) [F] is a clue that the material that follows is to be taken as supplementary. In addition, whereas the rest of M6:3–5 deal with the liability of the lessee for misuse of the animal or its equipment, M6:3 [F–J] is concerned with the liability of the lessor. However, the variance in the order of the sections of M6:3 (on which see the note to this pericope in Appendix I) is presumably to be explained on the basis of the great similarity in language between [K–R] and [A–E], rather than the "lateness" of [F–J].

[239] See, once again, *m. Ter.* 11:9, comparison of a lessee (*śôkēr*) and "receiver on estimation" (*šām*); T1:8; *t. B. Bat.* 11:6, both referring to "documents of land tenancy (*'arîsût*) and the receipt of animals (*qabbālat bĕhēmâ*)," and implying that these are analogous contracts.

however, the duty of the lessee ("borrower") to raise and care for the animal is also dealt with (M5:4 [H–I]; M5:5 [B–C]). Finally (and unaccountably), the Mishnah seems unwilling to let the same rules apply for tenant farming as for the raising of animals. The sharecropping tenant does not need to be paid a wage; moreover, loans involving a leasehold, which would under normal circumstances have been considered usurious (such as a loan of seed, to be paid back in kind, and ordinarily prohibited, M5:8; and loans of money for improvement of the property, and the concomitant exaction of a higher rent, M5:5 [E–F][240]) are permitted.

Even a cursory review of the traditions about the rental of dwellings in *m. Baba' Meṣi'a'* (M8:6–9) shows that its treatment of domestic leases is not evenly balanced. The only contractual issue applying to both lessor and lessee that is discussed is the question of payment for an intercalated month (M8:8): here the focus is on the implication of the agreement as it was stated (was the house leased for a year or for twelve months?).[241] Beyond this, there is not a single reference to the obligations of the lessee. On the other hand, we are told of a number of obligations of (or at least restrictions on) the lessor. The lessee is given a minimum term for a lease during which time his occupation is secure ("he is not allowed to remove him") (M8:6).[242] In this

---

[240] Although the exaction of a higher rent is not explicit in the Mishnah, this surely must be the implication of the qualifying "and he ought not hesitate because of interest" (M5:5 [F]). See also T5:13, which glosses M5:5 as follows: "How? He received a field from him at ten *kôrîn* of wheat, and said to him 'give me two hundred *dînārîm* and I will improve it (*'aparnĕsāh*), and I will give you twelve *kôrîn* of wheat for the year, it is permitted." Notably, this is followed with an explicit prohibition of this kind of loan in a lease for a shop or a boat, "or anything which does not produce from its body" (reading *'ôśeh bĕ-gûpô* as proposed by Lieberman, *TK*, 9, 216). (Since T5:13 attributes the words *maprîn 'et śādēhû* [=M5:5 [E]] directly to R. Simeon b. Gamaliel, the author of T5:13 apparently considered all of M5:5 [D–F] to belong to the tradition of R. Simeon b. Gamaliel.)

[241] This is a common Mishnaic preoccupation; consider M9:10 (for "seven years," or for "a week of years"?); M9:2 ("a field" or "this field"?).

[242] Compare, however, the tradition in T8:27 (cf. Y8:8 [11d]; B101b; and above Chapter II.B.2) that the time limits set (apparently in the Mishnah) do not refer to the duration of the lease, but "that he [must] inform him [of his eviction] before thirty days and that he inform him before twelve months." At any rate this passage reinforces the impression of a tendency to strengthen the position of the lessee: the lessee can only be evicted (even if the lease is formally up?) if the lessor informs the tenant that the lease would not be renewed. The same tendency is reflected by the material that precedes this tradition in T8:27: according to a tradition attributed to R. Judah, shopkeepers whose year lease is up at the end of Passover are to be given an additional "three festivals." Since the passage distinguishes between leases ending at the end of Tabernacles, which do not merit this special rule, and leases ending at the end of Passover, the force of "he gives him three festivals" may be to allow the lessee to hold the lease through Tabernacles, an additional six months (so Lieberman, *TK*, 9, 273, if I understood

connection it should be noted that the Mishnah is sensitive to the needs or expectations of city dwellers as opposed to village dwellers (M8:6[D–E]) and the special needs of shopkeepers [F–H]. The lessor is to supply certain basic equipment such as doors and bolts ("anything that is the work of an artisan") (M8:7).[243] Moreover, as with the lease of animals, where someone leased a house and it collapsed (through no fault of the lessee's) the lessor has to supply another house and allow the tenant to complete the term (M8:9).[244] The language of the pericope ("[If] it was small—let him not make it big; [if] it was big—let him not make it small .... Let him not increase the number of windows nor decrease ...." [D–H]) suggests, on the one hand, limits to what the lessor is liable to supply, but more importantly it stresses the right of the lessee to a dwelling of exactly the same quality (the lessee cannot be forced into taking a worse dwelling [even with a reduction in rent?] or a better one [with an increase in rent?]). It should be noted, however, that the lessee of a house is not entitled to the dung produced in the courtyard in which the house is situated (M8:7 [E–F]): although it is not formulated as such, there may be an implicit distinction here between a lease of a house for use, and for its productivity.

By contrast, the material on leases of agricultural land (M9:1–10) proceeds from the perspective of the lessor as landowner. Certain pericopae balance the interests of lessor and lessee. Since during the sabbatical year no work was to be done, M9:10 examines the implications of whether the agreement was made for seven years for a fixed sum (in which case the lessee pays for seven years of harvests) or whether it was made for a week of years (in which case the lease is up after seven years even though one of them was a fallow

---

him correctly). However, this interpretation is problematic since the extension is technically granted for leases terminating *after* Passover, in which case "three festivals" will extend to the end of the following Passover (i.e., a year's extension).

On the other hand, at the end of this pericope of the Tosepta are two traditions, one in which the requirement of the lessor to inform the lessee is balanced with that of the lessee, and one, attributed to R. Nehemiah, that dispenses with the minimum term (or notice period) of a year for potters of "white earth."

[243] Cf. D 33.7. 12.16–26 (Ulpian), on the *instrumentum* of a house (a rather broader concept than merely things that it takes a specialist to install).

[244] The Tosepta preserves a tradition that reflects some discomfort with the absolute formulation of the Mishnah (T8:33) "When [can the lessor not alter the quality of the house]? When he leased it from him for a long time; but if he leased it for a short time, he [the lessor] may say to him 'Lo yours is before you.'" Compare also the comment attributed to Resh Laqish in the Babli, apparently to be attached to M8:9 (B103a): "Where (*dĕ-*) he said to him the [Munich, Florence, and Rome B mss. "this"; see Rabbinovicz, *DS*, 300] house that I am leasing to you (*maśkîr lāk*) its length is such and such [etc.]."

year).²⁴⁵ In M9:1 the methods of cultivation of land are to be determined by custom [A–E], a rule that in principle works in the favor of either side. Moreover, where the contract was for a proportional rent in kind, ʾarîsût, both parties supply necessary products [H] and share in the produce of the leasehold [F–G].²⁴⁶ Finally, where payment was to be in kind (the pericope deals with a fixed payment, but the same should apply to a sharecropping arrangement as well) payment was to be from the produce of the field itself, whatever its quality (M9:7).

However, the bulk of the pericopae deal with the rights of the lessor or the duties of the lessee. In the case of failure of a field, the anonymous first view of M9:5 obligates the lessee (contracted to pay a proportional rent) to work as long as "there is in it enough to erect a pile in it" [C]. Whatever the quantity of a "pile" (and the objection in [E] may imply that it is not a specific quantity),²⁴⁷ the view attributed to R. Judah states that the lessee is obligated as long as the amount of seed grain can be recovered.²⁴⁸ Where a particular field has suffered (dryness, felling of trees, M9:2 [B]; blight or locusts, M9:6 [B]), the lessee is not thereby granted a reduction in rent; only where the locusts or blight were widespread (M9:6 [D–F]), or the lessee specified a specific field (because of its particular characteristics, M9:2 [E–G]) does the lessee merit a reduction. Moreover, the traditions presented in *m. Babaʾ Meṣiʿaʾ* take a specific interest in the management of the leasehold, in connection with both recalcitrant lessees and the selection of crops. M9:2 considers the case of a lessee (apparently a sharecropper) who has not worked the field. Of more interest is M9:4, in which the lessor can demand that the lessee carry out certain activities because of the owner's interest in maintaining the productivity of the field ("Tomorrow you leave and it grows grass before me"). M9:8–9 are of considerable interest because they shed a certain amount of light on assumptions about the effects of crops on soil and the proper rotation of crops. In contrast to the absolute position attributed to R. Simeon b.

---

²⁴⁵ See *TYṬ, TY ad loc.*

²⁴⁶ Compare, however, M9:9, which limits rights to sycamore prunings to leaseholds of seven years or more.

²⁴⁷ See the related traditions defining "a pile" in Y9:5 (12a) and B105a.

²⁴⁸ Presumably, the determination *kĕdê nĕpilâ*, literally "enough for falling" M9:5 [C], is the designation of the net (after deductions for taxes and expenses) and not gross production (this is the way the quantity of a "pile" in [C] is taken in the tradition attributed to R. Yose b. R. Hanina at Y9:4 [12a]; presumably the same applies to the amount given in [E]). If it is taken for granted that owners typically provided seed grain (cf. M5:8) and that this is repaid first before the division of the produce (neither of these is inherently unlikely, but they are assumptions on my part), the view attributed to R. Judah would seem to be that as long as the lessor can retrieve the invested seed grain, he can force the lessee to continue with the work, although the lessee derives no benefit from it (because there is nothing left to divide).

Gamaliel that prohibits any variation in the contract (M9:8; cf. M6:2 [F]), the anonymous view of M9:8 permits changes that are thought to improve the soil, or at least to damage the soil less (planting wheat instead of barley, legumes instead of grain),[249] but prohibit those that harm it. Similarly, the lessee is prohibited from planting flax unless the lease is for seven years (M9:9).[250] The issue in this rule is that the field must be restored to the lessor

---

[249] See M. Schnebel, *Die Landwirtschaft im Hellenistischen Ägypten* (Munich: C. H. Beck, 1925), 219–39; K. D. White, *Roman Farming* (Ithaca: Cornell, 1970), 111–24; Ben-David, 1974, 97–8; Y. Feliks, *Agriculture in Eretz-Israel in the Period of the Bible and Talmud* [Hebrew], rev. ed. (Jerusalem: Rubin Mass, 1990) 24–30 (who discusses only the alternating fallow and cultivation cycle). See also the synopsis of leases (including rotation of crops where specified) in Hennig, 1967, 56–72. For the harmfulness of barley see Columella, 2.9.14; on the enriching qualities of legumes, Pliny, *Natural History* 18.187.

The typical strategy of cultivation seems to be a two field system, e.g., T9:7: "... rather, he leaves half of it fallow and seeds half of it ..."; so, also, T9:8, 24–6. (However, "half" may be a simplification; it is not impossible that a three field system was known and used.) Other, supplementary forms of soil improvement are also referred to, as in the following expansion of M9:3 (T9:12): "But they do not estimate it [the field] against the fields that are on its sides, lest this one is fallow and this one is not fallow, this one is manured and this one is not manured, this one is improved [by multiple plowings during the fallow year] and this one is not improved."

There is some reason to think that crop rotation (as a supplement to or in place of fallowing), and not merely the "harmfulness" of certain kinds of crops is presupposed in M9:8–9. In Y9:9 (12a) (the entire text is quoted in the next note) a rule about restrictions on planting crops other than those specified is explained on the basis of the deleterious effects of planting "flax after flax" and "wheat after wheat." According to this explanation, the basis for the specification by the lessor depends at least in part on the crop of the previous year. In T9:25, one who leased a field for a fixed payment in kind for a short term may not let it lie fallow year after year nor may the lessee plant it year after year; by contrast, where the lease was for longterm the lessee may do so. This can be explained as the granting of more leeway to a longer term tenant, but only if we assume that there is a way of properly planting year after year without exhausting the soil. (This might, however, entail manuring and not rotation; but rotation is certainly possible.) Considering that hay (Greek *khortos*) was often rotated with grain in the Egyptian leases, the statement in M9:1 [F]: "Just as they split the grain, so let them split the hay and the straw," may presuppose a leasehold of two lots or a lease of more than one year.

[250] Cf. Columella 2.10.17, on the harmful qualities of flax. M9:9 [E–G] presupposes that the field will take seven years to recover ("If he received it from him for seven years he may plant flax in the first year" [E–F]). There are, however, other traditions. Compare T9:31: "In a place where it was the custom to seed it with flax even [every] five years, he may grow it in the second year ...." [Lieberman, *TK*, 294, takes the reference to five years as the term of the lease, and assumes (following the tradition from the Yerushalmi cited below) that flax is taken to cause three, and not seven, years worth of damage; but since T9:31 clearly amplifies M9:9 (which speaks of a contract of seven years) and the language of the Tosepta ("a place where it was the custom to seed it with flax") refers to the practice of seeding and not the term of the contract, this interpretation seems problematic.] Compare Y9:9 (12a):

Institutions and Relationships 231

in its original condition, and therefore sufficient time for recovery must be allowed. It is interesting to note that the longer the duration of the lease the greater the freedom allowed to the lessee in choosing the crops.

The divergence between the interests reflected in *śĕkîrût* leases (especially of dwellings, but also, through a process of revision, of animals) and those in *qablānût* leases (especially of agricultural land) requires explanation. It is not likely that these are the only rules available to the redactors (at whatever level) of the Mishnah. Indeed, if the Tosepta is any indication of the range of topics that might be covered in connection with these contracts, Rabbis were certainly capable of framing rules that concerned the obligations of the lessee of a house with respect to the property, and of the demands that the lessor might justifiably make of the lessee.[251] The presentation of the materials in *m. Baba' Meṣi'a'* is thus the result of a choice to present certain kinds of relationships in certain kinds of ways. In connection with the lease of agricultural property what is stressed is the owner's continuing interest in receiving the rents on the one hand, and the maintenance and productivity of the property on the other. Regarding leases of houses it is the right of the tenant to secure and uninterrupted possession that is emphasized. We should, of course, be cautious in drawing conclusions about the economic status or practices of Rabbis in late second-century Palestine from the contents of

---

(1) It is understood (*nîḥā'*) that "[If he contracted for] wheat, let him not seed it with flax,"
(2) [but why does the tradition state also] "flax, let him not seed it with wheat"?
(3) Flax damages the earth for three years, and you state thus?
(4) R. Menahem the brother of R. Gorion explained before R. La: "It is better to seed it with flax after flax than to seed it with wheat after wheat [so ms. Escorial; Leiden ms. and Venice *editio princeps*: "barley after barley"].

[251] T8:27 (end) has been cited above. Note also T8:29 (cf. B102a):
[A] One who leases a house from his fellow—
[B] [the landlord] prevents him with respect to the place of the oven,
[C] but he does not prevent him with respect to the place of the stove (*kîrâ*).
[D] [If] he leased a courtyard from him—
[E] he does not prevent him either with respect to the place of the oven or with respect to the place of the stove.
[F] Rather he places the oven where it belongs and the stove where it belongs.

[The Erfurt ms. read "shop" in [A], which Lieberman preferred, *TK*, 9, 276.] While it is possible that what is at issue in the case of the oven is whether the building was properly prepared to withstand the heat or weight of the installation (cf. *m. B. Bat.* 2:1), I am inclined to think that the significance of the contrast between courtyard [D] and house [A] is that the ovens belong outside (cf. *m. Ta'an.* 3:8), and the lessee has no rights to the use of the courtyard (just as the lessee has no rights to the refuse that accumulates there). (The problem of whether a tenant may have a fire in the house also occurs in Roman law, e.g., D 19.2.11 [Ulpian].)

legal traditions. However, if the above analysis is correct, the material discussed here reflects the interests of landholders. It is at least possible that in discussing leases in these terms Rabbis were reflecting their own interests as landowners as well.

C. Conclusions

The purpose of this chapter was to outline the way in which *m. Baba' Meṣi'a'* describes economic institutions and their functioning, and structures economic relationships. Of necessity, the treatment of this subject has focused considerably on terminological and legal issues of a technical kind. However, I have tried in my analysis of Rabbinic legal texts to keep the tractate's claims about society, and the possibility of locating those claims within a wider social, economic, and historical context, constantly in view.

Let me begin with the seemingly obvious. The Mishnah clearly presupposes an agrarian economy. The rhythms of that economy dictate when market prices emerge, for example, and therefore when one can make sales for delayed delivery (M5:7). The objects that people rent or borrow, we have seen, are connected either with agriculture or the preparation of food. Among other things, landed property is assumed to be a typical form of collateral for loans (M5:2–3). When the Mishnah considers the rights of workers, their privilege of eating in the fields is an important area of discussion because this is where workers are thought to be engaged in work.

Second, the Mishnah also presupposes an institutional framework in which economic transactions take place, consisting, at the very least, of money, markets, and banks. Rabbis are clearly comfortable with the notion of money, so much so that the Mishnah reports a dictum of Hillel that all loans of commodities (even a neighborly loan of a loaf of bread) should be made on the monetary value of the commodities (M5:8 [E–G]). This same dictum, and other passsages discussed above, also underscores the Rabbinic claim (surely not invented for ideological purposes) that commodities may vary in price in the marketplace. Money changers ("bankers") in *m. Baba' Meṣi'a'* serve to test and exchange coins and accept deposits.

More difficult, if not entirely impossible, is the evaluation of the depth or pervasiveness of this institutional framework. The common examples of transactions being carried out in kind rather than in coin may, I suggested above, reflect the limits of the reach of coinage. The rule that one might need several days to go to a nearby city to show a coin to a money changer assumes that (some) coinage is available in villages, but professional handlers of money are not. The failure of the Mishnah to regulate with respect to the rules of usury the kinds of loans or investments that "bankers" may engage in might arguably derive from the internal "systemic" reason that interest-bearing loans are prohibited and no special specifications for bankers are necessary. Yet the grouping of "bankers" with shopkeepers as money handlers seems to indicate instead the rather restricted scale of economic activities available to "bankers." That is to say, *m. Baba' Meṣi'a'* may well assume that it is householders who engage in substantial loans of produce or coin, and not professional handlers of money, the extent of whose credit capability (which should not be minimized) consists of being able to advance a day's wages to workers for a short term (M9:12 [G]). The various treatments of issues related to sale also raise the question of the limitations of the market system for organizing production and exchange. In *m. Baba' Meṣi'a'*, it seems to me, markets are addressed as places where householders purchase produce for consumption. By contrast, the descriptions of substantial sales of produce may locate them outside of the framework of the marketplace and as taking place between non-professionals.

Third, and more tentatively still, I have suggested in this chapter that the Mishnah regularly addresses the concerns of one particular group of people: substantial landowners whose wealth is sufficiently great that they need not engage in the labor of production themselves, but instead exploit their holdings through leases or hired labor; who live "in town"; and who sell off their produce and store their wealth (at least in part) in the form of money, and feed themselves from purchases in the marketplace. The claim that Rabbis themselves were wealthy landowners is largely beyond the limits of the evidence of the Mishnah itself, but this claim is consistent with occasional stories (see, e.g., M7:1, cited below), as well as material from outside of the Mishnah.[252] That *m. Baba' Meṣi'a'* addresses the concerns of the propertied

---

[252] On Rabbinic wealth in the Tannaitic period see S. J. D. Cohen, "The Place of the Rabbi in Jewish Society of the Second Century," in L. Levine ed., *The Galilee in Late Antiquity* (New York: JTSA, 1992), 169–71, nn. 52–7; and (for wealthy landholders among Rabbis in the late first and early second centuries) S. Applebaum, 1976, 697–8. L. Levine, *The Rabbinic Class of Roman Palestine in Late Antiquity* (Jerusalem and New York: Yad Izhak ben Zvi and JTSA, 1989), consistently classes Rabbis among the propertied but not very wealthy (e.g., p. 69); his description of standards of dress and comportment presupposes some wealth (pp. 52–3; for clothing as an expression of social status see Hamel, 1990, 73–92). Compare A. Büchler, *The Political and Social Leaders of the Jewish Community in Sepphoris in the Second and Third Centuries* (Oxford: Clarendon, 1909), 66–71; Alon, 1953–7, 1, 308–15 (who emphasizes the economic diversity and complexity of the Rabbinic movement); E. E. Urbach, "Class Status and Leadership in the World of the Palestinian Sages" [Hebrew], *Proceedings of the Israel Academy of Sciences* (Jerusalem, 1968) 2, 50–1; M. Goodman, *State and Society in Roman Galilee* (*Oxford Centre for Postgraduate Hebrew Studies*. Totawa: Rowman and Allanheld, 1983), 34, 93, all of whom presuppose widespread poverty among the early Rabbis.

helps to make sense of the way in which the tractate treats leases of dwellings and farm leases, in particular, the concern in connection with agricultural leases with retaining the long-term productivity of the land. Where there is some indication of the scale of transaction (e.g., in connection with sales of produce, leases, or deposits) these appear to reflect possession of lands, houses, livestock, and substantial stores of produce. The rules regarding the hiring and maintenance of labor, we have seen, were concerned to protect certain rights of workers within the framework of customary practice. However, an employer faced with financial loss due to recalcitrant workers is empowered to cheat (M6:1). The hypothesis that the Mishnah reflects the concerns of wealthier property owners helps explain the absence in discussions of civil law of much attention to how (or whether) small farmers brought their produce to market. By contrast, such questions are raised in the Mishnah in ritual contexts, where the permissibility of produce affects the householder as consumer.

In many respects, this picture of agrarian-based wealth is not specific to Jews or Rabbis. *m. Baba' Meṣiʿa'* constructs contracts in much the same way that documentary sources (primarily, but not exclusively, from Egypt) and Roman juristic texts do. This should not come altogether as a surprise: Rabbis, too, lived and worked in a province of the Roman empire and in an economy that was constrained by the same structural and material limitations as other areas in the empire. What is peculiar to the Mishnah (and to early Rabbinic culture more generally) is the way in which rules concerning money and contracts are utilized to articulate the boundaries of a Jewish society. The prohibition of usury, for instance, does not apply to gentiles. Sharply distinguished from "the gentiles," the community of Jews is imagined as an egalitarian one. It is in part for this reason, I suspect, that certain legal topics such as truly dependent labor or long-term traditional tenancy, although we have every reason to think that these existed, are not addressed in *m. Baba' Meṣiʿa'*.

The seemingly paradoxical tension between the consistent attention to the concerns of wealthier owners of property and status egalitarianism. at least for free adult Jewish males, is perhaps best expressed in a story in M7:1, in which a Rabbi is cast in the role of employer and householder:

> [G] A case happened in connection with R. Yohanan b. Mattya who said to his son: "Go out and hire workers for us."
> [H] And he agreed on food with them.
> [I] And when he came to his father [his father] said: "Even if you make them [a meal] like the meal of Solomon in his time, you have not fulfilled your obligation with respect to them, for they are sons of Abraham, Isaac, and Jacob.

[J] "Rather, before they begin working go out and tell them:
[K] "'On condition that you have [a claim to] only bread and pulse.'"

To be sure, there is an important contractual problem addressed in this pericope: when can one assume that conventional or traditional terms apply, and when must terms be made as explicit and clear as possible (in contrast with M7:1[A–F] and the view attributed to R. Simeon b. Gamaliel in [L–M], R. Yohanan b. Mattya holds that terms must always be specified). However, the language in which R. Yohanan b. Mattya's reproach to his son is cast is highly significant. To say that one's workers are Israelites, and therefore entitled to "the meal of Solomon in his time," certainly expresses their theoretical equality with their employers (and may be an expansive way of saying that at the very least they are entitled to the same meal their employers habitually eat). Yet there is something deeply ironic about this story, which describes how R. Yohanan, precisely because he recognizes this equality, requires his son to stipulate in a contract with the workers that as workers they will only receive that to which laborers ought to be entitled, bread and beans.

~ CHAPTER IV ~

Conclusions: Rabbinic Civil Law and the Social History of Roman Galilee

A reader who expected a detailed description of the social history of Roman Galilee will have been disappointed by this volume. This study of *m. Baba' Meṣiʿa'* has been unable to provide a map of the distribution of wealth, power, and authority in Roman Palestine. Ultimately the product of a religious elite, and reflecting the concerns of propertied householders, the tractate reveals the world of subalterns in only the most limited way. The reasons for these negative conclusions have been discussed in Chapter I. The Mishnah, and Rabbinic law more generally, do not simply describe the way in which Palestinian (or other) Jews lived their economic lives. The stories in *m. Baba' Meṣiʿa'* (and elsewhere) in which Rabbinic luminaries carry out these laws certainly suggest that in at least some strata within the Mishnah these laws were expected to be practicable. In addition, the similarities between the Rabbinic conceptions of how particular kinds of contracts were to be constructed and their counterparts in non-Rabbinic and non-Jewish sources suggest that a substantial portion of Rabbinic civil law does mirror social practice. Nevertheless, Rabbis do not appear to have had institutional authority in Galilee beyond their own adherents in the second or third centuries. Moreover, the legal program that the Mishnah outlines is ultimately an ideal one, in which the Temple still stands and in which high priest and king still function. Thus it is never clear to what extent people who might have followed rules corresponding to those of the Mishnah will have done so because Rabbis or their tradition require it.

The literary and redactional problems discussed in Chapter II have compounded the historiographical problem. In that chapter, I attempted to demonstrate the use of sources in the composition of *m. Baba' Meṣiʿa'*; their supplementation and revision; and, occasionally, the existence of outright contradictions. As a result of its complicated redactional history, we should not imagine that the Mishnah in general, or *m. Baba' Meṣiʿa'* in particular, constitutes a sort of "handbook" for landholders who wish to proceed according to God's law. There are too many gaps for the tractate to be used in this manner, such as the definition of a short-weight coin in M4:5 which leaves the matter in dispute (and which may in any case disagree with other pericopae), or the absence of a consistent definition of culpable negligence in the case of a depositary. If the tractate constitutes a "code" at all it is one that presupposes knowledge of principles left unstated (although these might be more self-explanatory to a contemporaneous nonspecialist than to a present-day student) and of rules to resolve contradictions or matters left in dispute.[1]

Instead, the tractate is better seen as the product of the Rabbinic community for its own specialist audience. Moreover, I have suggested (at the end of Chapter II) that the complex redaction of the tractate may reflect on a literary level a transition from an acephalous network of disciple circles to a centralized movement with authorized tradition. Thus, although the Mishnah may not "document" the social and economic life of Jews in Roman Palestine, it does indeed offer us an opportunity to examine how an articulate group of Jews within Palestinian society chose to depict that social and economic life. Some of the outlines of this depiction are elucidated in Chapter III.

As a collection of materials pertaining to civil law, the interests and problems that *m. Baba' Meṣi'a'* addresses most consistently are those of the landholding town dwellers. It is they, for instance, who had the greatest access to and need for coin, who marketed their goods through specialists (through large-scale sale or through agency), who were consumers of produce bought in the marketplace, who owned enough land to exploit it through tenancy or through hired labor, and who had large enough stores of produce to lend. At the very least, this suggests that to the extent that Rabbis wanted to be known as a group with an ancient and authoritative tradition about civil law, it is wealthy property owners to whom they wished to make this claim. Whether Rabbis as a group were themselves wealthy is beyond the evidence of the Mishnah itself. That a Rabbi might be a landowner is presupposed in M5:8 and M7:1, as well as in other material.[2] In addition, later Rabbinic sources, themselves the products of urban Rabbis and therefore perhaps disproportionately over-representing the traditions of the cities, nevertheless place Palestinian Rabbis predominantly in the cities of Palestine: Lydda,

---

[1] To be sure, later Rabbinic tradition had a set of rules that served exactly this purpose (see the brief discussion above, Chapter II.D.2). The question that remains is whether or not these are the product of later exegetical development (compare the development of the "law of citations" in later Roman law; see the brief discussion in H. J. Wolff, *Roman Law: An Historical Introduction* [Norman: University of Oklahoma, 1951], 159–61; and the *Codex Theodosianus* 1.4.1, 2, 3). That such rules formed a basis of the redactional strategy for the Mishnah is the view of D. W. Halivni, "*Mišnôt še-zāzû mi-mĕqômān*," *Sidra* 5 (1989), 86–8.

[2] See above, Chapter III.C., n. 252.

Caesarea, and especially Sepphoris and Tiberias.³ If this is correct, Mishnaic civil law does not only address the concerns of a provincial landed class, but is in fact the work of an urbanized, wealthy religious movement.

At the same time, in working out their rules and in presenting this claim, the framers of *m. Baba' Meṣi'a'* seem consistently to have stressed ethnic ties that link the collectivity of all of Israel across class or regional lines, rather than such categories as birth (e.g., priestly status) or civic affiliation that linked the upper classes at once to particular towns and to the broader aristocracy of the Roman empire.⁴ This stress on what is ostensibly an "egalitarian" society can be seen in a number of contexts, such as the general duty to care for lost objects (although an aspect of personal prestige is introduced in M2:8 [H]), or the assumption that such service, or the care of deposits and the lending of money, should be provided gratuitously. In connection with leases of agricultural land, and possibly the hiring of labor, *m. Baba' Meṣi'a'* avoids describing truly dependent relationships such as bound tenancy. This aspect of the social agenda of the tractate's rules is most clear in the case of loans, since it is not only explicitly usurious loans that are prohibited but also those loans in which the borrower provides money or services as "gifts." Here the laws of usury seem to be constructed to avoid systems of patronage based on wealth and power. At the same time, these same rules regarding usury reflect the inevitability of the differential relationship between lender and borrower (expressed, for instance, in the rules about the treatment of a pledge, and the obligations of a borrower who has borrowed a loan for "investment").

This tension inherent in the choice to present all Israelites as equal, but at the same time to accept social and economic inequalities between Israelites, is reflected repeatedly in *m. Baba' Meṣi'a'*, in particular in connection with rules concerning hiring of labor and loans. This acceptance may have been practical and realistic. However, it must be stressed that this was indeed a choice, and the ancient sources themselves suggest that it was not the only one available. For example, Rabbis might have chosen to quantify the entitlements of workers so as to guarantee them a certain standard of living (and perhaps create relations of dependence thereby), in the way that they did for poor people entitled to charity distributions and for wives. Furthermore, there is a long-standing communitarian tradition in ancient Palestinian

---

³ See above, Chapter I, n. 46.

⁴ See G. W. Bowersock, *Greek Sophists in the Roman Empire* (Oxford: Oxford, 1969), on the horizontal ties that linked the aristocracies of the cities of the Roman empire together. M. Goodman, *The Ruling Class of Judaea* (Cambridge: Cambridge, 1987), 47, points to an analogous failure on the part of the landholding classes of Judea in the first century to play the role of local aristocracies in the Greco-Roman world.

Judaism, hints of which can still be found in Rabbinic texts, that might have been utilized by these Rabbis.[5] In choosing to identify themselves with the wealthy Jewish landholders of Roman Galilee, Rabbis were also choosing, among other things, to sanction—and, to the extent that the image of "egalitarianism" is maintained, to mask—a set of unequal relationships between rich and poor.

In presenting this study I have attempted to use the text and concerns of *m. Baba' Meṣi'a'* as the framework for my analysis. To conclude, I wish briefly to locate the development of *m. Baba' Meṣi'a'* within a somewhat wider perspective. In the one hundred and fifty years between 50 and 200 CE, Palestinian Judaism had seen major political, social, and religious changes, not least of which were the suppression of two revolts, the destruction of the Jerusalem Temple, the garrisoning of the province with two legions, and increased urbanization. It is in the wake of a period of "pacification" and integration into the Roman empire that the Mishnah emerged, with its imagined world in which the Temple still stood. Mishnaic civil law is not best seen as a codification in the late second century of laws that by that time were of great antiquity.[6] Indeed, both from the literature of the second Temple period and from what Rabbinic texts themselves attribute to their earliest tradents, questions of contract and property appear to have been at best questions of secondary importance or, in the case of the Qumran sect, of sectarian governance. At precisely the time during which the economic practices of Palestinian Jews would have come increasingly under the direction of Roman provincial authorities, *m. Baba' Meṣi'a'* attempted to invent a "Jewish" civil law in which officials of any government (except for the *angareia*) are essentially absent.

It is in this context that the seemingly paradoxical tension between consistently speaking to and for all of Israel, for whom the sharpest divisions are those between Jew and gentile, or (outside of *m. Baba' Meṣi'a'*) between pious and impious, and the equally consistent addressing of the concerns of wealthy property owners, takes on particular significance. If my suggestions

---

[5] See, for instance, the Community Rule (1QS) VI.18–20 (upon completing a probationary year, the property of the examinee is merged with that of the "council of the community"); the Damascus Rule IX presupposes that property is privately held, but even here one can speak of "the property of the camp" (*mě'od ha-maḥaneh*), IX.11; see also Josephus's description of the Essenes, *War* 2. 122–4. The description of the Jerusalem community of Christians in Acts 4:32–5:11 surely comes out of this same tradition. Within Tannaitic literature, we can point to *t. Šebi.* 8:1 as an example of court-enforced pooling of resources, at least during the sabbatical year (this communalism is explicitly designated by the passage as something that happened *ba-ri'šoná*, "at first," but is no longer observed).

[6] H. Lapin, "Early Rabbinic Civil Law and the Literature of the Second Temple Period," *JSQ* 2 (1995), 149–83.

above with respect to the social origins of Rabbis are correct, the Rabbinic movement was one of wealthy intellectuals attempting to redefine who Israel was, its proper relationship with its God, and how that relationship should manifest itself in nearly every facet of human life, including economic practices. In doing so, the Rabbis who produced *m. Baba' Meṣi'a'* articulated an egalitarian ethic that incorporated all (male) Jews into "Israel," without regard to social status. It is important not to romanticize this notion. Rabbinic "egalitarianism" allowed Rabbis to make new social distinctions along the lines of piety and ritual practice. Moreover, *m. Baba' Meṣi'a'* tacitly embraces, and occasionally authorizes, the structural inequalities of poverty and wealth in its imagined Jewish society. Yet, in cultivating a rhetoric that addressed "Israel" and not the priests, the sons of light, or the *honestiores*, the Rabbinic movement constituted one voice (and the one that has been best preserved from antiquity) in an ongoing attempt to rearticulate Jewish ethnic identity in a world that had become, for Palestinian Jews, both smaller and more diffuse.

◆§ APPENDIX I ፦

Mishnah Tractate *Babaʾ Meṣiʿaʾ*: Text, Translation, and Annotation

The primary purpose of this appendix is to provide a text and translation of *m. Babaʾ Meṣiʿaʾ* that could be referred to in the body of this study. In order to do so, I have transcribed the text of the Kaufman manuscript, long regarded by scholars as a particularly good witness to the text of the Mishnah, although I have followed the conventional division of the text into pericopae (*mišnāyôt*) of standard printed editions. For convenience in annotating the text and in referring to it in the study itself, the text has been further subdivided into units that are marked by bracketed letters in the left-hand margin of the English text, and in the right-hand margin in the Hebrew text. (The subdivision and labelling of the text of the Mishnah follows a procedure systematically used by Neusner. However, the present subdivision and translation are entirely my own.) Much of the argumentation of this study, in particular Chapter II, emphasizes the complexity of Mishnaic rhetoric and diction. The present translation, therefore, attempts to stay close to the flow of the rhetoric of the Hebrew text, and to highlight this complexity, sometimes at the expense of English idiom.

Tractate *Babaʾ Meṣiʿaʾ* still awaits a critical edition, and neither the text nor the notes in this appendix are intended to fill this gap. Since they are based primarily on the major manuscripts of the Mishnah, and the evidence of Rabbinovicz, *DS* (although other sources were consulted) the notes are not complete, nor do they include every variant, especially where such variants merely reflect small variations in orthography. They are meant primarily to describe and elucidate the text of the Kaufman ms. (with reference to the other witnesses checked), to cover basic exegetical problems, and important (or potentially important) textual variants. (For a discussion of the manuscripts of the Mishnah see M. Krupp, "Manuscripts of the Mishnah," in S. Safrai, ed., *The Literature of the Sages [First Part]*, [*CRINT* 3: Philadelphia and Assen: Fortress and Van Gorcum 1987], 252–62. See also Epstein, *Nûsaḥ*; Y. Zussman, "Manuscripts and Text Traditions of the Mishnah" [Hebrew], in *Proceedings of the Eighth World Congress of Jewish Studies* [1977], vol. 3 [1981], 215–50 and D. Rosenthal, *Mišnâ ʿabôdâ zārâ: mahadûrâ biqortît bĕ-ṣērûp mābôʾ* [Diss.: Hebrew University, 1980].)

Manuscripts and Textual Signs

K	*Mischnacodex Kaufman A50*. Facsimile edition, The Hague, 1929.
G	L. Ginzberg, *Yerushalmi Fragments from the Genizah*. New York: JTSA, 1909, 254–5.
R	*Codex de Rossi (Parma)*. Facsimile edition. Jerusalem: Kedem, 1970.
L	*The Mishna Upon Which the Palestinian Talmud Rests*. Ed. W. R. Lowe. Cambridge, 1883. (Cambridge, University Library Add. 470 [II].)
M	*Mišnâ ʿim pērûš rabbēnû môšeh ben maymôn*. Ed. Y. Qafaḥ. 7 vols. Jerusalem: Mossad Harav Kook, 1963–8. (M designates the ms. Qafaḥ used as the basis of his text; Ma and Mq the texts designated א and ק respectively.)
P	*Codex Paris 328–9*. Facsimile edition. Jerusalem: Makor, 1973.
N	Naples *editio princeps* (1492). Facsimile edition. Jerusalem, 1969–79.
E	Ms. Escorial G1-3. *Yerushalmi Neziqin*. Ed. E. S. Rosenthal. Jerusalem: Israel Academy, 1983.
[ ]	Editorial addition to the text.
( )	Editorial deletion from the text.
[[ ]]	Scribal addition to the Kaufman ms.
(( ))	Scribal deletion from the Kaufman ms.

M1:1

[A]	Two people are holding a garment:	שנים אוחזים בטלת	[א]
[B]	this one says "I found it," and this one says "I found it,"	זה אום' אני מצאתיה וזה אום' אני מצאתיה	[ב]
[C]	this one says "It is entirely mine," and this one says "It is entirely mine,"	זה או' כולה שלי וזה או' כולה שלי	[ג]
[D]	let this one swear that he has no less than a one-half share in it and let this one swear that he has no less than a one-half share in it,	זה יישבע שאין לו בה פחות מחציה וזה ישבע שאין לו בה פחות מחצייה	[ד]
[E]	and let them split [it].	[ו]יחלוקו	[ה]
[F]	This one says "It is entirely mine," and this one says "It is half mine,"	זה אום' כולה שלי וזה אום' חצייה שלי	[ו]
[G]	let the one who says "It is all mine" swear that he has no less than three parts [of four] in it, and let the one who says "It is half mine" swear that he has no less than a quarter share in it,	האום' כולה שלי ישבע שאין לו בה פחות משלושה חלקים והאום' חצייה שלי ישבע שאין לו בה פחות מרביע	[ז]
[H]	let this one take three parts, and this one take a quarter.	זה נוטל שלושה חלקים וזה נוטל רביע	[ח]

M1:2

[A]	Two people are riding an animal, or one was riding and one was leading:	היו שנים רכובים על גבי בהמה או שהיה אחד רכוב ואחד מהלך	[א]
[B]	this one says: "It is all mine," and this one says: "It is all mine,"	זה אום' כולה שלי וזה אום' כולה שלי	[ב]
[C]	let this one swear that he has no less than a one-half share in it and let this one swear that he has no less than a one-half share in it,	זה ישבע שאין לו [[בה]] פחות מחצייה וזה ישבע שאין לו [[בה]] פחות מחצייה	[ג]
[D]	and let them split [it].	[ו]יחלוקו	[ד]
[E]	When they consent, or [when] they have witnesses,	בזמן שהן מודין או שיש להן עדים	[ה]
[F]	they split it without an oath.	חולקין ש[[לא]] בשבועה	[ו]

M1:1: 'מצא appears as line filler before the first מצאתיה in [B]. The ו in ויחלוקו in [E] is also absent in G. The reading with the conjunction is preferable: without it [D] would read as the protasis of a conditional sentence whose apodosis is found in [E], whereas [D–E] together clearly form the apodosis to [A–C].

M1:2: In [A], K uses the participle form רכוב; so too RMPNG; where E preserves the text of the Mishnah it uses the form רוכב but it retains רכוב in a citation of M1:3 within the text of the Yerushalmi itself.; cf. M1:3 below. (For the use of this form in Mishnaic Hebrew see Segal, 57–8, §113, E. Y. Kutscher, *The Language and Linguistic Background of the Isaiah Scroll* [Hebrew] [Jerusalem: Magnes, 1959], 268.) RM read מנהיג in [A] where KLGMaPN have מהלך. K omits בה twice in [C], and it has been added by a second hand. The words are present in the parallel clauses of M1:1, and in the present position in all the witnesses cited. The translation of מודין as "consent" in [E] follows D. W. Halivni, *Měqôrôt û-měsôrôt: bābāʾ měṣîʿāʾ* (forthcoming) and takes the clause to mean "if they each consent that the other not be required to take an oath ..." (see also H. M. Pineles, *Darkāh šel tôrâ* [Vienna,

M1:3

[A]	He was riding an animal	היה ר(ו)כב על גבי בהמה [א]
[B]	and he saw the found object:	וראה את המציאה [ב]
[C]	he said to his fellow: "Give it to me,"	אמ' לחבירו תנה לי [ג]
[D]	and he took it and said "I have gained possession over it,"	ונטלה ואמ' אני זכיתי בה [ד]
[E]	he has gained possession over it.	זכה בה [ה]
[F]	If after he gave it to him he said: "I have gained possession over it first,"	אם משנתנה לו אמ' אני זכיתי בה תחילה [ו]
[G]	he has not said anything.	לא אמ' כלום [ז]

M1:4

[A]	[If] he saw a found object and fell upon it,	ראה את המציאה ונפל(ו) לו עליה [א]
[B]	and another came and seized it,	ובא אחר והחזיק בה [ב]
[C]	the one who seized it has gained possession of it.	זה שהחזיק בה זכה בה [ג]
[D]	[If] he saw them running after a found object—	ראה אותן רצים אחר המציאה [ד]
[E]	after an injured gazelle, or after young pigeons that have not yet taken to flight—	אחר צבי שבור אחר גוזלות שלא פיריחו [ה]
[F]	and he said "My field has gained possession for me,"	ואמ' זכת לי שדי [ו]
[G]	it has taken possession for him.	זכת לו [ז]
[H]	[If] it was a gazelle running as it normally does, or if they were fledgling pigeons,	היה צבי רץ כדרכו או שהיו גוזלות מפרחין [ח]
[I]	and he said "My field has gained possession for me,"	וא[מר] זכת לי שדי [ט]
[J]	he has not said anything.	לא אמ' כלום [י]

M1:5

[A]	The object found by his minor son or daughter, Canaanite slave or maidservant, the object found by his wife—	מציאת בנו ובתו הקטנים עבדו ושפחתו הכנענים מציאת אשתו [א]
[B]	lo, they are his.	הרי אלו שלו [ב]

1861], 115, who comes to a similar conclusion, but follows the traditional understanding of מודין as "confess," "admit"). It is unclear what preceded the correction in [F]; the corrected text parallels the reading in GLPNM, but not RE, which have בלא שבועה.

M1:3: רוכב has been corrected and pointed to read רָכַב to agree with the spelling of M1:2 [A]. Cf. the note to M1:2 above.

M1:4: וא[מר] [I]: K reads ואו', in the participle (present), although the syntax of M1:3–4, as well as the agreement of the other mss., shows that the proper reading is in the perfect (past) tense, ואמר.

Appendix I: Text, Translation, and Annotation   247

[C] The object found by his adult son or daughter, or his Hebrew slave or maidservant, the object found by his wife whom he has divorced—   מציאת בנו ובתו הגדולים ועבדו ושפחתו העיברים מציאת אשתו [[שגירשה]] [ג]

[D] even though he has not yet given her her *kĕtûbbâ*—   אף על פי שלא נתן לה כתובתה [ד]

[E] lo, they are theirs.   הרי אלו שלהם [ה]

M1:6

[A] "[If] he found documents of indebtedness,   מצא שטרי חוב [א]

[B] "if a lien on property was in them,   אם יש בהם אחריות נכסים [ב]

[C] "let him not return [them];   לא יחזיר [ג]

[D] "[If] there was no lien on property in them,   אין בהם אחריות נכסים [ד]

[E] "let him return [them],   יחזיר [ה]

[F] "for the court does not exact payment from them,"   מפני שאין בית דין ניפרעים מהן [ו]

[G] the words of R. Meir.   דברי ר' מאיר [ז]

[H] And the sages say: "In any case let him not return them,   וחכמ' אומ' בין כך ובין כך לא יחזיר [ח]

[I] "for the court exacts payment from them."   מפני שבית דין ניפרעין מהם [ט]

M1:5: In [A] after הכנענים and in [C] after ושפחתו K fills the end of the line with first letters of the next word.

M1:6: With the exception of two manuscripts (mss. Hamburg and Florence), the Babli witnesses include מפני שבית דין נפרעין מהן, "because the court exacts payment from them," or a variant thereof (without מפני) also between [C] and [D] (see Rabbinovicz, *DS*, 29–30). The language of this explanatory clause is quite problematic. To begin with, the subject of the verb is not the creditor, as one might expect, but the court. Moreover, as far as I have been able to determine this is the only use of the phrase בית דין נפרעין in the Mishnah, Tosepta, Yerushalmi or Babli, and only once in a "Tannaitic" Midrash (*Sipre Num. Nāśoʾ* 2 [ed. Horovitz, p. 6]). Second, and more important, as antecedent of מהן we expect either the people from whom payment is exacted (e.g. *m. Ket.* 9:8; *m. ʿAb. Zar.* 1:1; figuratively, M4:2; *t. B. Bat.* 11:15; *Sipre Num. Nāśoʾ* 2) or the property itself (e.g. *m. Git.* 4:3; 5:2; *t. Ket.* 4:18), but neither of these are specifically mentioned. אחריות נכסים [B, D] refers to a lien clause, whereby the property that the debtor might alienate would be recoverable by the creditor. מהן might refer to precisely this property (cf. the formulation of analogous material in T1:5: שטר שיש (אין) בו אחריות נכסים גובה מנכסים משועבדים (בני חורין), "a document that has (does not have) a lien on property in it collects from property that is 'enslaved' [i.e., alienated] ('free' [i.e., still in the borrower's possession])" [cf. Y1:6 (8a); B13b]; compare forms of the nearly identical expression in *m. B. Bat.* 10:8, in which, however, גובה is dependent upon the lender, and not the document). This reading is made difficult by the fact that the negative formulation [F] corresponds to a case in which the deed made no mention of a lien, and hence of other property [D]. Neusner's reading, "on the strength of them," i.e., of the documents, is attractive but unsubstantiated

M1:7

[A] [If] he found the divorce documents of women, the emancipation documents of slaves, a will, [deed of] gift or a renunciation,
[B] lo, let him not return it—
[C] for I say: "They were written and he changed his mind so as not to give them."

[א] מצא גיטי נשים ושחרורי עבדים דייתיקי מתנה ושוברים
[ב] הרי זה לא יחזיר
[ג] שני אומ' כתובים היו ונימלך שלא ליתן

M1:8

[A] [If] he found letters of estimation [of property], or letters of alimony, documents of *ḥaliṣâ* or of refusal [of marriage], or documents of selection of judges, or any act of the court,
[B] lo, let him return it.
[C] [If] he found, in a bag or in a chest, a bundle of documents or a bunch of documents,
[D] lo, let him return it.
[E] And how much is a bunch of documents?
[F] Three documents tied one to another.
[G] Rabban Simeon b. Gamaliel says: "One borrowing from three lenders, let him return it to the borrower. Three borrowing from one lender let him return it to the lender."
[H] [If] he found a document among his documents,
[I] and it is not known what its nature is,
[J] let it be put aside until the advent of Elijah.
[K] If there are agreements with them, let him do what is in the agreement.

[א] מצא איגרות שום ואיגרות מזון שטרי חליצה ומאונים שטרי בירורים וכל מעשה בית דין
[ב] הרי זה יחזיר
[ג] מצא בחפיסה או בגלוסקמא תכריך של שטרות או אגודה של שטרות
[ד] הרי זה יחזיר
[ה] וכמה היא אגודה של שטרות
[ו] שלושה קשורות זה בזה
[ז] רבן שמעון בן גמליא' אומ' אחד לווה משלשה יחזיר (ללו) [ל]לווה שלושה לווים מן האחד יחזיר למלוה
[ח] מצא שטר בין שטרותיו
[ט] ואין ידוע מה טיבו
[י] יהא מונח עד שיבא אליהו
[כ] אם יש עמהן סימפו[[נות]] יעשה מה שבסימפון

M1:8 [ל]לווה: in [G] K reads ללו לווה, clearly an error. It has been corrected in the manuscript to read ((ל)לו)) לווה. K and R read the passive ידוע in [I]; PLE read ואינו יודע, "and he does not know;" N reads אין יודע, "no one knows," which is awkward. [[סימפו]]נות] in [K] may have originally read סימפון as in the last word of this clause. There is no agreement among the manuscripts for the spelling of the word, presumably because סימפון in its various forms is a loan word from the Greek (σύμφωνον):

R סימפונות / סימפונן
L M סימפון / סימפון
P סימפון / סימפונן
N סימפונין / סימפון
E סימפונות / סימפונות

Appendix I: Text, Translation, and Annotation

M2:1

[A]	Which found objects are his, and which is he obligated to proclaim?	אלו מציאות שלו ואלו חייב להכריז	[א]
[B]	Which found objects are his?	אלו מציאות שלו	[ב]
[C]	[If] he found scattered fruit or scattered money, small sheaves in the public domain, rounds of figs, and bakers' loaves, and strings of fish, and pieces of meat, and shorn wool having come from its district, and stalks of flax, and tongues of purple,	מצא פרות מפוזרים מעות מפוזרות כריכות ברשות הרבים עיגולי דבילה כיכרות של נחתום ומחרוזות שלדגים וחתיכות שלבשר וגיזי צמר הבאות ממדינתן ואניצי פישתן ולשונות שלארגמן	[ג]
[D]	lo, these are his.	הרי אלו שלו	[ד]
[E]	R. Judah says: "Anything that has a variation in it he is obligated to proclaim."	ר' יהודה או' כל דבר שיש בו שינוי חייב להכריז	[ה]
[F]	How?	כיצד	[ו]
[G]	[If] he found a fig-round and in it there was a potsherd, a loaf and in it there was money.	מצא עיגול ובתוכו חרס כיכר ובתוכו מעות	[ז]
[H]	R. Simeon ben Eleazar says: "All vessels of trade he is not required to proclaim."	ר' שמעון בן אלעזר אומ' כל כלי אנפוריא אינו חייב להכריז	[ח]

M2:2

[A]	And which [found objects] is he required to proclaim?	ואלו חייב להכריז	[א]

(See further D. Sperber, *Dictionary of Greek and Latin Legal Terms in Rabbinic Literature* [*Dictionaries of Talmud, Midrash and Targum* I: Ramat Gan: Bar Ilan, 1984], s.v.; R. Taubenschlag, *The Law of Greco Roman Egypt in Light of the Papyri* [Warsaw, 1955], 296 cites this term as a new one for a contract in fifth century Egypt.) In the present case, סימפון seems to mean a kind of codicil or supplementary agreement that modifies the terms of the primary agreement (see Maimoides, *ad loc*. Pineles, 1861, 116–7, Lieberman, *TK*, 9, 146–7 [to T1:9]). It is noteworthy that K was corrected to have the same reading as R.

M2:1: ומח appears as a line filler at the end of the line before ומחרוזות [C]. Between [D] and [E], E has דברי ר' מאיר, "the words of R. Meir," as in some versions of the Mishnah in the Babli (see Rabbinovicz *DS*, 52). The reading of KRLMPN is followed by the Munich and Florence mss. of the Babli (see also Ritba in *Šiṭṭâ měqubbeṣet, TYṬ* and *Měl'eket šělomoh ad loc*.), and is presupposed in the Babli's discussion, which consistently opposes R. Judah to the unnamed "first *tannā?*." This reading also retains the rhetorical structure of M2:1–2 as a single anonymous unit. It is not clear what כלי אנפוריא, lit. "vessels of trade" [H] means in context. כלי, "vessel" regularly means merely "object;" אנפוריא (L אמפוריא), is a loan word from Greek (ἐμπορία). Jastrow took the expression to mean "items used in the transport of merchandise" (*v. s.v.* אנפוריא); T2:1 implies that it refers to items produced in quantity for the marketplace, and that have no distinguishing marks (see also Albeck, *ad loc*. Lieberman, *TK*, 156).

[B]	[If] he found fruit in a vessel, or a vessel as it is, money in a pouch or a pouch as it is, bundles of fruit, bundles of money, three coins one on top of the other, small sheaves, and loaves of a householder and shorn wool from the artisan's house, (and) jars of wine and jars of oil,	מצא פירות בכלי או כלי כמות שהוא מעות בכיס או כיס כמות שהוא ציבורי פרות ציבורי מעות שלשה מטבעות זה על גבי זה כריכות ברשות היחיד וכיכרות שלבעל הבית וגיזי צמר הלקוחות מבית האומן ((ו))כדי יין וכדי שמן	[ב]
[C]	he is required to proclaim them.	חייב להכריז	[ג]

M2:3

[A]	[If] he found, behind a fence or behind a partition, bound fledglings, or on the paths that are in the fields,	מצא אחר הגפה או אחר הגדר גוזלות מקושרים או בשבילים שבשדות	[א]
[B]	lo, let him not touch them.	הרי זה לא יגע בהן	[ב]
[C]	[If] he found a vessel in the dung-heaps,	מצא כלי באשפות	[ג]
[D]	if it was covered, let him not touch it,	אם מכוסה לא יגע בו	[ד]
[E]	and if it was uncovered, he takes it and proclaims it.	ואם מגולה נוטל ומכריז	[ה]
[F]	[If] he found [it] in a rubble heap or an old wall, lo, they are his.	מצא בגל או בכותל ישן הרי אלו שלו	[ו]
[G]	[If] he found [it] in a new wall,	מצא בכותל חדש	[ז]
[H]	[if it was located] from the midpoint outward [it] is his,	מחציו ולחוץ שלו	[ח]
[I]	from the midpoint inward [it] is the householder's.	מחציו ולפנים של בעל הבית	[ט]
[J]	If he was leasing it out to others, even if he found it in the house, lo, they are his.	אם היה משכירו לאחרים אפילו מצא בתוך הבית הרי אלו שלו	[י]

M2:4

[A]	[If] he found [it] in the store, lo, they are his;	מצא בחנות הרי אילו שלו	[א]
[B]	between the chest and the shopkeeper, lo, they are the shopkeeper's;	בין תיבה לחנווני הרי הן שלחנווני	[ב]
[C]	In front of the moneychanger, lo, they are his;	לפני השולחני הרי אלו שלו	[ג]
[D]	between the chair and the moneychanger, lo, they are the moneychanger's.	בין כסא לשולחני הרי הן שלשלחני	[ד]

M2:3: In K מחציו [H] begins a new line; at the end of the preceding line the scribe has written the initial מ as filler. The implied object of the verb מצא in [F, G] as well as in M2:4 [A] seems to be the כלי mentioned in M2:3 [C]. However, note that the rulings in these pericopae use the plural pronouns הן and אלו (M2:3 [F, J], M2:4 [A–D]), whereas if the antecedent were כלי we would expect זה or הוא.

[E]	[If] he purchased produce from his fellow or [if] his fellow sent him produce, and he found money in it, lo, they are his;	לקח פרות מחבירו או ששילח לו חבירו פרות ומצא בתוכן מעות הרי אלו שלו	[ה]
[F]	if they were bound, he takes and proclaims them.	אם היו צרורים נוטל ומכריז	[ו]

M2:5

[A]	Even the garment was included among all these, and why did it go out [and was mentioned separately]?	אף השימלה היתה בכלל כל אילו ולמה יצאת	[א]
[B]	So that analogy may be made with it:	להקיש אליה	[ב]
[C]	Just as the garment is unique in that it has identifying marks, and has claimants,	מה השימלה מיוחדת שיש בה סימנין ויש לה תובעין	[ג]
[D]	so everything that has identifying marks and has claimants, he is required to proclaim.	ואף כל דבר שיש בו סימנין ויש לו תובעין (...) חייב להכריז	[ד]

M2:4: In [E] LN read ר׳ יהודה אומר אף הלוקח, "R. Judah says, 'Even one who acquires ....'" Epstein, *Nûsaḥ*, 1017, argued that since in the biblical account of Joseph's brothers finding bound money in the grain that they purchased (Gen. 42:35) the brothers report the find, and return it to Joseph upon their return (43:20–21), that the tradtion in [E–F] could not conceivably be the opinion of a single sage and must have been anonymous, thus favors the reading in K (and others). However, the circumstances of the Biblical story are hardly identical to those of our pericope: the brothers' action is based on Jacob's instructions (43:12), and are clearly designed to appease a perceived tyrant, whom the brothers know to be the legal owner of the money. Moreover, Epstein's thesis begins with the assumption that a rule to which all would agree would not be attributed to a single sage (which reflects, instead, an individually held and dissenting view). Yet, if the discussion in Chapter II.D.2 is correct, the inclusion of an attributed statement may (at least sometimes) have more to do with the redactional hands a passage has passed through than the authority of the statement (especially if, as in [E–F], the statement in question need not conflict at all, but is instead a supplement). Neusner's translation of [E]: " ... or sent produce to his fellow ..." (*Damages*, II, 30) is simply wrong. It is not clear what distinguishes bound money from loose money [E–F] since here, as opposed to M2:1–2, the produce may be presumed to have passed through the same hands whether the money found in it was bound or not. It seems that the present pericope assumes that bound money is considered to have distinguishing marks and that the owner can therefore prove ownership (see the discussion of M2:1–2, 5 in Chapter I).

M2:5: [A] presents a common midrashic formula for identifying an apparent anomaly in a verse: it asks why שמלה, "garment," is mentioned specifically in the list of lost items in Deut. 22:3. In the present pericope, however, the Mishnah omitted the verse. ואף (as in L) is perhaps not an error, but an example of *waw*-apodosis (cf. RMP, which have אף, N is lacking the entire clause [presumably due to the similarity in wording between [C] and [D]]), on which see Epstein, *Nûsaḥ*, 1076–90; I have omitted תובעין (!) ואף כל דבר שיש בו which K repeats in [D] due to dittography.

M2:6

[A] Until when is he required to proclaim?   [א] עד אמתי חייב להכריז

[B] "Until such time as the neighbors might have heard about it,"   [ב] עד כדי שידעו בו שכינים

[C] the words of R. Meir.   [ג] דב' ר' מאיר

[D] R. Judah says: "Three pilgrimage festivals and after the third pilgrimage festival seven days,   [ד] ר' יהודה אומ' שלשה רגלים ו[ו][אחר הרגל האחרון שבעת ימים

[E] so that he might go to his home [during] three, and return [during] three and proclaim for one day."   [ה] כדי שילך לביתו שלשה ויחזור שלשה ויכריז יום אחד

M2:7

[A] [If] he said the lost object but did not say its identifying marks, lo, let this one not give it to him.   [א] אמ' את האבידה ולא אמ' את סימניה הרי זה לא יתן לו

[B] The cheater, even though he said its identifying marks, lo, let this one not give it to him,   [ב] הרמיי אף על פי שאמר את סימניה הרי זה לא יתן לו

[C] for it is said: "Until your brother seeks (*děroš*) it" (Deut. 22:2),   [ג] שנ' עד דרוש אחיך אתו

[D] until you investigate (*še-tidrôš*) your brother [as to] whether he is a cheater or not.   [ד] עד שתידרוש את אחיך אם רמיי הוא אם אינו רמיי

[E] Let every thing that produces and eats produce and eat,   [ה] כל דבר שהוא עושה ואוכל יעשה ויאכל

[F] and let that which does not produce and eat be sold,   [ו] ודבר שאינו עושה ואוכל יימכר

[G] for it is said: "And you shall return it to him" (Deut. 22:2):   [ז] שנ' והש(ו)(ו)בותו לו

[H] see how [i.e., at what value?] you return it to him.   [ח] ראה היאך תשיבנו לו

[I] What shall be done with the proceeds?   [ט] כמה יהא בדמים

[J] R. Tarfon says: "Let him use them,   [י] ר' טרפון או' ישתמש בהן

[K] therefore, if they were lost he is liable for them."   [כ] לפיכך אם אבדו [חייב באחריותן

[L] R. Aqiba says: "Let him not use them,   [ל] ר' עקיבא או' לא ישתמש בהן

M2:6: In [D] שבעת begins a new line; שב appear at the end of the preceding line as filler. In [E] the subject of the verb יכריז, "(will) proclaim" appears to be identical to that of ילך and יחזור, that is, it is the owner who is expected to proclaim that he has lost an object unlike M2:1–4. (Compare Maimonides *ad loc.* who paraphrases "so that the man who has lost the lost object might go home ... and see what object he is missing, and return and find that he [the finder] is proclaiming ..."; cf. Rashi *ad loc.* [B28a]: "[The loser says:] 'I lost it and here are its distinguishing marks.'")

[M]	therefore, if they were lost he is not liable for them."	[מ] לפיכך אם אבדו] אינו חייב באחריותן

M2:8

[A]	[If] he found books, he reads them once in thirty days,	[א] מצא ספרים קורא בהן אחת [ל[]שלשים יום
[B]	and if he does not know how to read, he rolls them,	[ב] ואם אינו יודיע לקרות [[גוללן]
[C]	but let him not set out to learn from them, and let another not read with him.	[ג] אבל ((אם)) לא ילמד בהן כתחילה ולא יקרא אחר עמו
[D]	[If] he found a garment, he shakes it out once in thirty days,	[ד] מצא כסות מנערה אחת לשלושים יום
[E]	and he spreads it in accordance with its needs, but not for his honor.	[ה] ושוטחה לצ((ו))רכה אבל לא לכבודו
[F]	Silver vessels and copper vessels, he uses them in accordance with their needs, but not so as to wear them down.	[ו] כלי כסף וכלי נחושת מישתמש בהן לצ((ו))רכן אבל לא לשוחקן
[G]	Gold vessels and glass vessels, let him not touch them until Elijah comes.	[ז] כלי ((כסף)) [[זהב]] וכלי זכוכית אל יגע בהן עד שיבוא אליהו
[H]	[If] he found a sack or a basket, if it is not his habit to take up [such things], lo, let him not take [it] up.	[ח] מצא סק או קופה אם אין דרכו ליטול הרי זה לא יטול

M2:7: The verse explication in [C–D] takes אחיך as the object of דרוש: "Until the searching of your brother ...." In [G] K had והשובותו (perhaps an error for the *plene* השיבותו), which a second hand has changed to והשבותו in the ms. For the sale of the find compare M3:6 [C–D]; M9:13 [H–I]. [H] implies that the finder is not to diminish the value of the find for the owner by accruing expenses. Compare, e.g., *Mek. Mišpāṭîm* 20 (ed. Horovitz, p. 325), which clearly refers to the tradition of M2:7, and which glosses the same words in Deut. 22:2 as in M2:7 [G]: "a find that works and eats, and not a find that comes with (יש עמה) loss." (Compare the story brought in connection with M2:7 at Y2:9 [8c] about the finder who found five calves and sold off four to feed the fifth; and cf. a *bāraîtā'* at B28b. These passages deal with finds of multiple animals where sale of some is a practical, if prohibited, course of action.) The form כמה in [I] occurs also in L; RMPN have מה (N ומה). The material in brackets in [K–M] was omitted due to the close parallel between the two passages (i.e., by homoioteleuton). The corrector of K has essentially made the same correction as I have made in the above text by crossing out אינו after אבדו [K] and adding ר' עקיבא ... in the margin, to be added at the end.

M2:8: The correction in [A] is clearly correct. It is not clear what the reading of K was before the insertion of גוללן in [B]. אם [C], removed by a later hand, is an error (perhaps due to the conditional formulation of [B]). Also in [C], the scribe used the first two letters of כתחילה as filler at the end of the line, and began the word from the beginning again in the next line. כתחילה (as in RLMP; N appears to have בתחילה; Mq לכתחילה; see further Rabbinovicz, *DS*, 82; Epstein, *Nûsaḥ*, 1260–1) apparently means that one should not make use of the scroll for one's own study (i.e., the "reading" in [A] is not for the benefit of the finder but, like rolling in [B], for the care of the scroll); cf. Danby, "for the first time." The corrector has also crossed out the ו in לצורכה [E] and לצורכן [F]. The form occurs in R,

M2:9

[A]	What is a lost object?	[א] איזו(ה)[ו] היא אבידה
[B]	[If] he found an ass or a cow grazing on the road, this is not a lost object;	[ב] מצא חמור ופרה רועים בדרך אין זו אבידה
[C]	an ass and its accouterments turned over or a cow running among the vineyards, lo, this is a lost object.	[ג] חמור וכליו הפוכים ופרה רצה בין הכרמים הרי זו אבידה
[D]	[If] he returned it and it ran away, he returned it and it ran away, even four or five times, he is [still] obligated,	[ד] החזירה וברחה החזירה וברחה אפילו ארבעה וחמשה פעמים חייב
[E]	for it is said: "You shall indeed return them" (Deut. 22:1).	[ה] שנ' השב תשיבם
[F]	[If] he had given up a *selaʾ*, let him not say: "Give me a *selaʾ*,"	[ו] היה בטל מן הסלע לא יאמר לו תן לי סלע
[G]	but he gives him his wage as an idle laborer.	[ז] אלא נותן לו שכרו כפועל ((בטל))
[H]	If there is a court there let him stipulate with him before the court.	[ח] אם יש שם בית דין יתנה עמו לפני בית דין
[I]	If there is no [court] there before whom shall he stipulate?	[ט] אם אין שם לפני מי יתנה
[J]	[Rather,] his own [interest] comes first.	[י] שלו קודם

---

however, and presumably goes back to "Palestinian" pronunciation (see Epstein, *Nûsaḥ*, 1245f.; Segal, §§39, 282, pp. 25, 126–7; Kutscher, 1959, 261–2). The error in [G] stems from the opening words of the preceding clause. The words עד שיבוא אליהו in [G] are absent in one Babli ms. (Rome A), and Rabbinovicz, *DS*, 82, favors this reading because this expression generally refers to Elijah's coming to resolve doubts (cf. M1:8; 3:4, 5); the reasoning of Rabbinovicz (here the object may be presumed to have distinguishing marks, so doubt does not apply) may be overly fine.

M2:9: In K part of the ה of איזה [A] has been scratched out, leaving ו. The expression בטל מן הסלע [F] seems to mean the opportunity costs due to the time spent on the animal, and not out of pocket expenses. בטל [G] is missing in RM (as in K after the correction), as well as other witnesses (see the fuller list of variants in Epstein, *Nûsaḥ*, 956). Epstein argued on the strength of B31b that the inclusion of בטל reflects the emendation of the Mishnah on the basis of a *bāraîtāʾ*. All of the Mishnah texts checked have יתנה עמו (or a related form) in [H]. According to this reading, the ruling of [H] seems to be that the finder may take the owner to court and stipulate there that he will withhold the find until he receives payment. Thus, like [F–G], [H] is set at the time at which the owner wishes to recover his property. [H] is then further expanded by [I–J], which state that if there is no court available (when the finder first comes upon the object), he is exempt from dealing with the lost object. This temporal shift from after the fact to the moment of the find is awkward. The Babli mss. (with the exception of the Florence ms.) omit עמו, "with him" (see also *Nimûqê yôsēp* and the reading of R. Yehosep Ashkenazi in *Mĕlʾeket šĕlomoh ad loc.*) In that case, on analogy with T8:25 (see Lieberman, *TK*, 9, 271–2), the rule in [H] would be that the finder, before he undertakes to care for the object, may stipulate—even in the absence of the owner—that he only undertakes to care for the find if he will receive full compensation and not merely laborer's fees. This reading is still problematic in that [H–J] all take place at the moment of the find, whereas [G] is after the fact.

M2:10

[A]	[If] he found [it] in the cattle shed he is not obligated with respect to it,	[א] מצא בר((ו))פת אינו חייב בה
[B]	in the public space, he is obligated with respect to it.	[ב] ברשות הרבים חייב בה
[C]	[If] it was among graves let him not become unclean for it.	[ג] היתה בין הקברות אל ייטמא לו
[D]	[If] his father said: "Become unclean," or "Do not return it," lo, let this one not listen to him.	[ד] אמ' לו אביו היטמא או שאמ' לו אל תחזיר הרי זה לא ישמע לו
[E]	[If] he unburdened and loaded, unburdened and loaded [an animal] even four or five times, he is [still] obligated,	[ה] פרק וטען פרק וטען אפילו ארבעה וחמשה פעמים חייב
[F]	as it says, "You shall indeed help" (Ex. 23:5).	[ו] שנ' עזב תעזב
[G]	[If] he [the owner] went and sat himself down [and] said to him: "Since a commandment obligates you, if you wish to unburden [the animal], unburden," he is exempt,	[ז] הלך וישב לו אמ' לו הואיל ועליך מצוה אם רציתה לפרוק פרוק פטור
[H]	for it is said, "With him" (Ex. 23:5).	[ח] שנ' עמו
[I]	[If] he [the owner] was old or sick he is obligated.	[ט] היה זקן או חולה חייב
[J]	It is a commandment from the Torah to unburden but not to load.	[י] מצוה מן התורה לפרוק אבל לא לטעון
[K]	R. Simon says: "Even to load."	[כ] ר' שמעון אומ' אף לטעון
[L]	R. Yose the Galilean says: "If it had on it more than it could carry, he is not bound to it,	[ל] ר' יוסה הגלילי או' היה עליו יתר ממסואו אינו זקוק לו
[M]	"for it is said: 'Under its burden' (Ex. 23:5),	[מ] שנ' תחת מסאו
[N]	"a burden that it can stand."	[נ] מסוי שהוא יכול לעמוד בו

M2:11

[A]	His lost object and the lost object of his father, [the retrieval of] his own takes precedence.	[א] אבידתו ואבידת אביו שלו קודמת
[B]	His lost object and the lost object of his master, his own takes precedence.	[ב] אבידתו ואבידת רבו שלו קודמת
[C]	His father's lost object and the lost object of his master, his master's takes precedence over his father's,	[ג] אבידת אביו ואבידת רבו של רבו קודמת משלאביו

M2:10: The form רופת [A], occurs only in K (for the form cf. Kutscher, 1959, 41, 152, 285, 391–2, perhaps an Aramaicism); the other witnesses have רֶפֶת. All the texts checked have בין הקברות in [C]; the tradition in the Babli texts seems to have been בבית הקברות, "in the cemetery." See Rabbinovicz, *DS*, 91 and *TYṬ ad loc.*

[D] for his father brought him into the life of this world, and his master, who taught him wisdom, brought him into the life of the next world.	[ד] שאביו הביאו לחיי העולם הזה ורבו שלימדו חכמה הביאו לחיי העולם הבא
[E] If his father was equal to his master his father's lost object takes precedence.	[ה] אם היה אביו שקול כנגד רבו אבידת אביו קודמת
[F] [If] his father and his master were each carrying [a burden], he sets down that of his master, and afterwards sets down that of his father.	[ו] היה אביו (או) [ו]רבו נושאים משוא((ו))י מניח את של רבו ואחר כך מניח את של אביו
[G] [If] his father and master were in captivity he redeems his master and then redeems his father,	[ז] היה אביו ורבו בבית [[השבי]] פודה את רבו ואחר כך פודה את אביו
[H] but if his father was a sage he redeems his father and then redeems his master.	[ח] אבל אם היה אביו תלמיד חכם פודה את אביו ואחר כך פודה את רבו

M2:11: The text of [E] is confirmed in RLMPN and the Hamburg and Florence mss. of the Babli, as well as various commentaries, and is the preferred reading of *TYT*; the Babli Munich, Rome A and B mss. add the word חכם (Rabbinovicz, *DS*, 96), perhaps a corruption on the basis of [H]. Epstein, *Nûsaḥ*, 956–7, argued that [F–H] are a supplement to our Mishnah from a *bāraîtā* (see also Rabbinovicz, *DS*, 96). The text of [G], as well as the grammar and sense of [F] itself, support the correction of או to ו (from "or" to "and") in [F]. The marginal correction in [G] corrects a clear omission.

Appendix I: Text, Translation, and Annotation

M3:1

[A]	One who deposits with his fellow an animal or vessels—	המפקיד אצל חבירו בהמה או כלים	[א]
[B]	[and] they were stolen or lost:	[ו]]ניגנבו או שאבדו	[ב]
[C]	[if] he paid and did not want to swear—	שילם ולא רצה להישבע	[ג]
[D]	for lo, they have said: "An unpaid depositary swears and is exempt"—	שהרי אמרו שומר חנם נישבע ויוצא	[ד]
[E]	[if] the thief was found he pays the double payment;	נימצא הגנב משלם תשלומי כפל	[ה]
[F]	[if] he slaughtered it or sold it he pays the four- or fivefold payment.	טבח ומכר משלם תשלומי ארבעה [[ו]]חמשה	[ו]
[G]	To whom does he pay it?	למי הוא משלם	[ז]
[H]	To the one who had the deposit.	למי שהפיקדון אצלו	[ח]
[I]	[If] he swore and did not want to pay:	נשבע ולא רצה לשלם	[ט]
[J]	[if] the thief was found he pays the double payment;	נימצא הגנב משלם תשלומי כפל	[י]
[K]	[if] he slaughtered it or sold it he pays the four- or fivefold payment.	טבח ומכר משלם תשלומי ארבעה [[וחמשה]]	[כ]
[L]	To whom does he pay it?	למי הוא משלם	[ל]
[M]	To the owner of the deposit.	לבעל הפיקדון	[מ]

M3:1: The addition of ו in [B] makes for a smoother reading; but the conjunction is also missing in L. The translation "is exempt" for ויוצא [D] is dependent upon *TY*. Concerning the consistent omission in the Kaufman manuscript of the conjunction in the expression תשלומי ארבעה חמשה [F] (corrected by a later hand) see Epstein, *Nûsaḥ*, 1075, who saw its origin in a scribal error. The omission in [K] is a clear error (see not only the other witnesses to the text but also Ex. 21:37); ארבעה came at the end of a line and the scribe began [L], instead of completing the sentence. Filler at the end of lines occurs before the words נישבע [D] and כפל [J]. The text of L is quite idiosyncratic: after [H], L has the following text (numerals refer to the text as it is presented in L; bracketed letters mark the clauses to which these correspond in M3:1 [C–M]):

(1) =	[I]	נשבע אם לא רצה לשלם	[ט]
(2) =	[D]	שהרי אמרו שומר חנם נשבע ויוצא	[ד]
(3) =	[J]	נמצא הגנב משלם תשלומי כפל	[י]
(4) =	[K]	טבח ומכר משלם תשלומי ארבעה וחמשה	[כ]
(5) =	[L]	למי הוא משלם	[ל]
(6) =	[M]	לבעל הפקדון	[מ]
(7) =	[C]	שלם ולא רצה להישבע	[ג]
(8) =	[E]	נמצא הגנב משלם תשלומי כפל	[ה]
(9) =	[F]	טבח ומכר משלם תשלומי ארבעה (ארבעה) וחמשה	[ו]
(10) =	[G]	למי הוא משלם	[ז]
(11) =	[H]	למי שהפקדון אצלו	[ח]

In other words, L presents a version of [I–M] (1–6) that includes [D] (2) after [I] (1), and follows [M] (6) with a repetition of [C–H] (7–11) (without [D]). Could the scribe of L have conflated two versions of M3:1, of which one of the two versions had the reverse placement of [C–H] and [I–M]? (If such a version existed, it followed the order of the clauses of Ex. 22:6–7. Incidentally, the explanatory clause [D], (2) in L, makes quite a bit

M3:2

[A] One who leases a cow from his fellow— [א] הסוכר פרה מחבירו
[B] and has lent it to another and it died according to its manner [i.e., naturally]: [ב] והשאילה לאחר ומיתה כדרכה
[C] let the lessee swear that it has died according to its manner and the borrower pays to the lessee. [ג] ישבע השוכר שמתה כדרכה והשואל משלם לשוכר
[D] Said R. Yose: "How [can this be]? [ד] אמ' ר' יוסה כיצד
[E] "That one is doing business with the cow of this one! [ה] והלה עושה סחורה בפרתו שלזה
[F] "Rather let the cow [i.e., its value] return to its owners." [ו] אלא תחזור הפרה לבעלים

M3:3

[A] [If] he said to two people: "I robbed a *māneh* from one of you, but I do not know which one of you," [א] אמ' לשנים גזלתי את אחד מכם מנה ואיני יודע אי זה מכם
[B] [or:] "The father of one of you deposited a *māneh* with me, but I do not know which he is," [ב] אביו שלאחד מכם היפקיד אצלי מנה ואיני יודע אי זה הוא
[C] he gives a *māneh* to this one and a *māneh* to this one, [ג] נותן לזה מנה ולזה מנה
[D] because he has admitted it by his own mouth. [ד] מפני שהודה מפי עמו

M3:4

[A] [Two who deposited with one person—this one [depositing] a *māneh*, this one two hundred [*dînārîm*]: [א] שנים שהיפקידו אצל אחד זה מנה וזה מאתים
[B] this one says "The two hundred are mine," and this one says "The two hundred are mine." [ב] [[זה אומ' מאתים שלי]] וזה או' מאתים שלי
[C] He gives a *māneh* to this one and a *māneh* to this one, and let the remainder be set aside until Elijah comes. [ג] נותן לזה מנה ולזה מנה והשאר יהי מונח עד שיבא אליהו
[D] Said R. Yose: "If so what has the cheater lost? [ד] אמ' ר' יוסי אם כן מה הפסיד הרמיי

---

of sense following [I]: "If he swore and did not want to pay—for lo, they have said: 'An unpaid depositary swears and is exempt' ....")

M3:2: RM read הלה (without the ו) in [E] making [D–E] into a combined sentence: "How can that one do business with the cow of this one?"

M3:3: The *māneh* (cf. Gk. μνᾶ) equals 100 *dînārîm* or *zûzîm* (*denarii*). In [B], RLPM open with או, "or." In [A] P has אי זהו מכם, as in [B].

[E]	"Rather, let all of it be set aside until Elijah comes."	אלא הכל יהא מונח עד שיבא אליהו	[ה]

M3:5

[A]	And likewise two vessels one worth *māneh*, and one worth one thousand *zûz*,	וכן שני כלים אחד [[יפה]] מנה ואחד יפה אלף זוז	[א]
[B]	this one says "The valuable one is mine," and this one says "The valuable one is mine."	זה אומ' יפה שלי [וזה אומר יפה שלי]	[ב]
[C]	He gives the small one to one of them, and from the [proceeds of] the bigger one he gives the value of the smaller one to the second, and let the remainder be set aside until Elijah comes.	נתן את הקטן לאחד מהן ומתוך הגדול נותן דמי קטן לשני והשאר יהי מונח עד שיבא אליה	[ג]
[D]	Said R. Yose: "If so what has the cheater lost?	אמ' ר' יוסה אם כן מה הפסיד הרמיי	[ד]
[E]	"Rather, let it all be set aside until Elijah comes."	אלא הכל יהי מונח עד שיבא אליהו	[ה]

M3:6

[A]	One who deposits produce with his fellow—	המפקיד פרות אצל חבירו	[א]
[B]	even if it is perishing, lo, let this one not touch it.	אפילו הן אובדין הרי זה לא יגע בהן	[ב]
[C]	R. Simeon b. Gamaliël says: "Let him sell [it] before the court,	רבן שמעון בן גמליא' אומ' ימכור בפני בית דין	[ג]
[D]	"because of [the principle of] returning a lost object to its owners."	מפני השב אבדה לבעלים	[ד]

M3:4: [[זה ... שלי]] [B] is omitted in K and supplied in the margin in a different hand. Since what follows opens with ו it seems likely that it is the first clause that is lacking (however, cf. M2:5 [D] and note thereto). This omission appears to be due to homoioteleuton; however, an analogous omission occurs in M3:5 [B], which might suggest a different (if erroneous) textual tradition, or conscious abbreviation. Fillers at the ends of lines occur before והשאר [C] and אלא [E].

M3:5: In [A] יפה is required by context and is present in RLPNEM. In [B], it is the second clause that has been omitted by homoioteleuton; a second hand has restored K as if it were the first clause that was missing. (Cf. M3:4 [B] and note thereto.)

M3:6: In [C] R reads בבית דין, "in court." The idea of selling off another's property to protect that person's interests occurs also in M2:7 [E–I]. (See also M9:13 [H–I], also attributed to R. Simeon b. Gamaliel, in which a creditor is permitted to sell off a pledge after thirty days [presumably in his own interests, not in those of the debtor].) The rationale that one is returning a lost object also appears in M6:7 [E]; M7:4.

M3:7

[A]	One who deposits produce with his fellow—	[א] המפקיד פירות אצל חבירו
[B]	lo, let this one [the depositary] deduct losses:	[ב] הרי זה יוציא לו חסרונות
[C]	for wheat and rice nine half *qabbîm* to the *kôr*;	[ג] לחטים ולאורז תשעת חצאי קבים לכור
[D]	for barley and millet nine *qabbîm* to the *kôr*;	[ד] לשעורים ולדוחן תשעת קבים לכור
[E]	for spelt and linseed, three *sĕʾîn* to the *kôr*.	[ה] לכוסמים ולזרע פשתן שלש סאים לכור
[F]	All is [assessed] according to the measurement and all is [assessed] according to time.	[ו] הכל לפי המידה והכל לפי הזמן
[G]	Said R. Yohanan b. Nuri: "What does it matter to them? Mice eat [as much as they eat] whether from much or from little.	[ז] אמ' ר' יוחנן בן נורי וכי מה אכפת להם העכברים אוכלים בין מהרבה בין מקימאה
[H]	"Let him deduct losses only for a *kôr*."	[ח] אינו יוצ[י] א לו חסרונות אלא לכור בלבד
[I]	R. Judah says: "If the measure was large, he does not deduct losses because they increase."	[ט] ר' יהודה או' אם היתה מידה מרובה אינו יוציא לו חסרונות מפני שהן מותירות

M3:7: 1 *kôr* = 30 *sĕʾâ* (pl. *sĕʾîn*) = 180 *qab* (pl. *qabbîm*). העכברים [G] is preceded at the end of the preceding line by הע. RPN read לעכברים, in which case the passage reads "What do mice care, [for] they eat ..." (MP have והעכברים in the second clause, i.e., "for mice ..."). מותירות in [I] is taken in B40a (a tradition attributed to Rab Nahman) to mean increase in volume (by absorbing moisture over the winter); Albeck, *Nĕzîqîn, ad loc.* and p. 421, following Rabad (in *Šiṭṭâ mĕqubbeṣet* to B40a) understands it as referring to the use of heaped measures for large quantities: the percentage by which the amount of grain is underestimated when measured this way is taken to be equivalent to the approximated loss. A similar understanding may underlie R. Nahman's objection to the *bāraîtāʾ* cited at B40a that expands upon R. Judah's view in [I]:

A *tannāʾ* taught before R. Nahman: "When does this (M3:7 [A–F]) apply? When he [the depositor] measured for him from his threshing floor (*mi-tôk gornô*) [at the time of deposit], and [the depositary] returned it to him from his threshing floor. But [if] he measured for him from his threshing floor and he returned [it] from his house, he does not deduct losses because they increase." (Cf. T3:10.)

Said [R. Nahman] to him: "Are we dealing with fools who give with large measures and take with small ones?

"Perhaps it [the *bāraîtāʾ*] said: 'in the days of the harvest' (*bi-yĕmôt ha-gôren*) [rather than 'from the threshing floor (*mi-tôk gornô*)']:

"'When does this [A–F] apply? When he [the depositor] measured for him in the days of the harvest [at the time of deposit], and [the depositary] returned it to him in the days of the harvest. But [if] he measured for him in the days of the

M3:8

[A]	Let him deduct one sixth for wine.	[א] יוציא לו שתות ליין
[B]	R. Judah says, "One fifth."	[ב] ר' יהודה אומ' חומש
[C]	Let him deduct three *luggîm* of oil per hundred:	[ג] יוציא לו שלשת לוגים שמן למאה
[D]	one and one half *luggîm* for sediment; one and one half *luggîm* for absorption [by the casks].	[ד] לוג ומחצה שמרים לוג ומחצה בלע
[E]	If it was clarified oil, let him not deduct for sediment;	[ה] אם היה שמן מזווקק אינו יוצ[י][א] לו שמרים
[F]	[if] old casks, let him not deduct for absorption.	[ו] קינקנים ישנות אינו יוצ[י][א] לו בלע
[G]	R. Judah says: "One who sells clarified oil all year round, lo, this one accepts upon himself one and one half *luggîm* of sediment to the one hundred."	[ז] ר' יהודה אומ' המוכר שמן מזווקק לחבירו כל ימות השנה הרי זה מקבל עליו לוג ומחצה שמרים למאה

M3:9

[A]	One who deposits a jar with his fellow—	[א] המפקיד חבית אצל חבירו
[B]	[if] the owners did not single out a place for it, and he [the depositary] moved it and it broke:	[ב] [ו]לא ייחדו לה הבעלים מקום וטלטלה ונשברה
[C]	if it broke while in his hands, [if moved] for his need he is liable; for its need he is exempt;	[ג] אם מתוך ידו נשברה לצורכו חייב לצ(ו)[ו]רכה פטור
[D]	if it broke after he put it down, whether for his need or for its need he is exempt.	[ד] ואם משהינחה בין לצ(ו)[ו]רכו ובין לצ(ו)[ו]רכה פטור

---

harvest and he returned [it] in the rainy season, he does not deduct losses because they increase.'"

That is, the tradition attributed to Rab Nahman presupposes that one typically uses different kinds of measures when measuring "from his threshing floor" and "from his house," but objects that only a fool would fail to make sure the proper amount was returned due to the difference in measures. Albeck and Lieberman, *TK* 9, 173f. take R. Nahman's revision of the *bārâitā'* to be its actual meaning.

M3:8: RLPMN have וכו' אף המוכר, "even one who sells ...." in [G]. See Epstein *Nûsaḥ*, 1017–8. Since the subject of "accepts upon himself" (מקבל עליו) is not specified, it is not clear whether it refers to the seller (in which case the view attributed to R. Judah is that, unlike [E] where it is the one who receives the oil, i.e., the owner, who absorbs the loss, when one sells clarified oil it is the seller who must make up the volume of the sediments; so Epstein, *Nûsaḥ*, 1018) or the purchaser (in which case [G] extends the case of [E] to sale as well: in both cases the recipient of the oil makes allowance for the volume of the sediments; this is presupposed by the view attributed to R. Hoshaya [Y3:8 (9d)], the stammaitic expansion of the views of Abbaye and R. Pappa [B40b], and followed by Lieberman, *TK*, 9, 174–5). (The end of T3:10 and its relationship to M3:8 [G], over which Epstein and Lieberman disagreed, require further study.)

[E]	[If] the owners did single out a place, and he moved it and it broke:	[ה] ייחדו לה הבעלים מקום וטלטלה ונשברה
[F]	whether it broke while in his hands or after he put it down, for his need he is liable, for its need he is exempt.	[ו] בין מתוך ידו ובין משהיניחה לצו(ו)רכו חייב לצורכה פטור

M3:10

[A]	One who deposits money with his fellow—	[א] המפקיד מעות אצל חבירו
[B]	[If] he bound it and cast it behind him,	[ב] צררן והיפשילן לאחריו
[C]	[or] gave it to his minor son or daughter,	[ג] מסרן לבנו ולבתו הקטנים
[D]	and he locked [the door] before them in an inappropriate manner,	[ד] ונעל בפניהם שלא כראוי
[E]	he is liable,	[ה] חייב
[F]	for he did not watch [over it] in the manner of watchmen.	[ו] שלא שמר כדרך השומרים
[G]	And if he did watch in the manner of watchmen,	[ז] ואם שמר כדרך השומרים
[H]	he is exempt.	[ח] פטור

M3:9: In [B] KR read: לא ייחדו; a second hand has altered K to read ל[ו]לא as in LPNEM (cf M3:1 [B]). The spelling לצורכו/-ה in [C, D, F] (note that even where the ו is not crossed out, the צ is pointed ץ), as in K before the correction is also used in R, LN (except in [F]) and Mq. The spelling לצרכו/-ה is used in P (see above M2:8). The final ו in לצורכו in [D] looks very much like a ן (i.e., "their need;" however, the difference in appearance between ן and ו is slight).

M3:10: The antecedent of בפניהם in [D] could either be (1) the children [G], requiring that we take [C–D] together as a unit (i.e., the depositary's irresponsibility lay particularly in failing to make sure that the children to whom he had given the money to watch [for the expression מסר ל with the sense "give over to watch" cf. m. B. Qam. 4:9; 6:2], could not get out) (so, e.g., Rashi); or (2) the money [A], in which case [C] and [D] constitute different examples of inappropriate watching (note that the text of the Mishnah in Rif and Rosh has the disjunctive או, "or," at the beginning of [D] (see Nîmmûqê yôsēp to Rif ad loc.). In favor of (1) is the language ונעל בפניהם שלא כראוי, which implies that the thing before which one is locking the gate or door can move its own volition (as in m. B. Qam. 4:9; 6:1). In favor of (2) is the likelihood that handing a deposit over to minors is already negligent, so that we do not expect a clause [D] to specify even further negligence. The Yerushalmi presents a tradition, apparently echoing the language of M3:10 [B–F], which reads:

> When did they say "an unpaid depositary swears and is exempt?" (M3:1 [D]) When he watches in the manner of the watchmen (M3:10 [F]): [if] he locked it in the appropriate manner (נעל כראוי) (cf. M3:10 [D]), bound it in the appropriate manner ... [If] they were stolen or lost, he is required to swear and is exempt from payment .... (Y3:10 [9b])

The tradition goes on to outline the contrary case as well, in which the words נעל שלא כראוי are used. The language of this Yerushalmi passage implies that already in antiquity [D]

M3:11

[A]	One who deposits money with a banker—	המפקיד מעות אצל השולחני [א]
[B]	if it is bound let him not make use of it;	אם צרורים אל ישתמש בהן [ב]
[C]	if it is loose, let him use it.	ואם מותרין ישתמש בהן [ג]
[D]	[If he deposits] with a householder in any case let him not use it.	אצל בעל הבית בין כך ובין כך אל ישתמש בהן [ד]
[E]	"The shopkeeper is like a house-holder,"	החנווני כבעל הבית [ה]
[F]	the words of R. Meir.	דברי ר' מאיר [ו]
[G]	R. Judah says: "Like a banker."	ר' יהודה אומ' כשולחני [ז]

M3:12

[A]	One who appropriates a deposit—	השולח יד בפיקדון [א]
[B]	the House of Shammai says: "He is punished with depreciation and appreciation,"	בית שמי אומ' יילקה בחסר וביתר [ב]
[C]	and the House of Hillel says: "[He is liable for the value] at the time of taking it out,"	ובית הילל אומ' בשעת הוצאה [ג]
[D]	and R. Aqiba says: "According to [the value at] the time it is demanded."	ור' עקיבה אומ' כשעת התביעה [ד]
[E]	One who intends to appropriate a deposit—	החושב לשלוח יד בפיקדון [ה]
[F]	the House of Shammai deems liable;	בית שמי מחייבין [ו]
[G]	and the House of Hillel says: "He is not liable until such time as he has appropriated [it]"	ובית הלל אומ' אינו חייב אלא עד שעה ששילח יד [ז]
[H]	How?	כיצד [ח]
[I]	[If] he tipped the jar and took a *rĕbîʿit* from it and it broke, he pays only a *rĕbîʿit*.	היטה את החבית ונטל ממנה רביעית ונישברה אינו משלם אלא רביעית [ט]

---

could be taken to refer to the deposit and not to children, who are not mentioned in this passage. P is lacking clause [G]. D. Daube, "Negligence in the Early Talmudic Law of Contract (*Peshiʿa*)," *Festschrift Schulz* I, ed. H. Niedermeyer, W. Flure (Weimar, 1951), 143, suggested that (2) is correct ("before the money"), and that the awkward formulation reflects the influence of the law of delict (*m. B. Qam.* 4:9; 6:1) on the law of contract.

M3:11: הש appears at the end of the line preceding השולחני [A]. To this pericope compare M2:7 [J], [K]. After [B] LPNM have לפיכך אם אבדו אינו חייב באחריותן, "therefore if they were lost he is not liable for them;" after [C] PNM have לפיכך אם אבדו חייב באחריותן, " ... he is liable ..."; after [D] LNM repeat the first of these two clauses. Like K, R does not include these clauses. R. Yehosep Ashkenazi (cited in *Mĕlʾeket šĕlomoh ad loc.*) also deleted all three clauses.

[J] [If] he picked it up and took a *rĕbîʿît* from it and it broke, he pays for the whole. [י] היגביהה ונטל ממנה רביעית ונישברה משלם את הכל

M3:12: [H] is absent in some texts, although it is present in all the Mishnah texts checked for this study. In addition, a parallel to [I–J] could circulate separately, without reference to the Hillelite, Shammaite dispute (*t. B. Qam.* 10:34). For discussion and a list of variants see Epstein, *Nûsaḥ*, 1034f. Neusner, *Damages* II, 51, excises the word without any attention to the textual evidence.

Appendix I: Text, Translation, and Annotation 265

M4:1

[A]	Silver acquires gold, but gold does not acquire silver;	הכסף קונה את הזהב והזהב אינו קונה את הכסף	[א]
[B]	copper acquires silver, but silver does not acquire copper;	הנחשת קונה את הכסף והכסף אינו קונה את הנחשת	[ב]
[C]	bad money (*māʿôt*) acquires good [money], but good does not acquire bad;	מעות הרעות קונות את היפות והיפות אינן קונות את הרעות	[ג]
[D]	uncoined metal acquires the coin (*maṭbēʿa*), but the coin does not acquire uncoined metal;	אסימון קונה את המטביע והמטביע אינ[ו][[ן]] קונה את אסימון	[ד]
[E]	movable goods acquire the coin, but the coin does not acquire moveable goods.	המטלטלין קונים את המטביע והמטביע אינ[ו][[ן]] קונה את המטלטלים	[ה]
[F]	This is the rule: all moveable goods acquire one another.	זה הכלל כל המטלטלין קונים זה את זה	[ו]

M4:2

[A]	How?	כיצד	[א]
[B]	[If] he drew produce from him but did not give him money he cannot withdraw [from the sale].	משך ממנו פרות ולא נתן לו מעות אינו יכול לחזור בו	[ב]
[C]	[If] he gave money but did not draw produce he can withdraw.	נתן לו מעות [ו][[ו]]לא משך ממנו פירות יכול לחזור בו	[ג]
[D]	However, they said: "He who exacted payment from the men of the generation of the flood will in the future exact payment from him who does not stand by his word."	אבל אמרו מי שפרע מאנשי דור המבול עתיד להיפרע ממי שאינו עומד בדיבורו	[ד]

M4:1: PNEM read הזהב קונה את הכסף in [A] in accordance with the Babylonian tradition. See Babli and Yerushalmi *ad loc.* and see Epstein *Nûsaḥ*, 19–22; *Siprût*, 176–7; Lieberman, *TK* 9, 176 (to T 3:13). אסימון (Gk. ἄσημον, cf. LSJM *s.v.*) in [D] may refer either (1) to bullion (so apparently Lieberman, *TK* 2, 715 [to *t. Maʿaś Š.* 1:4], who cites *y. Maʿaś. Š.* 1:2 [52c]: "What is a pound (ליטרא, cf. Gk. λίτρα) of silver? אסימון"; and *Sipre Num.* 54 (ed. Horovitz, p. 55) referring to a temple vessel that was turned into סימון, and again into a vessel; and see S. Bolin, *State and Currency in the Roman Empire to 300 AD* [Stockholm: Almqvist and Wiskell, 1958], 89–90), or (2) to blanks that have not been stamped (so S. Krauss, *Griechische und lateinische Lehnwörter im Talmud, Midrasch und Targum* [Berlin, 1898–9], 2, 86, *s.v.*; see *Sipre Deut.* 107 [ed. Finkelstein, p. 167, which identifies אסימון, as opposed to a coin, as that which has no stamp [אין עליו צורה]]. אינ[ו][[ן]] in [D] and [E] seems to have been corrected, but it is not clear what was present in the ms. before the correction. RLMP have 'הכלל כל וכו at the beginning of [F]. The reading וכל (i.e., without הכלל, in N, the text of the Mishnah in Rif and Rosh, of R. Yehosep Ashkenazi [in *Mĕlʾeket šĕlomoh ad loc.*] and the Babli mss. Hamburg and Rome B) is favored by Epstein, *Nûsaḥ*, 1042, 1073.

| [E] | R. Simeon says: "Whoever has the money in his hand, his hand is in the superior position." | ר' שמעון אומ' כל שהכסף בידו ידו לעליונה | [ה] |

M4:3

[A]	*Hônāyâ* is four silver [coins] at twenty four silver coins to the *sela^c*—one sixth of the purchase.	ההוניה ארבע כסף מעשרים וארבע כסף לסלע שתות למקח	[א]
[B]	Until when can one return [an item bought at an inflated price]?	עד אמתי מותר להחזיר	[ב]
[C]	Long enough to show it to a merchant or to his relative.	כדי שיראה לתגר או לקרובו	[ג]
[D]	R. Tarfon ruled in Lod: "*Hônāyâ* is eight silver coins to the *sela^c*—one third of the purchase,"	הורה ר' טרפון בלוד ההוניה שמונת כסף לסלע שליש למקח	[ד]
[E]	and the merchants of Lod rejoiced.	ושמח[ו]ן תגרי לוד	[ה]
[F]	He said to them: "It is permitted to return the entire day."	אמ' להם מותר להחזיר כל היום	[ו]
[G]	They said: "Let R. Tarfon leave us our place."	אמרו יניח לנו ר' טרפון מקומינו	[ז]
[H]	And they went back to the words of the sages.	וחזרו לדברי חכמ'	[ח]

M4:4

[A]	Whether [it is] the buyer or whether [it is] the seller, they have *hônāyâ*.	אחד הלוקיח ואחד המוכר יש להם הוניה	[א]
[B]	Just as a non-professional has *hônāyâ*, so a merchant has *hônāyâ*.	כשם שהוניה להדיוט כך הוניה לתגר	[ב]
[C]	R. Judah says: "A merchant has no *hônāyâ*."	ר' יהודה או' אין [ל]תגר הוניה	[ג]
[D]	Whoever has been imposed upon, his hand is in the superior position.	משהוטל עליו ידו לעליונה	[ד]

M4:2: The conjunction ו was lacking in [C] and has been supplied by a second hand. For a discussion of the principles discussed in this pericope see Chapter III. B. 3.

M4:3: The "silver [coin]" referred to in [A] is the *mā^câ*, one sixth of a *dînār* (corresponding to the obol in Greek systems of coins). הוניה [A], [D], as well as M4:4, 5, 7, 9, 10, is variously spelled in the mss. (Segal, §67–8): K (except M4:9[A]) (and occasionally Ma) הוניה; M הוניה; NP אונאה; R is inconsistent (see I. Z. Feintuch, "On the Parma Ms." [Heb.] *BIA* 18/19 [1981], 196–217). I have chosen not to translate the term since it can have both its technical meaning of "over- (or under-) charge" and its root meaning of "oppression" as in M4:10 (see the brief discussion in H. Lapin, "Early Rabbinic Civil Law and the Literature of the Second Temple Period," *JSQ* 2 [1995], forthcoming). In [C] RLMPN read כדי עד, "until such time as," which answers the rhetorical question in [B] somewhat better. תגר in [C] and [E] has the root sense of "travel"; however in the context of both places in this pericope a recognized local merchant of some kind seems to be assumed by the term. It is not clear what, if anything, the correction in [E] has replaced. In [G] RLM read לו אמרו, "they said to him"; MqPN, like K, omit לו.

Appendix I: Text, Translation, and Annotation

[E]	For he says to him: "Give me my money or give me the amount whereby you have oppressed me (*še-hônētānî*)."	[ה] שהוא אומ׳ תן לי מעותי א[ו] תן לי מה שהוניתני

M4:5

[A]	And how much may a *sela'* be lacking and there [still] not be *hônāyâ* in it?	[א] וכמה תהא הסלע חסירה ולא יהי בה הוניה
[B]	R. Meir says "Four *'issārôt*—an *'issār* to the *dînār*."	[ב] ר׳ מאיר אומ׳ ארבעה אסרות מאסר לדינר
[C]	R. Judah says, "Four *pôndiônôt*— a *pôndiôn* to the *dînār*."	[ג] ר׳ יהודה אומ׳ ארבעה פונדיו(י)נות מפונדי[ו]ן לדינר
[D]	R. Simeon says, "Eight *pôndiônôt*—a *pôndiôn* to the *dînār*."	[ד] ר׳ שמעון אומ׳ שמונה פונדיונות משני פונדיונים לדינר

M4:6

[A]	Until when can one return [such a coin]?	[א] עד אמתי מותר להחזיר
[B]	In the towns, long enough to show [it] to a moneychanger;	[ב] בכרכים כדי שיראה לשולחני
[C]	and in the villages, until Sabbath eves.	[ג] ובכפרים עד ערבי שבתות
[D]	If he recognized it, even after twelve months he accepts it from him,	[ד] אם היה מכירה אפילו לאחר שנים עשר חודש מקבלה ממנו
[E]	but he has only anger against him.	[ה] ואין לו עליו אלא תרעומת
[F]	And he may give it for [redemption of] second tithe.	[ו] ונותנה למעשר שיני

M4:4: The expression יש (אין) לו הוניה could mean either (a) "he is (not) subject to the rules of *hônāyâ*"; or (b) "he has (no) right of *hônāyâ*," i.e., such a person may (not) undo a sale based on the claim of *hônāyâ*. Judging from the fact that in M4:3 [C] a תגר is deemed knowledgeable about true market prices (and therefore unlikely to make a mistake), M4:4 [C] would make more sense if it protected someone trading with a תגר, so (b) seems the more likely interpretation. Against M4:4 [B], the view attributed to R. Judah in [C] would then rule that a תגר may not bring a claim of *hônāyâ* (cf. the *bāraîtā'* at B51a [cited in support of a view attributed to Rab Nahman in the name of Rab] which adds to [C] the gloss "because he is an expert"). The correction in [C] follows the syntax of the similar expression in [B], as well as the other witnesses checked. Note, however, that against KRN the word-order in LMP is אין הונאה/אונאה לתגר. The translation of הוטל as "imposed upon" in [D] follows Danby, and reads משהוטל (KL) as identical to מי שהוטל (RMPN), and not "from the moment he has been been imposed upon ..." (see Epstein, *Nûsaḥ*, 1244). In [E], RM, like K, read שהוא; P has רצה, "[if] he wished [to do so] ..."; and N has both, a clear conflation. (L has כשהוא, "when he ...," which is quite awkward.) [ו]א replaces אמ׳ in K, a clear error.

M4:5: The Mishnah's monetary system is discussed in Chapter II.A.1. The coins correspond in name to Roman coins: *'issār*—*as* (cf. Gk. 'ασσάριον); *pôndiôn*—*dupondius*; *dînār*—*denarius* (1 *dînār* = 12 *pôndiônôt* = 24 *'issārîm*). KRLPE all open with וכמה in [A]; MN omit the conjunction (ו); some mss. of the Babli have עד כמה "up to how much" in the Mishnah and in a closely related *bāraîtā'* (see Rabbinovicz, *DS*, 144 notes ה, ט and כ, and, in connection with the *bāraîtā'*, Tos. B52a *s. v. Wĕ-tannā' bārā'*). The spelling in [C] is corrected on the basis of the spelling in [D], as well as other texts and witnesses.

[G]	And he ought not hestitate for this is only stinginess.	ואין חושש שאינה אלא נפש רעה [ז]

M4:7

[A]	*Hônāyâ* is four silver coins;	ההוניה ארבע כסף [א]
[B]	and a claim is two silver coins;	והטענה שתי כסף [ב]
[C]	and confession is a *pĕrûṭâ*-worth.	וההודיה שווה פרוטה [ג]
[D]	There are five *pĕrûṭôt*:	חמש פרוטות הם [ד]
[E]	confession is a *pĕrûṭâ*-worth;	וההודיה שווה פרוטה [ה]
[F]	and a woman is betrothed with a *pĕrûṭâ*-worth;	והאשה מתקדשת בשווה פרוטה [ו]
[G]	and one who derives a *pĕrûṭâ*-worth of benefit from consecrated [property], he has stolen sacred property;	והנהנה בשוה פרוטה מן ההקדש מעל [ז]
[H]	one who finds a *pĕrûṭâ*-worth he is required to proclaim it;	המוציא שווה פרוטה חייב להכריז [ח]
[I]	and one who steals a *pĕrûṭâ*-worth from his fellow and swears to him [that he did not], let him take it to him, even to Media.	והגזול את חבירו שווה פרוטה [[ו]]נשבע לו יוליכנו אחריו אפילו למדיי [ט]

M4:8

[A]	There are five [added] fifths:	חמשה ח(ו(ו))משים הן [א]
[B]	one who eats heave offering, or the heave offering from tithes, or the heave offering from tithes from produce suspected of not having been tithed, the priest's portion of the dough, or first fruits, they add a fifth;	האוכל תרומה ותרומת מעשר ותרומת מעשר שלדמיי החלה והביכורים מוסיפים חומש [ב]
[C]	one who redeems the fourth year fruits or his second tithe adds a fifth;	הפודה נטע רבעי ומעשר שני שלו מוסיף חומש [ג]
[D]	one who redeems his consecrated goods adds a fifth;	הפודה הקדישו מוסיף חומש [ד]
[E]	and one who derives a *pĕrûṭâ*–worth of benefit from consecrated goods adds a fifth;	והנהנה שווה פרוטה מן ההקדש מוסיף חומש [ה]

M4:6: In [B] RLMP have עד כדי; N עד (on analogy with [C]), as in M4:3 [C]. R has been corrupted on the basis of 4:4 [C] and corrected, apparently by the same scribe.

M4:7: [B] and [C] (which recurs in [E]) are linked: when the plaintiff claims an amount no less than two silver coins and the defendant claims that he only owes part of that amount, but not less than a *pĕrûṭâ*-worth (according to *m. Šebû.* 6:1, where [B] and [C] appear *verbatim* and are expanded upon, the plaintiff claims two silver coins plus a *pĕrûṭâ*, so that the difference between the claims equals two silver coins) the defendant pays the amount that he admits to owing and is exempt from paying the rest, on the strength of an oath which he takes in court. For the ו in נשבע[[ו]] in [I] compare the text of M4:8 [F]. For parallels between [D–I] and other passages in the Mishnah, see Chapter I. B. 1.

Appendix I: Text, Translation, and Annotation

[F] and one who robs a *pĕrûṭâ* worth from his fellow and swears to him adds a fifth.

[1] והגוזל את חבירו שווה פרוטה ונשבע לו מוסיף חומש

M4:9

[A] And these are things that do not have [the rule of] *hônāyâ*:

[א] ואילו דברי[ן] שאין להם הוניה

[B] slaves and documents and lands and consecrated goods.

[ב] העבדים והאשטרות והקרקעות וההקדשות

[C] They have neither [the rule of] two-fold payment nor four- or five-fold payment;

[ג] אין בהן לא תשלומי כפל ולא תשלומי ארבעה ו[ח]משה

[D] an unpaid depositary does not swear;

[ד] שומר חינם אינו נשבע

[E] a paid depositary does not pay.

[ה] נושא שכר אינו משלם

[F] R. Simeon says: "Sacrifices for which he is liable have *hônāyâ*, and for which he is not liable do not have *hônāyâ*."

[ו] ר' שמעון אומ' קדשים שהוא חייב באחריותן יש להן הוניה ושאינו חייב באחריותן אין להן הוניה

[G] R. Judah says: "Even a Torah scroll or an animal or a pearl do not have *hônāyâ*."

[ז] ר' יהודה אומ' אף ספר תורה ובהמה ומרגלית אין להם הוניה

[H] They said to him: "They only said these things."

[ח] אמרו [לו] לא אמרו אלא את אלו

M4:10

[A] Just as there is *hônāyâ* in purchase and in sale so there is *hônāyâ* in speech:

[א] כשם שהוניה במקח ובממכר כך הוניה בדברים

[B] Let him not say to him "How much is this article" and he does not wish to buy it.

[ב] לא יאמר לו בכמה חפץ זה והוא אינו רוצה ליקח

M4:8: In [A] K has been corrected to read חֲמֻ(ו)שִׁים (see the notes to M2:8, 10 above); RLM do not have ו. In [B] RLPNM all read מוסיף (in the singular), which fits the protasis better. The relationship between M4:8 and other passages in the Mishnah is discussed in Chapter I.B.1.

M4:9: The expression יש (אין) לו הוניה recurs here, this time in reference to the object and not to the parties (cf. M4:4). Here too I have taken it to mean "is (not) subject to the rules of *hônāyâ*." I have corrected דברי(ו) to read דברי[ן] in [A] (the difference between them is quite slight; notably, however, the plural form is regularly written דברים, with a final ם in K: cf. M4:10 [A] and 5:10 [O]). Note the form אשטרות in [B] (the other witnesses have שטרות; on the "prosthetic ʾaleph" see Epstein, *Nûsaḥ*, 1249). RLMPN all have ארבעה ו[ח]משה in [C] (see the note to M3:1). [A–F] circulated in different forms (see *m. Šebû.* 6:5; cf. *m. B. Qam.* 7:4); [F] refers to the distinction between sacrifices that, if lost or invalidated before being offered, the one who dedicated it is liable to make up (חייב באחריותן) and those that the dedicator is not obligated to make up (אינו חייב באחריותן) (e.g. if a specific animal was designated; see *m. Meg.* 1:6; *m. Qin.* 1:1; see also *m. Tem.* 2:1). Those which the dedication is liable to make up have in effect remained in the dedicator's possession (they do not fully belong to the Temple), and are therefore still subject to the rules of *hônāyâ* (Rashi, *ad loc.*). The absence of לו in [H] is probably due to haplography.

[C]	If he was a penitent let him not say to him: "Remember your former deeds."	[ג] אם היה בעל תשובה לא יאמר לו זכור [[מה]] היו מעשיך הראשונים
[D]	And if he was the son of converts (*ben gērîm*) let him not say "Remember the deeds of your ancestors."	[ד] ואם היה בן גרים לא יאמר לו זכור מה היו מעשה אבותיך
[E]	As it is said, "And you shall not oppress the stranger (*gēr*) and you shall not press him for you were strangers (*gērîm*) in the land of Egypt" (Ex. 22:2).	[ה] שנ' וגר לא תונה ולא תלחצנו כי גרים הייתם בארץ מצרים

M4:11

[A]	One does not mix produce with produce (for sale)—	[א] אין מערבין פירות בפירות
[B]	even new [produce] with new—	[ב] אפילו חדשים בחדשים
[C]	it goes without saying new [produce] with old—	[ג] אין צורך לומ' חדשים בישנים
[D]	Truly, in the case of wine they permitted one to mix harsh with mild because it improves it.	[ד] באמת ביין היתירו לערב קשה ברך מפני שהוא משביחו
[E]	One does not mix wine sediments with wine, but he gives him his sediments.	[ה] אין מערבין שמרי יין ביין אבל נותן לו את ש(ו)מריו
[F]	Whoever's wine has become mixed with water—	[ו] מי שנתערב מים ביינו
[G]	let him not sell it in a store unless he informs [the shopkeeper?]	[ז] לא ימכרנו בחנות אלא אם כן הודיע
[H]	and not to a merchant even though he informs him,	[ח] ולא לתגר אף על פי שהוא מודיעו
[I]	for it is only to cheat with it.	[ט] שאינו אלא לרמות בו
[J]	In a place where it was customary to put water [in the wine], let them put.	[י] מקום שנהגו להטיל מים יטילו

M4:12

[A]	The merchant takes from five threshing floors and puts them in one bin,	[א] התגר נוטל מחמש גרנות ונותן לתוך מגורה אחת

M4:11: The object of הודיע RLM in [G] is not specified (PN and the tradition of the Babli [Rabbinovicz, *DS*, 169] have הודיעו or מודיעו, "informed/informs him," but the antecedent of the pronominal suffix remains unspecified). Rashi took [G] to refer to a shopkeeper, who may not sell diluted wine unless he informs each of his customers. Cf. T3:27, in which the expression אלא אם כן הודיע, "unless he informs," clearly refers to informing customers. (Lieberman, *TK*, 9, 187–8, took this clause of T3:27 as referring to the case of mixing sediments with wine, M4:11 [E]; but it is possible that the passage in the Tosepta constitutes a new clause corresponding to [F–G]. In that case the evidence from the Tosepta for how the expression was taken in antiquity is even stronger.) The parallel construction between [G] and [H], however, makes it possible that both cases involve a householder giving property over to a market professional, and that אלא אם כן הודיע in [G] means "unless he [the owner] informed [the shopkeeper]," and that the expression לא ימכרנו בחנות refers to turning over one's produce to a shopkeeper to sell it. (For the shopkeeper as agent of the householder see Chapter III.A.2.)

Appendix I: Text, Translation, and Annotation

[B]	from five wine presses and puts them in one cask;	מחמש גיתות ונותן לתוך פית[ס] אחד	[ב]
[C]	so long as he does not intend to mix them.	[ו][ב]לבד שלא יתכוון לערב	[ג]
[D]	R. Judah says: "Let the shopkeeper not distribute parched grain and nuts to children because he accustoms them to come to him,"	ר' יהודה אומ' לא יחלק החנווני קליות ואגוזים לתינוקות מפני שהוא מרגילן לבוא אצלו	[ד]
[E]	and the Sages permit.	וחכמ' מתירין	[ה]
[F]	Let him not undercut the market price,	לא יפחות את השער	[ו]
[G]	and the Sages say, "He is remembered for good."	וחכמ' אומ' זכור לטוב	[ז]
[H]	Let him not pick over the pounded beans,	לא יבור את הגריסיס	[ח]
[I]	as according to the words of Abba Shaul;	כדברי אבא שאול	[ט]
[J]	and the Sages permit.	וחכמ' מתירים	[י]
[K]	[The Sages] concede that he should not pick over the mouth of the bin,	מודים שלא יבור על פי מגורה	[כ]
[L]	for this is only deceit [lit. "like stealing the eye"].	שאינו אלא כגונב את העין	[ל]
[M]	One does not paint a human, an animal or vessels.	אין מפרקיסים לא את האדם ולא את הבהמה ולא את הכלים	[מ]

M4:12: K read פיתם in [B], which was corrected to פית[ו]]ס; R פיטוס; MPN פיטס (see *RŠŠ, Měl’eket šělomoh ad loc.*). פיתס is properly a Greek loanword (πίθος). In [K] מגורה refers to the bin of produce that a marketer has in the markeplace. In [B], what is at issue is the mixing of wines in a single storage jar. This supports the possibility that מגורה in [A] should be taken as "bin" and not "storeroom" (see Jastrow *s.v.*). Both [A] and [B], then, which permit mixing, stand in some tension with [C], which glosses them (but cf. Rashi *ad loc*. [B60a], followed by Bertinoro and *TY ad loc.*, who reads [C] as if it said " ... and make it appear as if they were not mixed"). In [I] KRLMP read כדברי, "according to the words of" (in P the כ appears at the end of the preceding line; כדברי is also the reading in the Florence and Rome B mss. of the Babli, see Rabbinovicz *DS*, 168); EN (and the Munich ms. and other traditions of the Babli) read דברי, "[the preceding are] the words of."

M5:1

[A]	Which is *nešek* and which is *tarbît*?	[א] אי זה הוא נשך ואי זה הוא תרבית
[B]	Which is *nešek*?	[ב] אי זה הוא נשך
[C]	One who lends a *selaʿ* for five *dînārîm*, two *sāʾîn* of wheat for three,	[ג] המלוה סלע בחמשה דינרין סאתים חיטים בשלוש
[D]	because he bites (*nôšēk*).	[ד] מפני שהוא נושך
[E]	And which is *tarbît*?	[ה] ואי זה הוא תרבית
[F]	One who increases (*ha-marbeh*) by means of produce.	[ו] המרבה בפרות
[G]	How?	[ז] כיצד
[H]	He bought wheat from him at a golden *dînār* to the *kôr* and such was the market price.	[ח] לקח ממנו חיטים מדינר זהב הכור וכן השער
[I]	Wheat [later] stood at thirty *dînārîm* [to the *kôr*].	[ט] עמדו חיטים בשלושים דינר׳
[J]	He said to him: "Give me my wheat, for I am going to sell it and buy wine with it for myself."	[י] אמ׳ לו תן לי חיטיי שני מוכרן ולוקיח אני לי בהן יין
[K]	He said to him: "But lo, your wheat is valued with me at thirty *dînārîm*! And lo, you have a claim with me against them for wine"—	[כ] אמ׳ לו והרי חיטיך עשויות עלי בשלשים דינ׳ והרי לך אצל[י] בהן יין
[L]	but he does not have wine.	[ל] ויין אין לו

M5:2

[A]	One who lends to his fellow—	[א] המלוה את חבירו
[B]	let him not live in his courtyard for free, and let him not lease from him for less,	[ב] לא ידור בחצירו חינם ולא ישכור ממנו בפחות
[C]	because it is interest (*ribbît*).	[ג] מפני שהוא ריבית
[D]	One may increase (*marbîm*) upon the [rental] fee but one may not increase upon the sale [price].	[ד] מרבים על השכר ואין מרבין על המכר
[E]	How?	[ה] כיצד
[F]	He leased a courtyard to him.	[ו] השכיר לו את החצר

M5:1: One golden *dînār* (cf. Roman *aureus*) = 25 (or 24) silver *dînārîm* or *zûzîm*; one *selaʿ* = 4 *dînārîm* (i.e., a tetradrakhma). The inclusion of the pronoun לי in [J] seems unique to K based on the witnesses checked; LMP read: שאני מוכרן ולוקח אני בהן (RN have only ולוקח בהן); E here is rather different: שאני רוצה למוכרן וליקח בהן, "for I wish to sell it, and to buy with it ..." (see also Rabbinovicz, *DS*, 172). In [K] KRLMP read והרי; EN read הרי. The presence of the ו lends exclamatory force to the sentence. (בש appears as filler at the end of the line preceding בשלשים in [K]. [י]אצל(ו) is corrected on the basis of context (אצלו is meaningless here); אצלי is also the reading in RLMPEN. The point of [L] is that if the seller (the borrower) had had wheat the transaction would have been a legal sale, but since he has none he is lending produce that is liable to go up in value, and is therefore a form of usury (see Y5:1 [10a], on which see Lieberman's comments to the Escorial manuscript, *Yerushalmi Neziqin*, xxx; see also Maimonides; Rashi [B60b] *ad loc.*).

Appendix I: Text, Translation, and Annotation 273

[G]	He said to him: "If you give me [payment] now, lo, it is yours for ten *sĕlāʿin* per year, but if monthly, for a *selaʿ* per month—	אמ' לו אם מעכשיו אתה נותן לי הרי הוא לך בעשר סלעים לשנה ואם של חודש בחדש מסלע בחדש	[ז]
[H]	it is permitted.	מותר	[ח]
[I]	He sold him a field.	מכר לו את השדה	[ט]
[J]	He said to him: "If you give me [payment] now, lo, it is yours for one thousand *zûz*, but if at the threshing floor, twelve *māneh*"—	אמ' לו אם מעכשיו אתה נותן לי הרי היא לך באלף זוז ואם לגורן בשנים עשר מנה	[י]
[K]	it is prohibited.	אסור	[כ]

M5:3

[A]	He sold him a field and he [the buyer] gave him a part of the money.	מכר לו את השדה ונתן לו מקצת דמים	[א]
[B]	He said to him: "Whenever you wish bring money and take what is yours"—	אמ' לו אמתי שתירצה הבא מעות וטול את שלך	[ב]
[C]	it is prohibited.	אסור	[ג]
[D]	He lent him [money] against his field.	הילווהו על שדהו	[ד]
[E]	And he said to him: "If you don't give me [payment] from now until three years [from now], lo, it is mine"—	ואמ' לו אם אין אתה נותן לי מיכן ועד שלוש שנים הרי היא שלי	[ה]
[F]	lo, it is his.	הרי היא שלו	[ו]
[G]	So Boethos b. Zenon used to do in accordance with the sages.	כך היה בויתס בין זנון עו[[שה על פי]] חכמ'	[ז]

M5:4

[A]	One does not set up (lit. "seat") a shopkeeper [to sell merchandise] at half profit (*śākār*);	אין מושיבין חנווני למחצית שכר	[א]
[B]	let him not give him money with which to purchase produce for half profit;	לא יתן לו מעות ליקח בהן פירות למחצית שכר	[ב]
[C]	unless he gave him his wage (*śākār*) as an idle laborer.	אלא אם כן נתן לו שכרו כפועל בטל	[ג]

M5:2: Two line fillers appear: את/[F]את החצר, and [G] בש/לשנה. The latter case indicates that the scribe intended to write בשנה (compare the form בחדש in the last word in [G] and cf. L, which reads לחצר. A *māneh* [J] is equal to 100 *zuz*, so the seller receives 200 *zûz* more if the buyer delays in paying.

M5:3: It is unclear what stood before the correction in [G]. In K it is not clear whether the reading is בויתס or בויתם [G] (cf. M4:12). The name בויתס בין זנון (Boethos son of Zenon) is variously spelled in the mss.:

בויתס בן זינון RL
R (line-filler in the preceding וג' (זינון): perhaps presupposing the spelling זונן/
זונין?)
ביתוס בן דינון MqP
ביתוס בן זונין ME
ביתום בן זונין N

[D]	One does not set up chickens for half [profit];	[ד] אין מושיבין תרנגלין למחצה
[E]	and one does not assess the value of calves and foals for half;	[ה] ואין שמין עגלים וסייחים למחצה
[F]	unless he gave him the fee (*śākār*) for his labor and food.	[ו] אלא אם כן נתן לו שכר עמלו ומזונו
[G]	But one may receive calves and foals for half,	[ז] אבל מקבלים עגלים וסייחים למחצה
[H]	and one may raise them until they are three years old,	[ח] ומגדלים אותן עד שיהו [[מ]][ש(ו)]לשים
[I]	and an ass until it can bear burdens.	[ט] וחמור עד שתהא טוענת

M5:4: In all of these cases the terms of the contract are that the contractor receives half the profits in return for his labor; [C] and [F] require that the agent receive a wage in addition to his share so that the agent is not, in effect, offering free service to the owner of the raw material for the half of the value that is "on loan" to the contractor (since it must be returned). In [B] PE have ולא. With the conjunction, [C] clearly refers to both [A] and [B]; without the conjunction, [B–C] might be taken as a unit, with [C] glossing [B] specifically. In [C] ME lack בטל (as do RM in M2:9 [F]; cf. Epstein *Nûsaḥ* 956 who omits בטל; see also Tos. *s.v.* *Wĕ-nôtēn lô*, B68a). The translation "three years old" in [H] follows Albeck, *ad loc.* who cites Gen. 15:9 for this sense of משולש (see *BDB* *s.v.* [שלש]), and S. Lieberman, *Hellenism in Jewish Palestine* (*Texts and Studies* 18: New York: JTSA, 1952), 186. Lieberman understood [H] to give a rule for oxen parallel to that of [I] for asses, and cited Pliny *N.H.* 8.70.180 as proof that oxen were broken at three years. However, Lieberman favored the reading שלשים in K (uncorrected) and LN (see n. 53), "which can only mean three years old" (although the usage of Gen. shows that משולשים could mean exactly the same thing). The language used to describe these transactions is very terse. מושיבין חנווני [A], means to give merchandise to a shopkeeper for him to sell. The same participle, מושיבין, in [D] (but with the merchandise and not the agent as object) means to give someone hens (the Hebrew uses the masculine plural) to set up to lay eggs. The difference between contracts of "assessment" (שמין) [E] and of "receipt" (מקבלים) [G] is not made explicit, but since the former term implies assessment of value, it presumably presupposes a different way of assigning liability. T5:1–2 offers two pairs of cases dealing with the raising of cattle, in each of which the agent received a fixed amount per head and a share of the proceeds, but no wage as such (cf. M5:4 [C, F]). Each pair of cases opens with an initial assessment: קבל ... במאה של זהב, "he received ... for [i.e., at a liability of?] one hundred gold [coins]"), which Lieberman, *TK,* 9, 209, took as assigning liability for the entire amount of that initial assessment. The structure of the contract in T5:1–2 (including both a share and a fixed payment) may be the defining characteristic of *qablānût* (מקבלים) (cf. Chapter III, n. 163). However, if Lieberman is correct that the clause specifying assessment pertains only to the first, prohibited case of each pair, this differential assignment of liability may perhaps underlie the distinction between שמין and מקבלים in M5:4 as well. According to Rashi (*ad loc.*, B68a) מקבלים implies no liability for loss (as opposed to שמין in which the parties share liability) (cf. also Tos. *s.v.* *ʾAbāl*, B68a); Maimonides (*ad loc.*, in the edition of Qafaḥ; the medieval translation is not quite clear) took the case of קבלנות as one in which the agent received a fixed portion of the principal no matter what the loss. A similar view (i.e., that payment to the agent consisted of a fixed proportion of the final value, including the principal) was attributed to Rabad in Ritba, *Ḥiddûšîm, s.v. ʾAbāl* (who also attributes it to Tos.).

M5:5

[A]	One may assess the value of a cow or an ass and anything whose manner is to produce and to eat.	שמין פרה וחמור וכל דבר שדרכו לעשות ולאוכל [א]
[B]	In a place where it was the custom to divide the offspring immediately they divide;	מקום שנהגו לחלוק את הוולד מיד חולקים [ב]
[C]	and in a place where it was the custom to raise [the offspring], let them raise [them].	ומקום שנהגו לגדל יגדילו [ג]
[D]	R. Simeon b. Gamaliel says: "One may assess a calf with its mother, and a foal with its mother."	רבן שמעון בן גמליא' או' שמין עגל עם אמו וסייח עם אמו [ד]
[E]	One may enrich his field,	ומפרין על שדהו [ה]
[F]	and he ought not hesitate because of interest.	ואינו חושש משם רבית [ו]

M5:6

[A]	One may not receive "iron sheep" from an Israelite,	אין מקבלין צאן ברזל מישרא' [א]
[B]	because it is interest (*ribbît*).	מפני שהיא ריבית [ב]
[C]	But one may receive "iron sheep" from the gentiles,	אבל מקבלין צאן ברזל מן הגוים [ג]
[D]	and one borrows from them and lends to them at interest,	ולוים מהן ומלווים אותן ברבית [ד]
[E]	and so too with a resident alien.	וכן בגר תושב [ה]
[F]	An Israelite may lend [at interest] with the money of a foreigner,	מלווה הוא ישרא' על מעותיו שלנוכרי [ו]
[G]	with the knowledge of the foreigner, but not with the knowledge of the Israelite.	מדעת הנכרי אבל לא מדעת ישראל [ז]

M5:5: [E–F] could be taken as the continuation of R. Simeon b. Gamaliel's tradition or as an independent unit amplifying the rule in [A]. The reading מפרין [E] follows KRLMPEN; cf. Rashi *ad loc.* (B69b) who reads (emends?) מפריו, "extend (?)" (see also Rabbinovicz, *DS*, 196).

M5:6: The expression צאן ברזל, "iron sheep," [A, C] refers here (and perhaps originally) to a contract to raise animals in which the contractor assumes all the liability for loss or death of the animals (cf. *m. Bek.* 2:4; T5:14 [Y5:2 (10b)]); however, the expression has a broader application as a technical phrase for full liability (see *m. Yeb.* 7:1–2 [a husband's liability with respect to his wife's property]; T5:14 ["fields [let on terms of] צאן ברזל"]). Compare the late Greek expression ζῷον σιδήραιον (*Stud. Pal.* XX 217 [581 CE]); see A. Gulak, "*Ṣoʾn barzel bĕ-dînê ha-talmûd*," *Tarbiz* 3 (1932), 137–46; D. Daube, "Eisern Vieh," *ZRG, Röm. Abteilung*, 69 (1950), 388–92; A. L. Oppenheim, "A Note on the *Ṣon Barzel*," *IEJ* 5 (1955), 89–92; and, on the Greek document, A. Jördens, "Σιδήραιος = ἀθάνατος?" *ZPE* 71 (1988), 99–104. In all the witnesses examined the term used for the non-Jew in [C] is גוים, "gentiles," as opposed to [F, G], which have נכרי, "alien, foreign," although both terms are Biblical (see *BDB s.vv.*). וכן, "and so also" [E], may introduce a supplementary comment. The use of the expression "resident alien" (גר תושב) in [E] seems to be a conscious echo of

M5:7

[A]	One may not make a bargain for produce until the market price has gone out.	[א] אין פוסקין על הפרות עד שיצא השער
[B]	[If] he was the first of the reapers,	[ב] היה הוא תחילה לקוצרים
[C]	he may make a bargain for [the grain on] the threshing floor.	[ג] פוסק עמו על הגדיש
[D]	And [he may make a bargain] for the basket of grapes,	[ד] [ו]]על העבט שלענבים
[E]	and for the vat of olives,	[ה] ועל המעטן שלזיתים
[F]	and for the clay lumps of the potter,	[ו] ועל הביצים שליוצר
[G]	and for lime, from the time that his oven is filled,	[ז] ועל הסיד מי שישקע כיבשנו
[H]	and he may make a bargain with him for dung all year round.	[ח] ופוסק עמו על הזבל כל ימות השנה
[I]	R. Yose says: "He may not make a bargain with him for dung until he has dung in the dungheaps,"	[ט] ר' יוסה או' אין פוסק עמו על הזבל עד שיהא לו זבל באשפות
[J]	and the sages permit.	[י] וחכמ' מתירין

Lev. 25:35, which, in introducing the prohibition of interest to "your brother" states "and you shall uphold him as an alien and resident" (גר ותושב). If [E] implies that one may lend at interest to a resident alien (as one may to a gentile in [C–D]), this invocation of Lev. 25:35–6 goes against the apparently straightforward implication of those verses. A *barâitâ'* in the Babli, attributed to R. Judah the Patriarch, seems to address precisely this problem: "It was taught: R. [Judah the Patriarch] said: 'I do not know what [the meaning of] the righteous convert mentioned in connection with sale and [the meaning of] the resident alien mentioned in connection with usury are'" (B71a; cf. the rather different version in Y5:7 [10c]); at any rate the Babli connected R. Judah the Patriarch's statement with the apparent contradiction between Mishnah and Scripture (cf. the tradition attributed to R. Nahman b. Yishaq, cited below, which is brought in precisely this context in the Babli). The relevant words in Lev. 25:35 are difficult, and were variously treated in the ancient translations (see Lapin, 1995, forthcoming). It is possible that in permitting interest to the resident alien M5:6 [C] reflects an exegetical tradition parallel to that of the *Peshitta* or that of the Targumim, which, in different ways, may imply that a resident alien is not covered by the prohibition of interest. In the words of the Amoraic tradition attributed to R. Nahman b. Yishaq: "Is 'you shall not take ... from them' written here (Lev. 25:36)? 'You shall not take ... from him' is written: [i.e.] from the Israelite" (B71a). Cf. *Sipra, Bĕ-har* V:1 (ed. Weis, 109b), which glosses גר ותושב in a way that apparently includes non-Jewish aliens in the prohibition on interest. Following a *barâitâ'* given on B71b, which glosses [F–G] (compare T5:14; Y5:7 [10d] in which a similar tradition is presented independently of the Mishnah; but cf. Lieberman, *TK*, 9, 222–3) *TYT* (and, it seems, *TY*) took the first half of [G] to refer to a case in which a Jew who has borrowed from a gentile lends to another Jew, and the second half of [G] to a case of a gentile who has borrowed from a Jew and subsequently lent to another Jew. This is not a necessary reading of the *barâitâ'* (in which only the first half need be glossing M5:6, the second half may merely give an additional case governed by the same rules). [F–G] seem rather to refer to one case, where a Jewish borrower makes a subsequent loan of the gentile's money. (According to Albeck, *ad loc.*, [G] should be read: "but not with the knowledge of the Israelite [lender alone, i.e., without the knowledge of the non-Jew].")

Appendix I: Text, Translation, and Annotation

[K] He may make a bargain with him according to the lower market price.

[ב] פוסק עמו כשער הגבוה

[L] R. Judah says: "Even though he has not made a bargain with him [to always pay the lowest market price] he may say to him: 'Give me according to this [price] or give me my money.'"

[ל] ר' יהודה או' אף על פי שלא פסק עימו יכול הוא לומ' לו תן לי כזה או תן לי את מעותיי

M5:8

[A] A person may lend his tenants (ʾarisāyw) wheat against wheat for seed,

[א] מלוה אדם את אריסיו חיטין בחיטין לזרע

[B] but not for food.

[ב] אבל לא לאוכל

[C] For R. Gamaliel would lend his tenants wheat—

[ג] שהיה רבן גמליא' מלוה את אריסיו חיטין

[D] when expensive, and they became cheaper, [or] when cheap and they became more expensive—

[ד] ביוקר והוזלו או בזול והוקירו

[E] and he would take [repayment] from them according to the lower market price.

[ה] ונוטל מהן כשער הזול

[F] Not because such is the law (halākâ) but because he wanted to be strict with himself.

[ו] לא שהלכה כן אלא שרצה להחמיר על עצמו

M5:7: After [A] PE have: יצא השער פוסקים אע"פ שאין לזה יש לזה, "If the market price has gone out one may make a bargain, [for] even though this one does not have, this one does" (i.e., produce is readily available once the market price has been set); N has a version of this clause that begins אלא בשער, which is an error; R has the beginning of the clause (יצא ה) at the end of the line preceding [B] but the scribe has not continued it. (Tos. s.v. Wĕ-hāʾ tĕnan [B62b] was aware of the variant; see also Mĕlʾeket šĕlomoh ad loc.; Rabbinovicz, DS, 202; Epstein, Nûsaḥ, 962, gives a fuller list of variants than that presented here. Epstein saw the presence of this clause as due to the corruption of the text of the Mishnah from bāraîtôt [see, e.g., T6:3].) A letter appears as line filler at the end of the line preceding שליוצר [E]. The translation of [G] follows Epstein, Nûsaḥ, 543.

M5:8: R reads לוכל in [B], which may mean that the scribe took the word as an infinitive (cf. 5:5 [A], also an infinitive, where R has לוכל). The syntactical relationship between clauses [C–E] is somewhat awkward. As formulated in KRLMP (see also Mĕlʾeket šĕlomoh ad loc.) [D] interrupts the sentence [C+E] with qualifying details. However, in EN, [C], echoing [A] reads חיטין [בחיטין לזרע] (N has וזרע; see Lieberman, TK, 9, 197–8 to T3:27 for scribal confusion of ו and ל), and E lacks the initial conjunction ו in [E], so that [C] could be taken as the end of a sentence, and [D–E, F] as explanatory material ("Whether expensive, and they became cheaper ... he would take from them ...") qualifying what is meant by R. Gamaliel's activities in [C] (and the blanket rule in [A]). K has a character (?ר) between [B] and [C].

M5:9

[A] Let a person not say to his fellow: "Lend me a *kôr* and I will give it to you [at the time of] the threshing floor,"
[א] לא יאמר אדם לחבירו הלוויני כור חיטין ואני נותן לך לגורן

[B] but he says to him: "[Lend] ... until my son comes," [or] "... until I find the key."
[ב] אלא אומ' לו עד שיבא בני עד שאמצא מפתח

[C] Hillel prohibits.
[ג] הלל [אוסר]

[D] For thus Hillel used to say:
[ד] שכך היה הלל [[אומ']]

[E] "Let a woman not lend a loaf to her fellow until she has calculated its monetary value,
[ה] לא תלוה אשה ככר לחברתה עד שתעשינו דמים

[F] "lest wheat become more expensive,
[ו] שמא יוקירו החיטין

[G] and they will come to commit usury."
[ז] ונמצאו באות לידי ריבית

M5:10

[A] A person may say to his fellow: "Weed with me and I will weed with you," [or] "hoe with me and I will hoe with you,"
[א] אומר אדם לחבירו נכיש עמי ואנכיש עמך עדור עמי ואעדור עמך

[B] but let him not say to him: "Weed with me and I will hoe with you;" "hoe with me and I will weed with you."
[ב] אבל לא יאמר לו נכיש עמי ואעדור עמך עדור עמי ואנכיש עמך

[C] All the days of the dry season are one, and all the days of the wet season are one.
[ג] כל ימי גריר אחד כל ימי רביעה אחת

[D] Let him not say to him: "Plow with me in the dry season, and I with you in the wet season."
[ד] לא יאמר לו חרוש עמי בגריר ואני עמך ברביעה

[E] R. Gamaliel says: "There is interest (*ribbît*) in advance, and there is interest delayed."
[ה] רבן גמליא' או' יש ריבית מוקדמת ויש רבית מא[ו][ו]חרת

[F] How?
[ו] כיצד

[G] He wanted (lit. "set his eyes") to borrow from him;
[ז] נתן את עיניו ללוות ממנו

[H] he would send [gifts] to him,
[ח] היה משליח לו

[I] and said to him "So that he will lend to me":
[ט] ואמ' בשביל שילויני

[J] this is interest in advance.
[י] זו היא ריבית מוקדמת

[K] He borrowed from him and returned his money to him;
[כ] ((ל))לווה ממנו והחזיר לו את מעותיו

[L] he would send [gifts] to him,
[ל] [היה משלח לו

[M] and said to him: "For his money, which was idle with me":
[מ] ואמר בשביל מעותיו] שהיו בטילות אצלי

[N] this is interest delayed.
[נ] זו היא ריבית מאוחרת

[O] R. Simeon says: "There is verbal interest:"
[ס] ר' שמעון אום' יש ריבית דברים

M5:9: In [C] K has אסור, which has been corrected to אֹסְ(ו)ר by a second hand. [[אומ']] [D] was omitted, and supplied in the margin by a later hand.

[P]	let him not say to him: "Know that a cerain man is coming from a certain place [to borrow]."	לא יאמר לו דע אם בא איש פלוני ממקום פל'	[ע]

M5:11

[A]	And these transgress a negative commandment:	ואלו עוברים בלא תעשה	[א]
[B]	the lender, and the borrower, and the surety, and the witnesses.	המלווה והלווה והערב והעדים	[ב]
[C]	And the sages say: "Even the scribe."	וחכמ' אומ' אף הסופר	[ג]
[D]	They transgress: "... You shall not give him ... " (Lev. 25:37);	עוברים על בל תתן לו	[ד]
[E]	and "You shall not take from him ... " (Lev. 25:36);	ועל בל תקח ממנו	[ה]
[F]	and "... You shall not be as a creditor (nôšeh) to him ..." (Ex. 22:24);	ועל לא תהיה לו כנושה	[ו]
[G]	and "... You shall not put interest (nešek) upon him ..." (Ex. 22:24);	ועל לא תשימון עליו נשך	[ז]

M5:10: In LN the term for the dry season in [C] is גריר, as in K; in RMPE the spelling is גריד. In T6:16 as well both spellings are represented in the textual witnesses (גריד, Vienna ms.; גריר, Erfurt ms., and *editio princeps*); Lieberman, *TK*, 9, 242 *ad loc.* favored גריר. See the responsum attributed to the Gaon Paltoi (Pumbeditha, 9th century) which explicitly favors the spelling גריר (*ʾÔṣār ha-gĕʾônîm*, ed. B. M. Lewin [Jerusalem: Hebrew University, 1931; Rpt. 1984] vol. 4, *Mašqîn* [=*Môʿēd Qaṭ*.], responsa p. 10). E. Ben Yehudah, *Thesaurus totius hebraitatis* [Hebrew], rpt. (New York: Yoseloff, 1960), vol. 2, *s.v.* cites גריר as post-Talmudic usage. [היה ... מעותיו] in [L–M] was omitted due to homoioteleuton. I have supplied the text on the basis of RMP which have the closest parallels to the analogous material in [G–I] (see also E). Both [I] and [M] utilize a third person construction ("so that he lend me"; "for his money") as a polite periphrasis for the second person (this is also the reading of Yehosep Ashkenazi cited in *Mĕlʾeket šĕlomoh ad loc.*, who questions the reading, and in the the Babli Munich ms.; for the other Babli traditions see Rabbinovicz, *DS*, 210). Compare LN, which, for מעותיו in [M], read מעותיך, "your money." N is idiosyncratic in other ways as well: in [H] and [L] N reads והיה משגר לו דורון, "and he would send a gift." דורון (Gk. δῶρον) is not listed in C. Y. Kasovsky's *Thesaurus Mishnae* (Jerusalem: Massadah, 1957) vol. 2 (although it does occur in E and in the manuscript of Rif for M5:10, see Rabbiniovicz, *DS*, 210), and the use of the root שגר as a verb (an Aramaicism) occurs only in one other place in the Mishnah (*m. Pes.* 4:9). Perhaps the line entered the Mishnah from a marginal gloss attempting to explicate the slightly vague language of [H] and [L]. Finally, the attribution in [O] to R. Simeon appears in N as R. Ishmael. Like K, LMPE read דע אם בא in [P]; RN have דע בא. Commentaries are divided as to whether it is the borrower or the lender who speaks in this passage (see the discussions by *TYṬ*; *Mĕlʾeket šĕlomoh ad loc.*, and the variants and sources cited by them). The connection with [E–N] suggests that it is information offered to the lender as a gift that is meant. However, compare *Sipre Deut.* 262 (ed. Finkelstein, p. 284) in which the lender instructs the borrower: "Go out and greet ... או דע אם בא פלוני."

[H] and "Do not put a stumbling block in front of the blind man, and you shall fear your God, I am the Lord" (Lev. 9:14). [ח] ולפני עור לא תתן מכשול ויראתה מאלהיך אני ייי

M5:11: For the use of בל where the biblical verse uses אל [D, E], see Segal, 223f., §472.

M6:1

[A]	One who hires artisans—	[א] השוכר את האומנים
[B]	and they deceived one another:	[ב] והיטעו זה את זה
[C]	they have only anger against one another.	[ג] ואין לו זה על זה אלא תרעומת
[D]	He hired a donkey driver, or a potter, carriers of the [bridal] litter (?), flutes for the bride or for the dead; workers to take his flax out of the infusion,	[ד] שכר את החמר ואת הקדר פיריאון פרים חלילים לכלה או למת פועלים ל[ה][ע]לות פישתנו מן המישרה
[E]	and anything that might suffer loss,	[ה] וכל דבר שהוא אבד
[F]	and they withdrew:	[ו] וחזרו בהם
[G]	in a place where there is nobody [else], he hires [others] at their liability or deceives them.	[ז] מקום שאין אדם שוכר עליהם או מטען

M6:2

[A]	One who hires artisans—	[א] השוכר את האומנים
[B]	and they withdrew,	[ב] וחזרו בהן
[C]	their hand is in the inferior position.	[ג] ידן לתחתונה

M6:1: The meaning of הטעו in [B] is not quite clear. S. Friedman, *Talmud Arukh: BT Bava Meziʾa VI, Commentary* (Jerusalem: JTSA, 1990), 7, cited *m. Moʿed Qaṭ.* 2:1–2 as proof that it could (and does) mean "withdrew [from the contract]" as does חזרו in [F] (see also T7:1, which presents material closely related to that of M6:1 and echoes [B] but does not explicitly echo חזרו in [F]; this could mean that the author of T7:1 took the verbs as synonymous). The Yerushalmi's discussion takes הטעו to mean that one party misrepresents certain important information, such as the going rate for workers, or the expected duration of the job (Y6:1 [10d]; on the text of this passage see Lieberman, *Yerushalmi Neziqin*, 163 [to ll. 2–3]; Friedman, 1990, 4–5; and the discussion in Chapter III, n. 185, above; note also מטען in [G], where it clearly means "deceives them"). Both interpretations of the word are familiar to the stammaitic discussion of the Babli (B76a-b). The initial ו in [C], presumably a *waw*-apodosis, does not occur in the other witnesses (see Epstein, *Nûsaḥ*, 1076–90; but M6:1 is not listed in Epstein's examples from K, p. 1084). פיריאון פרים in [D] is a mystery and variously spelled:

RL   פרייה פרים (L פריה)
M   פריאפרין
Mq   פריאפירין
P   פריה פירין
N   פרייפרין.

Greek derivations have been proposed: φορειαφόρος, "carriers of the bridal litter" (Jastrow); περιφοράριος (Kohut). Rashi (and Albeck, *Nĕzîqîn*, 426) reads our word as derived from אפריון (Cant. 3:9; for this word *BDB* suggest a possible derivation from φορεῖον). Tos. apparently read פרייפרין [להביא] קרר in [D], "waggoners to bring the litter"; L, too, read קרר (on להביא, see Rabbinovicz, *DS*, 212; for קרר, see *TYṬ*; *TY* [citing German and Latin cognates]; note Greek κάρρον, Latin *carrum* (see S. Lieberman, *TR*, 1, 210; 3, 73). מקום שאין אדם [G] means that laborers are scarce and therefore expensive; the employer would thus suffer loss due to the withdrawal by the workers. The translation שוכר עליהן in [G] follows Rashi *ad loc.* (B75b).

[D]	And if the householder withdrew,	[ד] ואם בעל הבית חזר בו
[E]	his hand is in the inferior position.	[ה] ידו לתחתונה
[F]	And anyone who deviates [from the contract], his hand is in the inferior position,	[ו] וכל המשנה ידו לתחתונה
[G]	and anyone who withdaws, his hand is in the inferior position.	[ז] וכל החוזר בו ידו לתחתונה

M6:3

[A]	One who leases an ass—	[א] השוכר את החמור
[B]	to walk it on the mountain and he walked it in the valley, in the valley and he walked it on the mountain,	[ב] להוליכ(ו)\[[ה]] בהר והוליכה בבקעה בבקעה והוליכה בהר
[C]	even [if] this was ten miles and this was ten miles,	[ג] אפילו זו עשרת מילים וזו עשרת מילים
[D]	and it died,	[ד] ומיתה
[E]	he is liable.	[ה] חייב
[F]	He leased an ass,	[ו] שכר את החמור
[G]	and it was blinded or was carried off for the *angareia*,	[ז] והיבריקה או שנישאת \[[ב]]אינגרייא
[H]	he [the owner] says to him: "Lo, yours is before you."	[ח] אומ' לו הרי שלך לפניך
[I]	[If] it died or was broken,	[ט] מיתה או נשברה
[J]	he is liable to supply him with an ass.	[י] חייב להעמיד לו חמור
[K]	One who leases an ass—	[כ] השוכר את החמור
[L]	to walk it on the mountain and he walked it in the valley:	[ל] להוליכה בהר והוליכה בבקעה
[M]	if it slipped he is exempt,	[מ] אם החליקה פטור
[N]	but if it became overheated he is liable;	[נ] ואם הוחמה חייב
[O]	in the valley and he walked it on the mountain,	[ס] בבקעה והוליכה בהר
[P]	if it slipped he is liable,	[ע] אם החליקה חייב
[Q]	and if it became overheated he is exempt,	[פ] ואם הוחמה פטור
[R]	but if [it became overheated] due to the height he is liable.	[צ] ואם מחמת המעלה חייב

M6:2: [D–E] is lacking in the Mishnah text of the Munich ms. of the Babli, and Epstein, *Nûsaḥ*, 974 (among others) suspected it as a late addition; cf. Friedman, 1990, 85–6 and the literature cited there.

M6:3: The order of the units in M6:3 varies: (1) LMPN agree with K (as does the Hamburg ms. of the Babli); (2) R (uncorrected) and the Rome A and B mss. of the Babli place [K–R] before [A–E] (in R [A] has been labeled with an א, and [K] with a ב, to bring the order of the clauses into agreement with the tradition in K; Rome B has been similarly corrected in the margin); (3) other witnesses place [K–R] between [A–E] and [F–J] (for a fuller list of variants see Rabbinovicz *DS*, 219; Epstein, *Nûsaḥ*, 1004; Friedman, 1990, 131; on p. 135 n. 33, Friedman considers, and rejects, the possibility that the Yerushalmi, Y6:3 [11a], is not aware of M6:3 [K–R]). In [B] K initially read להוליכו, in agreement with the masculine חמור, but has been corrected to להוליכה (with a fem. pronominal ending) to

M6:4

[A]	One who leases a cow—	[א] השוכר את הפרה
[B]	to plow on the mountain and he plowed in the valley,	[ב] לחרוש בהר וחרש בבקעה
[C]	and the plow was broken,	[ג] ונשבר הקנקן
[D]	he is exempt;	[ד] פטור
[E]	in the valley and he plowed on the mountain,	[ה] בבקעה וחרש בהר
[F]	and the plow was broken,	[ו] ונשבר הקנקן
[G]	he is liable.	[ז] חייב
[H]	To thresh pulse and he threshed grain,	[ח] לדוש בקיטנית ודש בתבואה
[I]	he is exempt;	[ט] פטור
[J]	grain and he threshed pulse,	[י] בתבואה ודש בקיטנית
[K]	he is liable,	[כ] חייב
[L]	because pulse is slippery.	[ל] שהקיטנית מחלקת

M6:5

[A]	One who leases an ass—	[א] השוכר את החמור
[B]	to bring wheat and he brought barley,	[ב] להביא חיטים והביא שעורים
[C]	grain and he brought straw [and the animal was damaged]	[ג] תבואה והביא תבן
[D]	he is liable,	[ד] חייב
[E]	for volume is as difficult as load.	[ה] שהנפחה קשה כמשואי
[F]	To bring a *letek* of wheat and he brought a *letek* of barley,	[ו] להביא לתך חיטים והביא לתך שעורים
[G]	he is exempt;	[ז] פטור
[H]	and if he added to its load he is liable.	[ח] ואם הוסיף על משואו חייב
[I]	And how much shall he add to its load and [thus] be liable?	[ט] וכמה יוסיף על משואו ויהי חייב
[J]	Symmakhos says in the name of R. Meir: "A *sĕʾâ* for a camel; three *qabîm* for an ass.	[י] סומכס או' משם ר' מאיר סאה לגמל ושלושת קבים לחמור

---

bring the spelling into conformity with the other two occurrences of the word in [B] and in [L, O], and as in RLMPN throughout (see also the citation of R. Yehosef Ashkenazi in *Mĕlʾeket šĕlomoh, ad loc.* and Rabbinovicz *DS*, 219; note also the use of the feminine in [G, I, M, N, P, Q]). In [F] L reads השוכר, as in [A, K] (see the Babli variants in Rabbinovicz, *DS*, 219). On the basis of T8:10, Lieberman (*TK*, 3, 115) concluded that הבריקה [G] means "struck with an eye ailment (ברקית)"; cf. the Greek παράλαμψις ("a shining spot on the cornea," LSJM, *s.v.*). אינגרייא, ἀγγαρεία, "impressment for public service" (LSJM, *s.v.*) is variously spelled in the mss.: RLMqP אנגריא; M אנגוריא; N אנגריה; K (before the correction) N have no preposition; K (corrected) RMMq have ב-; LP have ל-. Preceding אינגרייא L has נעשית, "was made"; KRMPN have נישאת, "was carried off" (for the whole clause, and the possible implications of the נעשית/נישאת variant see Epstein, *Nûsaḥ*, 119; cf. Friedman, 1990, 157f.). On the institution of angareia see the literature cited by G. E. M. de Ste Croix, *The Class Struggle in the Ancient Greek World* (Ithaca: Cornell, 1981), 14–6, 539–40; B. Isaac, *The Limits of Empire* (Oxford: Clarendon, 1990), 291–7.

M6:5: 1 *kôr* = 2 *letek* = 30 *sĕʾâ* = 180 *qab*. This pericope assumes that a measure (by weight) of barley will take up a greater volume than a like amount of wheat (see Friedman,

M6:6

[A]	All artisans are [liable as] paid depositaries.	[א] כל האומנים שומרי שכר
[B]	And all who said: "Bring money and take what is yours"—[are deemend] an unpaid depositary.	[ב] וכולם שאמרו הבא מעות וטול את שלך שומר חינם
[C]	"Watch for me and I will watch for you"—a paid depositary.	[ג] שמר לי ואשמר לך שומר שכר
[D]	"Watch for me" and he said "Leave it before me"—an unpaid depositary	[ד] שמר לי ואמר לו הנח לפני שומר חינם

M6:7

[A]	One who lends against a pledge is a paid depositary.	[א] והמלווה על המשכון שומר שכר(ו))
[B]	R. Judah says: "[If] he lent him money he is an unpaid depositary,	[ב] ר' יהודה אומ' הילווהו מעות שומר חינם
[C]	"[if] he lent him produce he is a paid depositary."	[ג] הילווהו פירות שומר שכר
[D]	Abba Shaul says: "A person may lease out the pledge of a poor [debtor] in order to continually assign it to him [i.e., against his debt],	[ד] אבא שאול או' מותר אדם להשכיר משכונו שלעני להיות פוסק עליו והלך

---

223 n. 1, who, in turn, cites L. Foxhall and H. A. Forbes, "Σιτομετρεία: The Role of Grain as a Staple Food in Classical Antiquity," *Chiron* 12 [1982], 42–90). As in M6:3 [A–E], in this pericope liability is incurred in [A–E] simply because the renter did not comply with his contract narrowly construed. L reads שהנפה in [E] as does K; the other witnesses checked have שהנפח. Like K, RLMMqN all have the preposition כ in the expression קשה כמשואי [E] (N may have ב [on which see Friedman, 225]; ב and כ are sometimes difficult to distinguish in N) in [D]; P has ל, "difficult for bearing." This difference is the subject of a Talmudic dispute attributed to Raba (למשואי) and Abbaye (כמשואי) (B80a; see also *Nimûqê yôsēp* to this Mishnah, *TYṬ*; *Mĕl'eket šĕlomoh*; *RŠŠ*; and Epstein, *Nûsaḥ*, 380–1).

M6:6: KLN have שומר חנם in [B]; RMP read שומרי, in the plural,, which parallels the construction of [A] and may be preferable. KRLPN read הבא מעות וטול את שלך; M reads טול את שלך והבא מעות, following the tradition of the Babli (for more complete variants see Rabbinovicz, *DS*, 226; Friedman, 1990, 253 n. 22, 254 n. 24). The discussion of the Babli [in three parallel but different *sûgyôt*, requires the reading טול...והבא..., since it takes a case of הבא...וטול... as implying a different level of liability (B80b–81a; see the discussion of Friedman, 1990, 252–5). In [D] RLPMqMa (uncorrected) have: הנח לפניך, "leave it before yourself." Traditions attributed to Samuel ("[The Mishnah applies] when he said: 'Leave it before me,' but when he said: 'Leave it before yourself' he has not said anything"; Y6:7 [11a], following the Escorial ms. which reads שאמר שמו' against the Leiden ms. and the *editio princeps*, which have ששאל for שמואל; see Lieberman, *Yerushalmi Neziqin*, 165) and R. Huna ("If he said: 'Leave it before yourself' he is neither a paid nor an unpaid depositary," B81b) already seem to be aware of this variant (see Epstein, *Nûsaḥ*, 723–4; Friedman, 1990, 291–2).

[E]	"because he is like one returning a lost object."	מפני שהוא כמשיב אבדה	[ה]

M6:8

[A]	One who moves a jar from one place to another—	המעביר חבית ממקום למקום	[א]
[B]	and broke it:	ושברה	[ב]
[C]	whether he is an unpaid depositary or a paid depositary let him swear.	בין שומר חינם ובין שומר שכר יישבע	[ג]
[D]	Said R. Eliezer: "I question whether this one or this one can swear."	אמ' ר' אליעזר תמיה אני אם יכולים זה וזה להישבע	[ד]

M6:7: The initial ו in [A] (as in L as well) marks this clause as a continuation of the preceding pericope, in keeping with the division of the text in KRL, and of the Mishnah text in the Leiden ms. and the *editio princeps* of the Yerushalmi. The final ו in שכרו is meaningless and has been deleted by a second hand in K. Like K, RLP read פוסק עליו והולך (M has only פוסק והולך; the Rome A ms. of the Babli, פוסק עמו והולך; certain printed editions have פוסק והולך עליו [see Rabbinovicz, *DS*, 227]). The Munich and Florence mss. of the Babli have פוחת עליו והולך, "he continually deducts ..."; פוחת is also the reading of N. In N, however, the reading is the somewhat strange פוחת עליו והולך עמו. This reading may be the result of an erroneous addition of עמו to הולך, "walks with him," or of conflation (note the use of עמו in Rome A, and the expression פוסק עמו in M5:7, and the variation in word-order attested in the [admittedly later] printed editions of the Mishnah). See Friedman, 1990, 365.

M6:8: In KRMPN the name of the tradent in [D] is spelled אליעזר (L has ליעזר), i.e., Eliezer, of the late first to early second century; compare the versions of the Babli and commentaries, which read אלעזר, i.e., Eleazar b. Shamua of the mid- to late second century (this kind of variation is common: see Epstein 1162–82 deals with the shift between אליעזר/אלעזר alone). A *bāraîtā* at B82a supports the reading אלעזר since it attributes the language and view of [A–C] to R. Meir, also of the middle to late second century, to which R. Eleazar responds; see *Mĕl'eket šĕlomoh, ad loc.*; Epstein, *Nûsaḥ*, 1136; Friedman, 1990, 383–4; Neusner, *Damages* II, 107–8; V, 77 gives the name of the tradent as Eliezer, and attributes the pericope to Usha [i.e., 135–170], without comment). The word-order in KRLMPN is אמר ר' אלעזר (see further Epstein, *Nûsaḥ*, 1136). Note that in the Babli traditions (ms. Rome B excepted) R. Eleazar's tradition explicitly refers back to [C]: זה וזה ישבע...ותמיה; the additional three words are absent in KRLMPN (see Rabbinovicz, *DS*, 232).

M7:1

[A]	One who hires laborers—	השוכר את הפועלים	[א]
[B]	and told them to rise early or work late:	ואמ' להם להשכים ולהעריב	[ב]
[C]	in a place where it was customary not to rise early or not to work late he cannot force them;	מקום שנהגו שלוא להשכים ושלא להעריב אינו יכול לכופן	[ג]
[D]	in a place where it was customary to feed [the workers] let him feed;	מקום שנהגו לזון יזון	[ד]
[E]	to provide sweets, let him provide:	לספק במתיקה ייספיק	[ה]
[F]	all follows the custom of the province.	הכל כמנהג המדינה	[ו]
[G]	A case happened in connection with R. Yohanan b. Mattia who said to his son: "Go out and hire workers for us."	מעשה בר' יוחנן בן מתיה שא' לבנו צא ושכור לנו פועלים	[ז]
[H]	And he agreed on food with them.	ופסק עמהם מזונות	[ח]
[I]	And when he came to his father he [his father] said: "Even if you make them [a meal] like the meal of Solomon in his time, you have not fulfilled your obligation with respect to them, for they are sons of Abraham, Isaac and Jacob.	וכשבא אצל אביו אמ' לו אפילו את עושה להם כסעודת שלמה בשעתו לא יצאתך ידי חובתך עימהם שהן בני אברהם יצחק ויעקב	[ט]
[J]	"Rather, before they begin working go out and tell them:	אלא עד שלא יתחילו במלאכה צא ואמור להם	[י]
[K]	"'On condition that you have [a claim to] only bread and pulse.'"	על מנת שאין לכם אלא פת וקיטנית בלבד	[כ]
[L]	R. Simeon b. Gamaliel says: "He did not have to [specify this]—	רבן שמעון בן גמליא' אומ' לא היה צריך	[ל]
[M]	"[for] all follows the custom of the province."	הכל כמנהג המדינה	[מ]

M7:1: Where K has ופסק at the beginning of [H] (so too LM, and the Mishnah text in the Leiden ms. of the Yerushalmi), other witnesses read as follows:

R (and *Měl'eket šělomoh, ad loc.* citing Rosh): הלך והשכיר פועלים ופסק

N, Babli Munich ms. הלך ופסק

Babli Hamburg ms. הלך ושכר פועלים

Babli Florence ms. יצא ושכר פועלים

(See Rabbinovicz, *DS*, 236.) These readings fill a logical and syntactical gap ("[he went and hired workers] and agreed ..."), but none is necessary here. In [I] K has כס' at the end of the line preceding כסעודת. In [K] RN have the word עלי, "against (lit. on) me" (cf. *Měl'eket šělomoh, ad loc.*); for the expression יש (אין) לפלוני על ("so and so has a claim against ..."), see E. Y. Kutscher, "New Aramaic Texts," *JAOS* 74 (1954), 242; and compare: אין לו אלא תרעומת עליו, M4:6 [and the similar expression M6:1]). Instead of לכם in [K] P has להן and N has להם (both "to them"), i.e., taking [K] as indirect discourse. The Babli (B87a) preserves the suggestion (attributed to R. Aha b. R. Joseph) that פת קיטנית, "pulse-bread," be read in [K]. As the response in the Babli itself shows, however, the reading of K and of all the witnesses checked is preferable (see also Epstein, *Nûsaḥ*, 354). At the end of [L] K (paralleled by RN) again has a short version that is presented in a longer form in other witnesses: M צריך לומר, "have to say"; LP צריך לומר כן, "have to say thus" (cf. *Měl'eket*

M7:2

[A]	These [workers] eat according to the Torah:	אלו אוכלין מן התורה [א]
[B]	one who works on [produce while it is still] attached to the ground, at the time of the completion of the work;	העושה במחובר לקרקע בשעת גמר מלאכה [ב]
[C]	and on produce detached from the ground, so long as its work has not been completed,	ובתלוש מן הקרקע עד שלא ניגמרה מלאכתו [ג]
[D]	and as long as its growth is from the earth.	ובלבד שגידוליו מן הארץ [ד]
[E]	And these do not eat:	ואילו שאינן אוכלין [ה]
[F]	one who works on [produce while it is still] attached to the ground, at a time that is not the completion of the work,	העושה במחובר לקרקע בשעה שאינה גמר מלאכה [ו]
[G]	and on [produce] detached from the ground after its work has been completed,	ובתלוש מן הקרקע מאחר שניגמרה מלאכתו [ז]
[H]	and on something whose growth is not from the ground.	ובדבר שאין גידוליו מן הארץ [ח]

M7:3

[A]	[If] he was working with his hands but not his feet,	היה עושה בידיו אבל לא ברגליו [א]
[B]	with his feet, but not his hands,	ברגליו אבל לא בידיו [ב]
[C]	even [if only] on his shoulder,	אפילו על כתיפו [ג]
[D]	lo, let this one eat.	הרי זה יאכל [ד]
[E]	R. Yose b. R. Judah says: "[He may not eat] until he works with his hands and feet."	ר' יוסה ב ר' יהודה או' עד שיעשה בידיו ורגליו [ה]

M7:4

[A]	[If] he was working with figs, let him not eat from the grapes;	היה עושה בתאינים לא יאכל בענבים [א]
[B]	with grapes, let him not eat from the figs;	בענבים לא יאכל בתאינים [ב]
[C]	but he may hold himself back until he reaches the place of the nice ones, and eats [there].	אבל מונע הוא את עצמו עד שמגיע למקום היפות ואוכל [ג]

šĕlomoh, ad loc., citing R. Yehosef Ashkenazi, who deleted לומר). In addition, MPN have אלא, "rather," preceding [M], which fills the somewhat abrupt syntactical gap between the clauses (on the Babli traditions see Rabbinovicz, DS, 236).

M7:2: The expression גמר מלאכה, "completion of work," has two separate meanings in this pericope: in [C] and [G] it has the literal sense of completing the work necessary to make the produce a finished product (cf. m. Maʿaś. 1:5–7; 2:4); in [B] and [F] the expression connotes the ripening of the harvest (see e.g. TYT ad loc. who paraphrases: [sic] שנגמר מלאכת בשולן, "the work of their ripening has finished"; see also Tos. B87a, s.v. Bi-mĕḥubbār).

[D]	And [regarding] all of them, they said only "At the time of the completion of the work."	[ד] וכולם לא אמרו אלא בשעת גמר מלאכה
[E]	but because of [the principle of] returning lost objects to their owners they said:	[ה] אבל מפני השב אבידה לבעלים אמרו
[F]	"Workers may eat while walking from row to row,	[ו] הפועלים אוכלין בהליכתן מאומן לאומן
[G]	"and on their way back from the wine-press,	[ז] ובחזירתן מן הגת
[H]	"and an ass [may eat] until it is unburdened."	[ח] וחמור עד שתהא פורקת

M7:5

[A]	A worker may eat cucumber, even as much as a *dînār*,	[א] אוכל פועל קישות אפילו בדינר
[B]	and dates, even as much as a *dînār*.	[ב] וכותבת אפילו בדינר
[C]	R. Eleazar Hisama says: "Let the worker not eat more than his wage."	[ג] ר' אלעזר חסמא או' לא יאכל פועל יתר על שכרו
[D]	And the sages permit [this].	[ד] וחכמ' מתירין
[E]	But one teaches a person not to be a glutton,	[ה] אבל מלמדים את האדם שלא יהא רועבתן
[F]	and [thereby] shut the door in front of him.	[ו] ויהא סותם את הפתח לפניו

M7:4: [A–C] occurs in a somewhat different form at *m. Ma'aś.* 2:8 (where the opposition is between different kinds of dates). The first two letters of בתאינים in [B] appear at the end of the preceding line as filler; similarly, most of בחזירתן in [G] appears in the preceding line. In KRLMPN [D] reads בשעת גמר מלאכה (the Babli mss., by contrast, read בשעת מלאכה, "during work"; Nahmanides, *Ḥiddûšîm*, to B87b followed this reading but interpreted both versions identically; see also Rif; Ritba; *Nimûqê yôsēp* to B91b; *Mĕl'eket šĕlomoh, ad loc.*; Rabbinovicz, *DS*, 271; Lieberman, *TK*, 9, 262–3 and n. 6). If this text is correct, the expression takes on a third meaning, "at the time when they finish working," in addition to the two meanings in M7:2. Maimonides in his *Code* (*Śĕkîrût*, 12:2–3, but not his commentary *ad loc.*) seems to have followed the implications of this reading (i.e., that the "original" ruling only permitted workers to eat produce when they finished a discrete unit of work [D], e.g., filling a basket, but so as to prevent workers from taking extended breaks for eating, [F–H] permitted them to eat at other times; cf. Nahmanides, *Ḥiddûšîm*, to B87b). KLMq and Ma before correction have עד שתהא (i.e., for as long as the ass is carrying"; RMN have כשתהא; and P has כשהיא (both "while"; i.e., specifically when it is unburdened [but not other times, perhaps somewhat analogous to the rule for humans in [D], according to Maimonides]). The Babli explicitly questions the wording כשתהא and emends the text to עד שתהא (B92a). It is therefore possible that the texts of the Mishnah that read עד שתהא (K among them) conform to the emendation of the Babli (so Epstein, *Nûsaḥ*, 543–4, who supplies a fuller list of variants). Tos. *s.v.* 'Elā' 'ēmā' (92a; followed by *TY* and *TYT* to M7:4) took [H] (reading עד שתהא) as independent of [E–G] (see Albeck, *Nĕzîqîn*, 427). Incidentally, E places this pericope, together with its Talmudic discussion, after M7:8; it is marked as out of place.

M7:6

[A]	A person may stipulate [terms] for himself,	קוצץ אדם על ידי עצמו [א]
[B]	and for his adult sons and daughters,	ועל ידי בנו וביתו הגדולים [ב]
[C]	and for his Hebrew man- and maidservants,	ועל ידי עבדו ושפחתו העברים [ג]
[D]	and for his wife,	ועל ידי אשתו [ד]
[E]	because they have understanding.	מפני שיש בהם דעת [ה]
[F]	But he may not stipulate for his minor sons and daughters,	אבל אינו קוצץ לא על ידי בנו וביתו הקטנים [ו]
[G]	nor for his Canaanite man or maidservants,	ולא על ידי עבדו ושפחתו הכנענים [ז]
[H]	nor for his animal,	ולא על ידי בהמתו [ח]
[I]	because they have no understanding.	מפני שאין בהם דעת [ט]

M7:7

[A]	One who hires workers—	השוכר את הפועלים [א]
[B]	to work with him on his fourth-year produce,	לעשות עמו בנטע רבעי שלו [ב]
[C]	lo, let these not eat;	הרי אלו לא יאכלו [ג]
[D]	but if he did not inform them,	ואם לא הודיען [ד]
[E]	he redeems [the produce] and feeds them.	פודה [ה]
[F]	[If] his fig-rounds were broken up, or his jars were opened, or his gourds were cut,	ניתפרסו עיגוליו ניתפתחו חביותיו נתחתכו דילועיו [ו]
[G]	lo, let these not eat,	הרי אילו לא יאכלו [ז]
[H]	but if he did not inform them,	ואם לא הודיען [ח]
[I]	he separates the tithe and feeds them.	מעשר ומאכיל(י)(ן) [ט]

M7:6: This pericope, in context, rules that the head of a household may stipulate that members of his household with legally acknowledged "understanding" not eat produce while they work another's fields, and that in exchange they (and thus he) receive a higher wage from the employer. (M7:6 is thus understood by the Babli [B92b]. However, there is nothing in the pericope itself to link it specifically to the question of laborers and it could, in theory, apply more generally to negotiation by a *pater familias*.) The expression על ידי here has the meaning "for" (see, already, *Měl'eket šělomoh, ad loc.*, citing *m. Yoma'* 3:4: ומרק אחר שחיטה על ידו, and another [priest] finished the slaughtering for him"; C. Y. Kasovsky, *Thesaurus Mishnae* [Jerusalem: Massada, 1957] 2, 824 [col. 1]).

M7:7: In [A–E] the produce was the fourth harvest from fruit trees, which was to be taken to Jerusalem, or redeemed for money and the money taken to Jerusalem and used for food (Lev. 19:23–5). In [F–I] the fact that the figs were already in rounds (see *m. Ma'aś.* 1:8) and the wine in jars (cf., however, *m. Ma'aś.* 1:7) meant that they were liable to tithing and thus prohibited until the tithe is separated. The third case in [F], נתחתכו דילועיו, "his gourds were cut" if it is not a scribal error, is not immediately clear, since cutting gourds does not make them liable to tithes (although [I] implies that the rule of tithing is involved). (In addition to K, the words נתחתכו דילועיו are attested by Rif, Maimonides *Code*, *Šěkîrût* 2:6, Constantinople [1509] edition, and the text of the Mishnah in Meiri [ed. Dickman, *et al.*, 9, 338]; since the words do not appear in most traditions of the Mishnah,

M7:8

[A]	Watchers of produce eat according to local practice,	[א] שומרי פירות אוכלין מהלכת המדינה
[B]	but not according to the Torah.	[ב] אבל לא מן התורה
[C]	There are four watchmen:	[ג] ארבעה שומרים הן ((שומרים הן))
[D]	the unpaid depositary (lit. unpaid watchman) and the borrower, the paid depositary (lit. wage bearer) and the renter.	[ד] שומר חינם והשואל נושא שכר והשוכר
[E]	The unpaid depositary swears for everything;	[ה] שומר חינם נשבע על הכל
[F]	and the borrower pays for everything;	[ו] והשואל משלם את הכל
[G]	the paid depositary and the renter swear for the break, and the captured [animal] and the dead [animal].	[ז] נושא שכר והשוכר נשבעים על השבר ועל השבויה ועל המיתה
[H]	and they pay for the loss and for the theft.	[ח] ומשלמין את האבידה ואת הגניבה

M7:9

[A]	A single wolf is not ʾônes,	[א] זאב אחד אינו אונס
[B]	two wolves are ʾônes.	[ב] שני זאבים אונס

---

it is possible that the words are a corruption from, e.g., *m. ʿOrla* 3:8.) It may be that נתחתכו דילועיו refers to a case in which gourds liable to tithing have become mixed with permitted (tithed) gourds, and have prohibited the whole lot. It is in this context that the expression occurs in *m. ʿOrla* 3:8, which cites the cases of נתפתחו חביותיו נתחתכו הדילועים, among other cases in which produce of the first three years of a plant (ʿorlâ, cf. Lev. 19:23), which when "whole" prohibit any amount of like produce with which they become mixed, but which when no longer "whole" prohibit mixtures only in proportions of one to two hundred or more. If this is the case, however, it is difficult to see what relevance "cutting" has here: either way the mixture is prohibited until the whole is tithed [I] (see also *m. Ḥal.* 3:9 with Albeck, *Zĕrāʿîm*, 408–9; but cf. *t. Dem.* 5:12; *t. Ter.* 5:15 with Lieberman, *TK*, 1, 255–6, 374–5, in which tithing of the whole mixture does not seem to be possible). Perhaps the author of M7:7 has consciously applied the distinction between mixtures of "whole" or "broken" produce (which only occurs explicitly in reference to ʿorlâ, *m. ʿOrla* 3:7–8; *t. Ter.* 5:10) also to tithing, and has qualified the rule that untithed produce in mixtures prohibits the whole lot in any proportions (הטבל אוסר כל שהוא, *m. Ḥal.* 3:10; *t. Demai.* 5:12; *t. Ter.* 5:15). In both [A–E] and [F–I] the rule is that if the produce is prohibited the householder is not required to allow the workers to eat; but if there was no way for the workers to know that the food was prohibited (fourth-year produce is not distinguishable as such; nor are figs or gourds [but cf. *m. Maʿaś.* 1:5] necessarily identifiable as liable to tithes), and the householder did not inform them, it is the householder's obligation to make the produce permissible for the workers and to allow them to eat it.

M7:8: [C–H] appear in a different context in *m. Šebu.* 8:1. The correction in the manuscript made in [C] removes a clear dittography. KRLMPN all read השבר in [G], but on analogy with the form of שבויה and מיתה we expect a participle (in the feminine in agreement with the assumed בהמה); this, in fact, is the tradition of the Babli. הש׳ appears at the end of the line preceding השבויה [G].

Appendix I: Text, Translation, and Annotation

[C]	R. Judah says: "During an infestation of wolves even a single wolf is ʾônes."	ר' יהודה אומ' ((אף)) בשעת משלחת זאבים אף זאב אחד אונס	[ג]
[D]	Two dogs are not ʾônes.	שני כלבים אינן אונסין	[ד]
[E]	Yaddua the Babylonian said in the name of R. Meir: "From one direction it is not ʾônes,	ידוע הבבלי אמ' משם ר' מאיר מרוח אחת אינו אונס	[ה]
[F]	"from two directions it is ʾônes."	משתי רוחות אונס	[ו]
[G]	A brigand, lo, this is ʾônes.	הליסטיס הרי זה אונס	[ז]
[H]	The lion, and the bear, and the tiger and the leopard and the snake, lo, these are ʾônes.	הארי והדוב והנמר והפרדלס והנחש הרי אילו אנסים	[ח]
[I]	When?	אמתי	[ט]
[J]	When they have come of themselves.	בזמן שבאו מאליהם	[י]
[K]	But if he walked them to a place of bands of animals or brigands, they are not ʾônes.	אבל אם הוליכן למקום גדודי חיה וליסטיס אין אלו אנסים	[כ]

M7:10

[A]	It died according to its manner [i.e., naturally], lo, this is ʾônes;	מתה כדרכה [[הרי הן]] אונס	[א]
[B]	he afflicted it and it died, it is not ʾônes.	סיכפה ומיתה אינו אונס	[ב]
[C]	It went up to the tops of the peaks and it fell, lo, this is ʾônes;	עלתה לראשי ה(ו)((י))צוקים ונפלה הרי זה אונס	[ג]
[D]	he took it up to the tops of the peaks and it fell, it is not ʾônes.	העלה לראשי ה(ו)((י))צוקים ונפלה [[אינו]] אונס	[ד]

M7:9: In the present context, אונס, ʾônes, retains its root sense of violent force, as well as its more generalized meaning of unavoidable accident. Since in the next pericope the term is merely a technical term for unavoidable accident, I have left the word untranslated. In [C] the first occurrence of the word אף, "even" (also present in L), has been crossed out in K. The double אף in [C] is awkward, and surely mistaken. The logic of the supplement attributed to R. Judah [C] is that although normally damage done by a single wolf is not considered ʾônes, a single wolf during an infestation is classed as ʾônes (and all "watchers" but the borrowers are free from liablity in such a case). The force of the first אף, however, works against this logic: it implies that in an infestation liability is expected to be higher. I have written ליסטס in [G] (so also RL; MN have ליסטין), although the ס in this case is nearly indistinguishable from the ם in אנסים in [H]. In general, the difference between ם and ס is slight in K: thus the ם in משלם at the end of M7:10 looks very much like a ס (see also the note to M5:3 [G] above). The reading ליסטיס (as in PE; in this case, see also Rashi, ad loc., B93b) may be somewhat preferable since it conforms more closely to the Greek ληστής of which it is a loan word. However, the use ליסטים in [K], where the final letter is clearly a ם, and which, on analogy with חיה is a form of the singular, supports the reading ליסטים in [G]. At the head of the list of animals in [H] LMaE, and an insertion to R, have הזאב, which is somewhat problematic in light of [A], which rules that only two or more wolves constitute ʾônes (see Lieberman, TK, 9, 267 to T8:16, who suggested that זאב was added on analogy from, e.g., m. B. Qam. 1:4, or that [H] merely enumerates types and does not conflct with [A]). פרדלס (Greek πάρδαλις; Jastrow translated the Hebrew usage "leopard" or "hyena"; LSJM gave "leopard" for the Greek) is variously spelled: KR פרדלס; L ברדליס; MP ברדלס; Mq ברדלוס; N פרדליס (on this sort of consonantal shift see Epstein, Nûsaḥ, 1220–3).

[E]	An unpaid depositary may make a condition to be exempt from swearing;	מתנה שומר חינם להיות פטור משבועה [ה]
[F]	and the borrower to be exempt from paying,	והשואל להיות פטור מלשלם [ו]
[G]	and the paid depositary and the renter to be exempt from swearing or paying.	ונשא שכר והשוכר להיות פטורין משבועה ומלשלם [ז]

M7:11

[A]	Everyone who makes conditions on [i.e., contrary to] what is written in the Torah, his condition is invalid.	כל המתנה על הכתוב שבתורה תניו בטל [א]
[B]	And every condition that [involves] an act at the outset, his condition is invalid.	וכל תניי שהוא מעשה מתחילתו תניו בטל [ב]
[C]	And every [condition] that it is possible to fulfill at the end, and he made it a condition at the outset, his condition is valid.	וכל שאפשר לו לקיימו בסופו והיתנה עליו מתחילתו תניו קיים [ג]

M7:10: It is not clear precisely what has been erased and written over in [A] and [D]. The top of the ן in [A] appears to be the remnant of an earlier letter (perhaps of the ו of אינו). The remnants of a letter are visible to the left of the lacuna in [D]. The spelling סיכפה in [B] occurs in KR, LMPEN (and the parallel in T8:15) all have סיגפה (see Epstein, *Nûsaḥ*, 1226). ראשי היצוקים [C] is similarly spelled in R; LN have ראש הצוקים; MP, ראשי צוקים. At the end of the line preceding היצוקים in [D] the letters היצ׳ appear as filler.

M7:11: In [A] R parallels K; L has משכתוב בתורה (where משכתוב = שכתוב מה, see Epstein, *Nûsaḥ*, 1217); N שכתוב מה; MP הכתוב בתורה. The Babli found (correctly) that there seems to be a contradiction between [A] and M7:10 [E–G] which apparently permits a condition contrary to what is written in the Torah (B94a; Neusner, *Damages* II, 118, is probably wrong in claiming that "These stipulations [i.e., M7:10] are valid because they do not contradict the law of the Torah"). [B] and [C] are quite difficult to translate. In *t. Qid.* 3:7, M7:11 [B] is glossed: "How? 'I hereby perform *ḥaliṣâ* [i.e., the ritual procedure to end a levirate marriage obligation, Deut. 25:5–11] for you [now], on condition that my father agrees [after the fact],' even though [her] father was not willing, she is divorced." (The Vienna ms. lacks the words "she is divorced" as well as most of the next clause due to *homoioteleuton*; a Genizah fragment cited by Lieberman. *Tosefta, Nashim*, p. 287 in the apparatus reads חלוצה; see also Lieberman's introduction, p. v.) That is, if an act was performed but its legal force made conditional upon something that will take place after the fact, the condition is invalid, and the act itself (already performed) is valid (see Maimonides to M7:11; Albeck, *Nĕziqîn*, 427–8). Maimonides (*ad loc.* and Albeck *ad loc.*) sees the expression in [C] אפשר לו לקיימו בסופו as equivalent to אפשר לו לקיימו, "it can be fulfilled," and takes [C] as a whole as requiring (1) that the fulfillment of the condition be within the realm of the possible; and (2) that the statement of the condition precedes the act.

M8:1

[A]	One who borrows a cow—	השואל את הפרה	[א]
[B]	and borrowed its owners with it;	ושאל בעליה עמה	[ב]
[C]	borrowed the cow and hired (*śākar*) its owners with it,	שאל את הפרה ושכר בעליה עמה	[ג]
[D]	borrowed the owners or hired them, and afterwards borrowed the cow,	שאל את הבעלים או שכרן ואחר כך שׂ((ו))אל את הפרה	[ד]
[E]	and it died—he is exempt,	ומתה פטור	[ה]
[F]	for it is said: "If its owner is with it he shall not pay" (Ex. 22:14).	שנ׳ אם בעליו עמו לא ישלם	[ו]
[G]	But [if] he borrowed the cow, and afterwards borrowed the owners or hired them,	אבל שאל את הפרה ואחר כך שאל את הבעלים או שכרן	[ז]
[H]	and it died—he is liable,	ומתה חייב	[ח]
[I]	for it is said: "[If] its owners are not with it he shall surely pay" (Ex. 22:14).	שנ׳ ((אין)) בעליו [[אין]] עמו שלם ישלם	[ט]

M8:2

[A]	One who borrows a cow—	השואל את הפרה	[א]
[B]	he borrowed it for half a day and leased it for half a day,	שאלה חצי יום ושכרה חצי יום	[ב]
[C]	he borrowed it today, and leased it on the next day,	שאלה היום ושכרה למחר	[ג]
[D]	borrowed one and leased one:	שאל אחת ושכר אחת	[ד]
[E]	the lender says: "The borrowed one died," [or] "It died on the day it was borrowed," [or] "It died at an hour when it was borrowed,"	המשאיל אומ׳ שאולה מתה ביום שהיתה שאולה מתה בשעת שהיתה שאולה מתה	[ה]
[F]	and the latter says: "I do not know,"	והלה או׳ איני יודע	[ו]
[G]	he is liable.	חייב	[ז]
[H]	The renter says: "The leased one died," [or] "It died on the day it was leased" [or] "It died at an hour when it was leased,"	השוכר או׳ שכורה מתה ביום שהיתה שכורה מתה [בשעה שהיתה שכורה מתה]	[ח]
[I]	and the latter says: "I do not know,"	והלה או׳ איני יודע	[ט]
[J]	he is exempt.	פטור	[י]
[K]	This one says: "The borrowed one [died],"	זה אומ׳ שאולה	[כ]
[L]	and this one says: "The leased one,"	וזה או׳ שכורה	[ל]

M8:1: In [C] RP agree with K; ML שכר את הפרה: N has both readings (so also "other books" according to Yehosef Ashkenazi as attested in *Mĕleket šĕlomoh, ad loc.*): שכר את הפרה ושכר בעליה עמה שאל את הפרה ושכר בעליה עמה. The first two letters of שכרן in [D] appear as filler at the end of the preceding line. Also in [D], שואל has been corrected to match the verb form of all the other verbs in the passage (except the first), and in keeping with the tradition presented by the other mss. Incidentally, the first word in [D] is given by L as שכר, clearly an error in this context ("if he hired ... or hired them"). [I] has been corrected to conform to the word-order of the Biblical verse: first אין has been crossed out, and a mark (for insertion?) placed between בעליו and עמו.

[M]	let the renter swear that the leased one died.	ישבע השוכר שסכורה מתה	[מ]
[N]	This one says: "I do not know,"	זה או' איני יודיע	[נ]
[O]	and this one says: "I do not know,"	זה או' איני יודיע	[ס]
[P]	let them split [it].	יחלוקו	[ע]

M8:3

[A]	One who borrows a cow—	[השואל] את הפרה	[א]
[B]	and [the lender] sent it by the hand of his son or by the hand of his manservant or by the hand of his messenger,	ושילחה לו ביד בנו ביד עבדו ביד שלוחו	[ב]
[C]	or by the hand of the son, by the hand of the manservant, by the hand of the messenger of the borrower,	או ביד בנו ביד עבדו ביד שלוחו שלשואל	[ג]
[D]	and it died—he is exempt.	ומתה פטור	[ד]
[E]	The borrower said to him: "Send it to me by the hand of my son, by the hand of my manservant, by the hand of my messenger,	אמ' לו השואל שלחה לי ביד בני ביד עבדי ביד שלוחי	[ה]
[F]	"or by the hand of your son, by the hand of your manservant, by the hand of your messenger,"	או ביד בנך ביד עבדך ביד שלוחך	[ו]
[G]	or [if] the lender said to him: "Lo, I am sending it to you by the hand of my son, by the hand of my manservant, by the hand of my messenger,	או שאמר לו המשאיל הרי אני משלחה לך ביד בני ביד עבדי ביד שלוחי	[ז]
[H]	"or by the hand of your son, by the hand of your manservant, by the hand of your messenger,"	או ביד בנך ביד עבדך ביד שלוחך	[ח]
[I]	and the borrower said to send it,	[ואמר] לו השואל לשלח	[ט]
[J]	and he sent it to him,	ושלחה לו	[י]
[K]	and it died—he is liable.	ומתה חייב	[כ]
[L]	And so too at the time when he returns it.	וכן בשעה שהוא מחזירה	

M8:2: The first two letters of בשעת (a mistake for בשעה) in [E] appear as filler at the end of the previous line. The omission of the clause I have restored in [H] is presumably due to homoioteleuton, and has been supplied from the other texts examined, as well as by analogy with the parallel formulation in [E]. However, P lacks this clause in both [E] and [H]. Note that the order of the claims in [E] and [H] is in chiastic relationship with the description of the case in [B–D]: part of day, day, animal / animal, day, part of day.

M8:3: K has השוליח, "one who sends," as the first word of this pericope, an error stemming from the frequent recurrence of the root שלח in this Mishnah. The other texts consulted have השואל, which is also in keeping with the formulaic opening of the previous two pericopae. The first letter of שלוחו in [B] appears as filler at the end of the preceding line. M does not have the word שלוחו in [B] and adds של משאיל, "of the lender" at the end of that clause. R adds the conjunction או, "or," between each of the elements in [B] and [C]; M adds it in [B, C, F, H]. In K the word ואמר [I] is lacking (there is a correction mark in the

Appendix I: Text, Translation, and Annotation 295

M8:4

[A]	One who barters a cow for an ass and it gives birth—	[א] המחליף פרה וחמור וילדה
[B]	and so too, one who sells his maidservant and she gives birth—	[ב] וכן המוכר שיפחתו וילדה
[C]	this one says "[She gave birth] before I sold it,"	[ג] זה אומ׳ עד שלא עד שלא מכרתי
[D]	and this one says: "After I bought it,"	[ד] וזה אומ׳ משלקחתי
[E]	let them split [it].	[ה] יחלוקו
[F]	He had two manservants, one big and one small;	[ו] היו לו שני עבדים אחד גדול ואחד קטן
[G]	and so too, two fields one large and one small:	[ז] וכן שתי שדות אחת גדולה ואחת קטנה
[H]	the purchaser says: "I bought the big one,"	[ח] הלוקח אומ׳ [[ה]]גדול לקחתי
[I]	and the latter says: "I do not know,"	[ט] והלה אומ׳ אינ(ו)[י] יודיע
[J]	he has gained the big one.	[י] זכה בגדול
[K]	The seller says: "I sold the small one,"	[כ] והמוכר אומ׳ הקטן מכרתי
[L]	and the latter says: "I do not know,"	[ל] והלה או׳ איני יודיע
[M]	he only has the small one.	[מ] אין לו אלא קטן
[N]	This one says: "The big one [is mine],"	[נ] זה אומ׳ גדול
[O]	and this one says: "The small one,"	[ס] וזה או׳ קטן
[P]	let the seller swear that he sold the small one.	[ע] יישבע המוכר שהקטן מכר
[Q]	This one says: "I do not know,"	[פ] זה או׳ איני יודיע
[R]	and this one says: "I do not know,"	[צ] וזה אומ׳ איני יודיע
[S]	let them split [it].	[ק] יחלוקו

M8:5

[A]	One who sells his olive trees for wood—	[א] המוכר (ז)איתיו לעצים
[B]	and they produced less than a quarter-*lôg* [of oil] to the *sĕʾâ* [of olives]:	[ב] ועשו פחות מרביעית לסאה
[C]	lo, [these] belong to the owner of the olives.	[ג] הרי שלבעל הזתים
[D]	They produced a quarter-*lôg* to the *sĕʾâ*:	[ד] עשו רביעית לסאה
[E]	this one says: "My olive trees grew it,"	[ה] זה אומ׳ זיתיי גיד(ו)[ל]לו
[F]	and this one says: "My land grew it,"	[ו] וזה אומ׳ ארצי גידלה
[G]	let them split [it].	[ז] יחלוקו

---

manuscript), and it has been restored on comparison with LMNP (however, P is lacking all of [G–H]); R has שאמר או, "or if he said," which is a mistake.

M8:4: A י appears as filler at the end of the line preceding יחלוקו in [E]. [I] is corrected from context, and on the basis of comparison with other texts. The final letter is clearly a ו (a common and simple error to make; for examples in this ms. see M2:7 [G]; M8:5 [E]), but איני is clearly preferable (cf. [L, Q, R] and the analogous clauses in M8:2). K did not have the definite article in גדול in [H] and it was supplied in the ms. to match הקטן in [K]. However, RLMPN all give both nouns without the definite article.

[H]	A river swept away the olive trees, and deposited them in the field of his fellow:	שטף הנהר זתיו ונתנן לתוך שדה חבירו	[ח]
[I]	this one says: "My olive trees grew it,"	זה אומ' זתיי גידלו	[ט]
[J]	and this one says: "My land grew it,"	וזה או' ארצי גידלה	[י]
[K]	let them split [it].	יחלוקו	[כ]

M8:6

[A]	One who leases a house to his fellow—	המשכיר בית לחבירו	[א]
[B]	during the rainy season he is not allowed to remove him from the Festival [i.e., Tabernacles] until Passover;	[[ב]]ימות הגשמים אינו יכול להוציאו מן החג ועד הפסח	[ב]
[C]	and during the dry season—thirty days.	ובימות החמה שלשים יום	[ג]
[D]	And in the cities:	ובכרכים	[ד]
[E]	both the rainy season and the dry season—twelve months.	אחד ימות החמה ואחד ימות הגשמים שנים עשר חודש	[ה]
[F]	And in [the case of] shops:	ובחניות	[ו]
[G]	both cities and small towns—twelve months.	אחד כרכים ואחד עיירות שנים עשר חודש	[ז]
[H]	R. Simeon b. Gamaliel says: "A shop of bakers or dyers—three years."	רבן שמעון בן גמליא' או' חנות של נחתומים ושל צבעים שלש שנים	[ח]

M8:7

[A]	One who leases a house to his fellow—	המשכיר בית לחבירו	[א]
[B]	the lessor is obligated [to supply] the door, bolt and lock,	המשכיר חייב בדלת ובנגר ובמנעל	[ב]
[C]	and everything that is the work of an artisan.	ובכל דבר שהוא מעשה אומן	[ג]
[D]	But anything that is not the work of an artisan the lessee does.	אבל דבר שאינו מעשה אומן השוכר עושהו	[ד]
[E]	The dung belongs to the householder;	הזבל של בעל הבית	[ה]

M8:5: The initial letter of זיתיו appears to have been written as ו. In [C], RN, like K, have no pronoun; MP have הרי אלו; L הרי הן. The ו in גיד(ו)(ו)לו [E], excised by a later hand, is probably an error for י (i.e., *plene* spelling, without vowel reduction in *piʿēl*: *giddēlû* [here spelled *gi(y)ddē(y)lû*], not *giddēlû*; cf. the note to M2:7 above); but cf. the orthography in [F, J], and especially [I].

M8:6: It is not clear what K had before the correction in [B]; it may have read לימות (this is also the view of Epstein, *Nûsaḥ*, 338); the other witnesses all parallel the corrected text. Apparently, this Mishnah addresses the question of the presumed duration of a lease when the term was unstated (cf. however T8:27 [cited also in Y8:8 (11d); B101b], which discusses the cases of [C] and [E] [and presumably also [F–H]] as dealing with the issue of the amount of notice given for eviction, and see the discussion by Epstein, *Nûsaḥ*, 338f.). At the end of the line preceding ושל צבעים in [H] ושל צב' appears as filler.

[F]	The lessee has only what comes out of the oven and the stove.	אין לשוכר אלא היוצא מן התנור ומן הכירים בלבד	[ו]

M8:8

[A]	One who leases a house to his fellow—	המשכיר בית לחבירו	[א]
[B]	for a year:	לשנה	[ב]
[C]	[if] the year was made a leap year, it was made a leap year to [the advantage of] the lessee	[[ו]]ניתעברה השנה ניתעברה לסוכר	[ג]
[D]	He leased it to him on a monthly basis:	היסכיר לו לחדשים	[ד]
[E]	[if] the year was made a leap year it was made a leap year to [the advantage of] the lessor.	[[ו]]ניתעברה השנה ניתעברה למשכיר	[ה]
[F]	A case arose in Sepphoris concerning one who leased a bath from his fellow for twelve golden *dînārîm* for the year, at a golden *dînār* per month,	מעשה בציפורין באחד ששכר מרחץ מחבירו בשנים עשר [[דינר]] זהב לשנה מדינר זהב לחודש	[ו]
[G]	and the case came before R. Simeon b. Gamaliel and before R. Yose,	ובא מעשה לפני רבן שמעון בן גמליא' ולפני ר' יוסה	[ז]
[H]	and they said: "Let them divide the intercalated month."	ואמרו יחל((ו))קו את חודש העיבור	[ח]

M8:9

[A]	One who leases a house to his fellow—	המשכיר בית לחבירו	[א]
[B]	and it fell:	ונפל	[ב]
[C]	he must supply a house for him.	חיב להעמיד לו בית	[ג]
[D]	It was small, let him not make it big;	היה קטן (ו))לא יעשנו גדול	[ד]
[E]	it was big—let him not make it small;	גדול ((ו))לא יעשנו קטן	[ה]
[F]	one—let him not make it two;	אחד ולא יעשנו שנים	[ו]
[G]	two—let him not make it one.	שנים ((ו))לא יעשנו אחד	[ז]

M8:7: Note the spelling of the root שכר in M8:7–8. [E] does not make clear whose animal's dung is meant, and where it was found. The Babli understands it to mean that the tenant of a house on a courtyard has no claim to the dung that accumulates from animals that belong to neither the tenant nor the owner (i.e., the animals happened to be there, B102a).

M8:8: A ו has been added in K before the first word of both [C] and [E]. The force of this correction is to make the words [[ו]]ניתעברה השנה part of the protasis (e.g., "One who leases ... for a year, and the year was made a leap year, [then] ..."). According to the uncorrected reading in K, all of [C] and [E] each serve as single apodoses (constructed conditionally: "[then: if] it was made a leap year ..."). Of the witnesses checked the ו is attested in [C] only in P, and in [E] in MP. N agrees with the uncorrected text of K in [I], the other texts examined all read יחלקו as in the corrected text of K.

[H] Let him not decrease the number of windows nor increase it except with the knowlege of both of them.

[ח] לא יפחות מן החלונות ולא יוסיף עליהם אלא מדעת שניהם

M8:9: A reader of K has deleted three occurrences of ו [D, E, G], but left one [F]. Epstein, *Nûsaḥ*, 1076–7, 1081–6 (M8:9 is cited on p. 1084) considered these examples of *waw-apodosis*, which is common in K, but frequently corrected by a second hand.

M9:1

[A]	One who receives [i.e., in a lease] a field from his fellow—	המקבל שדה מחבירו [א]
[B]	in a place where it was customary to cut, let him cut;	מקום שנהגו לקצור יקצור [ב]
[C]	to uproot, let him uproot;	לעקור יעקור [ג]
[D]	to plow afterwards, let him plow;	לחרוש אחריו יחרוש [ד]
[E]	all follows the custom of the province.	הכל כמנהג המדינה [ה]
[F]	Just as they split the grain, so let them split the hay and the straw.	כשם שחולקים בתבואה כך חולקים בתבן ובקש [ו]
[G]	Just as they split the wine, so let them split the prunings and the stakes.	כשם שחולקים ביין כך חולקים בזמורת ובקנים [ז]
[H]	And both supply the stakes.	ושניהם מספקים את הקנים [ח]

M9:2

[A]	One who receives a field from his fellow—	המקבל שדה מחבירו [א]
[B]	and it is a field dependent on irrigation or a tree plantation	והוא בית שלחים או בית האילן [ב]
[C]	[if] the spring has dried up, or the tree was cut down,	יבש המעיין ניקצץ האילן [ג]
[D]	he does not deduct from his rent (ḥakôrô).	אינו מנכה לו (מחבירו?) [מחכורו] [ד]
[E]	If he said to him lease me this field dependent on irrigation, or this tree plantation,	אם אמ' לו השכר לי שדה בית שלחין זה או שדה בית האילן זה [ה]
[F]	[if] the spring has dried up, or the tree was cut down,	ייבש המעיין ניקצץ האילן [ו]
[G]	he deducts from his rent.	מנכה לו (מחבירו?) [מחכורו] [ז]

M9:1: The first two letters of the first word of [H] appear as filler at the end of the preceding line. One verb, קבל, "receive," (cf. M5:4 [G], 6 [A–C]) is used to describe all the cases in the series M9:1–10, but at least three types of contracts are referred to: (1) working for a share of the produce (אריסות), or in exchange for a fixed payment (2) in kind (חכירות; see next note) or (3) in money (שכירות, see Maimonides, to M9:2). While [A–E] deal only with the expected work of the tenant farmer, [F–H] may assume that the relationship is one of אריסות in which the tenant pays a percentage of the produce (and so shares both in by-products and in expenses). A statement attributed R. Pappa (B104a), that has been widely followed by the commentaries, claims that the first two pericopae (M9:1–2?) apply both to קבלנות ("receipt," interpreted by Rashi, Maimonides *et alii* as identical to אריסות) and חכירות, but that the remaining pericopae of this series apply either to the one or the other. The second part of the dictum works fairly well for M9:2–8 (see, however, the notes below to M9:2, which the commentaries have interpreted, perhaps unnecessarily, as referring to both types of contracts; and to M9:5, 7). However, Tos. *s.v. Hanî trê* (B104a), already noted a problem with this dictum of R. Pappa concerning the latter part of M9:1; nor is it clear how the formulator of the dictum divided the text of the Mishnah in referring to "these two first" pericopae.

M9:2: The first two letters of שלחים in [B] appear as filler at the end of the previous line. On the basis of the copy of the Kauman ms. that I have used, it appears that the scribe has

M9:3

[A] One who receives a field from his fellow—	[א] [המקבל שדה מחבירו]
[B] [if] from the time he has gained possession of it he has left it fallow,	[ב] מי שזכה בה הבירה
[C] they estimate how much it is fit to produce, and they give it to him,	[ג] שמין אותה כמה היא ראיה לעשות ונותנין לו
[D] for he says to him: "If I should leave it fallow and not work it I will pay at the highest value."	[ד] שהוא [[אומר]] לו אם אוביר ולא אעבי(ר)[ד] אשלם במיטבה

M9:4

[A] One who receives a field from his fellow—	[א] המקבל שדה מחבירו
[B] and he did not want to weed:	[ב] ולא רצה לנכש

---

written מחבירו ("from his fellow") in M9:2 [D, G], 6 [D], but not M9:6 [F, H], and that these have been subsequently corrected. Note also the apparent omission in M9:3 [A] (see the next note), and the spelling חבורו (M9:4 [C]) in KL. That the scribe wrote מחכורו in M9:6 [F, H] suggests that מחבירו is an error rather than an alternative text. However, it may also presuppose the form חכיר that appears in texts of the Babli (see, e.g., Rabbinovicz, *DS*, 302 (n. ח), 306 (n. צ). In all five cases LN have the odd text מן החכורו. In [E], RMPN all have the form השכיר) השכר in MPN); L has חכור. From the context (one may/may not deduct) and the use of חכורו in [D] and [G] (usually meaning a fixed payment in kind, see e.g., *m. Dem.* 6:1–5, and a record of leases from Wadi Murabaat, *DJD* II 24. B 8, 15; C 8, 13; E 10; F 7; but cf. M9:6[F–G] in which חכור is used in connection with rent paid in money), it seems clear that this Mishnah deals with חכירות, a contract for a fixed payment in kind. השכר in [E] might be taken to suggest that the contract is for a fixed monetary rental payment, although, as Maimonides, *ad loc.* points out, the terminology could be fluid. Albeck, *ad loc.*, understands this pericope as referring to both אריסות and קבלנות, following the medieval commentaries (Rashi, B104a [and apparently of Tos., *ibid.*]; Maimonides, *ad loc.*, based on the statement of R. Pappa cited in the previous note) but does not explain (cf. Albeck, *Nězîqîn*, 429, to M9:1). However, in the other pericope in this series in which the question of חכורו לו מן מנכה (אינו) ("does (not) deduct from his rent") arises, M9:6, Rashi states that it could only be a case of a fixed payment.

M9:3: [A] is missing in K, presumably due to homoioteleuton (מחכורו-מחבירו); see the preceding note. RN, like K have ונותנין in [C], although R has been corrected to read ונותן, the reading in the other witnesses checked. The variants involve a difference in both grammar and nuance: KRN: "and they [i.e the court, exact money from the tenant and] give it to him [the lessor]"; the others: "and he [i.e., the tenant] gives [that amount] to him." [D] in K presumably had כותב, "writes" as in MN (traces of the bottom of ב are visible in K); אומר is the reading in RLP. In the case of אעביר[ד] the scribe has inadvertently switched letters which are very close to one another. (I have corrected the text of K on the basis of T9:12 and the text of M9:3 [D] in RLMN; P reads אעביר.) The quote in [D] is in Aramaic, and ostensibly reproduces a clause from a standard lease. The form מיטבה appears in KN; in the other witnesses the form מיטבא is used (for the possible implications of the variant spellings see Albeck, *Nězîqîn*, 429, Lieberman, *TK*, 9, 284). The implication of [C] is that the contract is one of אריסות.

Appendix I: Text, Translation, and Annotation

[C]	he said to him: "What do you care, inasmuch as I am giving you your rent,"	אמ' לו מה אכפת לך הואיל ואני נותן לך (חבורך) [חכורך]	[ג]
[D]	one does not listen to him,	אין שומעין לו	[ד]
[E]	for he can say to him: "Tomorrow you leave and it grows grass before me."	שהוא או' לו למחר את יוצא ממנה והיא מעלה לפני עשבים	[ה]

M9:5

[A]	One who receives a field from his fellow—	המקבל שדה מחביר:	[א]
[B]	and it did not produce:	ולא עשת	[ב]
[C]	if there is in it enough to erect a pile with it,	אם יש בה כדי להעמיד בה כרי	[ג]
[D]	he is required to work with it.	חייב ליטפל בה	[ד]
[E]	Said R. Judah: "What amount is 'a pile'?	אמ' ר' יהודה מה קיצבה כרי	[ה]
[F]	"Rather: 'If there is in it sufficient for falling'"	אלא אם יש לה כדי ניפלה	[ו]

M9:6

[A]	One who receives a field from his fellow—	המקבל שדה מחבירו	[א]
[B]	and locusts ate it or it was blighted:	ואכלה חגב או נישדפה	[ב]
[C]	if it is a strike upon the whole province	אם מכת מדינה היא	[ג]
[D]	he deducts from his rent;	מנכה לו (מחבירו?) [מחכורו]	[ד]
[E]	and if it is not a strike upon the whole province,	ואם אינה מכת מדינה היא	[ה]
[F]	he does not deduct from his rent.	אינו מנכה לו (מחבירו?) [מחכורו]	[ו]
[G]	R. Judah says: "If he received it from him for money	ר' יהודה אומ' אם קיבלה ממנו במעות	[ז]
[H]	in any case he does not deduct from his rent.	בין כך ובין כך אינו מנכה לו מחכורו	[ח]

M9:4: For the correction in [C] see the note to M9:2 above. The first three letters of שומעין in [D] appear at the end of the preceding line as filler. The contract in question is, apparently, one involving a fixed payment in kind (חכירות).

M9:5: The second occurence of בה (i.e., "with it") in [C] is absent in RLMPN. Some texts of the Babli have בכרי in [E] (see Rabbinovicz, *DS*, 307(n. ש), which may alter the force somewhat: "Why is the amount set at a 'pile'? כדי ניפלה, "sufficient for falling," [F] apparently refers to the seed grain. The contract is apparently one of אריסות, since it is particularly in such contracts that the question of how much grain may be recovered by working becomes especially relevant. (However, in M9:4 the owner retains an interest in whether the property is worked or not even in fixed rate contracts, so arguably this pericope might be taken to apply to such contracts as well.)

M9:6: For the expression (אינו) מנכה לו מן חכורו, and its text, see the note to M9:2 above. In the present case, the contract seems to have been for fixed payment (חכירות), although in the last clause of this Mishnah, חכורו cannot mean payment in kind.

M9:7

[A]	One who receives a field from his fellow—	המקבל שדה מחבירו [א]
[B]	for ten *kôr* [yearly]:	בעשרת כורים חיטים [ב]
[C]	[if] it was struck [and had poor produce],	לקת [ג]
[D]	he gives him [payment] from it.	נותן לו מתוכה [ד]
[E]	[If] its produce was good,	היו חיטיה יפות [ה]
[F]	let him not say to him: "Lo, I am buying [grain for payment] for you from the market,"	לא יאמר לו הרי אני לוקיח לך מן השוק [ו]
[G]	but rather, he gives him from it.	אלא נותן לה מתוכה [ז]

M9:8

[A]	One who receives a field from his fellow—	המקבל שדה מחבירו [א]
[B]	to seed it with barley, let him not seed it with wheat;	לזו(ו)רעה שעורים לא יורעינה חיטים [ב]
[C]	wheat, let him seed it with barley,	חיטין יורעינה שעורים [ג]
[D]	R. Simeon b. Gamaliel prohibits.	רבן שמעון בן גמליא' אוסר [ד]
[E]	Pulse, let him not seed it with grain;	קיטנית לא יורעינה תבואה [ה]
[F]	grain, let him seed it with pulse,	תבואה יורעינה קטנית [ו]
[G]	R. Simeon b. Gamaliel prohibits.	רבן שמעון בן גמליא' אוסר [ז]

M9:7: In [B] RLMPN all add "of wheat" (R שלחיטים; L חיטין; P חטין; MN חטים); see also Rabbinovicz, *DS*, 310. The specification of an amount of grain shows that this Mishnah is dealing with a fixed-rate contract, but the logic should apply to אריסות contracts as well.

M9:8: The spelling לזורעה is retained in RP; לזרעה appears in MEN; L has ליזרענה. Concerning the text of [E–F]· compare M: קטנית יורעה תבואה תבואה לא יורעה קטנית this is the text of the Mishnah as it is represented in the Babli mss. as well, although the Hamburg and Florence and other mss. [and the Munich ms. after scribal correction] have the clauses in the reverse order [see Rabbinovicz, *DS* 313–4; Epstein, *Nûsaḥ*, 327–8, which presents a fuller list of variants]; cf. L which is corrupt: it reads לא יורענה in [E] as well as [F], an impossibility since the tradition of R. Simeon b. Gamaliel [G] prohibits something permitted in at least one of the clauses). The reading of K is attested also by Rif (early printed editions and mss.) and Maimonides *Code, Śěkîrût* 8:9; see also *TYṬ, Měl'eket šělomoh ad loc.* In the interchange in the Babli (B107a, following the version in Rif; see Epstein, *Nûsaḥ* 328, and 327 n. 4), R. Judah is said to have cited תבואה לא יורעה קטנית and Rabin is credited with the objection from the Mishnah, stating: תבואה יורעה קטנית (with the conclusion that one version corresponds to the agricultural conditions of Babylonia, and the other those of Palestine). This interchange may already presuppose both texts (i.e., a conflict between a Babylonian and Palestinian version of M9:8 already in antiquity; the expressions *matnê lêh* and *wě-hā' 'anan těnān* may imply this), although Epstein, and apparently Rashi as well , ook only one of the traditions as representing the Mishnah (Rashi *s.v. Hā' lān*: "The Mishnah deals with the land of Israel ... but we live in Babylonia ..."; that Rashi's text of the Babli [like that of the majority of witnesses] differed from that of the Rif ms. does not alter this conclusion; cf. Halivni, *Měqôrôt û-měsôrôt*, to *b. Baba' Meṣi'a'*, in preparation). At any rate, Epstein is presumably correct that it is the discussion of the Babli that lead to the "correction" of later printed editions of the Mishnah. (Rashi, although

M9:9

[A]	One who receives a field from his fellow—	המקבל שדה מחבירו	[א]
[B]	for few years:	[ל][שנים צעוטות	[ב]
[C]	let him not plant flax,	לא יזרענה פשתן	[ג]
[D]	and he has no [share] in sycamore beams.	ואין לו ((וב))קורת שקמה	[ד]
[E]	[If] he received it from him for seven years:	קיבלה ממנו שבע שנים	[ה]
[F]	he may plant flax in the first year,	זורעה שנה ראשונה פישתן	[ו]
[G]	and he has a share in the sycamore beams.	ויש לו ((וב))קורת שיקמה	[ז]

M9:10

[A]	One who receives a field from his fellow—	המקבל שדה מחבירו	[א]
[B]	seven years at seven hundred *dînārîm*:	שבע שנים בשבע מאות דינר	[ב]
[C]	the seventh [i.e., sabbatical] year is not counted among them;	ואין השביעית מן המינין	[ג]
[D]	a week [of years] at seven hundred *dînārîm*:	שבוע אחד בשבע מאות דינר	[ד]
[E]	the seventh [i.e., sabbatical] year is counted among them.	השביעית מן המינין	[ה]

---

following the text of the Mishnah as reflected in M and the Babli mss., explained in his commentary to B107a that despite the Mishnah, in Babylonia the lessee may plant legumes or grain as he wishes. Although this probably does not mean that Rashi thought that that there was a "Babylonian Mishnah" that read יזרענה in both [E] and [F], this is precisely the text of the Mishnah in the uncorrected Munich ms. If this is not merely a scribal error, it may reflect correction in accordance with Rashi's commentary.) The "Palestinian" version (reflected in K), which permits the planting of legumes rather than grain, but prohibits the reverse, fits the agricultural assumptions of the Greco-Roman (and modern) world about the "enriching" (nitrogen-fixing) properties of legumes (see the brief discussion in Chapter II.B.6). For a different discussion of the treatment of this pericope in the Babli see Halivni's discussion cited above).

M9:9: לשנים [B] is the reading in all the texts checked; cf. [E] ל is absent in L) and M9:10 [B] (ל is absent in RMN) and [D] (ל is absent in RLMPN) in which the preposition has not been added to K by a later hand. At the end of the line preceding יזרענה in [C], the first three letters of that word appear as filler. בקורת שקמה [D, G], as in K before the correction, is the reading in RPN (although P in both cases, and N only in the second, read בקורות); M has קורת שקמה; L has קורות של שקמה [D]; קורות שקמה [F].

M9:10: The order of the clauses in RLMPEN follows that of K (and is attested by Rif and Rosh, by the Babli mss. Rome A and B, Florence, and the fragment published by A. I. Katsch, *Ginze Talmud* [Jerusalem: Rubin Mass, 1979], 2, 208; and seems to be implied by Maimonides, *Code*, *Śĕkîrût*, 8:3). In the Hamburg ms. and the *editio princeps* of the Babli the order is [A + D–E], [B–C]. The Munich ms. has only [A–C]; [D–E], in whatever order it ought to have appeared, is lacking due to homoioteleuton. The *editio princeps* has קבלה הימנו at the beginning of [B] (in the position of [D]; cf. M8:8 [D]; M9:8 [E]), whence it was

M9:11

[A] A worker hired for a day collects all through the night,   שכיר יום גובה כל הלילה [א]

[B] and a worker hired for a night collects all through the day;   ושכיר לילה גובה כל היום [ב]

[C] and a worker hired to work for hours collects all through the night and all through the day.   ושכיר שעות גובה כל הלילה וכל היום [ג]

[D] A worker hired for a Sabbath [i.e., week], a worker hired for a month, a worker hired for a week [of years]:   סכיר שבת שכיר חודש שכיר שבוע [ד]

[E] [if] he left work during the day, he collects all through day,   יצא ביום גובה כל היום [ה]

[F] [if] he left [work] during the night he collects all through the night and all through the day.   יצא בלילה גובה כל הלילה וכל היום [ו]

M9:12

[A] Whether the wage of a man, or the wage of an animal, or the wage of utensils,   אחד שכ(וי)ר האדם [ו][אחד שכר הבהמה ואחד שכר הכלים [א]

[B] the law of "on that day you shall give him his wage" (Deut. 24:15) applies,   יש בו משם ביומו תתן שכרו [ב]

[C] and the law of "you shall not keep the wage of the hired worker with you over night until the morning" (Lev. 19:13) applies.   ויש בו משם לא תלין פעולת שכיר אתך עד בקר [ג]

[D] When?   אמתי [ד]

[E] When he has claimed [his wage] from him.   בזמן שתבעו [ה]

---

reproduced in the standard printed editions of the Mishnah and the Babli. The ו in ואין in [C] is not in any of the other Mishnah texts checked; see Epstein, *Nûsaḥ*, 1084, and cf. the note to M8:9 above.

M9:11: This pericope deals with the time during which a worker must have demanded payment before the employer has transgressed the Biblical injunction against keeping the worker's wage over night (Lev. 19:13; Deut. 24: 15). L reads כל היום in [A], and כל הלילה in [B], a reading that is unattested elsewhere. In [C] RLPN agree with K; M, the Leiden ms. of the Yerushalmi (and the *editio princeps*), and the Babli ms. Rome B have: כל היום וכל הלילה. Similarly, in [F] MP read כל היום וכל הלילה. [C] is interpreted in two ways in the Babli: (1) a worker hired for several hours during the day claims for the remainder of the day, and one hired for the night claims for the remainder of the night (based on the statement attributed to Rab); and (2) a worker hired for several hours during the day is like a day worker, but a worker hired for several hours during the night collects even during the next day (attributed to Samuel). The Babli is already aware of the fact that the first interpretation of [C] conflicts with [F] (cf. T10:2 in which a tradition parallel to [F] ends: יצא בלילה גובה כל הלילה, "he left ... all through the night," without the problematic "and all through the day").

Appendix I: Text, Translation, and Annotation

[F]	[If] he did not claim from him—he [the employer] does not transgress it.	לא תבעו אינו עובר עליו [ז]
[G]	[If] he sent him over to the shopkeeper or to the money changer he does not transgress it.	הימחהו אצל החנווני או אצל השולחני אינו עובר עליו [ז]
[H]	The hired worker, swears at his [proper] time and takes [his payment];	השכיר נשבע בזמנו ונוטל [ח]
[I]	[if] he passed over his time [without claiming] he does not swear and take;	עיבר זמנו אינו נשבע ונוטל [ט]
[J]	[but] if there are witnesses that he claimed from him, lo, this one swears and takes.	אם יש עדים שתבעו הרי זה נשבע ונוטל [י]
[K]	A resident alien,	גר תושב [כ]
[L]	the law of "on that day you shall give him his wage" (Deut. 24:15) applies;	יש בו משם ביומו תתן שכרו [ל]
[M]	but the law of "you shall not keep the wage of the hired worker with you over night until the morning" (Lev. 19:13) does not apply	ואין בו משם לא תלין פעולת שכיר אתך עד בקר [מ]

M9:13

[A]	One who lends to his fellow—	המלוה את חבירו [א]
[B]	let him not [come to] distrain [a pledge] from him except in court,	לא (ולא)) ימשכנינו אלא בבית [[דין]] [ב]
[C]	and let him not go into his house and take the pledge,	ולא יכנס לביתו ויטול את משכונו [ג]
[D]	as it is said: "You shall stand outside, and the man ...." (Deut. 24:17).	שנ' בחוץ תעמוד והאיש וגו' [ד]
[E]	[If] he had two utensils he takes one and returns one:	היו לו שני כלים נוטל אחד ומחזיר אחד [ה]
[F]	he returns the pillow at night and the plow during the day.	מחזיר את הכר בלילה ואת המחרשה ביום [ו]
[G]	But if he dies he does not return it to his heirs,	ואם מת אינו מחזיר ליורשיו [ז]

M9:12: The corrected form שכר, "reward, payment," in [A] is undoubtedly correct. The addition of the ו to אחד[ו]] corresponds to the text in all the witnesses checked. הימחהו [G] is difficult to translate. Jastrow (s.v. מחי) gives: "If he gave him an order to the store keeper." (See Chapter III.A.3.) [H–J] deal with the Mishnah's provision to allow certain individuals, among them workers, to collect from a defendant on the basis of an oath (cf. *m. Šĕbû.* 7:1). This provision is held to apply only during the time when a worker is supposed to collect (see M9:11). The reading נשבע בזמנו occurs in KRLMPN; later printed editions follow the versions in the Babli: בזמנו נשבע (the Leiden ms. of the Yerushalmi reads נשבע בזמנו in the text of the Mishnah preceding the chapter, but בזמנו נשבע in the lemma). The reading נשבע בזמנו makes it clear that the oath, too, must take place during "his time." This, at any rate, is the implication of the exception given in [J] (cf. T10:6). עיבר (*pi'el*) in [I], the form used in RLP as well, makes the worker the subject of the verb; עבר (MN), if it is *qal*, is part of an impersonal construction: "if the time passed ...." In [J] M reads שתבעו בזמנו, "he claimed it from him at his time" (cf. T10:6; and B113a, in which an Amoraic dispute may either dispute the meaning of בזמנו, or interpolate variants of the word into the Mishnah).

[H]	R. Simeon b. Gamaliel says: "Even to [the borrower] himself, he only returns it up to thirty days,	[ח] רב' שמעון בן גמליא' אומ' אף לעצמו אינו מחזיר אלא עד שלשים יום
[I]	"and from thirty days and thereafter he sells it in court."	[ט] ומשלשים יום ולהלן מוכרו בבית דין
[J]	A widow, whether she is poor or whether she is rich one does not [come to] distrain a pledge from her,	[י] אלמנה בן שהיא ענייה ובין שהיא עשירה אין ממשכנין אתה
[K]	as it is said: "You shall not seize the garment of a widow as a pledge" (Deut. 24:17).	[כ] שנ' לא תחבל בגד אלמנה
[L]	One who seizes the mill as a pledge—	[ל] החובל את הריחים
[M]	he transgresses a negative commandment,	[מ] עובר בלא תעשה
[N]	and is liable for two utensils,	[נ] וחייב משם שני כלים
[O]	as it is said: "You shall not seize the upper and lower millstone as pledge" (Deut. 24:6).	[ס] [[שנ' לא יחבל]] [ריחים ורכב]
[P]	Not the upper and lower millstone alone did they say,	[ע] לא]] ריחים ורכב בלבד אמרו
[Q]	but every thing with which one makes food for living (nepeš),	[פ] אלא בכל דבר שעושין בו אוכל נפש
[R]	as it is said: "For it is a life (nepeš) that he seizes as a pledge" (Deut. 24:6).	[צ] שנ' כי נפש הוא חובל

M9:13: After [C] N adds: ואם משכנו חייב להחזי' לו, "if he did distrain a pledge, he must return it" (attested in the Hamburg ms. of the Babli, attestations can also be found in commentaries; see Rabbinovicz, *DS*, 335; Lieberman, *TK*, 9, 300, n. 8). Epstein, *Nûsaḥ*, 969, argued that this line has been added on the basis of a *bāraîtāʾ* cited at B114b as corrected in a gloss attributed to R. Sheshet (the "corrected" version appears also at T10:8). In [E] KRLMPN all have ומחזיר (so also in the Florence, Rome B and Hamburg mss. of the Babli, and by various Rishonim [see the citations in *TYṬ*, *Mĕlʾeket šĕlomoh ad loc.*, and Rabbinovicz, *DS*, 335]); the variant ומניח, "and he leaves (deposits)" is attested in the Munich ms. of the Babli and other Babli traditions. A second hand has made two corrections in [B], one correcting a dittography, and the second inserting an omission. In addition, there are two corrections between [M] and [O]: one in the left hand margin of the text, and the second over an erasure in the next line. Although traces are visible underneath the correction, it is not clear from the photo-reproduction what this latter insertion in [N–O] replaces.

M10:1

[A]	The house and upper storey belonging to two people—	הבית והעליה של שנים [א]
[B]	that fell:	שנפלו [ב]
[C]	both split the wood and the stones and the earth.	שניהם חולקים בעצים ובאבנים ובעפר [ג]
[D]	They evaluate (lit. "see") which stones were most likely to have broken.	רואין אלו אבנים ראויות להישתבר [ד]
[E]	[If] one of them recognized some of his stones he takes them,	היה אחד מהן מכיר מקצת אבניו נוטל(ו)ין [ה]
[F]	and they are deducted from the tally.	ועולות לו מן החשבון [ו]

M10:2

[A]	The house and upper storey belonging to two people—	הבית והעליה של שנים [א]
[B]	[If] the upper storey was worn away,	ניפחתה העליה [ב]
[C]	and the owner of the house does not wish to fix it,	ואין בעל הבית רוצה לתקן [ג]
[D]	lo, the owner of the upper storey goes downstairs [and lives there] until he repairs the upper storey for him.	הרי בעל העליה יורד למטן עד שיתקן לו את העליה [ד]
[E]	R. Yose says: "The lower [resident] supplies the roofing [beams], and the upper supplies the plaster.	ר' יוסה או' התחתון נותן את תיקרא והעליון נותן את המעזיבה [ה]

M10:3

[A]	The house and the upper storey belonging to two people—	הבית והעליה שלשנים ((שנים)) [א]
[B]	that fell:	שנפלו [ב]
[C]	the owner of the upper storey told the owner of the house to build, but he [the owner of the house] does not want to,	אמ' בעל העליה לבעל הבית לבנות והוא אינו רוצה [ג]
[D]	lo, the owner of the upper storey builds the house,	הרי בעל העליה בונה את הבית [ד]
[E]	and lives in it until he [the owner of the house] gives him his outlay.	ויושב בתוכו עד שיתן לו את (( )) [י][צאותיו [ה]

M10:1: [D] supplements [A–C] with a rule that if it can be determined that the stones of one of the storeys were the ones that broke, the owner of that storey must take those, rather than simply dividing them. Similarly [E], if one party recognized his own stones he may take them. נוטל is clearly the correct reading in [D].

M10:2: של שנים [A] is omitted by Rashi *ad loc.* following the statement attributed to R. Ashi that in M10:2 the resident in upper storey was a tenant (B116b); cf. Tos. *s.v. Ha-bayît wě-ha-ʿaliyyâ* (B116b) who retain it. RLMPN all read יורד ודר, "goes down and lives" (N, inadvertently, ודר) in [D]. It is possible that the scribe of K left out ודר because of the similarity of letters in the two words.

[F]	R. Judah says: "But this one is dwelling in his fellow's [property], [and] must pay him a [rental] fee,	ר׳ יהודה או׳ אף זה דר לתוך שלחבירו צריך להעלות לו שכר	[ו]
[G]	"rather, the owner of the upper storey builds the house and the upper storey,	אלא בעל העליה בונה את הבית ואת העליה	[ז]
[H]	"and lives in the house until he gives him his outlay."	ויושב בבית עד שנותן לו את יצאותיו	[ח]

M10:4

[A]	And so too an olive press that was built in a rock, and there was another's garden on top of it,	וכן בית הבד שהוא בנוי בסלע וגינת אחר על גביו	[א]
[B]	and it became worn away,	וניפחת	[ב]
[C]	lo, the owner of the garden goes down,	הרי בעל הגנה יורד	[ג]
[D]	and plants below, until [the latter] makes a vault.	וזורע למטן עד שיעשה לבית בדו כיפים	[ד]
[E]	The wall and the tree that fell into the public domain—	הכותל והאילן שנפלו לרשות הרבים	[ה]
[F]	and did damage:	והיזיקו	[ו]
[G]	they are exempt from payment.	פטורין מלשלם	[ז]
[H]	They gave him time to remove the wall, and to cut down the tree, and they fell:	נתנו לו זמן לסתור את הכותל ולקוץ את האילן ונפלו	[ח]
[I]	during the time,	בתוך זמן	[ט]
[J]	he is exempt;	פטור	[י]
[K]	after that time,	לאחר זמן	[כ]
[L]	he is liable.	חייב	[ל]

M10:5

[A]	He who had a wall abutting the garden of his fellow and it fell:	מי שהיה כו(ו))תלו סמוך לגינת חבירו ונפל	[א]
[B]	he said to him: "Clear your stones,"	אמ׳ לו פנה את אבניך	[ב]
[C]	he said to him: "They are yours,"	אמ׳ לו היגיעוך	[ג]
[D]	one does not listen to him.	אין שומעין לו	[ד]

M10:3: The correction in [A] corrects a clear dittography. The correction in [D] may replace something like הוצאותיו, but what stood before the erasure is not clear. In any event יצאותיו is the form used in [H] and is attested in RLMPN. In [G] ומקרה את העליה is absent in K, but present in RLMPN. Although the sense of [G] is preserved without the words, it is possible that the omission in K is due to homoioteleuton. On the face of it, [H] reproduces the problem to which the tradition attributed to R. Judah [F] responded: The owner of the upper storey still lives in the lower storey rent-free. According to Rashi, *ad loc.*, the reason the owner of the upper storey needs to pay no fee is that "the one suffers no loss [the owner of the lower storey, who had no interest in rebuilding, receives a house], and the other receives no benefit [i.e., the owner of the upper storey, having built both, could just as easily live in the upper storey as in the lower]." Tos. *ad loc.*, suggest instead that [H] read בתוכה, "in it [i.e., in the upper storey]," instead of בבית, "in the house."

M10:4: L, like K, has פטורין מלשלם in [G], the subject of the verb (participle) being "the owners" (pl.). RMPN have the easier reading פטור מלשלם, in the singular, which fits somewhat better with [H, J, L], which all refer to a single owner.

[E]	[If] after he [the garden-owner] has accepted, he said to him here are your expenses, and I am taking what is mine,	משקבל עליו ואמ' לו הילך את יצאותך ואו(י)(ג)(ו)) נוטל את שלי	[ה]
[F]	one does not listen to him.	אין שומעין לו	[ו]
[G]	He who hires a worker—	השוכר את הפועל	[ז]
[H]	to work with him in hay and straw:	לעשות עמו בתבן ובקש	[ח]
[I]	he [the worker] said to him: "Give me my wage,"	אמ' לו תן לי שכרי	[ט]
[J]	he said to him: "Take from what you produced as your wage,"	אמ' לו ( ) טול מימה שעשיתה בשכרך	[י]
[K]	one does not listen to him;	אין שומעין לו	[כ]
[L]	[If] after he accepted he said to him: "Here are your wages, and I am taking what is mine,"	משקבל עליו אמ' לו הילך את שכרך ואני נוטל את שלי	[ל]
[M]	one does not listen to him.	אין שומעין לו	[מ]
[N]	One who is taking his dung out to the public domain:	המוציא זבלו לרשות הרבים	[נ]
[O]	the one taking out takes out, and the one putting dung [i.e., fertilizing] puts the dung.	המציא מוציא והמזבל מזבל	[ס]
[P]	One may not steep clay in the public domain,	אין שורין טיט ברשות הרבים	[ע]
[Q]	and one may not make bricks.	ולא לובנים ל[בנים]	[פ]
[R]	One may knead clay in the public domain,	גובלין טיט ברשות הרבים	[צ]
[S]	but not bricks.	אבל לא [[ל]]לבינים	[ק]
[T]	One who builds in the public domain—	הבונה ברשות הרבים	[ר]
[U]	the one bringing the stones brings, the builder builds,	המביא אבנים מביא [[ו]]הבונה בונה	[ש]
[V]	and if he does damage, he pays for what he has damaged.	ואם היזיק משלם מה שהיזיק	[ת]
[A']	R. Simeon b. Gamaliel says: "He may even prepare his work thirty days before [with no liability]."	רבן שמעון בן גמליאל אומ' אף מתקין הוא את מלאכתו לפני שלשים יום	[א']

M10:5: The scribal emendations in [E] correct a clear error (cf. [L]). There is a single character (filler?) between לו and טול in [J]. In [Q] the scribe has written only the first letter of לבנים, "bricks"; I have supplied the remainder on the basis of the other witnesses. According to the correction in [S] (which brings the text of K into line with that of RLMPN), [S] states that the clay that is permitted in [R] may not be used for bricks (according to *TY* this is because of the greater amount of time the clay must sit for the production of bricks). This is a possible reading of K without the correction as well. However, without the correction [R-S] might perhaps have a slightly different implication: one may knead clay, but not the material used for bricks (which, on the evidence of Rabbinic texts, need not necessarily be made of clay; see S. Krauss, *Talmudische Archäologie* [*Grundrisse der Gesamtwissenschaft des Judentums V*: Leipzig, 1911]. 1, 14–5), which may have a different method of preparation. On the word אף in [A'], see Epstein, *Nûsaḥ*, 1019. גמליאל [A'] appears to have been written גמליא', and subsequently corrected. For the

M10:6

[A]	Two gardens [on terraces] one above the other, and there are vegetables between them:	שתי גנות זו על גבי זו והירק בינתיים [א]
[B]	R. Meir says: "They belong to the upper";	ר' מאיר אומ' של עליון [ב]
[C]	R. Judah says: "They belong to the lower."	ור' יהודה אומ' שלתחתון [ג]
[D]	Said R. Meir: "What if the upper should want to remove his earth: there are no vegetables here!"	אמ' ר' מאיר ומה אם ירצה עליון ליטול את עפרו אין כאן ירק [ד]
[E]	Said R. Judah: "What if the lower should want to fill his garden: there are no vegetables here!"	אמ' ר' יהודה ומה אם ירצה התחתון למלאת גנתו עפר אין כאן ירק [ה]
[F]	Said R. Meir: "Inasmuch as neither can put off the other [along these lines], [consider] from whence these vegetables draw their sustenance!"	אמ' ר' מאיר וכי מאחר ששניהם יכולים למחות זה על ידי זה מנין ירק זה חייא [ו]
[G]	R. Simeon says: "Anything that the upper can reach out his hand and take, lo, this is his;	ר' שמעון או' כל שהעליון יכול לפשוט ידו וליטול הרי הוא שלו [ז]
[H]	"and the rest is the lower's."	והשאר שלתחתון [ח]

---

correction in [A] cf. M2:8 [E, F], M4:8 [A] and the notes thereto. My explanatory comment (in brackets) in [A'] follows Rashi and Maimonides *ad loc.*

M10:6: The form חייא in [F] is unusual.; cf. RL: חייה (L is pointed חַיָּיה; K has similar pointing); Mq: חיה; M: הייה; PN: היה (see also Rabbinovicz, *DS*, 357). Presumably, the forms in KRLMq (a Palestinian form of the sing. masc. participle of חיה?) stand before the forms in MPN, in which the problem of an unusual form has been avoided by "correcting" the text and replacing the verb in question with another, היה (see also *Měl'eket šělomoh ad loc.*).

✦ APPENDIX II ✦

Mishnah Tractate *Baba' Meṣi'a'* and Other "Tannaitic" Corpora

Throughout this study of *m. Baba' Meṣi'a'*, the focus has been on the Mishnah as an independent work that, by itself, reflects a particular world-view. Nevertheless, there is, in addition to the Mishnah, an extensive body of material that purports to be "Tannaitic" (i.e., its language is similar to that of Mishnaic Hebrew, and it cites as tradents individuals roughly contemporaneous with, or earlier than, the redaction of the Mishnah). For our purposes, this "Tannaitic" material falls into two categories: (1) the Tosepta and (2) the Halakhic midrashim (of particular relevance to this study of *m. Baba' Meṣi'a'* are the *Mekilta*, *Mekilta de-rašbi*, *Sipra*, and *Sipre* to Deuteronomy).[1] This appendix explores briefly both the question of the dependence of the Mishnah and the "Tannaitic" corpora upon one another (e.g., whether the texts not included in the Mishnah are dependent upon the Mishnah) and the implication of this material for our understanding of the redaction of the Mishnah against the background of a complex literary tradition. To the extent that it is possible to substantiate the claim that there was a body of material more or less contemporaneous

---

[1] A third category includes the *bāraîtôt* in the Babylonian and Palestinian Talmudim. These traditions are cited as fragments whose original context is uncertain. Thus, for instance, whether the Palestinian or Babylonian Talmud is citing from our Tosepta or midrashim when the wording is closely parallel is still subject to dispute (see, e.g., Epstein, *Siprût*, 245–6 [the Yerushalmi uses our Tosepta; the Babli an earlier version]; H. Albeck, *Introduction to the Talmud, Babli and Yerushalmi* [Hebrew] [Tel Aviv: Dvir, 1969], 63–7 [the Tosepta was not known to the redactors of the Talmudim]; for further bibliography and discussion of the dating of the Tosepta and midrashim see H. L. Strack, *Introduction to Talmud and Midrash*, ed. G. Stemberger, tr. M. Brokmuehl [Minneapolis: Augsburg-Fortress, 1992], 168, 174–5, 269, 272–3). Moreover, the *bāraîtôt* show the traces of the Amoraic Hebrew (MH2) (this is clearest in the case of the Babylonian Talmud, see D. Goodblatt, "The Babylonian Talmud," *ANRW* 2.19.2 [1974], 278, and bibliography thereto; for the Yerushalmi see B. Bokser, "An Annotated Bibliographical Guide to the Study of the Palestinian Talmud," *ANRW* 2.19.2 [1974], 176, and M. Moreshet, "Further Studies of the Language of the Hebrew Bārāytôt in the Babylonian and Palestinian Talmudim" [Hebrew], in M. Z. Kaddari ed., *Archive of the New Dictionary of Rabbinic Literature: Volume II* [Ramat Gan: Bar Ilan, 1974], 56–68). This material must therefore be studied in the context of both the redactional and the linguistic history of the Talmud, and is beyond the scope of the present project.

with the Mishnah and independent of it, it is also possible to begin to ask what makes the Mishnah unique within early Rabbinic tradition, and how it functioned as one text (and one textual community?) among others.

1. Tosepta.[2]

Because it is so extensive, and because it has such a close connection to *m. Baba' Meṣi'a'*, the Tosepta to *Baba' Meṣi'a'* demands special attention. Over all, the final form of the Tosepta follows the organization and structure of the Mishnah, showing that, as its name (*tôseptā', * "supplement") implies, it is a supplement to the Mishnah that post-dates the final redaction of the Mishnah. Indeed, much of the contents of *t. Baba' Meṣi'a'* glosses or supplements passages that appear in the Misnah. Thus, for example, T2:1–2 reads as follows:

T2:1

[A] R. Simeon b. Eleazar agrees in the case of vessels of trade that have been used[3] that he is obligated[4].
[B] And which are "vessels of trade"?
[C] Bunches of suspended (?)[5] needles and hooks, and strings of hatchets.
[D] And thus would R. Simeon b. Eleazar say: "All those [things] that they said: 'Lo, they are his,' when [is this the case]?
[E] "When he found them one by one, but if he found them two by two he is obligated to proclaim [them]."

T2:1

[A] And thus would R. Simeon b. Eleazar say: "One who saves from the mouth of the lion, or from the mouth of the wolf, or from the shore (?)[6] of the sea, or from the shore (?) of the river,

---

[2] For bibliography and discussion see Strack (ed. Stemberger), 1992, 167–81.

[3] Following the Schocken ms.: *še-ništāmmēš bā-hen*. The reading of the Vienna and Erfurt mss., *še-mistāmmēš* (*editio princeps*: *šmštmšw*), should mean "which one makes use of," here too referring to the use the owner has had of the object before it was lost. A *bāraîtā'* in the Babli (B24a) presents an analogue to this tradition, which is cast in terms of whether "the eye has sated itself" with respect to the lost object (i.e., whether the owner would be familiar enough with it to recognize and identify it). Recognition may be the issue in T2:1 as well (so Lieberman, *TK*, 9. 156), although the text of the *bāraîtā'* in the Babli may reflect specifically Babylonian Amoraic concerns (cf. the view attributed to R. Judah in the name of Samuel on B23b).

[4] Erfurt, Schocken mss., *editio princeps*: "he is obligated to proclaim [it]."

[5] Hebrew *bādê* (construct state). See Jastrow, s.v. *bd* V, who follows the gloss of the Babli, B24a, and translates "poles of peddlars for needles." The point here is that these are goods that are sold from bunches (and, as Lieberman *TK*, 9, 156, notes, are produced more or less uniformly) and hence, unlike the rule of T2:1 [A], one is not required to proclaim them.

[6] Here and in the next phrase "shore" translates *šûnîtô* (according to the Vienna ms. for the text of this passage see Lieberman, *TK*, 9, 157). Cf. *m. 'Ohal.*18:6: "And what is the *šûnît*? Any place that the sea rises forcefully (*bĕ-za'apô*)"; and see the literature cited by Lieberman, *TK*, 9, 157. Jastrow, sv. *šûnît*, "cliff, rocky bluff"; Sokoloff, s.v. *šûni*, "sea wall."

[B] "One who finds on the road (ʾisraṭiāʾ; cf. Latin *(via) strata*) or in the open place (*pĕlaṭayāʾ*; cf. Greek *plateia*),
[C] "lo, these are his,
[D] "for the owners have despaired of [finding] them."

These two passages present clear references to an antecedent text ("R. Simeon b. Eleazar agrees" T2:1 [A]; "All these [things] that they said" [D]), but that text does not appear in the Tosepta. The Mishnah (M2:1), however, does offer such a base text:

[A] Which found objects are his, and which is he obligated to proclaim?
[B] Which found objects are his?
[C] [If] he found scattered fruit or scattered money ....
[D] lo, these are his....

[H] R. Simeon ben Eleazar says: "All vessels of trade he is not required to proclaim."

Thus, T2:1 [A] qualifies the view of R. Simeon b. Eleazar as it is represented in M2:1 [H]; and T2:1 [D] may plausibly be taken to refer to M2:1 [B–D], and to explicitly cite M2:1[D]. T2:2 supplements the two preceding traditions attributed to R. Simeon b. Eleazar with a third on the subject of the acquisition of lost objects (introducing a principle, "despair" on the part of the owners, that is nowhere made explicit in the Mishnah in connection with lost objects).[7]

These two passages reflect the most common aspect of the Tosepta (at least of *t. Baba*ʾ *Meṣiʿa*ʾ) with respect to the Mishnah: that of glossing[8] and supplementing[9]

---

[7] See above, Chapter III, n. 77.

[8] I distinguish between glosses and supplements by using the former term to refer to examples where the Tosepta either cites and comments upon what appears to be our Mishnah, or in which there is a close paraphrase of the Mishnah. See, for example, the following (I include line-references to the edition of Lieberman for convenience): T1:2, ll. 3–6 (M1:1–2; extending the ruling of the Mishnah); T2:20, ll. 42–5 (M2:7 [E–H]); T2:22, ll. 52–4 (M2:8 [D–E]); T2:28, ll. 69–71 (M2:10 [J–K]); T2:29–30, ll. 75–9 (M2:11); T3:5, ll. 10–4 (M3:3–5; cf., however, the discussion in section II.B.2); T3:12, ll. 40–1 (M3:12 [A–B]); T3:17–9, ll. 59–66 (M4:5; cf. *m. Kel.* 12:7, and section III.A.1); T3:20–1, ll. 67–71 (M4:6); T3:24, ll. 75–8 (M4:9 [G–H]); T4:2, ll. 2–5 (M5:2 [D]); T5:13, ll. 30–3 (M5:5 [E]); T5:14, ll. 35–8 (M5:6 [A–C]); T6:8–9, ll. 21–5 (M5:8 [A–B]; see Lieberman, *TK*, 9, 237–8); T6:16, ll. 51–2 (M5:11 [B–C]; note, however, that where the Mishnah uses *sôpēr*, the Tosepta uses *liblār*; cf. the use of *liblarios*, from Latin, *librarius*, in Greek documents from the Judean Desert [*P. Babatha* 15.39 (and the note thereto, p. 64), 17.43, 18.37, 20.45, 21.33 (only partially legible), and 22.39]); T7:19, ll. 77–8 (M6:7 [D–E]); T8:13–5, ll. 36–44 (M7:8); T8:15, ll. 44–9 (M7:9 [I–K]; see Lieberman, *TK*, 9, 266 to l. 44); T8:20–1, ll. 57–64 (M8:1); T8:27, ll. 90–1 (M8:6); T9:31–2, ll. 75–8, 80–2 (M9:9, 8); T10:5–6, ll. 11–8 (M9:12 [G–J]); T11:1, ll. 1–3 (M10:1); T11:7, ll. 22–6 (M10:4 [E–L]).

[9] Supplementation through passages that may be alternative formulations of material found in the Mishnah will be discussed presently. Included below are some examples where *t. B.*

what appears to be the Mishnah. To that extent, at least, the Tosepta seems to reflect a post-Mishnaic "commentary" on the Mishnah.[10] However, I use the rather indefinite "what appears to be the Mishnah" and "seems to reflect" because, in fact, the relationship between the Mishnah and the Tosepta is quite complicated. In the first place, there are numerous passages that reflect alternative formulations to the material in the Mishnah, which cannot be accounted for solely as later commentary. Compare, for instance, T3:7 and T3:8 with M3:6. The Mishnah reads as follows:

[A] One who deposits produce with his fellow—
[B] even if it is perishing, lo, let this one not touch it.
[C] R. Simeon b. Gamaliel says: "Let him sell [it] before the court,
[D] "because of [the principle of] returning a lost object to its owners."

The two passages from the Tosepta both show distinct linguistic connections with the Mishnah (verbal parallels with the Mishnah are in italics):

T3:7	T3:8
[A] *One who deposits produce with his fellow—*	[A] "*One who deposits produce with his fellow—*
	[B] "and they rotted:
	[C] "wine and it went sour, oil and it went rancid,
[B] *Even if it is perishing, let him not touch it.*	[D] "*even if it is perishing, let him not touch it,*"
	[E] the words of R. Meir.

Meṣ. presents material that does not explicitly echo the Mishnah, but addresses legal issues raised in the Mishnah: T1:15, ll. 34–6 (cf. M1:6–8, as these issues are understood in T1:5–9); T2:24–7, ll. 61–7 (cf. M2:9–10); T2:31–2, ll. 79–82 (M2:11, and cf. *m. Hor.* 3:7); T3:1, ll. 1–3 (possibly amplifying M3:2, in which a renter transfers the object to another; cf. Y3:3 [9a]); T3:28–9 ll. 101–3 (cf. M4:12); T4:11–3, ll. 34–9 (M5:4 [A]); T4:14–22, ll. 38–70 (M5:4 [B]); T4:23, ll. 70–4 (cf. M5:1 [I–L], 9); T4:24–5, ll. 74–6 (cf. M5:4 [D]); T5:1–2, ll. 1–6 (cf. M5:4–5; see the notes to M5:4 in Appendix I); T5:15–20, ll. 39–51 (cf. M5:6 [F–G]); T6:10, ll. 25–6 (cf. M5:8); T7:2–7, ll. 16–39 (cf. M6:1, 2); T7:9, ll. 46–8 (cf. M6:2, 3, 5); T7:10–2, ll. 51–7 (cf. M6:3, 5); T8:29, ll. 107–10 (cf. M8:7); T9:7–8, ll. 16–9 (cf. M9:1–10); T9:22–30, ll. 57–75 (M9:1–9); 10:3, ll. 6–8 (cf. M9:12 [A–F]); T10:7, ll. 18–20 (cf. M9:12).

[10] For the strongest formulation of the the view of the Tosepta's dependence on the Mishnah and its significance see, e.g., J. Neusner, *The Tosepta: An Introduction* (*South Florida Studies in the History of Judaism* 147: Atlanta: Scholars, 1992), xviii–xvix, xxii–xxv. It should be noted, however, that here as elsewhere Neusner distinguishes between material in the Tosepta of varying degrees of closeness to or dependence on the text of the Mishnah. Cf. S. Friedman, "The Primacy of Tosefta in Mishnah-Tosefta Parallels—Shabbat 16, 1: *kol kitbê qôdeš*" [Hebrew], *Tarbiz* 62 (1993), 313–38, whose interest is in locating texts in which the Tosepta is primary.

Appendix II: Mishnah and Tannitic Corpora 315

[C] Therefore, the householder may make them tithes for produce in another place.

[D] *R. Simeon b. Gamaliel says:* "In [a case where] they are perishing, *let him sell [it] before a court,*

[E] "*because* he is like one *returning a lost object to its owners.*"

[F] And the Sages say: "He values it as money *in a court,*

[G] "[and] *he sells it* to others but he may not sell it to himself."

Either of these two formulations might arguably have constituted an expansion of the Mishnah (although in the case of T3:8 we would have had to account for the differences in the attributions between M3:6 and T3:8; cf. Chapter II.D.2, above). However, unless we suppose that the author of the Tosepta chose to rework M3:6 twice (and in rather different ways), T3:7–8 taken together, amd T3:8 in particular, suggest that other material, not included in the Mishnah but going over the same ground in similar language, was available for use in the Tosepta.[11]

The use of supplementary or alternatively formulated material is not limited to individual traditions, but to larger clusters of traditions as well. The use of nominative absolute ("article + participle") series in the Tosepta offers a case in point.[12]

---

[11] Precisely because the language and treatment of legal problems in the Tosepta are so similar to the Mishnah, true "alternative" material is difficult to differentiate from glosses. For possible examples, in addition to the preceding, see, e.g., T2:3–9, ll. 6–18 (M2:1–2; T2:3 disagrees with M2:2 in the case of jars of oil or wine); T2:15, ll. 30–33 (cf. M2:5; M4:7 [H]); T2:16, ll. 33–4 (cf. M2:7 [A–D]); T2:17, ll. 34–7 (cf. M2:6); T3:25, ll. 90–5 (cf. M4:11 [A–C]; what was anonymous in the Mishnah is attributed to R. Judah and the case of the proselyte is handled somewhat differently); T4:2, ll. 9–12 (cf. M5:3 [E–G]); T4:5, ll. 18–20 (cf. M5:2 [A–B]); T4:11, ll. 31–5 (cf. M5:4 [A–C]); T6:16, ll. 44–50 (cf. M5:7 [K–L]); T8:7, ll. 14–21 (cf. M7:2–3); T8:19, ll. 54–6 (cf. M7:10 [E–G]); T10:3–4, ll. 6–11 (cf. M9:12). (For T1:5–9, cf. n.15 below. See also T3:13–4, ll. 42–7, in which a different text for M4:1 [A] and apparently [F] is presupposed, and in which R. Simeon is said to agree with the rule that "a garment acquires a golden *dînār,* against M4:2 [E] and T3:16 [see further the note to M4:1 in Appendix I, and section III.A.1].)

[12] For these series see T4:11–3, ll. 31–9, *ha-môšîb 'et ḥăbērô* ... (for the formula cf. M5:4 [A]; T4:11 has an Ushan dispute, including R. Judah); T4:14–22, ll. 38–70, *ha-nôtēn māʿôt lĕ-ḥăbērô* ... (for the formula cf. M5:4 [B]; T4:18 has two statements attributed to R. Judah); T5:7–12, ll. 15–30, *ha-šām bĕhēmâ* ... (cf. M5:4 [E]; attributions to Symmakhos [L] in T5:7, 8 [cf. M6:5 [I–J]], one, T5:17, in dispute with R. Yose); T5:22–6, ll. 58–67, *ha-malweh 'et ḥăbērô bĕ-ribbît* (one [double] attribution to R. Meir, T5:22; T5:23, which does not share the opening formula, includes a statement attributed to R. Simeon b. Gamaliel); T7:1–12, ll. 1–57, *ha-sôkēr 'et ha-pôʿēl/pôʿalîm* (T7:1, 3, 4, 5, 7, 8)/*ḥămôr* (T7:7 [l. 39], 10, 11, 12)/*sĕpînâ* (T7:2) (for the formula cf. M6:1–5; 7:1–2; attributions: R. Dosa [L], T7:1 [for this dating of R. Dosa, see W. Bacher, *'Aggādôt ha-tannā'îm,* tr. A. Z. Rabbinowitz, 2 ed. (Dvir: Tel Aviv, 1928), vol. 2, pt. 2, p. 84]; R. Simeon b. Eleazar [L], T7:7; Symmakhos in the name of R.

These series tend to address cases not specifically referred to in the Mishnah. It is tempting, in light of the discussion of the series in *m. Babaʾ Meṣiʿaʾ* (above, section II.B.2), to see this as further confirmation that such a series on contracts was utilized by the redactor of *m. Babaʾ Meṣiʿaʾ* as a source, and to see in the series in the Tosepta analogues to or extensions of the same series used in the Mishnah.[13] Nevertheless, the *ha-ḥôkēr* series in T9:10–8 may imply otherwise. While some of this material may supplement chapter 9 of *m. Babaʾ Meṣiʿaʾ*, other passages in this series may well be reworkings of material in the Mishnah (compare, e.g., T9:11 and M9:3; T9:13 and M9:5).[14] If that is so, then the possibility must be allowed that at least some of the series in *t. Babaʾ Meṣiʿaʾ* have been constructed using the Mishnah as a model.

The relationship of *t. Babaʾ Meṣiʿaʾ* to *m. Babaʾ Meṣiʿaʾ* is further complicated by the fact that the Tosepta incorporates material that has no direct relationship to the subject matter of the Mishnah at all, but is included (presumably) for reasons particular to the redaction of the Tosepta.[15] The material that does not directly refer to the Mishnah (whether because it supplements, presents alternative formulations, or deals with material that is not in the Mishnah) cannot be assigned one date. On the one hand, there is at least one "alternative" passage that seems to reflect later (Amoraic) concerns, and that appears also in statements attributed to Amoraim.[16] On the

---

Meir, T7:10); T8:30–3, ll. 111–23 (for the formula cf. M8:6–9); T9:1–8, ll. 1–19, *ha-śôkēr śādeh* ... (reading *ha-śôkēr* in T9:7 as in the Schocken ms. (?); for the noun *ḥākôr* as referring to monetary rent, cf. M9:6 [F–G]; the Tosepta here includes one attribution to R. Simeon b. Gamaliel, T9:5, which is not part of the series); T9:10–8, ll. 23–51, *ha-mĕqabbēl śādeh* ...(for the formula cf. M9:1–10; attributions: R. Judah, 9:10; R. Simeon b. Gamaliel, T9:18); T9:22–30, ll. 57–75, *ha-ḥôkēr* (for the reading *ha-ḥôkēr* in T9:26 [according to the Schocken ms. and the *editio princeps*] and T9:29 see Lieberman, *TK*, 9, 291–3, to ll. 65–6 and 71–3); T9:31–2, ll. 75–81, *ha-mĕqabbēl śādeh* ... (cf., again, M9:1–10).

[13] This is partly borne out by the use of attributions in these series; see the preceding note. A fuller study of these series will also have to take into account places in which the Tosepta series seem to conflict with the assumed rule in the Mishnah, such as T7:7, in which the rule regarding *angareia* differs from that of M6:3 [F–H].

[14] Given the number of times in this series that the reference to customary practice occurs (T9:10, 11, 14, 18; all four invoke the formula *ʾēn mĕšannîn mi-minhag ha-mĕdînâ*, "one does not differ from the local custom"), it is not impossible that this series is dependent in part upon (and has consciously amplified) M9:1 as well.

[15] See. e.g., T1:10–2, ll. 21–9; T1:13, ll. 29–32; T1:16–7, ll. 36–50; T2:28, ll. 67–8 (if the general rule that follows in ll. 68–9 similarly applies to an obligation to prevent inadvertent damage to the property of another, that rule should also be grouped here); T2:28, ll. 71–4; T2:33, ll. 82–3; T3:9, ll. 23–5; T3:11, ll. 35–40 (cf., however, M3:7 [I]); T3:22–23, ll. 71–4 (for ll. 74–5 see Lieberman, *TK*, 9, 183, and the *bāraîtāʾ*, B51b); T4:7–9, ll. 21–8; T4:10, ll. 29–31; T5:21–6, ll. 51–67; T6:14, ll. 36–8; T6:15, ll. 42–4; T7:13–14, ll. 57–62; T7:16–7, ll. 66–72; T8:10–2, ll. 29–36; T8:25–6, ll. 83–90; T8:28, ll. 100–7; T9:5, ll. 12–3; T10:1, ll 1–2. See also T1:20–1, ll. 58–64, which offers an alternative formulation of *m. B. Bat.* 10:6, but is attached here because the immediate context deals with documents.

[16] See for instance, T1:5 (corresponding to M1:6; T1:5 is part of a series [T1:5–9] that is closely related to M1:6–8, but which presupposes a different list of documents, and so may

other hand, it is sometimes (although rather rarely) possible to suggest that the Mishnah presupposes material preserved in the Tosepta.[17]

---

not be a reworking of the Mishnah, but in fact may be based on an alternative formulation). Y1:6 [8a] cites the view of the Amora R. Eleazar that "If the borrower admits, lo, let this one [the finder] return it [to the lender]." This is precisely the clause that appears in T1:5 (in the view of R. Meir) and the equivalent appears repeatedly in T1:6–9. Whatever the relationship between the Tosepta and the Yerushalmi in general, here the Yerushalmi does not appear to be aware of the T1:5 in its entirety: the Yerushalmi quotes a *bāraîtā'* mentioning only a view attributed to R. Meir (*tĕnî bĕ-šēm r. mē'îr*) that deals only with the question of the effectiveness of documents without explicit liens but shows no knowledge that the distinction raised by R. Eleazar (i.e., whether or not the borrower confirmed the debt) is to be attributed to R. Meir. That distinction is only raised—and rejected—as an Amoraic opinion. (According to the text of the Leiden ms. and the *editio princeps*, R. Meir allows that, like T1:5, documents without explicit lien clauses can only be used to exact payment from non-alienated property [however, *Pĕnê mošeh, ad loc.*, understood this citation as implying that documents with explicit lien clauses too are limited to exaction from non-alienated property and therefore deemed this problematic; so too, apparently, Lieberman, *TK*, 9, 144, to l. 12, who refers to this version as corrupt]; in the Escorial ms. the views of R. Meir and the Sages are apparently reversed [cf., however, Lieberman, *Yerushalmi Neziqin*, 130, to ll. 66–8, who suggests that the Yerushalmi be emended to juxtapose two versions of R. Meir's view].) By contrast to the Yerushalmi, a close analogue to T1:5 is cited at B13b to resolve an Amoraic debate between R. Yohanan and R. Eleazar (B13b), as well as Samuel (B13a), about precisely the same issue: whether or not the dispute in M1:6 between R. Meir and the Sages refers to a case in which the borrower confirmed the debt (and this issue is given considerable anonymous discussion at B12b–14a). Hence Lieberman, *TK*, 9, 144, saw T1:5 as a Babylonian *bāraîtā'*. Perhaps, in light of the fact that in both the Babli and Yerushalmi Palestinian figures are said to refer to this issue, we should see T1:5 as reflecting Amoraic (even if Palestinian) tradition.

The view about "despair [on the part of] the owners" attributed to R. Simeon b. Eleazar, referred to above (T2:1 [D]), may reflect Amoraic concerns as well (cf. Chapter III.B.1). For further examples from elsewhere in the Tosepta see Epstein, *Siprût*, 252–3.

[17] I have not found convincing examples in *t. B. Meṣ*. Cf. S. Friedman, *Talmud Arukh: BT Bava Meẓi'a VI, Commentary* [Hebrew] (Jerusalem: JTSA, 1990), 225–7 who suggests that T7:10 has been modified in the formulation of M6:5 (cf. the discussion of M6:5 in Chapter II.B.2); *idem*, 1993, 313–8; and the arguments of B. De Vries, *Meḥqārîm bĕ-siprût ha-talmûd* (Jerusalem: Mossad Harav Kook, 1968), 15–20 (M4:10 and T3:16), 20–5 (M6:1 and T7:1, assuming that R. Dosa in T7:1 is Yabnean [cf. n. 11 above]); also 51–3 (M6:6–7 and T7:15, although De Vries himself admits that T7:15 could easily have been taken as glossing the Mishnah, pp. 52–3). One possible example may be M4:11 [A–C] and T3:26:

M4:11	T3:26
[A] One does not mix produce with produce (for sale)—	[A] One does not mix produce with produce (for sale)—
[B] even new [produce] with new—	[B] even new [produce] with new, or old with old—
[C] it goes without saying new [produce] with old.	[C] and it goes without saying new with old and old with new.

What this implies is that *t. Babaʾ Meṣiʿaʾ*, like the Mishnah, is constructed out of source material in order to supplement *m. Babaʾ Meṣiʿaʾ*. In practice, it may be difficult or impossible to isolate strata of the Tosepta that necessarily predate the redaction of the Mishnah. Nevertheless, the incorporation into the Tosepta of material that cannot merely be explained as later commentary is important, because it draws attention to the likelihood that there was more material available to the redactors of the Mishnah (at least of *m. Babaʾ Meṣiʿaʾ*) than that which appears in the Mishnah alone. To that extent we are justified in asking whether the final form of the Mishnah does not reflect conscious (as well as unconscious) choices of what to say and how to say it.

2. Halakhic midrashim.[18]

The relationship of the Halakhic midrashim to the Mishnah is more difficult to trace than that of the Tosepta. Unlike the Tosepta, which is organized around the Mishnah the midrashic texts are organized both formally and stylistically around verses in Scripture, and it is the Biblical text, at least on the surface, that provides the occasion for the midrashic comments and the context for the presence or absence of

	[D] Even [if he had produce that sells at] a *sĕʾâ* to the *dînār*, and [at] a *sĕʾâ* to a *dînār* and a *tĕrîsît* (cf. Latin *tressis*, a three-as coin),
	[E] let him not mix them and sell them at a *sĕʾâ* to the *dînār*.
	[F] One does not mix new wine with new or old with old, and it goes without saying new with old or old with new,
	[G] nor harsh [wine] with mild,
[D] Truly, in the case of wine they permitted one to mix harsh with mild because it improves it.	[H] and R. Judah permits harsh with mild because it improves it.
	[I] And thus would R. Judah say: "One kind that improves its fellow is permitted; two kinds that improve one is prohibited.

T3:26 [A–D] may plausibly be taken as expanding upon, and adding specificity to, M4:11 [A–B]. The immediate context suggests this as well, since what follows in T3:27 seems clearly to gloss M4:11 [E] ("One does not mix wine sediments [M4:11 [E]] .... How?... Even when they said: 'He gives him his sediments' [M4:11 [E]] ...."; see Lieberman, *TK*, 9, 187). However, what appears in M4:11 [D] as an abrupt note is rather clearer in T3:26. Is it possible that M4:11 [C] is the result of the abridgement of a fuller (if redundant) source reflected in T3:26 [F–H]? If so, that "source," as it appears in the Tosepta, occurs in a context that itself may have been reworked in terms of the Mishnah.

[18] For bibliography and discussion see Strack (ed. Stemberger), 1992, 269–99.

material. Hence, for instance, if a midrashic text engaged in exegesis of verses relevant to the topic of the Mishnah does not appear close to the Mishnah, it is not clear to what extent this may reflect a pointed relationship (e.g., conscious ignoring by author, redactor, or tradents of one text, of the other text) or a non-relationship (e.g., different schools with different traditions, or different texts pursuing different questions). Even the citation of non-exegetical traditions, frequently precisely or closely paralleled in the Mishnah—perhaps the best reason for seeing these collections as post-Mishnaic—do not in every case refer to the Mishnah.[19] Hence, exclusive focus on the evidence for the relationship of these Midrashic collections in their present form to our Mishnah may obscure what, from the point of view of both literary and social history, is the more important phenomenon: the existence of multiple forms of expression that, for all their commonalities, reflect multiple agendas.[20]

Among the midrashim, the *Mekilta* (and the *Mekilta de-rašbi*) offers the most extensive material for comparison to *m. Baba' Meṣiʿa'*. Strikingly, the relationship with the Mishnah is uneven, and depends upon the section of the *Mekilta*.[21] Although various pericopae of *m. Baba' Meṣiʿa'* regarding depositaries are manifestly dependent upon exegesis of Exodus 22:6–14 (see Chapter II.A.1 above), the *Mekilta* on these verses (*Nĕzîqîn* 15–6, pp. 298–307) overlaps remarkably slightly with *m. Baba' Meṣiʿa'*.[22] Strikingly, none of the material brought with an explicit citation formula derives from *m. Baba' Meṣiʿa'*.[23] The *Mekilta* certainly presupposes certain

---

[19] For citations (with formulae such as *mi-kā'n 'āmrû* or *mi-kā'n 'attâ 'ōmēr*) see Epstein, *Nûsaḥ*, 728–51; see further E. Z. Melamed, *The Relationship between the Halakhic Midrashim and the Mishna and Tosefta* [Hebrew] (Jerusalem, 1968); see further the discussion in *idem*, *An Introduction to Talmudic Literature* [Hebrew] (Jerusalem, 1973), 233–58. (On the basis of such citations S. Lieberman, *Siphre Zutta (The Midrash of Lydda)* [Hebrew] [New York: JTSA, 1968], 11–64 [see, already, Epstein, *Nûsaḥ*, 739–46], that *Sipre Zut.* cites a different mishnah collection.)

[20] See, e.g., the brief comments in D. W. Halivni, *Midrash, Mishnah and Gemara: The Jewish Predilection for Justified Law* (Cambridge: Harvard, 1986), 60–1.

[21] For the possibility of isolating sources based on attributions in the *Mekilta* see (the somewhat obscure) discussion in Epstein, *Siprût*, 580–1 (following 572–80), and J. Neusner, *A History of the Jews in Babylonia* (*Studia Post Biblica* VI: Leiden: Brill, 1965–70), 192–6. Both suggest a special connection between tractates *Nĕzîqîn* and *Pisḥā'*, in contrast (for our purposes) to *Kaspā'*. To some extent this is borne out by the connection with *m. B. Meṣ.* as well (compare *Nĕzîqîn* 15–6 with *Kaspa'* 19, 20, for which see below).

[22] A similar lack of connection may be argued for M4:10 and *Mek. Nĕzîqîn* 18 (ed. Horovitz-Rabin, p. 311), which shares with M4:10 the bare assumption that there is *hônāyâ* in connection with both words and money (p. 311, ll. 3–4). The entire Mishnaic construct of recision of sale for over- or under-charge (M4:3–10) is absent in the *Mekilta*. Exposition of what the Mishnah calls "verbal *hônāyâ*" is restricted in the *Mekilta* to the case of the proselyte (following Ex. 22:20: "... and the *gēr* shall you not oppress ..."), and is formulated rather differently than M4:10 [D–E] (cf. T3:25, for still another formulation).

[23] *Mek. Nĕzîqîn* 15, p. 299, l. 1 (cf. *m. Šebu.* 6:6); p. 301, l. 10 (cf. *m. Šebu.* 6:1); p. 302, ll. 2, 8 (cf. *m. Sanh.*. 1:1 [without the view of R. Judah the Patriarch cited in l. 9]; *t. Sanh.* 1:1; *t. Šebu.* 3:8, and see Epstein, *Nûsaḥ*, 738); *Nĕzîqîn* 16, p. 304, l. 6 (*m. Šebu.* 7:1); 304, l. 7 (cf.

principles that are also present in the Mishnah: that liability of "reaching out the hand" (šĕlîḥût yād) arises when the depositary made use of it only for "for his needs" (lĕ-sorĕkô);[24] that the liabilities of paid and unpaid depositaries are to be distinguished;[25] that loss (ʾabēdâ) is treated as equivalent to theft;[26] and that borrowers assume liability only when the object has entered their possession and are not liable for damages that occur with the owner present.[27] Yet, precisely because these are basic to the Rabbinic construction of civil law they need not imply that the Mekilta has utilized the Mishnah.[28]

Two units of material of this portion of the *Mekilta* require further discussion. The first involves the Hillelite-Shammaite dispute over whether the depositary is liable for intention alone (cf. M3:12 [E–G]). The *Mekilta* (*Nĕzîqîn* 15, p. 300, ll. 12–5) reads as follows:

[1] "That he did not reach out his hand to the work of his fellow" (Ex. 22:7):
[2] ["Reaching out"] for his need.
[3] You say it [Scripture refers to use] for his need?
[4] Perhaps it [refers to use] only for its (?) need and not for its (?) need?[29]

---

t. B. Qam. 1:1; and cf. *Mek. Nĕzîqîn* 12, p. 290, ll. 8–14). Beyond the prominence of material analogous to *m. Šebû.*, it is striking that only one of the citations with near parallels in the Mishnah (*Mek. Nĕzîqîn* 16, p. 304, l. 6) is sufficiently close to be a citation of the Mishnah (and this is a brief rule that could also be cited from elsewhere); the others differ from the Mishnah and may presuppose a different context than the Mishnah.

[24] *Mek. Nĕzîqîn* 15, p. 300, ll. 11, 12–5; 16, p. 304, ll. 1–5 (the text of these passages is difficult; see the apparatus of Horovitz, pp. 300, 304, and below, nn. 29–30); cf. M3:9.

[25] *Mek. Nĕzîqîn* 16, pp. 304, l. 8–305, l. 2; p. 307, ll. 1–8; cf. M7:8 [E, G]. See also *Mek. Nĕzîqîn* 15, p. 301, ll. 4–8 ("Scripture comes to distinguish between depositaries"), without specifying what distinction is implied.

[26] *Mek. Nĕzîqîn* 16, p. 305, ll. 3–5; cf. M3:1 [B]; M7:8 [G]. The formulaic "I have only theft [i.e., from Ex. 22:11, "And if it should be stolen ..."], whence [do I know] loss?" (ʾên lî ʾelāʾ ... minayin) asks for the derivation of a known rule. (E. Z. Melamed and, apparently, Epstein treated this as a citation formula: see Melamed's addenda to Epstein, *Siprût*, 739–40; the Epstein, Melamed edition of *Mekilta de-rašbi*, p. xxx; and Epstein's own listing of this formula, *Nûsaḥ*, 747. All these relate to *Mekilta de-rašbi*, but the same should apply to the other texts.)

[27] *Mek. Nĕzîqîn* 16, p. 306, ll. 10, 15–6; cf. M8:1, 3. The presence of the owner as removing liability is explicit.

[28] Since the Mishnah sometimes reflects further developments on these themes that are not dealt with in the *Mekilta* (e.g., M3:9: whether the owner designated a place and whether the object broke while in the hands of the depositary; M8:1, 3: in what way the owner is "with it/ him" (ʿimô) [M8:1]; the transfer of possession through agents of the owner or borrower [M8:3]), one might also argue that the Mekilta here is more "primitive" and therefore preserves the source from which the Mishnah is drawn. Nevertheless, these conceptions are basic and need not show literary dependence.

[29] The question marks reflect uncertainty as to whether to read lĕ-sorĕkāh ("its need") or lĕ-sorĕkô ("his need") (see the variants and notes by Horovitz, Rabin, ll. 11ff.). Nor is what is meant here clear. Perhaps what is at issue is use of the object in a way that does benefit the

[5] Therefore Scripture teaches (*talmûd lômar*): "For every matter of transgression" (Ex. 22:8).
[6] For the house of Shammai obligate [the depositary] for the thought of the mind (*lēb*) as for the deed,
[7] as it is said "For every matter of transgression;"
[8] and the house of Hillel only obligate from the moment he has reached out his hand.
[9] Therefore it is said: "That he did not reach out his hand to the work of his fellow:"
[10] ["Reaching out"] for his need.[30]

Formally, the citation of the Bible with the formula *še-neʾemar* ("as it is said" [7]) is typical of passages in the style of the Mishnah.[31] This, in and of itself, should raise the possibility that the *Mekilta* here quotes another text. The force of [1–5] is that "For every matter of transgression" (Ex. 22:8) specifically implies that that "transgression" consists of unauthorized use for the depositary's own benefit. The point of [6–10] seems to be to support this conclusion with the citation of a known "Houses" dispute ("*For* the house of Shammai obligate ..., but the house of Hillel only obligate ..." [6, 8]), on the assumption that it is the Hillelite view that is to be followed.[32] If the *Mekilta* quotes a "mishnaic" text here, however, it does not quote (or even paraphrase) M3:12 directly: to the extent that the "mishnaic" form is retained from source material, it is a source that attached the dispute to Scriptural verses that is presupposed. However, no verses appear in the Mishnah.[33] Whether the *Mekilta* quotes an "early" or "late" tradition here seems ultimately insoluble, but the possibility that a post-Mishnaic development is being quoted should be considered.[34]

---

depositary, but that is for the good of the object. See, e.g., T2:22, which apparently permits the use of lost objects [and this is theoretically extended afterwards to deposits] in a way that will not damage them. Unless we take the Tosepta to be in fundamental disagreement with M2:8 (and this remains a possibility; in that case, M2:8 permits "use" only when it is required for the object itself), perhaps we should interpret M2:8 [E–F] in this manner (cf. M2:8 [A], which may be taken as permitting one to read a found book since the finder must roll it anyway [B]).

[30] Reading *lĕ-ṣorĕkô* here (cf. M.Friedman (*ʾîš šālôm*), *Mĕkiltāʾ dĕ-rabbî yišmāʿēl ʿim pēruš mēʾîr ʿayyîn* [Vienna, 1870], 91b n. 25; J. Z. Lauterbach, *Mekilta de-Rabbi Ishmael* [Philadelphia: JPS, 1935], 3, 117, l. 55).

[31] See, e.g., Halivni, 1986, 34.

[32] Following the Hillelite view, Ex. 22:8 does not obligate the depositary for intention alone, but rather for an act, much like [1–5]. However, if Horovitz, p. 300, l. 4 (note) (see also Lieberman, *Yerushalmi Neziqin*, 144–5 and n. 18), is correct that the expression "come and swear to me that you did not have it in your mind (*libbĕkā*) to sell them" (*Mek. Nĕzîqîn* 15, p. 300, l. 4) presupposes the Shammaite view about intention, the assumption that the Hillelite view is correct is not inevitable in the *Mekiltāʾ*.

[33] See the note to M3:12 in Appendix I. Cf. Epstein, *Nûsaḥ*, 738, who lists this under the rubric of citations of the Mishnah (but notes that it is in "different language").

[34] Cf. Y3:13 (9b); *y. Šebu.* 8:1 (38c), in which the attachment to verses is carried out anonymously and in Aramaic, suggesting a late formulation; in B44a this is cited as a *bāraîtāʾ*.

The second passage relates to the conditions under which the loss or damage to an animal due to attack by wild beasts (M7:9 [A–F, H]) or brigands (M7:9 [G, K]), or to death "according to its manner" (kĕ-darkāh, M7:10 [A–E]) is deemed ʾônes (in the terminology of the Mishnah). Here the Mishnah seems to reflect an underlying exegesis of Exodus 22:9 ("... and it dies, or it is broken, or it is taken captive ...") that is also attested in the *Mekilta*:[35]

[1] "and it dies,"
[2] that its death be at the hands of heaven;
[3] "or it is broken,"
[4] that a beast broke it,
[5] "or it was taken captive,"
[6] that brigands took it captive.

Granting this fact, it is certainly possible (although not inevitable) that the Mishnah here is dependent upon a midrashic source preserved in the *Mekilta*. Even assuming that this is so, however, whether or not M7:9–10 depends upon the larger context of the *Mekilta* in its present form remains difficult to decide. It is possible that when the Mishnah considers how many dogs or wolves qualify as ʾônes (unavoidable accident), and what role the actions of the "depositaries" play in their own liability, it is developing the statement attributed to R. Ishmael[36] in the *Mekilta* that: "there is a tearing (tĕrēpâ [i.e., by wild animals]) that he pays and a tearing that he does not pay."[37] On the other hand, this passage in the *Mekilta*, in which R. Eliezer (in agreement with R. Aqiba) defines violent death or capture that could have been avoided "as a kind of theft," that is, for which the paid depositary is liable but an unpaid depositary is not, may go against the basic notion of ʾônes in M7:9–10 [D].[38] Arguably, this might mean that the redactor of the Mishnah used, but knowingly differed from, a text extant in the *Mekilta*. In fact, however, beyond the definitions of "death," "breaking," and "capture," there is little unambiguous evidence of knowledge and borrowing between the *Mekilta* and the Mishnah. It seems more likely that

---

[35] *Mek. Nĕzîqîn* 16 (Horovitz-Rabin, p. 303, ll. 4–5). For ʾones in M7:9–10 see the note to M7:9 in Appendix I. In context, M7:9–10 does not gloss Scripture, but rather the Scriptural terminology in M7:8 [G]. (See also Sections II.A.1, n. 34; II.C.1, n. 105; III.B.2, nn. 102, 104.)

[36] So, the Oxford ms. and the parallel in *Yalqût šimʿônî* (see the variants to Horovitz, Rabin, p. 303, l. 10); so also Friedman (ʾîš šālôm), 92b, n.

[37] If so, M7:9–10 does not appear to reflect the explicit development this rule is given below in *Mek. Nĕzîqîn* 16, p. 306, ll. 2–8, in which "a tearing that he pays" is glossed: "such as the tearing of a cat, a fox, or a marten (nĕmiyyâ [Jastrow, s.v.])," i.e., small animals; as opposed to "a tearing that he does not pay," glossed by a list of larger or deadlier animals (cf. M7:9 [H], a close parallel to this list, to be discussed below). By contrast, the Mishnah uses number as a criterion: e.g., one or more wolves (M7:9 [A–C]), two or more dogs (M7:9 [D–F]).

[38] See the discussion of negligence in Section III.B.2, n. 104. A further example of legal differences between the two texts is discussed in the preceding note.

for these definitions both the *Mekilta* and the Mishnah have utilized earlier common material.[39]

In tractate *Kaspaʾ* of the *Mekilta*, the relationship to the Mishnah is somewhat more pronounced but is not uniform. The *Mekilta* to Exodus 22:24–5 (*Kaspaʾ* 19, pp. 315–7) may be dependent upon the Mishnah. The material brought with the *mi-kāʾn ʾāmrû* formula is closely related to *m. Babaʾ Meṣiʿaʾ* and here appears to underlie the exegesis itself rather than to reflect a later redactional overlay.[40] In addition, where the *Mekilta* prohibits loans of produce to be repaid in produce, as well as loans of either money or produce to be repaid in the other medium, it does so with a generality that does not appear in the Mishnah.[41] In light of dependence on material much like the Mishnah here, it is possible that in this case the *Mekilta* generalizes the more nuanced rules, known from the Mishnah, into a legal maxim. (Since no clear literary relationship is demonstrable here, it is impossible to draw far-reaching

---

[39] It is often presumed that short glossing passages in the Tannaitic midrashim (such as the passage quoted above) form an early stratum to which the later dialectical discussion is added (see, e.g., Albeck, 87–93; Neusner, *Purities VII* (*Negaim. Sifra*), 197–202 considers this in connection with the Sifra: see also Halivni, 1986, 22–35, who discusses the antiquity of "simple" Scriptural exegesis in connection with the related question of the forms used for authoritative transmission of tradition). Even if this is not true as a general rule, here, at least, this presumption helps explain why common material exists in both texts but in rather different contexts. To this common material should perhaps be added the list of dangerous animals in M7:9 [H] and *Mek. Nĕzîqîn* 16, p. 306, ll. 5–6 (see also *m. B. Qam.* 1:4). The Mishnah disagrees with the *Mekilta* over the case of the wolf (see the note to M7:9 in Appendix I).

[40] (1) *Mek. Kaspaʾ* 19, p. 316, 8–11 (cf. M5:11; there is a closer parallel with T6:16 in terms of both terminology [*liblār*, against *sôpēr* in the Mishnah] and the continued parallel between ll. 11–2 and T6:17; the relevant material in T6:16, however, appears as a fragmentary gloss to the Mishnah; cf. Epstein, *Nûsaḥ*, 738). That there is a transgression on the part of the various parties to and facilitators of loans on interest is presupposed by the exegesis ("I only have a warning for the borrower and the lender; whence a warning for the guarantor, the witnesses and the scribe?"). (2) *Mek. Kaspaʾ* 19, p. 317, ll. 3–4 (cf. M9:13 [E–G]; however, where the Mishnah opposes items for day and night use [a plow, a pillow], the *Mekilta* stays closer to the language of Ex. 22:25–6, and refers only to a garment [*kĕsût*, as in Ex. 22:26] for day or night). Here, too, what is common with the Mishnah is presupposed in the exegesis ("I only have a day-garment .... whence a night garment ...?"). (For the formula *ʾēn lî ʾelāʾ* ... *minayîn*, cf. n. 26 above.)

[41] *Mek. Kaspaʾ* 19, p. 315, ll. 13–4. The most explicit statements in *m. B. Meṣ.* regarding loans of produce are one attributed to Hillel (M5:9 [D–G]) and another describing the customary practice of R. Gamaliel with his tenant farmers (M5:8 [C–F]). The latter, at least, is given as an example of supererogatory piety (and cf. the Amoraic conclusion about the view of Hillel, *b. B. Meṣ.* 75a). The Mishnah itself is somewhat more permissive: M5:8 [A–B] (loans of seed grain are permitted); M5:9 [A–B] (loans of produce of a kind that the borrower owns and can repay presently are permitted); the grey area between loans involving produce and sale are discussed in M5:1 and M5:7, and since the Mishnah permits contracts that can be construed as a sale, it is, again, more permissive than the bare rule of the *Mekilta*.

conclusions; among other alternatives, it is also possible that this reflects a common stock of basic legal traditions attested in the *Mekilta* but developed in the Mishnah.)

By contrast, the *Mekilta* to Exodus 23:4–5, incorporates material that runs parallel to the Mishnah.[42] Here it seems likely that we have an alternative formulation of material that also appears in the Mishnah, but the possibility that the *Mekilta* preserves material antecedent to the Mishnah, or even that it develops the Mishnah, cannot be ruled out.[43] At the same time, the exegesis of Exodus 23:4 in particular reflects material and concerns that do not appear in the Mishnah such as the distance the finder needs to travel in order to undertake the obligation, or the applicability of these rules to gentiles.[44]

---

[42] *Mek. Kaspāʾ* 20, pp. 324, l. 14–325, l. 3 (cf. M2:7 [A–F]); p. 325, l. 8 (cf. M2:10 [L–N]); p. 325, ll. 9–15 (M2:10 [A–D]); p. 326, ll. 1–8 (cf. M2:10, [J–K]).

[43] The case for direct influence is difficult to make. The strongest argument for dependence of the Mishnah on a midrashic substratum preserved in the *Mekilta* is the fact that it is precisely material that has an exegetical basis in Scripture that finds a parallel in the *Mekilta* here. (Cf. the suggestion, in Chapter II.A.1, that, on source critical grounds, M2:7 [together with M2:9–10] should be bracketed from M2:8 [and much of the rest of chapters 1–2 of the Mishnah], as dependent upon Scripture. Notably, however, none of M2:9, nor M2:10 [E–F] [which forms a unit with M2:9 [D–E]], finds a parallel in the *Mekilta*, suggesting a complex redactional history for M2:9–10. [For analogous material in *Sipre Deut.* §§222, 225 see below.]) The matter is not so simple, however. Part of the parallel material is based on exegesis of Deut. 22:2 (rather than Ex. 23:4) incorporated into the *Mekilta*, so that it is at least possible that what accounts for the parallels is the later expansion of the *Mekilta* (although not necessarily on the basis of the Mishnah). It is true the view of R. Yoshia (*Mek. Kaspāʾ* 20, p. 326, ll. 2–3) might arguably form the basis of the anonymous position in M2:10 [J] ("It is a commandment from the Torah to unburden, but not to load"). However, if this is so, that view was understood differently in the *Mekilta* in its present form than in the Mishnah. In the *Mekilta* the rule that both unburdening and loading are required underlies the entire present form of the dispute. Even the view of the R. Yoshia is glossed (p. 326, 3–6): "I have only unburdening, whence loading?..." (and although the derivation is based on reasoning, it is clear that loading also is "a commandment from the Torah": "For Scripture spoke in the case of the lesser [rule], to teach from it the case of the greater [rule]"). The dispute in the *Mekilta* is cross-referenced with a citation of the view of R. Simeon ("From here (*mi-kāʾn*) would R. Simeon b. Yohai say"; cf. the formula *mi-kāʾn ʾāmrû*), and this may imply a citation of the Mishnah (cf. M2:10 [K] for the same view in different language). Thus it is possible that a citation (possibly from the Mishnah) underlies the reworking in the *Mekilta* of earlier material. See also Chapter II, n. 21, above, in which I suggested that p. 325, l. 14 "'Do not unburden with him,' [or] 'Do not load with him,' [or] 'Do not return to him his lost object,'" may reflect exegesis of the Mishnah. The reverse is also possible, but in that case the Mishnah has utilized its "source" (which comments on a verse dealing with an animal struggling under its load) in a way that makes M2:10 [D] relate to lost animals alone, and in a context where it may make better sense in reference to struggling animals.

[44] See *Mek. Kaspāʾ* 20, pp. 323, l. 10–324, l. 14. Some of this has a parallel in the Tosepta: T2:25 (cf. *Mek.* pp. 323, l. 10–324, l. 2 and p. 325, ll. 4–6); T2:26–7 (cf. *Mek.* p. 324, ll. 3–10, where on the face of it T2:25 agrees with R. Natan in the *Mekilta* ["your enemy" in Ex. 23:4 refers to an Israelite, not a gentile], although T2:26 continues that one is nevertheless

The *Sipre* to Deuteronomy 22:1–4 offers an important counterpoint to this last section of the *Mekilta*, in part because, as it has come down to us, the *Sipre* closely overlaps with the *Mekilta* (as well as the Mishnah),[45] despite the fact that the two midrashic texts are conventionally held to come from different schools. Given the small size of the section under consideration and uncertainty as to the process by which this overlap came into being, it is not clear what the implications of this overlap are.[46] If it is not the result of medieval interpolations and "correction" it suggests once again that in antiquity similar material could circulate in more than one form without implying direct dependence.

In general, where Scriptural verses are relevant, the *Sipre* to Deuteronomy shows a substantial amount of overlap with the *m. Baba* Meṣiʿaʾ, even leaving aside outright citations (*mi-kāʾn ʾattâ ʾōmēr*),[47] but once again, the precise relationship with the Mishnah is not clear. Thus, for example, in the case of the *Sipre* to Deuteronomy 22:3 ("Even the garment (*śalmâ*) was included among these, and why did it go out ..." §224, p. 257) it might be argued that M2:5, which parallels this exegesis in classic "midrashic" style, finds its source here.[48] The matter is not so simple, however, since in what immediately precedes, the *Sipre* presents "mishnaic" material as "exegesis":

---

obligated with respect to the lost animal of a gentile; the Tosepta may reflect a simplification and collapsing of a more complex passage in the *Mekilta*). In addition, see *Mek. Kaspāʾ* 20, p. 325, ll. 7–8, 9, which have no parallel in the Mishnah.

In fact, the *Mekilta* may contradict the Mishnah at least one point. As noted above (previous note), M2:9 [D–E] and M2:10 [E–F] have no parallel in the *Mekilta*. Both passages base on Scripture the rule that if the lost (M2:9) or struggling (M2:10) animal needed to be dealt with repeatedly ("even four or five times"), the finder is still obligated. By contrast, the *Mekilta* specifies: "'falling (*rôbēṣ*)', but not one that habitually falls (*rabṣan*)" (p. 325, l. 9). This may mean that if the animal is already known to passersby as one that falls under its load (see, e.g., Rashi, B31a, *s.v. rôbēṣ*), they are exempt. This would imply, however, that the *Mekilta* assumes that one recognizes the animals that one happens upon on the road (not an impossible assumption, but cf. p. 324, ll. 11–2, in connection with lost animals: "whence [the obligation] even if he does not know him?"). Alternatively, the *Mekilta* may here exempt the passerby once the animal demonstrates itself to be "one that habitually falls" (see Y2:11 [8d]; and *Sipra Bĕ-har* V:1 [109b], below).

[45] *Sipre* §222, p. 255, cf. *Mek. Kaspāʾ* 20, pp. 323–4, repeated p. 325, (an exegesis of Ex. 23:4–5 in both); p. 256, ll. 3–5 (repeated §225, pp. 257–8), cf. *Mek.* p. 325, ll. 9–15 (notably, the language of the *Mekilta* is closer to that of the Mishnah here); §223, p. 256 (and §224, p. 257, l. 1?), cf. *Mek.* p. 324–5 (exegesis of Deut. 22:2 in both). See also §277 and *Mek. Kaspāʾ* 19 pp. 316, l. 14–317, l. 4.

[46] See, e.g., L. Finkelstein, "Prolegomena to an edition of the Sifre on Deuteronomy," *PAAJR* 3 (1931-2), 26–7 (and p. 32 for *Sipre* §222), who views this as a scribal process.

[47] See §222 (p. 255–6) (cf. M2:9); §225 (p. 257, 12–3) (cf. M2:10); §266 (p. 286, 10–2) (cf. M7:4 [A–C] [and *m. Maʿaś. Š.* 2:8]; a version of the dispute of M7:5 [C–D] follows immediately in ll. 12–3).

[48] Cf. Section II.A.1 above.

[1] "And so shall you do to his ass" (Deut. 22:3)—
[2] If it was an ass, it produces and eats (cf. M2:7 [E]);[49]
[3] [if it was] a garment (kĕsût), he shakes it out once in thirty days:
[4] he should spread it out in accordance with its needs, but not for his honor;
[5] silver vessels and copper vessels, he uses them according to their need, but not so as to wear them down ([3–5] = M2:8 [D–F]);
[6] [if] wooden vessels he makes use of them so that they do not rot.

None of this is either required by the Biblical verse itself or explicitly derived by the *Sipre* (cf. the dialectical exegesis of *śalmâ*, "garment," in the sequel), and seems to reflect the application of a list of rules, much like those of the Mishnah,[50] to the interpretation of the verse. If a hypothetical proto-*Sipre* serves as the source for M2:5, that exegetical work, too, appears to have been reworked. Perhaps it is more likely that here both the Mishnah and the *Sipre* draw on a stock of common material.[51] Nevertheless, there are passages that might be taken to reflect the influence of the Mishnah upon the *Sipre*.[52]

Where it does overlap with *m. Baba' Meṣi'a'* (in only a small number of passages), the midrashic collection that is closest is the *Sipra*, which includes extended blocks of material essentially parallel to the Mishnah.[53] While this may reflect the utilization

---

[49] In both the Mishnah (M2:7 [G–H]) and the parallel to *Sipre* in *Mek. Kaspā'* 20 (p. 325, ll. 2–3), this is attached to the end of Ex. 23:4 ("and you shall return it to him").

[50] With the presence of [6] (cf. B30a), the list does not derive (at least not in an unmediated way) from M2:8.

[51] Other possible examples include: §272 (p. 292) (cf. M9:13 [L–O, P–Q]); §277 (p. 295, ll. 8–9) (cf. M9:13 [E–F]); §278 (p. 295–6) (cf. M9:12); §287 (p. 305) (cf. M7:2–4, and see Section II.C.2).

[52] See, e.g., §262 (p. 284, ll. 13–5): "R. Simeon says: 'Whence [do we know] that he should not say to him ...'" (cf. M5:10 [O–P]). Although the statement is formulated exegetically, the use of "whence" (*minayîn*) suggests that this may be a citation (see above n. 26). Significantly, in §263 a parallel to M5:10 [E–N] is formulated exegetically with none of the markers of a citation. This looks suspiciously as though M5:10 [E–P] has been reused in *Sipre Deut.* §§262–3. Equally suspicious is the dispute of Eleazar Ḥisama and the sages, formulated exegetically and introduced with the formula *minayîn* (cf. M7:5 [C–D]), following immediately after the citation of a parallel to M7:4 (*mi-ka'n 'attâ 'ômēr*) (*Sipre* 266, p. 286). *Sipre Deut.* §279 (p. 296, ll. 10–1) (cf. M9:12) may be another example of this (utilizing *mĕlammēd* and *minayîn*). If my interpretation of these passages is correct, then, as noted above in connection with the *Mekilta* (n. 40 and the text thereto, and nn. 43–4), "citations" may function not merely as later appendages, but even as the material underlying the present form of the *Sipre*. (See also §276 [p. 294] which seems to be dependent upon *m. Šebu.* 7:1; cf. *Mek. de-rašbi*, p. 212.)

[53] *Sipra Qĕdôšîm* II:9–12 (88c–d) (cf. M9:11–2); 8:2 (91a) (cf. M4:10 [C–E]); *Bĕ-har* III:1–9 (107c–d) (M4:9, M4:3–6; III:8 includes the interpretive gloss to M4:6 [C], "for this is the manner of the market ...," that also appears in T3:20); 4:1–2 (107d) (cf. M4:10; T3:25); V:1–2 (109b–c) (M5:1; cf. M2:10 [E], M5:11 [B]).

of the Mishnah on the part of the *Sipra*,⁵⁴ in at least one set of passages it is clear that the *Sipra* disagrees with the ruling of the Mishnah.⁵⁵ Whatever its connection to *m. Baba' Meṣiʿa',* the *Sipra* is thus not in every case slavishly dependent upon the Mishnah.⁵⁶ At any rate, the sample of material from the *Sipra* is too small for any comprehensive conclusions about the relationship between the *Sipra* and the Mishnah.

Finally, in addition to the foregoing, mention should be made of the *Mekilta de-rašbi*, which is particularly problematic, and will not receive extended discussion here. The difficulties stem not least from the fact that the text is only partially reconstructed (from fragments, most notably from the Firkovitch collection).⁵⁷ Based on the extracts relevant to *m. Baba' Meṣiʿa',*⁵⁸ the *Mekilta de-rašbi* seems to postdate and make use of the Mishnah⁵⁹ and, it appears, the *Mekilta* as well.⁶⁰ This is in keeping

---

⁵⁴ This is clearest in connection with *Sipra Bĕ-har* III:1–3 (107c): "Whence [do we know] that there is no *hônāyâ* for lands?... for slaves?... for consecrated goods?... for documents?..." (see M4:9; cf. the discussion of *Mek. de-rašbi* to Ex. 22:8 and 9 below n. 59). The *Sipra* here derives the rules of *hônāyâ* from Lev. 25:14ff., which deals explicitly with the sale of land, and then excludes land from the rules of *hônāyâ*. This rather bizarre result may stem from the fact that the rules of *hônāyâ* (including the list of excluded items) precede the exegesis. (Cf. *Qĕdôšîm* II:9 [88c–d], which similarly derives the rule that other forms of "wage" must be paid on time, as in M9:12; but the *Sipra* includes "lands" on the list, unlike the Mishnah.)

⁵⁵ *Sipra Bĕ-har* V:1 (109b) (one does not pick up the load that has fallen off the animal five times) may be in pointed disagreement with M2:9 [D], 2:10 [E] ("even four or five times," cf. n. 43 above, on *Mek. Kaspā'* 20, p. 325, l. 9, "not a *rabsan*"; it should be pointed out that the legal problem here may be slightly different [the animal is not struggling under under a load; cf., however, the language of *Sipre* to Deut. §225, p. 258] and that the sequel states that one does support one's fellow [the case to which the fallen load is compared] "even four or five times"); V:2 (109b): although it is followed by a parallel to M5:1, the *Sipra* reads first: "from him you may not take [interest], but you may be a surety for him;" cf. M5:11 [A–B]: "And these transgress a negative commandment: the lender, and the borrower, and the surety, and the witnesses."

⁵⁶ See, e.g., J. Neusner, "Sifra and the Problem of the Mishnah," *Henoch* 11 (1989), 17–40, against his earlier view in *Purities VII* (*Negaim. Sifra*), 231, that the two texts draw from a common stock of material.

⁵⁷ For a description of the mss. used in the Epstein, Melamed edition see Melamed's introduction, xxxiii–xlv; literature on additional fragments is cited in Strack (ed. Stemberger), 1992, 282.

⁵⁸ I have only made use of those passages that are based on ms. Firkovitch: *Mek. de-rašbi* to Ex. 22:6–14 (ed. Epstein, Melamed, pp. 199–207); 22:20 (p. 210); 22:24 (pp. 211–2).

⁵⁹ In addition to the outright citations utilizing formulae, listed by Melamed on pp. xxviii–xxxi (nos. 41, 43, 64 (*kĕsad*), [66, from *Midraš ha-gadôl*]), see, e.g., *Mek. de-rašbi* to 22:8 (44a l. 19–44b l. 4, pp. 202–3), which derives exceptions from the rules of 22:8 for land, slaves, and documents, in precise correspondence to M4:9 [A–E] (cf. *m. Šebu.* 6:5): "These are things that do not have *hônāyâ*: slaves, documents, lands and consecrated goods.... an unpaid depositary does not swear, a paid depositary does not pay." The derivations have no clear exegetical basis in the verse itself, and it seems clear that the midrash is based on the existence of a list of exemptions and not the reverse (cf. Chapter II.A.2 above; and see *Mek. de-rašbi* p. 204, 45a ,18–23, where these are mechanically excluded again from Ex. 22:9). Moreover, the

with the characterization of Epstein (i.e., that the *Mek. de-rašbi* frequently utilizes other "Tannaitic" texts, and therefore is "late").[61] However, if the *Mekilta de-rašbi* is to be classified with the other Halakhic midrashim as essentially a Tannaitic text,[62]

Mek. de-rašbi continues with a near parallel to T2:15, which is, in turn, a variant of M2:5 (both are properly exegeses of Deut. 22:3 and relate to lost objects, here incorrectly attached to the word *śalmâ* in Ex. 22:8, suggesting that the verse exegesis, whatever the literary source, was available for citation). For the *Mek. de-rašbi* on Ex. 22:7, 10 (41b l. 21–44a l. 9 [pp. 201–2]; 45b l. 22–46a l. 1 [p. 205]) see C. Levine, "The Concept '*Sheliḥut Yad*' in the Mechilta De Rashbi" [Hebrew], *BIA* 18/19 (1981), 98–116, who argues that the midrashic text here reflects exegesis of M3:9 and 12 (cf. de Vries, 1968, 48–51). Like the *Mekilta*, the *Mekilta de-rašbi* presupposes the various rules for depositaries (see, e.g., p. 201, 41b ll. 2–17; p. 206, 46a ll. 13–8; 46a l. 20–46b l. 10); however, the *Mek. de-rašbi* presents a derivation of the rules only as an afterthought, in connection with Ex 22:14 (p. 207, 47a ll. 6–12; cf. *y. Šebu.* 8:1 [38b]). Here (unlike the *Mekilta*) the midrash may presuppose the wording of M7:8 [C–H]: the borrower "pays for everything" (as in M7:8 [F]); the unpaid depositary is "exempt from everything" (cf. M7:8 [E]); and the paid depositary "swears for part and pays for part" (cf. M7:8 [G–H]).

[60] There is substantial overlap in theme, and frequently in language between the two *Mekiltot*. See, e.g., p. 200, 40b. 25 (*Mek. Nězîqîn* 15, p. 299, 2); 41a, 1ff. (*Mek.* p. 299, 4); p. 201, 41b, 18–21 (*Mek.* p. 300, 7–12); pp. 201–2 (*Mek.* p. 300, 14–5); pp. 202–3 (*Mek.* pp. 300–1); pp. 203–4, 44b, 6–45a, 5 (*Mek.* p. 301, 9–10); p. 204, 45a, 5–13 (*Mek.* p. 302, 1–13); p. 205, 45b, 8–9 (*Mek. Nězîqîn* 16, pp. 302, 17–303, 3); p. 205, 45b, 16–7 (*Mek.* p. 303, 17–8); p. 205, 45b, 17–20 (*Mek.* p. 303, 18–9); pp. 205–6, 46a 6–13 (cf. 45b, 13–4) (*Mek.* p. 304, 6); p. 206, 46a, 13 (*Mek.* p. 305, 3); p. 206 46a, 18–20 (*Mek.* p. 305, 8–9); p. 206, 46a, 25–46b, 5 (*Mek.* p. 306, 9–11); p. 206, 46b, 5–10 (*Mek.* p. 306, 11–2); p. 210, 30a, 2–5 (*Mek. Nězîqîn* 18, p. 311, 3–5) . It is not always possible to tell whether this overlap reflects common exegetical tradition or the use by one text of the other. At least sometimes, however it appears that the *Mek. de-rašbi* has utilized the *Mekilta*. Thus, for instance, when the *Mek. de-rašbi* specifies the exceptions to Ex. 22:8 (pp. 202–3, 44a, l. 19–44b, l. 4; cf. preceding note), it may be amplifying the conclusion in *Mek. Nězîqîn* 15, p. 301, ll. 2–3, that the verse refers to "moveable property against which there can be no liens (*še-'ên lāhem 'aḥarāyût*)"; *Mek. de-rašbi* p. 204, 45a, ll. 5–9 may be a quotation of *Mek. Nězîqîn* 15, p. 302, ll. 1–5 (although, since the statement attributed to R. Nathan in *Mek. de-rašbi* does not fit with that attributed to R. Jonathan in the *Mekilta*, this is perhaps an independent formulation of similar material). The *Mek. de-rašbi* continues (ll. 9–12) with a statement attributed to R. Simeon, as does the *Mek*, ll. 10–3. The contents of these statements are different, but it may not be accidental that the *Mekilta* echoes the first part of *m. B. Qam.* 9:7, while the *Mek. de-rašbi* echoes the conclusion of *m. B. Qam.* 9:7 and 9:8. Both passages concude with similar exegeses of "to his fellow" (Ex. 22:8; *Mek.* l. 13; *Mek. de-rašbi* ll. 11–3).

[61] See Epstein, *Siprût*, 738 (=Epstein, Melamed edition, introduction, p. xxv), given, unfortunately, without substantiation. De Vries, 1968, 142–7, lists some seven examples in which, he argues, the *Mek. de-rašbi* depends upon the *Mek.*

[62] Cf. C. Levine, "Exegesis of the Mishna in the Mechilta de Rashbi and its Relation to Amoraic Teaching" [Hebrew], *BIA* 16–17 (1979), 59–69, who defines the *Mek. de-rašbi* as a kind of Amoraic text. If true, this would not, of course, exclude the possibility that the *Mek. de-rašbi* might preserve early Tannaitic material (even as the Babylonian or Palestinian Talmud

Appendix II: Mishnah and Tannitic Corpora   329

its close relationship with the Mishnah forms an important counterpoint to the *Mekilta*.[63]

In the preceding discussion of the Halakhic midrashim, I have noted a number of examples in which material in one or another of the exegetical collection is revised or juxtaposed with other material in the process of redaction. Beyond that, the results of this section confirm (in a general way and not without exception, see the discussion of *Mek. Kaspāʾ* 19, 20 above) the conventional distinction between so-called "Aqiban" midrashim (*Sipra*, the legal portions of *Sipre Deut.*; the *Mek. de-rašbi* is classed in this category as well) and the "Ishmaelite" midrashim (*Mekilta*), with the former deemed closer to the Mishnah.[64] There is some reason to think that in their final form all of the Halakhic midrashim discussed here reflect the influence of the Mishnah. This should not, however, obscure the existence—also noted in connection with the Tosepta, whose association with the Mishnah is unmistakable—of independent formulations of similar material whose existence cannot be attributed solely to borrowing from the Mishnah. To the extent that this is correct, this appendix points to "redaction" as a mode of Rabbinic text-production in general, and not merely of the Mishnah. Hence the argument made in the body of this study (especially Chapter II) that the question of sources and redaction is itself of central importance to understanding the Mishnah as both literary and social product. This question focuses attention on the Mishnah as produced in the context of a wider intellectual community, in which there may well have been considerably more material than that to which we have access, at the same time as it underscores the role of choice, juxtaposition and subtle redaction of traditional materials into a coherent Mishnah. At the same time, to the extent that influence of the Mishnah on other texts can be substantiated, it is also possible to attempt to trace the transformation of these "traditional materials" into the Tradition.

---

might preserve such material in the form of *bāraîtôt*); see, for instance, the argument of D. W. Halivni on *m. B. Qam.* 1:1, in *Meqôrôt û-mĕsôrôt: Babaʾ Qammaʾ* (Jerusalem: Magnes, 1993), 1–7 (essentially a revised edition of *idem*, "*ʿAl herkēbâ šel ha-mišnâ ha-riʾšonâ bĕ-bābāʾ qammāʾ*," in *Studies in Rabbinic Literature, Bible and Jewish History* [Hebrew; Festschrift for E. Z. Melamed], ed. M. Gilat *et al.* [Ramat Gan: Bar Ilan, 1982], 108–14).

[63] This is true not only of *m. B. Meṣ.* Thus, for instance, one may make a case for the dependence of the rather long and repetitive discussion of a depositary who appropriates the deposit but claims that it was stolen (*tôʿen taʿanat gānāb*) on *m. B. Qam.* 9:7–8 (*Mek. de-rašbi*, pp. 200–1); similarly, the *Mek. de-rašbi* to Ex. 22:10 (p. 205) may reflect knowledge of *m. Šebu.* 7:1 and 6:1, 3.

[64] For literature and a brief discussion of the history of this question see Strack (ed. Stemberger), 1992, 269–73.

⋄⟩ ABBREVIATIONS AND BIBLIOGRAPHY ⟨⋄

Abbreviations*

1. Rabbinic texts and editions.

m., M**	Mishnah (citations according to the division of the text in standard printed editions).
t., T**	Tosepta: S. Lieberman, ed. *Tosefta*. New York: JTSA, 1955–88; M. S. Zuckermandel, ed. *Tosephta*. Rept. Jerusalem: Wahrmann, 1975.
Mek.	*Mekilta*: H. S. Horovitz and I. A. Rabin, eds. *Mechilta d'Rabbi Ishmael*. Rpt. Jerusalem: Wahrmann, 1970.
Mek. dĕ-rašbi	*Mekilta de-rabbi šimʿon bar yoḥai*: J. N. Epstein and E. Z. Melamed, eds. *Mekhilta d'Rabbi Šimʿon b. Jochai*. 2ed. Jerusalem: Bet Hillel, n.d.
Sipra	*Sipra*: I. H. Weiss, ed. *Sifra D'Be Rav*. Vienna, 1882.
Sipre Num.	*Sipre to Numbers*: H. S. Horovitz, ed. *Siphre d'be Rab*. Rpt. Jerusalem: Wahrmann, 1966.
Sipre Deut.	*Sipre to Deuteronomy*: L. Finkelstein, ed., *Siphre ad Deuteronomium*. Berlin: 1939.
y., Y**	Palestinian Talmud (Yerushalmi) (citations by both chapter and *halākâ* and folio from the *editio princeps*, Venice, 1522–3).
b., B**	Babylonian Talmud (Babli) (citations by folio from the Vilna: Romm, 1880–6 edition).

2. Commentaries.

Bertinoro	Obadiah of Bertinoro (d. 1510)
Maimonides	(Rabbi) Moses b. Maimon (Rambam) (d. 1204)
Meiri	Menahem ha-Meiri (d. 1306), *Bêt ha-bĕḥîrâ*.

---

* In general, abbreviations follow the Society of Biblical Literature format. For abbreviations of published papyri I have followed J. F. Oates, W. H. Willis, R. S. Bagnall, K. A. Worp, eds. *Checklist of Editions of Greek and Latin Papyri, Ostraca and Tablets*, Electronic edition B (Packard Humanities Institute, CD-Rom 6, 1991). For a print version see the third edition, *BASP* Supplement 4, 1985.

** Note: M, T, Y, B are used as shorthand for references to passages from tractate *Babaʾ Meṣiʿaʾ*. Other tractates are referred to according to the Society of Biblical Literature format.

Mĕl᾿eket šĕlomoh	Solomon ha-Adani (d. 1625), *Mĕl᾿eket šĕlomoh.*
Nahmanides	(Rabbi) Moses b. Nahman (Ramban) (d. 1270)
Rabad	(Rabbi) Abraham b. David of Posquières (d. 1298)
Rashi	(Rabbi) Solomon b. Isaac (d. 1105)
Rif	(Rabbi) Isaac Alfasi (d. 1103)
Rosh	(Rabbi) Asher b. Yehiel (d. 1327)
Ritba	(Rabbi) Yom Tob b. Abraham (d. 1320)
RŠŠ	(Rabbi) Samuel Strashun (d. 1872)
Šiṭṭâ mĕqubbeṣet	Bezalel b. Abraham Ashkenazi (d. ca. 1691), ed., *Šiṭṭâ mĕqubbeṣet.*
Tos.	Tosafot
TY	Israel Lipschütz, *Tip᾿eret yiśrā᾿ēl* (1830–50).
TYṬ	Yom Ṭob Lipmann Heller, *Tosapôt yôm ṭôb* (1614–7, 1643–4)

3. References.

Albeck	Albeck, H. *Šišâ sidrê mišnâ.* Jerusalem: Bialik; Tel Aviv: Dvir, 1959. [When page numbers are included, the reference is to the supplements at the end of each volume.]
Albeck, *Mābô᾿*	H. Albeck, *Introduction to the Mishnah* [*Hebrew*]. Jerusalem and Tel Aviv: Bialik and Dvir, 1959.
BDB	Gesenius, W. *A Hebrew and English Lexicon of the Old Testament.* Ed. F. Brown, S. R. Driver, C. A. Briggs. Oxford: Clarendon, 1906.
CCSL	*Corpus Christianorum. Series Latina.* Turnhout, 1953–.
CIJ	*Corpus Inscriptionum Iudaicarum,* ed. J. B. Frey. Paris, 1936, 1952.
CIS	*Corpus Inscriptionum Semiticarum.* Paris, 1881-1962.
CJ	*Codex Iustinianus.*
CSEL	*Corpus Scriptorum Ecclesiasticorum Latinorum.* Vienna, 1866–.
CT	*Codex Theodosianus.*
D	*Digest of Justinian.*
Epstein, *Nûsah*	Epstein, J. N. *Mābô᾿ lĕ-nûsaḥ ha-mišnâ.* Jerusalem, 1948.
Epstein, *Siprût*	Epstein, J. N. *Prolegomena ad Litteras Tannaiticas* [Hebrew]. Ed. E. Z. Melamed. Jerusalem and Tel Aviv: Magnes and Dvir, 1957.
GCS	*Die griechischen christlichen Schriftsteller der ersten drei Jahrhunderten.* Berlin, 1897–.
IG	*Inscriptiones Graecae.* Berlin, 1873–.
IGR	*Inscriptiones Graecae ad Res Romanas Pertinentes.* Ed. R. Cagnat, et al. Paris, 1911–27.
Jastrow	Jastrow, M. *A Dictionary of the Targumim, the Talmud Babli and Yerushalmi, and the Midrashic Literature.* London, 1886–1903.
Lieberman, *TK*	Lieberman, *Tosefta Ki-Fshuṭa.* New York: JTSA, 1955–88.

Lieberman, TR	Lieberman, S. *Tosefeth Rishonin.* Jerusalem: Bamberger and Wahrmann, 1937–9.	
Lieberman, Yerushalmi Neziqin	Lieberman, S. *Yerushalmi Neziqin.* [Introduction and commentary; text ed. E. S. Rosenthal.] Jerusalem: Israel Academy of Sciences, 1983.	
LSJM	Liddell, H. G. and Scott, R. eds. *A Greek English Lexicon.* Rev. ed. with supplement, H. S. Jones, R. McKenzie. Oxford: Clarendon, 1968.	
M. Grz.; *M. Chr.*	Mitteis, L. *Grundzüge und Chrestomathie der Papyruskunde [II: juristische Teil].* Leipzig, Berlin, 1912.	
Neusner, Damages	Neusner, J. *A History of the Mishnaic Law of Damages.* SJLA 35: Leiden: Brill, 1982–5.	
Neusner, Purities	Neusner, J. *A History of the Mishnaic Law of Purities.* SJLA 6: Leiden: Brill, 1974–7.	
OGIS	*Orientis Graeci Inscriptiones Selectae.* Ed. W. Dittenberger. Leipzig, 1903–5.	
PG	*Patrologia graeca.* Ed. J.-P.Migne. Paris, 1857–66.	
PL	*Patrologia latina.* Ed. J.-P.Migne. Paris, 1878–90.	
Rabbinovicz, DS	Rabbinovicz, R. *Variae Lectiones in Mischnam et Talmud Babylonicum [Diqdûqê sôprîm].* Vol. 13. Munich, 1883.	
Segal	Segal, M. H. *A Grammar of Mishnaic Hebrew.* Oxford: Clarendon, 1927.	
*Syll.*³	*Sylloge Inscriptionum Graecarum.* Ed. W. Dittenberger. 3rd ed. Leipzig, 1915–24.	

Bibliography

Adan-Bayewitz, D. *Common Pottery in Roman Galilee: A Study in Local Trade.* Ramat Gan: Bar Ilan, 1993.

Adan-Bayewitz, D., Perlman, I. "The Local Trade of Sepphoris in the Roman Period." *IEJ* 40 (1990), 153–72.

Albeck, H. *Untersuchungen über die Redaktion der Mischna. Veröffentlichungen der Akademie für die Wissenschaft des Judentums. Talmudische Sektion* 2: Berlin, 1923.

——— . *Introduction to the Talmud, Babli and Yerushalmi* [Hebrew]. Tel Aviv: Dvir, 1969.

Alon, G. *Tôldôt ha-yĕhûdîm bĕ-ʾereṣ yiśrāʾēl bi-tĕqûpat ha-mišnâ wĕ-ha-talmûd.* Tel Aviv: Hakibutz Hameuchad, 1953–7. [=Alon, G. *The Jews in their Land in the Talmudic Age.* Tr. G. Levi. Jerusalem: Magnes, 1980–4.]

——— . *Meḥqārîm bĕ-tôldôt yiśrāʾēl.* Tel Aviv: Hakibutz Hameuchad, 1976. [=Alon, G. *Jews and Judaism in the Classical World.* Tr. I. Abrams. Jerusalem: Magnes, 1977.]

Anderson, B. *Imagined Communities*. Corr. ed. London: Verso, 1991.
Andreau, J. *La vie financière dans le monde romain. Bibliothèque des écoles françaises d'Athènes et de Rome* 265: Rome: École Française, 1987.
Applebaum, S. "Economic Life in Palestine." In S. Safrai, 1976, 631–700.
———. *Judaea in Hellenistic and Roman Times*. SJLA 40: Leiden: Brill, 1989.
Avi-Yonah, M. "The Foundation of Tiberias." *IEJ* 1 (1950–1), 160–9.
———. *The Jews of Palestine: A Political History from the Bar Kokhba War to the Arab Conquest. Blackwell's Classical Studies*: Oxford: Blackwell, 1976.
———. *The Holy Land*. Rev. ed. Grand Rapids: Baker, 1977.
Ayali, M. *Pôʿalîm wĕ-ʾûmānîm: mĕlʾaktām û-maʿamadām bĕ-siprût ḥzl. Yād la-talmûd*: Jerusalem: Masada, 1987.
Bacher, W. *ʾAggādôt ha-tannāʾîm*. Tr. A. Z. Rabbinowitz. 2 ed. Tel Aviv: Dvir, 1928.
Bagnall, R. S. "Price in 'Sales on Delivery.'" *GRBS* 18 (1977), 85–96.
———. *Currency and Inflation in Fourth Century Egypt*. BASP Suppl. 5: Atlanta: Scholars, 1986.
Bagnall, R. S., Bogaert, R. "Orders for Payment from a Banker's Archive: Papyri in the Collection of Florida State University." *Ancient Society* 6 (1973), 79–108.
Baldwin, J. W. "The Medieval Theories of the Just Price." *Transactions of the American Philosophical Society*. New Series. 49, part 4 (1959), 1–92.
Barnes, T. D. *Sources of the Historia Augusta. Collection Latomus* 155: Brussels, 1978.
Baron, S. W. *History and Jewish Historians*. Ed. A. Hertzberg, L. A. Feldman. Philadelphia: JPS, 1964.
Baras, T. *et al.*, eds. *Eretz Israel from the Destruction of the Second Temple to the Muslim Conquest* [Hebrew]. Jerusalem: Yad Izhak ben-Zvi, 1982.
Barth, F., ed. *Ethnic Groups and Boundaries*. Boston: Little, Brown, 1969.
Bellinger, A. R. *Dura Europus Final Report VI: The Coins*. New Haven: Yale, 1949.
Ben-David, A. "Jewish and Roman Bronze and Copper Coins: Their Reciprocal Relations in the Mishnah and Talmud from Herod the Great to Trajan and Hadrian." *PEQ* 103 (1971), 109–29.
———. *Talmudische Ökonomie*. Hildesheim: Georg Olms, 1974.
Ben Yehudah, E. *Thesaurus totius hebraitatis* [Hebrew]. Rpt. London and New York, 1960.
Birley, A. R. *The African Senator: Septimius Severus*. 2. ed. London: Batsford, 1988.
Bogaert, R. *Banques et banquiers dans les cités grecques*. Leiden: Sijthoff, 1968.
Bokser, B. M. "An Annotated Bibliographical Guide to the Study of the Palestinian Talmud." *ANRW* 2.19.2 (1979), 139–256.
———. "Talmudic Form Criticism." *JJS* 31 (1980), 46–60.
———, ed. *Jewish History: The Next Ten Years*. BJS 21: Chico: Scholars, 1980.
Bolin, S. *State and Currency in the Roman Empire to 300 AD*. Stockholm: Almqvist and Wiskell, 1958.
Bowersock, G. W. *Greek Sophists in the Roman Empire*. Oxford: Oxford, 1969.
Brooks, R. "Straw Dogs and Scholarly Ecumenism: The Appropriate Jewish Background for the Study of Origen." In C. Kannengiessen, W. L. Petersen, eds.

Origen of Alexandria: His World and Legacy. Notre Dame: University of Notre Dame, 1988, 63–95.
Broughton, T. R. S. *Roman Asia*. In *An Economic Survey of Ancient Rome* IV. Ed. T. Frank: Baltimore: Johns Hopkins, 1938.
Brown, P. "The Rise and Function of the Holy Man in Late Antiquity." In *Society and the Holy in Late Antiquity.* Berkeley: University of California, 1982, 103–52.
Buckland, W. W. *A Textbook of Roman Law.* 3 ed., P. Stein. Cambridge: University Press, 1963.
Büchler, A. *The Political and Social Leaders of the Jewish Community in Sepphoris in the Second and Third Centuries.* Oxford: Clarendon, 1909.
Cancian, F. "Economic Behavior in Peasant Communities." In *Economic Anthropology.* Ed. S. Plattner. Stanford: Stanford University, 1989.
Cassuto, U. *A Commentary on the Book of Exodus.* Tr. I. Abrahams. Jerusalem: Magnes, 1967.
Chiat, M. J. S. *Handbook of Synagogue Architecture.* BJS 29: Chico: Scholars, 1982.
Cohen, B. *Jewish and Roman Law: A Comparative Study.* New York: JTSA, 1966.
Cohen, E. *Athenian Banking.* Princeton: Princeton, 1992.
Cohen, G. D. *Sefer ha-Qabbalah: The Book of Tradition.* Philadelphia: JPS, 1967.
Cohen, S. J. D. "Epigraphical Rabbis." *JQR* 72 (1981), 1–17.
———. "The Significance of Yavneh: Pharisees, Rabbis and the End of Jewish Sectarianism." *HUCA* 55 (1984), 27–53.
———. "The Place of the Rabbi in Jewish Society of the Second Century." In Levine, 1992, 157–73.
Comaroff, J. *Body of Power, Spirit of Resistance: The Culture and History of a South African People.* Chicago: University of Chicago, 1985.
Comaroff, J., Comaroff J. L. *Of Revelation and Revolution.* Chicago: University of Chicago, 1991.
Cooke, G. A. *North Semitic Inscriptions.* Oxford: Clarendon, 1903.
Cotton, H. M. "Fragments of a Declaration of Landed Property from the Province of Arabia," *ZPE* 85 (1991), 263–7.
———. "Another Fragment of a Declaration of Landed Property from the Province of Arabia." *ZPE* 99 (1993), 114–21.
———. "Loan With Hypothec: Another Papyrus from the Cave of Letters?" *ZPE* 101 (1994), 53–60.
Cotton, H. M., Geiger, J., eds. *Masada: Final Reports II.* Jerusalem: IES, Hebrew University, 1989.
Crawford, M. H. "Money and Exchange in the Ancient World." *JRS* 60 (1970), 40–8.
———. "Finance, Money and Coinage from the Severans to Constantine." *ANRW* 2.2 (1975), 560–93.
Crook, J. A. *Law and Life of Rome.* Ithaca: Cornell, 1967.
Crouzel, H. *Origen.* Tr. A. S. Worall. San Francisco: Harper and Row, 1989.
Daube, D. "Civil Law in the Mishnah: The Arrangement of the Three Gates." *Tulane Law Review* 18 (1944), 352–407.

———. "Eisern Vieh." *ZRG (Röm. Abteilung)* 69 (1950), 388-92.
———. "Negligence in Early Talmudic Law of Contract (*Peshiʿa*)," *Festschrift F. Schulz* I. Ed. H. Niedermeyer, W. Flure (Weimar, 1951), 124–47.
———. *Studies in Biblical Law*. New York: Ktav, 1969.
de Lange, N. M. R. *Origen and the Jews*. Cambridge: Cambridge University, 1976.
de Ste Croix, G. E. M. *The Class Struggle in the Ancient Greek World*. Ithaca: Cornell, 1981.
de Zulueta, F. *The Roman Law of Sale*. Oxford: Clarendon, 1945.
De Vries, B. *Meḥqārîm bĕ-siprût ha-talmûd*. Jerusalem: Mossad Harav Kook, 1968.
Dickstein, P. "*Mĕḥîr ṣedeq wĕ-ʾōnāʾâ.*" *Ha-mišpāṭ ha-ʿibrî* 1 (1926) 15–55.
Douglas, M. *Purity and Danger*. London: Routledge, 1966.
Drewes, P. "*Die Bankdiagraphe in den gräco-ägyptischen Papyri.*" *JJP* 18 (1974), 95–156.
Drexhage, H. J. *Preise, Mieten/Pachten, Kosten und Löhne im römischen Ägypten bis zum Regierungsantritt Diokletians*. St. Katharin: Scripta Mercaturae, 1991.
Eilberg-Schwartz, H. *The Savage in Judaism*. Bloomington: Indiana, 1990.
Ejges, S. *Das Geld im Talmud*. Vilna/Vilnius, 1930.
Feintuch, I. Z. "On the Parma Ms." [Heb.] *BIA* 18/19 (1981), 196–217.
Feliks, Y. *Agriculture in Eretz-Israel in the Period of the Bible and Talmud* [Hebrew]. Rev. ed. Jerusalem: Rubin Mass, 1990.
Finkelstein, L. "Prolegomena to an Edition of the Sifre on Deuteronomy" *PAAJR* 3 (1931-2), 3–42.
Finley, M. I. *The Ancient Economy*. 2 ed. *Sather Memorial Lectures* 43: Berkeley: University of California, 1985.
Fishbane, M. *Biblical Interpretation in Ancient Israel*. Rpt. corr. ed. Oxford: Clarendon, 1985.
Flesher, P. V. M. *Oxen, Women or Citizens? Slaves in the System of the Mishnah*. BJS 143: Atlanta: Scholars, 1988.
Foerster, G. "The Ancient Synagogues of Galilee." In Levine, 1992, 289–320.
Foucault, M. *Discipline and Punish*. Tr. A. Sheridan. New York: Vintage, 1979.
———. *The Archaeology of Knowledge*. Tr. A. M. Sheridan Smith. New York: Pantheon, 1972.
Foxhall, L., Forbes, H. A. "$\Sigma\iota\tau o\mu\varepsilon\tau\rho\varepsilon\acute{\iota}\alpha$: The Role of Grain as a Staple Food in Classical Antiquity." *Chiron* 12 (1982), 41–90.
Frank, T. *Italy Under the Empire*. In *Economic Survey of Ancient Rome* IV. Ed. T. Frank. Baltimore: Johns Hopkins, 1940.
Frankel, Z. *Darkê ha-mišnâ* [Leipzig, 1859]. Rev. ed. I. Nusbaum. Tel Aviv: Sinai, n.d.
Freyne, S. *Galilee From Alexander the Great to Hadrian: 323 B.C.E. to 135 C.E. University of Notre Dame Center for the Study of Judaism and Christianity in Antiquity* 5: Wilmington and Notre Dame: Michael Glazier and Notre Dame, 1980.
Friedman, M. (*ʾîš šālôm*). *Mĕkiltāʾ dĕ-rabbî Yišmāʿēʾl ʿim pēruš mēʾîr ʿāyyîn*. Vienna, 1870.

Friedman, S. *A Critical Study of* Yevamot X *With a Methodological Introduction.* Jerusalem: JTSA, 1978.

———. *Talmud Arukh: BT Bava Meziʾa VI, Commentary.* Jerusalem: JTSA, 1990.

———. "The Primacy of Tosefta in Mishnah-Tosefta Parallels—Shabbat 16, 1: *kol kitbê qôdeš*" [Hebrew]. *Tarbiz* 62 (1993), 313–38.

Frier, B. W. *Landlords and Tenants in Imperial Rome.* Princeton: Princeton University, 1980.

Gapp, K. S. "A Lease of a Pigeon-House with Brood." *TAPA* 64 (1933), 89–97.

Garnsey, P. "Aspects of the Decline of the Urban Aristocracy in the Empire." *ANRW* 2.1 (1974), 229–52.

Garnsey, P., Saller, R. *The Roman Empire: Economy, Society and Culture.* Berkeley: University of California, 1987.

Geiger, A. *Ha-miqrāʾ we-targûmāyw.* Tr Y. L. Baruk from second ed. (1928). Jerusalem: Bialik, 1949. [=Geiger, A. *Urschrift und Übersetzungen der Bibel.* Breslau: Julius Hainauer, 1857.]

———. *Judaism and Its History.* Tr. from German (*Das Judenthum und seine Geschichte*), C. Newburgh. New York: Bloch, 1911.

Geiger, J. "The Last Jewish Revolt against Rome: A Reconsideration." *SCI* 5 (1979/80), 250–7.

Ginzberg, L. "*Tamid,* The Oldest Tractate of the Mishnah." *Journal of Jewish Lore and Philosophy* 1 (1919), 33–44, 197–209, 265–95.

Goldberg, A. "Purpose and Method in R. Judah Hannasi's Compilation of the Mishnah" [Hebrew]. *Tarbiz* 28 (1958–9), 260–69.

———. *Commentary to the Mishnah Shabbat* [Hebrew]. Jerusalem: JTSA, 1976.

———. "The Mishnah—A Study Book of Halakah," in S. Safrai, ed., 1987, 211–51.

———. *The Mishnah Treatise Eruvin* [Hebrew]. Jerusalem: Magnes, 1986.

Goldenberg, R. *The Sabbath Law of R. Meir.* BJS 6: Missoula: Scholars, 1978.

Goodblatt, D. "The Babylonian Talmud." *ANRW* 2.19.2 (1979), 257–336.

———. "The Title *Nasiʾ* and the Ideological Background of the Second Revolt" [Hebrew]. In Oppenheimer, Rappaport, 1984, 113–32.

Goodenough, E. R. *Jewish Symbols in the Greco-Roman Period.* Bollingen 27: Princeton: Princeton, 1954–68.

Goodman, M. *State and Society in Roman Galilee. Oxford Centre for Postgraduate Hebrew Studies.* Totowa: Rowman and Allanheld, 1983.

———. *The Ruling Class of Judaea.* Cambridge: Cambridge, 1987.

———. "The Roman State and the Jewish Patriarch in the Third Century." In Levine, 1992, 127–39.

Graetz, H. *Geschichte der Jüden.* Vienna, 1853–76. 3 ed. Fr. Rosenthal. Leipzig, 1893. [Hebrew ed. tr. S. P. Rabinovitz. Warsaw, 1890–1902.]

Green, W. S. "Palestinian Holy Men: Charismatic Leadership and the Rabbinic Tradition." *ANRW* 2.19.2 (1979), 619–47.

———, ed. *Law as Literature. Semeia* 25 (1983).

Groh, D. E. "The Stratigraphic Chronology of the Galilean Synagogue from the Early Roman Through the Early Byzantine Period (ca. 420 C.E.)." In Urman, Flesher, 1995, 51–69.

Gulak, A. *Lĕ-ḥēqer tôldôt ha-mišpāṭ ha-ʿibrî.* Jerusalem, 1929.

———. "Banking in Talmudic Law" [Hebrew]. *Tarbiz* 2 (1931), 154–75.

———. *"Soʾn barzel bĕ-dînê ha-talmûd."* *Tarbiz* 3 (1932), 137–46.

———. *Das Urkundwesen im Talmud.* Jerusalem: Rubin Mass, 1935.

Halivni, D. W. *Mĕqôrôt û-mĕsôrôt: Nāšîm.* Tel Aviv: Dvir, 1968.

———. *Mĕqôrôt û-mĕsôrôt: Môʿēd.* New York: JTSA, 1975–82.

———. "Methods of the Study of the Talmud." *JJS* 30 (1979), 192–201.

———. *"ʿAl herkēbâ šel ha-mišnâ ha-riʾšonâ bĕ-bābāʾ qammāʾ."* In *Studies in Rabbinic Literature, Bible and Jewish History* [Hebrew; Festschrift for E. Z. Melamed]. Ed. M. Gilat *et al.* Ramat Gan: Bar Ilan, 1982, 108–14.

———. *Midrash, Mishnah and Gemara: The Jewish Predilection for Justified Law.* Cambridge: Harvard, 1986.

———. *"Mišnôt še-zāzû mi-mĕqômān."* *Sidra* 5 (1989), 63–88.

———. *Mĕqôrôt û-mĕsôrôt: Bābāʾ qammāʾ.* Jerusalem: Magnes, 1993.

———. *Mĕqôrôt û-mĕsôrôt: Bābāʾ mĕšîʿāʾ.* In preparation.

Hamel, G. *Poverty and Charity in Roman Palestine, First Three Centuries C. E. Near Eastern Studies* 23: Berkeley, California, 1990.

Hanson, R. P. C. *Origen's Doctrine of Tradition.* London: SPCK, 1954.

Hanson, R. S. *Tyrian Influence in Upper Galilee. Meiron Excavation Project* 2: Cambridge: ASOR, 1980.

Harper, G. M. "Village Administration in the Roman Province of Syria." *YCS* 1 (1928), 103–68.

Harris, J. M. *Nachman Krochmal: Guiding the Perplexed of the Modern Age.* New York: NYU, 1991.

Heichelheim, F. M. "New Light on Currency and Inflation in Hellenistic-Roman Times From Inscriptions and Papyri." *Economic History* 10 (1935), 5–11.

———. *Roman Syria.* In *An Economic Survey of Ancient Rome* IV, ed. T. Frank: Baltimore: Johns Hopkins, 1938.

Heinemann, J. "The Status of the Labourer in Jewish Law and Society in the Tannaitic Period." *HUCA* 25 (1954), 263–325.

Hengel, M. *Judaism and Hellenism.* Tr. J. Bowden. Philadelphia: Fortress, 1974.

Hengstl, J. *Private Arbeitsverhältnisse freier Personen in den hellenistischen Papyri bis Diokletian.* Diss. Freiburg, 1971. Bonn: Habelt, 1972.

Hennig, D. *Untersuchungen zur Bodenpacht im ptolemäisch-römischen Ägypten.* Diss. Munich, 1967.

Hill, G. F. *Catalogue of Greek Coins in the British Museum: Palestine [BMC Palestine].* London, 1914.

Hoffman, D. "The First Mishnah and the Controversies of the Tannaim" (1882). In *The First Mishnah [and] the Highest Court.* Tr. fr. German P. Forscheimer. New York: Maurosho, 1977.

Hopkins, I. W. J. "City Regions in Roman Palestine." *PEQ* 112 (1980), 19–32.
Howgego, C. "Coin Circulation and the Integration of the Roman Economy." *JRA* 7 (1994), 5–21.
Hüttenmeister, F. G., Reeg, G. *Die antiken Synagogen in Israel.* Wiesbaden, 1977.
Isaac, B. *The Limits of Empire.* Oxford: Clarendon, 1990.
Jackson, B. S. *Essays in Jewish and Comparative Legal History.* SJLA 10: Leiden, Brill, 1975.
———. *Theft in Early Jewish Law.* Oxford: Clarendon, 1972.
Johnson, A. C. *Roman Egypt.* In *An Economic Survey of Ancient Rome* II. Ed. T. Frank: Baltimore: Johns Hopkins, 1936.
Jolowicz, H. F. "The Origin of *Laesio Enormis*." *Juridical Review* 49 (1937), 50–72.
———. *A Historical Introduction to Roman Law.* Rev. ed. B. Nicholas. Cambridge: Cambridge, 1972.
Jones, A. H. M. "The Urbanization of Palestine." *JRS* 22 (1931), 18–35.
———. *The Greek City from Alexander to Justinian.* Oxford: Oxford University, 1940.
———. "Inflation Under the Roman Empire." *Economic History Review* 5 (1953), 293–318.
———. "The Economic Life of the Towns of the Roman Empire." In *Receuils de la Société Jean Bodin* 6 (1954). Rpt. *The Roman Economy.* Ed. P. A. Brunt. Totowa: Rowman and Littlefield, 1974, 46–51.
———. *Cities of the Eastern Roman Empire.* Rev. ed. M. Avi-Yonah *et al.* Oxford: Clarendon, 1971.
Jördens, A. "Σιδήραιος = ἀθάνατος?" *ZPE* 71 (1988), 99-104.
Jost, I. M. *Geschichte des Israeliten.* Berlin, 1820–47.
July, H. H. *Die Klauseln hinter den Massangaben der Papyrusurkunden.* Diss. Cologne, 1966.
Juster, J. *Les Juifs dans l'empire romain.* Paris, 1914.
Kadman, L. *Corpus Nummorum Palaestinensium [CNP] II: Caesarea.* Tel Aviv: Schocken, 1957.
———. *Corpus Nummorum Palaestinensium [CNP] III: The Coins of the Jewish War.* Tel Aviv: Schocken, 1960.
Kasovsky, C. Y. *Thesaurus Mishnae.* Jerusalem: Massadah, 1957.
———. *Thesaurus Talmudis.* Jerusalem: JTSA, 1954–81.
Katsch, A. I. *Ginze Talmud.* Jerusalem: Rubin Mass, 1979.
Kedar, B. Z. *et al.* eds. *Commerce in Palestine Throughout the Ages* [Hebrew]. Jerusalem: Yad Izhak Ben Zvi, IES, 1990.
Keenan, J. G. "Two Loans from Tebtunis." *BASP* 7 (1970), 77–84.
Kehoe, D. *Management and Investment on Estates in Roman Egypt.* Bonn: Habelt, 1992.
Kimelman, R. "Rabbi Yohanan and Origen on the Song of Songs: A Third-Century Disputation." *HTR* 73 (1980), 567–89.
Kindler, A. *The Coins of Tiberias.* Tiberias: Hammat Tiberias, 1961.

Kleiman, E. "Bi-Metalism in Rabbi's Time: Two Variants of the Mishna 'Gold Acquires Silver'" [Hebrew]. *Zion* 38 (1973), 48–61.

———. "Were Fairs in Tannaitic and Amoraic Palestine Artificial or Redundant?" [Hebrew]. *Zion* 51 (1986), 471–84.

———. "'Just Price' in Talmudic Literature." *History of Political Economy* 19 (1987), 23–45.

Klein, M. L. *Genizah Fragments of the Palestinian Targum to the Pentateuch.* Cincinnati: HUC, 1986.

Klimowsky, E. W. "Monetary Function of City Coins." In A. Kindler ed., *International Numismatic Conference (1963).* Jerusalem: Schocken, 1967, 129–79.

Kohl, H., Watzinger, C. *Antike Synagogen in Galilaea.* Leipzig: J. C. Hinrichs, 1916.

Kraay, C. M. "Jewish Friends and Allies of Rome." *ANS Museum Notes* 25 (1980), 53–7.

Krauss, S. *Griechische und lateinische Lehnwörter im Talmud, Midrasch und Targum.* Berlin: 1898–9.

Krauss, S. *Talmudische Archäologie. Grundrisse der Gesamtwissenschaft des Judentums V.* Leipzig, 1911.

Krauss, S. *Qadmôniyôt ha-talmûd.* Berlin, Vienna, 1924.

Krochmal, N. *Môreh nĕbûkê ha-zĕman.* Ed. L. Zunz. Lemberg, 1851.

Kutscher, E. Y. "New Aramaic Texts." *JAOS* 74 (1954), 233–48. Rpt. in Kutscher, 1977, English section, 37–52.

———. *The Language and Linguistic Background of the Isaiah Scroll.* [Hebrew] Jerusalem: Magnes, 1959.

———. "Marginal Notes to the Biblical Lexicon [III]" [Hebrew]. *Leš.* 30 (1966), 18–24. Rpt. in Kutscher, 1977, Hebrew section, 348–54.

———. *Hebrew and Aramaic Studies.* Ed. Z. Ben-Hayyim *et al.* Jerusalem: Magnes, 1977.

Lane Fox, R. *Pagans and Christians.* New York: Knopf, 1989.

Lapin, H. "Rabbi." *Anchor Bible Dictionary.* New York: Doubleday, 1991.

———. *Text, Money and Law: The Social and Literary Background of Mishnah Tractate* Babaʾ Meṣiʿaʾ. Diss. Columbia University, 1994.

——— "Early Rabbinic Civil Law and the Literature of the Second Temple Period." *JSQ* 2 (1995), 149–83.

Lauterbach, J. Z. *Mekilta de-Rabbi Ishmael.* Philadelphia: JPS, 1935.

Levine, C. "Exegesis of the Mishna in the Mechilta de Rashbi and its Relation to Amoraic Teaching" [Hebrew]. *BIA* 16/17 (1979), 59–69.

———. "The Concept '*Shelihut Yad*' in the Mechilta De Rashbi" [Heb.]. *BIA* 18/19 (1981), 98–116.

Levine, L. I. *Caesarea Under Roman Rule.* SJLA 7: Leiden: Brill, 1976.

———. "The Patriarch (Nasi) in Third Century Palestine." *ANRW* 2.19.2 (1979), 649–88.

———. *Tĕqûpātô šel rabbî yĕhûdâ ha-nāśîʾ.*" In Baras, 1982, 1, 93–118.

---. "The Second Temple Synagogue: The Formative Years." In L. I. Levine ed. *The Synagogue in Late Antiquity*. Philadelphia and New York: ASOR and JTSA, 1987, 7–31.

---. *The Rabbinic Class of Roman Palestine in Late Antiquity*. Jerusalem and New York: Yad Izhak ben Zvi and JTSA, 1989.

---. ed. *The Galilee in Late Antiquity*. New York: JTSA, 1992.

Lewin, B. M., ed. *ʾIggeret rab šěrîrāʾ gāʾôn*. 1921. Rpt. Jerusalem: Makor, 1972.

---, ed. *ʾÔṣār ha-gěʾônîm*. Jerusalem: Hebrew University, 1928–43. Rpt. 1984.

Lieberman, S. "Palestine in the Third and Fourth Centuries." *JQR* 36 (1946), 329–70; 37 (1947), 31–66.

---. *Hellenism in Jewish Palestine*. Texts and Studies 18: New York: JTSA, 1950.

---. "ʿEśer milîn." *ʾEškolôt* 3 (1959), 73–89. Rept. in Lieberman, 1991, 440–56.

---. "The Importance of the Bar Kokhba Letters for Jewish History and Literature." In *Masada and the Finds from the Bar Kokhba Caves*. New York: Jewish Museum, 1967, 42–3. Rpt. in Lieberman, S. *Texts and Studies*. New York: Ktav, 1974, 208–9.

---. *Siphre Zutta (The Midrash of Lydda)* [Hebrew]. New York: JTSA, 1968.

---. "*Mišnat bābāʾ měṣîʿaʾ rēš ʾēzehû nešek û-pērûšāh*." In *Yad R. ʾ. M. Lifshitz*. Jerusalem, 1975, 217–23. Rpt. in Lieberman, 1991, 12–8.

---. *Studies in Palestinian Talmudic Literature* [Hebrew]. Ed. D. Rosenthal. Jerusalem: Magnes, 1991.

Lightstone, J. N. "The Rhetoric of the Mishnah and the Emergence of Rabbinic Social Institutions at the End of the Second Century." Paper presented at the SBL Annual Meeting, 1994.

Linder, A. "The Roman Imperial Government and the Jews under Constantine" [Hebrew]. *Tarbiz* 44 (1974–5), 95–143.

---. *The Jews in Roman Imperial Legislation*. Detroit: Wayne State, 1987.

MacMullen, R. "Market Days in the Roman Empire." *Phoenix* 24 (1970), 333–41.

---. *Roman Social Relations*. New Haven: Yale, 1974.

Mantel, H. *Studies in the History of the Sanhedrin*. Harvard Semitic Series 17: Cambridge: Harvard, 1961.

Mason, H. J. *Greek Terms for Roman Institutions*. ASP 13: Toronto: Hakkert, 1974.

Melamed, E. Z. "*Hitpatḥût dînê ha-ʾônāʾâ*." *Yabneh* 3 (1942–3), 33–56.

---. *The Relationship between the Halakhic Midrashim and the Mishna and Tosefta* [Hebrew]. Jerusalem, 1968.

---. *An Introduction to Talmudic Literature* [Hebrew]. Jerusalem, 1973.

Meshorer, Y. "The Coins of Sephorris (*sic*) as a Historical Source" [Hebrew], *Zion* 43 (1978), 184–200.

---. "Sepphoris and Rome." *Greek Numismatics and Archaeology: Essays in Honor of Margaret Thompson*. Brussels: Cultura, 1979, 159–71.

---. *The City Coins of Eretz-Israel and the Decapolis in the Roman Period*. Jerusalem: Israel Museum, 1984, 36–7.

Meyers, E. M. "Roman Sepphoris in Light of New Archeological Evidence and Recent Research." In L. I. Levine, ed., 1992, 321–38.
Meyers, E. M., Strange, J. F., *Archeology, the Rabbis and Early Christianity*. Nashville: Abingdon, 1981.
Mildenberg, L. *The Coinage of the Bar Kokhba War*. Araau: Sauerländer, 1984.
Milik, J. T. "*Deux documents inédits du Désert de Juda.*" *Biblica* 38 (1957), 245–68.
Milikowsky, C. "The *Status Quaestionis* of Research in Rabbinic Literature." *JJS* 39 (1988), 208–11.
Millar, F. G. B. "Local Cultures in the Roman Empire: Lybian, Punic and Latin in Roman Africa." *JRS* 58 (1968), 126–34.
———. "Paul of Samosata, Zenobia and Aurelian: The Church, Local Culture and Political Allegiance in Third-Century Syria." *JRS* 61 (1971), 1–17.
———. "The World of the *Golden Ass*." *JRS* 71 (1981), 63–75.
———. "Empire, Community and Culture in the Roman Near East: Greeks, Syrians, Jews and Arabs." *JJS* 38 (1987), 143–65.
———. *The Roman Near East*. Cambridge: Harvard, 1993.
Miller, S. S. *Studies in the History and Traditions of Sepphoris*. SJLA 37: Leiden: Brill, 1984.
Mitteis, L. "*Trapezitika*." *ZRG* (*Röm. Abteilung*) 19 (1898), 198–260.
Moore, G. F. "Christian Writers on Judaism." *HTR* 14 (1921), 197–254.
———. *Judaism in the First Centuries of the Christian Era*. Cambridge: Harvard, 1927.
Moreshet, M. "Further Studies of the Language of the Hebrew Bārāytōt in the Babylonian and Palestinian Talmudim" [Hebrew]. In M. Z. Kaddari ed. *Archive of the New Dictionary of Rabbinic Literature: Volume II*. Ramat Gan: Bar Ilan, 1974, 56–68.
Nautin, P. *Origène: sa vie et son oeuvre*. Paris, 1977.
Ne'eman, Y. "Sepphoris in the Period of the Second Temple, Mishna and Talmud." Diss. Hebrew University, 1987.
Netzer, E., Weiss, Z. "New Mosaic Art from Sepphoris." *BAR* 18 no. 6 (1992), 36–43.
Neusner, J. *A Life of R. Yohanan b. Zakkai*. SPB 6: Leiden: Brill, 1962.
———. *A History of the Jews in Babylonia*. SPB VI: Leiden: Brill, 1965–70.
———. *The Development of a Legend*. SPB 16: Leiden: Brill, 1970.
———. *Rabbinic Traditions About the Pharisees Before 70*. Leiden, Brill, 1971.
———. *The Idea of Purity in Ancient Judaism*. SJLA 1: Leiden, Brill, 1973.
———, ed. *The Modern Study of the Mishnah*. SPB 23: Leiden: Brill, 1975.
———. *Method and Meaning in Ancient Judaism*. First series: BJS 10: Missoula: Scholars, 1979. Second series: BJS 15: Missoula: Scholars, 1980. Third series: BJS 16: Chico: Scholars, 1980. Fourth series: BJS 168: Atlanta: Scholars, 1989.
———. "Dating a Mishnah Tractate." In *History, Religion and Spiritual Democracy: Essays in Honor of Joseph L. Blau*. Ed. F. A. Martin *et al*. New York: Columbia, 1980, 97–113.

———. *Judaism: The Evidence of the Mishnah*. Chicago Studies in the History of Judaism. Chicago: University of Chicago, 1981.

———, ed. *The Study of Ancient Judaism*. New York: Ktav, 1981.

———. *Oral Tradition in Judaism: The Case of the Mishnah*. New York and London, 1987.

———. *A Religion of Pots and Pans?* BJS 156: Atlanta: Scholars, 1988.

———. "Sifra and the Problem of the Mishnah" *Henoch* 11 (1989), 17–40.

———. *The Canonical History of Ideas*. South Florida Studies in the History of Judaism 4: Atlanta: Scholars, 1990.

———. *The Economics of the Mishnah*. Chicago Studies in the History of Judaism. Chicago: University of Chicago, 1990.

———. *The Philosophical Mishnah I*. BJS 163: Atlanta, Scholars, 1990.

———. *The Tosepta: An Introduction*. South Florida Studies in the History of Judaism 147: Atlanta: Scholars, 1992.

Ohrenstein, R. A. O. "Economic Thought in Talmudic Literature in the Light of Modern Economics." *American Journal of Economics and Society* 27 (1968), 185–96.

Oppenheim, A. L. "A Note on the Ṣôn Barzel." *IEJ* 5 (1955), 89-92.

Oppenheimer, A. "*Batei Midrash* in the Early Amoraic Period" [Hebrew]. *Cathedra* 8 (1978), 80–9.

———. *Galilee in the Mishnaic Period* [Hebrew]. Jerusalem: Zalman Shazar, 1991.

———. *The 'Am Ha-aretz: A Study in the Social History of the Jewish Period in the Hellenistic-Roman Period*. Arbeiten zur Literatur und Geschichte des hellenistischen Judentums 8: Leiden: Brill, 1977.

Oppenheimer, A., Rappaport, U. eds. *The Bar Kokhva Revolt: A New Approach* [Hebrew]. Jerusalem: Yad Izhak ben Zvi, 1984.

Pineles, H. M. *Darkāh šel tôrâ*. Vienna, 1861.

Plattner, S. M. "Periodic Trade in Developing Areas Without Markets." In Smith, 1976, 1, 72–81.

Porter F. C. "Judaism in New Testament Times." *Journal of Religion* 8 (1928), 30–62.

Pringsheim, F. *The Greek Law of Sale*. Weimar: Hermann Boelhaus, 1950.

Qimron, E., Strugnell, J. "An Unpublished Halakhic Letter from Qumran." *Biblical Archeology Today* 5 (1985), 400–7.

———. "An Unpublished Halakhic Letter from Qumran." *Israel Museum Journal* 4 (1985), 9–12.

Rabello, A. M. "The Legal Condition of the Jews in the Roman Empire." *ANRW* 2.13, (1979), 662–762.

Rathbone, D. *Economic Rationalism and Rural Society in Third-Century Egypt*. Cambridge Clasical Studies. Cambridge: Cambridge, 1991.

Rea, J. "P. Lond. Inv. 1562 Verso: Market Taxes in Oxyrynchus." *ZPE* 48 (1982), 191–209.

Ritterling, E. "Legio." *PW* 12, 1211–1829.

Rosenthal, D. *Mišnâ ʿabôdâ zārâ: mahadûrâ biqortît bĕ-ṣērûp mābô?*. Diss.: Hebrew University, 1980.
Rosenthal, L. A. *Über den Zusammenhang der Mischna.* Strasbourg, 1909.
Rostovtzeff, M. *Social and Economic History of the Roman Empire.* Rev. ed. P. M. Fraser. Oxford: Oxford University, 1957.
Rotenstreich, N. *Tradition and Reality: The Impact of History on Modern Jewish Thought.* New York: Random House, 1974.
Roth-Gerson. L. *The Greek Inscriptions from the Synagogues in Eretz-Israel* [Hebrew]. Jerusalem: Yad Izhak ben Zvi, 1987.
Sacks, N. ed. *The Mishnah.* Institute for the Complete Israeli Talmud: Jerusalem: Yad Harav Herzog, 1971–.
Safrai, S. *et al.*, eds. *The Jewish People in the First Century. CRINT* 1: Philadelphia and Assen: Fortress and Van Gorcum, 1976.
———, eds. *The Literature of the Sages. CRINT* 3: Philadelphia and Assen: Fortress and Van Gorcum, 1987.
Safrai, Z. "Urbanization in Israel in the Greco Roman Period" [Hebrew]. *Meḥqarîm* 5 (1980), 105–29.
———. "*Ha-kĕpār bi-tĕqûpat ha-mišnâ wĕ-ha-talmûd.*" In *Nation and History* [Hebrew]. Ed. M. Stern. Jerusalem: Zalman Shazar Center, 1983, 1, 173–95.
———. "*Lĕ-šĕʾēlat ha-mibneh ha-merḥābî šel ha-yiššûb ba-gālîl bi-tĕqupat ha-mišnâ wĕ-ha-talmûd.*" In *In the Lands of Galilee* [Hebrew]. Ed. A. Shemueli *et al.* Haifa: University of Haifa, 1983, 269–88.
———. "Fairs in Eretz Israel in the Mishnah and Talmud Period" [Hebrew]. *Zion* 49 (1984), 139–58.
———. *Pirqê galîl bi-tĕqûpat ha-mišnâ wĕ-ha-talmûd.* Tel Aviv: Maalot, 1985.
———. "The Fair as an Economic Institution—A Rejoinder" [Hebrew]. *Zion*, 51 (1986), 485–6.
———. "*Ha-mishar bĕ-ʾereṣ yiśrāʾēl ba-tĕqûpâ ha-rômît.*" In Kedar *et al.*, 1990, 108–39.
———. "*Ha-ṭippûl bĕ-maʿareket ha-dĕrākîm ha-kĕpāriyyôt bi-tĕqûpat ha-mišnâ wĕ-ha-talmûd.*" In Kedar *et al.*, 1990, 159–180.
———. *The Economy of Roman Palestine.* London: Routledge, 1994.
Said, E. *Orientalism.* New York: Pantheon, 1978.
Saldarini, A. *The Fathers According to Rabbi Nathan.* SJLA 11: Leiden: Brill, 1975.
Sanders, E. P. *Paul and Palestinian Judaism.* Philadelphia: Fortress, 1977.
Schäfer, P. "Das 'Dogma' des mündlichen Torah im rabbinischen Judentum." In *idem, Studien zur Geschichte und Theologie des rabbinischen Judentums.* Leiden: Brill, 1978, 153–97.
———. "Die Flucht Johanan b. Zakkais aus Jerusalem und die Gründung des 'Lehrhauses' in Jabne." *ANRW* 2.19.2 (1979), 43–101.
———. "Rabbi Aqiba and Bar Kokhba." In *Approaches to Ancient Judaism II.* Ed. W. S. Green. Chico: Scholars, 1980, 113–30.
———. *Die Bar Kokhba-Aufstand.* Tübingen: Mohr, 1981.

———. "Research into Rabbinic Literature: An Attempt to define the Status Quaestionis." *JJS* 37 (1986), 139–52.

———. "Once Again, the Status Quaestionis of Research in Rabbinic Literature: An Answer to Chaim Milikowsky." *JJS* 40 (1989), 89–94.

Schnebel, M. *Die Landwirtschaft im Hellenistischen Ägypten.* Munich: C. H. Beck, 1925.

Scholem, G. "The Science of Judaism—Then and Now." In *The Messianic Idea in Judaism.* New York: Schocken, 1971, 304–13.

Schorsch, I. "Ideology and History in the Age of Emancipation." In H. Graetz, *The Structure of Jewish History and Other Essays.* Tr., ed. I. Schorsch. New York: JTSA, 1975.

———. "Breakthrough into the Past: The Verein für Cultur und Wissenschaft der Juden." *Leo Baeck Institute Yearbook.* 33 (1988), 2–28.

Schulz, F. *A History of Roman Legal Science.* Oxford: Clarendon, 1946.

———. *Classical Roman Law.* Oxford: Clarendon, 1951.

Schürer, E. *A History of the Jewish People in the Age of Jesus Christ.* Tr. J. Macpherson *et al.* Edinburgh: T. and T. Clark, 1885–91.

———. *A History of the Jewish People in the Age of Jesus Christ.* Rev. ed. G. Vermes, *et al.* Edinburgh: T. and T. Clark, 1973–87.

Schwartz, S. *Josephus and Judaean Politics. Columbia Studies in the Classical Tradition* 18: Leiden: Brill, 1990.

Sider, G. "When Parrots Learn to Talk, and When They Can't: Domination, Deception, and Self-Deception in Indian-White Relations." *Contemporary Studies of History and Society* 29 (1987), 3–23.

Smallwood, E. M. "The Legislation of Hadrian and Antoninus Pius Against Circumcision." *Latomus* 18 (1959), 334–47.

———. *The Jews Under Roman Rule.* Corr. rpt. SJLA 20: Leiden: Brill, 1981.

Smith, C. A., ed. *Regional Analysis. Studies in Anthropology.* New York: Academic, 1976.

———. "Exchange Systems and the Spatial Distribution of Elites." In Smith, 1976, 2, 309–74.

———. "Regional Economic Systems: Linking Geographical Models and Socioeconomic Problems." In Smith, 1976, 1, 3–63.

Sokoloff, M. *A Dictionary of Palestinian Aramaic.* Ramat Gan: Bar Ilan, 1990.

Sperber, D. "Palestinian Currency Systems During the Second Commonwealth." *JQR* 56 (1965–6), 273–301.

———. *Roman Palestine, 200–400: The Land. Bar Ilan Studies in Near Eastern Languages and Cultures.* Ramat Gan: Bar Ilan, 1978.

———. *Dictionary of Greek and Latin Legal Terms in Rabbinic Literature. Dictionaries of Talmud, Midrash and Targum I.* Ramat Gan: Bar Ilan, 1984.

———. *Roman Palestine, 200–400: Money, Prices.* 2 ed. with supplement. Ramat Gan: Bar Ilan, 1991.

Stern, M. *Greek and Latin Authors on Jews and Judaism.* Jerusalem: Israel Academy of Arts and Sciences, 1976–84.

Strack, H. L. *Introduction to Talmud and Midrash.* Ed. G. Stemberger. tr. M. Brokmuehl. Minneapolis: Augsburg-Fortress, 1992.

Strack, H. L., Billerbeck, P. *Kommentar zum Neuen Testament aus Talmud und Midrasch.* Munich, 1922–8.

Strange, J. F. "Six Campaigns at Sepphoris: The University of South Florida Excavations, 1983–9." In Levine, 1992, 339–56.

Syme, R. *Emperors and Biography: Studies in the Historia Augusta.* Oxford: Clarendon, 1971.

Taubenschlag, R. *The Law of Greco Roman Egypt in Light of the Papyri.* Warsaw, 1955.

Tsafrir, Y. "On the Source of the Architectural Design of the Ancient Synagogues of Galilee: A New Appraisal." In Urman, Flesher, 1995, 70–86.

Tsafrir, Y. *et al. Tabula Imperii Romani: Iudaea, Palaestina.* Jerusalem: Israel Academy of Arts and Sciences, 1994.

Urbach, E. E. "Class Status and Leadership in the World of the Palestinian Sages" [Hebrew]. *Proceedings of the Israel Academy of Sciences.* Jerusalem, 1968, 2, 31–54.

———. *The Laws Regarding Slavery as a Source for the Social History of the Period of the Second Temple and the Mishnah and Talmud. Ancient Economic History.* New York: Arno, 1979.

Urman, D. "Jewish Inscriptions from Dabura in the Golan" [Hebrew]. *Tarbiz*, 40 (1970–1), 399–408 = *IEJ* 22 (1972), 1–23.

Urman, D., Flesher, P. V. M., eds. *Ancient Synagogues: Historical Analysis and Archeological Discovery.* SPB 47: Leiden: Brill, 1995.

Vermes, G. *Jesus the Jew.* Corr. ed. Philadelphia: Fortress, 1981.

Vogel, E. K. "Bibliography of Holy-Land Sites" I–III. *HUCA* 42 (1971), 1–96, 52 (1981), 1–92, 58 (1987), 1–63.

von Bolla, S. *Untersuchungen zur Tiermiete und Viehpacht in Altertum. Münchener Beiträge zur Papyrusforschung und antiken Rechtsgeschichte* 30: Munich: C. H. Beck, 1940.

Wegner, J. R. *Chattel or Person? The Status of Women in the Mishnah.* Oxford: Oxford, 1988.

Weiss, A. "*Lĕ-ḥēqer siprût ha-mišnâ.*" *HUCA* 16 (1941), 1–33.

Weiss, I. H. *Dôr dôr wĕ-doršāyw.* Vienna, 1871.

Welles, C. B., *et al. Dura Europus Final Report V, Part I: Parchments and Papyri.* New Haven: Yale, 1959.

Wellhausen, J. *Die Pharasäer und die Sadducäer.* Greifswald, 1874.

———. *Prolegomena to the History of Israel.* Tr. J. S. Black, A. Menzies. Edinburgh: A. and C. Black, 1885.

———. *The Arab Kingdom and its Fall.* Tr. M. G. Weir. London: Curzon, 1973.

———. *The Religio-Political Factions in Early Islam.* Tr. R. C. Ostle, S. M. Waltzer. Amsterdam: North Holland, 1975.

Wessely, C. *Mitteilungen aus der Sammlung der Papyrus Erzherzog Rainer [MPER].* Vienna, 1887-97.

White, K. D. *Roman Farming*. Ithaca: Cornell, 1970.
Wolf, E. R. "Closed Corporate Communities in Mesoamerica and Central Java." *Southwestern Journal of Anthropology*, 13 (1957), 1–18.
———. *Peasants*. Englewood Cliffs: Prentice Hall, 1966.
Wolff, H. J. *Roman Law: An Historical Introduction*. Norman: University of Oklahoma, 1951.
Yadin, Y. "Expedition D [to the Judean Desert]." *IEJ* 11 (1961), 37–52.
———. "Expedition D [to the Judean Desert]." *IEJ* 12 (1962), 227–57.
Yeivin, Z. "Survey of Settlements in Galilee and the Golan from the Period of the Mishnah in Light of the Sources." Diss. Hebrew University, 1971.
Zlotnick, D. *The Iron Pillar: Mishnah*. Jerusalem: Bialik, 1988.
Zuckermandel, M. S. *Gesammelte Aufsätze. Erster Teil. Zur Halachakritik*. Frankfurt, 1911.
Zussman, Y. "Manuscripts and Text Traditions of the Mishnah" [Hebrew]. In *Proceedings of the Eighth World Congress of Jewish Studies* [1977]. Vol. 3 [1981], 215–50

✧ Index of Primary Sources ✧

Hebrew Bible

Genesis
15:9—274
20:9—167
33:18—136
42:35—251
43:12—251
43:20–21—251

Exodus
21:37—53, 257
22:3—167
22:6–7—257
22:6–12—55
22:6–14—40, 40, 48, 164, 165, 168, 187, 224, 319
22:6—186
22:7—71, 164, 165, 166, 167, 172, 320, 328
22:8—44, 165, 166, 167, 168, 321, 327, 328
22:9–10—48
22:9–12—48
22:9–13—60
22:9—48, 165, 186, 322, 327
22:10—71, 164, 165, 166, 167, 168, 172, 328, 329
22:11—48, 320
22:12—169
22:13b–14a—44
22:13—60, 186
22:14—60, 79, 221
22:20—319
22:24–5—323
22:24—187, 190

22:25–6—200, 323
22:25—49
22:26—323
23:2—326
23:3—42
23:4–5—60, 324, 325
23:4—324
23:5—42, 43, 107
25:4—93

Leviticus
5:15–16—63
5:21–23—44
7:16—45
17:13—84
19:13—48, 153, 209, 212, 304
19:23–5—289
19:23—290
19:35–6—146
22:18—45
22:23—45
22:28—84
25:14—55
25:14ff.—327
25:29–30—193
25:35–6—47, 190, 276
25:35–7—47
25:35—276
25:36—46, 276
25:37—190
25:39–40—201
25:50—209
25:55—202

Numbers
15:3—45
18:16—127

29:39—45

Deuteronomy
12:6—45
12:17—45
14:22–7—150
22:1–3—42
22:1–4—60, 325
22:1—42, 43
22:2—42, 60, 253, 324, 325
22:3—42, 44–45, 158, 159, 162, 251, 325, 328
22:4—42, 43
23:20–1—190
23:21—47
23:25–6—210
24:6—49, 50, 60
24:10–3—200
24:10–5—60, 82
24:14–5—48, 212
24:15—153, 209, 304
24:17–18—60
24:17—49, 200
25:13–19—146
25:4—91, 92, 210
25:5–11—292

Ezekiel
18:7—49
18:8—46
18:12—49
18:13—46
18:16—49
18:17—46
22:12—46
33:5—49

Amos
2:8—49
8:11-2—27
Cantcles
3:9—281

Proverbs
20:16—49
27:13—49
28:8—46

Job
22:6—49
24:3-9—49

Qumran

Community Rule (1QS)
VI.18-20—240

Damascus Rule
IX.11—240

Mishnah

Berakot
2:4—204
9:3—175
Peʾa
1:6—186
3:3—137, 146
4:5—92
5:5—220, 222
5:6—203, 213
5:7—203
5:8—90
7:6—63
8:7—214
8:8—49, 199, 216
Demai
2:4—137
2:4—140, 143
3:1—210, 213, 217
3:2—137
3:4—164, 173, 174
5:7—137, 145, 147
6:1-5—218, 300
6:2—222
7:1—140
7:3—210, 217
8:3—137
Kilʾayim
7:6—203
Šebiʿit
4:5—44
5:3—44
5:6—204
5:8—150, 203

5:9—188, 189
6:1—44
7:3—137, 146
7:6—148
8:1—44
8:4—203, 214
8:5-6—188
9:7—218
10:1—209
10:2—199
10:5—49, 111
10:6—49, 199
10:9—175, 176
Terumot
1:10—90
3:4—203
6:3—210, 214, 217
11:9—218, 220, 224, 226
Maʿaśerot
1:5-7—90, 287
1:5—137, 146, 290
1:7—289
1:8—45, 59
2:1-3:4—56
2:3—140
2:4—90, 287
2:5-6—211
2:5—56
2:6—56
2:7-8—57
2:7-8—203
2:7-8—210

2:7—56. 57, 212, 217
2:8—56, 57, 288
3:1-3—203, 210, 212
3:2—56
3:3—212
3:4—56
4:2—148
5:1—186
5:5—175, 186, 203
7:8—211
Maʿaśer Šeni
1:1—49, 178, 199
1:5—175
1:7—186
2:2—137
2:7-8—150
2:8—150, 151, 325
2:9—137, 141, 150, 155
3:12—175, 188
3:6—90
4:1—151
4:2—137, 143, 150, 151, 155
4:4—203
5:3—63
5:9—218
Halla
1:6—137
2:7—137
3:9—290
3:10—290
4:1—175

Index of Sources

ʿOrla
  2:1—63
  3:7–8—290
  3:8—59, 290
Bikkurim
  1:5—203
  1:6—175
  1:11—175
  3:12—175, 186
Šabbat
  2:1–2—27
  9:7—140
  22:2—90
  23:1—187, 189
ʿErubim
  7:11—137
  7:6—203
  7:9—137
  8:2—214
Pesaḥim
  1:1—92
  2:5—137
  4:6—204
  4:7—204
  4:9—279
  7:2—203
  8:2—203
Šeqalim
  1:3—49, 148, 199, 203
  1:5—49
  2:1—150
  4:1—164
  4:9—76
  5:4—76
  7:5—49. 199
Yomaʾ
  3:4—289
Sukka
  5:4–5—37
  Beṣa
  1:10—204
  3:8—137, 141
  5:4—187, 188, 189
Roš Haššana
  1:8—46
  Taʿanit
  3:8—7, 231

4:8—188
Megilla
  1:6—269
  4:10—24
Moʿed Qatan
  1:8—204
  1:10—204
  2:1–2—203, 206, 281
  2:4—204
  3:3—57
  3:4—58
Ḥagiga
  2:1—16, 24
  2:2—100
Yebamot
  1–2—275
  10:1—44
  15:7—65
Ketubot
  4:1—44
  4:4—44
  5:5—215
  5:8–9—215
  5:8—216
  5:9—215
  6:1—44, 186
  8:3—186
  8:5—186
  8:7—186
  8:8—148
  9:1—40
  9:2—164
  9:4—140
  9:8—247
  11:3—49, 199
  11:4–5—186
  11:4—182
  11:5—182
  13:8—49, 199
Nedarim
  4:1—188, 189, 218
  4:2—44
  4:4—210
  4:7—141, 203
  5:3—218, 219, 220
  10:6—175
  11:2—137

Soṭa
  7:1—164
  8:1–7—60
  9:1–8—60
Giṭṭin
  3:5—164
  4:3—247
  5:2—247
  5:8—44
  5:9—188, 189
  8:5—44
Qiddušin
  1:1–5—175, 186, 62, 125, 175, 183, 184
  1:5—176, 183, 184
  1:6—131, 178, 186
  1:7—202
  3:2—148
  3:7—292
  4:14—142, 202
Babaʾ Qamma
  1:1—329
  1:4—291, 323
  2:4—45
  3—64
  3:1–3—64
  3:1—73
  3:2—64
  3:3—64
  4:1—126
  4:9—47
  4:9—164, 169, 172, 174, 187, 188, 218, 224, 262, 263
  5:7—44
  5:7—167
  6:1—262, 263
  6:2—262
  6:5—203
  6:6—137
  7:4—53, 54, 55, 56, 108, 188, 269
  7:5—113
  7:6—164, 174, 187, 218, 224
  8:1—137, 138, 147
  8:6—156

9:1-2—105, 172
9:2—73, 169
9:3—204
9:5—62
9:6-7—63
9:7-8—329
9:7—164, 165, 328, 328
9:8—164, 165, 328
10:1—150
10:2—158
10:5—73, 224
10:6—164
10:7—65, 164

Baba' Meṣiʿa'
1—4
1:1-2—95, 6, 313
1:1-4—94, 162
1:1—61, 94, 95, 162, 163, 245
1:2—61, 94, 95, 162, 246
1:3-4—68, 95, 96, 159, 246
1:3—44, 95, 159, 160, 245
1:4—42, 44, 95, 96, 160, 162, 163
1:5—44, 156,
1:6-8—57, 68, 162, 314, 316
1:6—68, 101, 109, 111, 112, 183, 316, 317
1:7—111, 112
1:8—68, 87, 101, 108, 109, 110, 111, 112, 219, 248, 254
2:1-2—45, 68, 87, 157, 158, 162, 249, 251, 315
2:1-4—252
2:1—44, 62, 68, 87, 100, 101, 108, 109, 112, 139, 157, 158, 313
2:2-4—41
2:2—41, 68, 157, 158, 204, 315
2:3-4—41, 160, 162

2:3—41, 42, 68, 158, 158, 218, 250
2:4—68, 99, 100, 101, 155, 160, 250
2:5—42, 44, 45, 45, 60, 109, 158, 159, 162, 251, 259, 315, 325, 326, 328
2:6—101, 109, 110, 315
2:7—41, 42, 43, 44, 52, 60, 101, 106, 107, 109, 152, 158, 160, 161, 162, 253, 259, 263, 295, 296, 313, 315, 324, 326
2:8—42, 68, 160, 161, 162, 163, 166, 239, 262, 269, 310, 313, 321, 324, 326
2:9-10—42, 43, 60, 162, 324, 314
2:9—42, 43, 44, 48, 68, 89, 161, 162, 197, 274, 324, 325, 327
2:10—42, 43, 68, 101, 106, 107, 108, 109, 163, 269, 313, 324, 325, 326, 327
2:11—44, 163, 313, 314
3:1—50, 60, 66, 69, 71, 92, 164, 166, 174, 257, 262, 269
3:2-5—65, 66, 67, 70, 71, 113, 187
3:2—65, 66, 69, 71, 102, 108, 109, 187, 188, 218, 224, 314
3:3-4—174
3:3-5—65, 66, 187, 313
3:3—65, 66, 218
3:4-5—65, 66
3:4—65, 66, 102, 108, 109, 254, 259
3:5—65, 66, 102, 108, 109, 174, 254, 259
3:6-7—74
3:6-8—74, 79, 115, 199

3:6-10—66
3:6-11—66
3:6—44, 52, 66, 67, 69, 71, 72, 73, 73, 74, 102, 109, 114, 145, 166, 170, 173, 253, 314, 315
3:7-8—74, 110, 173, 174
3:7—66, 67, 69, 71, 72, 73, 74, 102, 106, 107, 108, 109, 110, 114, 174, 216, 316
3:8—67, 71, 72, 73, 74, 102, 108, 109, 110, 115, 174, 185, 261
3:9—37, 45, 52, 66, 69, 71, 73, 106, 170, 171, 172, 320, 328
3:10—52, 66, 69, 156, 169, 262
3:11—51, 52, 66, 67, 69, 71, 102, 106, 107, 108, 109, 110, 114, 141, 148, 150, 152, 155, 161, 164, 173
3:12—45, 45, 52, 60, 69, 71, 73, 84, 102, 105, 106, 107, 167, 172, 313, 320, 321, 328
4:1-2—130
4:1—38, 87, 88, 89, 122, 124, 130, 131, 132, 134, 138, 175, 176, 177, 178, 179, 315
4:2—76, 87, 88, 89, 92, 102, 109, 122, 124, 130, 131, 134, 138, 176, 177, 178, 179, 247, 315
4:3-4—143
4:3-6—62, 63, 326
4:3-10—319
4:3—61, 117, 141, 143, 177, 180, 181, 268
4:4—102, 108, 109, 141, 145, 177, 178, 180,

m. Babaʾ Meṣiʿaʾ, cont.
  181, 266, 268, 269
4:5–6—40, 89, 122, 177, 180
4:5—40, 71, 102, 110, 111, 128, 129, 133, 141, 180, 238, 266, 313
4:6—40, 76, 89, 135, 143, 149, 180, 204, 286, 313, 326
4:7–8—61, 62, 63, 64, 65, 84
4:7—57, 61, 62, 63, 63, 68, 123, 131, 137, 158, 180, 266, 315
4:8—62, 63, 68, 268, 310,
4:9—47, 52, 53, 54, 55, 56, 92, 102, 108, 109, 110, 113, 139, 164, 172, 182, 183, 266, 313, 326, 327
4:10—60, 266, 269, 317, 319, 326, 326
4:11–12—138, 177, 185
4:11—138, 140, 141, 145, 181, 270, 315, 317, 318
4:12—59, 99, 102, 103, 109, 110, 138, 140, 142, 145, 273, 314
5:1–3—97
5:1—45, 46, 68, 87, 88, 96, 97, 98, 122, 123, 133, 138, 143, 145, 147, 178, 185, 191, 194, 195, 196214, 314, 323, 326, 327
5:2–3—97, 232
5:2–6—97
5:2–10—97, 98
5:2—46, 69, 88, 96, 97, 98, 122, 185, 192, 218, 221, 313, 315
5:3—96, 122, 138, 185, 192, 193, 198, 291, 315
5:4–5—47, 89, 196, 314
5:4–6—97, 152, 226
5:4—47, 48, 89, 97, 122, 138, 139, 152, 196, 197, 198, 218, 221, 227, 274, 299, 314, 315
5:5—42, 46, 47, 103, 108, 109, 145, 196, 197, 198, 220, 227, 313
5:6–10—98
5:6—46, 47, 89, 96, 97, 190, 196, 198, 218, 276, 299, 313, 314
5:7—97, 103, 108, 109, 110, 111, 122, 138, 143, 146, 147, 185, 194, 195, 232, 285, 315, 323
5:8–9—122, 123, 174, 199
5:8–10—97
5:8—97, 105, 117, 144, 198, 227, 229, 232, 238, 313, 314, 323
5:9—46, 90, 97, 103, 105, 106, 111, 123, 187, 189, 193, 194, 199, 314, 323
5:10—46, 87, 88, 97, 98, 103, 106, 111, 122, 192, 269, 279, 326
5:11—60, 97, 98, 103, 124, 149, 313, 323, 326, 327
5:12—124, 198
6:1–2—66, 74, 75, 204, 207, 208, 209
6:1–5—47, 64, 74, 75, 75, 75, 79, 83, 315
6:1—48, 69, 75, 83, 139, 203, 204, 205, 206, 207, 207, 234, 281, 286, 314, 317
6:2—69, 76, 77, 78, 108, 204, 205, 206, 207, 226, 230, 314
6:3, 5—314
6:3–5—66, 75, 79, 122, 224, 226
6:3—69, 73, 75, 76, 77, 78, 87, 115, 206, 218, 224, 225, 226, 282, 284, 314, 316
6:4—69, 76, 77, 218, 226
6:5—69, 75, 77, 78, 79, 86, 103, 112, 114, 115, 218, 225, 226, 314, 315, 317
6:6–7—47, 122, 164, 317
6:6–8—47, 47, 74, 75, 79, 84, 85
6:6—47, 74, 75, 77, 122, 173
6:7—44, 47, 69, 74, 75, 103, 108, 109, 122, 164, 199, 200, 218, 259, 313
6:8—47, 69, 73, 75, 103, 108, 109, 110, 170, 171, 172
7:1–2—315
7:1–7—49, 79, 84, 85, 86
7:1–8—57, 85, 122
7:1—48, 64, 66, 69, 74, 75, 77, 82, 83, 84, 85, 103, 108, 109, 110, 114, 117, 117, 201, 208, 210, 233, 234, 238
7:2–3—75, 315
7:2–4—57, 326
7:2–7—85, 203
7:2—45, 57, 68, 85, 89, 90, 92, 93, 164, 211, 212, 288
7:3—85, 104, 112, 211
7:4—44, 48, 56, 57, 68, 89, 90, 91, 92, 93,

m. Baba' Meṣi'a', cont.
    211, 212, 259, 288,
    325, 326
  7:5—48, 104, 106, 107,
    110, 122, 123, 211,
    214, 325, 326
  7:6—123, 156, 203, 289
  7:7—58, 59, 69, 74, 82,
    83, 217, 290
  7:8–10—50, 85, 79
  7:8–11—85, 86
  7:8—44, 47, 48, 50, 60,
    63, 79, 85, 86, 164,
    165, 166, 169, 170,
    172, 187, 188, 210,
    211, 212, 218, 224,
    224, 288, 313, 320,
    322, 328
  7:9–10—48, 48, 50, 60,
    85, 166, 168, 169,
    171, 224, 322
  7:9—40, 44, 48, 85, 104,
    109, 110, 112, 166,
    224, 313, 322, 323
  7:10—40, 44, 47, 48, 50,
    85, 86, 164, 166, 168,
    187, 188, 218, 291,
    292, 315, 322
  7:11—40, 58, 86, 292
  8:1–3—41, 66, 79, 80,
    82, 188
  8:1—44, 60, 69, 79, 164,
    188, 218, 221, 313,
    320
  8:2–3—44
  8:2—69, 79, 80, 81, 82,
    188, 218, 295
  8:3—69, 79, 188, 203,
    320
  8:4–5—41, 80, 81, 82
  8:4—40, 69, 80, 81, 82,
    122, 138, 178, 185
  8:5—69, 80, 81, 138,
    186, 2958:7—69, 204,
    218, 228, 314
  8:8—69, 77, 117, 122,
    218, 219, 227, 303
  8:9—69, 82, 221, 228,
    298, 304
  9–10—174
  9:1–2—299
  9:1–8—122
  9:1–9—314
  9:1–10—198, 82, 218,
    222, 228
  9:1—70, 75, 77, 122,
    218, 229, 230, 299,
    300, 314, 316
  8:6–9—66, 82, 227, 218,
    316
  8:6—69, 82, 104, 109,
    114, 164, 227, 228,
    313
  8:7–8—297
  9:2–8—299
  9:2—70, 109, 122, 218,
    227, 229, 299, 300,
    301
  9:3—70, 92, 109, 122,
    219, 230, 300, 316, 70
  9:4—229, 300, 301
  9:5—70, 104, 108, 109,
    110, 114, 229
  9:6—70, 104, 109, 110,
    114, 229
  9:7—70, 224, 229
  9:8–9—229, 230
  9:8—70, 77, 104, 108,
    109, 114, 230
  9:9—70, 222, 223, 229,
    230
  9:10—70, 77, 223, 224,
    227, 228, 303, 316
  9:11–12—48, 82, 209,
    326
  9:11–13—82, 83, 84
  9:11—41, 48, 209, 305
  9:11–12—48, 82, 209,
    326
  9:11–13—82, 83, 84
  9:12—48, 48, 58, 122,
    141, 153, 154, 155,
    209, 210, 213, 224,
    233, 313, 314, 315,
    326, 327
  9:12–13—60
  9:13—48, 49, 50, 70, 82,
    104, 109, 110, 114,
    122, 199, 200, 253,
    259, 323, 326
  10—64, 172
  10:1–3—64, 68
  10:1—64, 68
  10:2—64, 68, 89, 104,
    109
  10:3—64, 68, 104, 109
  10:4—64, 68, 84, 89,
    313
  10:4–6—64, 68
  10:4–5—64
  10:5—48, 64, 66, 70, 74,
    104, 109, 110, 122,
    209, 210
  10:6—64, 104, 110
Baba' Batra'
  1–2—64
  1:5—175
  2:1—231
  2:3—137, 139, 147
  2:5—186
  3:1–3—183
  3:3—183
  3:7–8—186
  4–6—83
  4:1–4—186
  4:1—114
  4:4—114
  4:5—114
  4:7—114
  4:9—114
  5:2—114
  5:4—175
  5:6–7—146
  5:7—146, 175, 176, 177,
    218
  5:8—114, 145, 146, 147
  5:9—114, 137
  5:10—114, 147
  5:11—114
  6:1–3—146
  6:1—114

Index of Sources

6:2—146
6:4—114
6:6—143
6:8—114
7:2-3—182
7:3—182
8:5—40, 58
10:2—128
10:3-4—219, 220
10:3—112, 183, 219
10:4—218
10:6—316
10:7—111, 198, 203
10:8—198, 247

Sanhedrin
1:1—319
1:9—319
3:3—46
10:4-6—60

Makkot
1:7—45

Šebuʿot
4:5—164
4:8—164, 174
5:1-3—164
6:1—61, 62, 131, 268, 319, 329
6:3—130, 329
6:5—47, 52, 53, 54, 55, 56, 108, 113, 164, 172, 269, 327
6:6—53, 319
6:7—74, 164, 174, 199
7:1—49, 58, 141, 209, 214, 216, 305, 319, 326, 329
7:2—49, 199
7:4—46, 164
7:5-6—137, 141
7:5—210
7:6—76, 155
8:1-6—165
8:1—47, 48, 50, 164, 172, 187, 218, 224, 290
8:2-6—174
8:5—187

8:6—47, 172, 218, 224

ʿEduyot
1:10—141, 150
1:4—112
1:5-6—112
1:9—150
2:5—90
3:1—88
3:8—148
4:3—63
4:7—62

ʿAboda Zara
1:1—186, 247
1:8-9—218
1:8—218
4:5—49, 199
5:1—203
5:4—137

ʾAbot
1:10—100, 203
1:12—100
1:3—202, 203
2:14-16—202

Horayot
3:7—44, 314

Zebaḥim
11:2—45

Menaḥot
9:8—203
10:5—137

Hulin
2:9—137
5:3—84
6:2—84

Bekorot
1:1—218
2:4—218, 275
5:1—136
8:7—127

ʿArakin
3:2—63
5:6—49
6:1—111
6:3—49, 204, 221
6:5—135, 136, 216
8:8—203
9:3—46, 193

Temura
2:1—269
3:5—136

Keritot
1:7—143
2:2—164
3:1—27
3:7—136

Meʿila
1:1—45
4:2—62
5:1—62
6:1-4—51
6:2—52, 137
6:3-4—137
6:4—126, 216
6:5—51, 52, 141, 148, 152, 155, 164
6:6—52

Qinnim
1:1—45, 269

Kelim
2:6—90
4:4—90
5:1—90
5:2—90
5:4—204
5:9—204
9:1—58
12:5—148
12:7—40, 128, 129, 130, 133, 313
17:11—214
20:7—90
26:1—204
26:8—158
27:12—44

ʾOhalot
3:1—88
18:1—137
18:7—203, 175
18:6—312

Negaʿim
1:1—88
7:2—88
14:12—203

Ṭohorot
3:5—44
4:12—44
5:7—44
8:2—164, 174

9:1—90
9:3—90
Nidda
5:4—175
5:7—44

9:3—188, 189
Makširin
6:2—137
6:3—164, 174

Tosepta

Peʾa
3:1—222
Demai
3:15—140
4:22—174
4:24—174
5:12—290
6:2—218
6:3—218
6:7—222
Šebiʿit
5:10—146
5:21—209
8:1—240
Terumot
1:6—209
2:11—222
5:10—290
5:15—290
Maʿaśerot
1:1—148
2:11—211
2:14—212
3:3—148
3:13—222
Maʿaśer Šeni
1:1—152
1:4—265
2:7—131
3:1—151
3:2–3—151
3:3—151
4:9—151
4:13—150
Šeqalim
1:8—148
2:8—216
2:13—148

Sukka
4:10—37
Beṣa
4:6—189
Moʿed Qaṭan
1:12—138, 139
Megilla
3:2—189
Yebamot
14:2—65, 66
15:7—66
Ketubot
2:1—184
4:10—219
4:18—247
6:5—133, 150
7:4—189
8:4—158
9:2—40
11:3—183
12(13):6—127
Nedarim
4:6—189
Nazir
2:2—40
Giṭṭin
9:1—40
Qiddušin
1:1–3—184
1:11—202
1:5—183
1:9—131
3:3—148
3:7—40
3:8—40
5:14–7—202
5:15—202
Babaʾ Qammaʾ
1:1—320

5:4—189
6:14—189
7:11—56
7:20—56
7:21—53
10:8–10—169
10:10—148
10:22—150
10:24—158
10:33—37
10:34—71, 264
10:35—37
11:1—174, 189
Babaʾ Meṣiʿaʾ
1:2—96, 313
1:3—95, 96
1:5–9—314, 315, 316
1:5—247, 316, 317
1:6–9—317
1:8—219, 226
1:9—249
1:10–2—316
1:13—316
1:15—314
1:16–7—316
1:20–1—316
2:1–2—312
2:1—249, 312, 313, 317
2:2—159, 313
2:3–9—315
2:3—315
2:7—158
2:12—41
2:14—62
2:15—315, 328
2:16—315
2:17—315
2:18—189
2:20—42, 160, 313

t. Baba' Meṣi'a', cont.
2:21–2—160, 161, 166, 313, 321
2:23—162
2:24–7—314
2:25—324
2:26–7—324
2:26—324
2:28—313, 316
2:29–30—313
2:31–2—314
2:33—316
3:1—314
3:5–6—66
3:5—65, 66, 313
3:6—66
3:7–8—315
3:7—40, 314
3:8—315
3:9—73, 316
3:10—72, 260, 261
3:11—316
3:12—313
3:13–4—315
3:13—88, 89, 131, 175, 176, 265
3:14—177, 178, 179, 181, 315, 317
3:17–8—128
3:17–9—313
3:17—129, 133
3:18—129, 133
3:19—133
3:20–1—313
3:20—149, 326
3:22–23—316
3:23—133
3:24—313
3:25—140, 315, 319, 326
3:26—317, 318
3:27—141, 270, 277, 318
3:28–9—314
4:2—153, 193, 313, 315
4:7–9—316
4:9—154

4:10—316
4:11–3—314, 315
4:11–25—196
4:11—197, 315
4:12–3—140, 198
4:14–22—152, 314, 315
4:18—315
4:19–21—198
4:23—195, 196, 314
4:24–5—314
5:1–2—196, 197, 221, 274, 314
5:1–14—196
5:1—220
5:2—220
5:7–12—315
5:7—315
5:8—315
5:10–2—168
5:10—168, 196
5:11–2—196
5:13—227, 313
5:14—198, 275, 276, 313
5:15–20—314
5:17—315
5:21–6—316
5:22–6—315
5:22—315
5:23—315
6:3—277
6:8–9—313
6:10—314
6:14—316
6:15—316
6:16—279, 313, 315, 323
6:17—323
7:1–12—315
7:1—55, 201, 204, 206, 207, 208, 281, 315, 317
7:2–7—314
7:2—315
7:3–4—201, 208
7:3—209, 315
7:4—210, 315

7:5—315
7:7—224, 225, 315, 316
7:8—315
7:9—314
7:10–2—314
7:10—78, 79, 315, 317
7:11—315
7:12—315
7:13–14—316
7:15—169, 317
7:16–7—316
7:18—201
7:19—313
7:20—221
8:1—209
8:4—221
8:7—90, 93, 211, 212, 217, 315
8:8—91, 212
8:10–2—316
8:10—283
8:13–5—313
8:15—224, 292, 313
8:16—224, 291
8:19—315
8:20–1—313
8:20–2—189
8:23—81
8:25–6—316
8:25—254
8:27—82, 227, 231, 296, 313
8:28—189, 316
8:29—231, 314
8:30–3—316
8:31—221
8:33—228
9:1–8—316
9:1—209
9:3—218
9:4—218
9:5—316
9:6—218
9:7–8—314
9:7—218, 230, 316
9:8—218, 230
9:10–8—316

t. Baba' Meṣi'a', cont.
9:10—316
9:11—316
9:12—230, 300
9:13—219, 316
9:14—316
9:18—316
9:22–30—314, 316
9:24–6—230
9:25—230
9:26—224, 316
9:29—316
9:31–2—313, 316
9:31—230
9:33—218
10:1—316
10:2—304
10:3–4—315
10:5–6—313
10:5—213
10:6—213, 305
10:7—209, 314
10:8—306
10:9—200
10:10—200
11:1—313
11:7—313
11:23—144
11:25–6—168
Baba' Batra'
1:8-9—220
1:8—219
2:5—209
2:12—184, 218
2:13—184
5:11–12—124, 125
5:11—125
5:12—125
6:26—182, 183
11:6–7—220
11:6—219, 226
11:15—247
Sanhedrin
1:1—319

Šebu'ot
3:8—319
6:7—189
'Aboda Zara
1:3—209
1:8—138, 139
2:8—218
2:9—218
Bekorot
6:13—216
'Arakin
4:3—216
Me'ila
1:23—216
2:10—216
2:11—51
Kelim Baba Meṣi'a'
5:3—189
Nidda
6:14—189
9:12—189

Yerushalmi

Berakot
2:4 (5a)—204
Demai
2:1 (22d)—113
3:1 (23a)—217
3:4 (23d)—174
Šebi'it
8:4 (38a)—187, 214
Ma'serot
2:6 (50a)—90, 91, 92, 93, 211, 212
2:7 (50a)—57
Ma'aser Šeni
1:2 (52c)—265
4:2 (54d)—150
Yoma'
2:3 (39d)—37
Ta'anit
2:14—113
Megilla Mo'ed
1:6—113

Mo'ed Qaṭan (Mašqin)
3:3 (82a)—58
Yebamot
4:11—113
Ketubot
11:4 (34 d)—182
Nedarim
5:2 (39a)—220
Giṭṭin
8:5 (39c)—38,
Qiddušin
1:1 (58b)—126, 183, 184
1:1 (58d)—124
1:1 (60c)—183
4:11 (66b)—142
Baba' Qamma'
5:7 (5c)—222
Baba' Meṣi'a'
1:6 (8a)—111, 112, 247, 317
2:1 (8b)—159

2:3 (8b)—158, 159
2:4 (8c)—41
2:9 (8c)—253
2:10 (8d)—160
2:11(8d)—325
3:1 (9a)—168
3:3 (9a)—314
3:8 (9b)—72, 261
3:10 (9b)—262
3:13 (9b)—321
4:1 (9c)—38, 84, 131, 132
4:2 (9c)—177
4:3 (9d)—177, 181, 194
4:4 (9d)—133, 177
5:1 (10a)—46, 272
5:2 (10b)—154, 192, 275
5:3 (10b)—193
5:6 (10b)—168
5:7 (10c)—198, 276
5:8 (10c)—195

Index of Sources

6:1 (10d)—205, 281
6:1 (10d–11a)—204, 207, 208
6:2 (11a)—202, 207
6:3 (11a)—76, 224, 225, 282
6:7 (11a)—199, 284

7:2 (11b)—90, 91, 93, 211, 212
7:6 (11b)—214
7:9 (11c)—85, 212
8:8 (11d)—82, 227, 296
9:5 (12a)—229
9:9 (12a)—230, 231

Šebuʿot
7:2 (37d)—222
8:1 (38b)—165, 328
8:1 (38c)—169, 321
ʿAboda Zara
1:1 (39b)—139
1:4 (39c)—139

Babli

Šabbat
92b—37
148a—187
Yomaʾ
14b—37
Moʿed Qaṭan
18b—58
Yebamot
13a—37
30a—84
32a—84
42b—113
Ketubot
67a—133
75b—37
Nedarin
46b—220
82a—38
Giṭṭin
56a–b—6
Qiddušin
2a—175
12a—124
25a—84
26a—183, 184
27a—184
28a—131
Babaʾ Qammaʾ
20b—37
45a—169
47a—37
48b—37
54b—167
76a—54, 56
102a—4, 113
107b—166
116b—168, 202

Babaʾ Meṣiʿaʾ
2a—162
3a—95
5a—168
6a—166
8a—162
8b—96
8b–9a—95
10a—202
12b–14a—317
13a—317
13b—247, 317
14b—111
23b—312
24a—312
25a—158
25b—41, 158
26a–b—159
28a—252
28b—160, 253
30a—160, 326
31a—325
32a—43
33b—166
37a—73
40a—72, 260
40b—261
40b–41a—37
41a—37
43a—51
44a—38, 176, 321
44a–b—84, 131
47b—55, 177
49b—194
50b—181
51a—181
51b—316

52a—40
52b—40
57a—182
60a—271
60b—272
61a—46
61b—46
62a—195, 277
62b–63a—124
63a—124, 193, 195
65a—192, 195
65b—55
66b—193
68a—197, 274
69b—275
71a—205, 276
73a—154
74a—111
74b—197
75a—193, 194, 323
75b—207, 281
76a—207, 208
76a–b—206, 281
76b—204, 207
77a—207
77a–b—202
78a—76, 224
78b—225, 226
79a—225
80a—77, 78, 284
80b–81a—284
81b—284
82a—171, 285
82b—37, 92, 108, 165, 170, 171
83a—165, 167, 170
84bff.—177

87a—286, 287
87b—91, 92, 212, 288
89a—90, 91, 212
89a–b—90
91b—288
92a—106, 288
92b—289
93a—85, 212
93b—168, 224
94a—40, 292
101b—82, 227, 296
102a—231, 297
103a—228
104a—299, 300
105a—229
105b—223

107a—302, 303
111a—41
112a—154
113a—305
114b—306
116b—307
Baba' Batra'
122b—113
Šebuʿot
4a—84
49a—50
ʿAboda Zara
2a—186
6b–7a—113
7a—4

13a—139
35b—84
Ḥulin
16a—37
32b—84
85a—84
116b—84
ʿArakin
31a—193
Temura
27b—182
Keritot
24b—37
Nidda
11b—113

Midrashim and Other Rabbinic Texts

Mekilta
Bo'
  15—209, 328
Nĕzîqîn
  12—320
  13—56
  15–6—319
  15—167, 319, 320, 321,
    325, 328
  16—48
  16—48, 165, 167, 168,
    169, 319, 320, 322,
    323, 328
  17—165
  18—319, 323, 328, 329
Kaspā'
  19—216, 319, 323, 325
  20—163, 253, 319, 324,
    325, 326, 327, 329
Sipra
'Emor
  4:17—209
Qĕdôšîm
  II:9–12—326
  II:9—327
  3:11—213
  8:2—326

Bĕ-har
  3:8—149
  III:1–3—55
  III:1–3—327
  III:1–9—326
  III:8—326
  4:1–2—326
  V:1–2—326
  V:1—276, 325, 327
  V:2—327
  7:3—201, 202
  8:7—209
Bĕ-ḥuqôtai
  3:3—222
Sipre Num.
  2—247
  54—265
Sipre Deut.
  13—148
  107—265
  222—43, 163, 325
  223—325
  224—45, 325
  225—43, 163, 325, 327
  262–3—326
  262—192, 279, 326
  263—326
  266—325, 326

272—326
276—326
277—325, 326
278—326
279—213, 326
287—90, 91, 92, 326
312—222
Mekilta de-Rašbi
  pp.199–207—327
  pp. 200–1—329
  p. 200—328
  pp. 201–2—328
  p. 201—328
  pp. 202–3—327, 328
  pp. 203–4—328
  p. 204—327, 328
  pp. 205–6—328
  p. 205—328, 329
  p. 206—328
  p. 210—327, 328
  p. 212—326
  pp. 211–2—327
Genesis Rabba
  79—136
Leviticus Rabba
  19.2 4
Canticles Rabba
  5:8—4

Lamentations Rabba
1:32—6

ʾAbot de Rabbi Nathan
A 11—203

A 18—38, 39, 84
B 21—203

New Testament

Matthew
6:25–33—202
20 1–16—106, 208
20:1ff.—214
20:4—208
20:12–15—208

21:12—148
25:14–30—152
Mark
11:15—148
Luke
12:22–31—202

19:12–27—152
19:45—148
John
2:15—148
Acts
4:32–5:11—240

Greek and Latin Authors

Ammianus Marcellinus,
  Res Gestae
  22.5.5—10
Aristotle
Econ.
  1343a—142
Nicomachean Ethics
  4.1124b.31–5a.2—201
Politics
  1256b–1258a—142
  8.1337b.19–21—201
Cassius Dio
  71.25.1—8
  71.27.3^2–9
  75.2.4,—10
  75.8.3–4—9
Cicero, *de Officiis*
  1.150–1—142, 201, 203
Codex Iustinianus
  1.9.3—15
  3.13.3—15
  4.44.2—179
  4.44.8—179, 184
Codex Theodosianus
  16.8.1—15
  16.8.2—15
  16.8.3—12
  16.8.4—15
  16.8.8—15
  16.8.13—15
  16.8.14—16
  16.8.29—16

Columella
  2.9.14—230
  2.10.17—230
Digest
  3.5.1—157
  3.5.3.pr.—157
  10.2.25.16—170
  12.1.9.9—107
  12.1.10—107
  13.6—187, 188
  13.6.18.pr.—170
  13.7—198
  16.1.24—107
  16.3.1.8–10—164
  16.3.18.1—187
  16.3.24—164
  16.3.25.1—164
  16.3.26.1—164
  16.3.28—164
  16.3.29.1—164
  18.1.1.pr.—124
  18.1.1.1—124
  18.1.2.1—124, 178
  19.2—201
  19.2.11—231
  19.2.19.9—201
  19.2.25.6—223
  19.2.25.7—170
  19 2.38.pr.—201
  20—198
  27.1.15.6—11
  33.7.12.16–26—228

  38.1—201
  38.1.50.1—201
  41.1.3.1—160
  41.1.31.1—160
  41.1.44—159
  41.1.5.1—160
  41.1.5.2–4—158–9
  41.1.57—159
  41.1.63—160
  41.2.3.3—160
  41.2.3.13—159
  41.2.3.14—160
  41.2.25.pr.—159
  41.2.44—160
  46.3.99—130
  47.2.90—201
  48.8.11—8
  48.19.11.1—201
  49.14.13.11—160
  49.14.3.10–11—160
  50.2.3.3—11
  50.15.1.7—9
  50.16.223.pr.—170
Epictetus, *Diss.*
  3.3.3—130
Epiphanius, *Panarion*
  15.2.1—17
  30.4.2—14
  30.7.2–3—14
  30.11.1–5—15
  33.9.4—17
  42.11—17

Eusebius
  Chronica—9
  Com. in Esaiam—16
Gaius, *Institutes*
  2.67–8—160
  3.135—178
  3.139–41—124
  3.206—173
Herodian
  3.2.7–9—9
  3.3—9
Homer, *Iliad*
  7.472–5—124
Jerome
  Com. in Esaiam—14, 17
  Com. in Abacuc 1—17
  Com. in Dan.—10, 11
  Com. in ep. ad Gal.—16
  Epistulae 121—17
Josephus
  War
  2.118—14
  2.122–4—240
  2.248–55—14
  3.399–408—6, 7

Antiquities
  4.287—166
  14. 175—100
  14.22–4—6, 7
  15. 3—100
  15.370—100
  15.292–8—99
  17.149–163—14
  18.4—14
Justin, *Dialogue with Trypho*
  112.4–5—16
Justinian, *Novellae*
  146.1, 553—17,
Libanius
  Epistulae—14
Lucian, *Apology*
  10—201
Origen
  Commentary to Song of Songs
  Prologue—16
  De principiis
  4.1.3—17
  Ep. ad Afric.
  7—17
  14—17

Frag. Com. on Psalms
  —17
Orosius
  7.17.3—10
Paul, *Sententiae*
  5.22.3–4l—8
Pliny, *N. H.*
  8.70.180—274
Scriptores Historiae Augustae
Ant. Pius
  5.4—8
M. Ant.
  25.6–11—9
Avidius Cassius
  8.1–4—9
Septimius Severus
  9.5—9
  4.6—9
  6.7—8
  7.1—11
  9.3–11—9
  22.4—11
Quadriga Tyrannorum
  8.4—15

Papyri and Inscriptions

BGU
  I 92—144
  I 114—173
  I 223—185
  I 260—192
  II 649—144
  III 730—144
  III 704—173
  III 729—173
  IV 1015—185
CIJ
  972—11
CIS
  III.3.I.3948—129
CPR
  I 29—173
DJD II
  18—149

  20—127
  22—139, 198
  23—127
  24—300
  25—139
  26—139
  27—139
  42—139
  114—128, 149, 191
  115—128
IG
  V.2 18—136
  XII.1 786—12
IGR
  III 1050—129
  IV 144—136
  IV 352—126, 150, 151

M.Chr.
  332—173
  333—173
  334—173
  335—173
  338—173
OGIS
  II 484—126, 150, 151
  II 515—129, 150, 151
P. Ath.
  21—198
P. Babatha
  [I] 7—128
  [I] 16—139
  [I] 44—127
  II 5—128, 173, 191
  II 11—128, 191
  II 14—191

Index of Sources 363

    II 15—191, 313
    II 16—127
    II 17—313
    II 18—313
    II 20—313
    II 21—313
    II 22—313
P. Bad.
    II 37—130, 144
P. Bour.
    13—140
P. Col.
    123—129
P. Coll. Youtie
    II 71—128
    II 72—128
P. Dura
    17—128
    20—192
    21—192
    25-8—139
P. Fouad
    44—192
P. Lond.
    II 193—199
    II 298—173
    II 310—173
P. Lond.
    Inv. 1562—138, 140, 143
P. Mich.
    III 188—192
    III 189—192
P. Ness.
    III 82—223
    III 83—223
P. Oslo
    III 118—192
P. Oxy.
    I 72—139
    I 83—144
    II 263—139
    III 485—198
    III 520—140
    III 530—199
    IV 728—143
    IV 729—223
    VII 1158—141
    XII 1411—130
    XII 1411—151
    XII 1454—144
    XII 1455—144
    XII 1461—140
    XIV 1630—223
    XIV 1631—223
    XVII 2134—198
    XXXI 2587—128
    XLI 2951—128
P. Ross. Georg.
    II 19—223
P. Sakaon
    71—196
P. Se'elim Gr.
    3—198
P. Stras.
    VI 557.20—128
P. Tebt.
    II 392—173
P. Vind. Bosw.
    12—128
P. Vind. Worp
    10—198
PSI
    III 202—144
    VI 692—140
SB
    IV 7468—223
    V 7814—196
Stud. Pal.
    XX 71—128
    XX 72—128
    XX 217—275
Syll.^{3}
    799—144
W. Chr.
    311-21—140

Index of Subjects

Amoraim, Amoraic, 3
    and source criticism of the Mishnah, 37–8
ʾĀmrû, 92
Ancient Judaism, modern study of, 20–2
Angareia, 224–6, 283
Attributions, 26–7, 98–115
    catalogue, 101–4
    Early (pre-70), 105–6
    Late, 112
    methodological problems, 98–101
    Neusner on, 99, 105–6
    nominative absolute series, 113–5
    supplementary, 106, 107–12
    Ushan, 107–12, 114
    Yabnean, 106–7
    See also: Source criticism (Mishnah), attributions and
Avidius Cassius, 8

Banks, *See* Moneychangers and banks

Codex Justinianus, See Index of Sources, *s.v.*
Codex Theodosianus, See Index of Sources, *s.v.*
Coins
    Gresham's Law, 132
    Mishnaic and Roman, 124–8
    "produce" and, 128–31, 133
    metallic vs. face value, 128–30
    relative values of, 126, 266, 267, 272
    "silver acquires gold," and "gold acquires silver," 131–3, 265
    "Tyrian," 128
    See also: Money
Crop rotation, 230, 302–3

Dead Sea Scrolls, 4, 240

Deposits
    depositum irregulare, See Roman law, *depositum irregulare*
    liability for, 164–73
    masking other transactions, 173–4
    negligence, 166–71
    oath of depositary, 166–4
    ʾônes and, 166–7, 171
    paid depositaries, 172–3
    produce, 71–4
Digest of Justinian, 4; *see also:* Index of Sources, *s.v.*
Diocletian, 15, 184
Deuterosis, 16–7

Ethnicity, study of, 34

Finders and Losers, *See* Found property
Found property
    care, 160–62
    despair (*yēʾûš*), 158–9
    intention, 159–60
    negotiorum gestio, See Roman law, *negotiorum gestio*
    status and, 163

Gentiles
    gēr tôšāb, 276
    interest, 46–7, 190, 275–6
    lost objects, 324–5
    ritual status of produce, 173–4
Glosses in *m. B. Meṣ., See* Source Criticism (Mishnah), glosses

Ḥakāmîm haynû tannāʾ qammāʾ, 106, 111
Halivni, 25–7, 106, 207
    m. Qid. 1:1, 175
    m. B. Qam. 1:1, 329

m. B. Meṣ. 1:2, 245
m. B. Meṣ. 4:9 (and parallels), 55–6
m. B. Meṣ. 9:8, 302
midrash and Mishnah, 45, 319, 321, 323
Ḥānût, henwwānî, See Shops, shopkeepers
Harmonization (in extra-Mishnaic literature), 40, 65, 73, 76, 128–9
Honi ha-Meʿagel, 7

Interest, 191–2
  contracts of "receipt" and "estimation" and, 196–8, 224–7, 274–5
  fluctuation of value of produce, 193–5
  gifts, 192
  labor contracts and, 196–8
  potentially usurious transactions, 96–8, 138
  rates, 191
  sale or rent of property, 192–3
  security, 198–201
  ṣoʾn barzel, 198, 275–6

Judah the Patriarch, R., 2

Kêṣad, 87–8

Laborers
  agricultural work, 203–4; see also: Slaves
  artisans (ʾumānîm), 204–8
  contracts of "receipt" and "estimation," See Interest, in contracts of ...
  customary contract, 210, 234–5
  deceiving the employer, 204–6, 281
  gĕmār mĕlʾākâ, šāʿat mĕlʾākâ, 90–3, 212, 287, 288
  payment, 209–10, 212–3
  right to eat in the fields, 84–6, 89–93, 210–2
  šākîr, 209
  servility, 201–3
  wages and standard of living, 213
Lease
  animals, 74–9
  deviation from contract, 76–76
  dwellings, 227–32
  qablānût (lease of productivity), 218–20, 299; see also: Interest, contracts of "receipt" and "estimation"
  śĕkîrût (lease for use), 218, 224–6, 299

tenant farming, See Tenant farming
Lien clause (ʾaharāyût), 247; see also: Slaves, documents, lands, and consecrated goods
Loans
  for consumption (milwâ), 190–3
  for use (šĕʾēlâ), 186–90
  interest: See Interest
  sale for deferred payment, for deferred delivery, 185, 192–3
Lost property, See Found property

Marcus Aurelius, 8, 10
Markets
  agricultural produce, 137–9
  agrarian societies and, 134–5
  fairs, 138–9
  ʾiṭlis, 136
  market price, 143–4; see also: Sale, hônāyâ
  specialization, 139–40
  šûq, 136–7
  tāgār, 141–3
Mekilta, 319–24
Mekilta de-rašbi, 327–9
Mishnah
  and Dead Sea Scrolls compared, 4, 240
  and Digest compared, 4
  as a literary artifact, 20–7, 115–7
  description of, 2–5
  disputes and authority, 112–3
  contents of, 3–4
  midrashic formulae in, 44–5, 251
  sources, See Source criticism (Mishnah)
  strophic composition, 87
Money, 122–34
  as commodity, 124–32
  distribution of, 134
  measure of value, 123–4
  transactions in kind and, 122–3
  See also: Coins
Moneychangers and banks
  "checks" in Mishnaic law, 153–4
  deposits, 151–2
  engaged in lending?, 148–9
  exchange of coins, 150–1
  pôrēṭ, meṣārēp, 150–1
  Pergamum, 126
  source of income, 151–3

Neusner, Jacob, 22–31, 99, 105–6
New Historicism, 34
Nominative absolute series
   attributions and, 113–5
   catalogue, 69–70
   formulae, 66
   ha-mapqîd, 70–4
   ha-maśkîr, 82
   ha-mĕqabbēl, 82–3
   ha-šô'ēl, 79–82
   ha-šôkēr, 74-9
   other possible series in *m. B. Meṣ.*, 68
   t. B. Meṣ., 315–6

Oaths, 52–5
Origen, 16–8

Palestine
   history, first to third centuries CE, 5–13
   recent discoveries, 32–3
Papyri
   See Index of Sources
Patriarchate (Jewish), 6, 14–8
Possessory acts, 95–6, 172
   See also: Sale, possessory acts

Rabbi (title), 13–4
Rabbinic civil law
   as historical source, 29–30, 214–9
   authority of, 2
   comparability to Greco-Roman evidence, 30
   landowners and, 31, 238–40
   reflective of practice?, 2
   social and economic background of, 232–5, 238–41
      egalitarianism and hierarchy, 189–8, 231–2
      deposit, 174
      interests of the propertied reflected, 134, 162–3, 216–7, 221–2, 228–32, 233–5
      laborers, 213–7
      money, 132–4
      markets, 146–7
      moneychangers, 155
      lost property, 162–3
      sale, 182–5, 186
      lease, 220–3, 228–32

Rabbinic literature
   historicity of, 6, 19–20, 29–30
   orality in, 5
Rabbis
   as judges, 18
   authority of, 13–9
   institutionalization, 116–7
   Second Temple period movements and, 13–4
   "tradition" and, 31–2
   wealth of, 18
Redaction as literary creation, 94–8
   See also: Source Criticism (Mishnah), redactional reuse of sources
Revolts against Rome, 7–8, 10, 28–9
Registration of real property, 139
Roman Law
   commodatum, 187, 188
   deposit, 164, 174
   depositum irregulare, 107, 152
   domestic leases, 222, 231
   labor, 201
   laesio enormis, 131
   locatio conductio, 203, 218
   mutuum, 187
   negligence, 170
   negotiorum gestio, 157
   Patriarch (Jewish), 15–6
   possession, 158–9, 160
   sale, 124, 128
   surety, 198
   thesauri inventio, 160
   See also: Index of Sources, *s.vv. Digest, Codex Justinianus, Codex Theodosianus*

Sale, 175–86
   barter and, 178
   for deferred payment, for deferred delivery, *See* Loans
   hônāyâ (*'ônā'â*), 52–5, 128, 139, 143–4, 179–85
   lqḥ, qny/h, 175–6, 176–84, 267–70
   possessory acts, 99–9
   withdrawal from, 175–9
Samaritans, 173–4
   putative war with Jews, 8
Scripture and *m. B. Meṣ.*, 60–1
   deposits, 40, 47–8, 164–6, 187

interest, 47, 190, 276
labor, 48, 93, 209, 212
loans, 186–7
lost objects, 42–5, 251, 253
security, 49, 199–200
struggling animals, 42–5
Septimius Severus, 8–9, 11
Severan emperors and Jews, 9–12
Shops, Shopkeepers
  agent of householder, 140–1
  ḥānût, ḥenwwānî, 136–7, 139–41
  shopkeeper as banker, 154–5
Sipra, 326–7
Sipre Deuteronomy, 325–6
Slaves
  domestic labor, 203
Slaves, documents, lands, and consecrated goods, 52–6, 113–5, 139
  See also: Trade and exchange, real property
Source criticism (Mishnah)
  attributions and, 66–7, 113–5; *see also:* Attributions
  associative clusters, 60–5, 86
  codas, 63, 64–5, 71, 74–5, 82, 84–6
  contradictions, 40–1, 71–4, 79–82
  glosses, revisions, and corrections, 86–93
  parallels, 50–9, 62–3, 152
  post-Mishnaic sources and, 37–9, 83–4, 84–6
  redactional reuse of sources, 52–6, 62–3, 75–9, 87, 226; *see also:* codas, Redaction as literary creation
  "schools" and, 66–7, 115–7
  series, *See* Nominative absolute series
  shifts in frame of reference, 40-2
  stylistic criteria, 44-5
  terminology, 44–9, 88
Šûq, *See* Markets, *šûq*

Tannaim, Tannaitic, 3
Tenant farming
  rates, 223
  traditional tenancy, 222
Tosepta, 312–18
Tractate *Nĕzîqîn*, 4, 83, 114–5
Trade and exchange
  producer to consumer, 144–6

large-scale sale, 146–7, 185–6
real property, 183–5
See also: Markets, Sale

Wissenschaft des Judentums, 21

Yabneh
  R. Yohanan b. Zakkai and, 6

Brown Judaic Studies

140001	*Approaches to Ancient Judaism I*	William S. Green
140002	*The Traditions of Eleazar Ben Azariah*	Tzvee Zahavy
140003	*Persons and Institutions in Early Rabbinic Judaism*	William S. Green
140004	*Claude Goldsmid Montefiore on the Ancient Rabbis*	Joshua B. Stein
140005	*The Ecumenical Perspective and the Modernization of Jewish Religion*	S. Daniel Breslauer
140006	*The Sabbath-Law of Rabbi Meir*	Robert Goldenberg
140007	*Rabbi Tarfon*	Joel Gereboff
140008	*Rabban Gamaliel II*	Shamai Kanter
140009	*Approaches to Ancient Judaism II*	William S. Green
140010	*Method and Meaning in Ancient Judaism I*	Jacob Neusner
140011	*Approaches to Ancient Judaism III*	William S. Green
140012	*Turning Point: Zionism and Reform Judaism*	Howard R. Greenstein
140013	*Buber on God and the Perfect Man*	Pamela Vermes
140014	*Scholastic Rabbinism*	Anthony J. Saldarini
140015	*Method and Meaning in Ancient Judaism II*	Jacob Neusner
140016	*Method and Meaning in Ancient Judaism III*	Jacob Neusner
140017	*Post Mishnaic Judaism in Transition*	Baruch M. Bokser
140018	*A History of the Mishnaic Law of Agriculture: Tractate Maaser Sheni*	Peter J. Haas
140019	*Mishnah's Theology of Tithing*	Martin S. Jaffee
140020	*The Priestly Gift in Mishnah: A Study of Tractate Terumot*	Alan. J. Peck
140021	*History of Judaism: The Next Ten Years*	Baruch M. Bokser
140022	*Ancient Synagogues*	Joseph Gutmann
140023	*Warrant for Genocide*	Norman Cohn
140024	*The Creation of the World According to Gersonides*	Jacob J. Staub
140025	*Two Treatises of Philo of Alexandria: A Commentary on* De Gigantibus *and* Quod Deus Sit Immutabilis	Winston/Dillon
140026	*A History of the Mishnaic Law of Agriculture: Kilayim*	Irving Mandelbaum
140027	*Approaches to Ancient Judaism IV*	William S. Green
140028	*Judaism in the American Humanities I*	Jacob Neusner
140029	*Handbook of Synagogue Architecture*	Marilyn Chiat
140030	*The Book of Mirrors*	Daniel C. Matt
140031	*Ideas in Fiction: The Works of Hayim Hazaz*	Warren Bargad
140032	*Approaches to Ancient Judaism V*	William S. Green
140033	*Sectarian Law in the Dead Sea Scrolls: Courts, Testimony and the Penal Code*	Lawrence H. Schiffman
140034	*A History of the United Jewish Appeal: 1939-1982*	Marc L. Raphael
140035	*The Academic Study of Judaism*	Jacob Neusner
140036	*Woman Leaders in the Ancient Synagogue*	Bernadette Brooten
140037	*Formative Judaism I: Religious, Historical, and Literary Studies*	Jacob Neusner
140038	*Ben Sira's View of Women: A Literary Analysis*	Warren C. Trenchard
140039	*Barukh Kurzweil and Modern Hebrew Literature*	James S. Diamond
140040	*Israeli Childhood Stories of the Sixties: Yizhar, Aloni, Shahar, Kahana-Carmon*	Gideon Telpaz
140041	*Formative Judaism II: Religious, Historical, and Literary Studies*	Jacob Neusner
140042	*Judaism in the American Humanities II: Jewish Learning and the New Humanities*	Jacob Neusner

140043	Support for the Poor in the Mishnaic Law of Agriculture: Tractate Peah	Roger Brooks
140044	The Sanctity of the Seventh Year: A Study of Mishnah Tractate Shebiit	Louis E. Newman
140045	Character and Context: Studies in the Fiction of Abramovitsh, Brenner, and Agnon	Jeffrey Fleck
140046	Formative Judaism III: Religious, Historical, and Literary Studies	Jacob Neusner
140047	Pharaoh's Counsellors: Job, Jethro, and Balaam in Rabbinic and Patristic Tradition	Judith Baskin
140048	The Scrolls and Christian Origins: Studies in the Jewish Background of the New Testament	Matthew Black
140049	Approaches to Modern Judaism I	Marc Lee Raphael
140050	Mysterious Encounters at Mamre and Jabbok	William T. Miller
140051	The Mishnah Before 70	Jacob Neusner
140052	Sparda by the Bitter Sea: Imperial Interaction in Western Anatolia	Jack Martin Balcer
140053	Hermann Cohen: The Challenge of a Religion of Reason	William Kluback
140054	Approaches to Judaism in Medieval Times I	David R. Blumenthal
140055	In the Margins of the Yerushalmi: Glosses on the English Translation	Jacob Neusner
140056	Approaches to Modern Judaism II	Marc Lee Raphael
140057	Approaches to Judaism in Medieval Times II	David R. Blumenthal
140058	Midrash as Literature: The Primacy of Documentary Discourse	Jacob Neusner
140059	The Commerce of the Sacred: Mediation of the Divine Among Jews in the Graeco-Roman Diaspora	Jack N. Lightstone
140060	Major Trends in Formative Judaism I: Society and Symbol in Political Crisis	Jacob Neusner
140061	Major Trends in Formative Judaism II: Texts, Contents, and Contexts	Jacob Neusner
140062	A History of the Jews in Babylonia I: The Parthian Period	Jacob Neusner
140063	The Talmud of Babylonia: An American Translation XXXII: Tractate Arakhin	Jacob Neusner
140064	Ancient Judaism: Debates and Disputes	Jacob Neusner
140065	Prayers Alleged to Be Jewish: An Examination of the Constitutiones Apostolorum	David Fiensy
140066	The Legal Methodology of Hai Gaon	Tsvi Groner
140067	From Mishnah to Scripture: The Problem of the Unattributed Saying	Jacob Neusner
140068	Halakhah in a Theological Dimension	David Novak
140069	From Philo to Origen: Middle Platonism in Transition	Robert M. Berchman
140070	In Search of Talmudic Biography: The Problem of the Attributed Saying	Jacob Neusner
140071	The Death of the Old and the Birth of the New: The Framework of the Book of Numbers and the Pentateuch	Dennis T. Olson
140072	The Talmud of Babylonia: An American Translation XVII: Tractate Sotah	Jacob Neusner
140073	Understanding Seeking Faith: Essays on the Case of Judaism II: Literature, Religion and the Social Study of Judiasm	Jacob Neusner
140074	The Talmud of Babylonia: An American Translation VI: Tractate Sukkah	Jacob Neusner
140075	Fear Not Warrior: A Study of 'al tira' Pericopes in the Hebrew Scriptures	Edgar W. Conrad

140076	Formative Judaism IV: Religious, Historical, and Literary Studies	Jacob Neusner
140077	Biblical Patterns in Modern Literature	Hirsch/Aschkenasy
140078	The Talmud of Babylonia: An American Translation I: Tractate Berakhot	Jacob Neusner
140079	Mishnah's Division of Agriculture: A History and Theology of Seder Zeraim	Alan J. Avery-Peck
140080	From Tradition to Imitation: The Plan and Program of Pesiqta Rabbati and Pesiqta deRab Kahana	Jacob Neusner
140081	The Talmud of Babylonia: An American Translation XXIII.A: Tractate Sanhedrin, Chapters 1-3	Jacob Neusner
140082	Jewish Presence in T. S. Eliot and Franz Kafka	Melvin Wilk
140083	School, Court, Public Administration: Judaism and its Institutions in Talmudic Babylonia	Jacob Neusner
140084	The Talmud of Babylonia: An American Translation XXIII.B: Tractate Sanhedrin, Chapters 4-8	Jacob Neusner
140085	The Bavli and Its Sources: The Question of Tradition in the Case of Tractate Sukkah	Jacob Neusner
140086	From Description to Conviction: Essays on the History and Theology of Judaism	Jacob Neusner
140087	The Talmud of Babylonia: An American Translation XXIII.C: Tractate Sanhedrin, Chapters 9-11	Jacob Neusner
140088	Mishnaic Law of Blessings and Prayers: Tractate Berakhot	Tzvee Zahavy
140089	The Peripatetic Saying: The Problem of the Thrice-Told Tale in Talmudic Literature	Jacob Neusner
140090	The Talmud of Babylonia: An American Translation XXVI: Tractate Horayot	Martin S. Jaffee
140091	Formative Judaism V: Religious, Historical, and Literary Studies	Jacob Neusner
140092	Essays on Biblical Method and Translation	Edward Greenstein
140093	The Integrity of Leviticus Rabbah	Jacob Neusner
140094	Behind the Essenes: History and Ideology of the Dead Sea Scrolls	Philip R. Davies
140095	Approaches to Judaism in Medieval Times III	David R. Blumenthal
140096	The Memorized Torah: The Mnemonic System of the Mishnah	Jacob Neusner
140097	Knowledge and Illumination	Hossein Ziai
140098	Sifre to Deuteronomy: An Analytical Translation I: Pisqaot 1-143. Debarim, Waethanan, Eqeb	Jacob Neusner
140099	Major Trends in Formative Judaism III: The Three Stages in the Formation of Judaism	Jacob Neusner
140101	Sifre to Deuteronomy: An Analytical Translation II: Pisqaot 144-357. Shofetim, Ki Tese, Ki Tabo, Nesabim, Ha'azinu, Zot Habberakhah	Jacob Neusner
140102	Sifra: The Rabbinic Commentary on Leviticus	Neusner/Brooks
140103	The Human Will in Judaism	Howard Eilberg-Schwartz
140104	Genesis Rabbah I: Genesis 1:1 to 8:14	Jacob Neusner
140105	Genesis Rabbah II: Genesis 8:15 to 28:9	Jacob Neusner
140106	Genesis Rabbah III: Genesis 28:10 to 50:26	Jacob Neusner
140107	First Principles of Systemic Analysis	Jacob Neusner
140108	Genesis and Judaism	Jacob Neusner
140109	The Talmud of Babylonia: An American Translation XXXV: Tractates Meilah and Tamid	Peter J. Haas
140110	Studies in Islamic and Judaic Traditions I	Brinner/Ricks

140111	Comparative Midrash: The Plan and Program of Genesis Rabbah and Leviticus Rabbah	Jacob Neusner
140112	The Tosefta: Its Structure and its Sources	Jacob Neusner
140113	Reading and Believing	Jacob Neusner
140114	The Fathers According to Rabbi Nathan	Jacob Neusner
140115	Etymology in Early Jewish Interpretation: The Hebrew Names in Philo	Lester L. Grabbe
140116	Understanding Seeking Faith: Essays on the Case of Judaism I: Debates on Method, Reports of Results	Jacob Neusner
140117	The Talmud of Babylonia: An American Translation VII: Tractate Besah	Alan J. Avery-Peck
140118	Sifre to Numbers: An American Translation and Explanation I: Sifre to Numbers 1-58	Jacob Neusner
140119	Sifre to Numbers: An American Translation and Explanation II: Sifre to Numbers 59-115	Jacob Neusner
140120	Cohen and Troeltsch: Ethical Monotheistic Religion and Theory of Culture	Wendell S. Dietrich
140121	Goodenough on the History of Religion and on Judaism	Neusner/Frerichs
140122	Pesiqta deRab Kahana I: Pisqaot 1-14	Jacob Neusner
140123	Pesiqta deRab Kahana II: Pisqaot 15-28 and Introduction to Pesiqta deRab Kahana	Jacob Neusner
140124	Sifre to Deuteronomy: Introduction	Jacob Neusner
140126	A Conceptual Commentary on Midrash Leviticus Rabbah: Value Concepts in Jewish Thought	Max Kadushin
140127	The Other Judaisms of Late Antiquity	Alan F. Segal
140128	Josephus as a Historical Source in Patristic Literature through Eusebius	Michael Hardwick
140129	Judaism: The Evidence of the Mishnah	Jacob Neusner
140131	Philo, John and Paul: New Perspectives on Judaism and Early Christianity	Peder Borgen
140132	Babylonian Witchcraft Literature	Tzvi Abusch
140133	The Making of the Mind of Judaism: The Formative Age	Jacob Neusner
140135	Why No Gospels in Talmudic Judaism?	Jacob Neusner
140136	Torah: From Scroll to Symbol Part III: Doctrine	Jacob Neusner
140137	The Systemic Analysis of Judaism	Jacob Neusner
140138	Sifra: An Analytical Translation I	Jacob Neusner
140139	Sifra: An Analytical Translation II	Jacob Neusner
140140	Sifra: An Analytical Translation III	Jacob Neusner
140141	Midrash in Context: Exegesis in Formative Judaism	Jacob Neusner
140142	Sifra: An Analytical Translation IV	Jacob Neusner
140143	Oxen, Women or Citizens? Slaves in the System of Mishnah	Paul V. Flesher
140144	The Book of the Pomegranate	Elliot R. Wolfson
140145	Wrong Ways and Right Ways in the Study of Formative Judaism	Jacob Neusner
140146	Sifra in Perspective: The Documentary Comparison of the Midrashim of Ancient Judaism	Jacob Neusner
140147	Uniting the Dual Torah: Sifra and the Problem of the Mishnah	Jacob Neusner
140148	Mekhilta According to Rabbi Ishmael: An Analytical Translation I	Jacob Neusner
140149	The Doctrine of the Divine Name: An Introduction to Classical Kabbalistic Theology	Stephen G. Wald
140150	Water into Wine and the Beheading of John the Baptist	Roger Aus
140151	The Formation of the Jewish Intellect	Jacob Neusner
140152	Mekhilta According to Rabbi Ishmael: An Introduction to Judaism's First Scriptural Encyclopaedia	Jacob Neusner

140153	Understanding Seeking Faith: Essays on the Case of Judaism III: Society, History, and Political and Philosophical Uses of Judaism	Jacob Neusner
140154	Mekhilta According to Rabbi Ishmael: An Analytical Translation II	Jacob Neusner
140155	Goyim: Gentiles and Israelites in Mishnah-Tosefta	Gary P. Porton
140156	A Religion of Pots and Pans?	Jacob Neusner
140157	Claude Montefiore and Christianity	Maurice Gerald Bowler
140158	The Philosophical Mishnah III: The Tractates' Agenda: From Nazir to Zebahim	Jacob Neusner
140159	From Ancient Israel to Modern Judaism I: Intellect in Quest of Understanding	Neusner/Frerichs/Sarna
140160	The Social Study of Judaism I	Jacob Neusner
140161	Philo's Jewish Identity	Alan Mendelson
140162	The Social Study of Judaism II	Jacob Neusner
140163	The Philosophical Mishnah I: The Initial Probe	Jacob Neusner
140164	The Philosophical Mishnah II: The Tractates' Agenda: From Abodah Zarah Through Moed Qatan	Jacob Neusner
140166	Women's Earliest Records	Barbara S. Lesko
140167	The Legacy of Hermann Cohen	William Kluback
140168	Method and Meaning in Ancient Judaism	Jacob Neusner
140169	The Role of the Messenger and Message in the Ancient Near East	John T. Greene
140171	Abraham Heschel's Idea of Revelation	Lawerence Perlman
140172	The Philosophical Mishnah IV: The Repertoire	Jacob Neusner
140173	From Ancient Israel to Modern Judaism II: Intellect in Quest of Understanding	Neusner/Frerichs/Sarna
140174	From Ancient Israel to Modern Judaism III: Intellect in Quest of Understanding	Neusner/Frerichs/Sarna
140175	From Ancient Israel to Modern Judaism IV: Intellect in Quest of Understanding	Neusner/Frerichs/Sarna
140176	Translating the Classics of Judaism: In Theory and In Practice	Jacob Neusner
140177	Profiles of a Rabbi: Synoptic Opportunities in Reading About Jesus	Bruce Chilton
140178	Studies in Islamic and Judaic Traditions II	Brinner/Ricks
140179	Medium and Message in Judaism: First Series	Jacob Neusner
140180	Making the Classics of Judaism: The Three Stages of Literary Formation	Jacob Neusner
140181	The Law of Jealousy: Anthropology of Sotah	Adriana Destro
140182	Esther Rabbah I: An Analytical Translation	Jacob Neusner
140183	Ruth Rabbah: An Analytical Translation	Jacob Neusner
140184	Formative Judaism: Religious, Historical and Literary Studies	Jacob Neusner
140185	The Studia Philonica Annual 1989	David T. Runia
140186	The Setting of the Sermon on the Mount	W.D. Davies
140187	The Midrash Compilations of the Sixth and Seventh Centuries I	Jacob Neusner
140188	The Midrash Compilations of the Sixth and Seventh Centuries II	Jacob Neusner
140189	The Midrash Compilations of the Sixth and Seventh Centuries III	Jacob Neusner
140190	The Midrash Compilations of the Sixth and Seventh Centuries IV	Jacob Neusner
140191	The Religious World of Contemporary Judaism: Observations and Convictions	Jacob Neusner
140192	Approaches to Ancient Judaism VI	Neusner/Frerichs
140193	Lamentations Rabbah: An Analytical Translation	Jacob Neusner
140194	Early Christian Texts on Jews and Judaism	Robert S. MacLennan
140196	Torah and the Chronicler's History Work	Judson R. Shaver

140197	Song of Songs Rabbah: An Analytical Translation I	Jacob Neusner
140198	Song of Songs Rabbah: An Analytical Translation II	Jacob Neusner
140199	From Literature to Theology in Formative Judaism	Jacob Neusner
140202	Maimonides on Perfection	Menachem Kellner
140203	The Martyr's Conviction	Eugene Weiner/Anita Weiner
140204	Judaism, Christianity, and Zoroastrianism in Talmudic Babylonia	Jacob Neusner
140205	Tzedakah: Can Jewish Philanthropy Buy Jewish Survival?	Jacob Neusner
140206	New Perspectives on Ancient Judaism I	Neusner/Borgen/Frerichs/Horsley
140207	Scriptures of the Oral Torah	Jacob Neusner
140208	Christian Faith and the Bible of Judaism	Jacob Neusner
140209	Philo's Perception of Women	Dorothy Sly
140210	Case Citation in the Babylonian Talmud: The Evidence Tractate Neziqin	Eliezer Segal
140211	The Biblical Herem: A Window on Israel's Religious Experience	Philip D. Stern
140212	Goodenough on the Beginnings of Christianity	A.T. Kraabel
140213	The Talmud of Babylonia: An American Translation XXI.A: Tractate Bava Mesia Chapters 1-2	Jacob Neusner
140214	The Talmud of Babylonia: An American Translation XXI.B: Tractate Bava Mesia Chapters 3-4	Jacob Neusner
140215	The Talmud of Babylonia: An American Translation XXI.C: Tractate Bava Mesia Chapters 5-6	Jacob Neusner
140216	The Talmud of Babylonia: An American Translation XXI.D: Tractate Bava Mesia Chapters 7-10	Jacob Neusner
140217	Semites, Iranians, Greeks and Romans: Studies in their Interactions	Jonathan A. Goldstein
140218	The Talmud of Babylonia: An American Translation XXXIII: Temurah	Jacob Neusner
140219	The Talmud of Babylonia: An American Translation XXXI.A: Tractate Bekhorot Chapters 1-4	Jacob Neusner
140220	The Talmud of Babylonia: An American Translation XXXI.B: Tractate Bekhorot Chapters 5-9	Jacob Neusner
140221	The Talmud of Babylonia: An American Translation XXXVI.A: Tractate Niddah Chapters 1-3	Jacob Neusner
140222	The Talmud of Babylonia: An American Translation XXXVI.B: Tractate Niddah Chapters 4-10	Jacob Neusner
140223	The Talmud of Babylonia: An American Translation XXXIV: Tractate Keritot	Jacob Neusner
140224	Paul, the Temple, and the Presence of God	David A. Renwick
140225	The Book of the People	William W. Hallo
140226	The Studia Philonica Annual 1990	David Runia
140227	The Talmud of Babylonia: An American Translation XXV.A: Tractate Abodah Zarah Chapters 1-2	Jacob Neusner
140228	The Talmud of Babylonia: An American Translation XXV.B: Tractate Abodah Zarah Chapters 3-5	Jacob Neusner
140230	The Studia Philonica Annual 1991	David Runia
140231	The Talmud of Babylonia: An American Translation XXVIII.A: Tractate Zebahim Chapters 1-3	Jacob Neusner
140232	Both Literal and Allegorical: Studies in Philo of Alexandria's Questions and Answers on Genesis and Exodus	David M. Hay
140233	The Talmud of Babylonia: An American Translation XXVIII.B: Tractate Zebahim Chapters 4-8	Jacob Neusner

140234	The Talmud of Babylonia: An American Translation XXVIII.C: Tractate Zebahim Chapters 9-14	Jacob Neusner
140235	The Talmud of Babylonia: An American Translation XXIX.A: Tractate Menahot Chapters 1-3	Jacob Neusner
140236	The Talmud of Babylonia: An American Translation XXIX.B: Tractate Menahot Chapters 4-7	Jacob Neusner
140237	The Talmud of Babylonia: An American Translation XXIX.C: Tractate Menahot Chapters 8-13	Jacob Neusner
140238	The Talmud of Babylonia: An American Translation XXIX: Tractate Makkot	Jacob Neusner
140239	The Talmud of Babylonia: An American Translation XXII.A: Tractate Baba Batra Chapters 1 and 2	Jacob Neusner
140240	The Talmud of Babylonia: An American Translation XXII.B: Tractate Baba Batra Chapter 3	Jacob Neusner
140241	The Talmud of Babylonia: An American Translation XXII.C: Tractate Baba Batra Chapters 4-6	Jacob Neusner
140242	The Talmud of Babylonia: An American Translation XXVII.A: Tractate Shebuot Chapters 1-3	Jacob Neusner
140243	The Talmud of Babylonia: An American Translation XXVII.B: Tractate Shebuot Chapters 4-8	Jacob Neusner
140244	Balaam and His Interpreters: A Hermeneutical History of the Balaam Traditions	John T. Greene
140245	Courageous Universality: The Work of Schmuel Hugo Bergman	William Kluback
140246	The Mechanics of Change: Essays in the Social History of German Jewry	Steven M. Lowenstein
140247	The Talmud of Babylonia: An American Translation XX.A: Tractate Baba Qamma Chapters 1-3	Jacob Neusner
140248	The Talmud of Babylonia: An American Translation XX.B: Tractate Baba Qamma Chapters 4-7	Jacob Neusner
140249	The Talmud of Babylonia: An American Translation XX.C: Tractate Baba Qamma Chapters 8-10	Jacob Neusner
140250	The Talmud of Babylonia: An American Translation XIII.A: Tractate Yebamot Chapters 1-3	Jacob Neusner
140251	The Talmud of Babylonia: An American Translation XIII.B: Tractate Yebamot Chapters 4-6	Jacob Neusner
140252	The Talmud of Babylonia: An American Translation XI: Tractate Moed Qatan	Jacob Neusner
140253	The Talmud of Babylonia: An American Translation XXX.A: Tractate Hullin Chapters 1 and 2	Tzvee Zahavy
140254	The Talmud of Babylonia: An American Translation XXX.B: Tractate Hullin Chapters 3-6	Tzvee Zahavy
140255	The Talmud of Babylonia: An American Translation XXX.C: Tractate Hullin Chapters 7-12	Tzvee Zahavy
140256	The Talmud of Babylonia: An American Translation XIII.C: Tractate Yebamot Chapters 7-9	Jacob Neusner
140257	The Talmud of Babylonia: An American Translation XIV.A: Tractate Ketubot Chapters 1-3	Jacob Neusner
140258	The Talmud of Babylonia: An American Translation XIV.B: Tractate Ketubot Chapters 4-7	Jacob Neusner
140259	Jewish Thought Adrift: Max Wiener (1882-1950)	Robert S. Schine
140260	The Talmud of Babylonia: An American Translation XIV.C: Tractate Ketubot Chapters 8-13	Jacob Neusner

140261	*The Talmud of Babylonia: An American Translation* XIII.D: *Tractate Yebamot Chapters 10-16*	Jacob Neusner
140262	*The Talmud of Babylonia: An American Translation* XV. A: *Tractate Nedarim Chapters 1-4*	Jacob Neusner
140263	*The Talmud of Babylonia: An American Translation* XV.B: *Tractate Nedarim Chapters 5-11*	Jacob Neusner
140264	*Studia Philonica Annual 1992*	David T. Runia
140265	*The Talmud of Babylonia: An American Translation* XVIII.A: *Tractate Gittin Chapters 1-3*	Jacob Neusner
140266	*The Talmud of Babylonia: An American Translation* XVIII.B: *Tractate Gittin Chapters 4 and 5*	Jacob Neusner
140267	*The Talmud of Babylonia: An American Translation* XIX.A: *Tractate Qiddushin Chapter 1*	Jacob Neusner
140268	*The Talmud of Babylonia: An American Translation* XIX.B: *Tractate Qiddushin Chapters 2-4*	Jacob Neusner
140269	*The Talmud of Babylonia: An American Translation* XVIII.C: *Tractate Gittin Chapters 6-9*	Jacob Neusner
140270	*The Talmud of Babylonia: An American Translation* II.A: *Tractate Shabbat Chapters 1 and 2*	Jacob Neusner
140271	*The Theology of Nahmanides Systematically Presented*	David Novak
140272	*The Talmud of Babylonia: An American Translation* II.B: *Tractate Shabbat Chapters 3-6*	Jacob Neusner
140273	*The Talmud of Babylonia: An American Translation* II.C: *Tractate Shabbat Chapters 7-10*	Jacob Neusner
140274	*The Talmud of Babylonia: An American Translation* II.D: *Tractate Shabbat Chapters 11-17*	Jacob Neusner
140275	*The Talmud of Babylonia: An American Translation* II.E: *Tractate Shabbat Chapters 18-24*	Jacob Neusner
140276	*The Talmud of Babylonia: An American Translation* III.A: *Tractate Erubin Chapters 1 and 2*	Jacob Neusner
140277	*The Talmud of Babylonia: An American Translation* III.B: *Tractate Erubin Chapters 3 and 4*	Jacob Neusner
140278	*The Talmud of Babylonia: An American Translation* III.C: *Tractate Erubin Chapters 5 and 6*	Jacob Neusner
140279	*The Talmud of Babylonia: An American Translation* III.D: *Tractate Erubin Chapters 7-10*	Jacob Neusner
140280	*The Talmud of Babylonia: An American Translation* XII: *Tractate Hagigah*	Jacob Neusner
140281	*The Talmud of Babylonia: An American Translation* IV.A: *Tractate Pesahim Chapter I*	Jacob Neusner
140282	*The Talmud of Babylonia: An American Translation* IV.B: *Tractate Pesahim Chapters 2 and 3*	Jacob Neusner
140283	*The Talmud of Babylonia: An American Translation* IV.C: *Tractate Pesahim Chapters 4-6*	Jacob Neusner
140284	*The Talmud of Babylonia: An American Translation* IV.D: *Tractate Pesahim Chapters 7 and 8*	Jacob Neusner
140285	*The Talmud of Babylonia: An American Translation* IV.E: *Tractate Pesahim Chapters 9 and 10*	Jacob Neusner
140286	*From Christianity to Gnosis and From Gnosis to Christianity*	Jean Magne
140287	*Studia Philonica Annual 1993*	David T. Runia
140288	*Diasporas in Antiquity*	Shaye J. D. Cohen, Ernest S. Frerichs
140289	*The Jewish Family in Antiquity*	Shaye J. D. Cohen
140290	*The Place of Judaism in Philo's Thought*	Ellen Birnbaum

140291	*The Babylonian Esther Midrash, Vol. 1*	Eliezer Segal
140292	*The Babylonian Esther Midrash, Vol. 2*	Eliezer Segal
140293	*The Babylonian Esther Midrash, Vol. 3*	Eliezer Segal
140294	*The Talmud of Babylonia: An American Translation V. A: Tractate Yoma Chapters 1 and 2*	Jacob Neusner
140295	*The Talmud of Babylonia: An American Translation V. B: Tractate Yoma Chapters 3-5*	Jacob Neusner
140296	*The Talmud of Babylonia: An American Translation V. C: Tractate Yoma Chapters 6-8*	Jacob Neusner
140297	*The Talmud of Babylonia: An American Translation XXII.D: Tractate Baba Batra Chapters Seven and Eight*	Jacob Neusner
140298	*The Talmud of Babylonia: An American Translation XXII.E: Tractate Baba Batra Chapters Nine and Ten*	Jacob Neusner
140299	*The Studia Philonica Annual, 1994*	David T. Runia
140300	*Sages, Stories, Authors, and Editors in Rabbinic Judaism*	Richard Kalmin
140301	*From Balaam to Jonah: Anti-prophetic Satire in the Hebrew Bible*	David Marcus
140302	*The History of Sukkot in the Second Temple and Rabbinic Periods*	Jeffrey L. Rubenstein
140303	*Tasting the Dish: Rabbinic Rhetorics of Sexuality*	Michael L. Satlow
140304	*The School of Moses: Studies in Philo and Hellenistic Religion*	John Peter Kenney
140305	*The Studia Philonica Annual, 1995*	David T. Runia
140306	*The Talmud of Babylonia, An American Translation IX, Tractate Rosh Hashanah*	Alan J. Avery-Peck
140307	*Early Rabbinic Civil Law and the Social History of Roman Galilee: A Study of Mishnah Tractate Baba Mesia*	Hayim Lapin

Brown Studies on Jews and Their Societies

145001	*American Jewish Fertility*	Calvin Goldscheider
145002	*The Impact of Religious Schooling: The Effects of Jewish Education Upon Religious Involvement*	Harold S. Himmelfarb
145003	*The American Jewish Community*	Calvin Goldscheider
145004	*The Naturalized Jews of the Grand Duchy of Posen in 1834 and 1835*	Edward David Luft
145005	*Suburban Communities: The Jewishness of American Reform Jews*	Gerald L. Showstack
145007	*Ethnic Survival in America*	David Schoem
145008	*American Jews in the 21st Century: A Leadership Challenge*	Earl Raab

Brown Studies in Religion

147001	*Religious Writings and Religious Systems I*	Jacob Neusner, et al
147002	*Religious Writings and Religious Systems II*	Jacob Neusner, et al
147003	*Religion and the Social Sciences*	Robert Segal

BM
497.8
.B33
L3
1995
39712s